D0172516

Israel
& the Palestinian
Territories

**Upper Galilee
& Golan**
p231

**Haifa & the
North Coast**
p156

**Lower Galilee &
Sea of Galilee**
p195

**Tel Aviv-
Jaffa (Yafo)**
p112

West Bank
p261

Jerusalem ◉
p46

**The Gaza
Strip**
p292

The Dead Sea
p297

The Negev
p315

○
**Petra
(Jordan)**
p341

Daniel Robinson, Orlando Crowcroft, Anita Isalska,
Dan Savery Raz, Jenny Walker

Contents

ST CATHERINE'S CHURCH P269

DYZIO/SHUTTERSTOCK ©

EFESENKO/SHUTTERSTOCK ©

HUMMUS P380

DANIEL REINER /SHUTTERSTOCK ©

WOMAN PREPARING FLATBREAD

Welcome to Israel & the Palestinian Territories

*At the intersection of Asia, Europe and Africa –
both geographically and culturally – Israel
and the Palestinian Territories have been
a meeting place of cultures, empires and
religions since history began.*

Holy Sites

Cradle of Judaism and Christianity and sacred to Muslims and Baha'is, the Holy Land invites visitors to immerse themselves in the variety of the region's religious traditions. Ancient Jewish sites include Jerusalem's Western Wall and Byzantine-era synagogues. The Roman-era synagogues around the Sea of Galilee may have been used by Jews and Christians before they diverged into separate faiths. Both Christian pilgrims and tourists can explore sites associated with Jesus's birth (in Bethlehem), ministry (in Nazareth and around the Sea of Galilee) and crucifixion (in Jerusalem). For Muslims, only Mecca and Medina are holier than Jerusalem's Al Haram Ash Sharif, known to Jews as the Temple Mount – perhaps the most contested site on earth.

Tel Aviv

Tel Aviv is a multicultural swirl of skyscrapers, bike paths, atmospheric cafes, stylish bistros and buff bods tanning on the sand. It may be a relatively new city by Israeli standards (it was first founded in 1909) but earned Unesco World Heritage status by virtue of its 1930s-style Bauhaus architecture. Israel's self-described 'start-up city', it is world-renowned as a tech hub and is home to some of the country's most happening firms – as well as myriad bars, pubs and clubs.

Archaeology

Thanks to the painstaking work of generations of archaeologists, modern-day visitors can explore the 10,000-year-old mud-brick relics of Jericho, enter into the world of David and Solomon in Jerusalem's City of David, and twin a visit to Masada, with its dramatic tale of resistance to the mighty legions of Rome, with a tour of the thoroughfares and theatres of Beit She'an, still pulsing with Roman opulence. Many of the country's most extraordinary finds are on display in Jerusalem's Israel Museum.

Adventures in Nature

Few countries have so much geographic variety packed into such a small space. Distances are short, so you can relax on a Mediterranean beach one day, spend the next floating in the mineral-rich waters of the Dead Sea, and the day after that scuba diving in the Red Sea. Hikers can trek the length of the country on the Israel National Trail, splash through seasonal streams as they tumble towards the Jordan, explore spring-fed oases tucked into the arid bluffs above the Dead Sea, and explore the multicoloured sandstone formations of Makhtesh Ramon. Many trails are ideal for mountain biking.

Contents

UNDERSTAND

SURVIVAL GUIDE

SPECIAL FEATURES

Why I Love Israel & the Palestinian Territories

By Orlando Crowcroft, Writer

Israel and the Palestinian Territories can be a difficult place, but when the call to prayer rings out in the streets of Jerusalem, the smell of spices hovers above the old city of Nablus or the sun sets over the hills of the Galilee, it can be a magical one too. It is as fascinating as it is frustrating, as tantalising as it is torn. But look close enough – with the right kind of eyes – and you get a glimpse of what unites all who live between the Jordan River and the Mediterranean: an unshakeable bond to the land.

For more about our writers, see p448

Above: Bethlehem (p266)

Israel & the Palestinian Territories

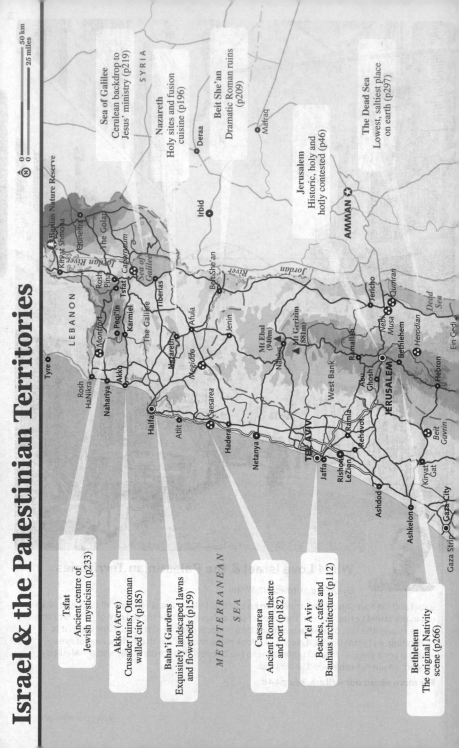

Tsfat
Ancient centre of Jewish mysticism (p233)

Akko (Acre)
Crusader ruins, Ottoman walled city (p185)

Baha'i Gardens
Exquisitely landscaped lawns and flowerbeds (p159)

Caesarea
Ancient Roman theatre and port (p182)

Tel Aviv
Beaches, cafes and Bauhaus architecture (p112)

Bethlehem
The original Nativity scene (p266)

Sea of Galilee
Cerulean backdrop to Jesus' ministry (p219)

Nazareth
Holy sites and fusion cuisine (p196)

Beit She'an
Dramatic Roman ruins (p209)

Jerusalem
Historic, holy and hotly contested (p46)

The Dead Sea
Lowest, saltiest place on earth (p297)

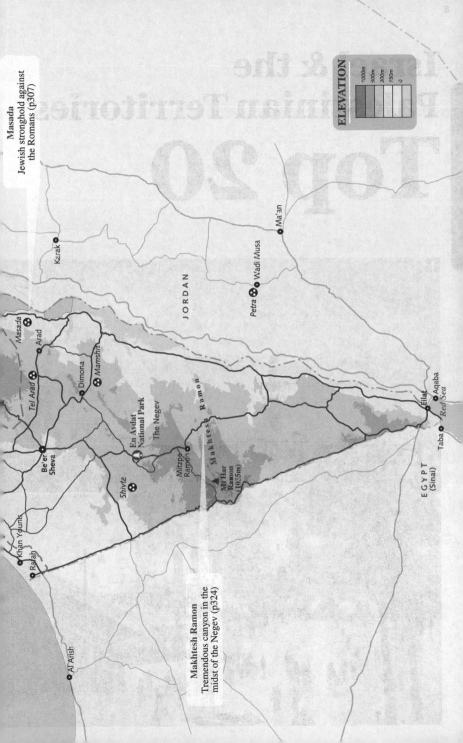

Masada
Jewish stronghold against
the Romans (p307)

Makhtesh Ramon
Tremendous canyon in the
midst of the Negev (p324)

ELEVATION

1000m
500m
300m
150m
0

Karak

JORDAN

Ma'an

Petra • Wadi Musa

Masada
Arad

Tel Arad

Dimona

Mamshit

En Avdat
National Park

The Negev

Be'er
Sheva

Shivta

Mitzpe
Ramon

Makhtesh Ramon

▲ Mt Har
Ramon
(1035m)

Eilat
Aqaba
Red Sea

Taba

EGYPT
(Sinai)

Khan Younis

Rafah

Al Arish

Israel & the Palestinian Territories'
Top 20

Dome of the Rock

1 The first sight of Jerusalem's Dome of the Rock (p58) – its gold top shimmering above a turquoise-hued octagonal base – never fails to take your breath away. Perhaps that's what the unknown architects had in mind more than 1300 years ago when they set to work on this impossibly gorgeous building. The best view, some say, is from the Mount of Olives, but don't miss the chance to see it up close by taking an early-morning walk up to the Temple Mount/Al Haram Ash Sharif.

The Dead Sea

2 You pass a sign reading 'Sea Level' and then keep driving downhill, eventually catching glimpses of the cobalt-blue waters of the Dead Sea (p297), outlined by snow-white salt deposits, reddish-tan cliffs and tufts of dark-green vegetation. At the oasis of Ein Gedi you can hike through steep canyons to crystal-clear pools and tumbling waterfalls before climbing to the Judean Desert plateau above – or heading down to the seashore for a briny, invigorating dip. To the south around Mt Sodom, outdoor options include adventure cycling along dry riverbeds.

MARK MILLAN / 500PX ©

RUSLANZASHINSKY / GETTY IMAGES ©

S J TRAVEL PHOTO AND VIDEO / SHUTTERSTOCK ©

Tel Aviv Beaches

3 Head to Gordon Beach (p124) in Tel Aviv and grab your spot either on the sand or on a sun lounger and watch sunbathers bronze their bods while the more athletic swim, surf, sail and play intense games of *matkot* (beach racquetball). Pick one of the bars or restaurants that brings food and beers to the sand and enjoy some lunch, then as evening falls do as the locals do and sink a few ice-cold Goldstars as the sun sets over the warm, deep-blue waters of the Mediterranean.

Ramallah

4 Home to most of the West Bank's best budget accommodation, as well as the bulk of its bars and clubs, Ramallah (p274) is an excellent base for visitors and an exciting, cosmopolitan and vibrant city in its own right. Since 2017, the city has also hosted the excellent Yasser Arafat Museum, located in the compound where the late Palestinian leader spent his final years under Israeli siege. Also in the de facto Palestinian capital is a museum to 'Palestine's poet laurette' Mahmoud Darwish.

Western Wall

5 For centuries Jews have come to the 2000-year-old western retaining wall (p65) of the Temple Mount to pray and to mourn the destruction of the First and Second Temples. The Western Wall's enormous stones, worn smooth by countless caresses, have an almost magnetic power, drawing close the hands and foreheads of the faithful, who come in search of a deep, direct connection with God. Look closely between the cracks to see prayers that have been written down and slotted between the ancient stones.

Church of the Holy Sepulchre

6 Built on what St Helena – Constantine the Great's mother – believed to be the site of Jesus's crucifixion and burial, Jerusalem's Church of the Holy Sepulchre (p60) is the holiest place in the world for many Christians. In darkened chambers infused with incredible spirituality, a variety of Christian denominations keep alive here some of the oldest traditions of their faith. Visitors are welcome to join the parade of resplendently garbed clergy and simply dressed pilgrims as they shuffle through candlelit corridors redolent with incense.

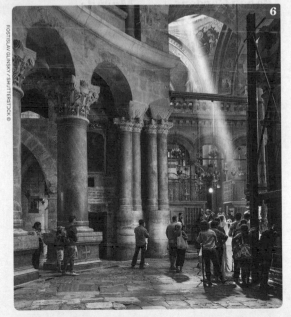

ROSTISLAV GLINSKY / SHUTTERSTOCK ©

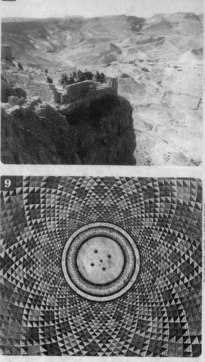

LEONID ANDRONOV / SHUTTERSTOCK ©

Baha'i Gardens

7 Fusing religious symbolism, breathtaking views and meticulous gardening, the 19 terraces of Haifa's Baha'i Gardens (p159) present visitors with a sublime expression of humankind's striving for beauty. The gold-domed Shrine of the Bab sits in the middle of the gardens, and tier after tier of geometric flower beds, immaculate lawns, sculptures and fountains cascade down the slopes of Mt Carmel, offering pilgrims and tourists alike a sense of incredible serenity. If you're fit enough, the view from the top over Haifa may take your mind off your burning calves.

Masada

8 The Romans had just destroyed Jerusalem when about a thousand Jewish Zealots took refuge on a remote hilltop overlooking the Dead Sea. As you peer down from their towering redoubt, you can still see the eight encircling Roman camps (p307), connected by a siege wall, making it easy to imagine the dramatic, tragic events that unfolded here in early 73 CE. Eventually the Romans built a ramp and breached the walls, but all they found were a handful of survivors – everyone else had committed suicide rather than submit to slavery.

Ancient Jericho

9 Walking among the ruins of ancient Jericho (p279) is an essential part of any traveller's itinerary in the West Bank, but there is a lot more here than the remains of the oldest city in the world (which is 10,000 years old according to some estimates). Take the time to check out the mosaics at Hisham's Palace and don't miss a cable-car ride to the epic Monastery of the Qurantul. Jericho is also home to one of the best youth hostels in the West Bank, Sami Youth Hostel. Above: Mosaic at Hisham's Palace (p280)

Tsfat (Safed)

10 The spirit of the 16th-century rabbis who turned Tsfat (p233) – the highest city in the Galilee, and in Israel – into the world's most important centre of Kabbalah (Jewish mysticism) lingers in the alleyways and ancient synagogues of the Synagogue Quarter and in the nearby Artists' Quarter, where intimate galleries offer creative, joyous Judaica (Jewish ritual objects). A Kabbalistic vibe is also palpable in the hillside cemetery, where some of Judaism's greatest sages – the Ari, Yitzhak Luria, Yosef Caro – lie buried.

Caesarea

11 Hugely impressive Roman ruins (p183) make it easy to imagine city life here two millennia ago, when crowds in the amphitheatre cheered wildly as slaves fought wild animals and the theatre hosted top musical talent – as it still does today. The remains of Herod's vast port, built to rival Alexandria, have been turned into one of the loveliest spots in Israel for a seaside meal or a cold beer. For a look underneath the harbour's turquoise waters, book an introductory scuba dive.

Akko (Acre)

12 The narrow alleys, domed mosques and colonnaded caravanserais of Akko's old city (p186) will transport you to the Ottoman era, but step underground and you're back in the time of the Crusaders, when this port city was the richest in the eastern Mediterranean and Marco Polo stopped here on his way to China. Wander through vaulted halls where Christian knights once dined, or follow in the footsteps of the Knights Templar through an amazing tunnel. The fishing port, lapped by the turquoise Mediterranean, is a great spot for a drink or a meal.

Nazareth

13 The village where Jesus grew up has also grown up and is now a bustling Arab city. In the Old City, alleyways are graced with churches commemorating the Annunciation and other New Testament events, and with Ottoman-era mansions. A new generation of restaurants has made Nazareth (p196) a star in Israel's gastronomic firmament. Alongside old-time specialities, served with traditional Arab hospitality, you can sample East-West 'fusion' dishes, such as fresh local herbs with artichoke hearts, or wild Galilean pine nuts with chopped beef.

Sea of Galilee

14. Before Judaism and Christianity became separate religions, Jesus and his earliest followers lived among the Jews of the Sea of Galilee (p219), in villages such as Capernaum – famed for its impressive synagogue – and Bethsaida. For breathtaking views of the area, head up the slope to the Mount of the Beatitudes, where Jesus delivered the Sermon on the Mount. A remarkably well-preserved wooden boat from the time of Jesus is on display at Kibbutz Ginosar. Swimming is possible at a variety of beaches, many linked by bike paths. Top right: Capernaum (p221)

Beit She'an

15. For a taste of the decadence and grandeur of Roman life in the centuries after Jesus, stroll through the column-lined Cardo (main boulevard), stone-paved streets, elaborate bathhouses and public toilets of ancient Beit She'an (p209), destroyed – like Pompeii – by a sudden natural cataclysm, in this case the great earthquake of 749 CE. The 7000-seat theatre and its arched entrances look much as they did in the 2nd century, when dramatic performances were staged here (these days it's used for concerts).

Makhtesh Ramon

16 Jerusalem is often described as 'ancient', but it's a veritable newcomer to the region when compared with this geological phenomenon in the midst of the Negev desert. An asymmetrical canyon (p324) that owes its existence to 200 million years of erosion, this majestic gash in the landscape features pink-hued rock formations, a sandstone floor studded with ammonite fossils, and local wildlife including oryx, gazelles, leopards, ibex and vultures. Sometimes windswept, always enigmatic, it's one of Israel's most underrated and compelling attractions.

Bethlehem

17 For nearly two millennia, pilgrims have been making their way to what Christians believe to be the birthplace of Jesus. In the streets around the Church of the Nativity (p267) and Manger Sq, you'll see ancient stone buildings and narrow alleyways that look much as they did centuries ago. But the past is only one side to Bethlehem: the city is also one of the best places in the West Bank to sample Palestinian food, both modern and traditional, and is home to a good few bars.

Tel Aviv Architecture

18 Jewish architects fleeing 1930s Germany brought a radical new style to Tel Aviv (p112): Bauhaus, also known as the International Style. Their legacy – some 4000 structures with clean horizontal lines, rounded balconies and 'thermometer' windows lighting the stairwells – constitutes the largest ensemble of Bauhaus buildings in the world, which is why the 'White City' was recognised as a Unesco World Heritage site in 2003. The preservation of Tel Aviv's Bauhaus gems is a work in progress – some have been gleamingly restored, but many others await TLC.

Israel Museum

19 Many museums claim to be 'world class', but here the accolade really does apply. Opened in 1965 and expanded in 2010, Israel's pre-eminent museum (p86) is one of two extraordinary cultural institutions in Jerusalem that owe their existence to a massive and mighty impressive program of international cultural philanthropy (the other is the Yad Vashem Holocaust museum). Exhibits include the Dead Sea Scrolls, a superb archaeological collection, rooms chock-full of Judaica and Jewish ethnographic displays, art galleries (Van Gogh! Monet! Renoir!) and a sculpture garden. Top right: Shrine of the Book (p87)

Nablus

20 The West Bank's second city (p286) sprawls between Mt Gerizim and Mt Ebal (known as the mountains of blessings and curses respectively). At its myriad market stalls, Palestinian shopkeepers hawk everything from fruit and vegetables to rich perfume and pungent spices. More sensory pleasure can be had at Al Aqsa *kunafeh* (warm, syrupy cheese-based pastry) stand, home of Nablus' most famous culinary delight, and at either of the city's two tourist-friendly hammams. On Mt Gerizim are ruins that the Samaritans consider to be the first piece of land created by God.

Need to Know

For more information, see Survival Guide (p407)

Currency

Israel and the Palestinian Territories: new Israeli shekel (NIS or ILS); Jordan and the West Bank: Jordanian dinar (JD or JOD)

Language

Israel: Hebrew and Arabic (official), English; Palestinian Territories, Jordan: Arabic (official), English

Visas

Israel and Jordan (at the Jordan River/Sheikh Hussein crossing) grant on-arrival visas to most nationalities.

Money

ATMs are widely available, except at border crossings with Jordan and Egypt. Credit cards almost universally accepted.

Mobile Phones

All but the remotest areas have excellent mobile and data coverage. Local prepaid SIM cards available.

Time

Two hours ahead of GMT/UTC.

When to Go

- Warm to hot summers, mild winters
- Dry climate
- Desert, dry climate

Tiberias
GO Oct–Jun

Tel Aviv
GO Oct–Jun

Jerusalem
GO Sep–Jun

Dead Sea
GO Oct–May

Eilat
GO Oct–Jun

High Season
(Jul & Aug)

➡ Warm in Jerusalem, muggy in Tel Aviv, infernal in Tiberias, Jericho, the Dead Sea and Eilat.

➡ Hotel prices spike and rooms are scarce.

➡ Jewish holidays of Passover, Rosh HaShanah and Sukkot are also high season.

Shoulder
(Sep–Nov & Mar–Jun)

➡ Sometimes rainy but more often warm and sunny.

➡ Spring wildflowers make March and April ideal for hiking.

Low Season
(Dec–Feb)

➡ Chilly or downright cold in the north, especially at higher elevations.

➡ Pilgrims flock to Bethlehem for Christmas.

➡ Popular time to head to the warmth of Eilat and the Dead Sea.

Useful Websites

Israel Nature & Parks Authority (www.parks.org.il) Nature reserves and archaeological sites.

Israel Ministry of Tourism (www.goisrael.com) Background, events and a virtual tour.

This Week in Palestine (www.thisweekinpalestine.com) Articles and cultural events.

ILH-Israel Hostels (www.hostels-israel.com) Independent hostels.

Lonely Planet (www.lonelyplanet.com/israel) Destination information, hotel bookings, traveller forum and more.

Important Numbers

Police	☑100
Ambulance	☑101
Fire	☑102
Israel country code	☑972
Palestinian Territories country codes	☑972 or 970

Exchange Rates

		NIS	JD
Australia	A$1	2.85	0.55
Canada	C$1	2.86	0.56
Euro zone	€1	4.31	0.87
Japan	¥100	3.29	0.65
NZ	NZ$1	2.60	0.51
UK	UK£1	4.64	0.98
USA	US$1	3.58	0.71

For current exchange rates see www.xe.com.

Daily Costs

Budget: Less than 350NIS

➡ Dorm bed: 100NIS

➡ Meals of falafel or hummus, and supermarket picnics: 100NIS (per day)

➡ Travel by bus or sherut (shared taxi): 50NIS

➡ Swim at free public beaches

Midrange: 350–600NIS

➡ Double room at midrange hotel (per person): 150–220NIS

➡ Meals at midrange restaurants: 100–150NIS

➡ Private taxi travel: 100–150NIS

Top end: More than 600NIS

➡ Luxury double room or B&B (per person): from 300NIS

➡ Meals at the finest restaurants: 300NIS

➡ Travel by midsize rental car or with guide: 400NIS

Opening Hours (Israel)

Banks 8.30am to 12.30pm, occasionally 4pm to 6.30pm Monday to Thursday. Many branches open on Sunday, some also open Friday morning.

Bars and clubs noon to midnight.

Post offices 8am to 12.30pm, occasionally 3.30pm to 6pm Sunday to Thursday, 8am to noon Friday. Earlier closing times during holidays and in July and August.

Restaurants 8am to 10pm, closed Shabbat. During Ramadan, almost all restaurants in Muslim areas, except in hotels, are closed during daylight hours.

Shopping malls 10am to 9.30pm Sunday to Thursday, until 2pm or 3pm on Friday.

Shops 9am to 6pm Sunday to Thursday, until 2pm or 3pm on Friday.

Arriving in Israel & the Palestinian Territories

Ben Gurion Airport (Tel Aviv) Taxi to Jerusalem/Tel Aviv (110/300NIS), shared sherut to Jerusalem (64NIS) or train to Tel Aviv (13.50NIS).

Jordan River/Sheikh Hussein Crossing (Jordan) Taxi to Beit She'an (40NIS, but you'll need to haggle hard).

Allenby/King Hussein Bridge (Jordan) Shared sherut to Jerusalem (35NIS, 30 minutes).

Yitzhak Rabin/Wadi Araba Crossing (Jordan) Taxi to Eilat (35NIS, 20 minutes).

Checkpoint 300 (Jerusalem-Bethlehem) Bus from near Damascus Gate, then taxi into Bethlehem (20NIS).

Qalandia Checkpoint (Jerusalem-Ramallah) Bus from near Jerusalem's Damascus Gate.

Getting Around

Israel has extensive public transport networks; for routes and schedules, head to www.bus.co.il. Buses and trains do not run on the Sabbath and Jewish holidays. The West Bank is served by frequent buses and shared taxis.

Bus Bus service is extensive.

Car A great way to tour the countryside, but parking can be a hassle in major cities.

Sherut (Servees) Service taxis leave when full and are generally quicker than buses on major routes.

Train Intercity and commuter lines run along the coast, to Ben Gurion Airport and up to Jerusalem.

For much more on **getting around**, see p422.

What's New

High-Speed Trains

A new line connecting Haifa and Beit She'an opened at the end of 2016, and a high-speed train between Jerusalem and Tel Aviv was due in the spring of 2018, slashing the distance between the two cities to just half an hour. There is also talk of a line that will connect Eilat with Tel Aviv.

Festivals

Israel has never been short of entertainment, and new offerings on the festival circuit include the Shutka Festival, bringing Balkan music to the Negev, and the Rising Spirit Festival, bringing dance music to the Golan.

Arab-Israeli Food

Arab-Israeli cuisine has become increasingly popular in cities such as Nazareth and Haifa, and the Galilee, with gourmet Palestinian and Levantine food cooked up by local celebrity chefs. (p228)

Ein Bokek Beach

The new public beach on the Dead Sea at Ein Bokek is one of only a few places where the water can be accessed in Israel (for free at least). Here you can also grab an essential post-swim shower. (p311)

Tel Aviv Tech

Always healthy, Tel Aviv's tech scene is now thriving with shared working spaces, including WeWork and Mindspace, opening in the coastal city in recent years.

Vegan Food

Once a rarity in Israel, vegan restaurants are popping up all over the country, many marked by 'Vegan-friendly' or 'HappyCow' (www.happycow.net) stickers.

Five-shekel Bakeries

Cheap bakeries where every item on the menu is just five shekels have become popular in Jerusalem in recent years and since spread to other cities – an excellent stop for a cheap lunch.

Apps

Smartphone apps in Israel for tracking everything from taxis to rocket attacks have taken Israel by storm. One essential app is Waze, which helps drivers navigate Israel-specific delays such as army checkpoints. Taxi booking apps have made life in Tel Aviv far easier.

Craft Beer

Like everywhere else in the world, Israel is craft-beer mad. Check out one of numerous breweries dotted throughout the country or a specific brew pub like Libira in Haifa. (p172)

Cycling

Not a year goes by in Israel without new cycle routes opening up, whether inside cities such as Tel Aviv or through deserts and forests. Check out Israel Ride for organised routes.

> For more recommendations and reviews, see lonelyplanet. com/israel and lonelyplanet. com/palestinian-territories.

If You Like...

Beaches

Hedonists preen and bronze along the Mediterranean, while at the Dead Sea they float and apply mud packs. At the Red Sea the most colourful creatures are under the water. The Sea of Galilee offers old-fashioned family fun.

Metzitzim Beach A family-friendly half-bay just south of the Tel Aviv Port dining and nightlife area. (p124)

Coral Beach Nature Reserve Eilat's best beach is a utopia for snorkellers. (p332)

Ein Bokek Beach Broad, clean and sandy – the Dead Sea's finest free beach. (p311)

Sea of Galilee Some are free, others come with fees and amenities, all are refreshing on a scorching summer's day. (p219)

Herzliya Fine Mediterranean sand between the marina and some of Israel's most expensive villas. (p151)

Hiking

Israel's hills and valleys burst into flower after the winter rains, making spring the ideal season to hit the hiking trails. Marked routes range from easy strolls for the whole family to multi-day treks requiring topographical maps.

Israel National Trail Israel's longest footpath links the Lebanese border with the Red Sea. (p33)

Ein Gedi Two spring-fed canyon oases are home to a profusion of plant and animal life. (p301)

Makhtesh Ramon Nature Reserve Hike through this vast desert crater, famous for its multicoloured sandstone. (p324)

Yehudiya Nature Reserve Canyons, waterfalls and pools on the western edge of the Golan. (p255)

Jesus Trail Walk from Nazareth to the Sea of Galilee. (p201)

Abraham Path Portions of this planned Iraq-to-Mecca route pass through Israel and the West Bank. (p265)

En Avdat National Park A hidden spring-fed oasis deep in the Negev Desert. (p321)

Wine Tasting

Grown here since biblical times, grapes thrive in Israel's varied microclimates, producing wines of surprising richness and subtlety that have won awards.

Zichron Ya'akov A winemaking centre since the late 1800s, this town has a typically Mediterranean climate. (p180)

Golan Heights High altitudes, a cool climate, well-drained volcanic soils and top-rate savoir faire. (p252)

Ramat Dalton High in the Upper Galilee, 'Israel's Tuscany' produces some of the country's top vintages. (p245)

Taybeh Winery Delicious reds and whites grown on a hillside near Ramallah. (p278)

Negev Highlands Hot daytime temperatures, cool nights and inspiration from the ancient Nabataeans. (p319)

Ancient Synagogues

Impressive ancient synagogues, some adorned with ornate stone carvings and gorgeous mosaics, have been unearthed all over the country.

Beit Alpha Synagogue Extraordinary mosaics depict a zodiac circle, a menorah, a shofar and a Torah ark. (p211)

Hamat Tverya National Park Mosaics in Tiberias feature two seven-branched menorahs and a zodiac. (p216)

Korazim National Park Decorated with exceptionally fine basalt carvings depicting floral and geometric designs. (p226)

Tzipori National Park Byzantine-era synagogue with an exceptional mosaic floor. (p205)

Bar'am National Park Solidly built of finely hewn limestone during the late Talmudic period. (p242)

New Testament Sites

The historical Jesus was born in Bethlehem, grew up in Nazareth, preached in Galilee and was crucified in Jerusalem. Many sites associated with his life and ministry have become places of Christian pilgrimage.

Church of the Holy Sepulchre The traditional site of Jesus's crucifixion, death and resurrection is Christendom's holiest site. (p60)

Church of the Nativity Believed to be the site of Jesus's birth since at least the 4th century. (p267)

Basilica of the Annunciation Where many Christians believe the Annunciation took place. (p196)

Capernaum Jesus's home base during most of his Galilean ministry. (p221)

Qasr Al Yahud Reputed site of Jesus's baptism by John. (p280)

Mt Tabor Traditional hilltop site of Jesus's Transfiguration. (p205)

Nightlife

Sip Galilee wine on the seashore, nurse a local microbrew in a dark pub, watch live music under the beams of an old warehouse, or dance the night away on the beach or inside a disco.

Tel Aviv Seafront cafes, fine dining, music venues and all-night boogying. (p112)

Ramallah Home to some of the West Bank's liveliest cafes and bars. (p274)

Cameri Theatre Stages contemporary Israeli plays in Tel Aviv, with English subtitles on some nights. (p145)

Haifa Haifa's trendy bars and clubs attract a young, studenty crowd. (p157)

Top: En Akev (p322), En Avdat National Park
Bottom: Basilica of the Annunciation (p196), Nazareth

Month by Month

TOP EVENTS

Purim, March

Midburn, May

Israel Festival, May/June

Gay Pride Parade, June

Lights in Jerusalem, June/July

Red Sea Jazz Festival, August

January

The coolest, wettest month of the year. Chilly in Jerusalem and the north; sometimes sunny along the coast; usually sunny at the Dead Sea and in Eilat. Occasional snow in Jerusalem and Tsfat. Low-season room prices.

Tu Bishvat

Tu Bishvat, otherwise known as the Jewish New Year for Trees, is celebrated worldwide, but here it has a special sense of renewal. People come to Israel's national parks from all over to plant trees and eat nuts and dried fruits. It makes a great excuse for hiking in the forests around Jerusalem. For tree-planting activities with the Keren Kayemet Fund, see www.

kkl-jnf.org (20–21 January 2019, 9–10 February 2020, 27–28 January 2021).

February

February marks the beginning of spring in Israel and the Palestinian Territories. Almond trees blossom with beautiful white flowers, and red poppies appear in the hills around Jerusalem. This month can still be cold and rainy, with the odd, unexpected desert wind.

Tel Aviv Marathon

A huge annual event held on a Friday morning in late February, the Tel Aviv Marathon takes over the city for a day. Tens of thousands of runners take part in this race along the seafront, main streets in town and HaYarkon Park. Many roads are closed for the event, so getting around town by foot or bicycle is advised.

March

Thanks to the winter rains, hillsides and valleys are green, wildflowers are in bloom and the hiking is great. Jerusalem can be cold and wet, but the weather on the coast is often perfect.

Purim

Purim is like no other Jewish festival. The emphasis is not on food but instead on fancy dress and alcohol. All over the country, people dress up in outlandish costumes and head out onto the streets. Particularly popular with children, the biggest Purim parade is in Holon, south of Tel Aviv. For adults, the best Purim street parties are held in Tel Aviv, usually around Kikar HaMedina or Florentin, where DJs blast the tunes to the crowds (20–21 March 2019, 9–10 March 2020, 25–26 February 2021).

April

Hillsides and valleys are alive with spring wildflowers – this is the best month for hiking. Accommodation prices spike during Passover and, near Christian sites, around Easter; coastal weather is still perfect.

Lailat Al Miraj

This holiday remembers the Prophet Muhammad's 'Night Journey' from Mecca to Jerusalem and from there to heaven. One of Islam's holiest days, thousands flock to the Dome of Rock in Jerusalem and the spot where Muhammad is believed to have left his footprint inside the Al Aqsa compound. Temple Mount/ Al Haram Ash Sharif is closed to visitors (2–3 April 2019, 21–22 March 2020, 10–11 March 2021).

◉ Passover

Passover (*Pesach* in Hebrew) is a week-long celebration of the Israelites' exodus from slavery in Egypt. Almost all shops and services are closed on the first and seventh days. Bread and other wheat products are forbidden and hidden behind plastic sheeting in supermarkets, though you'll find the odd Tel Aviv cafe still selling sandwiches. If you're in Israel, try to get invited to a Passover *seder* (ritual feast), where the Exodus story is read, songs are sung and much wine is drunk. Lots of Israelis go on holiday, so room prices skyrocket (19–26 April 2019, 8–15 April 2020, 27 March–3 April 2021).

◉ Good Friday

Commemorates Jesus's crucifixion in Jerusalem. This is an extremely busy but exciting time to be in Jerusalem. Just after midday, thousands of pilgrims pack the narrow streets for the Procession of the Way of the Cross on Via Dolorosa, and at night, you can watch the candlelit Funeral Procession at the Church of the Holy Sepulchre. Falls on the Friday before Easter Sunday (for Protestants and Catholics on 19 April 2019, 10 April 2020, 2 April 2021; for Orthodox Christians on 26 April 2019, 17 April 2020, 30 April 2021). (p60)

◉ Easter

Marks the resurrection of Jesus on the third day after the crucifixion and the end of Lent (40 days of penance and fasting). Easter is celebrated in the major churches in Jerusalem, Bethlehem and Nazareth. In Jerusalem, the most notable events are the parade of Armenian marching bands with bagpipes and drums on Easter Saturday and sunrise services at the Garden Tomb. Happens on 21 April 2019, 12 April 2020, 4 April 2021 for Catholics and Protestants, and on 28 April 2019, 19 April 2020, 2 May 2021 for Orthodox Christians.

🌠 Zorba Festival

Zorba (www.desertashram. co.il/en) is an annual five-day festival of music and spirituality in the Desert Ashram camp in the southern Negev desert. During the day, it offers a range of workshops from yoga, painting and meditation, plus activities for children, and as the sun sets, it turns into a huge dance party under the stars.

May

Sunny but not too hot, with nice long days. School is in session in Israel, Europe and North America, so few families are travelling. The last rains often fall in early May.

◉ Ramadan

Holy month of dawn-to-dusk fasting by Muslims. Celebratory break-fast meals are held after dark. Many shops and restaurants in East Jerusalem (including the Old City), the West Bank and Arab towns in Israel close during daylight hours, but sunset ushers in a lively atmosphere as Muslims head out to eat. In Arab areas, houses are decorated with lights, and there may be increased traffic as people travel to meet family in other towns (5 May to 4 June 2019, 23 April to 23 May 2020, 12 April to 11 May 2021).

✨ Israel Independence Day

Commemorating the declaration of the state of Israel in 1948, this is one of the major public holidays. Shops, restaurants and buses operate as normal. The day before Independence Day (8–9 May 2019, 28–29 April 2020, 14–15 April 2021) is Remembrance Day, when services are held around the country to honour fallen soldiers. The mood drastically changes at sunset as street parties and fireworks take place in all major city centres, such as Rabin Sq in Tel Aviv.

✨ DocAviv

Once a small fringe festival but now a major event for the city, DocAviv is the most comprehensive documentary film festival in the Middle East. Films covering a diverse range of topics are screened in English, Hebrew and Arabic at Tel Aviv's Cinematheque complex. (p132)

✨ Midburn

Midburn (www.midburn.org/en), Israel's answer to Burning Man, sees thousands of people descend on the Negev to celebrate art, music and radical self-expression. Like the original festival in the US, a temporary city is erected for six days in the desert near Sde Boker, where anything weird and wonderful is possible.

✨ Israel Festival

Three weeks of music, theatre and dance performances, some of them free, in and around Jerusalem in late May and early June. A great time to be in the Old City, where it feels like

there is a different band or performance of some sort around every narrow corner. (p91)

June

Long days and sunny, warm weather. The coast is not as hot and humid as in July and August. It rarely rains in June, and you can expect high-season room prices in some places.

◉ Eid Al Fitr

The end of Ramadan is marked by one to three days of celebrations with family and friends (4–5 June 2019, 23–24 May 2020, 12–13 May 2021). Most shops and services will be closed in Arab areas, as Muslims tend to go on holiday at this time.

◉ Shavu'ot

Shavu'ot is the last big Jewish festival before the summer kicks in. Travellers will notice a sharp rise in locals visiting the beaches and main tourist sites in Israel. Dairy products (including all kinds of cheesecake) are eaten, and there is a farmers market in Tel Aviv's Rabin Sq. As it's a religious festival that celebrates the Revelation at Mt Sinai, expect Shabbat-like closures of shops and public transport. Accommodation is scarce, and room prices are high (8–9 June 2019, 28–29 May 2020, 16–17 May 2021).

✨ Gay Pride Parade

In the second week of June, Tel Aviv is bedecked with rainbow flags for Israel's biggest and most colourful gay and lesbian extravaganza. Whether you are LGBT or not, Tel Aviv is an

incredible place for pride, with bars packed, the beach thumping and visitors from all over the world. (p132)

☆ White Night

Head to Tel Aviv for an all-night street party with free live music. Held each year on the last Thursday night of June, the White Night (*Laila Lavan* in Hebrew) sees the main streets, squares and beaches of Tel Aviv become impromptu stages for local bands, DJs, classical pianists and the occasional big act. (p132)

✨ Lights in Jerusalem

An extraordinary event in late June and early July, the totally free Lights in Jerusalem festival sees the ancient city lit up with colourful video projections and 3D light installations. Visitors can explore the Old City walls as they've never seen them before. (p92)

July

Sweltering along the coast but dry (albeit still hot) in Jerusalem. The warm sea also means it's jellyfish season. Sizzling at the Sea of Galilee, the Dead Sea and Eilat. Accommodation is pricey, especially in northern B&Bs.

✨ Jerusalem Film Festival

First held in 1984, the mid-July Jerusalem Film Festival features films and documentaries from all over the world every July. Alongside screenings are seminars, meet-and-greets and a lively awards ceremony. Book tickets well in advance. (p92)

☆ Opera in the Park

Nearly 100,000 people descend on Tel Aviv's Park HaYarkon at the height of the summer heat for a free performance by the Israeli Opera. Get there early to save a spot on the grassy hill, where thousands of locals picnic and drink wine while enjoying the performance.

August

The hottest month of the year. Sweltering along the coast, slightly cooler in Jerusalem, infernal at the Sea of Galilee, the Dead Sea and Eilat. Accommodation is expensive, especially in northern B&Bs.

◉ Eid Al Adha

During the Festival of the Sacrifice, Muslims commemorate the willingness of Ibrahim (Abraham) to sacrifice his son Ishmael. Marks the end of the hajj (annual pilgrimage to Mecca). Expect traffic jams if heading in or out of the West Bank, as many Palestinians are on holiday (11–15 August 2019, 30 July–3 August 2020, 20–24 July 2021).

🎷 Tsfat Klezmer Festival

Eastern European Jewish soul music high in the Galilee, when the town of Tsfat becomes a stage for musicians from across the country. Concerts begin at 9pm and go on well past midnight; camping is available for the three-night festival. (p239)

🎷 Red Sea Jazz Festival

Eilat sizzles with four nights of the coolest jazz during the last week of August. Now in its 31st year, the festival features artists such as Al McKay's Earth Wind & Fire Experience, Brian Blade & The Fellowship Band and dozens more. (p335)

🎷 Jerusalem Wine Festival

The Israel Museum opens its art garden up for four days each year for the Jerusalem Wine Festival. The event usually coincides with the Jewish calendar date of Tu B'Av (Israel's Valentine's Day). Tickets include unlimited samples from Israel's leading wineries and live music performances. (p92)

September

It's back to school for local children, so fewer families are travelling, though accommodation prices skyrocket at Rosh HaShanah and during Sukkot. Flights are often full around Rosh HaShanah and Yom Kippur.

◉ Rosh HaShanah

Rosh HaShanah, Jewish New Year, is a huge family event. Almost all shops and restaurants close from the first evening, so travellers need to prepare or get an invite to a family meal. Many locals go on holiday or visit folks out of town (29 September–1 October 2019, 18–20 September 2020, 6–8 September 2021). There are no big street parties, but in recent years, nightclubs such as Block in Tel Aviv have held special DJ nights. (p144)

October

The start of autumn, though most days are dry and sunny. Accommodation prices skyrocket if the Sukkot holiday season falls in this month. Can can be chilly in the north and in Jerusalem.

◉ Yom Kippur

The Day of Atonement is the most solemn day in the Jewish calendar. Traditionally a time for reflection and 25-hour fasting, synagogues are open all day for prayers, culminating in the blowing of the *shofar* (ram's horn). In Tel Aviv, it's a day where children cycle on the empty roads and tourists can experience a rare moment of silence without any cars. Yom Kippur has a huge effect on travellers: in Jewish areas, all businesses close (even the AM:PM stores), and transportation completely ceases. Make travel arrangements before or after, as Israel's airports and land borders close as well (8–9 October 2019, 27–28 September 2020, 15–16 September 2021).

◉ Sukkot

If you're in Israel during the week-long Feast of the Tabernacles, you'll see lots of foliage-roofed huts or tents temporarily erected on street corners, where you can stop by and even have a picnic. These tents represent the Israelites' 40 years of wandering in the desert. It's also the major autumn harvest festival, so the first and seventh days are public holidays with shop closures (13–20 October 2019, 2–9 October 2020, 20–27 September 2021).

The last day, Simhat Torah, marks the end of the Jews' annual cycle of reading the Torah and sees dancing in synagogues, particularly in Jerusalem. As Israelis are off work, many special exhibitions and musical festivals are held during Sukkot.

✨ Tamar Festival

One of Israel's biggest music festivals, Tamar is a gathering of some of the region's best-known acts each year during the Sukkot holiday week. Live concerts happen atop Masada late at night until sunrise with views over the red-rock desert and Dead Sea. Festival goers can camp or stay at one of the hotels along Ein Bokek beach. (p302)

✨ InDNegev Festival

InDNegev (nicknamed Indie Negev, www.ind negev.co.il) is a large annual music festival held in mid-October. Spread over three days in Mitzpe Gvulot, 30km west of Be'er Sheva in the Negev, more than 100 live gigs from Israel's best underground acts are on the roster. As the name suggests, there's plenty of indie rock bands but also hip hop, psychedelic, electronica and more.

🏃 Sovev TLV

The city of Tel Aviv goes bicycle-crazy for a few days leading up to Sovev TLV. The event culminates in a 42km bike ride that starts at dawn on a Friday morning in mid-October. Many inner-city roads and highways are closed for the main event, which welcomes cyclists and offers courses for children and skaters.

November

Sometimes rainy and chilly but frequently sunny, especially on the coast and at the Dead Sea and in Eilat. Jerusalem and highland areas can be cold and days are shorter. Low-season prices.

⊙ Yitzhak Rabin Memorial Day

A large peace rally at Tel Aviv's Rabin Sq every November commemorates the assassination of Prime Minister Yitzhak Rabin on 4 November 1995 by a far-right Israeli angered by the leader's efforts to secure peace with the Palestinians. The event has speeches in Hebrew, and music is performed. The tone is defiant but sad, as for many peace seems like a distant dream.

☆ Jerusalem International Oud Festival

This music festival is dedicated to the oud, a Middle Eastern guitar-like instrument. The Jerusalem International Oud Festival (www.confederationhouse.org) is held over 10 days at the Confederation House Centre for Ethnic Music and Poetry and other venues in the city.

December

Sometimes rainy and chilly but not infrequently sunny and even warm. Low-season accommodation prices except in Christian areas around Christmas, when rooms can be exceptionally hard to come by. Days are short.

⊙ Hanukkah

The Jewish Festival of Light is a beautiful time to visit. For eight nights, Jews celebrate by lighting candles using a nine-branched candelabra. In most city centres, there are candle-lighting services and bakeries are stocked full of doughnuts of all varieties. Shops and businesses are open throughout Hanukkah (2–10 December 2018, 22–30 December 2019, 10–18 December 2020).

✨ Holiday of the Holy Days

Haifa's Wadi Nisnas neighbourhood celebrates Hanukkah, Christmas and the season's Muslim holidays with art, children's plays and music over the last three weekends in December. Besides the concerts, usually held at Beit Hagefen Cultural Center, travellers can browse a unique Arab-style Christmas market. (p163)

⊙ Christmas

One of the most important pilgrimages for Christians is the journey to Bethlehem at Christmas. The main attraction is the Church of Nativity and the giant Christmas tree in Manger Sq. Elsewhere in Israel and the Palestinian Territories, it's a regular working day (unless on Shabbat), so all shops are open and transport is running. Pilgrims can also attend services at churches in Jerusalem and Nazareth. In recent years, some Israeli shops have put up Christmas decorations, and cafes sometimes serve mulled wine. Orthodox Christians celebrate in early January. (p128)

Itineraries

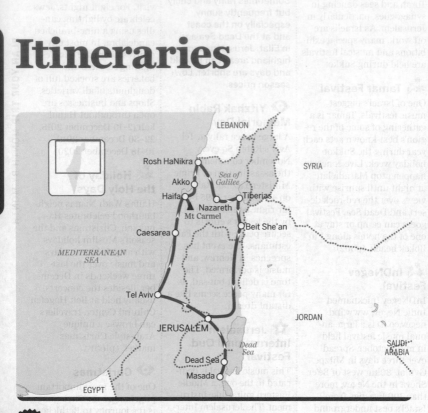

LEBANON

Rosh HaNikra

Sea of Galilee

Akko

Haifa

Nazareth

Mt Carmel

Tiberias

Caesarea

Beit She'an

MEDITERRANEAN SEA

Tel Aviv

JERUSALEM

JORDAN

Dead Sea

Dead Sea

Masada

EGYPT

SYRIA

SAUDI ARABIA

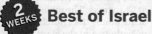

2 WEEKS **Best of Israel**

A whirlwind introduction to Israel's most important historical, religious and natural sights.

Spend your first four days in and around **Jerusalem**, including a couple of days wandering the alleys of the Old City, exploring the Western Wall and the adjacent Temple Mount/Al Haram Ash Sharif, and following the Via Dolorosa to the Church of the Holy Sepulchre. Break out your swimsuit and hiking shoes for a full-day excursion down to the **Dead Sea** and up the storied stronghold of **Masada**. Next, head to the Mediterranean coast for three days around **Tel Aviv**, dividing your time between strolling, cycling, lounging on the beach, fine dining and watching the world go by. Next, head up the coast for a peek at Roman-era **Caesarea** before pushing on to **Haifa**. Check out the views from atop Mt Carmel and the Baha'i Gardens before a day trip to the walled city of **Akko** and the grottoes of **Rosh HaNikra**. After a day in **Nazareth**, concluded with a tongue-tingling 'fusion' dinner, head to **Tiberias** for a day exploring the storied shores of the **Sea of Galilee**. On the drive back to Jerusalem, stop at the Roman ruins in **Beit She'an**.

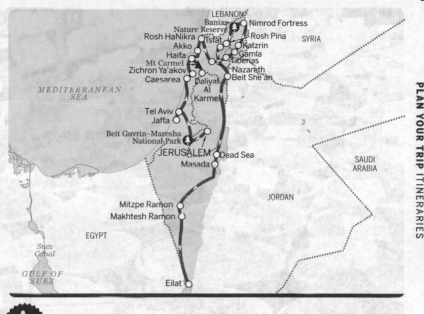

4 WEEKS Israeli Odyssey

Explore the best Israel has to offer from the Lebanese border to the Red Sea.

After four or five days in and around **Jerusalem**, including a couple of days exploring the Old City and a half-day visit to the Israel Museum, take a trip down to the wondrous caves at **Beit Guvrin–Maresha National Park**, stopping at a winery on the way. Next, stir it up in **Tel Aviv** for a few days, strolling along the beachfront promenade to historic **Jaffa**, biking along the Yarkon River and working on your Mediterranean tan. On your way north to **Haifa**, stop at the Roman ruins of **Caesarea** and the quaint old town of **Zichron Ya'akov**, famed for its vintage winery. After touring Haifa's sublime Baha'i Gardens, visit Mt Carmel and the Druze village of **Daliyat Al Karmel**. The next day, continue north to **Akko**, with its enchanting mixture of Crusader ruins and Ottoman relics. Next, go as far north as politics permit, to the subterranean grottoes of **Rosh HaNikra**, before heading inland for a couple of days in **Nazareth**, exploring Christian sites and dining on traditional Arab delicacies and East-West fusion dishes. Based in **Tiberias** for a couple of days, relax around the Sea of Galilee, combining ancient synagogues and Christian sites with quiet beaches and, perhaps, white-water rafting on the Jordan River. Loop east to the Golan Heights, visiting the hilltop ruins of **Gamla**, the Golan Archaeological Museum in **Katzrin** and towering **Nimrod Fortress**. Circle west via the lush vegetation of **Banias Nature Reserve** to the wetlands of the Hula Valley, beloved by migrating birds; the quaint, cobbled streets of **Rosh Pina**; and **Tsfat**, suffused with the spirituality of the Kabbalah (Jewish mysticism). Finally, head south through the Jordan Valley, strolling the colonnaded Roman thoroughfares of **Beit She'an**. After a starlit night on the shores of the **Dead Sea**, rise early to catch the sunrise from high atop **Masada**. Continue south into the Negev Desert for a day or two around **Mitzpe Ramon**, including a hike into **Makhtesh Ramon**. The last stop, for a spot of sea, sun and snorkelling, is **Eilat**.

Above: Spices, Mahane Yehuda Market (p81), Jerusalem

Left: Tomb of Yasser Arafat (p275), Ramallah

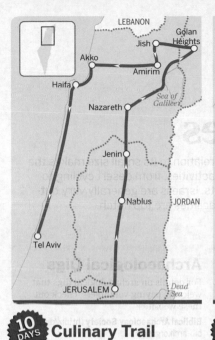

10 DAYS Culinary Trail

From simple hummus to Arab- and French-inspired gourmet meals, this tour of gastronomic hot spots takes in the Holy Land's most delicious dishes.

Start in **Jerusalem**, where contenders for the 'best hummus' title can be found in the Old City, and the foodie scene around the Mahane Yehuda produce market is worth exploring. For the country's best gooey-hot, cheesy-sweet *kunafeh* pastry, head north to the West Bank city of **Nablus** and then sample extra-virgin olive oil in **Jenin**. Make a beeline for **Nazareth**, where the buzzword is fusion. Continue your culinary pilgrimage on the shores of the **Sea of Galilee** with a lunch of St Peter's fish and then head to the **Golan Heights** for perfectly aged steak – paired, of course, with Golan-grown red wines. Looping west, stop in **Jish** for Galilee-style Arab cuisine or drop by the all-vegetarian settlement of **Amirim** for meat-free treats. Finally, head to the Mediterranean coast, sampling seafood and hummus in **Akko**, creative Arab cuisine in **Haifa**, and modern Israeli cuisine in **Tel Aviv**, where glamorous restaurants run by celebrity chefs vie for attention with traditional eateries serving hummus, falafel and the local fast-food favourite, *sabich*.

1 WEEK Welcome to the West Bank

This route takes you to the major Palestinian cities and sights.

Start off at the Yasser Arafat Museum in **Ramallah** before jumping on a sherut up to **Taybeh** to check out the West Bank's oldest brewery for an hour or two. Spend your first evening either bar-hopping in Ramallah or hanging out with the locals in the cafes close to Manara Sq. The next day jump on a bus to **Nablus** for a day of shopping in its enchanting market, scrubbing up at an ancient hammam and visiting the Samaritans atop **Mt Gerizim**. Up early the next day, grab a service to **Jenin** and check out the Freedom Theatre and then either head back to Ramallah or spend a day staying with farmers near the northern village of Burqi'in. Take a service to **Jericho** for a full day of sightseeing (perhaps two, if you want to see everything). End your trip with a couple of nights **Bethlehem**, with its winding lanes and ancient churches, and a day trip to the troubled city of **Hebron**, profoundly sacred to both Jews and Muslims.

Plan Your Trip
Activities

Israel's diverse topography in relation to its small size makes the country an excellent place for activities, from desert cycling to mountain hiking to water sports. Israelis are generally very outdoorsy, so infrastructure and facilities are top notch.

Top Short Hikes

Ein Gedi Nature Reserve (p301)

Thanks to year-round springs, two canyons overlooking the arid Dead Sea are lush with vegetation. A great place to spot ibex.

Banias Nature Reserve (p258)

Gushing springs, waterfalls and tree-shaded streams - plus a Roman palace complex.

Majrase Nature Reserve (p228)

Tramp through water and dense reeds in the Sea of Galilee's north-eastern corner.

Wadi Qelt (p281)

Hike through a spring-fed canyon to St George's Monastery, built into the cliff face in the 5th century.

Yehudiya Nature Reserve (p254)

A variety of day hikes, from two park entrances, take you through dramatic wadis on the Golan.

Montfort Castle (p192)

An impressive Crusader castle overlooking the Western Galilee and the Mediterranean.

Archaeological Digs

For details on archaeological digs that welcome paying volunteers, check out these websites:

Biblical Archaeology Society (http://digs.bib-arch.org/digs)

Hebrew University of Jerusalem (http://archaeology.huji.ac.il/excavations/excavations.asp)

Israeli Foreign Ministry (www.mfa.gov.il) Search for 'archaeological excavations'.

Birdwatching

The Mediterranean coast, the Galilee's Hula Valley and the Eilat area are some of the world's foremost venues for birding. Gatherings of twitchers (birdwatchers) include the Hula Valley Bird Festival and the Eilat Bird Festival (www.birds.org.il).

Cycling

Mountain biking has become hugely popular in Israel in recent years. Many cycling trails go through forests managed by the Jewish National Fund (www.kkl.org.il); for details, click 'Cycling Routes' on its website. Shvil Net (www.shvilnet.co.il) publishes Hebrew-language cycling guides that include detailed topographical maps.

Races are regularly held in locales such as the Dead Sea; many are sponsored by the Israel Cycling Federation (www.israel

cycling.org.il). There is also a variety of annual long-distance rides, such as the Arava Institute & Hazon Israel Ride (https://israelride.org) and the ALYN Hospital International Charity Bike Ride (www.alynactive.org). Israel Spokes (www.israelspokes.com) is a cycling organisation that runs group rides. Companies and cycling groups that organise rides and tours around Israel:

Cyclenix (www.cyclenix.com)

EcoBike Cycling Vacations (www.ecobikes.co.il)

Genesis Cycling (www.genesiscycling.com)

Israel Cycling Tours (www.israelcycling.com)

Israel Pedals (www.israelpedals.co.il)

Urban cycling is highly developed in Tel Aviv thanks to 130km of dedicated bike paths and lanes.

Hiking

With its unbelievably diverse terrain, Israel offers some truly superb hiking. The country gets little or no precipitation for at least half the year so Israelis can plan outings without having to worry about getting rained on. Whenever you hit the trails, don't forget to bring a hat and plenty of water, and plan to make it back before dark.

At many national parks and nature reserves (www.parks.org.il), basic walking maps with English text are handed out when you pay your admission fee. In other areas, the best maps to have – in part because they indicate the precise boundaries of minefields and live-fire zones used for army training – are the 1:50,000-scale topographical maps produced by the Society for the Protection of Nature in Israel (SPNI), sold at bookshops, SPNI field schools and some nature reserves.

The website www.tiuli.com has details in English on the hiking options around the country.

In the Palestinian Territories, for security reasons it's generally not a good idea to wander around the countryside unaccompanied. Consult local organisations such as Walk Palestine (www.walkpalestine.com) to find a guide and for up-to-date information on areas considered safe; Jericho and environs are usually a good bet.

Popular long-distance trails (from north to south):

Israel National Trail (Shvil Yisra'el; www.israelnationaltrail.com) Rambles for 940km through

Israel's least-populated and most-scenic areas, from Kibbutz Dan in the north to Taba on the Red Sea.

Sea-to-Sea Hike (Masa MiYam l'Yam; www.touristisrael.com/yam-lyam-hike) A 70km route from the Mediterranean (Achziv Beach) to the Sea of Galilee (near Ginnosar).

Jesus Trail (www.jesustrail.com) A 65km route from Nazareth's Church of the Annunciation to Capernaum, on the Sea of Galilee.

Gospel Trail (www.goisrael.com) The Israeli Ministry of Tourism's 63km-long version of the Jesus Trail runs from Nazareth's Mt Precipice to Capernaum, avoiding built-up areas.

Sea of Galilee Circuit (Shvil Sovev Kineret, Kinneret Trail) Circumnavigates the Sea of Galilee. Of the planned 60km, 45km have so far been marked with white-purple-white trail blazes.

Nativity Trail Stretches 160km from Nazareth to Bethlehem. Must be done with a guide – for details, contact Hijazi Travel (http://hijazih.wordpress.com), Walk Palestine (www.walkpalestine.com) or Green Olive Tours (www.toursinenglish.com).

Abraham Path (Masar Ibrahim Al Khalil; www.abrahampath.org) It may be many years before this trail is fully operational, but one section that's already open goes from Nabus via Jericho to Hebron.

Jerusalem Trail A 42km circuit that connects the Israel National Trail with Jerusalem, meandering through the Jerusalem Hills and around the Old City.

Scuba Diving

The Red Sea has some of the world's most spectacular and species-rich coral reefs. Good-value scuba courses and dive packages are available in Eilat, but the underwater life is a lot more dazzling across the Egyptian border in Sinai – however, the US, the UK and Australia recommend avoiding all travel to Sinai, except by air to Sharm El Sheikh. The waters of the Mediterranean aren't nearly as colourful, but at places like Caesarea you can explore Atlantis-like ancient ruins.

Windsurfing

Windsurfer Gal Fridman won Israel's only ever Olympic gold medal at the 2004 Athens games, so it comes as no surprise that the country offers world-class sailing conditions. Popular venues include the Mediterranean coast, the Red Sea and even the Sea of Galilee.

Plan Your Trip
Shabbat

For Jews both religious and nonreligious, Shabbat, the day of rest, is a time for family. Across the country, Israeli Jews will sit down together on Friday evening for the lighting of candles, the blessing of wine and a festive dinner. For tourists, the Shabbat can range from mild inconvenience (not being able to find anywhere to eat) to potential disaster (finding yourself unable to get public transport back to your accommodation). But it is also a memorable part of any visit.

The Laws of Shabbat

On the Sabbath, observant Jews refrain from performing 39 'creative activities', including lighting or extinguishing fires, using electricity, travelling by motorised vehicle, writing, cooking, baking, sewing, harvesting, doing business, handling money, and transporting objects between private and public spaces.

Airports & Public Transport

Israel's airports operate as usual on Shabbat. However, most inter- and intra-city buses and trains – including transport to/from the airports – cease operation from Friday afternoon until sometime on Saturday afternoon (bus services often begin several hours before sundown). Some local buses operate in mixed Jewish-Arab cities such as Haifa.

Border Crossings & West Bank Checkpoints

Checkpoints between Israel and the West Bank and border crossings with Jordan and Egypt remain open on Shabbat, but can be busy because of heavy traffic (particularly at Jalameh in the West Bank). The Allenby Crossing with Jordan closes early on Friday and Saturday afternoons so arrive early to avoid getting stuck on either side of the border.

Shabbat Observance

Shabbat begins 18 minutes before sundown on Friday (36 minutes in Jerusalem) and ends an hour after sundown on Saturday night (technically, until three stars can be seen in the heavens, according to Jewish law). During this time, the streets of many Israeli cities – including mostly secular Tel Aviv – have noticeably less traffic, but few Israeli Jews, except for the Orthodox, follow Sabbath prohibitions.

Because Israel is both religiously and culturally diverse, the impact of Shabbat varies from place to place. In Tel Aviv, Friday is one of the biggest nights for dining out, cultural events and bar-hopping. Majority-Arab cities and areas such as Nazareth, Akko and Jaffa are unaffected (although Friday is the Muslim day of rest so it can be quieter than usual), as is Arab East Jerusalem.

The best places to observe a traditional Shabbat are in Tsfat and Jerusalem, where it is ushered in by a long blast on a horn that reverberates throughout the city. It is a fascinating time to be in the Old City, where Haredi men and boys, with their black suits and ringlets, rush to the Western Wall in time for sunset prayers.

Because the impact of Shabbat isn't universal across the country, we've ranked how strictly Shabbat is observed in each region, with 5 being the most observant and 1 being the least.

Jerusalem

Shabbat is when the division between kosher and nonkosher (observant vs nonobservant) restaurants in Jerusalem really comes to the fore: the former will close their doors mid-afternoon on Friday and in some cases will not open until Sunday. This includes most eateries in West Jerusalem, including on Jaffa St, although there are some exceptions. In some hotels, the front desk will shut down (to avoid the restrictions on working and handling money) and staff may ask you to settle your bill before sunset on Friday.

There are no buses on Shabbat, although sheruts still run. Taxis are relatively plentiful but official fares are 25% higher than on weekdays, and drivers are even less likely than usual to use the meter. It is advisable to catch a cab in the east of the city to get a reasonable price. The Nesher service between Jerusalem and Ben Gurion Airport runs on Shabbat, as do the sheruts to Tel Aviv, but they leave from Jaffa St, to the west of the Jerusalem Hostel.

Be warned that driving through Orthodox neighbourhoods on Shabbat is not only ill-advised but can be dangerous: many of the streets are barricaded and youths have been known to throw stones at cars.

Score 5/5

Tel Aviv

Although the city is proudly secular, visitors to Tel Aviv will still feel the impact of Shabbat. The streets are noticeably quieter, and some bus lines are replaced with sheruts. Getting to the airport usually involves taking a taxi (250NIS), worth bearing in mind if you book a flight on a Saturday.

Most bars and restaurants remain open and Jaffa is almost entirely unaffected.

Score 2/5

North Coast

In Haifa and Akko, it is possible to not even notice Shabbat, with Haifa's nightlife pounding on regardless and Akko's large Muslim population meaning there is little interruption to services. On the other hand, Zichron Ya'akov will feel strongly observant, and the Holocaust memorials at Kibbutz Lohamei HaGeta'ot are closed.

Score 2/5

WHAT'S OPEN ON SHABBAT
••••••••••••••••••••••••••••••••••••
For practical information on how to handle Shabbat in Jerusalem and around the country, see p96 and p416.

Lower Galilee

Everything in Nazareth is open, but Tiberias mostly shuts down except for a handful of restaurants. All the tourist sites around the Sea of Galilee (Christian sites, national parks, nature reserves, paid-for and free beaches) are open, though beaches can be crowded. Heading to Nazareth for dinner on Friday night is a good option, but traffic jams can be a nightmare.

Score 3/5

Upper Galilee & Golan

Tsfat is completely closed on Shabbat, as are the wineries of the Dalton Plateau. Rosh Pina is mostly open and so are the nature reserves of the Hula Valley and along the Lebanese border. Most restaurants are also open. On the Golan, Katzrin is shut except for two restaurants, but the many nature reserves and almost all tourist sites are open, as are the Druze villages.

Score 3/5

Dead Sea

Virtually everything is open, including nature reserves, restaurants, shops and beaches.

Score 1/5

The Negev

Virtually everything in Eilat is open (Israelis hardly come to beach-party central to rest), and visitors are unlikely to notice Shabbat on the Red Sea coast. In Be'er Sheva, while most tourist sites are open, the city itself, including shops, public transport and some restaurants, is closed. Mitzpe Ramon has a fair bit to do on Friday night and Saturday. Nature reserves are open.

Score 2/5

Plan Your Trip
Crossing Borders

Israel may be at peace with two of its four Arab neighbours (Egypt and Jordan), but its border crossings are still heavily militarised and can be intimidating and challenging places to enter and exit the country. They can also be surreal: at the Allenby Bridge crossing with Jordan, for example, visitors take a bus across a desolate no-man's land, passing through minefields littered with bombed-out buildings and abandoned military vehicles. Most visitors receive a visa on arrival when entering Israel by land from Jordan and Egypt, but regulations going the other way (particularly entering Jordan from Israel) change frequently. It's always best to check with your hotel or hostel before turning up at the border. It is not possible or advisable to cross by air, land or sea into Lebanon or Syria.

Peaceful Borders

The borders between Israel and the two countries with which it has signed peace treaties, Egypt and Jordan, are open to both tourists and locals. Note that most Western governments advise against all travel to northern Sinai because of recent attacks against tourists by radical Islamists.

Blue, Purple & Green Lines

The UN-certified international border between Israel and Lebanon is known as the Blue Line; the Israeli-Syrian ceasefire line of 1974 is known as the Purple Line; and the pre-1967 border between Israel and the West Bank is known as the Green Line.

Border History

Britain and France determined the future borders of Palestine, Syria, Lebanon, Transjordan (Jordan) and Iraq in the secret Sykes-Picot Agreement of 1916.

Planning Your Crossing
Visas, Security & Entry Stamps

For details on visas to Israel and Jordan, see p418. For tips on Israeli security measures, see p408.

Israel no longer stamps tourists' passports – instead, it issues you with a playing-card-sized slip of paper. If you lose this slip, it can make life very difficult when leaving the country. Tourists with multiple stamps from Arab nations should expect a robust grilling when entering (and leaving) the country.

Land Crossings: Your Options

Israel–Jordan: Jordan River/Sheikh Hussein crossing, south of the Sea of Galilee; Yitzhak Rabin/Wadi Araba crossing, just north of Eilat/Aqaba

West Bank–Jordan: Allenby/King Hussein Bridge, just east of Jericho (controlled by Israel)

Israel–Egypt: Taba crossing, on the Red Sea just south of Eilat

Fees for land border crossings (not including visa fees, if applicable) are as follows:

COUNTRY	ARRIVAL	DEPARTURE
Israel	None	101NIS (175NIS at Allenby/King Hussein Bridge)
Sinai, Egypt	None	None
Rest of Egypt	US$25 visa fee	None
Jordan	JD42	JD8 at Jordan River/Sheikh Hussein, JD10 at Allenby/King Hussein

Border Closings

Yom Kippur All Israeli land borders and airports closed.

Eid Al Hijra/Muslim New Year Land crossings with Jordan closed.

Eid Al Adha Taba crossing with Egypt and Palestinian wing of the Allenby/King Hussein Bridge closed.

Ramadan All crossings may close early.

Northern Frontiers

Unless you're a UN peacekeeper, Israel's borders with Syria and Lebanon are shut tight.

To/From Jordan

While the two land crossings between Israel and Jordan are quick and efficient, the Allenby/King Hussein Bridge crossing between the Israeli-controlled West Bank and Jordan is not always as smooth.

Israeli exit fees can be paid at the border in a variety of currencies or by credit card. To save a handling fee of 5NIS, pay in advance at any Israeli post office (cash only) or online (http://borderpay.co.il).

Jordan River & Sheikh Hussein Crossing

Generally far less busy than Allenby/King Hussein Bridge, this crossing is in the Jordan Valley 8km east of Beit She'an, 30km south of the Sea of Galilee, 135km northeast of Tel Aviv and 90km northeast of Amman. Jordan issues on-arrival visas for many nationalities. The crossing is open from 7am to 8.30pm Sunday to Thursday and 8.30am to 6.30pm Friday and Saturday, but it's closed on Yom Kippur and Al Hijra (Muslim New Year).

The Israeli side lacks an ATM, but you can get a cash advance at the currency-exchange window, whenever the terminal is open.

For travellers heading to Jordan, getting through Israeli border formalities usually takes no more than half an hour. You then have to take a bus to cross to the Jordanian side of the river (walking across is forbidden).

Getting There & Away

Taxis that wait at the border can take you to Beit She'an (40NIS, but you'll need to haggle hard) and destinations around Israel, including Tiberias, Jerusalem and Tel Aviv. Kavim bus 16 connects Beit She'an with Kibbutz Ma'oz Haim (7NIS, 10 minutes, five or six daily Sunday to Friday), 3km west of the crossing.

On the Jordanian side, regular service taxis travel to/from Irbid's West bus station.

Nazarene Tours (p204) links Nazareth with Amman via the Jordan River/Sheikh Hussein crossing on Sunday, Tuesday, Thursday and Saturday. Departures are at 8.30am from the company's Nazareth office, near the Bank of Jerusalem and the Nazareth Hotel (not to be confused with the office of Nazarene Transport & Tourism in the city centre) and at 2pm from Amman's Royal Hotel (University St). Reserve by phone at least two days ahead.

Yitzhak Rabin & Wadi Araba Crossing

Located just 3km northeast of Eilat, this crossing is handy for trips to Aqaba, Petra and Wadi Rum. But Jordanian visas are no longer issued on arrival here, so get it in advance. Most hotels and hostels in Eilat offer day trips to Petra. The crossing is open 6.30am to 8pm Sunday to Thursday, and from 8am Friday and Saturday.

Getting There & Away

You can take a 10-minute taxi to/from Eilat (35NIS, 20 minutes). If you're coming by bus from the north (eg Jerusalem, Tel Aviv or the Dead Sea), it may be possible to get

BANNED: ISRAELI PASSPORT STAMPS

Arab and Muslim countries have widely varying policies on admitting travellers whose passports show evidence of their having visited Israel. Jordan and Egypt, with which Israel has peace treaties, have no problem at all, and the same goes for Turkey, Tunisia, Morocco and many of the Gulf emirates, as well as for Malaysia and Indonesia.

On the other hand, Lebanon and Iran have been known to put travellers on the next plane out if they find even circumstantial evidence of travel to Israel, for example a passport freshly issued in Amman or a chewing-gum wrapper written in Hebrew. Saudi Arabia is also known to be very strict on occasion.

If there's any chance you'll be heading to Arab or Muslim lands during the life of your passport, your best bet is to make sure that it shows no indication that you've been to Israel. Simplifying matters is the fact that Israel no longer stamps tourists' passports, instead issuing a loose-leaf visa, and Jordanian officials generally do the same. Egypt, however, is not so flexible, although an Egyptian stamp from Taba is as much a testament to your having visited Israel as an Israeli one. If you need to get from Eilat to Sinai without a Taba stamp, one option is to cross to Jordan and then take a ferry from Aqaba.

Some countries, including the United States, allow their citizens to carry more than one passport: one for Israel and its neighbours, the other for the rest of the world.

---

off on Rte 90 at the turn-off to the border or at Kibbutz Eilot, but from there it's 2km on foot through the desert (along Rte 109).

Once you're in Jordan, you can take a cab to Aqaba, from where you can catch a minibus for the 120km ride to Petra; minibuses leave when full between 6am and 7am and 11am and noon. Alternatively, bargain for a taxi all the way from the border to Petra.

Allenby & King Hussein Bridge

Linking the Israeli-controlled West Bank with Jordan, this busy crossing is 46km east of Jerusalem, 8km east of Jericho and 60km west of Amman. It is the only crossing that people with Palestinian Authority travel documents, including West Bank Palestinians, can use to travel to and from Jordan and the outside world, so traffic can be heavy, especially on Sunday, around holidays and on weekdays from 11am to 3pm.

Try to get to the border as early in the day as possible – times when tourists can cross may be limited and delays are common. Israeli citizens (including dual citizens) are not allowed to use this crossing.

Jordan does not issue on-arrival visas at the Allenby/King Hussein crossing – you'll have to arrange a visa in advance at

a Jordanian embassy, such as the one in Ramat Gan, near Tel Aviv. However, if your visit to the Palestinian Territories and/or Israel started in Jordan, you won't need a new visa to cross back into Jordan through Allenby/King Hussein Bridge, provided you do so within the period of validity of your Jordanian visa – just show your stamped exit slip.

The bus across the frontier costs JD7, plus JD1.50 per piece of luggage. Jordan has doubled the cost of Jordanian visas from JD30 to JD60.

Bring plenty of cash (Jordanian dinars are the most useful) and make sure you have small change. There are no ATMs, but both sides have exchange bureaux.

This crossing can be frustratingly delay-prone, especially if you're travelling into the West Bank and/or Israel. Chaotic queues, intrusive security, luggage X-rays (expect to be separated from your bags) and impatient officials are the norm; expect questions from Israeli security personnel if your passport has stamps from places such as Lebanon or you're headed to less touristed parts of the West Bank. There are separate processing areas for Palestinians and tourists.

The border is (officially) open from 8am to midnight Sunday to Thursday and 8am until 3pm on Friday and Saturday, but arrive after 6pm and you risk not being able to cross.

Getting There & Away

Shared taxis run by Abdo (02-628 3281) and Al Nijmeh (02-627 7466), most frequent before 11am, link the blue-and-white bus station opposite Jerusalem's Damascus Gate with the border (40NIS, 30 minutes); the charge per suitcase is 5NIS. Private taxis can cost as much as 300NIS, with hotel pick-up as an option.

Egged buses 948, 961 and 966 from West Jerusalem's Central Bus Station to Beit She'an (and points north) stop on Rte 90 at the turn-off to Allenby Bridge (12.50NIS, 40 minutes, about hourly). Walking the last few kilometres to the crossing is forbidden, so you'll have to take a taxi (50NIS).

For travel to/from Jerusalem, shuttle-bus services such as Amman 2 Jerusalem (www.amman2jerusalem.com) can ease some of the organisational pain (four-/seven-seater car transfer US$250/350), though the same time-consuming security and immigration checks apply.

To get to/from Amman's Abdali or South bus stations, you can take a *servees* (shared taxi) or minibus (JD8, 45 minutes); a taxi costs about JD22. JETT (www.jett.com.jo) runs a daily bus to the border from Abdali (JD8.50, one hour, departure at 7am).

To/From Egypt

Taba Crossing

Taba crossing, on the Red Sea 10km south of Eilat, is the only border post between Israel and Egypt that's open to tourists. The crossing is open 24 hours. There's an exchange bureau on the Egyptian side. Check travel advisories before taking this route as the security situation in Sinai is changeable.

You can get a 14-day, Sinai-only entry permit at the border, allowing you to visit Red Sea resorts stretching from Taba to Sharm El Sheikh, plus St Katherine's.

It's no longer possible to travel overland to Cairo via Sinai because of the security situation. One option is to travel to Sharm El Sheikh and then fly to Cairo, but you will need to get an Egyptian visa in advance, either at the Egyptian consulate in Eilat or the embassy in Tel Aviv.

Getting There & Away

Local bus 15 links Eilat's central bus station with the Taba crossing (30 minutes, hourly 8.10am to 9.10pm Sunday to Thursday, 8.10am to 4.10pm Friday and 9.10am to 7.10pm Saturday). On the way back to Eilat this line is known as bus 16; departures are 50 minutes later. A taxi costs about 30NIS.

Israeli Border Control

Israel's rigorous entrance procedures are a source of annoyance for some and a breeze for others. Don't be surprised if you are asked questions about your reasons for travelling, trips you've recently made, your occupation, your acquaintances in Israel and the Palestinian Territories, and possibly your religious or family background.

If you are meeting friends or family, you might want to have their full name, address and phone number handy (a letter confirming you're staying with them is ideal). If you have hotel reservations, a printout may help – or be completely superfluous.

If border officials suspect that you're coming to take part in pro-Palestinian political activities or if you have an Arab or Muslim name, they may ask some probing questions; on occasion they have even searched laptops. Sometimes they take an interest in passport stamps from places such as Lebanon or Iran, but often they don't. The one sure way to get grilled is to sound evasive or to contradict yourself – the security screeners are trained to try to trip you up. Whatever happens, remain calm and polite.

Israeli airport security is the strictest in the business. It unabashedly uses profiling, but not necessarily in the way you think. In 1986, a pregnant Irish woman, Anne Mary Murphy, almost boarded an El Al 747 in London with Semtex explosive hidden in her luggage – it had been placed there without her knowledge by her Jordanian boyfriend, Nezar Hindawi, who is still in prison in the UK. Ever since then, Israeli security officials – at Ben Gurion Airport and at airports abroad – have been on the lookout for anyone who might unwittingly serve as a suicide bomber, with young, unmarried Western women near the top of the profiling list.

Plan Your Trip
Travel with Children

Travelling with children is generally a breeze: the food's varied and tasty, the distances are short, there are child-friendly activities at every turn and the locals absolutely love children. For general tips, see Lonely Planet's Travel with Children.

Top Activities for Kids

Underwater Observatory Marine Park (p332) Take in scuba-quality reef views without getting wet; there's also a petting pool.

Rosh HaNikra (p193) Kids will love the cliffside cable car and the deep blues of the sea-battered grottoes.

Water Hikes A hike along – and through – a spring-fed stream is especially glorious during the hot, dry days of summer (try the Ein Gedi, Banias, Yehudiya and Majrase Nature Reserves).

Desert Cycling Tweens and teens will enjoy mountain biking through the desert along a dry wadi bed. There are many routes in the Judean Desert, but it is best to go on an organised tour.

Gan-Garoo Australian Park (p211) Pet kangaroos and feed lorikeets in the Jezreel Valley.

Mini Israel (p110) Midway between Jerusalem and Tel Aviv, this park shrinks 350 of Israel's best-known attractions to scale-model size.

Play Areas in Malls Most shopping malls have a *meeschakiya* (play area) for babies and toddlers – a great place to meet local kids (and on occasion their colds), especially on rainy days.

Israel for Kids

Israeli society is very family-oriented, so children are welcome pretty much everywhere. At every turn, your children will encounter local children out and about with their parents, especially on Saturday and Jewish holidays and in July and August.

Israel's beaches are usually clean and well equipped with cafes and even playgrounds. Make sure you slather on the sunblock, especially in summer, and stay out of the midday sun. (The Dead Sea, because it's so far below sea level, poses less risk of sunburn, but kids have to be extra careful to keep the water out of their eyes.)

Most nature reserves are fantastic for kids, and older children will enjoy the hikes – some gentle, some more challenging – on offer throughout the country. As park wheelchair access has improved in recent years, so has the ease of getting around with a stroller.

Tel Aviv, Jerusalem, Mitzpeh Ramon and Eilat offer a wide variety of things kids will love, though the alleys of Jerusalem's Old City are tough for strollers.

Planning

Disposable nappies (diapers; *chitulim*), wet wipes *(magavonim)*, baby formula *(formoola)*, baby bottles *(bakbukim l'tinok)* and pacifiers (dummies; *motzetzim*) are available in supermarkets and pharmacies, but prices are higher than in most Western countries. If your baby is picky, it pays to bring familiar powdered milk from home. Jars of baby food are also available, though in fewer flavours than in the UK or USA; organic baby food is available in some places. Medicines for children are easily obtained; almost all pharmacists speak English and are happy to assist.

A lightweight, collapsible (ie umbrella-style) stroller is convenient for travelling, but for the narrow cobblestone alleys and staircases in places such as Jerusalem's Old City, Akko and Tsfat it's a good idea to bring a wearable kid-carrier.

Sleeping

With the exception of a few B&Bs (tzim-merim) that cater exclusively to couples (eg in Rosh Pina), children are welcome to stay almost everywhere. In the vast majority of hotels, guesthouses and B&Bs, babies and toddlers can sleep in their parents' room for free (let management know if you'll need a cot); older children sometimes incur an extra charge. Most rooms in HI hostels and SPNI field schools have at least four beds, making them ideal for families.

Eating

Virtually all restaurants welcome children, with both the servers and other diners taking the disruptions of kiddie mealtime in their stride. Almost all have high chairs, and some also offer special kids' portions for child-sized prices. Most eateries, except the most upscale, are open all day long, so mealtimes can be flexible. Israeli breakfasts are famously copious and usually include at least a couple of breakfast cereals.

Many children take an instant liking to falafel, hummus, sabich (aubergine, boiled egg and potato, and salads in a pita) and shawarma, but as these fast foods (including their sauces and salads) are more likely than most meals to play host to microbes unknown back home, you might want to go easy, at least at first.

CHILDREN'S DISCOUNTS

At nature reserves, archaeological sites and museums, children generally get in free up to the age of four, and receive significant discounts from age five to 17 or 18. Young children qualify for moderate discounts on buses and trains. Places where the main clients are children, such as amusement parks, tend to charge full price from age three.

Travelling by Car

➡ Babies up to one year old (recommended through age two) or who weigh less than 9kg must sit in a rear-facing child seat (moshav b'tichut). A portable baby seat that can attach to both a car seat and a stroller is known in Hebrew as a salkal.

➡ For toddlers aged two and three (recommended through age four), a child seat (rear or forward facing) is required.

➡ Children up to age eight must sit on a booster seat.

➡ Car seats are not required for children who are riding in a taxi.

➡ A child seat must not be placed in any passenger seat equipped with an airbag.

The Palestinian Territories for Kids

Children receive a warm welcome in the West Bank and will often be whisked away to meet local children or treated to cakes and cookies. But travelling in the area has its own special challenges. Pushing a stroller around West Bank cities such as Ramallah, Nablus and Bethlehem can be laborious, and then there's the matter of getting through checkpoints.

Remember to bring your kids' passports as well as your own.

Regions at a Glance

Jerusalem

History
Religion
Culture

Old City

Explore the Old City's Christian, Armenian, Jewish and Muslim quarters, including the Citadel (Tower of David) and the Via Dolorosa.

Sacred Sites

The Western Wall, the Church of the Holy Sepulchre, the Dome of the Rock: Jerusalem's many religious sites could keep you busy for weeks.

Diversity

Ultra-Orthodox Jews wearing *shtreimels* (fur hats), secular Jews in short shorts and tank tops, Palestinian Muslims on their way to Al Aqsa Mosque, Christian clergy in long robes, feminist Orthodox Jews, gay-rights activists, free-spirited artists – you'll run into them all on Jerusalem's wonderfully diverse streets.

p46

Tel Aviv-Jaffa

Food
Shopping
Nightlife

Fine Dining

Yes, Tel Aviv has fantastic beaches, but the city's real passion is food. From falafel stalls and hummus joints to gelato parlours, European-style cafes, sushi bars and restaurants run by celebrity chefs, you won't go hungry here.

Boutiques

Tel Aviv has Israel's best shopping. Shop 'til your credit card groans in bazaars, modern malls and designer boutiques on Sheinken, Dizengoff and Shabazi Sts.

Nightlife

Head to uber-trendy Rothschild Boulevard or the bars and clubs that line Tel Aviv's dual arteries of Ben Gurion St and Dizengoff St to take in the city's world-famous nightlife.

p112

Haifa & the North Coast

History
Sacred Sites
Scenery

Ancient Ports

Caesarea was one of the great ports of antiquity and, 1000 years later, a walled Crusader stronghold. Akko, visited by Marco Polo on his way to China, is brimming with medieval and Ottoman history.

Spiritual Gardens

Haifa's incredible Baha'i Gardens are a spiritual highlight for people of all faiths. Elijah's Cave in Haifa is sacred to Jews, Christians and Muslims.

Sea Grottoes

The sea grottoes of Rosh HaNikra feature hues of blue you never knew existed. For stunning panoramas of the Mediterranean, head to Haifa's eagle's-eye promenade, high atop Mt Carmel.

p156

Lower Galilee & Sea of Galilee

Christianity
Archaeology
Food

Jesus's Ministry

Mary is said to have experienced the Annunciation in Nazareth, later Jesus's childhood home. It is believed that the Transfiguration took place at Mt Tabor, and Jesus spent much of his ministry around the Sea of Galilee.

Roman Sites

Top excavations include the Roman and Byzantine city of Beit She'an, ancient synagogues at Hamat Tverya, Korazim, Capernaum and Tzipori, and the Belvoir Crusader castle.

World Food

Nazareth is known for its East-West fusion cuisine, with many excellent restaurants in the Old City. The best is Al-Reda, in the grounds of a 200-year-old Ottoman-era mansion.

p195

Upper Galilee & Golan

Hiking
Bird Life
Wine

Wild Trails

Trails for all fitness levels abound, from the alpine summit of Mt Hermon (elevation 2000m) to the banks of the Jordan River (elevation -200m), and through the cliff-lined canyons of the Banias and Yehudlya Nature Reserves.

Migrations

Half a billion birds migrate through the Hula Valley – you can spot local and migrating species in the wetlands of the Hula Nature Reserve and Agamon HaHula, especially in spring and autumn.

Winery Visits

Many of the region's finest wineries, some of them boutique, can be visited at Katzrin, Ein Zivan and Odem on the Golan and on the Dalton Plateau northwest of Tsfat.

p231

West Bank

Shopping
Food
Religion

Bazaars

West Bank cities revolve around their lively bazaars. Shop for fresh fruit, taste sweets and haggle over handicrafts in the colourful markets of Hebron, Nablus and Bethlehem.

Local Cuisine

Once difficult to find in West Bank restaurants, traditional Palestinian food is now far more common on the menus in Bethlehem and Ramallah. If you're in Nablus, don't miss the famous local dessert, *kunafeh*.

Holy Sites

For Jews and Muslims, the Cave of Machpelah is an important pilgrimage site. Christian sites include the Church of the Nativity and the Mount of Temptation. No spiritual exploration of the West Bank is complete without a trip to the Samaritans of Mt Gerizim.

p261

The Gaza Strip

Inaccessible

Gaza is definitely not a tourism destination right now. Almost impossible to enter unless you're a journalist, aid worker or diplomat, this thin strip of land remains a danger zone. Although billions of dollars were pledged to reconstruct Gaza after the 2014 war with Israel, it is likely to be many years before the strip's heavily bombed cities and crippled infrastructure is capable of supporting its 1.8 million people – let alone tourists. Until then, its politically charged cities, beautiful beaches, historic sites and unique culture will remain off limits to all but a few.

p292

The Dead Sea

Beaches
Archaeology
Hiking

Dead Sea

Float on your back
while reading the
newspaper – a
cliché but eminently
doable in the hyper-
saline waters of the
Dead Sea, which
will relax your
nerves and soothe
your skin.

Masada

The Romans had
already destroyed
Jerusalem, but high
atop Masada, 1000
Jews resisted the
besieging might of
Legion X, in the end
preferring death to
slavery.

Desert Oases

Year-round springs
feed the dramatic
desert oases of
Ein Gedi and Ein
Bokek, where hikers
encounter cool
streams, luxuriant
vegetation, Edenic
waterfalls and rare
wildlife such as the
majestic Nubian
ibex.

p297

The Negev

Hiking
Diving
Archaeology

Desert Trails

The Negev Desert is
filled with life. Hike
through the wilder-
ness of Makhtesh
Ramon, Sde Boker
or Ein Avdat and
you'll likely spot
camels, ibexes and
soaring birds of
prey.

Coral Reefs

Keen to explore
coral reefs and
swim with schools
of tropical fish? Go
to the Red Sea to
snorkel or dive. Just
dip your head un-
derwater and enjoy
the show.

Nabataean Sites

Home to biblical ru-
ins such as Tel Be'er
Sheva and Tel Arad,
plus the ancient
Nabataean cities of
Avdat, Shivta and
Mamshit, the desert
is slowly revealing
its secrets.

p315

Petra

Ancient Ruins
Hiking
Stunning
Scenery

Rose-Red City

The ancient city
of Petra is a world
wonder. Allow
enough time to
reach the Treasury
in early morning,
picnic at a High
Place by noon,
watch the sunset
at the Monastery
and walk the Siq by
candlelight at night.

Desert Hikes

Petra has some of
the best and most
accessible hikes in
Jordan. Engaging a
local Bedouin guide
will help bring the
recent history of
Petra to life.

Natural Decor

Outrageously col-
ourful sandstone,
wind-eroded
escarpments and
oleander-trimmed
wadis make the
landscape of Petra
a worthy consort
of the ancient
architecture.

p341

On the Road

Jerusalem ירושלים القدس

02 / POP 865,721

Best Places to Eat

➡ Machneyuda (p101)

➡ Abu Shukri (p98)

➡ Modern (p102)

➡ Pinati (p99)

➡ Anna Cafe (p100)

Best Places to Stay

➡ American Colony Hotel (p94)

➡ Abraham Hostel (p94)

➡ Austrian Hospice (p92)

➡ Post Hostel (p95)

➡ YMCA Three Arches Hotel (p96)

Why Go?

Jerusalem's Old City is a spiritual lightning rod, sacred to Jews, Muslims and Christians. Wide-eyed with awe, pilgrims flood into the walled city to worship at locations linked to the very foundation of their faith. Church bells, Islamic calls to prayer and the shofar (Jewish ram's horn) electrify the air with a beguiling, if not harmonious, melody. Fragrances of incense, coffee and candle smoke drift through the thrumming souqs (markets). Muslim, Christian, Jewish and Armenian quarters each add their own spice, but Jerusalem's diversity grew from millennia of bloody sieges and transfers of power, leaving deep wounds.

West of the Old City is a treasury of world-class attractions, including the Israel Museum and Yad Vashem memorial, while bars and restaurants crowd Jerusalem's downtown. Meanwhile, East Jerusalem endures the strain of an uncertain outlook, claimed as capital of a future Palestinian state while Israeli settlements and building projects continue to be developed.

When to Go
Jerusalem

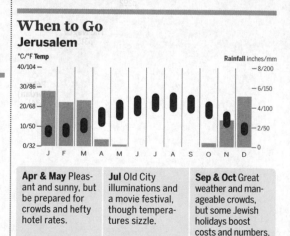

Apr & May Pleasant and sunny, but be prepared for crowds and hefty hotel rates.

Jul Old City illuminations and a movie festival, though temperatures sizzle.

Sep & Oct Great weather and manageable crowds, but some Jewish holidays boost costs and numbers.

History

First Temple

Jerusalem's earliest settlements surrounded the Gihon Spring, in the Kidron Valley just southeast of the present-day Jewish Quarter. A small Canaanite city is mentioned in Egyptian texts of the 20th century BCE, and biblical sources say it was conquered around 1000 BCE by the Israelites under King David, who made the city his capital.

Biblical sources say that, under King Solomon (David's son), the boundaries of the city were extended north to enclose the spur of land that is now Temple Mount/Al Haram Ash Sharif. The construction of the First Temple began around 950 BCE.

According to the Bible, some 17 years after Solomon's death, the 10 northern tribes of Israel split off to form the separate Kingdom of Israel and Jerusalem became the capital of the Kingdom of Judah. In 586 BCE Jerusalem fell to Nebuchadnezzar, king of Babylon, and both the city and the First Temple were destroyed; the people of Jerusalem were exiled to Babylonia. Three generations later, the king of Persia, Cyrus II, allowed them to return and even gave money for the reconstruction of the temple, in the hope that the exiled Judeans would become his allies.

Second Temple

The Second Temple was constructed from 516 BCE, and from 445 BCE Nehemiah, governor of Judah, led the decades-long rebuilding of the city walls.

The next notable stage in the history of Jerusalem came with Alexander the Great's conquest of the city in 332 BCE. On his death in 323 BCE, the Seleucids eventually took over until the Maccabean Revolt 30 years later. This launched the Hasmonean dynasty, which resanctified the Temple in 165 BCE after it had been desecrated by the Seleucids.

Romans

Under the leadership of General Pompey, Jerusalem was besieged and conquered by the Romans around 63 BCE. Then Herod the Great marched into Jerusalem in 37 BCE, to rule what would become the Roman province of Judaea (Iudaea). A tyrant's tyrant, Herod had his wife and children, as well as rabbis who opposed his rule, put to death. But he is also known for his ambitious construction and infrastructure projects, including expansion of Temple Mount.

Upon the death of Herod, the Romans resumed direct control, installing a procurator to administer the city. Pontius Pilate, who is best known for ordering the crucifixion of Jesus in Jerusalem around 30 CE, was the fifth procurator.

The Great Jewish Revolt against the Romans began in 66 CE, but after four years of conflict, the Roman general (and later emperor) Titus triumphed. Rome's Arch of Titus, with its famous frieze of Roman soldiers carrying off the contents of the Temple, was built to celebrate his victory.

With the Second Temple destroyed and Jerusalem burnt, many Jews became slaves and more fled into exile. The ruined city continued to serve as the administrative and military headquarters of the Roman province of Judea; meanwhile Jerusalem was also becoming an early centre for Christianity.

Around 130 CE, Emperor Hadrian decided to rebuild it – not as a Jewish city (he feared renewed Jewish national aspirations) but as a Roman city complete with pagan temples. This provoked the Jews' unsuccessful and bloody Bar Kochba Revolt (132–35 CE), led by Simon Bar Kochba. After the uprising was crushed, Jerusalem was renamed Aelia Capitolina and Judea became Syria Palaestina. The Romans rebuilt Jerusalem, but Jews were banned from the city.

Byzantines & Muslims

In 313 CE, the Western Roman Emperor, Constantine, and Eastern Roman Emperor, Licinius, met in Milan and agreed on an edict requiring tolerance of all previously persecuted religions. Eleven years after this, Constantine defeated Licinius in a civil war and became sole Emperor of the Roman Empire (later known as the Byzantine Empire). He legalised Christianity and his mother, Helena, visited the Holy Land in 326–28 CE searching for Christian holy places and claiming to have discovered the 'True Cross', on which Jesus was crucified. This sparked off the building of basilicas and churches, and the city quickly grew to the size it had been under Herod the Great.

The Byzantine Empire was defeated by the Persians, who conquered Jerusalem in 614 CE. Their rule lasted just 15 years before the Byzantines succeeded in retaking the city. That victory, however, was short-lived, for within another 10 years an Arab army, led by Caliph Omar under the banner of Islam, swept through Palestine. In 688 CE the Dome of the Rock was constructed on the site of the destroyed Temple. Under the early Islamic leaders, Jerusalem was a protected centre of pilgrimage for Jews and Christians

Jerusalem Highlights

❶ Temple Mount/ Al Haram Ash Sharif (p53) Gazing at the architectural magnificence built on this site sacred to Muslims and Jews.

❷ Western Wall (p65) Feeling the spiritual power of Judaism's holiest prayer site.

❸ Church of the Holy Sepulchre (p60) Marvelling at soaring vaults and candlelit chapels in one of Christianity's most sacred shrines.

❹ Mahane Yehuda Market (p81) Weaving between mounds of fresh fruit, halvah (sesame-paste nougat) stalls and hole-in-the-wall cafes.

❺ Yad Vashem (p88) Pondering tragedy, evil, human resilience and reconciliation.

❻ Israel Museum (p86) Admiring an extraordinary collection of art and artefacts.

❼ Muslim Quarter (p68) Wandering through the wonderfully aromatic and colourful souqs of the Old City.

❽ Citadel (p59) Learning about the city's long and eventful history at the Museum of the History of Jerusalem.

❾ Via Dolorosa (p60) Following in Jesus's footsteps.

❿ City of David (p75) Going underground in a tunnel-laced archaeological site.

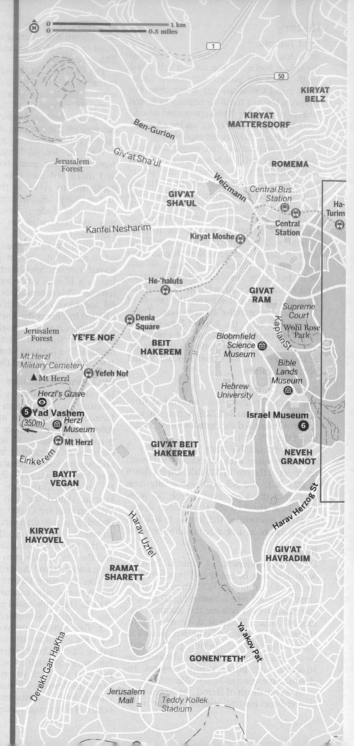

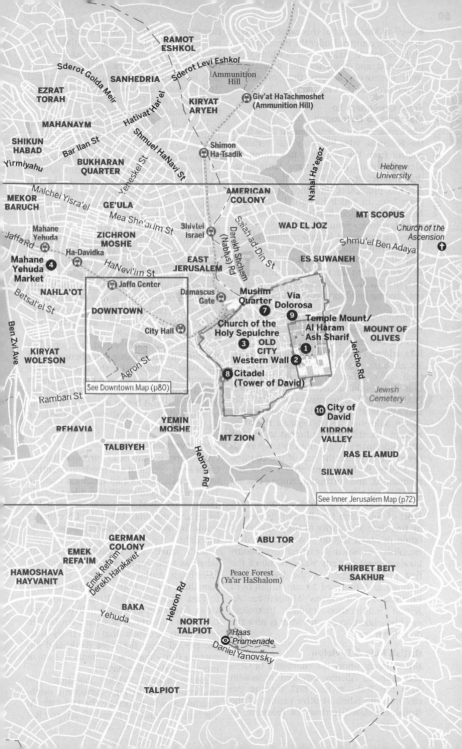

as well as Muslims, but this came to an end in the 10th century. Under the mercurial Fatimid Caliph Al Hakim, non-Muslims were persecuted and churches and synagogues were destroyed, actions that eventually helped provoke the Crusades.

From Crusaders to Mamluks to Ottomans

The Crusaders took Jerusalem in 1099 from the Fatimids, who had only just regained control from the Seljuks. After ruling for almost 90 years, the Christians' Latin Kingdom was defeated in 1187 by Saladin (Salah Ad Din), prompting the Third Crusade two years later, in which Richard I ('the Lionheart') of England fought to regain Holy Land territories from Saladin; Richard had many successes, but Jerusalem eluded him.

Meanwhile Saladin's efficient administration allowed Muslims and Jews to resettle in the city. From the 13th to the 16th centuries, the Mamluks constructed a number of outstanding buildings dedicated to religious study.

Although a Muslim academic centre, Jerusalem became a relative backwater. In 1517 the Ottoman Turks defeated the Mamluks, adding Palestine to their large empire. Yet although they too are remembered for their lack of efficiency in local administration, their initial impact on the city is still lauded today. The impressive Old City walls that were built in the mid-1500s by order of Sultan Süleyman, aka Süleyman the Magnificent, are still much admired today. But after Süleyman's reign, the city's rulers allowed the city, like the rest of the country, to decline. Buildings and streets were not maintained, and corruption among the authorities was rife.

In the wake of the Turkish sultan's 1856 Edict of Toleration for all religions, Jews – by this time a majority of the city's population of about 25,000 – were allowed to establish Jerusalem's earliest neighbourhoods beyond the city walls. Some of the first projects, begun in the 1860s, were inspired and financed by an Italian-born Englishman, Sir Moses Montefiore. As Jewish immigration rapidly increased, neighbourhoods grew into what is now the downtown area.

British Rule & Division

British forces under the command of General Edmund Allenby captured Jerusalem from the Turks in late 1917, turning the city into the administrative capital of the British-mandated territory of Palestine. In these times of fervent Arab and Jewish nationalism, the city became a hotbed of political tensions, and the city was the stage for terrorism and, occasionally, open warfare, between Jews and Arabs, among rival Arab factions (eg between supporters of the Nashashibi and Husseini families) and between Zionists and the British.

Under the United Nation's 1947 Partition Plan, Jerusalem was to be internationalised, kept separate from the two states – one Jewish, the other Arab – that the United Nations proposed Palestine be divided into. Accepted in principle by the Zionist leadership but rejected by the Arab and Palestinian leaderships, the Partition Plan was outpaced by events as the 1948 Arab–Israeli War engulfed the city and the country.

During the 1948 war, the Old City and East Jerusalem, along with the West Bank, were captured by Jordan, while the Jews held onto most of what now forms the downtown area. Patches of no man's land separated them, and the new State of Israel declared its part of Jerusalem as its capital.

For 19 years Jerusalem – like Berlin – was a divided city. Mandelbaum Gate, north of the western edge of the Old City, served as the only official crossing point between East and West Jerusalem for the few who were permitted to move between them. In the Six Day War of 1967, Israel captured the Old City from Jordan and began a massive program of restoration, refurbishment, landscaping and construction.

Controversial Capital

Controversy continues to surround the status of Jerusalem, and as a result all countries with embassies in Israel maintain them in Tel Aviv. In December 2017 President Donald Trump recognised the city as the capital of Israel and announced that the US embassy would be moved to Jerusalem at some future date.

Both Israelis and Palestinians see Jerusalem as their capital city. At present, the Palestinian Authority is based in nearby Ramallah, but it hopes one day to move to East Jerusalem. The Israeli government views Jerusalem as Israel's indivisible capital. It has constructed a separation barrier, on security grounds, that effectively seals the city off from the West Bank, and has continued to expand settlements in spite of international condemnation.

Approximately 300,000 Palestinian Jerusalemites live in East Jerusalem neighbourhoods, which include the Old City; At Tur on the Mount of Olives; Silwan and Ras

JERUSALEM IN...

Four Days

Start day one with an enriching overview of the Old City on the 8.45am **Sandemans** (p91) free walking tour. Wander around Saleh El Din St and then grab a bottle of water and queue for **Temple Mount/Al Haram Ash Sharif** (p53; there are two limited access periods per day for non-Muslims). Sample exceptional hummus at **Abu Shukri** (p98) and meander to the majestic **Church of the Holy Sepulchre** (p60). Leave the Old City by **Jaffa Gate** (p59) and bar-hop around Jaffa Rd.

On day two, approach the **Western Wall** (p65; pre-book for the Western Wall Tunnels tour). Head for lunch at the atmospheric **Armenian Tavern** (p98). Lose the afternoon in labyrinthine **Jewish Quarter** alleys, pausing for panoramic views from **Hurva Synagogue** (p68), and shopping at the **Muslim Quarter's** souqs.

On day three, board the light rail for a sobering trip to **Yad Vashem** (p88). Returning, disembark at **Mahane Yehuda Market** (p81) for a smorgasbord of Middle Eastern produce, and people-watching over iced coffee or beer. In the evening, attend the **sound-and-light show** at the **Citadel** (p59; you'll need to pre-book).

On day four, begin early at the expansive **Israel Museum** (p86), enjoying lunch at sleek **Modern** (p102) restaurant. Back in the centre, bus it to the **City of David** (p75) and tour its archaeological excavations. Toast your day in the bars around Horkanos St.

Al Amud near the southern edge of the Old City; and Sheikh Jarrah and Shuafat north of the Old City. A 2013 report on the Palestinian economy in East Jerusalem compiled by the United Nations Conference on Trade and Development stated that Israeli authorities pursue a policy of physical, political and economic segregation of East Jerusalem from the West Bank and that its residents face official impediments with regard to housing, education, employment, taxation and representation. The report also stated that East Jerusalem receives a disproportionately small share of municipal services such as water, sewerage, road maintenance, postal services and garbage collection.

Israel has greatly expanded the municipal borders of Jerusalem, annexing parts of the West Bank to the city and developing numerous Israeli settlement neighbourhoods in East Jerusalem. The annexation is widely seen as illegitimate and Palestinians, some Israelis and almost the entire international community criticise settlements as obstacles to the peace process. Around 200,000 Israelis live in East Jerusalem.

Various peace plans propose that the city be partitioned, with Jewish neighbourhoods in Israel and Arab neighbourhoods in Palestine. There is little agreement on exactly how to handle the Old City, especially Temple Mount/Al Haram Ash Sharif (p53), Judaism's holiest site and Islam's holiest site after Mecca and Medina.

Incidents of violent, often fatal, confrontation between extremist factions in both communities have been tragically common over recent years. After the killing of two Israeli police officers in July 2017, metal detectors were introduced at entry points to Al Aqsa Mosque (p59). Following widespread protests and violent clashes in which several Israelis and Palestinians were killed, the metal detectors were removed and proposed alternative security measures hotly debated. Controversial measures by the Israeli government to revoke the Jerusalem residency permits of Palestinian assailants (and even their families) have met with condemnation from the international community.

Cooperative initiatives between Israelis and Palestinians in Jerusalem – in areas as diverse as tourism, handicrafts, religious 'exchanges' and social clubs – attempt to heal wounds but the divide between the residents of East and West Jerusalem seems to be growing.

◎ Sights

Jerusalem's major sights can be broken down geographically, with the highest concentration in the Old City. East Jerusalem's downtown, the City of David and Mt Zion are all within easy walking distance of the Old City.

In West Jerusalem, the downtown area contains a number of sights, while others – including the Israel Museum, Mt Herzl, Yad Vashem and Ein Kerem – are spread out and are best reached by Jerusalem Light Rail (JLR), bus or taxi.

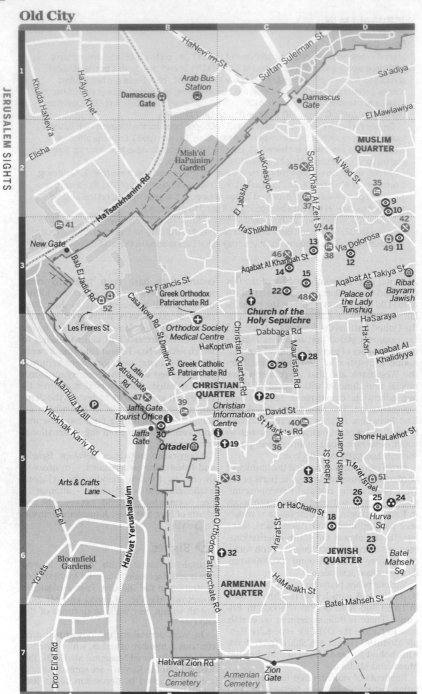

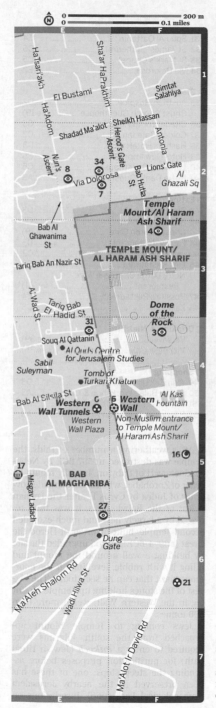

Old City

Busy roads roar around the Old City, but within its majestic walls life continues in many ways as it has done for centuries. Mornings crackle with energy as pilgrims from around the globe arrive to worship at the Western Wall (p65), Dome of the Rock (p58) or Church of the Holy Sepulchre (p60). Tourists explore its four quarters (Christian, Muslim, Jewish and Armenian) and barter (or think they are bartering!) in the souqs until the late afternoon. This is when the Old City is at its loveliest, its stone walls bathed in coppery sunlight. Before twilight the markets close, shops are shuttered, and only a few restaurants remain active.

There are four major entry points to Jerusalem's Old City: Jaffa Gate (p59), Damascus Gate (p68), Dung Gate (Old City) and Lions' (St Stephen's) Gate (p69). Most visitors enter through Jaffa Gate, which leads straight into the Christian and Armenian Quarters and from where the rest of the Old City is a short downhill walk. Damascus Gate leads straight into the Muslim Quarter; Lions' Gate to the start of the Via Dolorosa; and Dung Gate to the Jewish Quarter (Western Wall) and to the tourist entry for Temple Mount/Al Haram Ash Sharif. Inside, most of the streets are pedestrian only (and can be quite slippery!).

Temple Mount/ Al Haram Ash Sharif

★Temple Mount/
Al Haram Ash Sharif   RELIGIOUS SITE
(Map p52; ⊙8.30-11.30am & 1.30-2.30pm Sun-Thu Apr-Sep, 7.30-10am & 12.30-1.30pm Sun-Thu Oct-Mar) **FREE** There are few patches of ground as holy – or as disputed – as this one. Known to Muslims as Al Haram Ash Sharif (The Noble Sanctuary) and to Jews as Har HaBayit (Temple Mount), this elevated cyprus-planted plaza in the southeastern corner of the Old City is home to two of Islam's most sacred buildings – the Dome of the Rock (p58) and Al Aqsa Mosque (p59) – and is revered by Jews as the location of the First and Second Temples. Queue early and dress appropriately.

Note that opening hours for non-Muslims are limited and security checks are thorough.

The Talmud states that it was here, on a large slab of rock protruding from the ridge of Mt Moriah, that God gathered the earth that was used to form Adam and that

Old City

biblical figures such as Adam, Cain, Abel and Noah all performed ritual sacrifices. The most well-known account appears in Genesis (22:1–19): as a test of faith, Abraham was instructed by God to sacrifice his son Isaac, but at the 11th hour an angel appeared and a ram was sacrificed instead. The Bible states that David later erected an altar here (Samuel 24:18–25).

Although no archaeological traces have been found in situ (and it is unlikely that any will ever be found, as excavations are out of the question due to religious sensitivities), Solomon is said to have erected the First Temple on the site of David's altar. The Talmud says that Solomon's temple took 7½ years to complete, but for reasons unknown it stood unused for 13 years. When it was finally consecrated, Solomon placed the Ark of the Covenant inside and celebrated with a seven-day feast.

After weathering a number of raids, the Temple was destroyed in 587 BCE by Nebuchadnezzar II of Babylon. Initially rebuilt by order of Zorobabel, who had been made governor of Judea by Cyrus II after the Persian defeat of the Babylonians, it was then replaced by a largely new and much-extended Second Temple, built by order of Herod the Great (r 39–4 BCE). Herod upgraded the site by building a wall around the mount and filling it with rubble, levelling off the enormous plaza that can be seen today. The biggest of the stones holding up Temple Mount (eg in the Western Wall) weigh more than 500 tonnes.

Jews coming to Temple Mount approached from the south. Pilgrims were required to enter a *mikveh* (Jewish ritual bath) for purification purposes before ascending the steep steps; one of these has been preserved in the nearby Jerusalem Archaeological Park (p66). Inscriptions on stones warned that any gentile entering the mount would do so on pain of death. Only the high priest could enter the inner sanctum of the Temple; he did so once a year on Yom Kippur.

Any civic improvements made by Herod were for naught, however, as the Second Temple was almost totally destroyed by the Romans in 70 CE.

Despite the destruction they had wrought, the Romans, too, felt a spiritual affinity for Temple Mount and erected a temple to Zeus that was later turned into a Christian church.

Fast forward to the mid-7th century in Mecca, where the Prophet Muhammad is believed to have announced to his fellow Meccans that in a single night he had travelled to the 'farthest mosque' and led other prophets in prayers. Although Muhammad did not mention Jerusalem by name, the farthest mosque was interpreted to be at Al Haram Ash Sharif, thus making Jerusalem a holy place for Muslims (in fact, Islam's third-holiest place after Mecca and Medina). The site was left desolate under the Byzantines, for whom its religious significance was waning. But when Caliph Omar accepted the surrender of the city in 638 CE, his interest in Temple Mount was immediately obvious, and he set about erecting a simple mosque. This was later replaced by the Dome of the Rock (c 691 CE) and Al Aqsa Mosque (c 705–15 CE).

Below the surface of the pavement 19th-century explorers discovered more than 30 cisterns, some of them 15m to 20m deep and up to 50m long. Because of religious prohibitions, no one is is allowed into these today.

Immediately following the 1967 Six Day War, Israeli commander Moshe Dayan handed religious control of Temple Mount/ Al Haram Ash Sharif to Jerusalem's Muslim leaders. Their control of the mount has never gone down well with fervently nationalist Jews, and there have been a number of protests and violent incidents, including failed plots to blow up Muslim holy sites in the early 1980s. Many Orthodox Jewish authorities forbid Jews to visit Temple Mount because they may inadvertently tread on the sacred ground on which the Temple's innermost sanctuary once stood. Non-Muslim prayer remains forbidden.

For visitors uninvolved in the politics of the site, Temple Mount/Al Haram Ash Sharif is a place for silent awe – after the initial queues and security checks, that is. The flat, paved area spreads across 140 acres, fringed with attractive Mamluk buildings and with the Dome of the Rock positioned roughly in its centre. Walking around this storied site is a true contrast to the noise and congestion of the surrounding alleyways. Today, the compound is the biggest public space in East Jerusalem, so along with praying, children come to play football and adults come to relax.

ⓘ VISITING THE TEMPLE MOUNT/AL HARAM ASH SHARIF)

There are nine gates connecting Temple Mount/Al Haram Ash Sharif to the surrounding narrow streets, but non-Muslims are allowed to enter only at the Bab Al Maghariba/ Sha'ar HaMugrabim (Gate of the Moors), reached via a covered wooden walkway on the southern side of the Western Wall plaza. Line up early (if you don't, you're unlikely to get inside), and bear in mind that the site closes on Muslim holidays and is only open in the morning during Ramadan. You'll need to have your passport to make it through the security check. Note that it's possible to exit the enclosure by all open gates, not just Bab Al Maghariba.

Caretakers at the enclosure force any visitors deemed to be insufficiently clothed to purchase a shawl and wear it sarong-style. Needless to say, sarongs are overpriced and receipts are unavailable. To avoid being subjected to this, both men and women should wear long pants or skirts (definitely no shorts) and have their shoulders, elbows, backs and décolletages covered.

Bag searches at the entrance are thorough and anything deemed to be a non-Islamic religious object will not be allowed on the site. Don't bring religious texts or wear religious symbols; even tourist pamphlets about the Western Wall have been known to be confiscated.

It is not possible for non-Muslims to enter the Al Aqsa Mosque or the Dome of the Rock; trying to do so is both disrespectful and unwise.

Note that the enclosure is often closed to visitors during times of political unrest.

Al Haram Ash Sharif/ Temple Mount

A TOUR OF THE TEMPLE MOUNT

The Temple Mount encompasses multiple sites that span an area the size of one or two city blocks. A visit requires a little planning and may need to be accomplished over a couple of days.

Ascend the rickety wooden ramp at the Western Wall plaza to reach the Temple Mount at the Bab Al Maghariba (Gate of the Moors). Passing through the gate, continue ahead to view the understated facade of the ❶ **Al Aqsa Mosque** and the sumptuous detail of the ❷ **Dome of the Rock**. Take a slow turn around the Dome to admire its surrounding structures, including the curious ❸ **Dome of the Chain** and the elegant ❹ **Sabil of Qaitbay**. Don't miss the stunning view of the Mount of Olives seen through the stone arches known as the ❺ **Scales of Souls**.

Exit the Temple Mount at the ❻ **Bab Al Qattanin (Gate of Cotton Merchants)**; and return to the Western Wall plaza where you can spend some time at the ❼ **Western Wall** and visit the ❽ **Jerusalem Archaeological Park & Davidson Centre**.

TOP TIPS

➡ Opening hours for the Temple Mount are limited and lines can be long during the busy summer season, so queue early (gates open at 7.30am).

➡ An interesting way to reach the Jerusalem Archaeological Park is to take the underground tunnel that starts 600m away in the City of David (tickets for the park are sold at the City of David).

Scales of Souls
Muslims believe that scales will be hung from the column-supported arches to weigh the souls of the dead.

Bab Al Atim

Bab Al Ghawanima

Bab Al Nazir

Small Wall

❺
Dome of the Ascension

Bab Al Hadad

❻

Bab Al Silsila

Bab Al Qattanin (Gate of Cotton Merchants)
This is the most imposing of the Haram's gates. Make a point of departing through here into the Mamluk-era arcaded market of the Cotton Merchants (Souq Al Qattanin).

Sabil of Qaitbay
This three-tiered, 13m-high structure was built by Egyptians in 1482 as a charitable act to please Allah and features the only carved-stone dome outside Cairo.

Dome of the Rock

The crown jewel of Jerusalem's architectural heritage, the Dome famously contains the enormous foundation stone that Jews believe is the centre of the earth and Muslims say is the spot where Mohammed made his ascent.

Dome of the Chain

Some believe this structure was built as a model for the Dome of the Rock. Legend has it that Solomon hung a chain from the dome and those who swore falsely while holding it were struck by lightning.

Al Aqsa Mosque

One of the world's oldest mosques, Al Aqsa (the Furthest Mosque) is 75m long and has a capacity for more than 5000 worshippers. The Crusaders called it Solomon's Temple and used it as a royal palace and stable for their horses.

Bab Hitta

Solomon's Throne

2

3

Summer Pulpit

4

5

Dome of Learning

Mamluk Arcade

Bab Al Maghariba

Al Kas Fountain

Musala Marwani Mosque (Solomon's Stables)

1

7

Western Wall Plaza

8

Western Wall

Today it's the holiest prayer site on earth for Jews and an important cultural nexus on Shabbat, when Jews from around the city come to sing, dance and pray by the Wall.

Jerusalem Archaeological Park & Davidson Centre

This is the place to see Robinson's Arch, the steps that led up to the Temple Mount and ancient *mikvehs* (Jewish ritual baths) where pilgrims washed prior to entering the holy temple.

COMING CLEAN

Al Kas Fountain, located between Al Aqsa Mosque and the Dome of the Rock, is used for ritual washing before prayers.

TEMPLE MOUNT/AL HARAM ASH SHARIF: WHO'S IN CHARGE?

Administrative and security control of Temple Mount/Al Haram Ash Sharif is a touchy subject with both Jews and Muslims. After the 1967 Six Day War, Israel ceded administrative control of the Temple Mount compound to the Jordanian-controlled Jerusalem Islamic Waqf, a trust overseen by the Grand Mufti of Jerusalem and the Supreme Muslim Council.

Then, in 1994, Israel and Jordan signed the Wadi Araba Peace Treaty, under which Jordan was given administrative control of all Muslim sites in Jerusalem. This agreement is still in force, although the Israelis maintain overall security in the Muslim Quarter and on Temple Mount/Al Haram Ash Sharif. Under Israeli rules, non-Muslims are unable to pray in the compound (something that infuriates ultra-nationalistic Jews) and Muslim men under the age of 45 are denied access when the security situation is judged to be unsettled. West Bank Palestinians need an Israel-issued permit and are allowed easier access during Islamic holidays, and even at these times only males aged over 35 and women of all ages may enter. The short-lived introduction of Israeli metal detectors in July 2017 sparked an outcry and ignited deadly clashes, reviving the thorny issue of control over this holy site.

★ **Dome of the Rock**   RELIGIOUS SITE
(Map p52; Qubbet Al Sakhra) The jewel in the crown of Temple Mount/Al Haram Ash Sharif is the gold-plated Dome of the Rock, the enduring symbol of the city and one of the most photographed buildings on earth. As its name suggests, the dome covers a slab of stone sacred to both the Muslim and Jewish faiths. According to Jewish tradition, it was here that Abraham prepared to sacrifice his son. Islamic tradition has the Prophet Muhammad ascending to heaven from this spot.

Only Muslims can enter, though modestly attired visitors of all creeds can see it as part of their walk around the plaza.

The building was constructed between 688 and 691 CE under the patronage of the Umayyad caliph Abd al Malik. His motives were shrewd as well as pious – the caliph wanted to instil a sense of pride in the local Muslim population and keep them loyal to Islam. He also wanted to make a statement to Jews and Christians: Islam was both righteous and all-powerful, so it could build a structure more splendid than any Christian church on a location that was the location of the Jewish Holy of Holies, thus superseding both religions.

Abd Al Malik had his Byzantine architects take as their model the rotunda of the Holy Sepulchre. But not for the Muslims the dark, gloomy interiors or austere stone facades of the Christian structures; instead, their mosque was covered inside and out with a bright confection of mosaics and scrolled verses from the Quran, while the crowning dome was covered in solid gold that shone as a beacon for Islam.

A plaque was laid inside honouring Abd al Malik and giving the date of construc-tion. Two hundred years later the Abbasid caliph Al Mamun altered it to claim credit for himself, neglecting to amend the original date. Briefly repurposed as a church under the Crusaders, it promptly became an Islamic shrine again in the 12th century under Saladin. In 1545, Süleyman the Magnificent ordered that the much-weathered exterior mosaics be removed and replaced with tiles. These were again replaced during a major restoration in the 20th century. The original gold dome also disappeared long ago and the dome you see today is covered with 5000 gold plates donated by the late King Hussein of Jordan. The 80kg of gold cost the king US$8.2 million – he sold one of his homes in London to pay for it.

Essentially, what you see today is the building as conceived by Abd Al Malik. Inside, lying centrally under the 20m-high dome and ringed by a wooden fence, is the rock from which it is said Muhammad began his *miraj* (ascension to heaven). According to the Quran, Muhammad pushed the stone down with his foot, leaving a footprint on the rock (supposedly still visible in one corner). Jewish tradition also has it that this marks the centre of the world. Steps below the rock lead to a cave known as the Well of Souls, where according to medieval legends the voices of the dead are said to be heard falling into the river of paradise and on to eternity. The *mihrab* (niche indicating the direction of Mecca) in the sanctuary is said to be the oldest in the Islamic world.

Note that the whole Temple Mount/Al Haram Ash Sharif enclosure is often closed to visitors during times of political unrest.

Al Aqsa Mosque

MOSQUE

(Map p52) While the Dome of the Rock serves more as a shrine than a mosque, Al Aqsa is a functioning house of worship, accommodating up to 5000 worshippers at a time. The name Al Aqsa means 'farthest mosque', a reference to the journey Muhammad is believed to have made on his way to heaven to receive instructions from Allah. It's off-limits to non-Muslims, though tourists can admire it from the outside.

Originally built by order of the Umayyad caliph Al Walid (r 705–15 CE), Al Aqsa stands on what the Crusaders thought to be the site of the First Temple and what others believe was a marketplace on the edge of the Temple. Some Christians revere it as the location where Jesus turned over the tables and drove out the moneychangers (Matthew 21:13).

Rebuilt at least twice after earthquakes razed it, the mosque was converted into the residence of the kings of Jerusalem after the Crusaders took the city in 1099 CE. On the death of Baldwin II in 1131 the building was handed over to an order of soldier-monks, whose members soon began referring to themselves as the Templars after their new headquarters. The order added a number of extensions, including the still-remaining refectory along the south wall of the enclosure. The other Crusader structures were demolished by Saladin (Salah ad Din; 1137–93), the first of the Sunni Ayyubid dynasty, who added an intricately carved *mihrab* (prayer niche indicating the direction of Mecca).

Tragic events have repeatedly struck the mosque during the last century. King Abdullah of Jordan (1882–1951) was assassinated while attending Friday prayers here. In 1969, an arson attack by an Australian visitor irreparably damaged priceless religious objects. Israeli metal detectors were temporarily established at entrances to Al Aqsa in July 2017, as a response to the shooting of two Israeli police officers; this prompted bloody clashes and several deaths.

◉ Jaffa Gate

Jaffa Gate

GATE

(Map p52) One of the city's six original gates built by order of Süleyman the Magnificent, Jaffa Gate has an imposing entryway that bends at an abrupt right angle as you enter (a design feature to slow down charging enemies). The breach in the wall was made in 1898 to permit German Kaiser Wilhelm II to ride with full pomp into the city; these days taxis, rather than imperial parades, trundle in.

★ Citadel

MUSEUM

(Tower of David; Map p52; ☑ info 02-626-5333, tour reservations 02-626-5347; www.tod.org.il; Omar Ibn Al Khattab Sq; adult/student/child 40/30/18NIS; ⊙ 9am-4pm Sat-Thu, to 5pm Jul & Aug, 9am-2pm Fri) First things first: despite being referred to as the 'Tower of David', the citadel dominating views as you enter Jaffa Gate started life as a palace of Herod the Great. Also used by the Romans and Crusaders, the structure was extensively remodelled by the Mamluks and the Ottomans. Today it's home to the impressive **Museum of the History of Jerusalem**, which tells the city's story in a series of chronologically arranged exhibits starting in the 2nd millennium BCE and finishing in 1948.

A megalomaniacal builder, Herod furnished his palace with three enormous towers, the largest of which was reputedly modelled on the Lighthouse of Alexandria, one of the Seven Wonders of the Ancient World. The chiselled-block remains of one of the lesser towers still serve as the base of the Citadel's main keep. Following Herod's death the palace was used by the Roman procurators, so it's highly possible that this was the location where Pontius Pilate judged Jesus (John 18:28–19:16). The building was largely destroyed by Jewish rebels in 66 CE, and the Byzantines, who came along some 250 years later, mistook the mound of ruins for Mt Zion and presumed that this was David's palace – hence the name Tower of David. They constructed a new fortress on the site.

As Jerusalem changed hands, so too did possession of the Citadel, passing to the Muslim armies and then to the Crusaders, who added the moat. It took on much of its present form in 1310 under the Mamluk sultan Malik an-Nasir, with Süleyman the Magnificent making further additions between 1531 and 1538. Süleyman is responsible for the gate by which the Citadel is now entered. The Citadel's erroneous association with David continued in the 19th century, when Europeans mistook its Ottoman minaret for David's tower. It was on the Citadel steps that General Allenby accepted the surrender of the city on 9 December 1917, ending 400 years of rule by the Ottoman Turks.

The citadel offers 360-degree views across Jerusalem, as good a primer on the city as the museum exhibits; it's worth visiting when you first arrive in Jerusalem. A useful audio guide is available at no charge at the museum, or you can download a mobile app (iOS and Android) from the museum website before you arrive. There's a **cafe** (open

9am to 4pm Sunday to Thursday, to 2pm Friday) with wi-fi in the garden courtyard.

The popular **Night Spectacular** (adult/student and child 55/45NIS), a 45-minute sound-and-light show about the history of Jerusalem, is staged in the Citadel's internal courtyard and cloaks the ancient stone in vivid projections. It takes place twice per night, five nights per week; start times vary depending on what time the sun sets. See the website for details. The Night Spectacular is accessible to visitors with disabilities, as is some of the museum.

Ramparts Walk   HISTORIC SITE
(Map p52; adult/child 18/8NIS; ⊙ both sections 9am-4pm Sat-Thu Oct-Mar, to 5pm Apr-Sep, southern ramparts 9am-2pm Fri year-round) This shade-free walk atop the Old City ramparts can feel gruelling in the midday sun, but otherwise it's a popular way to survey this timeless city along two stretches of the old walls: from Jaffa Gate (p59) south to Dung Gate (p53), and from Jaffa Gate north and west to Lions' (St Stephen's) Gate (p69). Temple Mount's ramparts are off-limits. Buy tickets from the tourist office (p107) near Jaffa Gate.

One ticket allows access to both lengths of the ramparts within a single day. The northern stretch is closed on Friday, while the southerly ramparts can be strolled until 10pm during July and August. The section between Jaffa and Damascus Gates provides the best views, but lovelier panoramas (with protection from the sun) can be enjoyed from the Citadel (p59) and the Lutheran Church of the Redeemer (p65), as well as a number of hostel and restaurant roof terraces.

⊙ Christian Quarter

The 0.18-sq-km Christian Quarter is an attractive blend of narrow streets filled with souvenir shops, artisans' workshops, hospices, hostels and religious institutions belonging to 20 Christian denominations. At its centre stands the venerable Church of the Holy Sepulchre, one of the world's most important pilgrimage destinations. If you enter the Old City through Jaffa Gate, the first two streets to the left – Latin Patriarchate Rd and Greek Catholic Patriarchate Rd – lead to a quiet area around New Gate where the local Christian hierarchy resides.

Heading straight across Omar Ibn Al Khattab Sq from Jaffa Gate, you'll find a narrow passage that leads down David St, a tourist bazaar dedicated to filling up travellers' suitcases with overpriced tourist tat (bargain hard). About halfway down the street, to the left, is Christian Quarter Rd, another narrow passage lined with souvenir shops. Head down here to access the Church of the Holy Sepulchre.

David St ends at a chaotic intersection that leads on the left to Souq Khan Al Zeit St, one of the main thoroughfares of the Muslim Quarter, and on the right to the Cardo Maximus (p67), which leads into the Jewish Quarter. Continuing downhill via a dog-leg turn is Bab Al Silsila St, which leads to the Western Wall (p65) and the Al Silsila entrance to Temple Mount/Al Haram Ash Sharif (p53).

On Fridays, Franciscan fathers lead a cross-bearing procession along the route of the **Via Dolorosa** (Way of the Sorrows; Map p52), leaving the Pilgrims Reception Centre 300m inside St Stephen's (Lions') Gate at 3pm (October to March) or 4pm (April to September). Unfortunately, crowds make the experience less than satisfying, so you will be better off following the Via Dolorosa walking tour (p62) at a different time.

For a handy guide to Christian sites, see www.cicts.org.

★**Church of the Holy Sepulchre**   CHURCH
(Map p52; ☑ 02-626-7000; ⊙ 5am-9pm Easter-Sep (until 8pm Sun), 4am-7pm Oct-Easter) Four magnificent arches, their lintels richly decorated with Crusader crosses, herald the entrance to one of Christianity's most sacred sites. The church is believed by many Christians to be built over the biblical Calvary, or Golgotha, where Jesus was nailed to the cross, died and rose from the dead. For the past 16 centuries pilgrims have travelled far to worship here; expect crowds rather than quiet contemplation, unless you arrive early. The easiest access is via Christian Quarter Rd.

Tightly enclosed within a courtyard at the edge of the Christian and Muslim Quarters, the church appears to rise out of nowhere. It is perennially packed with tourists and pilgrims, largely because it incorporates the final five Stations of the Cross (stops 10 to 14 of the Via Dolorosa).

The decision to erect a church here is said to have been the result of lobbying on the part of Helena, the mother of Emperor Constantine, 300 years after the crucifixion. While on pilgrimage in the Holy City, she took note of Hadrian's pagan temple and shrine to Venus (built in 135 CE), and believed it had been placed here to thwart early Christians who had worshipped at the site. She joined the Bishop of Jerusalem, Macarius, in petitioning the emperor to

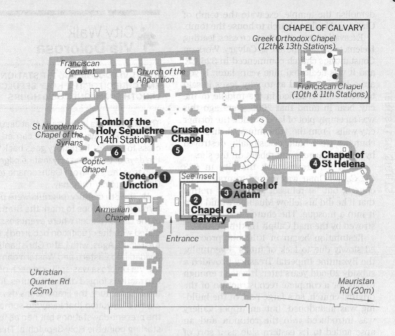

CHAPEL OF CALVARY
Greek Orthodox Chapel
(12th & 13th Stations)

Franciscan Chapel
(10th & 11th Stations)

Franciscan Convent
Church of the Apparition

St Nicodemus Chapel of the Syrians

Tomb of the Holy Sepulchre (14th Station)

Crusader Chapel **5**

Chapel of St Helena **4**

Coptic Chapel

Stone of Unction **1**

See Inset

Chapel of Adam **3**

Armenian Chapel

Chapel of Calvary **2**

Entrance

Christian Quarter Rd (25m)

Mauristan Rd (20m)

Church Tour
Church of the Holy Sepulchre

START STONE OF UNCTION
END TOMB OF THE HOLY SEPULCHRE
LENGTH ONE HOUR

On entering the church, you will see the **1 Stone of Unction** directly in front of you. This commemorates the place where the body of Jesus is said to have been anointed before burial. The current stone dates from 1810; emotional pilgrims often lie across it.

Climb the steep staircase directly to the right of the front entrance. The **2 Chapel of Calvary** at the top is divided into two naves. The 10th Station of the Cross, where Jesus is said to have been stripped of his clothes, is at the entrance to the first (Franciscan) chapel, and the 11th Station, where it is said that Jesus was nailed to the cross, is also there. The 12th Station, in the second (Greek Orthodox) chapel, is said to be the site of Jesus's crucifixion; at its centre is the Rock of Calvary, on which an altar has been built (a hole in the altar allows pilgrims to touch the rock below). Brisk attendants keep the line moving. The

13th Station, where the body of Jesus is said to have been taken down and handed to Mary, is located to the left of the altar.

Walk down the stairs facing the Greek Orthodox chapel and turn right. The **3 Chapel of Adam** to your right was the original burial place of the first two Crusader rulers, Godfrey de Bouillon and Baldwin I (their tombs were removed in 1809). Further on, down a staircase, is the **4 Chapel of St Helena**. Legend has it that Helena dug into the ground here and discovered three crosses – the True Cross was identified after a sick man touched the crosses and was healed by one of them.

Continue around the eastern wall of the central **5 Crusader Chapel** (undergoing renovation on our visit) to eventually reach a wooden rotunda housing the the 14th Station of the Cross, the **6 Tomb of the Holy Sepulchre**. Pilgrims queue to enter the tiny space and are given a few moments inside before being hurried along by a priest on door duty.

demolish the temple, excavate the tomb of Christ and build a church to house the tomb.

Excavations revealed three crosses, leading Helena to declare the site as Calvary. Work on Constantine's church commenced in 326 CE, and it was dedicated nine years later. If you are a little confused as to why Jesus is said to have been crucified in the middle of the city, bear in mind that 2000 years ago this was an empty plot of land outside the former city walls. From the 4th century, shrines and churches were built, occasionally destroyed by invading armies and rebuilt on the site.

When his armies took the city in 638 CE, Caliph Omar was invited to pray in the church, but he refused, generously noting that if he did his fellow Muslims would turn it into a mosque. The church was later destroyed by the mad Caliph Hakim in 1009.

Restoration began in 1010 but proceeded slowly due to lack of funds. Eventually, the Byzantine Imperial Treasury provided a subsidy 20-odd years later. It wasn't enough to pay for a complete reconstruction of the original church, so a large part of the building was abandoned, but an upper gallery was introduced into the rotunda and an apse added to its eastern side as a sort of compensation. This was the church that the Crusaders entered on 15 July 1099 as the new rulers of the city. They made significant alterations, and so the church as it exists today is more or less a Crusader structure of Byzantine origins. At that time the main entrance had two access points: the current entry door and another at the head of the Crusader-era staircase on the exterior, which led into a small chapel built to provide a ceremonial entrance to the site of Calvary. This chapel was walled up after the Crusaders' defeat in 1187; its carved lintel is now exhibited in the Rockefeller Museum (p79).

A fire in 1808 and an earthquake in 1927 caused extensive damage, and serial disagreements between the Christian factions who share ownership (Catholic, Greek Orthodox, Armenian Orthodox, Syrian, Coptic and Ethiopian) meant that it took until 1959 for a major repair program to be agreed upon. It also took decades to agree on the most recent renovations in 2016, when the tomb enjoyed a US$4-million injection of funding to stabilise the shrine. To avoid clashes over control of the church, the keys to it have been in the possession of the Nusseibehs, thought to be the oldest Muslim family in Jerusalem, since the days of Saladin, and it's still their job to unlock the doors each morning and secure them again at night.

🏃 City Walk
Via Dolorosa

START VIA DOLOROSA, 1ST STATION
END CHURCH OF THE HOLY SEPULCHRE
LENGTH 600M; ONE TO 1½ HOURS

The Via Dolorosa is the route that Jesus is believed to have taken as he carried his cross to Calvary. Its history goes back to the days of the earliest Byzantine pilgrims, who trod the path from Gethsemane to Calvary on Holy Thursday.

By the 8th century, pilgrims were performing ritual stops to mark the Stations of the Cross (places where events associated with the crucifixion occurred). In the Middle Ages, with Latin Christianity divided into Eastern and Western camps, the Via Dolorosa was split and each of the two factions forged different routes. In the 14th century, the Franciscans devised a walk of devotion that included some of the present-day stations but had as its starting point the Holy Sepulchre. This became the standard route for nearly two centuries, but it was eventually modified by the desire of European pilgrims to follow the order of events of the gospels, finishing at the believed site of the crucifixion. Today, the popularly recognised stations are marked by round metal plaques.

The ❶ **1st Station**, where Pontius Pilate is said to have condemned Jesus, is inside the working Islamic Al Omariyeh school near St Stephen's (Lions') Gate. The entrance is the brown door at the top of the ramp on the southern side of the Via Dolorosa, next to the Ecce Homo Arch. Entry is not always permitted (don't be surprised if you are asked to leave), and many pilgrim groups simply pray outside. Your best chance of entering is after school hours, from 3pm to 5pm.

The ❷ **2nd Station** is located across the street in the Franciscan Church of the Condemnation, to the left after you enter the church compound. This is where it is believed Jesus received the cross; the Chapel of the Flagellation to the right is where he is said to have been flogged. Built in 1929, the design on the chapel's domed ceiling over the altar incorporates the crown of thorns, and the windows around

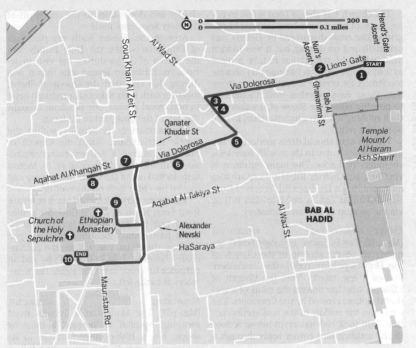

the altar show the mob who witnessed the event. For an extra 15NIS, a multimedia show tells the full story.

Continue down a short hill until you reach Al Wad St. Turn left on Al Wad and walk just a few steps to the ❸ **3rd Station**, where it is believed Jesus fell for the first time. The station is in the small chapel to the left of the entrance to the Armenian Catholic Patriarchate Hospice; walk down to the crypt. The ❹ **4th Station**, which marks the spot where Jesus is said to have faced his mother in the crowd of onlookers, is an area of paving stones found at the entrance to the chapel.

As Al Wad St continues south towards the Western Wall, the Via Dolorosa breaks off to climb to the west; right on the corner is the ❺ **5th Station**, where it is said that the Romans ordered Simon the Cyrene to help Jesus carry the cross. The station is marked by a Latin inscription above a stone door frame.

Further along the street, the ❻ **6th Station** is marked by a brown wooden door on the left. This is where Veronica is believed to have wiped Jesus's face with a cloth.

A bit further along you'll enter bustling Souq Khan Al Zeit St. The ❼ **7th Station**,

where it is believed Jesus fell for the second time, is a small chapel marked by signs on the wall of the souq. In the 1st century, this was the edge of the city and a gate led out to the countryside, a fact that supports the claim that the Church of the Holy Sepulchre is the genuine location of Jesus's crucifixion, burial and resurrection.

Cut straight across Souq Khan Al Zeit St and ascend Aqabat Al Khanqah St. A short distance up this street, embedded in the stone wall on the left and marked with a red sign, is the stone and Latin cross marking the ❽ **8th Station**, where it is said Jesus told some women to cry for themselves and their children, not for him.

Backtrack to Souq Khan Al Zeit St and turn right (south). Head up the stairway on your right and follow the path around to the Coptic church. The remains of a column in its door mark the ❾ **9th Station**, where it is believed Jesus fell for the third time.

Retrace your steps to the main street or head through the Ethiopian Monastery to reach the ❿ **Church of the Holy Sepulchre** (p60), home to the remaining five stations.

The church has always been home to relics, many of which have been coveted by pilgrims. The cross discovered by Helena was originally put on display, but it was hidden away when the temptation to take a piece as a memento (or even bite one off) became too strong for certain ardent pilgrims to resist. These days, pilgrims limit themselves to pouring oil on the Stone of Unction and then rubbing it off on a handkerchief to take home as a relic.

Visitors here should dress modestly – the guards refuse entry to those with bare legs, shoulders or backs. The main entrance is via Christian Quarter Rd, but there are also entry points via Dabbaga Rd (accessed from Souq Khan Al Zeit St or Mauristan Rd) or via the rooftop Ethiopian Monastery.

Ethiopian Monastery RELIGIOUS SITE
(Map p52; Deir Es Sultan; ⊘daylight hours) Sequestered on the rooftop of the Church of the Holy Sepulchre (p60), this monastery houses a few monks from the Church of Ethiopia who live among the ruins of a medieval cloister erected by the Crusaders. The cupola in the middle of the roof section admits light to St Helena's crypt below. A door in the southeastern corner leads through a chapel and downstairs to the courtyard of the Holy Sepulchre itself.

Around the cloister walls are paintings of Ethiopian saints, the Holy Family and the Queen of Sheba during her visit to Jerusalem. Ethiopian legend tells that it was during this visit that the Queen of Sheba, together with King Solomon, produced heirs to both royal houses, one of whom brought the Ark of the Covenant to Ethiopia.

The monastery is actually within the Coptic Patriarchate. When the Church of Ethiopia became a self-governing organisation in the early 20th century, its monks were kicked out of the Coptic monastery and moved into huts here on the rooftop.

The monastery is reached via a staircase from Souq Khan Al Zeit St (look for a juice stand and the ramshackle entrance to famous pastry shop Zalatimo; p98). As you walk up the stairs, you will see the patriarchate chapel straight in front of you and an entrance to a cistern on the right. The monastery is to the left.

Mauristan HISTORIC SITE
(Map p52) The Mauristan, a Persian word meaning 'hospital' or 'hospice', is lined by shops, has a 19th-century fountain in its centre and leads to two souqs (one full of

JERUSALEM SYNDROME

Each year millions of tourists descend on Jerusalem to walk in the footsteps of the prophets, and a handful come away from the journey thinking they *are* the prophets. This medically recognised ailment, called Jerusalem Syndrome, occurs when visitors become overwhelmed by the metaphysical significance of the Holy City.

The ailment was first documented in the 1930s by Jerusalem psychiatrist Dr Heinz Herman. Sufferers of all faiths have been documented, with cases spiking around Passover and Christmas. Their symptoms tend to begin with anxiety and disorientation, culminating with delusions of divine purpose. Over recent years visitors have believed they were the biblical Samson, a pregnant Virgin Mary, and too many horsemen of the Apocalypse to count.

Most sufferers are harmless, occupying themselves with impromptu sermons and erratic behaviour. But in 1969, in the most serious case so far, a mentally ill Australian Christian set fire to Al Aqsa Mosque, believing he was on a mission from God to clear Temple Mount/Al Haram Ash Sharif of non-Christian buildings to prepare for the Messiah's Second Coming.

Doctors estimate that Jerusalem Syndrome affects more than 50 people each year. Many have mental health conditions but some – referred to as 'type III' – have no recorded history of mental illness.

Most of the afflicted are taken to the state psychiatric ward, Kfar Shaul, on the outskirts of West Jerusalem. Patients are monitored and usually sent straight home, provided they are no risk to themselves or others.

The time-trapped quality of Jerusalem's Old City is thought to act as a trigger, imparting a sense of profundity in visitors passing through. Neuroscientists explain the phenomenon as an overstimulated limbic system, where the emotional centre of the brain goes into overdrive. The syndrome usually subsides as quickly as it arose, usually with the patient's departure from Jerusalem.

butcher shops) that link to David St. The plaza was an urban market under the Romans. The Crusaders established churches with attached hospices here; one of them, St John the Baptist, still exists, although its hospice is long gone. Today it's kept lively by colourful clothing and souvenir stalls.

Lutheran Church of the Redeemer   CHURCH
(Map p52; ☑02-626-6800; Mauristan Rd; crypt & tower adult/child under 14yr 15/7.50NIS; ⊙10am-5pm Mon-Sat) The square bell tower of this Protestant church, the second built in Jerusalem, has ornamented the Old City's skyline since 1898. The Church of the Redeemer was commissioned by Kaiser Wilhelm II and built on the site of an 11th-century sanctuary. It's worth buying a ticket to access the tower – hold your breath: its winding stairs are a squeeze – for 360-degree views over the Old City.

Christ Church   CHURCH
(Map p52; ☑02-627-7727; www.cmj-israel.org; Omar ibn al Khattab Sq) Completed in 1849, this Gothic Anglican church has stained-glass windows decorated in Jewish symbols, and it faces Temple Mount/Al Haram Ash Sharif, as do all of Jerusalem's synagogues. The blurring of Jewish and Christian lines is deliberate: Christ Church's founders were inspired by the belief that Jews would return to what was then Turkish Palestine, and that many would acknowledge Jesus Christ as the Messiah. Today, Christ Church is careful to insist that its mission is interfaith dialogue rather than wholesale conversion.

English-language Sunday services take place at 9.30am and 7pm.

◉ Jewish Quarter

The Jewish Quarter (0.12 sq km) was heavily shelled by the Arab Legion during the 1948 fighting and later demolished by the Jordanians, so most of the quarter had to be totally rebuilt after 1967. Living among the pleasant stone streets, which spider from central **Hurva Sq** (Map p52), are more than 2000 inhabitants – around one-10th of the quarter's population in the early 20th century. A number of interesting archaeological finds have been uncovered below street level, some of which are said to date back to the time of the First Temple (around 1000 to 586 BCE); see some of the best exhibited in the Herodian Quarter Museum (p67).

The Jewish Quarter is the one of the best parts of the Old City for wheelchair users to explore; there's a marked trail beginning

at the car park south of Hurva Sq. Enquire at the tourist office (p107) for further information. For more information about Jewish sites, see www.rova-yehudi.org.il.

★**Western Wall**   JEWISH SITE
(Map p52; www.thekotel.org; ⊙24hr) The air is electric at Judaism's holiest prayer site, where worshippers recite scriptures, lay their hands on 2000-year-old stone and utter impassioned prayers. The Western Wall supports the outer portion of Temple Mount, upon which the Second Temple once stood. Its builders could never have fathomed that their creation would become a religious shrine of such magnitude. Rabbinical texts maintain that the Shechina (divine presence) never deserted the Wall. It's open to members of all faiths 365 days a year; dress modestly.

Following the destruction of the Temple in 70 CE, Jews were sent into exile and the Temple's precise location was lost. Upon the Jews' return they purposely avoided Temple Mount, fearing that they might step on the Holy of Holies: the ancient inner sanctum of the Temple, barred to all except the high priest. Instead they began praying at this remaining element of the original structure.

The Wall became a place of pilgrimage during the Ottoman period and Jews would come to mourn and lament the destruction of the Temple – that's why the site is also known as the Wailing Wall, a name that Jews tend to avoid. At this time, houses were pressed right up to it, leaving just a narrow alley for prayer.

In 1948 the Jews lost access to the Wall when the Old City was taken by the Jordanians and the population of the Jewish Quarter was expelled. Nineteen years later, when Israeli paratroopers stormed in during the Six Day War, they fought their way directly here and their first action on securing the Old City was to bulldoze the neighbouring Arab houses to create the sloping plaza that exists today.

The area immediately in front of the Wall now operates as a great open-air synagogue, exerting a pull discernible even to nonreligious visitors. It's divided into two areas: a small southern section for women and a much larger northern section for men. Here, black-garbed ultra-Orthodox men rock backwards and forwards on their heels, bobbing their heads in prayer, occasionally breaking off to press themselves against the Wall and kiss the stones. Women face greater challenges to freely worship at the

JEWISH QUARTER COMBO TICKET

Save cash on four attractions in the Jewish Quarter with a **combined ticket** (adult/child 60/45NIS). The ticket covers entry to the Herodian Quarter Museum, Hurva Synagogue (p68), Burnt House and Archaeological Park & Davidson Centre. Buy the ticket at any of the sites; it's valid for 48 hours.

Wall, whose Orthodox custodians remain deeply uncomfortable with female voices reciting here. Mooted plans for a mixed-sex worship area at the Wall remain hotly debated. One movement, Women of the Wall, opposes the segregation of genders and the smaller space given to women at the Wall, and holds prayers and protests. The issue of gender segregation at the Wall is particularly important to American Jews, though it rarely registers for Israeli Jews. The Israeli government recently backtracked on a much-lauded and sought-after compromise to create an egalitarian prayer space.

To celebrate the arrival of Shabbat, there is always a large crowd at sunset on Friday. The plaza is a popular site for bar mitzvahs, which are usually held on Shabbat or on Monday and Thursday mornings. This is a great time to visit, as the area is alive with families singing and dancing as they approach.

Notice the different styles of stonework composing the Wall. The huge lower layers are made up of Herodian-era stones, while the stones above them date from the time of the construction of the Al Aqsa Mosque. Also visible at close quarters are the wads of paper stuffed into the cracks in between the stones. Some Jews believe that prayers and petitions inserted between the stones have a better-than-average chance of being answered. Prayers posted into the crevices are never thrown away; periodically the Wall attendants will gather all the notes that have fallen onto the prayer plaza, and they are interred along with the next deceased person to be buried on the Mount of Olives. Prayers are also accepted in digital form: an online form on the Kotel website allows you to send a prayer to be printed by the Wall custodians and taken there.

On the men's side of the Wall a narrow passage runs under Wilson's Arch, which was once used by priests to enter the Temple. Look down the two illuminated shafts to get an idea of the Wall's original height. Women are not permitted into this area.

Modest dress is recommended for visitors (if in doubt, cover from shoulders to knees), and a head covering is required for men (paper kippot are available if you don't have one). Photography is prohibited on Shabbat; point your lens respectfully at other times. If you're visiting on Shabbat and want to plant a paper prayer in the Wall, write it before you arrive as writing isn't permitted in the plaza during this time.

★**Western Wall Tunnels**   ARCHAEOLOGICAL SITE
(Map p52; ☑02-627-1333; www.thekotel.org; adult/student & child 35/19NIS; ⊗ by tour only 8.30am-5pm) Guided tours of the Western Wall tunnels offer an entirely different perspective on Herod's epic construction: visitors are led along a 488m passage following the northern extension of the Wall. The excavated tunnel burrows down to the original street level, allowing visitors to tread the same ground as the ancients. Guides give fascinating insights into how these mighty walls were erected – Herod's stone masons chiselled blocks up to 14m long and weighing almost 600 tons apiece.

You can only visit the tunnels on guided tours (Hebrew and English multiple times a day; French, Spanish and Russian less regularly in summer only), which take about 75 minutes and must be booked in advance. These tours are very popular and fill up fast – try to book at least a week ahead.

**Jerusalem Archaeological
Park & Davidson Centre**   HISTORIC SITE
(Map p52; ☑02-627-7550; www.archpark.org.il; adult/student & child 30/16NIS, guided tour 160NIS, audio guide 5NIS; ⊗ 8am-5pm Sun-Thu, to 2pm Fri) Pore over the remains of streets, columns, gates, walls, plazas and *mikve'ot* (Jewish ritual baths) at this archaeological site near Dung Gate (p53). An audio guide is a helpful accompaniment at the open-air portion of the site; meanwhile, video presentations (in Hebrew and English) at the visitor centre give an overview of the main excavations in the 1970s and reconstruct the site as it looked 2000 years ago.

As you enter, you'll notice on your left the remains of what was once Jerusalem's main street, which ran the length of the Temple's Western Wall. Note the remains of an arch protruding from Herod's wall. This is **Robinson's Arch** (named after a 19th-century American explorer), once part of a bridge that connected Temple Mount and the city's main commercial area. The piles of stones on the Herodian-era street below the arch are said to be part of the Western Wall, hurled down by Roman soldiers as they destroyed the Temple in 70 CE. Nearby is a divided staircase leading down to a *mikveh* from the same period; one side was for bathers on the way to the bath and the other was for bathers who had been purified.

At the back of the site (ie closest to the Mount of Olives) are the **Huldah Gates**, also built in the Second Temple period. These originally gave access to tunnels that led up to the Temple Mount enclosure. Nearby is a largely reconstructed staircase that was once the main entry for pilgrims headed to Temple Mount. Near the bottom of the steps you can spot more *mikve'ot*.

Book in advance for guided tours.

Cardo Maximus   HISTORIC SITE
(Map p52) Originally, the Cardo was a 22m-wide colonnaded avenue flanked by roofed arcades, the main artery of Roman and Byzantine Jerusalem. Following excavations in 1975, a southern swath of the broad avenue, 2.5m below present street level, was reconstructed, while another section has been reshaped into an arcade full of art boutiques.

At one time the Cardo would have run the whole breadth of the city, up to what's now Damascus Gate, but in its present form it starts just south of David St, the tourist souq, serving as the main entry into the Jewish Quarter from the Muslim and Christian areas. There are wells to allow visitors to see down to the levels beneath the street, where there are strata of a wall from the days of the First Temple and the Second Temple.

Four Sephardi Synagogues   SYNAGOGUE
(Map p52; ☑02-628-0592; 2 Mishmerot HaKehuna; adult/child 10/7NIS; ☺9.30am-3.30pm Sun-Thu, to 1pm Fri) This synagogue complex offers a taster of four places of worship, tightly packed together and able to be visited with a single ticket. The two oldest synagogues date from the late 16th century and all four were in ruins following the Arab–Israeli War; they were restored between 1967 and 1972. With their associated study houses and charitable institutions, the synagogues were at the centre of the local Sephardi community's spiritual and cultural life until the late 19th century.

The synagogues remain active places of worship and celebration today.

In accordance with a law of the time stating that synagogues could not be taller than neighbouring buildings (and certainly not higher than mosques), these synagogues were embedded deep into the ground – a measure that saved them from total destruction during the bombardment of the Jewish Quarter in 1948. Instead, the synagogues were looted by the Jordanians and used as sheep pens. They were restored using the remains of Italian synagogues damaged during WWII.

The first synagogue in the grouping (closest to the ticket desk) is **Eliahu Hanavi** synagogue, the oldest of the four; its arches and dome reference Byzantine buildings. The early-17th-century **Yokhanan Ben Zahai** synagogue is named after a renowned Jewish sage, whose Second Temple study hall is believed to have stood on this spot. The elongated **Emtza'i (Middle) Synagogue** is the smallest of the four, created when a roof was built over a courtyard between two of the synagogues in the mid-18th century, creating a synagogue in between.

Doors in the Emtza'i lead to a small exhibit about the history of the synagogues, and to the **Istanbuli Synagogue**, which is the largest of the four and was the last to be built. It was constructed in the 1760s by immigrants from the Turkish city of the same name.

Burnt House   MUSEUM
(Map p52; The House of Kathros; ☑02-626-5921; Tiferet Israel St; adult/concession 29/15NIS; ☺9am-5pm Sun-Thu, to 1pm Fri) Buried under rubble for centuries and only recently excavated, this house was destroyed in 70 CE when the Romans put the city to the torch. The archaeological remains on display include Roman-era coins, stone tablets, ovens, cooking pots and a spear that were found at the site, as well as a stone weight with the name 'Kathros' on it (Kathros was a priestly family living in the city at this time).

Piecing together the house's history, the museum has created a multimedia presentation shown in a number of languages, including English. Movies (25 minutes long) begin every 40 minutes; showing times vary, so be prepared to wait around. Burnt House is included in the 60NIS Jewish Quarter ticket, which also accesses the tower at Hurva Synagogue and the Herodian Quarter Museum.

**Herodian Quarter
Museum**   ARCHAEOLOGICAL SITE
(Map p52; Wohl Archaeological Museum; ☑072-393-2833; 1 HaKara'im St; adult/concession 20/10NIS; ☺9am-5pm Sun-Thu, to 1pm Fri) Descend to Jerusalem's ancient bones at this small, subterranean museum. Among its impressively intact archaeological sites is a 600-sq-metre Herodian-era mansion, complete with ritual baths, thought to have belonged to a high priest. Other displays

provide a tantalising portal to the past: one mosaic shows evidence of fire damage, thought to date to the conflagration at the First Temple site. It's worth grabbing an audio guide (5NIS).

Hurva Synagogue

SYNAGOGUE

(Map p52; Ruin Synagogue; ☑02-626-5900; www.rova-yehudi.org.il; Hurva Sq; adult/student 20/10NIS; ⊗9am-5pm Sun-Thu, to 1pm Fri winter, to 7pm Sun-Thu, to 1pm Fri summer) To the local Jewish community, the reconstructed Hurva Synagogue is a symbol of resilience. The earliest synagogue on this spot was wrecked in the early 18th century, and its 19th-century successor fell during the 1948 Arab–Israeli War. The broad-domed edifice standing today was dedicated in 2010, and the best reason to visit is to clamber up the tower for peerless views of the Jewish Quarter's rooftops.

Zion Gate

GATE

(Map p52) This weathered entryway on the Old City's southern wall was a pivotal location during the 1948 Arab–Israeli War, and its bullet-eaten facade gives an indication of the fighting's ferocity. Note the *mezuzah* (box containing extracts from the Torah) on the doorpost; it was fashioned from bullet casings collected after the fighting. To Jews, the gate is Sha'ar Tziyon (Zion Gate), while in Arabic it's Bab Haret Al Yahud (Gate of the Jewish Quarter).

⊙ Muslim Quarter

The largest of the Old City's neighbourhoods (0.3 sq km), the Muslim Quarter has the power to exalt and exasperate you within the space of a minute. Pilgrims process along the Via Dolorosa's Stations of the Cross, merchants beckon towards their stalls, and children scamper and play football in between. The odours of incense, spices and fresh pastries mingle in the air.

The quarter, which has a resident population of 22,000, runs from permanently congested Damascus Gate to Bab Al Silsila St near Temple Mount/Al Haram Ash Sharif (p53). About 100m in from the gate, the street forks; bearing to the left is Al Wad St, lined with shops selling everything from belly-dancing scarves to burqas, and pastries to pomegranate juice – not to mention innumerable Palestinian-themed souvenirs ranging from old-school travel posters to slogan T-shirts. This route crosses the Via Dolorosa (p60) and leads directly to the Western Wall (p65). Bearing to the right at the fork is Souq Khan Al Zeit St, which is even busier than Al

Wad St; here you'll find shops selling fruit, vegetables, sweets, clothing, spices and nuts.

For an interesting perspective on this part of town, try to visit around midday on Friday. Position yourself near Damascus Gate St and watch the streams of Muslim faithful flood through the quarter towards Al Haram Ash Sharif on their way to prayers.

Damascus Gate

GATE

(Map p52) The sights and sounds of the Muslim Quarter intensify on the approach to Damascus Gate, on the northern wall of the Old City. The gate's triangular crenellations give it the appearance of a crown; for the best view, walk through the gate to a small stone plaza, surveyed by armed Israeli soldiers, facing Derekh Shchem (Nablus) Rd.

The gate's present form dates from the time of Süleyman the Magnificent, although there had been a gate here long before the arrival of the Turks. This was the main entrance to the city as early as the time of Agrippa, who ruled in the 1st century BCE. The gate was considerably enlarged during the reign of the Roman emperor Hadrian. Excavations in the 1960s revealed the remains of a triple-arched Roman gate.

A long-disappeared column erected by Hadrian once stood in the square, which is why the gate is known in Arabic as Bab Al Amud (Gate of the Column). In Hebrew it is known as Sha'ar Shchem (Damascus Gate).

Today it's a fascinating place to people-watch. Vendors catcall their wares to passers-by, locals and tourists barter over produce from vegetables to SIM cards, and elderly Palestinian women dart in and out of the gate with surprising speed.

St Anne's Church

CHURCH

(Map p72; Sha-ar HaArayot Rd; adult/student & child 10/8NIS; ⊗8am-noon & 2-6pm Apr-Sep, to 5pm Mon-Sat Oct-Mar) The finest example of Crusader architecture in Jerusalem, St Anne's was completed in 1138 on a site thought to have been the home of Joachim and Anne, the parents of the Virgin Mary. One of the sunken pools accessed from the rear of the church compound is traditionally thought to be the biblical **Pool of Bethesda** where Jesus is said to have healed a sick man (John 5:1-18).

Inside this enigmatic Romanesque structure, slender vaults lift the gaze and the church's renowned acoustics spur countless visitors (in particular Christian pilgrim groups) to burst into song.

MAMLUK ARCHITECTURE

The Muslim Quarter possesses a wealth of buildings constructed during the golden age of Islamic architecture. Most of these are in a sadly dilapidated state but retain vestiges of their original grandeur.

This part of the Old City was developed during the era of the Mamluks (1250–1517), a military dynasty of former slaves ruling out of Egypt. Driving the Crusaders out of Palestine and Syria, they followed up with an equally impressive campaign of construction, consolidating Islam's presence in the Levant with masses of mosques, *madrassas* (religious schools), hostels, monasteries and mausoleums. Mamluk buildings are characterised by the banding of dark and light stone (a technique known as *ablaq*) and by elaborate carvings and patterning around windows and in recessed portals.

All of these features are exhibited in the **Palace of the Lady Tunshuq** (Aqabat Al Takiya St), built in 1388 and found halfway down Aqabat Al Takiya. Though the facade is badly eroded, the uppermost of the three large doorways still has beautiful inlaid marble work and the third door down is decorated with a Mamluk trademark: the stone 'stalactites' known as *muqarnas*. You can admire from the outside only, as this noblewoman's palace now houses an orphanage school. Opposite the palace is the 1398 **Tomb of the Lady Tunshuq** – look for the carved panel above the locked green door.

Down the hill, towards the junction with Al Wad St, you will see on your right the last notable piece of Mamluk architecture built in Jerusalem, the 1540 **Ribat Bayram Jawish** (Aqabat Al Takiya), which has a facade featuring handsome *ablaq* and shallow *muqarnas*. Compare this with the buildings on Tariq Bab an-Nazir St, straight across Al Wad St, which are Jerusalem's earliest Mamluk structures, built in the 1260s before the common use of *ablaq*. This street is named after the gate at the end, which leads through into Temple Mount/Al Haram Ash Sharif (entry for Muslims only).

Continuing south on Al Wad St, the road passes the Souq Al Qattanin and then, on the same side, a *sabil* (public fountain) dating from Ottoman times, Sabil Suleyman. Built by order of long-reigning Ottoman ruler Süleyman the Magnificent, this door-shaped fountain was crafted from the repurposed ruins of Crusader (and even earlier) buildings; its base is a Roman sarcophagus. The road terminates in a police checkpoint at the mouth of the tunnel down to the Western Wall plaza. However, the stairs to the left lead up to the busy Bab Al Silsila St and the Bab Al Silsila Gate (which leads to Temple Mount/Al Haram Ash Sharif). Just before the gate is the tiny, kiosk-like 1352 **Tomb of Turkan Khatun** (Bab Al Silsila St), with a facade adorned with uncommonly asymmetrical carved geometric designs. Bab Al Silsila St has a number of other handsome Mamluk buildings with *muqarnas* and *mashrabiyyas* (projecting oriel windows featuring carved-wood latticework).

The earliest traces at this site have hinted at a Roman-era pagan shrine, and ruins can still be seen in St Anne's gardens. When Jerusalem fell to the armies of Saladin, St Anne's became a Muslim theological school – an inscription above the church's entrance testifies to this. Successive rulers allowed the church to fall into decay, so that by the 18th century it was roof-deep in refuse. In 1856 the Ottoman Turks presented the church to France in gratitude for its support in the Crimean War against Russia, and it was reclaimed from the garbage heap. It is still French owned.

Lions' Gate   GATE
(St Stephen's Gate; Map p72) This easterly gate of Jerusalem's Old City points towards the Mount of Olives and Gethsemane. Although originally called Bab Al Ghor (Jordan Valley Gate), it became known as St Stephen's Gate after the first Christian martyr, who was stoned to death at a spot nearby. The Hebrew name, Sh'ar Ha'Arayot (Lions' Gate), is a reference to the two pairs of heraldic lions carved on the exterior side of the archway.

It is thought that the feline figures (actually leopards) originated with Süleyman the Magnificent, who interpreted his dreams of fearsome beasts as a warning to fortify Jerusalem's Old City. Historians have suggested that the carved cats predate the gate and were repurposed from an older Mamluk building.

This gate is also where Israeli paratroopers fought their way into the Old City on 7 June 1967.

On Palm Sunday, a Christian procession from the Mount of Olives enters the Old City through St Stephen's Gate.

Souq Al Qattanin   MARKET

(Cotton Market; Map p52; ⊙ daylight hours) Food and clothing vendors are framed by soaring vaults in this mid-14th-century shopping arcade. The part closest to Al Wad St dates from the Crusader period; the Mamluks extended it in the middle of the 14th century. A cotton bazaar once stood here, though these days lamps, souvenirs, snacks and bric-a-brac are on sale, creating an atmospheric diversion for visitors to the Muslim Quarter.

◉ Armenian Quarter

Sequestered behind high walls and enormous wooden doors, life in the Armenian Quarter (0.1 sq km) plods along unnoticed, as it has for nearly two millennia.

Armenia was the first nation to officially embrace Christianity, after its king converted in around 300 CE. Armenians established themselves in Jerusalem sometime in the following century, and when the Kingdom of Armenia disappeared at the end of the 4th century, Jerusalem was adopted as its spiritual capital. Armenians have had an uninterrupted presence here ever since, at one stage numbering 25,000.

Originally, their presence was purely religious, but a large secular element arrived early last century to work on retiling the Dome of the Rock (p58) and to escape Ottoman Turkish persecution. Many residents are committed to spreading awareness among tourists regarding atrocities suffered by Armenian people under the Ottomans between 1915 and 1918; you'll see plenty of multilingual posters detailing the Armenian genocide. Though many scholars and governments describe it as such, the term 'genocide' remains disputed by some governments, such as Turkey. The community today numbers fewer than 2000 and is still very insular, having its own schools, library, seminary and residential quarters arranged within the gated Armenian compound (not open to visitors).

St James' Cathedral   CHURCH

(Couvent Armenien St-Jacques; Map p52; ♪ religious-service info 02-628-2331; https://armenian-patriarchate.com; Armenian Orthodox Patriarchate Rd; ⊙ morning prayers 6.30am, vespers 3pm, Mass 8am Sat & 8.30am Sun) Accessible only for services, the interior of this 12th-century cathedral is infused with incense smoke. Blue-and-white tiles and glittering icons adorn its walls, and richly patterned carpets are strewn across the floor. At other times, you can enter the courtyard to see the exterior, which is decorated with *khatchkars*

ARMENIAN CERAMICS

In 1919, the restoration of the magnificent Dome of the Rock (p58) prompted the establishment of the first Armenian ceramics workshop in the city, a crafts tradition that continues strongly to this day.

Armenian ceramic techniques reached their height in Turkey during the 17th and 18th centuries, when many Armenian families operated workshops in the important ceramic centres of Kütahya and İznik. After the events of 1915–18, following mass killings, property confiscation and deportation of Turkey's Armenian population, a number of Armenian potters and their families were brought to Jerusalem by David Ohannessian (1884–1953), an Armenian ceramics master who had worked in Kütahya and who had fled Turkey for Jerusalem in 1919. On arriving, he was able to establish a ceramics workshop on the Via Dolorosa with the assistance of the Pro Jerusalem society, set up in 1918 by Sir Ronald Storrs, the military governor of Jerusalem, and Charles Robert Ashbee, an architect and leading designer of the Arts and Crafts Movement. Ohannessian and his Armenian master craftsmen went on to produce new tiles to replace the worn originals on the Dome of the Rock.

Local artisans claim that Jerusalem is now the only place in the world where genuine Armenian pottery is still produced. Old, hand-painted techniques have changed little over the centuries and are used to produce richly coloured ceramics featuring floral, animal and geometric patterns.

To see wonderful examples of Armenian tiles, head to a service at St James' Cathedral, with its profusion of blue-and-white tiles, or to the more easily visitable St Andrew's Church (p82), which features tiles at the entrances to the church and its guesthouse. To purchase ceramics to take home, browse the Sandrouni Armenian Art Centre (p105) in the Old City, Armenian Ceramics (p105) in East Jerusalem or Arman Darian (p106) in West Jerusalem.

(Armenian stone crosses surrounded by intricate tracery) and tiled murals depicting the Last Judgement and the Apostles.

It was actually the Georgians who first constructed a church here in honour of St James, believing the site to be the place where he was beheaded and became the first martyred disciple. In the 12th century, the Armenians, in favour with the ruling Crusaders, took possession of the church and undertook its restoration. The tiles in the interior date from the 18th century.

Modest dress is required to attend services; women should cover their heads.

St Mark's Chapel   CHURCH
(Map p52; ⊘ 9am-noon & 2-5pm Mon-Sat Apr-Sep, 7am-4pm Mon-Sat Oct-Mar, 11am-4pm Sun) This medieval chapel is the home of the small Syrian Orthodox congregation in Jerusalem, who believe that it occupies the site of the home of St Mark's mother, Mary. Peter is said to have come here after he was released from prison by an angel (Acts 12:12-17).

Inside the small 12th-century sanctuary, look for the painting on leather of the Virgin and child, which is attributed to St Luke.

◉ Mt Zion

Home to a room venerated by Christians as the location where Jesus and his disciples had their Last Supper, as well as to a small prayer room marking the place where many Jews believe King David is buried, this cluster of buildings is an important pilgrimage site for peoples of both Jewish and Christian faiths. Although it once encompassed the entire ridge of the upper Old City (including the Citadel), 'Mt Zion' is used to refer to the hill south of the Old City beyond Zion Gate.

King David's Tomb   RELIGIOUS SITE
(Map p72; ⊘ 8am-5pm Sun-Thu, to 1pm Fri) FREE
Erected by Crusaders two millennia after King David's death, this ground-floor tomb is of dubious authenticity but is nonetheless a holy place for Jews and Christians. The prayer hall is divided into sides for men and women, both leading to the velvet-draped tomb. Behind is an alcove believed to be a synagogue dating back to the 5th century CE.

The Bible references David's burial with his ancestors in the City of David (1 Kings 2:10), and most archaeologists and historians believe that it is likely that David is buried under the hill of the original Mt Zion, east of the City of David (p75).

The tomb is off the courtyard in front of the Franciscan Monastery, which is accessed through a doorway on the left-hand side of the path into the main complex, past an arch and the stairway leading to the Room of the Last Supper.

Room of the Last Supper   CHRISTIAN SITE
(Cenacle, Coenaculum; Map p72; ⊘ 8am-6pm) FREE Medieval beliefs about the location of the Last Supper have embedded the Coenaculum (Latin for dining hall) in Christian tradition. Most historians agree that this hall is unlikely to be built on the spot where Jesus ate his final meal. Nonetheless, this elegantly rib-vaulted chamber (formerly part of the 4th-century Holy Zion church) usually teems with pilgrims. Retained in the 14th-century Crusader structure that replaced the original church, it was converted to a mosque during the Ottoman period.

The building features stained glass and a 16th-century *mihrab* (niche indicating the direction of Mecca), forming an intriguing contrast against its Gothic-style Christian framework.

A more widely accepted belief about this site is that it was where Jesus's disciples received the Holy Spirit on the Pentecost and gained the ability to speak foreign languages (Acts 2), enabling them to spread Christianity.

The room is above King David's Tomb, reached by a staircase nearby.

Church & Monastery
of the Dormition   CHURCH
(Map p72; ☑ 02-565-5330; www.dormitio.net; ⊘ 9am-5pm Mon-Sat, from 10am Sun) FREE
With its round sandstone tower and graceful Romanesque-style arches, the Dormition Church is one of Jerusalem's most recognisable landmarks. The church occupies the site traditionally believed to be where the Virgin Mary died (the word 'dormition' means a peaceful sleep or painless death). The current church and monastery, owned by the German Benedictine order, was consecrated in 1906. Turn left upon entering for the stairs down to the womb-like **crypt**, where carved pillars surround a shrine to Mary. Dress modestly.

The site's Latin name is Dormitio Sanctae Mariae (Sleep of Holy Mary). The building suffered damage during the battles for the city in 1948 and 1967. During the latter, Israeli soldiers occupied the church's tower overlooking Jordanian army positions on the Old City ramparts below. The soldiers nicknamed the tower 'bobby' because it resembles the helmet worn by London police officers.

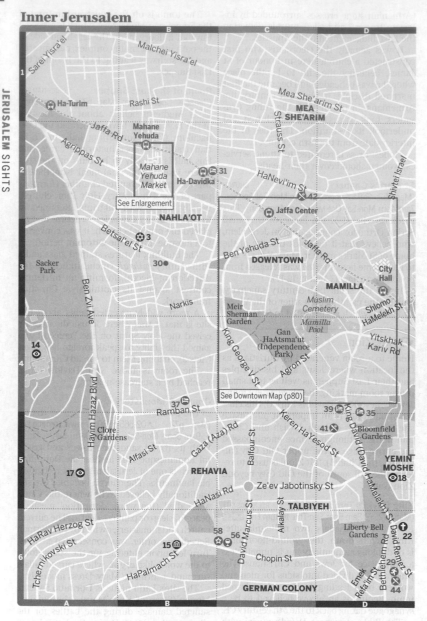

The church's interior features a golden mosaic of Mary with the baby Jesus in the upper part of the apse; below are the prophets of Israel. The chapels around the hall are each dedicated to a saint or saints: St Willibald, an English Benedictine who visited the Holy Land in 724; the Three Wise Men; St Joseph, whose chapel is covered with medallions that feature kings of Judah as Jesus's forefathers; and St John the Baptist. The floor is decorated with the names of saints and prophets, as well as zodiac symbols.

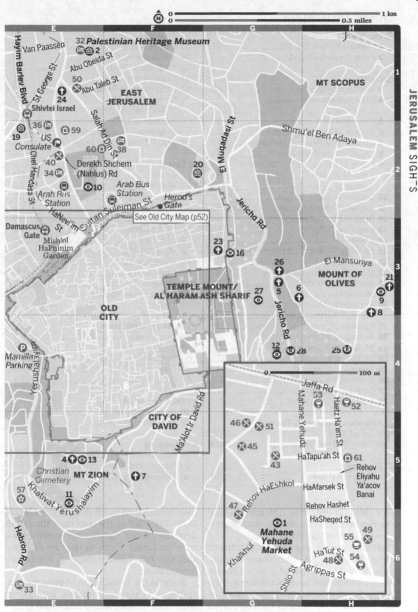

Grave of Oskar Schindler MEMORIAL
(Map p72; ⏰8am-noon Mon-Sat) Austrian
industrialist Oskar Schindler (1908–74)
earned the honorific of Righteous Among
the Nations, awarded by Israel to non-Jews
who risked their lives to save Jews during

the Holocaust. Schindler rescued more
than 1200 Jews from the gas chambers by
employing them in his factory. His grave is
in the Christian cemetery on Mt Zion. From
Zion Gate walk directly ahead, downhill.
Once inside the Christian cemetery, descend

Inner Jerusalem

to the third (lowest) level. The grave is easy to recognise as it is covered in small stones (a Jewish custom signifying respect).

Schindler's story was told by filmmaker Steven Spielberg in the Oscar-winning *Schindler's List* (based on Thomas Keneally's historical novel *Schindler's Ark*); the famous 'list' contained the names of Jews Schindler arranged to be transported to Brünnlitz, out of harm's way.

Church of St Peter of Gallicantu CHURCH
(Map p72; ☎02-673-1739; www.stpeter-gallicantu. org; adult/child 10/5NIS; ⊗8.30am-5pm Mon-Sat) Looking almost as though it might wobble from its rocky perch, St Peter of Gallicantu occupies the site where Jesus is said to

have been denied by his disciple Peter (Mark 14:66–72) – 'before the cock crow thou shalt deny me thrice' (*gallicantu* means 'cock crow' in Latin). Views of the City of David and the Palestinian village of Silwan are breathtaking.

Built on the foundations of previous Byzantine and Crusader churches, the modern structure's bulging domes and broad arches (completed in 1930) were built with an eye to Byzantine style. The church interior has some unusual stained-glass windows; below, the foundations and mosaics of earlier churches (including the site where three Byzantine-era crosses were found) are exposed. The site is managed by a French Catholic order.

Reach the church by turning east as you descend the road leading from Mt Zion down and around to Sultan's Pool. Roman steps lead down from the church garden to the Gihon Spring in the Kidron Valley.

◉ Kidron Valley

East of the Old City, the Kidron Valley and its western slopes form the oldest section of Jerusalem, laced with archaeological remnants and tombs that date back more than 4000 years. This is the site of the legendary City of David, which was actually a city long before David slung any stones, and there are a number of graves and tombs in the area, particularly in the Valley of Jehoshaphat. Steep topography has isolated the valley from the rest of the city (the best access is via Dung Gate or Lions' Gate). For archaeology fans with sturdy walking shoes, it's definitely worth trekking down here.

City of David   ARCHAEOLOGICAL SITE
(Map p52; ☑info 02-626-8700, tour reservations 077-996-6726; www.cityofdavid.org.il; adult/child 29/15NIS, movie 13NIS, biblical city tour adult/child 60/45NIS; ⊙8am-5pm Sun-Thu, to 2pm Fri Oct-Mar, to 7pm Sun-Thu, to 4pm Fri Apr-Sep; ▣1, 2, 38) As teeming with controversy as ancient history, the City of David is one of Jerusalem's most active archaeological sites. The oldest part of Jerusalem, it was a settlement during the Canaanite period; David is said to have captured the city and to have brought the Ark of the Covenant here 3000 years ago. Excavations began in the 1850s and are ongoing, as are arguments over the development and expansion of the site (in Silwan, East Jerusalem). Allow at least three hours.

From Dung Gate (p53), head east (downhill) and take the road to the right; the entrance is then on the left. At the visitors centre you can buy water (in summer, you'll need it) and watch a 15-minute 3D movie about the city. If you intend to walk through Hezekiah's Tunnel – and we suggest that you do – you can change into a swimming costume in the bathrooms and leave your gear in a locker (10NIS); alternatively, wear shorts. You will also need suitable footwear (flipflops or waterproof shoes). Key-chain lights can be purchased from the ticket office, but it's better to bring a torch (flashlight).

Note that the entrance fee covers admission to the underground areas of the site (Warren's Shaft, Hezekiah's Tunnel, the Pool of Siloam, Temple Road Ascent); admission should be free if you only explore aboveground areas. At this active dig site with

ongoing works, it can be difficult to know what you're looking at – many visitors find it useful to join a guided tour.

Once you reach the bottom of the hill you can walk back up through the Temple Road Ascent or via the road that passes through the Palestinian village of Silwan.

➡ **Royal Quarter (Area G)**
Area G, also called the Royal Quarter, was first constructed in the 10th century BCE, most likely as a fortification wall for a palace on the ridge. During the First Temple period an aristocrat's home (Achiel's House) was built against the wall, but it was destroyed along with the Temple in 586 BCE. Judean and Babylonian arrowheads were found in one of the chambers, called the **Burnt Room** because of its coating of ash, vivid reminders of the bloody battle waged here. Archaeologists have also located 51 royal seals (in ancient Hebrew script), including one thought to be that of the prophet Jeremiah's scribe, Gemaryahu Ben Shafan (Jeremiah 36:10).

➡ **Warren's Shaft**
The long, sloping Warren's Shaft was named after Sir Charles Warren, the British engineer who rediscovered it in 1867. The tunnel, which runs underneath the City of David to the Gihon Spring, allowed the Canaanites to obtain water without exposing themselves to danger in times of siege. It's just inside their city's defence wall and is possibly the tunnel described in 2 Samuel 5 as the means by which David's soldiers entered and captured the city. Modern archaeologists, however, tend to doubt this theory, suggesting the invaders used a different tunnel. From Warren's Shaft, you can proceed down to Hezekiah's Tunnel at the bottom of the hill. The shaft closes one hour before the City of David's official closing time.

➡ **Hezekiah's Tunnel**
This 500m-long underground watery passage ends at the Pool of Siloam, where it is said that a blind man was healed after Jesus told him to wash in it. The purpose of the tunnel was to channel water flowing from the Gihon Spring, a temperamental source that acts like a siphon, pouring out a large quantity of water for some 30 minutes before drying up for several hours.

Gihon means 'gushing', and the spring is the main reason the Canaanites settled in the valley rather than taking to the adjacent high ground. The tunnel was constructed around 700 BCE by King Hezekiah to bring the water of the Gihon into the city and store it in the Pool of Siloam, so preventing invaders, in

ONGOING CONTROVERSY

Controversy surrounds many of Jerusalem's ancient sites, but the City of David has especially bitter points of contention. Visitors will notice that the site feels like something of a Jewish island amid largely Palestinian neighbourhoods. The City of David is managed by Elad, an organisation that promotes tourism to Jerusalem and funds archaeological excavations. The group promotes the expansion of Israeli settlements into East Jerusalem, so its management of the City of David has many critics. Historians have raised doubts, too, about the objectivity with which archaeological discoveries are used to confirm biblical stories. Visitors may find the official narrative presented by some of the guides in the City of David to be partial and Jewish-centric.

particular the Assyrians, from locating the city's water supply and cutting it off (an account of this is in 2 Chronicles 32:30).

Although the tunnel is narrow and low in parts, you can wade through it; the water is normally between 50cm and 1m deep. The tunnel is as little as 60cm wide at some points. About 20m into the tunnel, the cavern turns sharply to the left, where a chest-high wall blocks another channel that leads to Warren's Shaft. Towards the tunnel's end the roof rises. This is because the tunnellers worked from either end and one team slightly misjudged the other's level. They had to lower the floor so that the water would flow. A Hebrew inscription was found in the tunnel (a copy can be seen in the Israel Museum, p86): carved by Hezekiah's engineers, it tells of the tunnel's construction.

The walk through Hezekiah's Tunnel takes about 20 minutes (or 40 minutes if it's busy). If you don't want to get wet, there's a second tunnel without water, which takes about 15 minutes to walk through. To find the entrance to the dry tunnel, go left just before the opening to Hezekiah's Tunnel. Older children can walk through Hezekiah's Tunnel, but ask about the water levels before going inside. You must begin the tunnel walk one hour before the City of David's official closing time.

➡ **Pool of Siloam**

As you exit from Hezekiah's Tunnel there is a small pool with round stones. Mindful of

Jesus's healing of the blind man (John 9), the Byzantines built this pool in the 5th century. They were unable to find the Shiloach Pool, which was buried under debris.

➡ **Shiloach Pool**

From the Byzantine Pool of Siloam, head up the stairs and out to an open area with crumbling steps that lead down to a pond. This is the Shiloach Pool. Discovered during excavations in 2004, the pool was built during the Second Temple period and was used for purification rituals. Archaeologists and historians have theorised that this is the pool where Jesus is said to have healed a blind man.

➡ **Eastern Stepped Street**

From the Shiloach Pool head up the flight of wooden steps to the Eastern Stepped Street, an ancient flight of stone steps. The stair pattern – pairs of short steps with a long gap between them – is thought to have been designed for animals, so sacrifices could be led upwards with ease. A drainage ditch is located under the steps and it was here that archaeologists found Roman-era coins and pottery, leading historians to believe that the ditch served as a hideout for Jews while the city was being sacked in 70 CE.

➡ **Temple Road Ascent**

This recently discovered 650m-long tunnel is a drainage ditch that channelled water out of the Temple Mount area. The bottom of the tunnel is near the Shiloach Pool; from here it's possible to walk uphill back to the Old City, exiting near Dung Gate. The tunnel ceiling is low and the walls are narrow in spots, so if you are particularly tall or wide (or claustrophobic) give this one a miss.

Valley of Jehoshaphat RELIGIOUS SITE
(Map p72; Jericho Rd; by donation; ⊙ daylight hours) The word *jehoshaphat* (*yehoshafat* in Hebrew) means 'God has judged', and this narrow furrow of land located between Temple Mount/Al Haram Ash Sharif and the Mount of Olives is where it is said the events of Judgment Day will take place (Joel 3:12) and all nations will be judged. At the southern end is a series of tombs dating from the Second Temple period. The northernmost tomb is that of **Jehoshaphat**; this 1st-century burial cave is notable for the impressive frieze above its entrance. Just in front of it is **Absalom's Pillar**, which legend says is the tomb of David's son (2 Samuel 18:17). Just beyond Absalom's Pillar is the **Grotto of St James**, where St James is believed to have hidden when Jesus was arrested nearby. Next to the grotto, carved out of the rock, is the **Tomb of Zechariah**, where

Jewish tradition holds the prophet Zechariah is buried (2 Chronicles 24:25).

Despite their names, the tombs most likely belong to wealthy noblemen of the Second Temple period.

⊙ Mount of Olives

With a mountain-splitting rumble, this is where God will start to redeem the dead when the Messiah returns on Judgment Day, according to the Book of Zechariah (14:4). Many Jews have chosen to be buried here, and to date some 150,000 people have been laid to rest on these slopes. (Rumour has it that the best plots cost upwards of US$100,000.) Aside from being likely the world's oldest continually used cemetery, the area has many churches and sites commemorating the events that led to Jesus's arrest and, as the faithful believe, his ascension to heaven.

Church of the Ascension   CHURCH

(www.evangelisch-in-jerusalem.org; cnr Anbar St & Martin Buber St; 5NIS; ⊙8am-1pm Mon-Sat; 🚍275) In 1898, the Ottomans granted Germany 8 hectares of land on the Mount of Olives. This was set aside for a church and hospice, and the complex was named after Augusta Victoria, wife of Kaiser Wilhelm II. Completed in 1910, the church is decorated with mosaics and frescoes, and has a 60m-high bell tower that can be climbed by visitors (there are 203 steps). The Turkish army occupied the hospice during WWI and the British later converted it into a military hospital – it's still a hospital today.

Dome of the Ascension/
Chapel of the Ascension   RELIGIOUS SITE

(Map p72; ⊙7.30-10.30am & 1.30-2.30pm) It's easy to overlook this chapel, which is diminutive and decrepit. Thought to mark the site where Jesus ascended to heaven (Luke 24:50-51), it was built in the Byzantine era, reworked by the Crusaders and then converted to a mosque by Saladin in 1198. In its present form, it is a rotunda set inside an octagonal compound whose walls incorporate a squat stone minaret. Hours are irregular, but there's usually someone around in the morning to open it up.

Inside, the stone floor bears an imprint said to be the footstep of Jesus. Perhaps the reason for its unconvincing appearance today is that pilgrims in the Byzantine period were permitted to take bits of it away. Only the right footprint is now visible, as the left footprint was taken to Al Aqsa Mosque (p59) during the Middle Ages.

Church of the Pater Noster   CHURCH

(Map p72; ☎02-626-4904; 8NIS; ⊙8.30am-noon & 2.30-4.30pm Mon-Sat Apr-Sep, from 8am Mon-Sat Oct-Mar) Tiled panels bearing the Lord's Prayer beam from the walls of this church and cloister. Queen Helena, mother of Emperor Constantine, believed this to be the location where Jesus taught the Lord's Prayer to his disciples, and she arranged for a church to be built here. It was destroyed, but the Crusaders rebuilt a church at this site in 1152 (itself razed by the Mamluks). The current building is a partial reconstruction of the Byzantine church with a 19th-century cloister. The tiles are decorated with the Lord's Prayer in 132 languages, though it depends on how you count: a number of languages are also represented in Braille.

Tomb of the Prophets   TOMB

(Map p72; by donation, per person 5NIS; ⊙9am-3pm Mon-Thu) Head into the section of cemetery below the panoramic viewpoint, via

JERUSALEM SIGHTS

ⓘ PRACTICAL TIP: TOURING THE MOUNT OF OLIVES

Tackling the Mount of Olives on foot can be hard work, especially during summer. If you treat yourself to one guided tour, make it the Mount of Olives; Sandemans (p91) offers an excellent three-hour excursion (€21 including transfer). Travelling independently, take Arab bus 275 (5NIS) from the bus station opposite Herod's Gate on Sultan Suleiman St in East Jerusalem or hail it outside Damascus Gate. When you see the 'Augusta Victoria Hospital' sign, you can disembark for the Church of the Ascension. Alternatively, stay on board for a couple more stops to bring you closer to the Mount of Olives' most storied sights: walking downhill, they include the **Russian Church of the Ascension** (Map p72; ☎02-628-4373; ⊙hours vary, usually 9am-noon), the Dome of the Ascension, the Church of the Pater Noster, and the Tomb of the Prophets. When you ascend back towards Lions' Gate (p69) and the Old City, you'll pass the Garden of Gethsemane (p78) and the Tomb of the Virgin Mary (p78).

Most of the churches and gardens open in the morning, close for at least two hours around noon and reopen again mid-afternoon.

a staircase, to find this set of ancient rock-cut tombs. Jewish tradition holds that they house the graves of the prophets Haggai, Zachariah and Malachi, who lived in the 5th and 6th centuries BCE, but modern archaeologists tend to dispute this, dating the tombs to later centuries.

Church of Mary Magdalene CHURCH

(Map p72; ⊘10am-noon Tue & Thu) A glint of St Petersburg on the Mount of Olives, this shapely church was constructed in the style of a 17th-century Russian Orthodox church. Built in 1888 by Alexander III in memory of his mother, the church is now a convent and guards the relics of two Russian saints. Its seven golden onion-shaped domes form one of Jerusalem's most attractive landmarks.

Church of All Nations CHURCH

(Basilica of Gethsemane; Map p72; ⊘8am-5.50pm Apr-Sep, to 4.50pm Oct-Mar) Built above the remains of two previous churches, a Franciscan basilica crowns the site where Jesus is believed to have prayed through the night before he was betrayed (Matthew 26:36). Inside the church, also referred to as the Sanctuary of the Agony of Jesus, light is muted by stained-glass windows and the vaulted ceiling spangled with stars, to evoke the mood of Jesus's nocturnal prayers in the Garden of Gethsemane.

The exposed rock near the altar is believed to be where Jesus prayed.

DANGERS & ANNOYANCES
....

Most travellers to Jerusalem enjoy their visit without incident, but be cautious: ongoing tensions can escalate quickly, sometimes violently.

➡ Demonstrations by Jews and Arabs are common. Many are peaceful, but steer clear of protests. Damascus Gate, Lions' Gate and Temple Mount/Al Haram Ash Sharif are common flashpoints.

➡ Many travellers report feeling unsafe around the Mount of Olives, and some women travellers have reported harassment. If possible, visit in pairs.

➡ Ultra-Orthodox Jewish groups sometimes stone buses and violently confront the police in the neighbourhood of Mea She'arim. Hostilities can also erupt when tourists (especially those deemed to be immodestly dressed) saunter in.

Garden of Gethsemane GARDENS

(Map p72; ⊘8.30am-noon & 2.30-5pm Mon-Wed, Fri & Sat, to 4pm Sun & Thu) FREE After a night of feverish prayer, Jesus is believed to have been arrested in this garden (Mark 14:26, 32-50), now attached to the Church of All Nations. It has some of the world's oldest olive trees (in Hebrew *gat shmanim* means 'oil press'), though testing has failed to prove conclusively that these were the same trees beneath which Jesus prayed and his disciples slept. A railing protects the remaining trees from visitors (scotching pilgrims' attempts to snap off branches). Enter from the narrow alleyway leading up to the Mount of Olives.

Tomb of the Virgin Mary CHRISTIAN SITE

(Map p72; ⊘5am-noon & 2.30-5pm Apr-Sep, from 6am Oct-Mar) FREE Centuries of candle smoke have blackened the walls of this subterranean shrine, one of Christianity's holiest sites. According to tradition, this is the resting place of Mary, mother of Jesus. Though strung with countless lanterns and crowded with icons worth millions of shekels, the space is faintly lit. A central shrine is cloaked in velvet and pilgrims can duck inside.

A monument was first constructed at this site in the 5th century but was repeatedly destroyed. The facade of the current structure dates to the Crusader period of the 12th century, but the crypt is Byzantine. An ancient cistern lies beneath the floor.

The eggs atop the shrine's pendulous oil lamps aren't an Easter decoration: they form an obstacle course that makes it difficult for rats to clamber down the chain.

◉ East Jerusalem

Predominantly Arab, East Jerusalem is subject to intense dispute. The land was held by Jordan as part of the 1949 Armistice Agreements that followed the Arab–Israeli War. The Green Line (demarcation line 1948–67) between the Israeli- and Jordanian-overseen sections of the city ran along Chel Handasa St (now part of the JLR route). After the Six Day War in 1967, East Jerusalem came under Israeli control, and most of the international community considers it territory occupied by Israel.

Confusingly for newcomers, 'East Jerusalem' can refer to neighbourhoods north, east and south of the Old City. East Jerusalem locations around the Old City are flashpoints for tension (and violence) between the predominantly Arab population and omnipresent Israeli security forces.

When exploring this area, consider stopping for a drink or meal at the historic American Colony Hotel (p94). Legend has it that when the Ottomans surrendered the city to British rule, the Turkish governor of Jerusalem snatched a sheet from one of the beds (it was a hospital at the time) and used it as a flag to surrender. The 'flag' is now in the Imperial War Museum in London.

⭐**Palestinian Heritage Museum**　MUSEUM
(Dar Al Tifel Al Arabi Foundation; Map p72; ☑02-627-2531; www.dta-museum.org; American Colony, Al Jarrah St; adult/child 20/10NIS; ⊙8am-4pm Mon-Thu & Sat) Within the American Colony complex in a 19th-century building, this museum provides a useful primer on ancient and modern Palestinian culture. Displays on embroidery, basket weaving and agrarian implements offer a glimpse into age-old village traditions. The museum also details the displacement of the Palestinian people, including lists of formerly Arab villages, and memorialises events such as 1948's Deir Yassin massacre.

St George's Cathedral　CHURCH
(Map p72; www.j-diocese.org; Derekh Shchem/Nablus Rd; ⊙hours vary; ⓐShivtei Israel) Named after the patron saint of England, who is traditionally believed to have been martyred in Palestine early in the 4th century, St George's Cathedral was consecrated in 1898 and has a mixed Arabic- and English-speaking congregation. The church compound is a piece of the British Mandate frozen in time, featuring symbols of the British presence in Jerusalem.

Museum on the Seam　GALLERY
(Map p72; ☑02-628-1278; www.mots.org.il; 4 Chel Handasa St; adult/student 30NIS/25NIS; ⊙10am-5pm Mon, Wed & Thu, to 2pm Fri, 2-8pm Tue; ⓐShivtei Israel) Located on the 'seam' (border) between East and West Jerusalem, this gallery presents rotating contemporary art exhibitions, often exploring themes of identity, multiplicity and faith. Expect anything from neon multimedia installations to searing recreations of biblical scenes; whatever is on display is sure to be thought provoking. The building itself served as a forward military position for the Israeli army from 1948 to 1967 and still bears the scars of war.

There is a rooftop cafe, and a downstairs gift shop. Note that some of the work shown here may not be suitable for small children.

Garden Tomb　GARDENS
(Map p72; ☑02-539-8100; www.gardentomb.org; East Jerusalem; ⊙8.30am-5.15pm Mon-Sat; ⓐDamascus Gate) **FREE** Away from the din

of Derekh Shchem (Nablus) Rd is a tranquil patch of green, considered by its trustees to be the garden and sepulchre of Joseph of Arimathea, and possibly the place where Jesus was resurrected. The claims are strongly disputed, but this walled and attractively landscaped space is more conducive to contemplation than the teeming Church of the Holy Sepulchre (p60), the site more widely believed to be that of the crucifixion. There are some interesting archaeological excavations here, too.

Biblical significance was first attached to this location by General Charles Gordon (aka Gordon of Khartoum) in 1883. Gordon did not believe that the Church of the Holy Sepulchre could occupy the site of Calvary, and on identifying a skull-shaped hill just north of Damascus Gate (p68) he began excavations. The ancient tombs he discovered under the mound, including a chamber sealed with a rolling stone, further strengthened his conviction that this was the true site.

Archaeologists have since challenged the theory by dating the tombs to the 7th to 5th centuries BCE, though believers counter that old tombs were often reused in the Holy Land. Several cynics suggest that the continued championing of the Garden Tomb has more to do with the fact that it's the only holy site in Jerusalem that the Protestants, its owners, have any stake in.

To get there from Sultan Suleiman St head north along Nablus Rd and turn right at Schick St, opposite the bus station. The site is wheelchair accessible.

Rockefeller Museum　MUSEUM
(Map p72; ☑02-670-8074; 27 Sultan Suleiman St, East Jerusalem; ⊙10am-3pm Sun, Mon, Wed & Thu, to 2pm Sat; ⓐDamascus Gate) **FREE** The Rockefeller Museum doesn't ride high on must-see lists for Jerusalem, but it's calm, uncrowded and only a short walk from Herod's Gate. The atmosphere is as enjoyable as the contents; make for the Cloisters, where Roman-era antiquities are arranged around a gushing water feature.

◉ Downtown

Jerusalem's downtown (or city centre) is the area northwest of the Old City. Its central axis is Jaffa Rd, running from Tzahal Sq to the Mahane Yehuda Market area. Between the square and the market is Zion Sq, a handy landmark and meeting point. Despite its status as Jerusalem's downtown, the area is easy to navigate on foot.

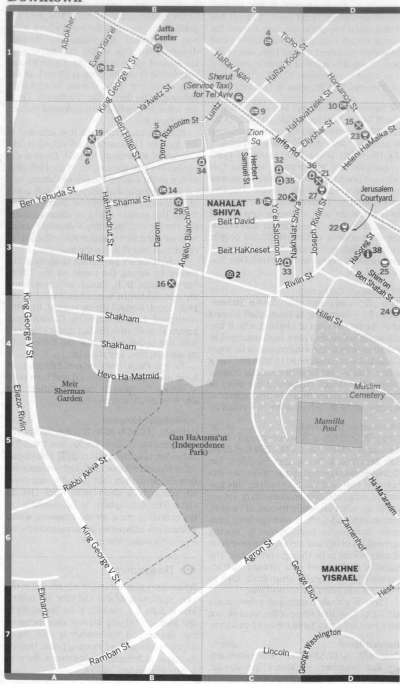

Jaffa Center

Albokher

Even Yisra'el

King George V St

Ya'Avetz St

HaRav Agan

Ticho St

HaRav Kook St

Horkanos St

HaHavatzelet St

Eliyshar St

Heleni HaMalka St

Sherut (Service Taxi) for Tel Aviv

Luntz

Zion Sq

Jaffa Rd

Jerusalem Courtyard

Ben Hillel St

Dorot Rishonim St

Herbert Samuel St

Yo'el Salomon St

Nakhalat Shiv'a

Joseph Rivlin St

HaSoreg St

Shim'on

Ben Shatah St

Ben Yehuda St

HaHistadrut St

Shamai St

Darom

Angelo Bianchini

Hillel St

NAHALAT SHIV'A

Beit David

Beit HaKneset

Rivlin St

Hillel St

Shakham

Shakham

Hevo Ha-Matmid

Muslim Cemetery

Meir Sherman Garden

Mamilla Pool

Eliezor Rivlin

King George V St

Gan HaAtsma'ut (Independence Park)

Ha-Ma'aralim

Rabbi Akiva St

Zamenhof

Agron St

George Eliot

MAKHNE YISRAEL

Hess

Elkhar'zi

King George V St

Ramban St

Lincoln

George Washington

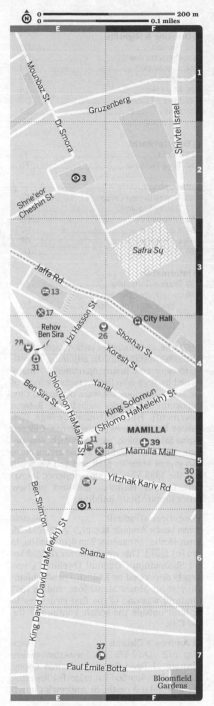

★ **Mahane Yehuda Market**   MARKET
(Map p72; www.machne.co.il; Jaffa Rd, Downtown; ⊗8am-7pm Sun-Thu, 9am-3pm Fri; 🚊Mahane Yehuda) All of Jerusalem meets in Mahane Yehuda, from first-time visitors to residents loading their trolleys with fruit and veg. Market tables are laden with wheels of halva (sesame-paste nougat), olives larger than thumbs, glistening poppy-seed pastries and almost everything that can be made or grown locally. At night, it reinvents itself as a restaurant and bar hub where local foodies and tourists hang out.

The market has two major streets: Mahane Yehuda St, the open-air market, is more suited to loading up on produce from butchers and veg sellers, while Etz Chayim St, the covered market, has a proliferation of places to sample pastries, pancakes, juices and more.

A market has stood here since Ottoman times. During the British Mandate period, attempts to streamline its layout fell by the wayside, allowing Mahane Yehuda to preserve its straggling appearance to this day. Historically, the names of the market's alleyways related to the products available, but these days it's a moveable feast: HaAfarsek ('Peach St') has linens, HaTut ('Berry St') has a butcher and Ha'Egoz ('Walnut St') is busy with sweet, coffee and flower sellers.

The market is at its bustling best on Thursday and Friday during the pre-Shabbat scramble, though you'll be elbow to elbow with shoppers.

Russian Compound   HISTORIC SITE
(Map p80; Shivtei Israel St, Downtown; ⊗Church of the Holy Trinity 9am-1pm Mon-Sat Apr-Sep, 9am-1pm Mon-Fri, to noon Sat Oct-Mar; 🚊City Hall) Dominated by the green domes of its **Church of the Holy Trinity**, this compound was acquired by the Russian Orthodox Church in 1860 to strengthen the Russian imperial presence in the Holy Land. In the last years of the British Mandate, it and nearby streets were turned into a fortified administrative zone nicknamed 'Bevingrad' by Palestinian Jews after the reviled British foreign secretary Ernest Bevin. Today it's home to Jerusalem's central police station and law courts.

Museum of Italian Jewish Art   MUSEUM
(Map p80; 🖉02-624-1610; http://ijamuseum. org; 25 Hillel St, Downtown; adult/child 25/15NIS; ⊗10am-5pm Sun, Tue & Wed, noon-9pm Thu, 10am-1pm Fri; 🚊Jaffa Center) A baroque-style synagogue, twinkling with gold vine leaves and decorative arches, is the focal point of this overlooked museum. Transported across the

Downtown

◎ Sights
1 Hebrew Union College.............................E5
2 Museum of Italian Jewish Art.............. C3
3 Russian Compound.................................E2

🛏 Sleeping
4 7 Kook Hotel & Suites..............................C1
5 Arthur Hotel...B2
6 City Center Hotel....................................A2
7 David Citadel Hotel.................................E5
8 Harmony Hotel..C3
9 Jerusalem Hostel & Guest House........C2
10 Jerusalem Inn...D2
11 Mamilla Hotel..E5
12 Palatin Hotel...A1
13 Post Hostel...E3
14 Shamai Suites...B2

✖ Eating
15 Darna...D2
16 Focaccia Bar...B3
17 Hamarakia...E3
18 Mamilla Rooftop Restaurant.................E5
19 Pinati..A2
20 T'mol Shilshom......................................C2
21 Village Green..D2

◎ Drinking & Nightlife
22 Barood..D3
23 Cassette Bar...D2
24 Jabotinski..D4
25 Kadosh...D3
26 Mazkeka...E4
27 Mike's Place..D2
28 Sira...E4
    Videopub...(see 23)

❂ Entertainment
29 Bimot...B3
30 Time Elevator..F5

🛍 Shopping
31 Arman Darian Ceramic...........................E4
32 Danny Azoulay...C2
33 Greenvurcel..C3
34 Kippa Man..B2
35 Lametayel..C2
36 Steimatzky..D2

❶ Information
37 French Consulate....................................E7
38 Jerusalem Open House for
    Pride and Tolerance..............................D3
39 Super-Pharm...F5

Mediterranean piece by piece from its place of origin, Conegliano Veneto, the synagogue was reconstructed here in 1951. Within the same building is a collection of objects associated with Jewish life in Italy from the Renaissance period through to the present day.

Ades Synagogue SYNAGOGUE
(Map p72; cnr Be'ersheva & Shilo Sts; ⊘ hours vary) Built by the Syrian Halebi Congregation in 1901, this synagogue was named for Ovadia and Yosef Ades, the Aleppo brothers who financed the project. It quickly became a centre for Syrian *hazzanut* (Jewish liturgical singing) and saw the training of many a Jerusalem cantor. Today it maintains the rare tradition of *bakashot*, a set cycle of Kabbalistic poetry sung in the early hours of Shabbat during the winter months.

The synagogue is primarily for worshippers (though some tourists visit). It hosts two morning services and a combined afternoon/evening service, which visitors can attend; times are posted outside.

◉ King David Street

The most coveted stretch of real estate outside the Old City lies along King David (David HaMelekh) St, on a hillside west of Jaffa Gate. Dominated by the King David Hotel

(p97), the area includes parks, gardens and upmarket restaurants. In adjoining **Mamilla**, rows of new luxury apartments – many owned by Jews who live overseas for most of the year – overlook the walls of the Old City. Important landmarks include the Reform Movement's **Hebrew Union College** (Beit Shmuel; Map p80; www.beitshmuel.co.il; 6 Eliyahu Shama St) complex, part of which was designed by Moshe Safdie (whose architecture also graces Mamilla Mall and Yad Vashem), and the 1933 YMCA (p96), designed by Arthur Loomis Harmon, architect of New York's Empire State Building.

Montefiore Windmill LANDMARK
(Yemin Moshe Windmill; Map p72; ☑02-625-1258; Yemin Moshe; ⊘museum 9am-4pm Sun-Thu, to 1pm Fri) **FREE** This neighbourhood, Mishkenot Sha'ananim ('Tranquil Dwellings'), was largely developed by English Jewish philanthropist Sir Moses Montefiore, and its 1857 windmill was one of the first structures to be built outside the secure confines of the Old City.

St Andrew's Church CHURCH
(Map p72; ☑02-673-2401; www.standrewsjeru salem.org; 1 David Remez St, German Colony; ⊘church 9am-4pm Sun-Thu, to 1pm Fri) Towering like a Highland castle, St Andrew's Church

has been a small corner of Scotland ever since its first stone was laid in 1927. The so-called 'Scottish Church' was built in memory of the Scottish soldiers killed in action in the Holy Land during WWI. Scots continued to make use of the church during WWII, but these days a multitude of nationalities pass through, in particular to stop over at the excellent guesthouse (p96).

The building fuses Eastern and Western styles: note the Crusader-style church windows, with blue Hebron glass, the Armenian tiles and the broad Byzantine-style dome.

◉ Rehavia & Talbiyeh

These neighbourhoods were built in the early 20th century and are among the city's more fashionable places to live – Talbiyeh was built by wealthy Christian Arabs and Rehavia by Jewish intellectuals. These days the official residences of the prime minister and president are here. The upper (north-eastern) section of Gaza (Aza) Rd – the old route to Gaza – and Ramban St are particularly busy bar and cafe strips.

Both areas lie south of Bezalel St and west of King George V and Keren HaYesod Sts.

LA Mayer Museum
for Islamic Art   MUSEUM
(Map p72; 02-566-1291; www.islamicart.co.il; 2 HaPalmach St, Rehavia; adult/student/child 40/30/20NIS; 10am-3pm Mon-Wed, to 7pm Thu, to 2pm Fri & Sat; 13) Ornate artwork invites a close look within this gallery on Rehavia's southern fringe. The LA Mayer Museum exhibits treasures across the Islamic art world: 11th-century glassware and Mamluk pottery are worthy of attention, though the Iranian tile work steals the show. The museum serves as a useful primer on Islamic art's themes and development, and you can tour its three floors of inlaid wood and bejewelled weaponry in the space of an hour-long visit.

Opened in 1974, the museum also features a multimedia 'Introduction to Islam' hall that contextualises Islamic art within the faith's primary tenets while also delving into subjects including the life of Muhammad and Sufi mysticism.

Elsewhere, the museum's world renowned collection of clocks and watches includes many of the timepieces stolen in 1983 in Israel's most spectacular heist and recovered in 2008.

There are guided tours in English upon request (call ahead).

◉ German Colony

Despite the name, you'll hear just as much English, French and Hebrew as German spoken in this genteel neighbourhood, which begins just south of the Ottoman-era First Station complex (p102). Only occasional Gothic-style German lettering gives away the roots of the German Colony, founded by the Templars, a Protestant splinter group, in the 1880s. In this manicured, cosmopolitan area, life appears to revolve around reading the *Ha'aretz* newspaper and sipping coffee on cafe terraces. Evenings are a pleasant time to stroll here as there is a range of restaurants and cafes to spend time in.

Buses 7 and 34 travel to Emek Refa'im St from King George V St downtown.

◉ Talpiot

Haas Promenade   VIEWPOINT
(Talpiot) The Haas Promenade offers cypress-framed views across Jerusalem: its Old City, with tower blocks rising behind, and village-speckled valleys rolling into the distance. Several walking paths allow for a variety of angles on this expansive view. Go in the late afternoon, when the picturesque ensemble is bathed in coppery light.

Take bus 78 from the Central Bus Station and get off at the corner of Daniel Yanovski and HaAskan Sts.

◉ Givat Ram & Museum Row

The political seat of the Israeli government and two important museums are located in the government and university neighbourhood of Givat Ram, south of the Central Bus Station.

NAHLA'OT

Founded in the 1860s, this neighbourhood south of the Mahane Yehuda Market is a warren of narrow alleys where a number of old synagogues and *yeshivas* (Jewish religious seminaries) are hidden, many set in large stone-walled compounds. The most interesting street is HaGilboa, where you'll find a number of historic homes; each contains a plaque that describes the family that built the home. One street over, on HaCarmel, look for the attractive synagogue Hased veRahamim, with its unmistakable silver doors.

1. Western Wall (p65)
This 2000-year-old wall is Judaism's holiest prayer site.

2. Dome of the Rock (p58)
This shimmering dome is venerated by Muslims as sheltering the stone from where Prophet Muhammad ascended.

3. Church of the Holy Sepulchre (p60)
Built on what is believed to be the site of Jesus' crucifixion, burial and resurrection, this is one of Christianity's most sacred shrines.

4. Mahane Yehuda (p81)
Sample local produce and Middle Eastern delicacies at this lively market.

MEA SHE'ARIM

Walk north from Jaffa Rd along Strauss St and you'll soon enter a neighbourhood with squat, stone-fronted buildings, balconies adorned with drying laundry, bearded figures in black, and long-skirted mums trailed by a gaggle of formally dressed children. If you have the sense that you've stumbled upon an Eastern European *shtetl* (ghetto) of the 1880s then you are probably standing somewhere near Kikar Shabbat, the main intersection of Mea She'arim, Jerusalem's oldest ultra-Orthodox Jewish (Haredi) neighbourhood.

A throwback to older times, Mea She'arim was developed by ultra-Orthodox Eastern European immigrants who modelled their Jerusalem home on the ones they remembered from Poland, Germany and Hungary. Despite their transition to the Holy Land, residents have maintained the customs, habits and dress of 19th-century Eastern Europe. Fashions are conservative, including black suits and hats for men and floor-scraping dresses for women; even in the height of the Middle Eastern summer it's still customary among many Hasidic men to wear *shtreimels* (fur hats) on Shabbat and holidays.

Families are typically large and this fact has made Mea She'arim one of the fastest-growing neighbourhoods in Jerusalem, as well as contributing to the increasingly religious nature of the city. Yiddish is the preferred language on the street, as the ultra-Orthodox believe Hebrew to be a holy language suitable for religious purposes only. Days are often spent in prayer and business is a secondary pursuit – religious study is frequently financed by a combination of Israeli government subsidies and ultra-Orthodox communities abroad.

In the most conservative families, married women shave their heads and cover their bald scalp with a scarf or wig, in the name of modesty. For some, though, this is not enough, and in 2011 extremist groups tried to segregate some of Mea She'arim's sidewalks – men on one side, women on the other. The campaign, opposed by many mainstream ultra-Orthodox Jews, was declared unconstitutional by Israel's Supreme Court.

As this is a religious neighbourhood, visitors are expected to dress and act in a conservative manner. Large signs loom bearing the dress code, which includes knee-length skirts for women, and covered shoulders and elbow-length sleeves for both sexes. Don't take pictures of the residents (they resent being treated as a touristic curiosity) or speak to children or members of the opposite sex. Do not walk arm in arm or even hand in hand with anyone; kissing is definitely taboo. Disobeying local customs will lead to verbal objections or even stone throwing. If a confrontation with the police seems to be brewing, steer clear – at the time of research there had been a spate of aggressive encounters between police and locals, some violent.

Friday is the liveliest day to visit, as you'll see families heading to and from market in their preparations for Shabbat. On Friday nights the streets are awash with people taking a break from their Shabbat dinners. On Shabbat, don't drive into these areas: barriers put up by the municipality blocking the roads make it easier not to do so. If you do wander into one of these neighbourhoods, don't pull out your phone to figure out how to navigate your way out, as that could anger local residents who see using technology as a violation of the Sabbath.

Mea She'arim is within 15 minutes' walk of both Damascus Gate and the Jaffa Rd/King George V St junction.

★**Israel Museum**   MUSEUM
(☑02-670-8811; www.imj.org.il; 11 Ruppin Blvd, Museum Row; adult/student/child 5-17yr 54/39/27NIS; ☺10am-5pm Sat-Mon, Wed & Thu, 4-9pm Tue, 10am-2pm Fri; 🚍7, 9, 14, 32) More than 5000 years of cultural treasures are assembled around the vast Israel Museum's indoor and outdoor galleries. Highlights are the titanic statues of the **Archaeological Wing**, while the **Fine Arts Wing** showcases 20th-century Israeli art from carpet weaving to sculpture. Newcomers to Jewish culture will appreciate the **Rhythm of Life Room's** lavish displays on birth, marriage and death ceremonies. The prize exhibit is the **Dead Sea Scrolls**: housed in a distinctive shrine, these are among the world's oldest biblical manuscripts.

Before starting your tour (dedicate at least half a day), pick up a complimentary audio guide from the visitor centre. If you decide to spend a full day – and many visitors do – the excellent Modern (p102) restaurant serves lunch. There are also two (cheaper) cafes on site.

➡ Shrine of the Book

The distinctive lid-shaped roof of this pavilion was designed to symbolise the pots in which the Dead Sea Scrolls were kept. The first of the scrolls, more than 900 in all, were found in 1947 and date back to the time of the Bar Kochba Revolt (132–35 CE). Dealing with both secular and religious issues, they were thought to have been written by an ascetic group of Jews called the Essenes, who inhabited the area for about 300 years. The most important is the Great Isaiah Scroll, the largest (7.3m) and best preserved – it is reproduced in facsimile at the museum. The exhibit tells the story of the scrolls and the Essenes and displays some of the original documents.

➡ Archaeology Wing

Forming the most extensive collection of biblical and Holy Land archaeology in the world, the exhibits here are organised chronologically from prehistory to the Ottoman Empire. A group of 13th-century-BCE human-shaped clay coffins greets visitors in the first room, and other impressive displays include a 3rd-century mosaic floor from Nablus depicting events in the life of Achilles. Also notable is the 'House of David' Victory Stele, a fragmentary inscription from the First Temple period discovered at Tel Dan. This is the only contemporary, extrabiblical reference to the Davidic dynasty to have come to light thus far.

➡ Jewish Art & Life Wing

The prize exhibits here are four complete synagogues brought from various locations and reconstructed. One, the 18th-century Vittorio Veneto Synagogue, is adorned with gilt and plaster and was transported from Vittorio Veneto in Italy in 1965. The others are from Cochin in India, Paramaribo in Suriname and Horb am Main in Germany. Also worth seeking out is the painted Deller family sukkah (temporary wooden dwelling erected during the harvest festival of Sukkot), which dates from the 19th century and was smuggled out of Germany to Jerusalem in 1935. The rooms at the rear of the wing focus on Jewish costume and jewellery.

➡ Fine Arts Wing

The highlight here is the Impressionist and Post-Impressionist Gallery, which showcases work by Renoir, Pissarro, Degas, Sisley, Monet and Cézanne among many others. The Modern Art Gallery has works by Schiele, Rothko, Motherwell, Pollock, Modigliani and Bacon, and Israeli art is well represented in the Israeli Art pavilion, with striking paintings by Reuven Rubin and Yosef Zaritsky.

➡ Art Garden

A paved promenade leads from the Shrine of the Book to this sprawling sculpture garden, which was designed by Japanese artist and landscape architect Isamu Noguchi and includes works by 19th-, 20th- and 21st-century artists including Moore, Kapoor, LeWitt, Oldenburg, Serra, Rodin and Picasso.

Show your Bible Lands Museum ticket to get 10% off the entry price.

Bible Lands Museum
MUSEUM

(🖉02-561-1066; www.blmj.org; 21 Stefan Wise St, Museum Row; adult/student & child 44/22NIS; ☺9.30am-5.30pm Sun-Tue & Thu, to 9.30pm Wed, 10am-2pm Fri & Sat; 🚍7, 9, 14, 35, 66) Attempting to join the dots between archaeological finds and events related in the Bible, this sizeable museum has a trove of sculpture and everyday objects from various ancient civilisations. The museum layout is confusing, so use the audio guide or join the free guided tours between Sunday and Friday at 10.30am (English) and 11am (Hebrew), on Wednesday at 5.30pm (English) and 6pm (Hebrew), and on Saturday at 11.30am (Hebrew).

Among the most interesting displays are the Egyptian collection, including richly decorated sarcophagi and blue-glazed jewellery, Syrian fertility figures from the Neolithic period and a vessel whose carved lettering enabled historians to unlock cuneiform scripts.

Children under 18 are given free entrance on Saturday and Wednesday afternoons.

Knesset
LANDMARK

(Map p72; 🖉02-675-3337; www.knesset.gov.il; Ruppin Rd, Givat Ram; 🅿; 🚍7, 7A, 14, 35) **FREE** Israel's 120 lawmakers convene at the Knesset, a 1966 building belonging to the unfortunate multistorey-car-park school of architecture. Visitors can take a free one-hour guided tour of the committee rooms, plenary chamber, Chagall Hall (featuring three tapestries and several mosaics by the great 20th-century Jewish artist) and a display of the Declaration of Independence. The building is part of Kiryat Ben Gurion, the governmental district.

Tours are conducted on Sunday and Thursday in Hebrew, Arabic, English, French, Spanish, German and Russian (and Amharic, with advance notice); check the website for times. Tours for kids themed around Jewish symbols and customs take place on Sunday; enquire ahead. It's also possible to observe Knesset plenary debates from the public gallery on Monday and Tuesday from 4pm and Wednesday from 11am.

Visitors must have a passport and be modestly dressed (no shorts, sleeveless shirts, T-shirts bearing political slogans, or flip-flops). Be prepared for a swift interrogation (even if you're only walking past the site).

Next to the bus stops opposite the Knesset is a giant **bronze menorah**, a gift from the British Labour Party in 1956. It's decorated with panels representing important figures and events in Jewish history.

Monastery of the Cross　　　MONASTERY
(Map p72; ☑054-520-2281; 15NIS; ◷10am-4pm Mon-Sat Oct-Mar, to 6pm Apr-Sep; ☐15) The origins of this fortified monastery are cloaked in mystery. It is believed that Jesus's cross was constructed from wood grown in this valley, leading to a monastery being founded here in the 4th century; some historians link its construction to Empress Helena, mother of Constantine the Great. In the 11th century, the present structure was built under the instructions of King Bagrat IV of Georgia; the chapel remains faithful to Georgian style.

◉ Har Hazikaron

On the far western fringe of the city, between rows of housing blocks and the Jerusalem forest, is an area of wooded slopes and spectacular views known as Har Hazikaron (Mount of Remembrance). It is home to Mt Herzl, a military cemetery, and Yad Vashem.

★ Yad Vashem　　　MEMORIAL, MUSEUM
(☑info 02-644-3749, tour reservations 02-644-3802; www.yadvashem.org; Hazikaron St, Har Hazikaron; ◷9am-5pm Sun-Wed, to 8pm Thu, to 2pm Fri; ☐Mt Herzl) **FREE** Israel's official memorial to the six million Jews who died at the hands of the Nazis is powerful, poignant and a masterpiece of design. The museum's name was taken from Isaiah 56:5 and means

---

VARIETIES OF JEWISH DRESS

Wearing 'modest' (non-revealing) clothing is a central tenet in the lives of the Haredi community, commonly referred to as 'ultra-Orthodox' Jews (though some prefer the term 'traditional Orthodox'). Women wear long skirts or dresses (never trousers) and shirts or blouses with long sleeves. Men commonly wear black suits and white shirts with no tie. Married Haredi women cover their heads, usually with a wig, snood or scarf. All Haredi men wear some type of head covering, such as the following:

Kippa (yarmulke in Yiddish, skullcap in English) Worn by all Jewish men in synagogues and at holy sites, and by most observant Jewish men all of the time, the kippa is a reminder that God is constantly above the wearer. Knitted or crocheted kippot are worn by modern Orthodox or religious Zionist men; Haredi men tend to wear black velvet or cloth kippot, often under a hat, though some groups, such as the Braslavers, prefer white. In recent decades, women members of the Reform and Conservative movements have begun wearing kippot.

Shtreimel Said to be of Tartar origin, these large round fur hats are worn on Shabbat and holidays by married Hassidic and 'Yerushalmi' Jews (those belonging to the old-line Ashkenazi community of the city). Traditional fox- or marten-fur shtreimels can cost thousands of dollars, which is why their owners sometimes cover them in huge plastic shower caps when it rains.

Spodik Another fur hat worn by some Haredim on Shabbat or holidays, and also of Eastern European origin, but taller and thinner than the shtreimel.

Fedoras Haredi men and boys wear black hats during the weekdays. These usually take the form of a wide-brimmed fedora made using rabbit fur, or a round, wide-brimmed hat.

Other regularly worn religious clothing includes the **tallit katan**, a four-cornered undershirt with knotted tassels called tzitziot (usually the only part you can see). The knots are tied according to a formula spelled out in the Talmud and some are coloured with a special blue dye called t'chelet (Numbers 15:38).

The side curls that many Hasidic and traditional Yemenite men and boys wear are called **payot** (peyes in Yiddish). These reflect an interpretation of the biblical injunction against shaving the 'corners' (payot) of one's head (Leviticus 19:27), interpreted by the Mishnah as incumbent only on men.

'A Memorial and a Name'; as well as honouring the names of those killed, Yad Vashem's research centre continues to work tirelessly to record the names of victims who were not survived by anyone to mourn them. Allow at least three hours to visit this 18-hectare site.

Yad Vashem's main building is a vast concrete ark sunk into the earth, containing the **Holocaust History Museum**. Nine underground galleries in this prism-like hall detail the events leading up to the Shoah (the Holocaust), as well as the disturbing, deep-rooted history of anti-Semitism in Europe. With explanations in English and Hebrew, the galleries trace the story chronologically and thematically, and use artefacts, films, personal testimonies on video, photographs and art installations, leading visitors gradually out of darkness to a terrace overlooking the Jerusalem Forest.

Photos of those who perished cover the ceiling of the **Hall of Names**, and books filled with their names are arranged all around. A hole in the floor symbolises the lost unknown, victims whose names will never be recorded because they, their entire families, all their friends and everyone who had known them was killed, leaving no one to testify or say the mourning Kaddish (Jewish prayer).

Near the exit of the museum is a separate building housing the **Museum of Holocaust Art**, a collection of works created in ghettos and camps. Nearby there is an **Exhibitions Pavilion** housing temporary displays and a **synagogue** that visitors can use for private prayer; it is decorated with items from European synagogues that were destroyed.

In the **Hall of Remembrance** on the ground level an eternal flame burns near a crypt containing the ashes of victims brought from the death camps; the floor is inscribed with the names of 22 of the most infamous camps. Behind the hall are a number of other memorials, including the **Cattle Car Memorial**, one of the original train cars used to transport Jews from the ghettos to the camps. Also here is the **Garden of the Righteous Among the Nations**, established in honour of the thousands of non-Jews who risked their lives to rescue Jews during the Holocaust.

Closer to the visitors centre is the poignant **Children's Memorial**, dedicated to the 1.5 million Jewish children who died in the Holocaust. Dug into the bedrock, the sombre underground memorial contains a solitary flame reflected infinitely by hundreds of mirrors. Recorded voices read the names of children who perished. Be careful as you enter as it will take a while for your eyes to adjust to the darkness. Close by, **Warsaw Ghetto Square** contains an imposing red-brick memorial to the fierce resistance of fighters in the Warsaw Ghetto Uprising of 1943.

The JLR Mt Herzl stop is a short walk away; the journey from City Hall takes 15 minutes. When you alight from the tram, cross the road towards the forest and walk for 10 minutes up gently sloping Hazikaron St. Alternatively, wait at the bus stop en route for a free shuttle, which runs every 20 minutes.

Note that on Thursday, many of the memorials close at 5pm (the Holocaust History Museum, Museum of Holocaust Art, Exhibitions Pavilion and the synagogue remain open until 8pm). Entrance to the Holocaust History Museum is not permitted for children under the age of 10.

Herzl Museum MUSEUM
(☑ 02-632-1515; www.herzl.org.il; Herzl Blvd, Har Hazikaron; adult/student & child 25/20NIS; ⊙ 8.30am-5pm Sun-Wed, to 7pm Thu, to 12.15pm Fri; ⊒ Mt Herzl) The history of the Zionist dream is detailed in the Herzl Museum, a multimedia journey into the life of Theodor Herzl, the father of modern Zionism. A one-hour guided tour in various languages including English tells Herzl's story; bookings are essential.

Herzl's quest began in fin de siècle Paris, where the secular, Budapest-born journalist was working as a correspondent for a Vienna newspaper. After witnessing violent outbreaks of anti-Semitism in the wake of the 1894 Dreyfus treason trial, he dedicated himself to the creation of a Jewish state where Jews would not be subject to such hatred. Three years of campaigning culminated in the first World Zionist Congress, held in Basel, Switzerland, in 1897. Herzl continued campaigning over the next seven years, until his death in 1904. His grave, a simple black marker with his name etched upon it, is on a small knoll west of the museum. Nearby are the graves of several Israeli prime ministers and presidents, including Golda Meir and Yitzhak Rabin.

A short walk north leads to the military cemetery, or you can continue west down a path that leads to Yad Vashem.

RELIGIOUS SERVICES IN JERUSALEM

Experience a slice of holiness in Jerusalem by attending Shabbat services, Friday prayers or a Sunday-morning church service. Dress modestly.

Shabbat services are typically held on Friday evening shortly after candle lighting (36 minutes before sunset) and on Saturday morning starting between 8.30am and 9.30am (Sephardic and especially Yemenite synagogues may begin earlier). Every Jewish neighbourhood has a variety of synagogues, the vast majority of them Orthodox or ultra-Orthodox. Nahla'ot is famous for the diversity of its scores of tiny houses of prayer, including one that follows the traditions of Aleppo (Syria).

Jerusalem synagogues that aren't traditionally Orthodox:

Har El (www.kharel.org.il) Israel's first Reform synagogue, founded in 1958.

Kol HaNeshama (www.kolhaneshama.org.il) Sizeable Reform congregation.

Moreshet Yisrael (www.moreshetyisrael.org) Conservative/Masorti.

Shira Hadasha (www.shirahadasha.org.il) A feminist Orthodox community.

For details on church services, see the Christian information centre website (www.cicts.org) and click the 'Masses and Services' link.

Muslims can join Friday prayers in the Al Aqsa Mosque (p59), providing there are no security restrictions in place; check with the tourist office (p107) at Jaffa Gate.

◉ Ein Kerem

Hidden in a valley on Jerusalem's western outskirts is this pretty village of Arab-built stone houses surrounded by Lebanese cedars and native pine trees. The small community is home to several churches related to John the Baptist, and the Chagall Windows are not too far away. The history of the town was rather ordinary until the middle of the 6th century, when Christian pilgrims identified it as the likely home of Elizabeth, mother of John the Baptist. Inevitably, shrines and churches were built over holy sites. The 1948 Arab–Israeli War caused the local Arab residents to flee the town; their homes were later taken over by immigrants from Morocco and Romania. A growing student population has breathed new life into the community.

To reach the village, take bus 28 from the Central Bus Station or Mt Herzl.

Church of St John the Baptist   CHURCH
(☏ 02-632-3000; Ein Kerem; ◷ 9am-noon & 2.30-5pm Sun-Fri Apr-Sep, to 4.45pm Oct-Mar) The blue-and-white tiled interior of the Franciscan-owned Church of St John is reminiscent of European churches – not surprising, as it was funded by the Spanish monarchy in the mid-19th century. The paintings are by Spanish artists, and there is a royal coat of arms above the entrance. Towards the front of the church is the grotto where it is believed John the Baptist came into the world (Luke 1:5-25, 57-80); a small marble circle under the altar marks the spot.

The church is located on a street just east of Ein Kerem's main road; follow the bell tower.

Church of the Visitation   CHURCH
(☏ 02-641-7291; Ein Kerem; ◷ 8-11.45am & 2.30-5pm Oct-Mar, to 6pm Apr-Sep) This modern Franciscan church is built over what is said to have been the home of Zacharias and Elizabeth; it's named for Mary's visit to Elizabeth (Luke 1:39-49) when both women were pregnant. The prayer that Mary is said to have uttered ('My soul exalts the Lord'; Luke 1:46-56) is inscribed on the walls in more than 40 languages.

From Ein Kerem's main intersection, walk along the narrow road heading south; the church will appear on the left after about 10 minutes.

Chagall Windows   SYNAGOGUE
(☏ 02-677-6271; www.hadassah-med.com; Ein Kerem; ◷ 8am-1pm & 2-3.30pm Sun-Thu) [FREE] Intended as a gift of love and peace to the Jewish people, modernist artist Marc Chagall created 12 stained-glass panels for the synagogue of the Hadassah Medical Centre, Ein Kerem (not to be confused with the Hadassah-Mt Scopus Medical Centre across town). Chagall's dreamlike images depict the tribes of Israel, referenced in Genesis 49 and Deuteronomy 33.

To get here, take the tram west from the Central Bus Station and get off at the last stop (Mt Herzl), where you can transfer to bus 27. This will bring you to the hospital.

📚 Courses

Ulpan Or LANGUAGE
(📞02-561-1132; http://ulpanor.com/hebrew-courses/hebrew-learning-jerusalem; 2nd fl, 43a Emek Rafa'im St, German Colony) This *ulpan* (Hebrew-language school) is proud of its 'rapid language acquisition' teaching techniques. Indeed, it says that after a 90-minute one-on-one 'Cup O'Hebrew' session (US$116), which is conducted over coffee, you will have acquired basic conversational skills. It also offers programs tailored to families and groups.

Ulpan Beit Ha'Am LANGUAGE
(Map p72; 📞02-545-6891, 02-624-0034; ulpanheithaam@gmail.com; Gerard Behar Center, 11 Betsal'el St, Downtown; 2/3/5 days a week per month 394/613/920NIS; ⊗8am-12.30pm Sun-Thu) Run by the Jerusalem municipality, this city-centre program offers rolling admission to its Hebrew classes.

Hebrew University Ulpan LANGUAGE
(📞02-588-2603; https://overseas.huji.ac.il/heb programs; Rothberg International School, Boyar Bldg, Hebrew University of Jerusalem, Mt Scopus; course fees US$1730-$2385) Offers intensive Hebrew summer courses (late June to late September) of up to 11 weeks. The approach is more academic than in non university *ulpanim*. Fees don't include accommodation.

Ulpan Etzion LANGUAGE
(📞02-636-7310, 02-636-7326; www.jewishagency.org/ulpanetzionjerusalem; General Pierre Koenig St; per person 7200NIS) Founded in 1949, Israel's first Hebrew-language school is a convivial experience, offering Hebrew study to university graduates aged 22 to 35. Five-month courses begin in January and July. The fee covers shared accommodation and meals.

Al Quds Centre for Jerusalem Studies LANGUAGE
(Map p52; 📞02-628-7517; www.jerusalem-studies.alquds.edu; Muslim Quarter, Old City) Classes at this institute are held on the atmospheric campus of Al Quds University in the Old City. The centre offers 60- and 75-hour courses (US$495 to US$860) in spoken Arabic and Modern Standard Arabic for those at beginner, intermediate and advanced levels.

🧭 Tours

The municipality's website offers free maps and apps for 15 self-guided audio walking tours of the Old City (www.itraveljerusalem.com/trs/old-city-self-guided-audio-tours). Five tours in the Jewish quarter are accessible for visitors in wheelchairs. Tours are in English,

Russian and Hebrew and are available for download to both Apple and Android devices.

Tour guides offering their services outside the Jaffa Gate are often unlicensed and may claim they can give you free entry to various monuments (none of the monuments they visit charge for entry). If you need a guide, ask the tourist office or opt for a reputable operator such as Abraham Tours (www.abrahamtours.com; affiliated with Abraham Hostel, p94, or Green Olive Tours.

⭐ Sandemans New Jerusalem Tours WALKING
(www.newjerusalemtours.com; ⊗8.45am, 11am & ?pm) FREE Well organised, friendly and with an impressive wealth of knowledge, Sandemans' free tours take place three times a day and are an ideal introduction to Jerusalem's Old City. Bookings aren't usually necessary (except in high season). Tips are appreciated (50NIS per person is appropriate). Most tours begin at Jaffa Gate (p59); look for the guides in red T-shirts.

Green Olive Tours WALKING
(📞03-721-9540; www.greenolivetours.com) This well-regarded company has Israeli and Arab owners and offers a daily walking tour of the Old City (three hours, 165NIS), a twice-weekly walking and light-rail day tour of West Jerusalem including Yad Vashem (260NIS) and a weekly walking tour of the East–West divide (three hours, 140NIS). It also runs a number of tours into the West Bank, including a Banksy tour of Bethlehem and a visit to Hebron.

Free Saturday Tours WALKING
(📞050-593-1450; www.itraveljerusalem.com/free-saturday-tours; ⊗10am-1pm Sat) FREE Exploring a different neighbourhood each week, these three-hour tours are offered by the municipality and led by licensed guides. They begin from Safra Sq (26 Jaffa St), near the palm trees, and are usually conducted in English.

City Tour Jerusalem WALKING
(📞054-930-1499; www.citytourjerusalem.com; from US$100) Offers guided excursions around Jerusalem's Old City as well as Mahane Yehuda Market (p81), the City of David (p75) and the Israel Museum (p86).

🎊 Festivals & Events

Israel Festival PERFORMING ARTS
(http://israel-festival.org; ⊗late May–mid-Jun) Music, dance and theatre performances by Israeli and international artists span a three-week period for this renowned festival founded in 1961.

Jerusalem Film Festival   FILM
(www.jff.org.il; ⊙mid-Jul) One of the largest film festivals in the Middle East. Screenings are held in July in indoor and outdoor venues.

Jerusalem Sacred Music Festival   MUSIC
(http://en.mekudeshet.com; ⊙late Sep) With a unifying theme of peace between different faiths, this musical extravaganza hosts performances from around the world over four joyous days. The festival includes an all-night performance in the Citadel.

★ **Lights in Jerusalem**   ART
(www.lights-in-jerusalem.com; ⊙late Jun–mid-Jul) Huge video projections and 3D light installations on streets and landmark buildings heighten the fairy-tale atmosphere of the Old City, bathing its ancient walls in coloured lights.

Balabasta   FOOD & DRINK
(⊙various dates in Jul) As if Mahane Yehuda (p81) wasn't lively enough already, this raucous event adds free nibbles, DJ sets, eating games and gourmet tours to Jerusalem's favourite market, plus cafes and stalls open late. Ask at the tourist office (p107) for specific dates.

Jerusalem Wine Festival   WINE
(www.imj.org.il; ⊙late Aug-early Sep) Held over four genteel evenings, this festival in the garden of the Israel Museum (p86) is probably the most important Israeli wine event of the year. Boutique wineries join international names in showcasing their wares through sophisticated tasting evenings, accompanied by nibbles from cheese and olives to sushi.

Jerusalem Opera Festival   MUSIC
(http://jerusalem-opera.com; ⊙late Jun) Opera performances unfold in dramatic outdoor settings around Jerusalem at this highly acclaimed event. Book ahead.

Jerusalem International Oud Festival   MUSIC
(www.confederationhouse.org; ⊙Nov) International and Israeli performers showcase the oud, a traditional Middle Eastern stringed instrument, over 10 days at this winter festival. It's organised by the Confederation House Centre for Ethnic Music and Poetry and held in venues around town.

Jerusalem Beer Festival   BEER
(www.jerusalembeer.com; tickets from 40NIS; ⊙Aug) More than 120 local and international beers are poured for this hoppy event in Gan HaAtsma'ut (Independence Park).

🛏 Sleeping

Downtown and the Old City have the biggest selection of places to stay, though decent midrange options are thin on the ground. The Old City is atmospheric, but downtown offers proximity to restaurants, bars, cafes and public transport.

Rates can fluctuate wildly between seasons and in response to political disturbances. High-season rates usually apply from April to June and from September to October, as well as during Easter, Christmas and New Year.

🛏 Old City

Budget and high-end hotels are plentiful in the Old City, with little of quality in between. If you arrive in Jerusalem by taxi or sherut (shared taxi) and are staying in the Old City, you'll need to alight at one of the city gates and walk to your hotel. (If you have your own car, you'll need to stay outside the Old City.) Note that the call to prayer can be a problem for light sleepers in the Muslim Quarter – bring earplugs.

Citadel Youth Hostel   HOSTEL $
(Map p52; ☏02-628-5253; www.citadelyouthhostel.com; 20 St Mark's Rd, Armenian Quarter; mattress on roof 50NIS, dm 63NIS, d 207NIS, s/d with shared bathroom 123/177NIS; @🛜) Seconds away from the markets, steeped in history, yet somewhat shabby, the Citadel is a perfect example of a hostel with unrealised potential. Parts of the building date back 700 years and while the stone-walled rooms have atmosphere, the beds are worn and the bathrooms poorly maintained.

Golden Gate Inn   GUESTHOUSE $
(Map p52; ☏02-628-4317; www.goldengate4.com; 10 Souq Khan Al Zeit St, Muslim Quarter; r from 250NIS; 🛜) Set within an atmospheric building that has existed in one form or another since 1155, this family-run guesthouse near Damascus Gate (p68) feels threadbare. There are en-suite double and family rooms with slightly mildewed bathrooms, and ceiling fans may not be enough to keep you cool. But it's cheap, there's a rooftop with views, and you can tumble straight into the souq.

Note that wi-fi only works in the lobby, and alcohol is forbidden on the premises.

★ **Austrian Hospice**   GUESTHOUSE $$
(Map p52; ☏02-626-5800; www.austrianhospice.com; 37 Via Dolorosa, Muslim Quarter; dm/s/d/tr €32/97/140/198; @🛜) Stepping into this gated complex feels like discovering a

treasure. This castle-like guesthouse first opened in 1863 and its gardens, archways and stone walls ooze history. Private rooms are simply furnished but large, with good beds. Single-sex dorms are in the basement, where there are also squeaky-clean shared bathrooms. There's a €7 surcharge for stays of one night. Half-board is available for an additional €16 per person.

The hospice is on the corner of Al Wad St and Via Dolorosa. Ring the intercom to enter (reception is open 7am to 11pm).

Hashimi Hotel
HOTEL $$

(Map p52; ☑02-628-4410; www.hashimihotel.com; 73 Souq Khan Al Zeit St, Muslim Quarter; s/d/tr from US$80/110/280; @ 🛜) An oasis in the Old City, this hotel in a 400-year-old building has light-flooded, floral-patterned rooms (ask for a corner room with a view). There are a few rules (no alcohol anywhere, and no unmarried couples in the same room), but they'll be nothing as you sip mint tea on the rooftop overlooking extraordinary views of the Dome of the Rock (p58).

Lutheran Guesthouse
GUESTHOUSE $$

(Map p52; ☑02-626-6888; www.luth-guesthouse-jerusalem.com; St Mark's Rd, Armenian Quarter; s/d/tr/q €71/109/142/185; 🛜) Beyond the heavy steel door are a variety of rooms, a courtyard garden and a rooftop reading room and lounge, built over mid-19th-century foundations. Smallish rooms are simply furnished but comfortable, and there's a generous buffet breakfast. From Jaffa Gate, walk down David St, then take the first right up a narrow staircase; the guesthouse is 100m down on the left.

Add lunch or dinner for an extra €18. Book ahead: this place is popular.

Hotel New Imperial
HOTEL $$

(Map p52; ☑02-628-2261; www.newimperial.com; cnr Demetrius Hakadosh & Omar El Hatab St, Old City; s/d/q from US$75/140/240; 🛜) The elegantly weathered facade of the New Imperial, a few steps from Jaffa Gate, harks back to the 1880s. Its common areas from reception to the breakfast room are a trove of Islamic art curios. However, the rooms are a lottery: some are poky and misshapen (with an attic-style sleeping space above the bathroom) and others are tidily renovated.

Christ Church Guesthouse
GUESTHOUSE $$$

(Map p52; ☑02-627-7727; www.cmj-israel.org; Omar Ibn Al Khattab Sq, Old City; s/tw/ste/q 430/645/710/985NIS; P @ 🛜) This wonderfully maintained guesthouse gets high marks for its period atmosphere, multilingual staff, prime location and garden setting. The simply furnished rooms have stone floors, domed ceilings and comfortable beds, and there are lounges where guests can relax over free tea and coffee.

JERUSALEM FOR CHILDREN

Tisch Zoological Gardens (Jerusalem Biblical Zoo; ☑02-675-0111; www.jerusalemzoo.org.il; 1 Derech Aharon Shulov, Malcha; adult/child 55/42NIS; ⊗9am-7pm Sun-Thu, to 4.30pm Fri, 10am-6pm Sat; P; 🚌26) A welcome break from archaeological sites and suitable for all ages. There's a special emphasis on species mentioned in the Bible, arranged around a pretty artificial lake.

Bloomfield Science Museum (☑02-654-4888; www.mada.org.il; Hebrew University, Ruppin Rd, Museum Row; adult/child under 5yr 49NIS/free; ⊗10am-6pm Mon-Thu, to 2pm Fri; 🚻; 🚌9, 14) Halls of mirrors and a host of science-themed games, with the suitable age groups flagged, plus a play area and snacks out back.

Time Elevator (Map p80; ☑02-624-8381; www.time-elevator-jerusalem.co.il; 6 Yitzhak Kariv Rd, Downtown; 54NIS, internet bookings 46NIS; ⊗10am-5pm Sun-Thu, to 2pm Fri, noon-6pm Sat; 🚻; 🚌City Hall) An interactive cinema experience for over-fives, with panoramic screens and special effects synchronised to the action of the film. Book in advance.

City of David (p75) Older kids can wade through spooky, water-filled Hezekiah's Tunnel (the water level is around 70cm).

Israel Museum (p86) Older children and teens may enjoy the Youth Wing, which brims with historic toys and work by child artists.

Smart Tour (Map p72; ☑02-561-8056; http://smart-tour.co.il; 4 David Remez St, First Station; electric bike per day 199NIS; ⊗9am-6pm Sun-Thu, to 12.30pm Fri) Discovering Jerusalem is a lot more fun on a Segway or electric bike, and this operator can lead guided cycling tours tailored for families.

As it's part of the same complex as the first Protestant church in the Middle East, Christ Church (p65), the majority of guests are pilgrims seeking to participate in church services or enjoy prayerful reflection. The cafe (p99), on the other hand, is a lively meeting point for all stripes of tourists in Jerusalem.

East Jerusalem

The area immediately east of the Old City's Damascus Gate is predominantly Palestinian. East Jerusalem is considered occupied territory, so unsurprisingly there are additional considerations when staying here: many taxis will refuse to bring you from west to east, streets are less manicured than their West Jerusalem equivalents, and many locals will urge you not to walk East Jerusalem's streets after dark. Nonetheless, there is a mix of Arab- and multinational-owned hotels here, from midrange (like the pleasant Legacy Hotel) to lavish (such as the famed American Colony Hotel).

★**American Colony Hotel** HISTORIC HOTEL **$$$**
(Map p72; ☑02-627-9777; www.americancolony. com; 1 Louis Vincent St; s from US$320, d US$320-550, ste US$675-875; P@🕲🕲) East Jerusalem's VIP choice is this luxurious complex based around a mid-19th-century building. The American Colony Hotel retains much of its historic charm – think mother-of-pearl inlaid furniture and intricate tile work – though rooms sprinkle just the right amount of modernity into the mix. Standard rooms have a classic style (hardwood beds, flowing drapes), while some suites have chandelier windows and four-posters.

National Hotel HOTEL **$$$**
(Map p72; ☑02-627-8880; www.nationalhotel -jerusalem.com; As Zahra St; s/d/tr/f US$125/ 185/250/300; P🕲; 🖫Shivtei Israel) This venerable hotel has come a long way since it was a two-room guesthouse in 1948. Guests have included King Hussein of Jordan and former US president Jimmy Carter, and the National's faded glamour is beguiling. Five minutes' walk from Herod's Gate, the hotel's 121 rooms have smart navy-and-white beds, cooling tiled floors, safes and fridges. The staff is exceptionally friendly.

St George's Guesthouse GUESTHOUSE **$$$**
(Map p72; ☑02-628-3302; www.stgeorgesguest house.org; 20 Derekh Shchem/Nablus Rd; s/d standard US$110/150, deluxe US$150/180;

P@🕲; 🖫Shivtei Israel) Within a century-old Anglican church, this tranquil guesthouse has been welcoming pilgrims since 1923 (the buildings previously housed the choir school and clergy). Twin guest rooms, with crisp linens, satellite TV and kettle, are set around a courtyard garden; the deluxe versions, with stone walls, extra space and modernised bathrooms, are worth the extra charge.

Jerusalem Hotel HOTEL **$$$**
(Map p72; ☑02-628-3282; www.jrshotel.com; Derekh Shchem/Nablus Rd; s/d/f US$130/160/240; @🕲; 🖫Shivtei Israel) Decorated glass and a tangle of vines adorn the entrance to the 19th-century mansion housing the small, family-run Jerusalem Hotel. Its 14 high-ceilinged rooms are uniquely decorated with embroidered throws and antique furnishings such as huge mirrors and Andalusian side tables. Some rooms have air-con, others fans. It's five minutes' walk from Damascus Gate.

Legacy Hotel HOTEL **$$$**
(Map p72; ☑02-627-0800; www.jerusalemlegacy. com; 29 Derekh Shchem/Nablus Rd; s/d from US$150/185; P@🕲; 🖫Shivtei Israel) Elegant cream-coloured rooms fill this refined hotel in a former YMCA building. Bathrooms would benefit from a spot of maintenance and the breakfast buffet is a shadow of those in other hotels, but the cordial multilingual staff and chic, large rooms compensate. The rooftop terrace is an excellent place to watch the sun set as Jerusalem sparkles below.

Facilities include a 5th-floor restaurant with great views over the Old City, a lobby bar and a garden cafe. Guests are given free entry to the YMCA gym and indoor pool in the building next door.

Downtown

The commercial heart of predominantly Jewish West Jerusalem is full of sleeping options to suit all budgets and has a thriving hostel scene.

★**Abraham Hostel** HOSTEL **$**
(Map p72; ☑02-650-2200; https://abrahamhos tels.com; 67 HaNevi'im St, Davidka Sq; dm 85-115NIS, s 270-330NIS, d 300-420NIS, f 490-620NIS; @🕲; 🖫Ha-Davidka) Lively Abraham Hostel has earned its popularity. Its friendly crew easily covers traveller essentials – 24-hour reception, laundry (12NIS), shared kitchen – and ups the ante with a sweet bar and lounge, nightly events and culturally enriching tours. Choose from men's, women's

or mixed dorms, or basic but clean en-suite rooms. Mingle with the international crowd and sigh at the rooftop views: you've arrived.

If you're here on Shabbat, the hostel holds a dinner for up to 40 people (40NIS). You should also take advantage of the language exchange (Monday), enjoy happy hour (6pm to 8pm) at the bar and sign up for at least one event, whether it's the excellent pub crawl or the hummus-making class.

Shared bathrooms have 24-hour hot water, but in private rooms there's a timer that takes 20 minutes to make the water toasty.

The entrance is on HaNevi'im St near the bus stop.

★ Post Hostel   HOSTEL $
(Map p80; ☑ 02-581-3222; http://theposthostel. com; 23 Jaffa Rd; dm US$24-32, d US$105-125, tr US$145; ☎; ☐ City Hall) On the 3rd floor of an old post office is this airy and well-run hostel. Bold red and navy decor and postal-themed murals pay homage to the building's past, and the digs are simple but spotless, ranging from private rooms to dorms (single sex and mixed). The bar, roof terrace and chill-out area with pool table promote a relaxing, convivial vibe.

Jerusalem Hostel & Guest House   HOSTEL $
(Map p80; ☑ 02-623-6102; www.jerusalem-hos tel.com; 44 Jaffa Rd, Zion Sq; dm 80-90NIS, d 240-330NIS; @☎; ☐ Jaffa Center) An old-school backpacker ambience infuses the well-maintained Jerusalem Hostel. Rooms might be plain, but the common areas are given a lift with antiques, old photos, Judaica and (in the entrance vestibule) huge columns. There's a choice of en-suite rooms and single-sex and mixed dorms, as well as a communal kitchen and a roof terrace with couches to chill on.

City Center Hotel   APARTMENT $$
(Map p80; ☑ 02-650-9494; www.citycentervaca tion.com; 17 King George St, cnr HaHistadrut St; studios 512-640NIS, ste 695-824NIS; P@☎; ☐ Jaffa Center) 'Plenty of character but looking a bit worn' is a common descriptor for accommodation in this ancient city. And that's why the existence of this spick-and-span modern hotel should be wholeheartedly celebrated. Spread over two buildings in a conveniently located part of the modern city centre, it offers 38 comfortable rooms with kitchenette.

Shamai Suites   APARTMENT $$
(Map p80; ☑ 02-579-7705; www.shamaisuites.com; 15 Ben Hillel St; studios US$120-150, ste US$135-

220; ☎; ☐ Jaffa Center) With mod cons and minimalist design, these suites are a superb option for self-caterers. Gleaming studios and one- and two-bedroom suites all feature flat-screen TVs, nicely equipped kitchenettes and balconies, and they're tended by a daily housekeeping service. Attentive, multilingual staff complete the picture.

Jerusalem Inn   HOTEL $$
(Map p80; ☑ 072-256-6964; http://smarthotels. co.il; 7 Horkanos St; d from US$110; ☎) It may look a little IKEA, but the pint-sized rooms at this chain hotel have excellent beds, mini-fridges and glass-fronted bathrooms (admittedly not ideal if you and your travel companion are shy). But the ensemble is cosy and the hotel has a superb location for wining and dining: it's only 150m from Jaffa Rd.

Palatin Hotel   HOTEL $$
(Map p80; ☑ 02-623-1141; www.palatinhotel.com; 4 Agrippas St; s/d/ste from US$105/130/180; ☎; ☐ Jaffa Center) Located near the hub of Jerusalem's shopping and cafe district, homey, family-run Palatin has 33 small but reasonably comfortable rooms with writing desks and antique tiled floors (though the bathrooms aren't ageing gracefully). The friendly service and superb location almost compensate for the lack of soundproofing and the polyester sheets.

★ Harmony Hotel   HOTEL $$$
(Map p80; ☑ 02-621-9999; www.atlas.co.il/harmo ny-hotel-jerusalem; 6 Yo'el Salomon St; s/d from US$180/200; P@☎; ☐ Jaffa Center) We love Harmony as much for its ethos as for the quality of its rooms. Photos extend across the lobby ceiling representing Jerusalem's various religions, and accommodating staff and a free happy hour (5pm to 7pm Sunday to Friday) enhance the welcoming ambience. Rooms have a kingly colour scheme of purple and emerald, and bathrooms dazzle with ultramodern fittings and chessboard tiles.

★ Arthur Hotel   BOUTIQUE HOTEL $$$
(Map p80; ☑ 02-623-9999; www.atlas.co.il/ arthur-jerusalem; 13 Dorot Rishonim St; d from US$184; P@☎; ☐ Jaffa Center) Rooms at the nostalgic Arthur Hotel employ fur-lined cushions, embroidered headboards and antique furnishings to conjure the 1920s. Jewel-toned rooms vary in style, but bathrooms are glossy and well maintained; try to get a balcony room in the rear of the building. The breakfast here is impressive, and there's a happy hour with gratis snacks and drinks.

7 Kook Hotel & Suites

BOUTIQUE HOTEL $$$

(Map p80; ☑02-580-8068; http://7-kook-bou tique-hotel.jerusalem-hotels-il.com/en; Ticho St; excl breakfast d US$160-570, studios from US$600; 🛜; 🚇 Jaffa Center) Part of an upmarket apartment development, 7 Kook offers crisp parquet-floored and white-walled double rooms and studios, all with great soundproofing, excellent bathroom, espresso machine and kettle. Prices vary enormously by season and room: the simplest have no windows, the best are huge and include sofa beds, but all are elegant.

Notre Dame Guest House

GUESTHOUSE $$$

(Map p52; ☑02-627-9111; www.notredamecenter. org; 3 Paratroopers Rd, near Old City; d from US$300, ste from US$430; 🛜; 🚇 City Hall) Most of the rooms at this splendidly located Vatican-owned guesthouse have wonderful views of the Old City and the Mount of Olives. The building dates from 1904, and its rooms have been refurbished with a refined, classic feel. The guesthouse also has a Mediterranean restaurant with a garden terrace downstairs, and a cheese and wine restaurant (p100) on the rooftop.

🛏 Mamilla & Yemin Moshe

St Andrew's Scottish Guesthouse

GUESTHOUSE $$

(Map p72; ☑02-673-2401; www.scotsguesthouse. com; 1 David Remez St, Yemin Moshe; s/d/ste US$135/170/380; 🅿🛜) A lofty location and a stone exterior combine to give St Andrew's an edifying air. Accommodation has a school-dormitory feel, but rooms are sizeable, with high ceilings and surgically clean bathrooms, and Scottish flavour has been infused throughout (including generous use of tartan). More expensive rooms include balconies; ask for room 1 for spectacular views towards the Old City.

YMCA Three Arches Hotel

HOTEL $$

(Map p72; ☑02-569-2692; 26 King David/David HaMelekh St, Yemin Moshe; s/tw/tr/ste from US$137/166/174/200; 🅿@🛜🏊) Stay at the Three Arches and be happy in the knowledge that your hotel is one of modern Jerusalem's most recognisable landmarks. Beneath the soaring, 46m clock tower, the main building has ornate ceilings and huge, brassy chandeliers; rooms are creak-

---

JERUSALEM ON SHABBAT

Thirty-six minutes before sunset on Friday you can hear the drone of a siren vibrating across the Jerusalem hills. This signifies the start of Shabbat and with it comes a pronounced spiritual vibe that permeates the streets. All across the city you can see Jewish Jerusalemites dressed in their Shabbat best, drawn to the Western Wall or carrying backpacks full of food as they head to the home of a friend or relative for the customary Friday-night dinner.

Put on the best clothes you've got and follow the crowds down to the Western Wall to marvel at the singing, dancing and prayer that ignite this magical place. Alternatively, visit a synagogue for Friday-night Kabbalat Shabbat services.

If given the opportunity, be sure to join a local family for their Shabbat meal. If you're staying at the Abraham Hostel (p94) downtown, you can join its Shabbat dinner. Otherwise, you'll need to scope out a restaurant ahead of time, as most restaurants in West Jerusalem close on Friday night. Restaurants that remain open include Adom (p102) in the German Colony, and Focaccia Bar (p100) and the Notre Dame Cheese & Wine Restaurant (p100) downtown. Later in the evening, much to the chagrin of ultra-Orthodox Jews, some of the downtown bars will be open for business.

While the downtown area and the Jewish Quarter of the Old City are closed on Saturday, this is just another day for Jerusalem's Arab population, and most of the sights are open in the rest of the Old City, Mt Zion, the Mount of Olives and East Jerusalem.

On Saturday you can join two free walking tours: the three-hour walking tour (p91) offered by the municipality and the Sandemans tour of the Old City (p91).

There are no services on Egged buses and the light-rail system on Shabbat, but some taxis continue to operate. The Arab bus network and service taxis operate from the Damascus Gate area, and Shabbat is as good a time as any to visit a West Bank city such as Jericho or Bethlehem. Ein Gedi, Masada and the Dead Sea are other popular day-trip options – all-inclusive tours are offered by tour operators and hostels in the city. You can also catch a shared minibus to Tel Aviv from Neveim St.

ier but classily attired (quality bedlinen, crimson trimmings and the occasional flash of gold).

King David Hotel

HOTEL $$$

(Map p72; ☑02-620-8888; www.danhotels.com; 23 King David/David HaMelekh St; r US$550-800, ste US$1020-2700; P@奈) One of Jerusalem's grandest addresses is the 1930s-era King David, whose art-deco stylings, from velvet couches and gold drapery to marble-top tables, will floor you from the moment you enter. And that's just the reception area: rooms have throne-like beds, large marble bathrooms and every modern convenience. Standard rooms aren't huge, but deluxe rooms have dainty velveteen sofas and writing desks.

Mamilla Hotel

DESIGN HOTEL $$$

(Map p80; ☑02-548-2222; www.mamillahotel. com; 11 King Solomon/Shlomo HaMelekh St; r US$400-475, ste US$585-860; P@奈; City Hall) For the fashionable set, this swish hotel couldn't be better located: east is pedestrianised Mamilla Mall, while the restaurants and bars of Hillel St (and the 'Downtown Triangle') are just west. The building's peach-coloured stone mimics that of the Old City, inside, sizeable rooms seem even larger thanks to glass-walled bathrooms, while maroon, navy and white decor bestows a classic feel. Suites enjoy views of the Old City.

Completing the glamorous picture are a spa with hammam, a gym, an indoor pool, two bars, a cafe and a rooftop Mediterranean restaurant (kosher).

David Citadel Hotel

HOTEL $$$

(Map p80; ☑02-621-1111; www.thedavidcitadel.com; 7 King David/David HaMelekh St; r US$510-634, ste US$1000; P奈; City Hall) Some large hotels resemble microcities, with enough leisure facilities and dining choices that you never need to leave. The 400-room David Citadel fits this description, providing a city within a city for its pampered guests. Rooms are spacious and beautifully appointed, there are three restaurants, and facilities include executive lounge, outdoor pool, children's play centre, spa and gym.

🛏 Rechavia

Little House in Rehavia

HOTEL $$

(Map p72; ☑02-563-3344; www.jerusalem-hotel. co.il; 20 Ibn Ezra St; s/d/q/f US$139/153/190/243; 奈) A midrange gem in a pretty residential neighbourhood, Little House's 1929 stone

building has plenty of character, and the staff is just as charming. Twenty-eight simple but clean rooms have well-kept, beige-tiled bathrooms. The hotel's a little bare but great value, especially with the roof terrace, free coffee, and a kosher Israeli breakfast buffet, best eaten in the cat-patrolled garden.

🛏 German Colony, Abu Tor & Baka

Jerusalem Garden Home

B&B $$

(☑050-524-0442; www.jerusalemgardenhome. com; 74 Derech Beit Lehem, German Colony; s from US$95, d US$120-150, tr from US$150; P奈; 7, 71, 72, 74, 75) Jerusalem-born owners Roni and Adi extend an effusive welcome to guests at their homey B&B. Simple but spacious rooms are given a hint of elegance with touches such as antique tiles and hand-embroidered throws and yes, there's a pretty garden and a tiled patio to relax on. It's five minutes' walk from the German Colony's main drag.

Ariela's Place

APARTMENT $$

(☑052-380-7077; 49 Hebron Rd, Abu Tor; ste from 355NIS; 奈) These quaint suites come with kitchenettes and decent wi-fi, and they're much cheaper than you'll pay closer to town. It's a full 20-minute walk to the Old City (though less to the German Colony and nightlife in the First Station (p102)), but the homey welcome and ambience – tiny balconies, lacy trimmings, antique tiled floors – create a comforting retreat.

Arcadia Ba'Moshava

BOUTIQUE HOTEL $$$

(☑02-542-3000; www.arcadiahotels.co.il; 13 Yehoshua bin-Nun St, German Colony; d/f midweek from US$205/240, weekend from US$255/290; P奈; 14, 18) This 23-room hotel within a romantic sandstone building occupies a placid spot on a residential street in the German Colony. Standard rooms aren't huge, but it's hard to mind: rooms have high ceilings, rain showers and mini-fridges, and they're regally attired with gilt drapes. Don't sleep through the high-quality breakfast buffet. The hotel provides bikes for guests to use.

Dan Boutique Hotel

HOTEL $$$

(Map p72; ☑02-568-9999; www.danhotels.co.il; 31 Hebron Rd, Abu Tor; d from US$210; P奈) Within this unmistakable building, which rather resembles a big concrete thumbs-up, are 128 modern rooms with brooding colour schemes. The mustard and oxblood decor is a little dark, but rooms are well equipped and feature coffee makers and plump beds, plus there are excellent city views from the bar and the small gym.

🚌 Central Bus Station Area

Allenby 2 B&B   B&B $
(☑052-396-3160; http://allenby2.com; Allenby Sq 2, Romema; s with shared bathroom US$55, d from US$95, with shared bathroom from US$80, f from US$130; @ 🛜; 🚇 Central Station) One of the most popular B&Bs in Jerusalem, Allenby 2 combines a warm and convivial atmosphere with excellent service. With 11 rooms spread over a few properties, it's also one of the larger B&Bs in the city. The shared kitchen and the location close to the Central Bus Station and JLR line are definite draws. There's no reception, so call ahead.

✖ Eating

Jerusalem is an exceptional place for gourmands of all budgets. At the right falafel-and-hummus joint an authentic Middle Eastern dining experience will only cost about 15NIS; Abu Shukri and Lina are two favourites. Mahane Yehuda Market (p81) provides a lively primer on local produce. Alternatively, splash cash at rooftop cheese tastings in Notre Dame (p100), fusion cuisine at Yudale (p101) or creative plates at Modern (p102).

✖ Old City

Most Old City restaurants stick to hummus, kebabs, shawarma and other Middle Eastern fare. The only exceptions are around Jaffa Gate, where there are a few Mediterranean-style places, and in Hurva Sq in the Jewish Quarter, where there are American-style fast-food joints. Finding a meal after dark can be challenging, as the Old City shuts down when the crowds go home.

Note that many places in the Muslim Quarter close during Ramadan.

★ Abu Shukri   MIDDLE EASTERN $
(Map p52; ☑02-627-1538; 63 Al Wad St, Muslim Quarter; hummus 20NIS; ⊗9am-4pm; 🖉) Abu Shukri is so popular that it's spawned imitators around Jerusalem. The standard platter includes a bowl of rich, smooth hummus – topped with chickpeas, tahina (sesame-seed paste), *fuul* (stewed fava beans) or pine nuts – crunchy veg and a basket of pita bread. Be sure to add a side order of falafel (10NIS). Cash only.

Lina Restaurant   MIDDLE EASTERN $
(Map p52; ☑02-627-7230; Aqabat Al Khanqah St, Muslim Quarter; hummus 20NIS; ⊗9am-5pm) The main rival to legendary Abu Shukri is this excellent Middle Eastern place, whose moreish hummus – usually glistening with olive oil – is among Jerusalem's best. There are two dining rooms on opposite sides of the street, though this unassuming spot is easy to miss. A good place to recover after battling the crowds at the nearby Church of the Holy Sepulchre (p60).

Ja'far Sweets   DESSERTS $
(Map p52; 40-42 Souq Khan Al Zeit St, Muslim Quarter; desserts from 15NIS; ⊗8am-7pm Sat-Thu) It's a hypnotic sight, watching pieces of bright-orange, syrup-soaked *kunafeh* (soft cheese topped with shredded pastry) carved from a huge tray. *Kunafeh* is the signature sweet of this well-established Palestinian dessert vendor. Ja'far is also noteworthy for selling well-wrapped trays of baklava and Turkish delight (also unusually, they're labelled with fixed prices); handy for a takeaway. If you're staying to eat dessert, order a glass of tea to offset the sweetness.

Zalatimo   DESSERTS $
(Map p52; Souq Khan Al Zeit St, Muslim Quarter; mutabbaq 20NIS; ⊗ hours vary) Hidden in a vault underneath the Ethiopian Monastery, Zalatimo is famous for its *mutabbaq*, created using a family recipe finessed over 150 years. After elaborate massaging and twirling (watching the process is part of the fun), pastry is stuffed with clarified butter, cinnamon and walnuts or sheep's cheese, baked and drizzled with sugar syrup. Check the price when you order; calculation errors aren't unknown.

There is no obvious shop sign, so look for the grey metal door halfway up the stairs (behind a juice stand). Opening hours are changeable, so you may need to try a few times.

Armenian Tavern   ARMENIAN $$
(Map p52; ☑02-627-3854; 79 Armenian Orthodox Patriarchate Rd, Armenian Quarter; mains 65-80NIS; ⊗11am-10.30pm Tue-Sun) The atmosphere is enough to lure you to the Armenian Tavern. Step down into the Crusader-era building, and pearl-embossed mirrors glitter, iron chandeliers dangle and antiques impede the path to your table. Service isn't warm, but the house wines are drinkable and the food is more than decent; try the *khagoli derev* (lamb mince in vine leaves, stewed in yoghurt).

Family Restaurant MIDDLE EASTERN $$
(Map p52; 02-628-3435; Souq Khan Al Zeit St, Muslim Quarter; mains from 30NIS) A Middle Eastern grill and hummus restaurant that ticks all the boxes. As the name suggests, you'll see families galore crowding this canteen-style joint in the Muslim Quarter. Established in 1942, it's clean and consistent, and serves grilled skewers and half-chickens, spreads of hummus, pita and salads, best washed down with mint-infused lemonade. No alcohol served, and no credit cards accepted.

Christ Church Cafe CAFE $$
(Map p52; 02-627-7727; Omar Ibn Al Khattab Sq, Old City; mains 20-60NIS; meals served 10.30am-3.30pm, cafe to 8pm;) Decorated with Bible quotes, this cafe near Jaffa Gate nurtures a cosy, collegiate atmosphere and is usually brimming with excitable residents of the adjoining guesthouse (p99). Pizza, salads and sandwiches are served until 3.30pm, though we keep returning for soft-serve ice cream and the selection of cheesecakes, carrot cake and lemon loaf. A merry retreat in the Old City.

Rossini's Restaurant INTERNATIONAL $$
(Map p52; 02-587-7423; www.rossini-rest.com; 42 Latin Patriarchate Rd, Christian Quarter; mains 45-130NIS; noon-11pm; ; City Hall) Various factors place this rather average steak and pasta place directly in the sights of tourists: it's open on Shabbat, it serves alcohol, and it's steps from Jaffa Gate. Rossini's feels modern and welcoming, and the meaty main courses, including musakhan (Palestinian-style chicken, onions and sumac on bread) hit the spot after a day of rambling of the Old City.

✗ East Jerusalem

Al Mihbash MIDDLE EASTERN $$
(Map p72; 02-628-9185; www.facebook.com/AlMihbashRestaurantAndCafe; 21 Derekh Shchem/Nablus Rd; mains 50-75NIS; 10am-late; Shivtei Israel) Perch on an overhanging balcony table for a feast of Palestinian-style dishes, from fish kebabs and falafel to stuffed chicken, along with enough Mediterranean salmon fillets and steaks to keep homesick expats happy. Smashed avocado and almond smoothies also feature on the somewhat scattered menu. Service is perfunctory, but food (and views) are great.

Sarwa Street Kitchen CAFE $$
(Map p72; www.facebook.com/sarwarstreetkitchen; 42 Salah Ad Din St; mains 15-60NIS; 11am-11pm; ; Shivtei Israel) Sarwa Street Kitchen is

a chill place for a quiet coffee, meal or beer. The kitchen offers a range of dishes, from homemade pizzas and burritos to Palestinian favourites such as *makloubeh* (chicken, rice, vegetables and spices cooked together and turned 'upside down'), as well as vegan and vegetarian options. With wi-fi and lots of natural light, the cafe invites you to loiter as long as you like.

Al Diwan Restaurant MIDDLE EASTERN $$$
(02-541-2222; www.jerusalemambassador.com; Ambassador Hotel, 5 Derekh Shchem/Nablus Rd; mains 70-120NIS; noon-11pm; Shimon Ha-Tsadik) It feels pricey if you've been snacking on street food all day, but the Ambassador Hotel's restaurant is one of East Jerusalem's best places to eat. Puffy pita breads emerge from the charcoal-fired oven and are heaped onto tables alongside smoky grilled meats, green wheat soup and great pizzas. Rather than the so-so dining room, enjoy this bounty on the verandah.

✗ Downtown

The downtown area – especially on and near the Ben Yehuda St pedestrian mall – is jampacked with restaurants and cafes. Many are kosher, which means they're closed on Shabbat and Jewish holidays.

Hamarakia SOUP $
(Map p80; 02-625-7797; 4 Koresh St; mains 30NIS; 12.30pm-midnight Sun-Thu, from 8pm Sat; ; City Hall) Somewhere between homey and ramshackle, this Jerusalem institution specialises in nourishing soups, which change daily. Leek, lentil and tomato are in frequent rotation and there are always vegan options. For more than a liquid lunch, Hamarakia serves aubergine salads, hummus and other veggie dishes. The long shared table and open kitchen create a sociable atmosphere, and there's a patio out back.

★ Pinati MIDDLE EASTERN $$
(Map p80; 02-625-4540; http://pinati.co.il; 13 King George V St; mains 25-60NIS; 8am-7pm Sun-Thu, to 3pm Fri; ; Jaffa Center) Locals swear by the hummus, served with pita and piquant garlic-chilli paste, but Pinati's well-seasoned mains are worth sampling, too: slow-stewed moussaka, schnitzels, bean soups and shakshuka (egg and tomato bake). Casual dining and comforting kosher food are a winning formula, so you may have to battle crowds at lunchtime (note the photos of loyal customers from across 30 years).

T'mol Shilshom

CAFE $$

(Map p80; ☑02-623-2758; www.tmol-shilshom.co.il; 5 Yo'el Salomon St; mains 40-55NIS; ⊗8.30am-11pm Sun-Thu, to 2pm Fri; ☎☑; ⬛Jaffa Center) Whether you settle into the book-lined interior or the shaded courtyard, T'mol Shilshom is one of Jerusalem's most relaxing brunch spots. This friendly kosher joint is best known for its shakshuka: classic, spicy or cheese-laden versions of the Middle Eastern egg-and-tomato bake are on offer, always with a mountain of fresh bread, salad and olive tapenade. It's a little tricky to find: follow signs through the stone arch on Yo'el Salomon St, walk down the passageway, turn left and head to the end of the courtyard – the cafe is upstairs.

Village Green

VEGETARIAN $$

(Map p80; ☑053-944-3273; www.villayegreen. rest-e.co.il; 33 Jaffa Rd; salad bar from 45NIS, mains 30-70NIS; ⊗9am-10pm Sun-Thu, to 3pm Fri; ☑; ⬛Jaffa Center) Cleanse your palate at a nourishing veggie and vegan joint. This kosher cafe offers soups, quiches and DIY salads (from beetroot and leaves to more filling root veggies and spiced chickpeas). Even the cake selection has a health kick, featuring low-sugar brownies, quinoa-flour muffins and other virtuous treats.

Village Green is more of a canteen than a restaurant; head up to the counter whether you're dining in or ordering takeaway.

Focaccia Bar

ITALIAN $$

(Map p80; ☑02-625-6428; http://bar.focaccia.co; 4 Rabbi Akiva St; focaccia & pizza 30-60NIS, pasta 45-65NIS, mains 57-109NIS; ⊗9am-midnight; ☑; ⬛Jaffa Center) Hauled from a taboun (clay oven), crisp focaccia, laden with goat cheese, aubergine, smoked goose and more, are top of the menu at this popular place. You can also tuck into pizzas, pasta dishes, salads or steaks. There's a delightful terrace; inside, things get lively (rowdy, even), but the bar is great for solo diners.

★ Anna Cafe

ITALIAN $$$

(Map p72; ☑02-543-4144; www.annarest.co.il; Ticho House, 10 HaRav Hagan; pizza & pasta 50-70NIS, mains 80-90NIS; ⊗9am-11pm Sun-Thu, to 2pm Fri; ☑; ⬛Jaffa Center) 🍴 On the upper floor of elegant Ticho House, Anna Cafe is a stylish spot for a coffee or an Italian meal. Nibble pastries, pizza bianca or artichoke omelette, satisfied by the knowledge that it's for a good cause: the cafe employs and trains local youth in distress.

Darna

MOROCCAN $$$

(Map p80; ☑02-624-5406; www.darna.co.il; 3 Horkanos St; mains 75-155NIS, set menus 175-240NIS; ⊗noon-3pm & 6.30pm-midnight Sun-Thu, after Shabbat-10pm Sat; ⬛Jaffa Center) Aromatic and delicious dishes from Morocco – including plenty of tagine and couscous choices – are served in atmospheric surrounds at this long-standing kosher favourite. Be sure to try the pastilla fassia (filo pastry stuffed with poussin and almonds) and consider the mechoui (slow-cooked lamb shoulder).

Notre Dame Cheese
& Wine Restaurant

FRENCH $$$

(Map p52; ☑02-627-9177; www.notredamecenter. org; 4th fl, Notre Dame Centre, 3 Paratroopers Rd, near Old City; platters from 80NIS; ⊗noon-11pm; ⬛City Hall) The scent of ripe brie and pungent gruyère tickles your nostrils the moment you step out of the elevator to this 4th-floor rooftop restaurant. The view is jaw dropping, the soundtrack is chiming church bells, and the cheese platters greatly outshine the main courses (European fare from scallops to rack of lamb); come for a sunset apéritif.

✖ Mahane Yehuda

The alleys around Mahane Yehuda Market (p81) are home to some of the city's most creative and interesting eateries.

Sabayos

CRÊPES $

(Map p72; ☑050-301-9708; Haetz Ha'em St; crêpes 25NIS; ⊗8am-sunset Sun-Thu, 9am-2pm Fri; ☑; ⬛Mahane Yehuda) Whopping crêpes are crammed with fillings such as olive, tomato and various cheeses at this kosher crêperie. Dessert options are just as filling, with crushed halva (sesame-paste nougat) and seasonal fruits to tempt you away from the savoury menu. Choose from wheat or buckwheat batters. Excellent value.

Pasta Basta

ITALIAN $

(Map p72; http://pastabasta.co.il; 8 HaTut Alley; pastas 25-38NIS; ⊗11am-10pm Sun-Thu, to 1.30pm Fri; ⬛Mahane Yehuda) This carb-loading canteen in Mahane Yehuda Market isn't well signposted, but you'll catch sight of penne, fettucine and fusilli being energetically tossed in a choice of nine sauces. Filling and fast.

Mousseline

ICE CREAM $

(Map p72; ☑02-500-3601; www.mousseline-jeru salem.com; HaArmonim 2; ice cream from 15NIS; ⊗10am-midnight Sun-Wed, 9am-midnight Thu, 7.30am-3pm Fri, 1hr after Shabbat-midnight Sat;

🅰 Mahane Yehuda) This grab-and-go ice-cream spot is ideally positioned near the edge of Mahane Yehuda Market to refresh you after a morning dodging shopping trolleys and vendors flinging plastic crates. Pomegranate hits the spot on a hot day, while black sesame or grapefruit and basil sorbet are delightfully original.

Azura   MIDDLE EASTERN $$
(Map p72; 🖉 02-623-5204; Iraqi Market; hummus 22-40NIS; mains 22-100NIS; ⊙9.30am-4pm, closed Shabbat; 🖋; 🅰 Mahane Yehuda) With slow-cooked comfort food and efficient service, this Turkish-influenced kosher restaurant off Rehov HaEshkol St near Mahane Yehuda Market is one of Jerusalem's best loved. The fragrance of goulash and meatballs is enough to set stomachs rumbling, while the signature dish – aubergine stuffed with cinnamon-scented minced beef and pine nuts – is peppery, filling and served at lightning speed.

Ishtabach   KURDISH $$
(Map p72; 🖉 02-623-2997; cnr Shikma St & Beit Ya'akov St; mains 40-65NIS; ⊙noon-1am; 🅰 Mahane Yehuda) Ishtabach is nestled on the outskirts of the Mahane Yehuda Market on a street bustling with other restaurants, but nowhere else offers the same delicious (and filling) *shamburak*, Kurdish pastry stuffed with various meats or vegetables and served with unique sauces (like garlic jam) for added flavour. Come hungry for the *siske* filling – beef that's been slow cooked for more than 15 hours.

⭐ **Machneyuda**   INTERNATIONAL $$$
(Map p72; 🖉 02-533-3442; www.machneyuda.co.il; 10 Beit Ya'akov St; mains 86-175NIS, tasting menu 295NIS; ⊙12.30-4pm & 6.30-11pm Sun-Thu, to 3pm Fri; 🅰 Mahane Yehuda) Is it New York comfort food, Italian fine dining or haute cuisine? This superb restaurant near Mahane Yehuda Market has won local acclaim for its playful menu, which offers Catalan-style calamari, black linguine with crab and good ol' fashioned steak and potatoes. Book well in advance, and pray there's semolina cake.

Yudale   ISRAELI $$$
(Map p72; 🖉 02-533-3442; 11 Beit Ya'akov St; starters 46-71NIS, mains 77-175NIS; ⊙6.30pm-late Sun-Thu; 🅰 Mahane Yehuda) The precocious sibling of Machneyuda looks like a Hawaiian beach shack and serves the same exciting modern fusion cuisine as its big bro – Thai-style beef tartar, Kurdish pastries, truffled polenta –

but it's more raucous and more fun. Sitting at the bar and watching chefs work their arak-fuelled magic is highly entertaining (if you can score a seat, that is).

It's open on Friday until two hours before Shabbat and starts up again on Saturday a couple of hours after Shabbat ends.

🍴 Mamilla & Yemin Moshe

Angelica   INTERNATIONAL $$$
(Map p72; 🖉 02-623-0056; www.angelicarest.com; 4 George Washington St, Yemin Moshe; mains 92-158NIS; ⊙12.30-10.30pm Sun-Thu, 8.30-11pm Sat) Sandstone arches and stone-framed windows establish a worldly tone at Angelica, but the menu is sheer invention. Appetisers marry a medley of cuisines: awaken your taste buds with aioli-drizzled fish shawarma served in a taco, or smoked-almond and nectarine salad doused in champagne vinaigrette. Mains borrow bistro classics from across Europe, such as goose breast with beans, hanger steak, and mushroom ravioli.

Mamilla Rooftop Restaurant   INTERNATIONAL $$$
(Map p80; 🖉 02-548-2230; www.mamillahotel.com; 11 King Solomon/Shlomo HaMelekh St, Mamilla; mains 90-186NIS; ⊙6-11pm Sun-Thu, noon-2.30pm Fri, 7.30-11pm Sat; 🅰 City Hall) Not keen on bumping elbows with fellow diners in the Old City hummus restaurants? This sleek rooftop brasserie is a refined place to

AN OTTOMAN TRAIN STATION TRANSFORMED

First Station (Map p72; ☑02-653-5239; www.firststation.co.il; 4 David Remez St, German Colony; snacks from 20NIS, mains from 55NIS; ◷7am-late; ☑🚗), a dining and entertainment complex housed in a handsome 19th-century railway station, is an atmospheric place for a sit-down meal or a few beers. There are boutiques, cafes and an ice-cream stand, plus several restaurants, including kosher steak (Bread & Meat), Italian (Fiori) and Asian (Station 9) joints. It's popular with families during the day and gets lively after dark.

Built in 1892 as the Jerusalem terminus of the Jaffa–Jerusalem railway line, the station was in almost continuous use until 1998, when the line from Tel Aviv to Jerusalem closed. Recently restored, it opened in its present guise in 2013.

Pilates classes, jazz concerts, stand-up comedy and folk dancing each find a place on First Station's busy entertainment program, and many events and activities are free. It's worth popping by from 4pm on summer Thursdays, when an arts-and-crafts market takes up residence. For kids aged two to 12, there's usually a miniature train and a carousel, among other games. Check the website for details of events, including plenty of summer concerts.

retreat. Meals (all kosher) are designed for distinguished palates, with citrus salmon sashimi, gnocchi with black olives and roast goose accented with chocolate and caramel sauce. Reserve.

✖ German Colony

There are plenty of chain cafes and burger joints along Emek Refa'im St, and its gradually improving restaurant scene features French-style bistros and Italian cuisine.

Adom   MEDITERRANEAN $$$
(Map p72; ☑02-624-6242; www.adom.rest/en; First Station, 4 David Remez St; mains 70-135NIS; ◷12.30pm-midnight; ☑; ☐71) Decked out like a glamorous train-station waiting room, this trendy bistro spills into the First Station courtyard. A sophisticated pan-European menu features tempting grilled entrecôte and salmon tartar with date honey, while vegetarian options offer unexpected flavour pairings such as chestnut gnocchi, or artichoke, goat-cheese and fig salad. It's a satisfying warm-up to a night out in Jerusalem.

✖ Givat Ram

★Modern   ISRAELI $$$
(☑02-648-0862; www.modern.co.il; Israel Museum, Ruppin Rd; mains 70-120NIS, tapas platter 110NIS; ◷11.30am-5pm Sun-Thu, to late Tue; ☑; ☐7, 9, 14, 35, 66) The main restaurant at the Israel Museum (p86) is as swanky as its setting demands, with a refined array of dishes: artichoke sofrito, stuffed ravioli and chicken kadaif so elaborately presented that it could grace a Jackson Pollock canvas. Local fla-

vours are given an unexpected twist (Israeli tapas, beef and apricot kebabs) and it's all served with bread straight from the oven.

☕ Drinking & Nightlife

Jerusalem's downtown is well endowed with bars. The best are in the Mahane Yehuda Market area and in the vicinity of Zion Sq, on Rivlin, Ben Shatah, Hillel, Heleni HaMalka and Dorot Rishonim Sts. East Jerusalem bars tend to be inside hotels, while the Old City is almost as dry as the Negev.

☕ Old City

Viennese Café   CAFE
(Map p52; Austrian Hospice, 37 Via Dolorosa; cakes 23NIS, mains 50-70NIS; ◷10am-10pm) Baroque music and Sachertorte attempt to carve out a corner of Vienna within Jerusalem's Austrian Hospice. Make no mistake: this is a canteen, but with apple strudel, good cups of tea and schnitzel. It's a guilty pleasure within the tranquil confines of the Austrian Hospice.

To find the cafe, ring the bell at the gate at the corner of Al Wad St and Via Dolorosa. When you're given entry, walk into the charming guesthouse foyer and turn left; the cafe is at the end of the corridor. There's indoor and outdoor seating.

Versavee   BAR, CAFE
(Map p52; ☑02-627-6160; www.versavee.com; Greek Patriarchate Rd; ◷10am-late; 🛜) Whether you're sipping mint-infused lemonade or a glass of wine, Versavee's courtyard seating and location by Jaffa Gate make it a convenient spot for quick refreshment. It's right

next to the Hotel New Imperial (p93) and is styled with the same pleasant mix of shabbiness and 19th-century grandeur.

🍸 Downtown

Cassette Bar
BAR

(HaCasetta; Map p80; 1 Horkanos St; ⏰8pm-5am Sat-Thu, 2pm-6am Fri; 🚉Jaffa Center) Accessed from the street (look for the metal door covered with old cassette tapes) or through the rear of the Record Bar next door, this pint-sized bar is a long-standing hipster haunt. The crowd drinks well into the night, serenaded by alternative tracks. Upstairs is Videopub, a popular gay bar.

Kadosh
CAFE

(Map p80; 📞02-625-4210; 6 Shlomzion HaMalka St; ⏰7am-12.30am, closed Shabbat; 🛜; 🚉City Hall) Since 1967, Kadosh has been cultivating an uncanny miniature Paris, from the burnished colour scheme and outdoor seating to the intimate chit-chat mingling with French *chansons* on the sound system. The espresso on ice with vanilla is a refresher with bite, and coffee cups are swapped for cocktail flutes when the sun goes down.

Videopub
GAY

(Map p80; https://sites.google.com/site/videopub jerusalem; 1st fl, 1 Horkanus St; ⏰8pm-4am Mon-Thu, Sat & Sun, from 10pm Fri; 🚉Jaffa Center) The local LGBT community flocks to this teensy space above Cassette Bar for drinking, dancing and the occasional drag show (Thursday and Saturday are particularly busy). Expect nostalgic electronica, '80s pop tunes and a crowd welcoming of LGBT patrons and their hetero friends.

Barood
BAR

(Map p80; 📞02-625-9081; 31 Jaffa Rd; ⏰noon-late; 🚉Jaffa Center) A solid selection of local wine, Guinness on tap, and delicious Balkan-meets-Italian nibbles, pass the time beautifully at this intimate bar-restaurant in a courtyard behind Jaffa Rd. Red-checked tablecloths and stone walls decorated with wistful European posters make you imagine, for a split second, that you're in a Parisian bistro – though why would you want to be anywhere else?

Sira
BAR, CLUB

(Map p80; 📞02-623-4366; 1 Ben Shatakh St; ⏰4pm-3am; 🚉City Hall) This tiny bar off Ben Sira St is dark, crowded and loud, reverberating with anything from jazz to electronica depending on the night. There's a mini dance floor ruled by DJs with eclectic tastes, and the beer flows fast and well into the night, guzzled by a student-heavy crowd.

Mazkeka
BAR

(Map p80; www.mazkeka.com; 3 Shoshan St; ⏰9pm-2am; 🚉City Hall) Mazkeka bustles late into weekend nights with people gathering for a drink and enjoying the sounds and sights of the city's emerging and independent artists. Check www.facebook.com/Mazkeka to see what movies are being screened and which artists are performing throughout the week, or just stop by and watch the hip side of Jerusalem go by.

Jabotinski
PUB

(Map p80; 2 Shim'on Ben Shalah St, ⏰7pm-2am Sun-Fri, 1pm-late Sat; 🛜; 🚉City Hall) Named after the Russian-born Zionist Ze'ev Jabotinsky (1880–1940), this pub and traveller hang-out is one of a number of popular watering holes on Shim'on Ben Shatah St. The food is forgettable (ribs, burgers and the like), but the beer is cold, and there's plenty of streetside seating.

Mike's Place
SPORTS BAR

(Map p80; 📞054-799-1220; www.mikesplacebars. com; 33 Jaffa Rd; ⏰noon-late Sun-Thu, to 5pm Fri, from 9pm Sat; 🚉Jaffa Center) Guinness on tap, sports on screen and traveller-friendly staff. Yup, you've seen the same formula in a dozen other bars, but this Israeli chain pub is an easy place to start or finish a night out in Jerusalem. Choose from streetside seating or the reassuringly worn pub interior (including a surprisingly cavernous downstairs).

The best time to show up is 10pm, when the night's entertainment usually kicks off: there's open-mic night on Monday, live music on Tuesday and Thursday, and jazz on Wednesday.

🍸 Mahane Yehuda

Beer Bazaar
CRAFT BEER

(Map p72; 📞02-671-2559; www.facebook.com/ Beer.Bazaar.Jerusalem; 3 Haetz Ha'em St; ⏰11am-late Sun-Thu, to 5pm Fri, from 8pm Sat; 🚉Mahane Yehuda) Glug your way through more than 100 craft beers (including dozens of Israeli brews) at this enormously friendly bar in Mahane Yehuda Market (p81). The popular Jerusalem location of a Tel Aviv microbrew chain, Beer Bazaar rotates both the beers on tap and the entertainment, which ranges from 'beer yoga' to live music.

LGBTIQ JERUSALEM

Owing to Jerusalem's religious nature, the city's lesbian, gay, bisexual and transgender scene is much more subdued than its Tel Aviv equivalent. Public displays of affection, especially between same-sex couples, will be unwelcome in Jewish Orthodox areas and East Jerusalem.

Videopub (p103) is a spangleicious gay bar with a tiny dance floor. Email the **Jerusalem Open House** (Map p80; ☑02-625-3191; www.joh.org.il; 1st fl, 2 HaSoreg St; ⊠City Hall) ahead of time to learn about community events, some of which are English-speaker friendly.

In late July or early August, the LGBT community takes to the streets in the **Jerusalem March for Pride and Tolerance**. More a human rights demonstration than a carnival, the march remembers those killed and injured in 2009's Bar-Noar shootings, as well as Shira Banki who was stabbed to death by an ultra-Orthodox man at the parade in 2015, and urges tolerance of the LGBT community.

Roasters COFFEE
(Map p72; ☑054-671-0296; Haetz Ha'em St; ⊗8am-sunset Sun-Thu, 9am-2pm Fri; ⊠Mahane Yehuda) Perch on a wobbly stool (or an even wobblier metal barrel) at this immensely popular coffee spot in the thick of Mahane Yehuda Market. Sip a foamy cappuccino or silky-smooth iced coffee, with a swirl of sugar water for added kick.

Casino de Paris BAR
(Map p72; ⊗noon-2am Sun-Thu, from 9pm Sat; ⊠Mahane Yehuda) During the British Mandate, this building was an Officers Club for British soldiers. The Brits left in 1948, and this place promptly fell into disrepair until local entrepreneurs decided to recreate those gin-soaked glory days. Today the Casino de Paris houses an indoor-outdoor bar serving tapas, pizza, Israeli boutique beers and nostalgic cocktails themed around its 1920s heyday.

Etrog Man JUICE BAR
(Map p72; www.etrogman.com; Ha'Egoz St; ⊗8am-sunset Sun-Thu, 9am-2pm Fri; ⊠Mahane Yehuda) Part smoothie bar, part medicine man, Etrog Man aims to cure your ills with a chilled glass of goat milk and passion fruit, or its 'etrogat', whose amazing health properties include the power to bring you peace on Shabbat. With cups from 5NIS, it's hard to say no to this refreshing and friendly stand.

🍴 Talbiyeh & German Colony

Talbiye WINE BAR
(Map p72; ☑02-581-1927; www.talbiye.com; 5 Chopin St, Talbiyeh; ⊗9.30am-4.30pm & 5pm-midnight) Israeli and international wines flow freely at this bohemian-feel bar, whose antique furnishings and location by the Jerusalem Theatre pull a worldly, moneyed crowd of revellers

and literati. As you'd expect of the sibling of edgily gourmet Machneyuda (p101), Talbiye also has a superb pan-European menu of light snacks and full-blown feasts.

Coffee Mill CAFE
(☑02-566-1665; 23 Emek Refa'im St, German Colony; ⊗7am-11pm Sun-Thu, to 3pm Fri, 7-11pm Sat; ⊠4, 18, 21) Bustling and bookish, Coffee Mill draws a multilingual crowd to sip lattes between walls lined with coffee beans and covers of the *New Yorker*.

☆ Entertainment

Theatre buffs, movie lovers and music fans will feel right at home in Jerusalem. The city's events calendar is especially busy in summer (June to August). Major international acts tend to go to Tel Aviv, but the local music scene in Jerusalem's downtown is varied and vibrant. Check what's on at www. itraveljerusalem.com or in Friday's *Jerusalem Post*; book tickets through **Bimot** (Map p80; ☑02-623-7000; https://tickets.bimot.co.il; 8 Shamai St, Downtown; ⊗9am-7pm Sun-Thu, to 1pm Fri; ⊠Jaffa Center).

Cinematheque CINEMA
(Map p72; ☑02-565-4333; www.jer-cin.org.il; 11 Hebron Rd, near Old City; tickets 39NIS) The Jerusalem Cinematheque, with its quality foreign films and miniature festivals on themes from gay cinema to China on the silver screen, is a hang-out for true movie connoisseurs. It's a favoured haunt of secular, left-leaning Jerusalemites and the home of the respected Jerusalem Film Festival (p92).

Yellow Submarine LIVE MUSIC
(☑02-679-4040; www.yellowsubmarine.org.il; 13 HaRechavim St, Talpiot) Does Middle Eastern dance music or Balkan pop sound like your

jam? How about soft jazz or Jewish spiritual song, or stand-up comedy (in English)? An impressively diverse program of musical and spoken-word talent takes the stage at Yellow Submarine; browse the website for upcoming events.

Zappa in the Lab   LIVE MUSIC
(☑box office 03-762-6666; www.zappa-club.co.il; 28 Hebron Rd, Abu Tor; ☉box office 9am-9pm) Crafted out of a disused railway warehouse, this venue has an industrial feel and an attractive bar backlit against weathered stone. Zappa stages jazz, folk, rock and pop concerts, with a smattering of tribute bands and comedy. Events are almost nightly; check the website for details (it's worth booking).

Jerusalem Theatre   PERFORMING ARTS
(Jerusalem Centre for the Performing Arts; Map p72; ☑02-560-5755; www.jerusalem-theatre.co.il; 20 David Marcus St, Talbiyeh; ☉box office 9.30am-7.30pm Sun-Thu, to 1pm Fri) This complex includes a concert hall, a cinema, theatres and a cafe. This is the place to catch a performance by the Jerusalem Symphony Orchestra, as well as comedy, music, children's theatre and dance performances.

Its **Sherover Theatre**, the largest stage, has simultaneous English-language surtitles during certain performances.

🛍 Shopping

Jerusalem is an excellent place to shop for Judaica: browse the Cardo (p67) in the Old City or downtown's Yo'el Salomon St. Avoid David St in the Old City, as products here are generally of inferior quality. Elsewhere, best buys include delicate Armenian ceramics and foodie souvenirs such as coffee, spices and wrapped sweets from the Muslim Quarter and Mahane Yehuda Market (p81).

🛍 Old City

Sandrouni Armenian
Art Centre   CERAMICS
(Map p52; ☑02-626-3744; www.sandrouni.com; 4 HaAhkim St; ☉9.30am-7pm Mon-Sat) After you stroll through New Gate into Jerusalem's Old City, it's hard to resist taking a peek inside the colourful ceramics workshop of Armenian brothers George and Dorin Sandrouni. Since setting up their atelier in 1983, they have been crafting traditional Armenian ceramic designs: pomegranate-shaped ornaments, decorative plates, and tiles patterned with fish, flowers and peace symbols.

Heifetz   GIFTS & SOUVENIRS
(Map p52; ☑02-628-0061; www.bennyheifetz.com; 24 Tiferet Israel Rd; ☉10am-5pm Sun-Thu, to 2pm Fri) Traditional Jewish ritual items are given a fresh, contemporary overhaul at Benny Heifetz' studio, where he crafts silver Torah pointers, jaggedly geometric candelabra and a lovely range of jewellery with Jewish themes (such as sparkling Stars of David and chais).

Bint Al Balad
Workshop & Café   ARTS & CRAFTS
(Map p52; ☑02-627-7333, 02-628-1377; www.araborthodoxsociety.com; HaAhkim St; ☉9am-3pm Mon-Sat; 🚌City Hall) 🌱 Operated by the Arab Orthodox Society, this shop sells embroidered clothing, bags, purses and pillows made by West Bank women working to preserve Palestinian handicraft traditions. Also on offer are Palestinian-style pastries and coffee.

Alan Baidun   ANTIQUES
(Map p52; ☑02-626-1469; www.baidun.com; 28 Via Dolorosa; ☉10am-7pm Sat-Thu) Dedicated antiques-lovers will be disappointed by their rummaging in the Old City...until they reach Alan Baidun's store. All antiques – from Egyptian amulets to exquisite Islamic art – are sold with export certificates and papers proving their provenance.

🛍 East Jerusalem

Educational Bookshop & Cafe   BOOKS
(Map p72; ☑02-628-3704; www.educationalbookshop.com; 19 Salah Ad Din St; ☉8am-8pm; 📶; 🚌Shivtei Israel) The ideal starting point for exploring East Jerusalem, the Educational Bookshop attracts journalists, aid workers, activists and art-lovers. There's a range of books and DVDs pertaining to the Arab–Israeli conflict, and a good selection of magazines and Palestinian music CDs. Linger in the tiny upstairs cafe for tea, a sandwich or impromptu debate with one of the clued-in, multilingual patrons.

Armenian Ceramics   CERAMICS
(Map p72; ☑02-628-2826; www.armenianceramics.com; 14 Derekh Shchem/Nablus Rd; ☉8am-5pm; 🚌Shivtei Israel) The longest-established Armenian-style ceramics studio in Jerusalem, this family business is run by Neshan Balian, grandson of a master potter from Turkey. Founded in 1922, the factory was destroyed in the Six Day War but later revived and still sells beautiful hand-painted tiles.

It's opposite the US consulate in East Jerusalem. Look for the sign that says 'Palestinian Ceramics'; you may have to buzz or phone to get in.

JERUSALEM INFORMATION

Sunbula
ARTS & CRAFTS

(☑02-672-1707; www.sunbula.org; cnr Derekh Shchem/Nablus Rd & Sheikh Jarah; ⊘noon-6pm Mon-Thu & Sat; ⓠShimon Ha-Tsadik) ✎ This not-for-profit outfit empowers Palestinian artisans by promoting and selling traditional handicrafts, including embroidery, basketry, weaving, carving and olive-oil soap. It runs two shops in Jerusalem, one of which is inside the St Andrew's Guesthouse (p96) and the other here in East Jerusalem. All of the items for sale are handmade.

🛍 Downtown

Greenvurcel
GIFTS & SOUVENIRS

(Map p80; ☑02-622-1620; www.greenvurcel. co.il; 27 Yo'el Salomon St; ⊘10am-10pm Sun-Thu, to 2pm Fri, 1hr after Shabbat-11pm Sat; ⓠJaffa Center) Sleek, minimalist designs characterise the metalwork of versatile artist Yaakov Greenvurcel. His gleaming challah trays and dreidels are among the Judaica on offer; meanwhile, the jewellery – featuring Tahitian pearls, semi-precious gems and abstract designs – feels very contemporary.

Arman Darian Ceramic
CERAMICS

(Map p80; ☑02-623-4802; www.facebook.com/ arman.darian.ceramic; 12 Shlomzion HaMalka St; ⊘hours vary; ⓠCity Hall) Yerevan-born Arman Darian might be the best-known ceramicist in Israel, having installed his designs in many public buildings. Skilfully decorated ceramic vases, plates and tiles fill his 1986-founded workshop and boutique, as well as larger pieces such as tables topped with Armenian blue-and-white tiles.

Danny Azoulay
GIFTS & SOUVENIRS

(Map p80; ☑02-623-3918; www.ketubahazoulay art.com; 5 Yo'el Salomon St; ⊘10am-7pm Sun-Thu, to 2.30pm Fri; ⓠJaffa Center) Drawing inspiration from European and Middle Eastern design, Morocco-born artist Danny Azoulay creates *ketubahs* (Jewish wedding contracts) with lacy paper-cut designs. Also on sale are pretty ceramic honey jugs, framed pictures and other Judaica.

Kippa Man
FASHION & ACCESSORIES

(Map p80; ☑02-622-1255; 5 Ben Yehuda St; ⊘hours vary Sun-Thu; ⓠJaffa Center) An astonishing range of kippot (yarmulkes or skullcaps; from 15NIS) bulge from the entryway to this comprehensive shop on pedestrianised Ben Yehuda St. There are classic designs (like the Star of David), but why not mix it up with a smiley face or a Chicago Bulls logo?

Steimatzky
BOOKS

(Map p80; www.steimatzky.co.il; 33 Jaffa Rd; ⊘8.30am-8pm Mon-Thu, to 3pm Fri; ⓠJaffa Center) Chain bookshop with several branches around town, including this one in Jaffa Rd and another in the German Colony (43 Emek Refa'im St; ⊘8.30am-10pm Sun-Thu, to 3pm Fri, 9-10.30pm Sat). It has a good range of English-language books.

Lametayel
SPORTS & OUTDOORS

(Map p80; ☑077-333-4504; www.lametayel.co.il; 5 Yo'el Salomon St; ⊘10am-8pm Sun-Thu, to 2pm Fri; ⓠJaffa Center) Sells maps and travel guidebooks (including Lonely Planet), as well as quality camping supplies and outdoor gear.

🛍 Mahane Yehuda

★ Halva Kingdom
FOOD

(Map p72; 12 Haetz Ha'em St; ⊘8am-sunset Sun-Thu, to 2pm Fri; ⓠMahane Yehuda) Grinding sesame into paste since 1947, this irresistible stall is hard to miss thanks to its crown-shaped sign, huge wheels of halva and attendant offering samples. Once you've tasted it, you'll likely be hooked. Choose from flavours including rose, pistachio and chocolate, then await the sugar rush.

ℹ Information

MEDICAL SERVICES

Hadassah Medical Centre Ein Kerem
(☑emergency room 02-677-7222, info 02-677-6333; www.hadassah.org.il; Kiryat Hadassah) The Ein Kerem campus of this venerable hospital has a 24-hour emergency department and staff who speak English and Russian. Board a westbound train from the Central Bus Station and disembark at the last stop (Mt Herzl), where you can transfer to bus 27.

Hadassah Medical Centre Mount Scopus
(☑emergency room 02-584-4333, info 02-584-4222; www.hadassah.org.il; ⓠ19) The Mt Scopus campus of this nonprofit hospital has a 24-hour emergency department and a specialist paediatric emergency department that is also open 24 hours.

Orthodox Society Medical Centre (☑02-627-1958; Greek Orthodox Patriarchate Rd; ⊘9am-2pm Mon-Fri, to 1pm Sat) In the Old City's Christian Quarter, the Orthodox Society operates a low-cost medical and dental clinic that welcomes travellers.

Super-Pharm (Map p80; ☑077-888-1450; 9 Mamilla Mall, Downtown; ⊘9.30am-10pm, closed Shabbat) Pharmacy located between Jaffa Gate and downtown.

Terem (☑1-599-520-520; www.terem.com; 80 Yirmiyahu St, Romema; ⊘24hr; ⓠCentral Station) Efficient multilingual walk-in medical clinic that handles everything from minor ailments to emergencies. It's a five-minute walk from the Central Bus Station.

MONEY

The best deals for changing money are at the private, commission-free exchange offices in the downtown area (around Zion Sq), East Jerusalem (Salah Ad Din St) and in the Old City (Jaffa Gate). Note that in Jewish areas many close early on Friday and remain closed all day Saturday.

ATMs are found across the city, including at Zion Sq.

TOURIST INFORMATION

Call **Tourist Line** on *3888 (note the asterisk) for immediate answers regarding tourist services as well as assistance from the Israel Police, Ministry of Interior Services and Airport Authority. Operates 24/7.

Christian Information Centre (☑ 02-627-2692; www.cicts.org; Omar Ibn Al Khattab Sq, Old City; ☺ 9am-5.30pm Mon-Fri, 8.30am-12.30pm Sat) This office opposite the entrance to the Citadel is operated by the Franciscans and provides information on the city's Christian sites.

Jaffa Gate Tourist Office (☑ 02-627-1422; www.itraveljerusalem.com; Jaffa Gate; ☺ 8.30am-5pm Sat-Thu, to 1.30pm Fri) Main tourist office in Jerusalem. It supplies free maps, organises guides and provides information and advice. It's the second office after Jaffa Gate.

USEFUL WEBSITES

Go Jerusalem (www.gojerusalem.com) Handy tourist website with info on events, festivals, tours and attractions.

i Travel Jerusalem (www.itraveljerusalem.com) Extremely useful website operated by the municipality, including itineraries.

Jerusalem.com (www.jerusalem.com) Overview of the city, its attractions and events; includes virtual tours of important sites.

ℹ️ Getting There & Away

BUS

Buses to major cities and towns across Israel leave from the **Central Bus Station** (www.bus.co.il; Jaffa Rd). Book your ticket to Eilat in advance, as these services are often full.

DESTINATION	BUS NUMBER	COST (NIS)	DURATION (HR)	FREQUENCY
Be'er Sheva	446, 470	27	1¾	2 hourly
Eilat	444	70	5	4 daily
Haifa	940, 947	37.50	2½-3	every 15min
Masada	444, 486	37.50	2½	almost hourly
Tel Aviv (Arlozorov Bus Station)	480	16	1	every 15min
Tel Aviv (Central Bus Station)	405	16	1	every 15min
Tiberias	961, 962	37.50	2½	almost hourly

If you are headed into northern areas of the West Bank such as Ramallah (bus 18, 7NIS), use the **Arab bus station** (East Jerusalem Central Bus Station; Map p72) on Derekh Shchem (Nablus) Rd, the street straight in front of Damascus Gate. The buses that leave from here are green and white.

For Bethlehem, take bus 21 (8NIS) from the **Arab bus station** (Sultan Suleiman St, East Jerusalem) west of the Damascus Gate next to the tram stop. The buses that leave from here are blue and white. For Hebron, take bus 21, alight at Bab Al Zqaq and then take a Hebron bus (5NIS).

Check the latest info with the East Jerusalem Transport Association (02-627-2881). The general rule is that blue-and-white buses go to southern West Bank destinations and green-and-white buses go to northern West Bank destinations.

SHERUT

Sheruts (shared taxis) depart more frequently than buses and often cost only a few shekels more; on Shabbat they're the only public transport to destinations in Israel. **Sheruts for Tel Aviv** (Map p80; from 24NIS per person on weekdays, 30NIS on weekends and after midnight) depart from the corner of HaRav Kook St and Jaffa Rd, near Zion Sq; in Tel Aviv, they stop just outside the Central Bus Station.

TRAIN

Jerusalem's **train station** (Jerusalem Malcha; ☑ 02-577-4000; www.rail.co.il; Yitzhak Moda'i St, Malcha; ☺ ticket booth 6-10am & 3.15-7.45pm Sun-Thu, 8.45am-2pm Fri) is located in the southwest of the city, near the Jerusalem Mall. Hourly trains reach Tel Aviv's Savidor HaHagana and HaShalom stations (20NIS, 1½ hours). At the time of research, trains departed between 6.17am and 9.17pm from Sunday to Thursday; the last train on Friday left at 2.46pm and one Saturday train operated at 9.45pm. Trains from Haifa and the coast change in Tel Aviv.

The train station is reached on bus 18 from King George St or bus 6 from the Central Bus Station (allow 45 minutes). Ring *5770 (note the asterisk) for more details.

ⓘ Getting Around

Jerusalem's Old City is walkable and the rest of its neighbourhoods are well connected by buses and a reliable light-rail system. Metered taxis can fill in any gaps. Car hire isn't required if you plan to limit your travel to the wider metropolitan area, but it's an efficient way to day-trip to the Judean Hills.

TO/FROM THE AIRPORT

Ben Gurion Airport is 52km northwest of Jerusalem, just off Rte 1 to Tel Aviv. **Nesher Service Taxis** (☑ 02-625-7227, 072-264-6059; www. neshertours.co.il) operates 24-hour minibuses to Jerusalem from Ben Gurion, which depart from the rank in front of the international arrivals hall and charge 64NIS per passenger. The sherut leaves when full (you might have to wait). Tell the driver which part of Jerusalem you're going to and then the driver will decide in what order passengers are dropped off (depending on where your fellow riders are going, it can take a while). To get to Ben Gurion from Jerusalem, call Nesher a day in advance to schedule your shared taxi pick-up. Service can be gruff, but airport sheruts are reliable and good value.

There is also now a bus (485) that goes every hour between Ben Gurion and Jerusalem's Central Bus Station (p107) for 16NIS. You can't book in advance, but wait for it on the road outside the bus station by the stand showing its number. A private taxi costs 268NIS on weekdays, 320NIS at weekends.

BICYCLE

With many steep areas and a hectic downtown, Jerusalem is best suited to experienced cyclists. The tourist-information office at Jaffa Gate has a list of bike-hire and cycle-tour companies. **Bike Jerusalem** (☑ 02-579-6353; www. bikejerusalem.com; rental per day 90NIS) offers rental bikes with downtown pick-up (including helmet and repair kit), while Smart Tour (p93) takes some of the effort out of pedalling the city hills by offering electric-bike rental. The Arcadia Ba'Moshava (p97) hotel in the German Colony offers bikes for its guests.

BUS

Jerusalem is laced with a good network of bus routes (5.90NIS per ride), which cover all West Jerusalem neighbourhoods (and reach into a few in East Jerusalem). For routes, schedules and transport maps, see www.jet.gov.il.

Be aware that East Jerusalem's bus routes are privately run, and Rav-Kav cards, which can be used on most buses in the Greater Jerusalem area, are not valid for East Jerusalem buses. At the time of writing, there were plans to introduce a Rav-Kav equivalent for the East Jerusalem network.

To get to parts of East Jerusalem such as the Mount of Olives (bus 75, 5NIS), use the **Arab bus station** (Map p72; Sultan Suleiman St, East Jerusalem), near Herod's Gate. The buses that leave from here are blue and white.

CAR

Traffic congestion is common, drivers are impatient, and parking is painful – so consider carefully whether you need a car in Jerusalem. Paid street parking available to non-residents is marked by a blue-and-white kerb; purchase a ticket from a nearby machine (5.70NIS per hour) and display this on your dashboard. Street parking is usually free in the evening and during Shabbat. Alternatively, register with Pango (http://en.pango.co.il) to locate spaces and pay for parking through an app on your phone (in some places, your only option is to pay through Pango). Parking fines are applied readily, and cars are towed swiftly if illegally parked.

For convenient and secure parking near Jaffa Gate, head to **Mamilla Parking** (17 Kariv St, Downtown; 1st hour free, each subsequent hour 12NIS, full day 50NIS; ⊙ 6am-2am).

LIGHT RAIL

Jerusalem Light Rail (www.citypass.co.il) consists of a single line that runs from Mt Herzl in the west of the city to Heyl HaAvir in Pisgat Ze'ev, in the city's far northeast. There are 23 stops along a 13.9km route, including the Central Bus Station, Mahane Yehuda Market and Damascus Gate. The service runs every 10 minutes or so from 5.30am to midnight daily except on Shabbat: on Friday services stop 90 minutes before Shabbat begins, and Saturday services start one hour after Shabbat concludes. Tickets (5.90NIS) can be purchased from the machines on tram stops and must be validated on-board the tram. Multiple journeys can be loaded onto a Rav-Kav card.

ⓘ RAV-KAV CARDS

For easy travel around the city, get a reusable Rav-Kav card, valid on the light rail and all buses within the Greater Jerusalem area (but not East Jerusalem). Obtain an 'anonymous' card for 5NIS from any bus driver, or get one for free on presentation of your passport at the Egged desk (open 7am to 7pm Sunday to Thursday, to 2pm Friday) near platform 22 at the Central Bus Station.

Pre-load the card with rides (5.90NIS each, no transfers) or passes (per day/ week from 13.50/64NIS), and scan it each time you board a light-rail or bus service. Recharge the card at ticket machines by tram stops, on any bus, or at the Central Bus Station's Egged desk. One child under five years of age can travel free with every paying customer.

TAXI

Plan on spending between 25NIS and 50NIS for trips anywhere within the central part of town. Insist that the driver use the meter; between 5.30am and 9pm (except Shabbat), the meter should start on 12.30NIS. Call **Hapalmach Taxi** (02-679-3333), or find taxi services by neighbourhood (and sample fares) on JerusalemTaxis (http://jerusalemtaxies.com).

Drivers at Jaffa Gate are notorious for refusing to use the meter and then overcharging – if you need a taxi from this location, ask the nearby tourist information office to call one for you. Drivers waiting next to the Tomb of the Virgin Mary on the Mount of Olives have a similar reputation.

AROUND JERUSALEM

For millennia, pilgrims have travelled across the Judean Hills to the Holy City, building and endowing monasteries, churches and shrines along the way. Caves and tombs are secreted within this landscape of rock-strewn plains, low hills and valleys; for visitors it's a rewarding combination of natural splendour and archaeological riches. All major sites can be reached on a day trip by car from Jerusalem.

Abu Ghosh   אבו גוש   ابو غوش

02 / POP 7000

Historic churches and hilly views entice travellers to rough-hewn Abu Ghosh, 12km west of Jerusalem. Spliced across a steep and busy main road, Abu Ghosh is a lively Arab town with a slew of hummus restaurants and cafes to stop in before exploring its two main sights, a Crusader-era church and a magnificent basilica. An earlier settlement nearby is known in the Bible as Kiryat Ya'arim (Town of Forests), where the Ark of the Covenant was said to have been located for 20 years until David moved it to Jerusalem (1 Chronicles 13:5–8).

☉ Sights

**Our Lady of the
Ark of the Covenant**   CHURCH
(Notre Dame de l'Arche d'Alliance; cnr Kvish Ha-Shalom & Notre Dame St; ☉8.30-11.30am & 2.30-5pm Mon-Sat; P) Crowned with a statue of Mary carrying the infant Jesus, this hilltop church was built on the site of Kiryat Ya'arim, believed by many Christians to be where the Ark of the Covenant remained during the reigns of kings Samuel, Saul and David.

A 5th-century mosaic can be seen on the church floor, beautifully preserved from the original Byzantine basilica that was destroyed and rebuilt multiple times. Standing today is a 1924 rebuild, decorated in lustrous art-deco style.

Benedictine Abbey   ABBEY
(Rashid St; ☉8.30-11.30am & 2.30-5.30pm Mon-Sat) The centrepiece of this Benedictine complex is the grand, vaulted Church of the Resurrection, which dates to the mid-12th century. This Crusader-era church, one of the best preserved in the country, was acquired by the French government at the turn of the 20th century. Today it is enclosed within a small French Benedictine community, from whom you can buy olive oil and religious icons.

🛏 Sleeping

Most travellers day-trip from Jerusalem, but staying the night in Abu Ghosh is worth considering if a more low-key experience appeals. Aside from the very good **Jerusalem Hills Inn** (077 557-0948; http://jerusalemhillsinn.com; Rehov HaTut 9; s/d from US$65/95; P🛜), there are a few quality places to stay. Travellers with deeper pockets (and a rental car) might want to splurge for a stay at luxurious **Cramim Resort** (08-638-7797; www.isrotel.com/cramim; r from US$330; P🖥🛜🏊) in Kiryat Anavim, 2.5km east.

🍴 Eating

Kvish Ha-Shalom, the main road, has a handful of cafes, mini-marts and restaurants. These include two average hummus places, both named Abu Shukri (though neither is related to the famous restaurant in Jerusalem's Old City).

★ Sultan Sweets & Cafe   DESSERTS $
(Haj Musa 8; sweets from 10NIS; ☉9am-8pm Mon-Sat) Decorated with musical instruments, this jaunty cafe with a soundtrack of Arabic pop is a relaxing place to puff on a nargileh (water pipe) or tuck into desserts like baklava, wedges of sesame halva or a wonderfully syrupy *kunafeh* (vermicelli-topped cheesecake), best accompanied by strong coffee.

❶ Getting There & Away

Abu Ghosh is 12km west of Jerusalem along Rte 1. Superbus 185 and 189 travel to Abu Ghosh from a stop on Shazar Blvd opposite the Jerusalem International Convention Center, close to the Central Bus Station (9.60NIS, 30 minutes, half-hourly).

Around Jerusalem

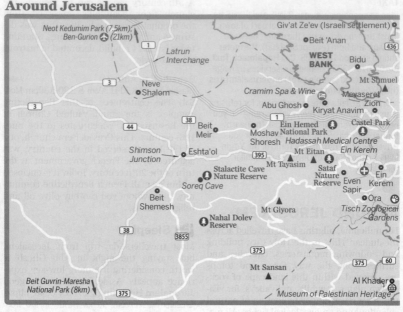

Latrun

לטרון اللطرون

Latrun is equal parts bustle and calm. Just west of Rte 1 between Tel Aviv and Jerusalem, Latrun is less a town, more a knot of roaring highways. It's flanked by olive groves and vineyards, which have inspired local monks to press oil and make wine since the foundation of Latrun Monastery. The monastery and nearby amusement park Mini Israel are the main attractions and make an enjoyable day trip from Jerusalem or Tel Aviv – though there's little reason to dawdle after that.

◉ Sights

Latrun Monastery   MONASTERY
(www.holy-wine.com; ⊗church 8.30-11.30am & 2.30-4pm Mon-Sat winter, 8.30am-noon & 3.30-5pm Mon-Sat summer, shop 8am-5pm Mon-Sat winter, 8.30am-5.30pm Mon-Sat summer; P) Visitors arrive at Latrun Monastery not only for peaceful contemplation and a peep into the church, but also the chance to buy olive oil and wine made by its monks. French Trappist monks founded the site in 1890 and set about cultivating the land. They left during WWI but returned in 1926 to build the sandstone monastery complex that stands today, its elegant archways, cathedral-style windows and flower gardens all enclosed behind high, brick walls. The gift shop sells a superb range of the monks' produce, including oils, wine and olive oil soaps.

Mini Israel   AMUSEMENT PARK
(☑1-700-559-559; www.minisrael.co.il; adult/student & child 69/59NIS; ⊗10am-5pm Sun-Thu & Sat year-round, to 10pm Fri Jul & Aug, to 2pm Fri Sep-Jun; P) More than 380 of Israel's major sights are shrunk to Lilliputian proportions at this cheerful and child-friendly amusement park. Pathways lead you among scale models of cities such as Tel Aviv and Haifa, the ancient ruins of Caesarea, and (curiously) a Coca-Cola factory. Best of all are the moving models of skiers on Mt Hermon and worshippers swaying at the Western Wall.

❶ Getting There & Away

Buses 404, 433, 434 and 435 travel from Jerusalem's Central Bus Station to/from Latrun (16NIS, 30 minutes, frequent).

Neot Kedumim

The 2.5-sq-km **Neot Kedumim** (Biblical Landscape Reserve; ☑08-977-0777; www.neot-kedumim.org.il; off Rte 443; adult/child 25/20NIS; ⊗8.30am-4pm Sun-Thu, to 1pm Fri; P) is the

Beit Guvrin-Maresha National Park

حديقة وطنية بيت جبرين ماريشا

בית גוברין-מרשה

פארק לאומי

Covering 5 sq km of the Judean Hills, Beit Guvrin-Maresha National Park's (☑08-681-1020; www.parks.org.il; off Rte 35; adult/child 28/14NIS; ⊗8am-4pm Sat-Thu, to 3pm Fri) rocky valleys and low hills are home to mountain gazelles, hyenas and songbirds – but most visitors pour in to see the remains of biblical city Maresha and to step inside tombs within bone-white limestone caves. Driving anticlockwise from the entrance, it takes a couple of hours to complete a circuit of the Unesco-listed sites, with time to stop at tombs along the way; allow half a day if you want to embark on walking trails.

On a 30m-high hill, the Tel Maresha site (near car park B) shows the remains of city walls that stood for more than eight centuries, between the 9th and 1st centuries BCE, plus the foundations of a large villa (dating to the end of that period). Continuing along the park road to car park C you'll reach the breathtaking Sidonian Caves, where ancient Maresha's most illustrious citizens were buried. Stepping inside, you'll see meticulously restored wall paintings of animals, fish and urns. Among the tantalising archaeological discoveries here is the much-debated inscription, 'I am sleeping with someone else, but it is you I love'.

Further along the road, a walking trail leads to the ruin of Crusader-era St Anne's Church, whose name was preserved as 'Sandahanna' by local Arabic peoples. Towards the exit of the park are the Bell Caves, whose voluptuous shapes were chiselled by quarriers during the Byzantine and early Islamic periods. Leaving the park, just west on the opposite side of the highway is a petrol station; nearby are the weather-beaten remnants of a Roman amphitheatre and a 4000-sq-metre bathhouse.

Archaeological Seminars VOLUNTEERING
(www.archesem.com; adult/child US$30/25; ⊗by arrangement) Does digging, sifting and crawling through unexcavated caves sound appealing? Volunteers can indulge their inner 'Tomb Raider' on three-hour 'Dig for a Day' experiences at Beit Guvrin-Maresha National Park. The sessions are run by Archaeological Seminars, and suit older children and adults.

best place in Israel to get a sense of what the natural and agricultural landscapes of the Holy Land looked like back in biblical times. Armed with a guide to native fauna and flora, visitors follow self-guided tours along four nature trails (up to 3½ hours) via old oil presses and date palms.

The reserve is located 9km southeast of Ben Gurion airport and 17km north of Latrun.

Soreq Cave

مغارة سوريك

מערת שורק

Thousands of spindly stalactites hang within the 4800-sq-metre Soreq Cave (Stalactite Cave, Avshalom Cave; ☑02-991-1117; www.parks.org.il; Beit-Shemesh; adult/student/child 29/25/15NIS; ⊗8am-5pm Sat-Thu, to 3pm Fri Apr-Sep, 8am-4pm Sat-Thu, to 2pm Fri Oct-Mar), with illuminations in blue and violet adding to the sense of enchantment. A short film tells about the cave's formation and accidental discovery in 1967 by a quarrying crew.

Regular walking tours of paved trails around the cave take around 45 minutes, pointing out some of the more intriguing rock formations.

Tel Aviv-Jaffa (Yafo)

תל אביב–יפו   تل ابيب-يافا

🎵 03 / POP 432,892

Best Places to Eat

➡ Dalida (p140)
➡ Kalamata (p142)
➡ Miznon (p137)
➡ Ouzeria (p141)
➡ Port Sa'id (p139)

Best Places to Stay

➡ Abraham Hostel (p136)
➡ Cinema Hotel (p133)
➡ Hotel Montefiore (p136)
➡ Mendeli Street Hotel (p133)
➡ Shenkin Hotel (p136)

Why Go?

Tel Aviv could not be more different to its older sibling, Jerusalem. Modern, vibrant and cosmopolitan: hedonism is the main religion in this hip, bustling Mediterranean 'Manhattan'. In Hebrew, the city's name means 'Hill of Spring', and it does have an air of perpetual renewal. All over the city, flowers blossom, new restaurants open, and there's always a party going on somewhere.

TLV's biggest draw is its strip of fine beaches, but it's also home to Unesco-listed Bauhaus buildings, historic Jaffa (Yafo) with its fascinating Arab heritage, the quiet Neve Tzedek quarter and trendy Florentin. Expect everything from art galleries to military museums, upmarket bistros to simple hummus joints, peaceful parks to pumping bars. Cranes and skyscrapers may point the way forward, but it's still a city with its feet firmly on the ground. A few days here is fun, but a week can be a revelation – don't miss it.

When to Go
Tel Aviv

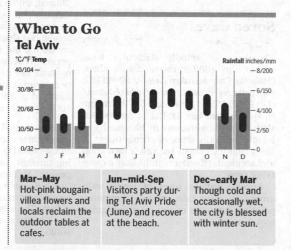

Mar–May
Hot-pink bougainvillea flowers and locals reclaim the outdoor tables at cafes.

Jun–mid-Sep
Visitors party during Tel Aviv Pride (June) and recover at the beach.

Dec–early Mar
Though cold and occasionally wet, the city is blessed with winter sun.

History

Ancient Jaffa

For thousands of years, while Tel Aviv was nothing more than sand dunes, it was Jaffa that stood as one of the great ports of the Mediterranean. According to archaeologists, Jaffa was a fortified port at least as far back as the 18th century BCE. An Egyptian document from around 1470 BCE mentions the city's conquest by Pharaoh Thutmose III.

The ancient Israelite port of 'Joppa' (as mentioned in the Hebrew Bible) came to prominence during the reign of King Solomon, while the temple was being built in Jerusalem. Over the centuries, Jaffa was conquered by, among others, the Assyrians (701 BCE), the Babylonians (586 BCE), Alexander the Great (332 BCE), the Egyptians (301 BCE) and the Maccabees (mid-1st century BCE) but was neglected by the Romans, who had their own port up the coast at Caesarea. In Greek mythology, Andromeda was chained to a rock just off the coast of Jaffa.

Byzantine Jaffa fell to Arabs in 636 CE. In 1100 the Crusaders captured the city and then held it for most of the period until 1268, when the Egyptian Mamluks arrived (the exception was between 1187 and 1191, when Salah Ad Din took the city and then lost it to Richard I 'The Lionheart' of England). Four centuries of Ottoman rule (1515–1917) were briefly interrupted by Napoleon, who in 1799 conquered the city.

19th-Century Revival

In the early 1800s Jaffa was hardly more than a village, but reconstruction began in 1807 under Muhammad Abu Nabbut. Jews returned in the 1820s, and by the end of the century Jaffa had become a major gateway for boatloads of Jewish pilgrims and immigrants. Palestinian farmers cultivated a new type of orange, later known as the Jaffa (Shamouti) orange and exports grew significantly from 1845 to 1870.

Several new neighbourhoods were established northeast of Jaffa's walled city during the latter half of the 1800s. A group of American Christians from Maine founded the American Colony in 1866; followed by the Templers, messianic Protestants from Germany, who were the first to label the oranges. In the late 1800s, groups of Jews tired of the cramped conditions in Jaffa's Old City established two new neighbourhoods on the sand dunes, Neve Tzedek (1887) and Neve Shalom (1890).

The New City of Tel Aviv

In 1906, 60 Jewish families – led by the dynamic Meir Dizengoff (1861–1936), a Zionist pioneer and the city's first mayor – from Kishinev and Odessa met in Jaffa to lay out plans to establish an entirely new Jewish city. They purchased 12.8 hectares of empty sand dunes north of the city, divided much of it into 60 lots and in 1909 held a lottery – using seashells – to divvy up the land around what is now the intersection of Herzl St and Rothschild Blvd. They took as a model the English 'garden city' (a planned, self-contained community with plenty of public parks and open spaces). By the time WWI broke out in 1914, 140 homes had been built.

The name of the new city, Tel Aviv (Hill of Spring), comes from the title of the Hebrew translation of Theodor Herzl's utopian novel *Altneuland;* it's also mentioned in Ezekiel 3:15.

The Mandate Period

Tel Aviv's development ground to a halt during WWI, and in the spring of 1917 the Ottoman administration expelled the entire Jewish population from both Tel Aviv and Jaffa. But after WWI, the British Mandate in Palestine made it possible for the city to resume its exponential growth. Arab riots in Jaffa in 1921 sent many Jews fleeing north to Tel Aviv, helping to bring the new city's population to around 34,000 by 1925.

The 1930s saw waves of new arrivals, many fleeing Nazi Germany. A boycott of Jewish passengers and cargo by Jaffa's Arab port workers, begun in 1936, led Tel Aviv to build its very own port. By 1939 Tel Aviv's population had reached 160,000, meanwhile, a few kilometres to the northeast in the Templer settlement of Sarona, the patriotically German residents were flying the Nazi flag.

Jewish architects who had fled Nazi Germany set about designing apartment houses in the clean-lined, modernist Bauhaus style that would soon become the city's hallmark.

With the outbreak of WWII in 1939, many local Jews volunteered for the British army, and Tel Aviv played host to Allied troops while simultaneously serving as a centre of Zionist opposition to Britain's anti-immigration policies. The city was bombed by Mussolini's air force in 1940.

In late 1947 and into 1948, as the British prepared to pull out of Palestine, Jewish-Arab tensions rose, with Arab snipers firing at Jewish neighbourhoods from the

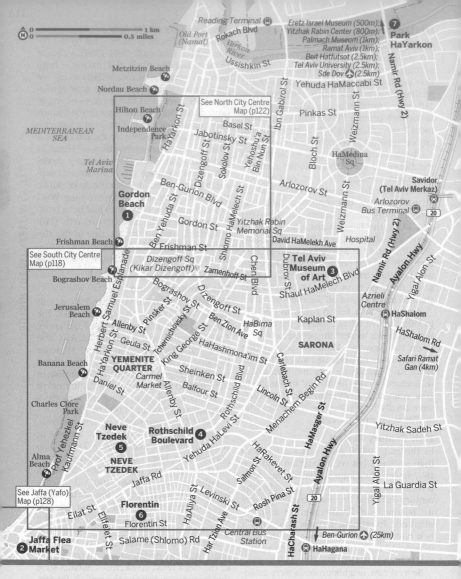

Tel Aviv-Jaffa (Yafo) Highlights

1 Gordon Beach (p124)
Joining swimmers, sunbathers and beach volleyballers on the sands of TLV's famous beach.

2 Jaffa Flea Market (p129)
Investigating the bohemian bars and Arabic antiques.

3 Tel Aviv Museum of Art (p116) Contemplating impressionist masterpieces

and cutting-edge contemporary artworks.

4 Rothschild Boulevard (p117) Checking out stylish cafes and Unesco-listed Bauhaus buildings.

5 Neve Tzedek (p121) Exploring the narrow, peaceful streets of the city's oldest quarter.

6 Florentin (p121)
Discovering underground bars and street art in this hipster hang-out.

7 Park HaYarkon (p126)
Walking, jogging or cycling through this huge green expanse.

minaret of beachfront Hassan Bek Mosque. The Haganah and the Irgun (Jewish underground forces) responded by laying siege to Jaffa. In April 1948, Jaffa was captured by Jewish forces and the vast majority of the 70,000 Arab residents were expelled or fled, most for Gaza or Beirut.

From City to Metropolis

On 14 May 1948, David Ben-Gurion declared the State of Israel from Mayor Dizengoff's house on Rothschild Blvd. In April 1949 Tel Aviv and Jaffa were joined to create a single municipality. The previous Arab residents were not allowed to return to their homes, and many of the vacant properties in Jaffa were taken over by Jewish immigrants, many from the Balkans. During the 1950s, Old Jaffa was once more neglected and became a retrogressive crime area, nicknamed 'The Wasteland'.

Yet, the decades after the establishment of the State of Israel saw metropolitan Tel Aviv expanding in every direction, turning neighbouring towns such as Ramat Gan and Givatayim to the east and, to the south, Bat Yam and Holon into bustling inner suburbs. The city flourished as Israel's main centre of newspaper publishing, Hebrew literature, theatre and the arts. Early restrictions on the height of buildings had to be modified when authorities realised that the only place to go was up.

During the First Gulf War (1991), greater Tel Aviv was hit by about three dozen Iraqi Scud missiles, damaging thousands of apartments. On 4 November 1995, Prime Minister Yitzhak Rabin was assassinated by a right-wing Orthodox Jew during a peace rally at what is now Rabin Sq. The following year the city centre was hit by a wave of Palestinian suicide bomb attacks. The confident optimism of the Oslo Peace Process years was over.

Into the 21st Century

The start of the new millennium brought more hard times, with more than a dozen suicide bombings in downtown Tel Aviv during the Second Intifada. But the early 21st century also saw a rejuvenated economy based largely on high-tech innovation. In 2003 the city accepted Unesco World Heritage status for its 'White City' Bauhaus buildings; restoration of these is proceeding, albeit slowly. Young Israelis started to move back to TLV, and older neighbourhoods such as Neve Tzedek and parts of Jaffa underwent gentrification.

In summer 2011, as the Arab Spring continued to dominate headlines, Tel Aviv was at the heart of a wave of protests as people took to the streets demanding social justice and affordable housing. But the protests gradually faded, and in recent years Tel Aviv has gone even further upmarket. Derelict areas such as the Old Railway Station and Sarona were transformed into deluxe shopping and entertainment zones. Tel Aviv's infrastructure is also being updated and expanded, including a planned light-rail system, a new seafront promenade and futuristic skyscrapers. Today, Tel Aviv is heavily reliant on tourism and its growing reputation as one of the world's hippest beach cities.

◎ Sights

This is a city that is best explored by foot or bicycle. You should spend most of your time wandering through the colourful and diverse neighbourhoods in and around the city centre and relaxing on the wonderful beaches on the city's western edge. In summer, there's a simple rule: spend your days at the beach and your nights investigating one of the best eating and drinking scenes in the Middle East. In winter, there are enough museums and shopping opportunities to keep you busy during the day, and the nighttime eating and drinking scene is just as vibrant as its warm-weather equivalent.

◎ City Centre

The area running from Arlozorov St south to Sheinken St is generally referred to as the city centre (*Merkaz ha-Ir* or *Lev ha-Ir*). It includes the cultural precinct around HaBima Sq; the upper stretch of the city's favourite promenade, Rothschild Blvd; the shopping hubs of Dizengoff Centre, Sarona (p124) and Carmel Market (p117); and the popular retail and cafe strips along Dizengoff, Allenby and King George Sts.

Rabin Square   SQUARE

The biggest public square in the city, this huge expanse of paving stones was repaved and upgraded in recent years. It has an ecological pond filled with lotus flowers and koi, a fountain that's lit up at night, and some cool cafes around the perimeter. On the northern edge towers City Hall, which looks like a 1960s communist-style block (though not when it's lit up with laser beams).

Rabin Sq used to be called Malchei Israel (Kings of Israel) Sq but was renamed after

TEL AVIV IN...

Two Days

With only two days at your disposal, you'll need to get cracking! Have breakfast at **Benedict** (p139) or another cafe around Rothschild Blvd and then wander around this area, admiring its Bauhaus buildings. Next, browse the boutiques in the historic Neve Tzedek (p121) quarter before heading to even-more-historic Jaffa, where you can have lunch in the **flea market** (p129) before wandering around Old Jaffa. In the evening, sample some new Israeli cuisine at the buzzing **Port Sa'id** (p139) or upmarket **North Abraxas** (p140).

On day two, get a warm bowl of the world's best hummus at **Ali Caravan** (p141), walk along the beachside promenade and then head up through the **Carmel Market** (p117) to the city centre before making your way to the wonderful **Tel Aviv Museum of Art** (p116). At night, eat Greek at **Ouzeria** (p141) and then enjoy drinks on the tree-covered patio of the ultra-cool **Kuli Alma** (p143).

Four Days

An extra couple of days will make a world of difference, and you may find yourself slipping into a laid-back Tel Avivian lifestyle. Spend a morning at **Hilton Beach** (p125) in the north and another at **Alma Beach** (p126) in the south. Hire a bicycle from **O-Fun** (p149) or book a Segway tour with **SmartTour** (☑02-561-8056; http://smart-tour.co.il; per person 195NIS) from Jaffa's Port along the seafront, stopping at cafes along the way. Check out the comprehensive **Beit Hatfutsot** (p126) museum at Tel Aviv University and walk through the green **Park HaYarkon** (p126) back to town to get a cheeky frozen yoghurt at **Tamara** (p138). If time allows, stroll around the redeveloped **Sarona** (p124) centre, join a walking tour with **Delicious Israel** (p131) and simply take your time sampling the late night bar and cafe culture.

---

the assassination of Prime Minister Yitzhak Rabin in 1995. Rabin Sq is also the site for most of Tel Aviv's big events, from Independence Day celebrations in May to mass protests and peace vigils. On Ibn Gabirol St next to City Hall, a small memorial marks the spot where Rabin was shot.

Ben-Gurion Museum MUSEUM
(Map p122; ☑03-522-1010; www.bg-house.org; 17 Ben-Gurion Blvd; ◉8am-3pm Sun & Tue-Thu, to 5pm Mon, to 1pm Fri, 11am-2pm Sat) FREE Built between 1930 and 1931, this modest house on the way to the seafront was the Tel Aviv home of David Ben-Gurion, Israel's first prime minister. Built in a workers' neighbourhood, it is maintained more or less as it was left on the great man's death. Downstairs visitors can view photographs of Ben-Gurion meeting figures such as Nixon, Kennedy and Einstein, while upstairs is home to the former PM's library and thousands of books in different languages.

★ **Tel Aviv Museum of Art** GALLERY
(Map p118; ☑03-607-7020; www.tamuseum.com; 27 Shaul HaMelech Blvd; adult/student/child under 15yr 50/40NIS/free; ◉10am-6pm Mon-Wed & Sat,

to 9pm Tue & Thu, to 2pm Fri; 🅿🚻; 🚌7, 9, 18, 38, 42, 70, 82) The modern 'envelope' building by American architect Preston Scott Cohen is one of many reasons to visit this impressive gallery located on the eastern edge of the city centre. There's a huge amount to see here (including art activities for kids), but undoubtedly the highlight is the superb collection of impressionist and post-impressionist art on the 1st floor of the main building, which includes works by Renoir, Gauguin, Degas, Pissarro, Monet, Picasso, Cézanne, Van Gogh, Vuillard, Matisse, Soutine and Chagall.

Helena Rubenstein Pavilion GALLERY
(Map p118; ☑03-528-7196; www.tamuseum.com; 6 Tarsat Blvd; 10NIS; ◉10am-6pm Mon, Wed & Sat, to 9pm Tue & Thu, to 2pm Fri) FREE Endowed by the cosmetics entrepreneur of the same name, this contemporary art space is an annexe of the Tel Aviv Museum of Art. There's a permanent collection of decorative arts on the top floor, but the main draw is the temporary exhibition space downstairs, which showcases work by both Israeli and international artists. The International-style building, which opened in 1959, is just off HaBima Sq, home to Israel's national theatre.

Jabotinsky Institute
MUSEUM

(Map p118; ☑ 03-528-6523; www.jabotinsky.org; 38 King George St; ☺ 8am-4pm Sun-Thu) **FREE** This historical research organisation has a small museum on the 1st floor presenting the history and activities of the Etzel (Irgun), an underground militia founded by Ze'ev Jabotinsky in 1931. Exhibits concentrate on Jabotinsky's political, literary and journalistic activities, and also document the creation of the Jewish Legion (five battalions of Jewish volunteers who served in the British army during WWI).

Gan Meir Park
PARK

(Map p118) To escape the city pace, head to Gan Meir Park, on the western side of King George St, where dog walkers release their four-legged friends in a specially designated dog run, and parents do the same to their two-legged charges at the playground. There's plenty of tree-shaded space and picnic benches for some lunchtime lounging.

In the middle of the park there is the Tel Aviv Gay Center (p143) and a branch of Landwer Cafe.

Beit Ha'ir
CULTURAL CENTRE

(Town House, Map p118, ☑ 03-724 0311; http;// beithair.org; 27 Bialik St; adult/student & child 20/10NIS, incl Bialik Museum adult 30NIS; ☺ 9am-5pm Mon-Thu, 10am-2pm Fri & Sat) Located in a cul de sac at the end of Blalik St, which is full of significant Bauhaus-style buildings, this cultural centre comprises two galleries where temporary exhibitions are held, as well as a permanent exhibition of historical photographs and documents about the city. The building, which dates from 1925, was used as Tel Aviv's city hall until 1965 and visitors can see a reconstruction of the office once used by Meir Dizengoff.

Bialik Museum
MUSEUM

(Map p118; ☑ 03-525-3403; http://eng.shimur.org/ Bialik; 22 Bialik St; adult/student & child 20/10NIS, incl Beit Ha'ir adult 30NIS; ☺ 11am-5pm Mon-Thu, 10am-2pm Fri & Sat) Israel's national poet Chaim Nachman Bialik lived in this handsome 1920s villa, which is designed in the style of the Arts and Crafts movement. Its richly decorated downstairs interiors include custom-made furniture, a vivid colour scheme and ceramic tiles representing the Twelve Tribes of Israel, the Star of David and the signs of the zodiac. Bialik's private library, study and bedroom are preserved upstairs, and there's an archive of his papers in the basement.

Rubin Museum
GALLERY

(Map p118; ☑ 03-525-5961; www.rubinmuseum. org.il; 14 Bialik St; adult/child 20NIS/free; ☺ 10am-3pm Mon, Wed, Thu & Fri, to 8pm Tue, 11am-2pm Sat) Sometimes referred to as the 'Gauguin of Palestine' but more reminiscent of Matisse, Romanian-born Reuven Rubin (1893–1974) immigrated to Palestine in 1923 and painted wonderful landscapes and scenes of local life in his adopted country. Set in his former home, there are a number of scenes of Jaffa and plenty of portraits, providing a fascinating account of Jewish immigration and the early years of Israel.

◎ South City Centre

Tel Aviv is a vibrant and cultured city with many art galleries, cafes, bars and boutiques. But it's here, on the southern fringe of the city centre, where the culture is most pronounced and where the city's avant-garde and hipster communities congregate.

Although the main stretch of Allenby St can be somewhat sleazy, its adjoining streets are littered with upmarket restaurants, stylish cafes and boutique hotels. The lower part of Rothschild Blvd is rich in Bauhaus building stock (p120) and plush new skyscrapers, and on weekends, Tel Avivians flock here to meet friends and enjoy the highly social street scene.

★Carmel Market
MARKET

(Shuk HaCarmel; Map p118; ☺ 8am-late afternoon Sun-Thu, to mid-afternoon Fri) Squeezed between the dishevelled streets of the Yemenite Quarter and the pedestrianised section of Nahalat Binyamin St, Tel Aviv's busiest street market is, in many ways, the heart of the city. The total opposite of the characterless air-conditioned shopping malls and supermarkets found elsewhere in the city, it's a crowded and noisy place where vendors hawk everything from cut-price beachwear to knock-off designer accessories, and where locals come to buy olives, pickles, nuts, fruit, vegetables, cheese and freshly baked bread.

Independence Hall
HISTORIC SITE

(Beit Haatzmaut; Map p118; ☑ 03-510-6426; http:// eng.ihi.org.il; 16 Rothschild Blvd; adult/student/ child 24/18/16NIS; ☺ 9am-5pm Sun-Thu, to 2pm Fri) This building, still in need of some restoration work, was originally the home of Meir Dizengoff, one of the city's founding fathers and its first mayor. It was here, on 14 May 1948, that David Ben-Gurion declared

South City Centre

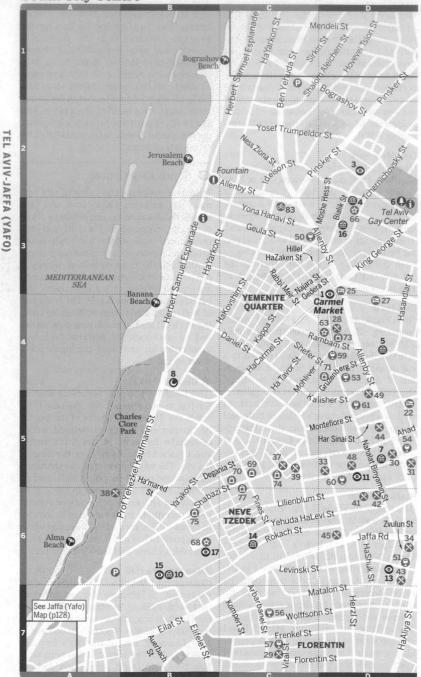

Mendeli St

Bograshov Beach

Herbert Samuel Esplanade

HaYarkon St

Sirkin St

Shalom Aleichem St

Ben Yehuda St

Hovevei Tsion St

Bograshov St

Pinsker St

Yosef Trumpeldor St

Jerusalem Beach

Ness Ziona St

Idelson St

Pinsker St

Tchernichovsky St

Fountain

Allenby St

3

Moshe Hess St

Bialik St

4

6

Tel Aviv Gay Center

Yona Hanavi St

83

66

16

Geula St

50

Allenby St

King George St

MEDITERRANEAN SEA

Herbert Samuel Esplanade

HaYarkon St

Hillel HaZaken St

Rabbi Meir St

Najara St

Gedera St

Hasandlar St

Banana Beach

Hakovshim St

YEMENITE QUARTER

1

Carmel Market

25

27

Kappa St

63

28

73

Daniel St

HaCarmel St

Rambam St

59

5

8

Shefer St

Ha Tavor St

Mohliver St

71

Gruenberg St

Allenby St

53

Kalisher St

61

49

Montefiore St

22

Charles Clore Park

Prof Yehezkel Kaufmann St

Har Sinai St

44

Ahad

54

Nahalat Binyamin St

7

30

31

Degania St

69

37

33

48

Ya'akov St

70

39

74

60

11

38

Shabazi St

77

Pines St

Lilienblum St

41

42

75

NEVE TZEDEK

Yehuda HaLevi St

Zvulun St

Alma Beach

68

14

Rokach St

45

Jaffa Rd

34

17

Levinski St

HaShuk St

51

43

15

10

13

See Jaffa (Yafo) Map (p128)

Matalon St

Herzl St

HaAliya St

Eilat St

Elifelet St

Kompert St

Arbabanel St

56

Wolffsohn St

Auerbach St

Frenkel St

57

29

Vital St

FLORENTIN

Florentin St

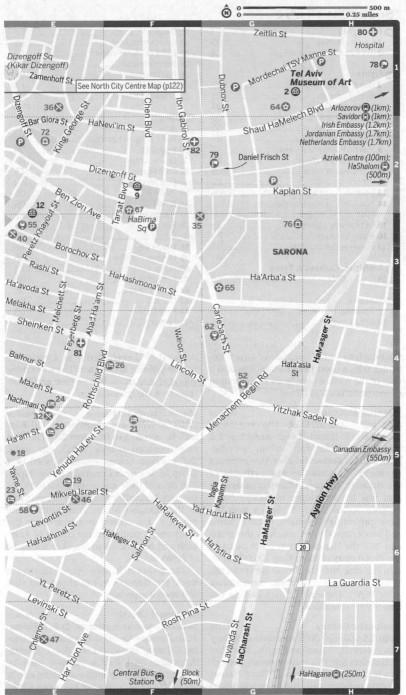

N

0 ———————————— 500 m
0 ———————————— 0.25 miles

Zeitlin St

Hospital

80

78

Dizengoff Sq
(Kikar Dizengoff)

Zamenhoff St

See North City Centre Map (p122)

Mordechai TSV Manne St

Dubnov St

**Tel Aviv
Museum of Art**

2

Dizengoff St

36

Bar Giora St

King George St

HaNevi'im St

Chen Blvd

Ibn Gabirol St

64

Shaul HaMelech Blvd

Arlozorov (1km);
Savidor (1km);
Irish Embassy (1.2km);
Jordanian Embassy (1.7km);
Netherlands Embassy (1.7km)

72

82

79

Daniel Frisch St

Azrieli Centre (100m);
HaShalom (500m)

Dizengoff St

Ben Zion Ave

Tarsat Blvd

9

Kaplan St

12

55

HaBima
Sq

67

35

76

40

Peretz Khayout St

Borochov St

HaHashmona'im St

SARONA

Ha'Arba'a St

Rashi St

Melchett St

Ahad Ha'am St

65

Ha'avoda St

Feierberg St

Carlebach St

Melakha St

Wilson St

HaMasger St

Sheinken St

62

Balfour St

Lincoln St

Hata'asia
St

81

26

52

Rothschild Blvd

Menachem Begin Rd

Yitzhak Sadeh St

Mazeh St

24

Nachmani St

32

20

21

Canadian Embassy
(550m)

Ha'am St

18

Yehuda HaLevi St

HaMasger St

Avalon Hwy

23

Yavne St

19

Mikveh Israel St

46

Yagia
Kapaim St

58

Levontin St

Yad Harutzim St

HaRakevet St

HaHashmal St

HaNegev St

Salmon St

HaTsfira St

YL Peretz St

20

Levinski St

La Guardia St

Chlenov St

47

Rosh Pina St

Har Tzion Ave

Central Bus
Station

Block
(50m)

Lavanda St

HaCharash St

HaHagana (250m)

South City Centre

the establishment of the State of Israel. Entry includes a short introductory film and a tour of the room where Israel's Declaration of Independence was signed.

Haganah Museum · MUSEUM
(Map p118; ☑03-560-8624; http://eng.shimur.org/hagana; 23 Rothschild Blvd; adult/student & child 15/10NIS; ⊙8am-4pm Sun-Thu) Splendidly located on Rothschild Blvd, this museum chronicles the formation and activities of the Haganah, the paramilitary organisation that was the forerunner of today's Israel Defence Forces (IDF). A civilian guerrilla force protecting kibbutzim (Israeli farms and cooperatives) from attack in the 1920s and '30s, the Haganah went on to assist in the illegal entry of more than 100,000 Jews into Palestine after the British government's 1939 white paper restricting immigration. After WWII, Haganah fighters carried out anti-British operations.

Chelouche Gallery · GALLERY
(Map p118; ☑03-620-0068; www.chelouchegallery.com; 7 Mazeh St; ⊙11am-7pm Mon-Thu, 10am-2pm Fri, 11am-2pm Sat) This contemporary art gallery is set in the neoclassical 'Twin House', a 1920s building with two identical wings

designed by Joseph Berlin as a residence for himself and his brother. The welcoming Tola'at Sfarim (Book Worm) Cafe and Bookshop is on the ground floor.

Maine Friendship House · MUSEUM
(☑03-681-9225; www.jaffacolony.com; 10 Auerbach St; ⊙noon-3pm Fri, 2-4pm Sat) The first neighbourhood outside Jaffa's city walls, the American Colony was established by a group of American Christians in the 1860s. The story of their star-crossed (some would say hare-brained) settlement scheme is told at the engaging Maine Friendship House museum. The colony area, run-down but charming, is centred on the corner of Auerbach and Be'er Hoffman Sts, 1km northeast of Jaffa's old city.

The museum is only open two days a week, but visitors can call ahead and staff will open it especially.

Immanuel Church · CHURCH
(www.immanuelchurch-jaffa.com; 15 Be'er Hofman St; ⊙10am-2pm Tue-Fri) This small but charming German Templer church, now Lutheran, dates from 1904. Its fine organ is used for concerts. Completely unlike anything else in Tel Aviv, it's a little piece of European Chris-

TEL AVIV-JAFFA (YAFO) SIGHTS

tian architecture in the Middle East. It holds services at 11am on Saturday and 10am on Sunday.

Levinski Spice Market MARKET
(Shuk Levinski; Map p118; www.shuktlv.co.il; Levinski St, between Herzl St & HaAliya St) Beloved by celebrity chefs, this aromatic market is a mini-neighbourhood of pantries and stores. Set along Levinski St (the block between HaAliyah and Herzl Sts) it was established in the 1920s by Balkan immigrants. This is where local cooks come to source fresh herbs and spices, dried fruit, stuffed chilli peppers, olive oil, cheese and other goodies.

👁 Neve Tzedek

Tel Aviv's first neighbourhood has its own unique atmosphere. Somehow separate from the bustle and *balagan* (chaos in Hebrew) found in the rest of the city, the bohemian enclave of Neve Tzedek quietly passes the time away.

Founded in 1887, Neve Tzedek is the oldest quarter in the new city. Centred on Shabazi St, a gentle slope running downhill to Tel Aviv Promenade, it is a hugely atmospheric tangle of narrow streets lined with bars, cafes and edgy artisan boutiques with old stone walls, as well as the Suzanne Dellal Centre for dance.

Suzanne Dellal Centre ARTS CENTRE
(Map p118; ☎03-510-5656; www.suzannedellal. org.il; 5 Yechiely St, Neve Izedek) The first school built outside the city walls of Jaffa, this 1892 building set in leafy surrounds was converted into a cultural centre between 1984 and 1989, triggering the gentrification of the formerly dishevelled Neve Tzedek neighbourhood. A popular venue for festivals and cultural events, it has a focus on dance and is home to the internationally recognised Batsheva troupe. Even if you've not got tickets to a performance, it's worth visiting just to stroll around its idyllic courtyard.

Nachum Gutman Museum of Art MUSEUM
(Map p118; ☎03-516-1970; www.gutmanmuseum. co.il; 21 Shimon Rokah St, Neve Tzedek; adult/child 24/12NIS; ⊙10am-4pm Mon-Thu, to 2pm Fri, to 3pm Sat) Found on a quiet, picturesque street in the Neve Tzedek quarter, this museum displays 200 works by the 20th-century Israeli artist Nachum Gutman (1898–1980). The Gutmans were among the first Jewish families to settle in Tel Aviv and Nachum became one of the country's most celebrated painters and children's book illustrators.

👁 Florentin

Named after David Florentin, a Greek Jew who purchased this area in the 1920s, Florentin is the city's artistic, shabby-chic

North City Centre

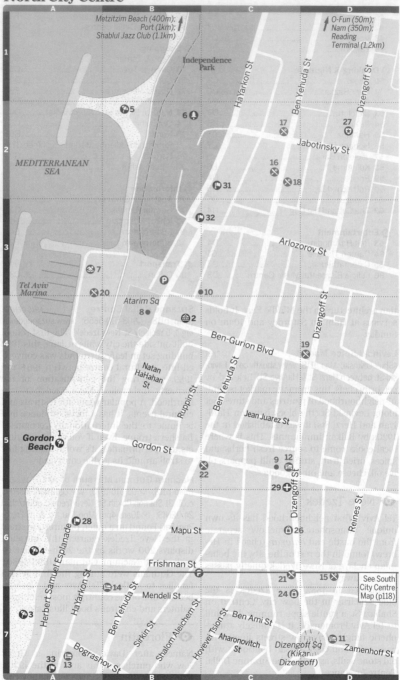

TEL AVIV-JAFFA (YAFO) SIGHTS

Metzitzim Beach (400m);
Port (1km);
Shablul Jazz Club (1.1km)

O-Fun (50m);
Nam (350m);
Reading
Terminal (1.2km)

Independence Park

HaYarkon St
Ben Yehuda St
Dizengoff St

MEDITERRANEAN SEA

Jabotinsky St

Arlozorov St

Tel Aviv Marina

Atarim Sq

Ben-Gurion Blvd

Dizengoff St

Natan HaHahan St

Ruppin St

Ben Yehuda St

Jean Juarez St

Gordon Beach

Gordon St

Dizengoff St

Reines St

Herbert Samuel Esplanade

Mapu St

Frishman St

See South City Centre Map (p118)

HaYarkon St
Ben Yehuda St
Sirkin St
Shalom Aleichem St
Hovevei Tsion St
Mendeli St
Ben Ami St
Aharonovitch St

Dizengoff Sq
(Kikar
Dizengoff)

Zamenhoff St

Bograshov St

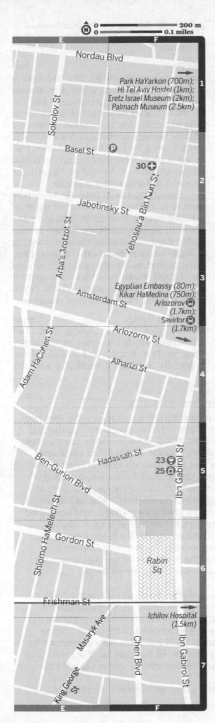

North City Centre

◉ **Top Sights**
1 Gordon Beach A5

◉ **Sights**
2 Ben-Gurion Museum B4
3 Bograshov Beach.............................A7
4 Frishman Beach................................A6
5 Hilton Beach.....................................B2
6 Independence Park B2

⊕ **Activities, Courses & Tours**
7 Gordon Swimming Pool A3
8 Surf House.......................................B4
9 Tel Aviv Art Studio C5
10 Ulpan Gordon..................................B3

▭ **Sleeping**
11 Cinema Hotel...................................D7
12 Dizengoff Avenue Hotel C5
13 Lusky Hotel......................................A7
14 Mendeli Street Hotel D7

✕ **Eating**
15 Anastasia D6
16 Barbunia...C2
17 Benedict...C2
18 Dosa Bar...C2
19 Goocha D4
20 Landwer Café A3
21 Sabich Frishman C6
22 Tamara..C5

◉ **Drinking & Nightlife**
23 Kanta F5

◉ **Shopping**
24 Bauhaus Centre C7
25 Gan Ha'ir Mall F5
26 Steimatzky.......................................C6

ⓘ **Information**
27 Dizengoff Police Station D2
28 French Embassy A6
29 Superpharm C5
30 Tel Aviv Doctor F2
31 Turkish Embassy C2
32 UK Embassy B3
33 US Embassy A7

neighbourhood, home to designers, musicians, photographers and a few talented graffiti artists. Head to a bar or cafe on Vittal St to hang out in hipsterville.

◉ **Tel Aviv Beach & Port**

In hot weather, Tel Avivians flock to the city beach, a 14km-long stretch of golden sand divided into individual sections, each with its own character. You'll find young and old soaking up the Mediterranean rays, swimming and playing fierce games of *matkot* (paddle ball).

The water here is clean, and there are changing rooms and freshwater showers scattered along its length. Swimmers, however, must heed lifeguard warnings when conditions become rough; a black flag means that swimming is forbidden, a red flag means that swimming is dangerous and a white flag means that the area is safe. Beaches are patrolled between May and October until around 6pm.

The beaches are packed in summer, especially on Saturday, when crowds descend early to nab a prime spot. The prices of beach-furniture hire are regulated by the municipality: beach chairs cost 6NIS, an umbrella 6NIS and a lounge bed 12NIS. The municipality provides free wi-fi for beachgoers. Look out for the occasional guy shouting 'Arctic' (he's not crazy, he's selling ice lollies).

★ **Gordon Beach**   BEACH
(Map p122; P) South from Hilton Beach, this is Tel Aviv's main beach. Well equipped with sun loungers, ice-cream shops, an outdoor gym and beach restaurants, it's popular with Tel Avivians, tourists and *matkot* (paddle ball) players. On Saturdays, you'll likely see group folk dancing on the boardwalk. The Gordon Swimming Pool (p131) is at the nearby marina.

Old Port   PORT
(Namal; www.namal.co.il; P) The Old Port is popular with families wandering around its waterfront shops, restaurants and cafes while planes swoop in low overhead to land at nearby Sde Dov airport. A covered organic farmers market (p147) also attracts locals looking for their fresh vegetables, pasta and seafood. After dark and on weekends, hordes of clubbers descend on the strip of bars and nightclubs after midnight.

Originally opened in 1936, Tel Aviv's port went into decline with the construction of a better, deeper harbour at Ashdod in the 1960s. In the early 2000s, the Tel Aviv municipality finally overhauled the area, creating a wide wooden boardwalk, adding playgrounds and bike paths, and transforming the derelict warehouses into a commercial centre with big-name stores (Crocs, Levi's, Steve Madden, etc) to draw local shoppers.

Metzitzim Beach   BEACH
Named after a 1972 comedy film, Hof Metzitzim (which translates as the sleazy 'Peeping Tom Beach') is actually a family-friendly bay with a small play area for

---

SARONA, OLD & NEW

In 1871 a group of Pietist Christians from southwestern Germany known as the Templers (not to be confused with the medieval Knights Templar) established a small agricultural colony 4km northeast of Jaffa, on the banks of the Ayalon River, and called it Sarona. The technologies, agricultural and otherwise, that they brought with them had a profound impact on the early Zionists, with whom they had good relations. Exiled to Egypt by the British at the end of WWI, they returned in 1921, constructing Bauhaus-style buildings.

As the Nazi party rose to power in Germany, some of Sarona's residents became enthusiastic supporters, leading, unsurprisingly, to friction with their Jewish neighbours. At the outbreak of WWII, the Templers were declared 'enemy aliens', and Sarona was turned into an internment camp; in 1943 most of the Templers were deported to Australia.

After the war, the fortified camp became a military base for the British forces and a target for attacks by the various Jewish undergrounds – the Haganah, Etzel and Lehi. In December 1947, as they were about to leave, the British turned over the camp to the Jewish leadership. After 1948, the Israeli government turned the old Templer buildings into government offices.

In recent years, more than 30 of the colony's historic buildings were restored and redeveloped as a commercial centre. Set in lush green surrounds, Sarona includes offices, restaurants, bars, cafes, fashion stores, art galleries and a visitor centre where the colony's fascinating history is told. Today the biggest attraction is the indoor **Sarona Market** (Map p118; ✔ centre 03-609-9028, market 03-624-2424; http://saronamarket.co.il/en; Eliezar Kaplan St, Sarona; ⊙9am-10pm Sun-Thu, 8am-5pm Fri, 9am-11pm Sat; 🛜📶), an arcade featuring global street-food stands, celebrity-chef restaurants and shops to buy fresh meat, fish, cheese and more.

Sarona is on Eliezer Kaplan St, 1km east of the Dizengoff Center and just east of Habima Sq.

TEL AVIV WITH CHILDREN

Despite its party reputation, Tel Aviv is as family-friendly as cities get. A baby boom in recent years has seen more families with children living in the city, and thanks to its beaches, parks and tree-lined avenues, TLV is now a top destination for kids.

Most children will be entertained for hours on Tel Aviv's beaches (p123), which have lifeguards and are well equipped with ice-cream vendors and beach cafes. But if it's a grassy expanse you're after, try Park HaYarkon (p126), equipped with a small farm, pedal boats and playgrounds. Nearby, the **Meymadion Water Park** (☑03-642-2777; www.meymadion.co.il; Ganei Yehoshua Park, Rokah Ave; 117NIS, after 1pm 97NIS; ☺9am-4.30pm Jun-Aug, Sat 1st half Sep) offers water rides that little kids like but teenagers will consider pretty tame. Across the street, the **Luna Park** (☑03-642-7080; www.lunapark.co.il; Rokach Ave; adult/child under 2yr 117NIS/free; ☺10am-8pm Jul & Aug, 10am-6pm Sat only rest of year; ☒113, 48, 47, 28, 27, 21) is a compact theme park with rides for teenagers and little ones. Its opening hours change by the month, so call ahead. **Safari Ramat Gan** (☑03-632-0222, www.safari.co.il; Sodorat Hatsvi St, Ramat Gan; adult/student/child under 2yr 70/63NIS/free; ☺9am-5pm Sat-Thu & to 2pm Fri May-Aug, reduced hours Sep-Apr; Ⓟⓖ; ☒67, 55), as close as you'll get in Israel to the Serengeti plains, is both a drive-through safari and a large zoo with a petting farm and workshops for kids.

But best of all is the sheer range of playgrounds with swings, slides and climbing frames. There are small playgrounds all over town, but some of the larger ones include Independence Park, Gan Meir Park (p117), located at the northern end of the Old Port, Dubnov St behind the Tel Aviv Museum of Art (p116), and at the end of Shabazi St in Neve Tzedek.

Many shopping malls, including Gan Ha'ir (p147) and the Dizengoff Centre (p147) have popular soft play areas (mischakiyot) for toddlers and young children.

Outside of town, the educational Israel Children's Museum (p152) and the **Yamit 2000** (☑03-650-6500; www.yamit2000.co.il; 66 Mifratz Shlomo St; adult/child under 2yr 100NIS/free; ☺9am-4pm Sun-Thu to 4.30pm Fri & Sat; ☒Dan 89, 96, 163, 172, 201) waterpark in Holon make for a fun day out for kids.

Dining with children, at all times of the day, couldn't be easier. Many restaurants and cafes cater for tiny clients and are equipped with high chairs. Most branches of **Landwer Café** (Map p122, ☑03-681-8699; www.landwercafe.co.il; 14 Fliezer Peri St , Marina; breakfasts & mains from 52NIS; ☺8am-midnight; ☎ⓖ) offer crayons and colouring-in menus. It's common to see kids dining with their parents well into the night.

children. It also hosts Friday afternoon beach parties during summer.

Hilton Beach   BEACH
(Map p122) Named after the nearby hotel, Hilton Beach is divided into three parts: the city's unofficial gay beach is in the middle, the dog-walkers' beach is to the north (it's the only beach where dogs are officially allowed) and surfers hang 10 near the breakwater in the south. This bay is also used for kayaking and windsurfing activities and lessons.

Independence Park   PARK
(Gan Hatzma'ut; Map p122) Nothing to do with Independence Hall on the other side of town, this is a beautiful seafront park with Mediterranean views and plenty of grass to run around, throw a frisbee or have a picnic. Like most of Tel Aviv's public spaces, it's popular with dog walkers and the venue

for children's birthday parties on weekends. Next to the Hilton Hotel, it also has a well-equipped children's play area with swings, slides and climbing frames.

Frishman Beach   BEACH
(Map p122; Ⓟ) Frishman Beach is perhaps the widest stretch of sand in Tel Aviv. There's plenty of space on the sand and good access to the swimming area. It's located in front of the rainbow-coloured Dan Hotel building and has large wooden gazebos for shade.

Bograshov Beach   BEACH
(Map p122) One of Tel Aviv's most popular beaches, Bograshov is part of a party-central strip along with Gordon and Frishman beaches. Relatively quiet during the week, on Friday and Saturday it overflows with a mix of bronze-bodied locals and slightly sunburnt tourists.

Alma Beach BEACH

(Charles Clore Beach; Map p128; P) This is probably the coolest beach in the city, with spectacular views across the water to Jaffa. It's home to the hugely popular Manta Ray (p141) restaurant and fills up with hipsters sipping their Goldstar beers on the beach on Shabbat.

◉ Park HaYarkon & Ramat Aviv

North of the city centre, across the Yarkon River, is the huge green space of Park Ha-Yarkon and the upmarket residential suburb of Ramat Aviv, location of Tel Aviv University and a number of museums and cultural institutions.

★**Park HaYarkon** PARK

(Ganei Yehoshua; www.park.co.il; Rokach Blvd; P) Park HaYarkon is Tel Aviv's answer to Central Park or Hyde Park. Joggers, cyclists, skaters, footballers and frisbee-throwers should head for this 3.5-sq-km stretch of grassy parkland, Tel Aviv's largest green space, along the Yarkon River. The **Sportek Centre** here has a climbing wall, basketball courts, a skate park and trampolines. Starting from Tel Aviv's Old Port, the park opens out into wide fields and a large lake as you get closer to Ramat Gan.

Beit Hatfutsot MUSEUM

(Museum of the Jewish People; ☑03-745-7808; www.bh.org.il; Gate 2, Tel Aviv University, 2 Klausner St, Ramat Aviv; adult/child under 5yr 45NIS/free; ⊙10am-7pm Sun-Wed, to 10.30pm Thu, 9am-2pm Fri, to 3pm Sat; P; ☐Dan 7, 13, 25, 45) Once known as the Diaspora Museum and recently revamped as the Museum of the Jewish People, Beit Hatfutsot is located on the leafy campus of Tel Aviv University. Opened in 1978, the museum recounts the epic story of the Jewish exile and global Jewish di-

---

TEL AVIV'S BAUHAUS HERITAGE

Central Tel Aviv has more 1930s Bauhaus-style buildings than any other city in the world, which is why the area known as the 'White City' (roughly the streets of the city centre and south city centre) was declared a Unesco World Heritage site in 2003.

Tel Aviv's White City heritage is easy to spot, even through the modifications of the past 70 years. Look for structures characterised by horizontal lines, flat roofs, white walls and an almost complete absence of ornamentation.

Founded by the architect Walter Gropius and later led by Ludwig Mies van der Rohe, Bauhaus was an enormously influential art and design school active in the German cities of Weimar, Dessau and Berlin from 1919 to 1933. The Nazis detested the Bauhaus style, considering it 'cosmopolitan' and 'degenerate' and forced the school to close when they came to power.

The modernist ideas and ideals of Bauhaus were brought to Palestine by German-Jewish architects fleeing Nazi persecution; 19 of these had studied at the Bauhaus, two had worked with Erich Mendelsohn (a pioneer of the streamline moderne style) and at least two others had worked with the great modernist Le Corbusier. As Tel Aviv developed in the 1930s (following a street plan drawn up in the late 1920s by the Scottish urban planner Sir Patrick Geddes), some 4000 white-painted Bauhaus buildings – the quintessence of mid-20th-century modernism – were built. Approximately 1000 of these are identified in the Unesco listing.

Today, many of these buildings are in a state of disrepair (the heat and desert winds are particularly tough on the concrete), but several hundred have been renovated and each year more are being restored to their former glory. Superb examples of the Bauhaus style can be found along the length of Rothschild Blvd and on the streets running across it (such as Mazeh and Nahmani Sts) and on Bialik St near Gan Meir Park.

The **Bauhaus Centre** (Map p122; ☑03-522-0249; www.bauhaus-center.com; 99 Dizengoff St; ⊙10am-7.30pm Sun-Thu, to 2.30pm Fri; ☎) sells a variety of architecture-related books and plans of the city. It also has two Bauhaus walking-tour offerings: hire of a headset outlining a self-guided Bauhaus walk in the streets around the centre; and a two-hour guided walking tour of the same streets starting every Friday at 10am. Each option costs 80NIS per person. Another alternative is the free English-language guided **Bauhaus tour** run by the Tel Aviv Tourist Office. This departs from 46 Rothschild Blvd (corner Shadal St) every Saturday at 11am.

aspora using objects, photographs, audio-visual presentations and databases. New permanent exhibitions include Heroes, an interactive exhibit on Jewish greats such as Einstein (for children) and Hallelujah!, displaying intricate models of synagogues from past and present.

The museum includes the Feher Jewish Music Centre, the Douglas E Goldman Jewish Genealogy Centre (where visitors can register their family tree) and a Visual Documentation Centre, the largest database of Jewish life in the world. There are temporary exhibitions in the lobby; the core exhibition is also being renovated (scheduled to be completed in 2019).

A testament to the faith and courage that has preserved Judaism for centuries, Beit Hatfutsoth is one of Israel's most comprehensive museums and visitors will need a few hours to get around. The museum can be reached by taking a train to Tel Aviv University and walking to Gate 2.

Eretz Israel Museum　MUSEUM
(Land of Israel Museum; ☑03-641-5244; www.eretzmuseum.org.il; 2 Chaim Levanon St, Ramat Aviv; adult/student 52/32NIS, child under 18yr free, incl planetarium adult/child 84/35NIS; ☺10am-4pm Sun-Wed, to 8pm Thu, to 2pm Fri, to 3pm Sat, planetarium shows 11.30am & 1.30pm Sun-Thu, 11am & noon Sat; ℗; ☐Dan 7, 13, 24, 25, 45, 127) Incorporating the archaeological excavations of Tel Qasile, an ancient port city dating from the 12th century BCE, this museum sports a huge and varied range of exhibits and deserves at least half a day. Sights include pavilions filled with glass and coins, a reconstructed flour mill and olive-oil plant, an ethnography and folklore collection, and a garden built around a gorgeous Byzantine bird mosaic. A planetarium is among the other attractions.

Palmach Museum　MUSEUM
(☑03-643-6393; www.palmach.org.il; 10 Haim Levanon St, Ramat Aviv; adult/child 30/20NIS; ☺by appointment only Sun-Fri; ℗) The story of the Palmach from its establishment in 1941 until the end of the Arab–Israeli War of 1948 is the focus of this multimedia museum. Starting in a memorial hall for Palmach members who died fighting for the establishment of the State of Israel, a Hebrew-speaking guide takes visitors on a tour that focuses on the stories of individual members who fought with this elite Haganah strike force. Headphones provide translations into other languages.

KEEPING FIT WITH THE LOCALS

The city's parks and seafront promenade become a giant gym every day, so join the Tel Avivians as they head out to get fit.

Gordon Swimming Pool (p131) Grand outdoor saltwater pool on Tel Aviv's Marina.

Gordon Beach (p124) Central beach for volleyball, cycling along the promenade or a workout at the outdoor gym.

Park HaYarkon (p126) Basketball courts, climbing walls, soccer fields and more.

Hilton Beach (p125) Bay with crashing waves for surfers and windsurfers.

Kayak4All (p132) Centre for kayaking on Old Jaffa's Port.

Yitzhak Rabin Centre　MUSEUM
(☑03-745 3358; www.rabincenter.org.il; 14 Chaim Levanon St; self-guided tour adult/student & child 50/25NIS, guided tour adult/student & child 60/35NIS; ☺9am-5pm Sun, Mon & Wed, to 7pm Tue & Thu, to 2pm Fri; ℗; ☐Dan 7, 85, 29) Established in 1997 to promote democratic values, narrow socio-economic gaps and address social divisiveness, this centre is also home to the Israeli Museum, which includes 150 films and 1500 photographs telling the story of modern Israel's struggle for peace with its neighbours. Visitors can take a self-guided tour using a multi-language audio device or book in advance to join a guided tour in Hebrew or English. The museum's central narrative is interwoven with the story of former Prime Minister Yitzhak Rabin (1922–95), assassinated by a radical right-wing Orthodox Jew because of his work devising and implementing the Oslo Accords, which created the Palestinian National Authority and granted it partial control over parts of the Gaza Strip and West Bank.

⊙ Jaffa (Yafo)

Jaffa, a separate enclave with its own ancient history, has more Arab residents and a different atmosphere to Tel Aviv. Its three major draws are a flea market (p129) near Jaffa's landmark 1903 clock tower, the hilltop Old City (p128) enclave and the shopping and entertainment centre at the old Jaffa Port.

South of the Old City and port is the Ajami district, where Ottoman-era homes still exist side by side with ramshackle fisherfolk's shacks. Once notorious for crime and drugs, its seafront opens out into a large green park and a boardwalk that connects Old Jaffa to Bat Yam. Most buses from the city centre stop on Sderot Yerushalayim, the southern extension of the seafront Herbert Samuel Esplanade.

Clock Tower LANDMARK

(Map p128; Yefet St) Not quite Big Ben, this Ottoman clock tower was funded by residents to mark the 25th anniversary of the reign of Sultan Abdulhamid II (1876–1909). The tower – one of seven built around Ottoman Palestine – was completed in 1903, a time when few of the sultan's subjects had watches. It's a good meeting point for tour groups.

Old Jaffa Visitors Centre ARCHAEOLOGICAL SITE

(Map p128; ☑03-603-7686, 03-603-7000; www. oldjaffa.co.il; Kedumim Sq, Old Jaffa; adult/student 30/15NIS; ◷9am-8pm Sat-Thu, to 5pm Fri summer, 9am-5pm Sat-Thu, to 3pm Fri winter) Sometimes called 'Jaffa Tales', this small visitor's centre is actually an archaeological excavation site in a chamber underneath Kedumim Sq. Here, you can view partially excavated remains from the Hellenistic and Roman era and learn about more than 4000 years of Jaffa's colourful history in a virtual experience.

St Peter's Monastery CHURCH

(Map p128; Kedumim Sq; ◷8-11.45am & 3-5pm Oct-Feb, to 6pm Mar-Sep) The most prominent building in Jaffa, this beautiful cream-painted Franciscan church was built in the 1890s on the ruins of the Crusader citadel and is still used as a place of worship. In December it's one of the few places in town where you'll find a giant Christmas tree.

HaPisgah Gardens PARK

(Map p128) This pleasant grassy knoll has a panoramic view of the Tel Aviv seafront

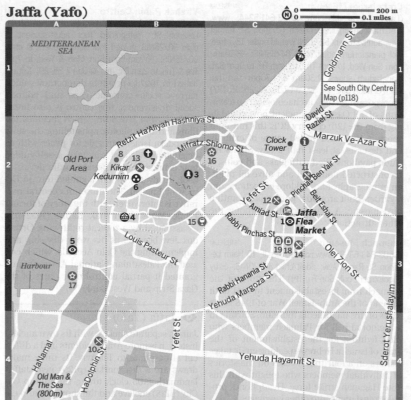

Jaffa (Yafo)

as its backdrop. The small amphitheatre in the centre of the park hosts free music concerts every Saturday in July and August after 9pm. The bizarre white neo-Mayan sculpture on one of the hills depicts the fall of Jericho, Isaac's sacrifice and Jacob's dream.

Ilana Goor Museum
GALLERY

(Map p128; ☎03-683-7676; www.ilanagoor museum.org; 4 Mazal Dagim St; adult/student/child 30/25/20NIS; ☺10am-4pm Sun-Fri, to 6pm Sat; ☒Dan 10, 18, 25, 41) Built in the 18th century, this imposing stone building just south of Kedumim Sq originally served as a hostel for Jewish pilgrims arriving at Jaffa and later was converted into a soap and perfume factory. Now the residence of local artist Ilana Goor, it is open to the public as a gallery. The collection here won't be to all tastes, being dominated by tribal art and works by Goor, but the interior spaces and panoramic terrace are extremely attractive.

Jaffa Port
PORT

(Map p128; www.namalyafo.co.il; ☺10am-10pm Mon-Wed, to 11pm Thu, 9am-11pm Fri & Sat; ℗; ☒Dan 10, 18, 25, 41) One of the oldest known harbours in the world, the port of Jaffa was mentioned in the Bible (as 'Joppa') and was once the disembarkation point for pilgrims to the Holy Land. Up until recent decades, it was also where Jaffa Oranges were stored and exported all over the world. These days it's predominantly an entertainment facility incorporating a boardwalk and warehouses hosting bars, fish restaurants, shops and the not-for-profit Nalaga'at Centre (p146), home to a deaf-blind theatre company.

The port is busiest on summer evenings, when free entertainment is sometimes staged and the boardwalk restaurants are packed with local diners. There is a large free car park to the south of the port.

★ Jaffa Flea Market
MARKET

(Shuk HaPishpeshim; Map p128; ☺stalls 10am-3pm Sun-Fri, to late Thu; ☒Dan 10, 18, 25, 41) In recent years, lots of energy has gone into giving Jaffa's Old City a tourism-triggered makeover, and the results are undeniably attractive. However, the real draw in this part of the city is considerably more dishevelled. Spread over a grid of streets south of the clock tower, Jaffa's much-loved *pishpeshuk* or *shuk ha-pishpeshim* (flea market) is full of boutiques, laid-back cafes, pop-up bars and colourful street stalls selling vintage clothes, objects and furniture.

Some of the items sold are junk (such as old TVs or irons), but within the rough you'll also find genuine antiques, wood crafts, Arabic drums and more. Note that stalls and shops are closed on Saturday, but cafes, bars and restaurants are open. On summer nights, outdoor entertainment is sometimes staged in the main stall area and on Thursdays the market is open until late.

Hassan Bek Mosque
MOSQUE

(Hasan Bey Mosque; Map p118) Built in 1916 by Jaffa's Ottoman governor of the same name, this white limestone mosque built on the border of Tel Aviv and Jaffa has always had symbolic significance for Jaffa's Arab population. In the 1948 Arab–Israeli War, its minaret was used by Arab snipers. Although not open to visitors, it is one of the city's best-preserved old buildings.

Jaffa (Yafo)

Old Railway Station   HISTORIC SITE
(HaTachana; Map p118; www.hatachana.co.il;
Neve Tzedek; ⊙10am-10pm Sat-Thu, to 5pm Fri;
🅿; 🚌18, 10, 100) Once the terminus of the
Jerusalem–Jaffa train line, this station near
the southern end of the beachfront promenade operated between 1892 and 1948
and was subsequently used by the IDF as a
storage facility before being converted into
a retail and entertainment complex. Now
the old station houses are home to shops,
cafes, bars and a branch of the popular ice-
cream chain Vaniglia, it's known locally as
HaTachana (The Station). Its parking lot is
also handy for a visit to the Neve Tzedek

(p121) neighbourhood. Note that cafes and
restaurants are open Friday evening, but the
shops in the complex close at 5pm.

IDF History Museum   MUSEUM
(Map p118; 📞03-517-2913; http://eng.shimur.
org/batey-osef; Prof Yehezkel Kaufmann St, Tel
Aviv Promenade; adult/student & child 15/10NIS;
⊙8am-4pm Sun-Thu) FREE Thirteen pavilions and sheds in the Old Railway Station
complex now house tanks, armoured fighting vehicles, anti-aircraft guns, rifles and
machine guns used by the Israel Defence
Forces since its establishment in 1948. Most
kids seem to love clamouring over the vehi-

THE REVIVAL OF HEBREW

Many Israelis feel that one of the supreme cultural achievements of the Zionist movement was the resurrection of the Hebrew language, which had not been used for everyday living for a couple thousand years.

During the Diaspora, Jews adapted to local cultures and picked up the local lingo
wherever they settled, combining it with Hebrew to create uniquely Jewish languages
such as Yiddish (based on medieval German) and Ladino (based on medieval Spanish).
Classical Hebrew was preserved in sacred texts and synagogue prayers but was rarely
heard on the street.

The turning point came when early Zionists began publishing secular literature in
Hebrew in the mid-1800s and, in the latter decades of the 19th century, settling in Palestine. Among them was Eliezer Ben Yehuda, newspaper editor and author of the first
modern Hebrew dictionary, born in Lithuania in 1858. Like most Jewish children of his era,
he was introduced to biblical Hebrew as part of his religious upbringing. When he arrived
in Palestine in 1881, he was determined to turn Hebrew into a secular tool of everyday
communication, thus enabling Jews from all over the world to communicate with each
other. (Herzl, the founder of modern Zionism, never spelled out what language he thought
would be spoken in the Jewish state, but it appears that he assumed it would be German.)

When Ben Yehuda began living a Hebrew-speaking life, he found himself at a loss when
trying to describe modern inventions such as trains and light bulbs. He began updating
the language while simultaneously spreading it, as a spoken language, among his peers.

Ben Yehuda's persistence and the work of generations of Hebrew-language ulpanim
(language schools) for new immigrants paid off, and today there are some nine million Hebrew speakers worldwide, including quite a few Palestinian Arabs. By contrast, on the eve
of WWII there were around 11 million speakers of Yiddish; today there are fewer than one
million. People working to preserve shrinking minority languages often look to Hebrew –
the only case of a 'retired' language having been completely resurrected – for inspiration.

Over the decades, a rich Hebrew literature has been cultivated – from the early Israeli
poet Bialik to modern storytellers such as Amos Oz, David Grossman and Etgar Keret. In
just one century, Hebrew was transformed from a language of the Torah to a universe of
children's stories, songs and day-to-day speech.

As in ancient times, when all sorts of Greek, Aramaic, Persian and Egyptian words
crept into Hebrew, latter-day globalisation has resulted in an influx of words and concepts from languages such as English, German, French, Russian and Arabic. A classic
case of word adoption is the @ symbol, which Israelis call a shtrudel because it looks like
the Austrian pastry.

On the streets of Tel Aviv – which proudly bills itself as 'the first Hebrew city' – you may
hear some 'Hebrish', as Israelis tend to drop English (including obscenities) into the middle of Hebrew sentences. Much Israeli slang comes from Arabic – for instance, you'll often
hear the words sababa (cool, OK) and achla (excellent). A classic Hebrew-Arabic-English
hybrid phrase, used when people say goodbye, is 'Tov, yallah, bye' (OK, let's go, bye).

cles, but the lack of signage or interpretative panels in languages other than Hebrew is a problem for adult visitors who aren't military equipment enthusiasts. It's accessed through the parking lot next to the Old Railway Station centre.

Activities

Gordon Swimming Pool
SWIMMING

(Map p122; ☑03-762-3300; www.gordon-pool.co.il; Tel Aviv Marina; adult/student & child Sun-Fri 69/59NIS, Sat 79/70NIS; ☺6am-9pm Mon-Thu, to 7pm Fri, 7am-6pm Sat, 1.30-9pm Sun; ⊞) Originally opened in 1956, the outdoor Gordon Swimming Pool was rebuilt in 2009. Next to the marina and surrounded by palm trees, it has a 50m saltwater pool whose water is frequently changed, plus dedicated pools for children and toddlers. Pay extra and you can also use the sauna, hot tub or gym.

Courses

Tel Aviv Art Studio
ART

(Map p122; ☑052-786-3483; www.telavivartstudio.com; 31 Gordon St; classes from 120NIS; ⊞) Run by Natasha and Michal, trained art therapists and teachers, this unique space welcomes singles, couples and children for a mix of English-language painting classes. Paint Night (7pm to 9pm Thursday) makes for a fun excuse to get creative and enjoy some wine.

Citizen Cafe
LANGUAGE

(Map p118; www.citizencafetlv.com; 45 Rothschild Blvd; courses from 3320NIS) A new kind of *ulpan* (Hebrew language school), Citizen Cafe offers courses for those wanting to speak like a local Israeli. Set in Mindspace, an uber-hip co-working space on Rothschild Blvd, it offers 10-week courses, meeting twice a week and, delightfully, no textbooks! If you're in town for a while, it's a fun way to learn some 'street' Hebrew, such as 'Yalla' (that's Arabic for 'come on').

Surf House
WATER SPORTS

(Map p122; ☑09-957-4522; www.surfhouse.co.il; 169 HaYarkon St; lessons from 250NIS; ☺10am-7pm Sun-Thu, 10am-3pm Fri) Conveniently located near Gordon Beach, this school offers kitesurfing, windsurfing, paddleboard and surfing lessons for beginners. Check the website for course details.

Tel Aviv University Ulpan
LANGUAGE

(☑03-640-8639; www.international.tau.ac.il; Ramat Aviv) The city's most prestigious university has an *ulpan* offering students the

opportunity to develop their Hebrew skills. Courses include a seven-week Hebrew program and a four-week intensive course. On-campus accommodation is available.

Ulpan Gordon
LANGUAGE

(Map p122; ☑03-522-3181; www.ulpangordon.co.il; 7 LaSalle St) The most popular *ulpan* in Tel Aviv charges around 750NIS per month for tourists; classes meet for 2½ to 4½ hours a day, two or three times a week.

Tours

Free walking tours are offered by Tel Aviv's official tourism office (www.visit-tel-aviv.com). One focuses on Sarona and starts at 11am every Friday at 34 Kaplan St. Another concentrates on the city's Bauhaus heritage, starting at 11am every Saturday from 46 Rothschild Blvd. There are also tours of Old Jaffa. Bookings aren't necessary, but contact the Jaffa Tourist Information Office (p148) for details. For high-end, bespoke tours of the city for big or small groups, contact Pomegranate Travel (https://pomegranate-travel.com).

Delicious Israel
WALKING

(☑052 569-9499; www.deliciousisrael.com; per person from US$110) American-born Inbal Baum immigrated to Israel in 2009 and soon established a successful business conducting culinary tours around the country. Her Tel Aviv offerings include a 4½-hour walking tour through Jaffa and the city centre, a 2½-hour walking tour around the Levinski Spice Market (p121), a shorter Carmel Market (p117) tour, a hummus crawl and a street-food hop.

Alternative Tel Aviv
WALKING

(www.hasayeret.co.il; private tour for 2/6 people 800/1200NIS) Alternative Tel Aviv runs a variety of street-art and contemporary-gallery walking tours, mostly in the Florentin neighbourhood. Tel Aviv has some pretty astounding street art, and on the tour you'll learn about the people behind the tags. Tour duration is around an hour and a half; it also runs occasional pay-as-you-like tours on Fridays at 11am.

Sandemans Tours
WALKING

(www.newtelavivtours.com) FREE Two tours – one of Old Jaffa at 11am daily and a second of Jaffa and the new city at 2pm on Monday, Wednesday and Saturday – are conducted by freelance tour guides working with this well-regarded company. The first is free and relies on tips (50NIS per person is standard); the second costs 76NIS per person. Check the website for details.

Kayak4All KAYAKING
(Map p128; ✆054-775-7076; www.kayak4all.com; tours from 150NIS) Offering sea-kayaking trips for experienced rowers and novices, Kayak4All is located on the Old Jaffa Port. Check the website for a full list of activities and prices.

✯ Festivals & Events

Tel Aviv Pride LGBT
(www.visit-tel-aviv.com; ☉Jun) Held in the second week of June, this celebration of Israel's LGBT community draws a huge number of international visitors and is the country's biggest festival. Its centrepiece is the Pride Parade, starting from Gan Meir Park, but other events include parties at Hilton Beach (p125) and the LGBT International Film Festival (www.tlvfest.com).

★White Night CULTURAL
(Laila Lavan; www.visit-tel-aviv.com; ☉Jun) Each June, the city has one sleepless night when the city's cultural venues stay open and free music events are staged across town, including the HaTachana, Sarona Colony, Jaffa Port, beaches, HaBima Sq and Nachalat Binyamin Market. Head to Rothschild Blvd to catch the atmosphere.

Opera in the Park MUSIC
(www.israel-opera.co.il; Park HaYarkon, Rokach Ave; ☉Jul/Aug) One of the highlights of the Tel Aviv calendar, Opera in the Park is a free event attended by nearly 100,000 people from all over the country. Each July

or August, the Israeli Opera gives a full performance of a classic opera, while crowds picnic with wine and food on the grassy hill in the middle of Park HaYarkon. Check the opera's website for details and arrive early to get your spot.

DocAviv FILM
(www.docaviv.co.il/org-en; 5 Ha'Arba'a St; ☉May) DocAviv is the leading documentary film festival in the Middle East, held over 10 days in May at the Tel Aviv Cinematheque (p144). Featuring a full program of the best Israeli and international documentaries in English and Hebrew, it's not to be missed if you're in town.

Tel Aviv Jazz Festival MUSIC
(www.visit-tel-aviv.com; ☉Nov) Annual jazz music festival at the end of November, usually hosted at the Cinematheque (p144) and one of the Zappa clubs. Second only to the Red Sea Jazz Festival, it features top Israeli and international jazz performances for three nights.

Israeli Beer Festival BEER
(www.hatachana.co.il; Neve Tzedek; admission incl tastings 70-100NIS; ☉Jun) Held over two days in the second week of June, the Israeli Beer Festival is now a regular event at the Old Railway Station (p130). Featuring more than 200 Israeli craft beers, drinkers can take their time tasting the top brews in the Holy Land.

⌴ Sleeping

The best area to look for charming boutique hotels is around Rothschild Blvd. Jaffa, with its vibrant, Arab-inflected street life, also makes for a great base. Several popular

---

THE ART SCENE

Tel Aviv is a creative place, home to artists, art students and its fair share of boutique galleries.

Alternative Tel Aviv (p131) Walking tours of Florentin's shockingly good graffiti.

Chelouche Gallery (p120) One of the best showcases for TLV's contemporary art set in a beautiful Bauhaus building.

Nachum Gutman Museum of Art (p121) Houses work by this 20th-century Israeli painter and illustrator in Neve Tzedek.

Rubin Museum (p117) Filled with dreamy oil paintings by Mediterranean master Reuven Rubin.

Tel Aviv Museum of Art (p116) A world-class collection of modern art, design and architecture.

Tel Aviv Art Studio (p131) A fun way to learn painting in a relaxed environment.

TLV TECH

Once upon a time in a galaxy not so far away, travellers wanting to get online used to login at internet cafes. But in Tel Aviv these so-called 'cyber cafes' are fading out fast as wi-fi is readily accessible in cafes, hotels and even on beaches.

And then came the birth of the 'digital nomad', a more sophisticated tech traveller looking to earn some cash while on the road. Overnight, working remotely no longer applied to just those flying in business class, but freelance designers, developers, bloggers and all sorts of startup-ers.

With its startup nation spirit, Tel Aviv was one the earliest cities to establish co-working spaces. These tech hubs offer drop-in desks at different rates and meeting rooms for hire, a creative environment to collaborate with like-minded talents and, most importantly, free coffee. Here are some of the best co-working spaces in town:

Mindspace (http://mindspace.me/tel-aviv) Has two buildings very near to each other on Rothschild Blvd and Ahad Ha'am St. With its uber-cool designer decor, Mindspace is a real hipster hub.

Urban Place (http://urbanplace.me) The latest co-working space in town with a large open-plan office on 3 Rothschild Blvd.

WeWork (www.wework.com/l/tel-aviv) Four locations in Tel Aviv, including one at Sarona, which is fast-becoming Israel's new startup centre.

hostels can be found near Yehuda HaLevi St, an area currently being redeveloped for the light rail. The major hotel chains tend to locate their towers overlooking the beach, along busy HaYarkon St. On site parking is rare; instead, most hotels have deals with nearby car parks for around 70NIS per day.

You'll need to book ahead at most times of the year, particularly on weekends and during July, August and festival periods such as Rosh HaShanah, Sukkot, Hanukkah and Passover. During Tel Aviv Pride Week, every hotel in the city is full – reserve as far ahead as possible.

City Centre

★ **Mendeli Street Hotel**   BOUTIQUE HOTEL **$$$**
(Map p122; ☑03-520-2700; www.mendelistreet hotel.com; 5 Mendeli St; d US$250, superior/deluxe US$300/360; @🛜) In summer, the living is both easy and glamorous at this hotel close to Frishman Beach. The hotel lobby and restaurant are design magazine chic, and the rooms are similarly stylish, with contemporary fittings and good amenities. The standard room is compact, so consider opting for a deluxe or superior version. Staff are young, charming and extremely helpful.

Dizengoff Avenue Hotel   BOUTIQUE HOTEL **$$$**
(Map p122; ☑03-694-3000; www.d-avenue. co.il; 133 Dizengoff St; s/d 550/732NIS; 🛜) This pretty, urban hotel is bang in the middle of Dizengoff, one of the main shopping streets, but you'd be forgiven for missing it. A simple doorway with a side entrance leads to this simple boutique hotel that's slightly cheaper than its counterparts. Nice touches include free ice popsicles at reception and a happy hour with Israeli wine for guests.

Cinema Hotel   HOTEL **$$$**
(Map p122; ☑03-520-7100; www.atlas.co.il; 1 Zamenhoff St; s/d/ste from US$196/216/300; P🛜) Fans of the silver screen will appreciate the decor of this converted Bauhaus-era cinema. Public spaces feature old projectors and cinema memorabilia, and the 83 rooms have movie posters and lights made from tripods. The feel is functional rather than glamorous, though the complimentary early-evening aperitif on the roof terrace strikes a Hollywood note. There's free parking and bike hire.

Lusky Hotel   HOTEL **$$$**
(Map p122; ☑03-516-3030; www.luskyhtl.co.il; 84 HaYarkon St; s/d/ste US$165/180/300; P🛜) This family-run choice offers well-appointed rooms featuring large windows letting in lots of light. Most of these have kitchenettes, and a number have balconies with sea view – the pick of the bunch is undoubtedly the one-bedroom penthouse, which has a huge balcony overlooking the beach. Drivers will appreciate the free underground parking.

3

1. Tel Aviv Museum of Art (p116)
This museum is impressive both inside and out, with its superb collections and modern architecture.

2. Gordon Beach (p124)
Locals flock to this city beach for sports and sunbathing by the sparkling Mediterranean Sea.

3. Neve Tzedek (p121)
Wander the the narrow, atmospheric streets of Tel Aviv's oldest neighbourhood.

4. Rothschild Boulevard (p126)
Wine and dine in stylish cafes and admire Unesco-listed Bauhaus buildings.

🛏 South City Centre

★ Abraham Hostel   HOSTEL $

(Map p118; ☑03-624-9200; https://abraham hostels.com; 21 Levontin St; dm/s/d/ste from 95/460/470/520NIS; 🛜) This mammoth hostel is one of the best places to meet other travellers, and it has some of the cleanest and best-kept hostel rooms you'll find. It also offers excellent suites for couples or families with bathroom, kitchenette and TV. Friendly, multicultural and multilingual staff (we met Palestinian and Swiss receptionists), also operates tours in Tel Aviv and around Israel. The huge dining hall doubles as a venue for (often loud) live bands and comedy.

Little Tel-Aviv Hostel   HOSTEL $

(Map p118; ☑03-559-5050; www.littletlvhostel. com; 51 Yehuda HaLevi St; dm/d 130/450NIS; 🛜) A hostel that sets high standards, Little Tel-Aviv is not so little once inside. Housed in a renovated building in the heart of the action, it offers mixed dorms or female-only dorms, plus very clean private rooms. Guests can enjoy hanging out in the hostel's cute garden, common kitchen and bar. The age limit for dorms is under 35.

Florentine Hostel   HOSTEL $

(☑03-518-7551; www.florentinehostel.com; 10 Elifelet St, Florentin; dm/d from 94/280NIS, d with shared bathroom 240NIS; 🖳🛜) On first view, the less-than-pictureque district this hostel is located in can be off-putting. However, it doesn't take backpackers long to appreciate the location, which is close to Neve Tzedek, Florentin, Jaffa and the beach. Eight six-bed dorms and nine private rooms are on offer (all small), as is a rooftop bar and busy entertainment program. Be warned: the hostel has an age restriction of 18 to 40 years.

★ Poli House   DESIGN HOTEL $$$

(Map p118; ☑03-710-5000; http://thepolihouse. com; 1 Nahalat Binyamin St; s/d from 900/1300NIS; 🛜🖳) Boldly bursting onto the TLV scene in 2017, the 40-room Poli House is the latest creation from the owners of Brown TLV. Slightly different from the other Browns, Poli turns up the volume, brightness and colour. Expect yellow, blue and green walls, black and white zebra flooring and neon lights – all concepts of designer Karim Rashid.

★ Norman Hotel   BOUTIQUE HOTEL $$$

(Map p118; ☑03-543-5555; www.thenorman. com; 23-25 Nachmani St; deluxe/loft/ste from US$570/840/1090; 🛜🖳) The most royal of Tel Aviv's boutiques (rooms include the King Albert Suite), the Norman is housed in two restored 1920s Bauhaus buildings. No detail is overlooked here; accommodation ranges from loft apartments to garden suites. Facilities include a fitness room, wellness area and rooftop infinity pool, and it offers fine dining in its library and brasserie.

★ Rothschild Hotel   BOUTIQUE HOTEL $$$

(Map p118; ☑03-957-8888; www.rothschild-hotel. co.il; d/ste/tr from US$272/382/510; 🛜) 🍃 Ofra Zimbalista's sculpture of choral singers on the exterior is but one of many whimsical features at this exemplary boutique hotel. Pre-dating Tel Aviv's recent boutique-hotel boom, the Rothschild's decor has worn extremely well, and this place still leads the pack when it comes to service. The in-house restaurant serves what it describes as 'Zionist cuisine with a French accent'.

★ Hotel Montefiore   BOUTIQUE HOTEL $$$

(Map p118; ☑03-564-6100; www.hotelmontefiore. co.il; 36 Montefiore St; s/d 1420/1560NIS; 🛜) A truly classy choice, the Montefiore occupies a heritage-listed 1920s villa in a tree-lined street running between Rothschild Blvd and Allenby St. The 12 elegant rooms have high ceilings, wooden floors, an armchair, a generously endowed bookshelf, double-glazed windows and spacious bathrooms. As is the case in the fashionable downstairs bar and restaurant, contemporary Israeli art adorns the walls.

★ Shenkin Hotel   BOUTIQUE HOTEL $$$

(Map p118; ☑03-600-9400; www.shenkinhotel.com; 21 Brener St; s/d from US$196/270; 🅿🖳🛜) Its mantra is 'Locals Know Best', and the excellent recommendations supplied by the Shenkin's friendly staff certainly prove the point. A small and stylish place in a great location behind Sheinkin St, it offers four attractive room types, common areas showcasing local contemporary art, a roof terrace and a lovely rear terrace where complimentary tea, coffee and biscuits are available.

Alma Hotel   BOUTIQUE HOTEL $$$

(Map p118; ☑03-630-8777; www.almahotel.co.il; 23 Yavne St; s/deluxe/executive from US$260/280/550; 🛜) The lovely light-green 1920s building, theatrical decor and on-site restaurant and tapas bar are the main draws at this boutique choice just off Rothschild Blvd, but the rooftop bar and pretty rear courtyard garden provide additional inducement. Both room types offer plenty of space, a huge bed, an espresso machine and a lovely bathroom with luxe Sabon toiletries.

Diaghilev BUSINESS HOTEL $$$
(Map p118; ☑03-545-3131; www.diaghilev.co.il; 56 Mazeh St; d/ste excl breakfast from US$235/340; ☎) Paintings, prints and sculptures decorate every wall and common area in this 'Live Art Hotel', which occupies a handsome Bauhaus-style building off Rothschild Blvd. The spacious rooms have sitting area, kitchenette and separate bedroom. Top marks go to the quiet location, on-site parking and helpful front-desk staff. It also offers family suites.

🛏 Jaffa (Yafo)

Beit Immanuel HOSTEL $
(☑03-682-1459; www.beitimmanuel.org; 8 Auerbach St, American Colony; dm/s/d 225/285/410NIS; ☑☎) This convent-style hostel is located in an 1884 building opposite a pretty Lutheran church. Operated by an evangelical congregation, its rooms are clean and comfortable, and it has a private garden and a free car park. Although only a 10-minute walk from Old Jaffa or the hip Florentin neighbourhood, it's incredibly peaceful around here.

The building once housed a fashionable hotel – German Kaiser Wilhelm II stayed here in 1898 – owned by Baron Plato von Ustinov, grandfather of the actor Peter Ustinov. It's located on a quiet street just off Eilat St (the continuation of Jaffa Rd).

Old Jaffa Hostel HOSTEL $
(Map p128; ☑03-682-2370; www.telaviv-hostel. com; 13 Amiad St; dm/s/d 90/250/280; ☑☎; ☐Dan 10, 18, 25, 41) Occupying an Ottoman-era house in the flea market, this hostel is the most atmospheric option in its price range in Tel Aviv, but it's not the most comfortable. Dorm beds are reasonably priced and there is a generous number of communal bathrooms, a communal kitchen and a large roof terrace with sea glimpses.

🛏 Tel Aviv Port

Port Hotel BOUTIQUE HOTEL $$
(☑03-544-5544; www.porthoteltelaviv.com; 4 Yirmiyahu St; s/d US$175/185; ☑☎) This self-titled 'mini hotel' near the Old Port offers something that is very rare in Tel Aviv – stylish accommodation for those on a budget. Though small and without views, rooms are clean and comfortable. The roof terrace and proximity to the beach are major assets.

🛏 Park HaYarkon

HI Tel Aviv Hostel HOSTEL $
(☑02-594-5654; www.iyha.org.il; 36 B'nei Dan St; dm/s/d 162/321/410NIS, child 94NIS; @☎) Formerly known as the B'nei Dan Guest House, this clean and spacious hostel was recently refurbished. It is the only guesthouse located next to the peaceful Park HaYarkon and is within walking distance of the Old Port, though you may prefer to take a sherut (number 5) or hire a bicycle to get into town.

🍴 Eating

Tel Aviv is all about the food. Because of its location smack bang in the middle of the Middle East, it mixes Mediterranean, Balkan, Arab and Asian influences, and it's also one of the most vegan-friendly cities on earth.

🍴 City Centre

★Miznon ISRAELI $
(Map p118; www.facebook.com/miznon; 30 King George St; pitas 25-49NIS; ☺noon-1am Sun-Thu, to 3pm Fri, from 7pm Sat; ☑) The vibe here is bustling, the prices are (very) reasonable, and the staff are friendly and full of energy. And let's not forget the most important thing: the food is exceptionally delicious. Huge pitas stuffed with your choice of veggies, chicken, offal or meat await, as do fish and chips or roasted spiced yam and cauliflower (yum!).

You'll need to line up to order and give your name. Then make your choice from the tahina, *labneh*, green chilli sauce and pickle spread, claim a seat and wait for your order to be announced. Drinks include lemonade, beer and arak.

★Dosa Bar INDIAN $
(Map p122; ☑03-659-1961; www.facebook.com/ Dosabar; 188 Ben Yehuda St; mains from 35NIS; ☺noon-11pm Sun-Thu, 11am-4pm Fri; ☑) Indian, kosher, vegan and gluten-free – Dosa Bar is all of the above. This small restaurant with friendly staff specialises in *dosa*, Indian pancakes, served sweet or savoury. The masala *dosa* is particularly good. It also does Indian breakfasts on Friday if you fancy starting the weekend with some spice.

CHOWING DOWN IN TEL AVIV

There really is something for all tastes in Tel Aviv, from great seafood to Greek-inspired restaurants, and more recently a boom in Asian eateries, with Thai at **Nam** (☑03-670-8050; www.facebook.com/namrest; 275 Dizengoff St; mains 67-75NIS; ⊙12.30-5pm & 6pm-midnight; 🐾) and Vietnamese at Vong (p140) worthy examples. For truly global cuisine, head to the indoor street-food markets of Sarona (p124) and Rothschild-Allenby.

Coinciding with the boutique makeover that the city is undergoing, there is a rising crop of celebrity chef restaurants, as well as an ever-growing number of swanky brasseries. The best known of these culinary celebrities is Eyal Shani. A devotee of simple, seasonal cuisine, he seems to have the magic touch when it comes to putting together casually chic eateries – he started Miznon, Port Sa'id, Romano (p141) and North Abraxas (p140) – where having fun is as much of a priority as enjoying the food.

If you're on a budget, there are plenty of cheap street-food eateries and kiosks to choose from. Classics include the Israeli national dish, falafel, and *sabich* (hard-boiled eggs, fried aubergine and tahini in a pita). Hummus may be more synonymous with Abu Ghosh or Akko, but Jaffa can more than hold its own with Ali Caravan (p141).

If you're self-catering, the best fresh fruit and vegetables in town are sold at the Carmel Market (p117). Supermarkets offering a good selection of products, reasonable prices and late-night hours can be found all over the city.

Between Sunday and Friday, many restaurants offer 'business lunch' deals where diners get a free starter, or sometimes even a starter and a glass of wine, when ordering a main course.

★Tamara
ICE CREAM $

(Map p122; 96 Ben Yehuda St; small/medium/large cup 22/27/32NIS, tapioca 15NIS; ⊙9.30am-12.30am Sun-Fri, from 10.30am Sat) Indulgent but delicious, Tamara, near Gordon Beach, is the best frozen yoghurt in town (and there are a few to contend with). Enjoy your cup plain or choose from a range of indulgent toppings. Besides yoghurt, it also sells refreshing fruit tapioca and *paletas* (Mexican fruit ices). Kids can sit on swings while adults queue for their yoghurt.

HaKosem
MIDDLE EASTERN $

(Map p118; 1 Shlomo HaMelech St; falafel from 18NIS; ⊙10.30am-11.30pm Sun-Thu, to 3pm Fri; 🖉) One of the friendliest falafel stalls in town, HaKosem (the Magician) is a popular snack stop on the corner of King George St. Aside from its trademark green, fried chickpea balls in pita, it also offers *sabich* (egg, aubergine and salad in pita*)* and shawarma (meat sliced off a spit and stuffed in a large bread wrap with tomatoes and garnish).

Sabich Frishman
MIDDLE EASTERN $

(Map p122; 42 Frischmann St; sabich 18NIS; ⊙9am-11.30pm Sun-Thu, to 4pm Fri, from 8pm Sat; 🖉) This tiny stall specialises in *sabich*, an Iraqi-derived snack consisting of fried aubergine, boiled egg, cabbage, salad, potato, hummus and spicy *amba* (mango) sauce, all stuffed into a pita. It's on the

corner of Dizengoff and Frishman Sts; just look for the long lines and the falafel stall next door.

Ha'achim
ISRAELI $$

(Map p118; ☑03-691-7171; www.facebook.com/haachim; 12 Ibn Gabirol St; mains 39-62NIS; ⊙noon-midnight Sun-Thu, from 9am Fri & Sat; 🖉) Ha'achim, 'The Brothers' in Hebrew, has a distinctly Mediterranean menu of hummus, *labneh*, tahini, olives and complimentary pita breads with olive oil. Much more than a hummus joint, there are chef specials and grilled meat and fish, plus the business lunch menu offers diners two salads (such as beetroot or eggplant) of their choice with all mains.

Goocha
SEAFOOD $$

(Map p122; ☑03-522-2886; www.goocha.co.il; 171 Dizengoff St; mains 64-92NIS; ⊙noon-1am; 🐾) Not to be confused with its newer sibling restaurant, the Goocha Diner on Ibn Gabirol St, Goocha is the original and better. Locals and tourists flock here for dishes such as *moules* and *frites*, shrimp burger and seafood risotto. Thanks to its fab spot on the corner of Ben-Gurion Ave, it's always packed, and advance booking is advised.

Barbunia
SEAFOOD $$

(Map p122; ☑03-527-6965; 163 Ben Yehuda St; mains 58-86NIS; ⊙noon-11pm) Going strong for nearly three decades, Barbunia is older than most of Tel Aviv's residents. The no-frills, paper tablecloths add to the charm of this family fish restaurant. All mains come with a seemingly endless stream of small salads, fried vegetables, bread basket and hummus. Sea bream or mixed fried shrimps and calamari win our vote, washed down with a local beer.

Benedict
BREAKFAST $$

(Map p122; ☑03-686-8657; www.benedict.co.il; 171 Ben Yehuda St; breakfasts from 69NIS; ⊗24hr; ☎☑) Those craving blueberry pancakes, bacon and eggs, shakshuka or eggs Benedict at five in the afternoon – or, for that matter, in the morning – need go no further than this constantly crowded all-night breakfast place. Bring a big appetite: servings are huge and come with a bread basket. There's another branch on **Rothschild Blvd** (Map p118; 29 Rothschild Blvd; breakfasts from 62NIS) and one in **Herzliya** (☑09-958-0701; 1 Haetzel St; breakfast 45-98NIS).

Anastasia
VEGAN $$

(Map p122; ☑03-529-0095; www.facebook.com/cafeanastasia; 54 Frischmann St; sandwiches/breakfasts from 39/52NIS; ⊗8am-11.30pm Sun-Thu, to 5pm Fri, 9am-11pm Sat; ☑) A veritable dream for vegans, Anastasia has it all – breakfasts, salads, soups, sandwiches and more. Set on the leafy corner of Frischmann and Reines Sts, it's also a shop with vegan products. The menu features corn omelettes with hummus, homemade gluten-free bread, plus vegan cakes and cookies. Worth a visit just for the banana, date, cocoa and almond milkshake.

✖ South City Centre

★ Port Sa'id
MIDDLE EASTERN $

(Map p118; 5 Har Sinai St; small plates 22-52NIS, mains from 34NIS; ⊗noon-late; ☑) The mothership for inner-city hipsters, this restaurant-bar next to the Great Synagogue is decorated with a library of vinyl records on wooden shelves and has a coterie of heavily tattooed regulars. There's good Middle Eastern–accented food on offer (no English menu, so you'll need to consult with the waiters) and lots of drink choices.

Get here early to score a table. Try the hummus made from lima beans.

★ Arte
GELATO $

(Map p118; ☑055-895-4868; http://arteglideria.com; 11 Nahalat Binyamin St; ice cream from 22NIS; ⊗11am-11pm Mar-Oct, 1-7.30pm Sun-Wed & to 11pm Thu-Sat Nov-Feb; ☑) ✎ No ordinary ice-cream shop, Arte sells bona fide gelato in the heart of the Nahalat Binyamin Crafts Market (p147). Run by chefs Stefania Pagani and Marco Camorali, professional ice-cream makers from Tuscany and Sicily, Arte is as sustainable as it gets. It does not use food colouring or chemicals and sources ingredients locally, where possible.

Bunny Chow
SOUTH AFRICAN $

(Map p118; ☑054-260-8850; www.facebook.com/bunnychowtlv; 36 Rothschild Blvd; mains from 35NIS; ⊗noon-late) Despite its name, Bunny Chow doesn't serve rabbit food. Instead, it specialises in fine South African street food, its signature dish of course called 'Bunny Chow' – a hollowed-out loaf of bread filled with curry. It also offers mighty beef sandwiches served in homemade challah bread.

Previously a stand at the Carmel Market, it's now a fixture of the indoor **Rothschild-Allenby Market** (Map p118; 36 Rothschild Blvd; ⊗8am-11.30pm).

Tenat
ETHIOPIAN $

(Map p118; ☑054-749-9538; www.facebook.com/tenatvegan; 27 Chlenov St; mains 35NIS; ⊗11am-11pm Mon-Thu, to 4pm Fri; ☑) Take a trip to Africa with this small, funky Ethiopian vegan restaurant. It may be situated in a rundown area of the city, but the food here is well worth the trip. Specialities include the *injera* (Ethiopian flatbread with a spongy texture) plates, served with salad, fava beans and spices, plus the freshly squeezed beet root and carrot juices.

SHAKSHUKA

Many cultures claim this dish as their own (Tunisia being the main contender), but only in Israel has it attained the status of national treasure. Eggs baked in a rich sauce of tomatoes, onions and spices (usually paprika, cumin and chilli powder), it is sometimes customised with peppers, sausage, cheese, spinach or other ingredients.

Baked and served in a flat cast-iron, copper or terracotta pan and accompanied by crusty white bread, it's delicious at all times of the day but is most popular at breakfast and brunch. The most famous version in the city is served at Dr Shakshuka (p142) in Jaffa.

TEL AVIV-JAFFA (YAFO) EATING

A CITY IN FLUX

Wherever you go in TLV, you'll be sure to come across some large-scale construction work. Tel Aviv is a city in flux, and the municipality is constantly upgrading its decaying Bauhaus buildings, most of which are more than 50 years old and in need of a facelift.

To ease the traffic and legendary parking issues, a futuristic light-rail system is being built, with the first line from Petah Tikva to Bat Yam tentatively scheduled to open in 2021. But don't hold your breath – Israel has a habit of missing deadlines for ambitious transportation projects. In town, the areas around Savidor Train Station (p149) and Yehuda HaLevi St are most affected by the tunnelling work.

Other areas undergoing major redevelopment include Dizengoff Sq and parts of the seafront promenade.

Skyscrapers with luxury apartments and offices for high-tech companies are shooting up, particularly around the Sarona Colony (p124) area. Indeed, all over town, the skyline is dotted with cranes. But somehow that's part of the thrill – it's a city that doesn't stand still. In fact, there are so many changes in Tel Aviv–Jaffa that even locals find it hard to keep up with the pace.

Taqueria
MEXICAN $

(Map p118; ☑03-600-5280; www.taqueria.co.il; 28 Levontin St; mains 29-39NIS; ☺noon-midnight Sun-Tue, to 1am Wed-Sat; ☜) Popular with young Tel Avivians, Taqueria is a down-to-earth Mexican joint with very reasonably priced tacos and burritos, plus probably the best nachos in town. It doesn't take advance bookings (except for Friday nights), so you may have to join those waiting outside for a table with a refreshing frozen margarita in hand.

Vong
VIETNAMESE $$

(Map p118; ☑03-633-7171; www.vong.co.il; 15 Rothschild Blvd; mains 57-65NIS; banhs from 42NIS; ☺noon-midnight; ☜🍴) If you're looking for huge bowls of Vietnamese food, then Vong is for you. Located on Rothschild Blvd, opposite Independence Hall, it's now an institution of its own. Dishes include bok choy (Chinese cabbage), spicy dien-dien noodles and bahns, soft rolls with beef, fish, curry or tofu fillings. Check out the cocktails with names such as Forrest Jump and Lady Ga.

Zakaim
VEGAN $$

(Map p118; ☑03-613-5060; 20 Simtat Beit Hashoeva; mains 49-62NIS; ☺6pm-late Sun-Thu, noon-late Fri & Sat; 🍴) Despite its 100% vegan menu, chef Harel Zakaim's restaurant – hidden down an alleyway off 98 Allenby St – is a taste-fest for non-vegans. Dishes range from Persian rice (cooked with crispy potatoes on top) to red peppers stuffed with vegetables and lentils, to vegan pizzas, to chips served in a brown paper bag. There are even cocktails and chocolate truffles.

North Abraxas
ISRAELI $$

(Map p118; ☑03-516-6660; 40 Lilienblum St; small plates 22-52NIS, mains 34-120NIS, pizza 54NIS; ☺noon-midnight Sun-Thu, from 1pm Fri & Sat) The food at this flamboyant place is relegated to secondary importance – here, it's all about the vibe. Sitting at the bar and watching the chefs and waiters chop, flambée, plate, sing and down arak shots with customers is fabulous fun, and the modern Israeli menu with its pizzas, colourful vegetable dishes and flavourful slow-cooked meats will please most diners.

Nanuchka
VEGAN $$

(Map p118; ☑03-516-2254; http://nanuchka.co.il/en/; 30 Lilienblum St; mains 49-68NIS; ☺noon-late; 🍴) A vegan Georgian restaurant? Surely not. But that is indeed what Nanuchka – once a traditional Georgian eatery – has transformed itself into. There's a bohemian buzz about the place and occasional live music that explains its popularity. Dishes include filo pastry filled with spinach, tofu and green onions, slow-cooked rice with lentils and root vegetables and roasted aubergine with tahini.

★ Dalida
FUSION $$$

(Map p118; ☑03-536-9627; http://en.dalidatlv.co.il; 7 Zvulun St; mains 84-142NIS; sharing platters 159NIS; ☺5pm-2am Sun-Thu, from noon Fri & Sat; ☜🍴) One of Florentin's finest, Dalida is named after and inspired by the former Miss Egypt and iconic '60s singer who, like the food here, blended Arab, Italian and French styles. High-class but homely, Dalida offers a half-price menu from 5pm to 7pm

Sunday to Thursday. Try the Arabic cabbage with seared calamari or lamb, pistachios and halloumi kebab.

Café Noir FRENCH $$$

(Map p118; ☑03-566-3018; www.cafenoir.co.il; 43 Ahad Ha'am St; brunch 34-64NIS, mains 70-128NIS; ⊙noon-midnight Sun-Wed, to 1am Thu, 8am-1am Fri, 9am-midnight Sat; ☎) This bustling French-style brasserie is known locally for two things: weekend brunches and its signature schnitzels. We're big fans of the first but prefer the consistently excellent salads or pastas over the schnitzel. It's worth paying extra for a bread basket.

Manta Ray BREAKFAST SEAFOOD $$$

(Map p118; ☑03-517-4773; www.mantaray.co.il; southern Tel Aviv Promenade; breakfast 39-45NIS, mains 75-175NIS; ⊙9am-11pm; ☎) It's stylish, casual and at the beach – the perfect Tel Avivian triumvirate. On the slope directly above Alma Beach, this is the summer breakfast and lunch venue of choice for locals and tourists alike, so be sure to book (specify an outside table with a view). Try an omelette at breakfast and fish at other times of the day.

✖ Neve Tzedek

Meshek Barzilay CAFE $$

(Map p118; ☑03-516-6329; www.meshekbarzilay. co.il; 6 Ahad Ha'am St, Neve Tzedek; breakfast 38-64NIS, mains 46-68NIS; ⊙7am-4pm Sun, to midnight Mon-Fri, from 9am Sat; ☎⚹) Vegetarians and vegans are well catered for in Tel Aviv, but this place goes that extra mile when it comes to making them happy. One of only two restaurants we found serving organic free-range eggs (bravo!), it has plenty of interesting Indian- and Asian-influenced dishes on its menu and some great breakfast choices. Regulars swear by the vegan farm breakfast.

Lulu CAFE $$

(Map p118; ☑03-516-8793; www.lulucafe.co.il; 55 Shabazi St, Neve Tzedek; breakfast 38-58NIS, sandwiches 44-48NIS, mains 64-96NIS; ⊙7.30am-11.30pm; ☎) A perfect example of Neve Tzedek's laid-back but carefully curated style, this cafe-bar-restaurant has a vaguely arty ambience, Mediterranean menu and fashionable clientele. The food is a notch or two up the quality scale from standard cafe fare, and the indoor-outdoor seating arrangement suits all weather.

✖ Florentin

Beit Lechem Hummus MIDDLE EASTERN $

(Map p118; 5 Florentin St; hummus 18NIS; ⊙10am-9pm Sun-Thu, to 4pm Fri; ☑) The free self-service *tshai nana* (mint tea) is a nice touch, but Florentin regulars are drawn here solely on the strength of the hummus. Choose from fuul (with mashed and spiced fava beans) or *masabacha* (with chickpeas and warm tahina) versions, and consider ordering an egg topping (2NIS). Beit Lechem, means 'House of Bread' in Hebrew, the name of the town of Bethlehem.

Casbah Cafe CAFE $

(Map p118; ☑03 510 2144; 3 Florentin St; mains from 34NIS; ⊙8am-2am Mon-Sat, to midnight Sun; ☎☑) One of the most popular cheap eateries in the hip neighbourhood of Florentin, Casbah is run by the same people behind the equally cool Hoodna Bar (p144), just around the corner. It has a lazy laid-back feel and has many dishes for veggies such as the Balkan shakshuka, cauliflower curry or the vegan burger with sweet-potato fries.

Ouzeria GREEK $$

(Map p118; ☑03-533-0899; 44 Matalon St, Florentin; mezze 35 60NIS, ⊙noon-midnight Sun-Fri; ☑) Popular with locals of every age and style, this exuberant corner restaurant in the Levinski Spice Market precinct is busy every night but is absolutely hopping on Friday after the market closes. It doesn't accept bookings, so you may need to queue. Greek mezze showcase vegetables and seafood and are both tasty and well priced.

Romano FUSION $$

(Map p118; ☑054-317-7051; www.facebook.com/romanotlv; 9 Jaffa Rd; mains 41-74NIS; ⊙6pm-2am Mon-Sat; ☎) A hidden hipster gem, the entrance to Romano is deceiving. Behind the graffiti and gates, through a courtyard and up a staircase, this restaurant is one of the hottest spots in south TLV. Another of chef Eyal Shani's quirky creations, posters of Bruce Lee films adorn the walls as the young and hungry tuck into experimental and classic dishes.

✖ Jaffa (Yafo)

★Ali Caravan MIDDLE EASTERN $

(Abu Hassan; Map p128; 1 HaDolphin St; hummus portions 20NIS; ⊙8am-3pm Sun-Fri; ☑; ⬚Dan 10, 18, 25, 41) If hummus is a religion, then this could well be its Mecca. This tiny restaurant

V IS FOR VEGAN

Some reports claim that Israel has more vegans per capita than any other country. Though that may be difficult to prove, it's nevertheless true that Tel Aviv has caught the vegan vibe. Eateries approved by Vegan Friendly (www. vegan-friendly.co.il), an Israeli-based index, and HappyCow (www.happycow. net), an international online community, can be recognised by stickers in their windows.

near Jaffa Port offers a limited menu of three hummus choices: plain, fuul (with mashed and spiced fava beans) or *masabacha* (with chickpeas and warm tahina). It's always busy, so you'll probably need to queue.

★ **Kalamata** GREEK $$
(Map p128; ☑03-681-9998; www.kalamata.co.il; 10 Kedumim Sq; mains 62NIS; ☺5pm-late Sun-Wed, from noon Thu-Sat; 🐾) A real Tel Aviv *taverna*, this cute restaurant, set in a 500-year-old house on the main tourist square in Jaffa, offers a predominantly Greek and Cypriot menu but with an Israeli twist. Every dish here is delicious, but tasty starters include stuffed vine leaves and Arab-style ceviche; mains range from black seafood pasta to lamb or fish kebabs.

Casino San Remo MEDITERRANEAN $$
(☑03-504-2003; 2 Nehama St; mains 46-58NIS; ☺8am-2am; 🐾☑) On the border of Jaffa, in the hip Noga quarter, Casino San Remo is a chilled-out cafe, bar and restaurant. Aside from the cool music, dishes range from the meaty Bolognese and hamburgers to veggie leek patties and salads. The falafel platter served with mint leaves, tahini and eggplant is a tasty upmarket version of the street-food favourite.

Puaa CAFE $$
(Map p128; ☑03-682-3821; www.puaa.co.il; 8 Rabbi Yohanan St; breakfast 39-48NIS, sandwiches 38NIS, mains 44-58NIS; ☺9am-1am Sun-Fri, from 10am Sat; 🐾; 🚌Dan 10, 18, 25, 41) The thrift-shop-chic decor is truly authentic here – every piece of furniture and decorative knicknack is for sale. In the midst of the flea-market action, laid-back Puaa serves an all-day breakfast and is particularly busy on weekends, when the shakshuka, *sabich* and

bundash (fried challah served with jam and halva or with sour cream and cucumber) are must-order treats.

El Jamila MIDDLE EASTERN $$
(Map p128; ☑03-550-0042; 4 Olei Zion St, Jaffa; mains 60-120NIS; ☺noon-midnight; 🚌Dan 10,14, 25, 41) Traditional fish dishes from the Ajami district are on offer at this Arab-run restaurant in the flea market. The stone-walled dining space has a high ceiling and attractive tiled floor, and is a lovely place to park your shopping bags after a busy morning in the souq. Try the *ta'ashima* (fish fillets baked in dough and served with almond tahina).

Dr Shakshuka MIDDLE EASTERN $$
(Map p128; http://shakshuka.rest.co.il; 3 Beit Eshal St, Jaffa; shakshuka 38-45NIS, couscous 45-58NIS, shawarma 52-58NIS; ☺8am-midnight Sun-Fri; ☑) Set in an atmospheric Ottoman-era building in the flea market, the doctor has been working his shakshuka magic since 1991 and shows no sign of giving up. The eponymous egg dish is great, of course (his secret is loads of spice, particularly paprika), but locals tend to prefer the shawarma and couscous. Dine inside or in the shaded courtyard.

★ **Old Man & the Sea** SEAFOOD $$$
(☑03-681-8699; 85 Kedem St; mains from 99NIS; ☺11am-1am) As classic as the Hemingway novel of the same name, this Old Man is still at the top of his game. Spacious enough for dozens of waiters to serve hundreds of people, its terrace overlooks the sea in southern Jaffa. Huge portions of fish or seafood come with 20 or so small mezze, such as falafel balls and hummus.

🍷 **Drinking & Nightlife**

The city has a fantastic bar scene, with drinking dens to suit every taste, style and budget. Some are hipster hot spots, while others range from wine bars to craft breweries, and from rooftop bars to uber-chilled neighbourhood joints.

When it comes to clubbing, dance bars and bars hosting live gigs dominate the scene. There aren't too many mega-clubs here. Dress codes are relaxed – you can enter almost any pub or club in sport shoes or sandals, and it's not unusual to see people out in vests, shorts or bikinis in the summer.

City Centre

★ Kanta
ROOFTOP BAR

(Map p122; http://kanta.co.il; 71 Ibn Gabirol; ☻8pm-3am; 🛜) On the rooftop of the Gan Ha'Ir (City Garden) shopping mall, behind Rabin Sq, trendy Kanta has one of the finest outdoor terraces in Tel Aviv. Surrounded by plants and lit up at night, this urban garden is great for summer but also in winter, when it gets enclosed and the outdoor heaters take residence. Check out culinary delights from renowned Israeli chef Yaron Malka and enjoy cocktails such as Lion in Zion, a strange but refreshing mix of gin, lime and fresh basil. If the mall entrance is closed, it can be reached by climbing the large outdoor steps at the Gan Ha'Ir park from Ben Gurion Blvd.

HaMaoz
BAR

(Map p118; 📞03-620-9458; 32 King George St; ☻5pm-late Sun-Thu, noon-3am Fri & Sat; 🛜) Locals and tourists love HaMaoz, which has three main areas – an outdoor garden deck, an indoor bar and a backroom that deliberately looks like someone's apartment. It is particularly popular on Friday afternoons and evenings, when drinkers enjoy watching the passing parade along King George St.

BuXa
BAR

(Map p118; 📞058-511-1558; http://buxatlv.com/bar; 31 Rothschild Blvd; ☻9pm-6am) BuXa is a unique venue – part art gallery displaying designer toys, part high-end cocktail bar and part underground DJ den. It hosts regular live music events on its basement dance floor, and its top-floor balcony is the spot to mingle with a young, artsy crowd. The bar also serves Asian fusion dishes such as the Bombay Sloppy Joe.

The Cat and the Dog
CLUB

(Map p118; 📞03-561-5595; www.facebook.com/thecatandthedog; 23 Carlebach St; entry from 50NIS; ☻11pm-7am Thu & Fri) Leading the city's underground dance scene for years, The Cat and the Dog is top dog for thumping, sweaty trance and progressive house. Located in the heart of Tel Aviv, it has played host to the biggest international and local DJs, including John Digweed, Sven Vath, Sasha and Infected Mushroom. Check out its Facebook page for the latest events.

South City Centre

★ Bicicletta
BEER GARDEN

(Map p118; 📞03-643-3097; www.facebook.com/BiciclettaTLV; 29 Nahalat Binyamin St; ☻6pm-1am Sun-Thu, from noon Fri & Sat; 🛜) A vibrant, young bar on Nahalat Binyamin St, Bicicletta (Italian for bicycle) has one of the best patio gardens in town. The food is great – eclectic dishes include the smoked turkey sandwich with brie, pork belly with cauliflower and date honey, and its signature homemade aubergine fries. Happy hour is 5.30pm to 8pm. Look for the bicycle in the window.

★ Kuli Alma
BAR

(Map p118; 📞03-656-5155; http://kulialma.com; 10 Mikveh Israel St; ☻10pm-5am; 🛜) Mystical and just downright cool, Kuli Alma is a TLV nightlife institution with an emphasis

TEL AVIV-JAFFA (YAFO) DRINKING & NIGHTLIFE

GAY & LESBIAN LIFE

Tel Aviv has a reputation as one of the world's great destinations for LGBTIQ travellers. In June it plays host to the week-long Tel Aviv Pride (p132), the region's biggest and most flamboyant gay and lesbian festival. Rainbow flags can be found in cafes and on beaches and the city's hotels are almost all LGBT-friendly.

LGBT-focussed venues include the hip gay bar Shpagat (Map p118; 📞03-560-1785; 43 Nahalat Binyamin St; ☻7pm-late Sat-Thu, noon-5pm Fri); and the male-only hook-up bar-club Apolo (Map p118; 📞03-774-1106; www.apolo.co.il; 46 Allenby St; ☻10pm-4am). To keep updated on the latest happenings, check Atraf (www.atraf.com), which has a smartphone app, and the official Tel Aviv Gay Vibe (www.visit-tel-aviv.com/gayvibe).

Beachgoers might also want to visit Hilton Beach (p125), Tel Aviv's unofficial gay beach. Check events and club nights (many held at the HaOman 17 venue on Arbarbanel St) when planning your trip at www.gaytelavivguide.com.

The Tel Aviv Gay Center (Map p118; 📞03-525-2896; www.gaycenter.org.il; Gan Meir Park) off King George St hosts gay- and lesbian-themed events, lectures, sports groups and pot-luck picnics.

on art and music. Behind the unimposing entrance, locals and not-so locals mingle in the patio dotted with plants, graffiti and an outdoor gallery. There's a vegetarian menu, and it hosts an eclectic mix of DJ and live music nights.

★ **Prince** ROOFTOP BAR

(Map p118; 058-606-1818; www.facebook.com/theprincetlv; 18 Nahalat Binyamin St; ⊙5pm-late Sat-Thu, noon-6pm Fri) For years this place was one of Tel Aviv's best-kept secrets: an amazing rooftop bar on the corner of the Nahalat Binyamin Crafts Market. But now the secret's out and the Prince (*HaNasich* in Hebrew) is packed to the brim with people. Like all good Tel Aviv bars, it has a dark and dingy entrance (with some pretty weird graffiti).

But after climbing the stairs, you're greeted by a rooftop that's hard to beat. Unpretentious and without plush design, expect a hippie, rather than hipster, vibe.

★ **Rothschild 12** BAR

(Map p118; 03-510-6430; www.rothschild12.co.il; 12 Rothschild Blvd; ⊙7am-late) One of our favourite breakfast stops (pastries and bread are French-style and delicious), it's equally good for lunch (burgers, *sabich*, toasted sandwiches), afternoon coffee, aperitifs or late-night drinks. The soundtrack comes courtesy of jazz discs during the day and live bands and DJs at night. The website is in Hebrew only.

★ **Block** CLUB

(www.block-club.com; 157 Shalma/Salame Rd, Neve Sha'anan; early arrivals 50-70NIS, late arrivals 70-90NIS; ⊙11pm-late Thu-Sat) In the Central Bus Station building, Block is known as Tel Aviv's best club for good reason, hosting big-name international DJs playing anything from funk, hip-hop and Afrobeat to drum 'n' bass, house and trance. There's an impressive sound system and a smoker's lounge.

Beit Maariv CLUB

(Map p118; www.facebook.com/BeitMaariv; 51 Menachem Begin Rd; entry 70-100NIS; ⊙11.30pm-late Thu-Sat; 26, 89, 189) It's all about the sound at Beit Maariv, one of the best clubs in the city's underground dance scene. A total astral experience with lasers and huge speakers, this club is housed in the building that was once used for the Israeli newspaper Maariv. It's now home to some of the top local and international house DJs.

Florentine

Beer Bazaar CRAFT BEER

(Map p118; 03-917-4590; https://beerbazaar.co.il; 13 Zvulun St; ⊙noon-midnight Sun-Thu, to 6pm Fri, 8pm-midnight Sat) What began as a craft-beer stand in the Carmel Market has now turned into an empire. Well, maybe a mini-empire. Beer Bazaar has four locations in Tel Aviv and one in Jerusalem's Mahane Yehuda Market. In this bar, try tastings from an impressive range of 100 Israeli craft beers before choosing your pint. The shop also sells bottles.

Jackson Bar BAR

(Map p118; 6 Vital St, Florentin; ⊙7pm-late; 📶) On Wednesday night, there's only one truly hip (hop) place to be, and that's here. Owned by the well-known Tel Aviv rapper Axum (aka Mr Jackson), this street art–decorated bar has DJ sets every night but really goes off midweek.

Hoodna Bar BAR

(Map p118; 13 Arbarbanel St, Florentin; ⊙6pm-late Sun-Thu, from 1pm Fri & Sat; 📶) Hoodna ('truce' in Arabic) is a carpenter's workshop zone by day but transforms itself at night, when tables and sofas are dragged into the street to create a chilled-out drinking space. Inside there are almost daily live or DJ sets. In the last week of February, it hosts the Southern Wind indie rock festival.

Jaffa (Yafo)

Anna Loulou Bar BAR

(Map p128; www.annaloulou.com; 1 HaPninim St, Old Jaffa; ⊙9pm-3am Mon-Sat; Dan 10, 18, 25, 41) Describing itself as a cross between underground bar and cultural centre, this is a gay- and smoker-friendly hipster bar. The music is predominantly electro-Arab, African or Middle Eastern, although there's the occasional wild-card event (country, hip-hop, drag shows). Wednesday is the night to party.

☆ Entertainment

Tickets to many major events can be pre-purchased online at Eventim (www.eventim.co.il/en).

★ **Cinematheque** CINEMA

(Map p118; 03-606-0800; www.cinema.co.il/english; 1 Ha'Arba'a St; from 30NIS; ⊙10am-midnight Sun-Fri, from 11am Sat) The flagship in a chain of Israeli cinemas featuring classic,

THE GREAT ESCAPE

Being trapped in a strange room for 60 minutes may sound like punishment to some, but for many young Tel Avivians it's a fun night out. Yes, the escape room (or 'exit room') craze is firmly part of Tel Aviv's fabric. Popular with tech-savvy millennials, these rooms are more like adventure games, quests and puzzles, where players must solve clues to exit and 'save the world'.

Not surprisingly, many of the escape rooms here have a high-tech, military feel. There are dozens of exciting escape rooms dotted all over the city, housed in seemingly run-of-the-mill buildings. Below are three of the main networks with games in English. Admission costs 80NIS to 120NIS per person, depending on the size of the group.

Brainit's (https://brainit.co.il/en) Escape rooms include a serial-killing doctor in Old Jaffa, a virtual reality shoot-out and a space station. It also has games in Herzliya and Netanya.

Escape Rooms (www.escaperoom.co.il/en/tel-aviv) Lists exit rooms for two to six people with themes ranging from doomsday to the paranormal, Mossad (Israeli intelligence) to *Titanic*.

Locked Games (www.locked-games.com/english) Has two locations – 26 Tchernihovsky St (near Meir Park) and 3 HaPelech St (in the south). Prices start from 200NIS.

retro, foreign, avant garde and experimental films. It often holds film festivals, such as DocAviv (p132).

★ **Barby** LIVE MUSIC
(☑ 03-518-8123; www.barby.co.il; 52 Kibbutz Galuyot St) This Tel Aviv institution at the south ernmost point of the city is a favourite venue for reggae, electronica, funk and alternative bands. Occasionally hosts big-name acts and the vibe is always positive with a capital 'P'. Check the website for lineups.

Goldstar Zappa Club LIVE MUSIC
(☑ 03-762-6666; www.zappa-club.co.il; 24 Raoul Wallenberg St, Ramat HaChayal) Local and international music luminaries play at this intimate all-seated club named after the legendary Frank Zappa. Situated 8km northeast of central Tel Aviv, it's best reached by car or taxi. Call or look out for listings to find out who's on while you're here.

Shablul Jazz Club JAZZ
(☑ 03-546-1891; www.shabluljazz.com; Hangar 13, Old Port) Cool jazz, blues, salsa and world music takes centre stage at this intimate venue on the Old Port. Shablul hosts nightly live music. Check the Facebook page (www. facebook.com/shabluljazz) for an events calendar.

Beit HaAmudim JAZZ
(Map p118; ☑ 03-510-9228; www.facebook.com/ BeitHaamudim; 14 Rambam St; ⊗noon-2am Sun, Mon, Wed & Thu, 9am-3am Tue & Fri, 7pm-3am Sat) Tel Aviv's intimate live jazz venue welcomes

a disparate crowd to its almost nightly gigs, which kick off at 9.30pm. Entry fee for gigs is 5NIS per musician, so if you see a band of five people, you pay 25NIS. Close to Carmel Market, it functions as a cafe during the day. Check the Facebook page for details.

Felicja Blumental Music Centre CLASSICAL MUSIC
(Map p118; ☑ 03-620-1185; www.fbmc.co.il; 26 Bialik St) Named in honour of Polish-born Brazil ian pianist Felicja Blumental, this regal but intimate 115-seat auditorium hosts classical, jazz and chamber music concerts.

Suzanne Dellal Centre DANCE
(Map p118; ☑ 03-510-5656; www.suzannedellal. org.il; 5 Yechieli St) The leading dance school in the country and set in a building dating from 1892 in Neve Tzedek, Suzanne Dellal is also a theatre. Opened in 1989 by the Dellal family of London, it stages a variety of performing arts including modern dance, music and ballet, and is home to the world-famous Bat Sheva dance company.

Cameri Theatre THEATRE
(Map p118; ☑ 03-606-0960; www.cameri.co.il; 30 Leonardo da Vinci St) Hosts first-rate theatre performances in Hebrew, on some nights with simultaneous English translation or English-language subtitles.

Habima National Theatre THEATRE
(Map p118; ☑ 03-629-5555; www.habima.co.il; 2 Tarsat Blvd, HaBima Sq) Home to Israel's national theatre company, Habima stages

SHABBAT IN TEL AVIV

If you've already experienced the hush that descends on Jerusalem as Shabbat is welcomed in – and wondered what on earth you're going to do without public transport, ATMs, restaurants and shops for a full 24 hours or so – don't despair: simply go to Tel Aviv and spend Shabbat the secular way.

Here, most shops close on Friday afternoon and don't open again until Saturday evening or Sunday morning, but that seems to be the extent of the city's nod to the holy day of rest. On Friday evening, bars, restaurants and clubs are packed to the rafters until dawn. Saturday sees locals thronging to the beach, lazing at cafes, dining at restaurants and generally being active throughout the day. And although municipal laws make it illegal to operate retail stores on Shabbat, there are also plenty of AM:PM, Tiv Ta'am, Super Yuda and mini-supermarkets that remain open 24/7.

You will notice less noise on the streets as there are no buses, but there are sheruts and taxis if you need to get around.

weekly performances in its impressive, modern, restored dome-shaped building. Most have simultaneous subtitles in English.

Jaffa Theatre　　　　　　　　　THEATRE
(Arab-Hebrew Theatre; Map p128; www.arab-hebrew-theatre.org.il; 10 Mifratz Shlomo St) Founded in 1998 in a multi-arched building in Old Jaffa to bring two cultures together, this stage showcases Hebrew and Arabic-language plays, sometimes with English translations. Not afraid to run plays that tackle the Israeli–Palestinian conflict, it also holds musical performances and festivals such as the Arab-Hebrew Women's Festival.

Nalaga'at Centre　　　　　　　THEATRE
(Map p128; ☑03-633-0808; www.nalagaat.org.il; Jaffa Port) A unique nonprofit organisation set in a renovated shipping hangar, Nalaga'at (meaning 'Do Touch') is the only deaf-blind theatre company in the world. While watching a show here, it's easy to forget that the people on stage cannot see or hear, as the actors tell stories, play musical instruments and even perform choreographed dances. Aside from the theatre, it houses the BlackOut restaurant, where diners eat in darkness, assisted by blind waiters.

🛍 Shopping

🛍 City Centre

Lametayel　　　　　　SPORTS & OUTDOORS
(Map p118; ☑077-333-4501; www.lametayel.co.il; top fl, 50 Dizengoff St, Dizengoff Center; ☺10am-9pm Sun-Thu, to 2.30pm Fri) Israel's largest camping and travel-equipment shop carries a full range of Lonely Planet guides and is a prime source of information for Israeli backpackers. It's a worthwhile stop – for kit or tips – if you'll be doing any camping, for example along the Jesus Trail, around the Sea of Galilee or in the Dead Sea area.

Steimatzky　　　　　　　　　　BOOKS
(Map p122; ☑03-522-1513; www.steimatzky.co.il; 109 Dizengoff St; ☺9am-8pm Sun-Thu, to 4pm Fri) This branch of the chain bookstore has helpful staff and a decent array of English-language titles and children's books.

🛍 South City Centre

Contour　　　　　　　　　　　JEWELLERY
(Map p118; ☑03-654-2270; www.contour-studio.com; 25 Gruzenberg St; ☺10am-6pm Sun-Thu, to 3pm Fri) Contour was founded by two award-winning Israeli designers, Lior Shulak-Hai and Galit Barak, in 2015. Located near Nahalat Binyamin Crafts Market, Contour creates bespoke handmade jewelry that's unique in its bold and beautiful shapes.

🛍 Neve Tzedek

Sipur Pashut　　　　　　　　　BOOKS
(Map p118; ☑03-510-7040; www.sipurpashut.com/english; 36 Shabazi St, Neve Tzedek; ☺10am-7pm Sun-Thu, 9.30am-4pm Fri) Book stores don't get much cuter than this. Sipur Pashut (meaning 'simple story') is a tiny shop filled from floor to ceiling with quality Hebrew and English literature. Set in the heart of Neve Tzedek, it is also a venue for poetry readings, book launches and children's stories. It publishes the Israeli version of the world-renowned *Granta* magazine.

Chomer Tov   CERAMICS
(Map p118; ☑03-516-6229; www.chomertov.co.il;
27 Shabazi St, Neve Tzedek; ☉10am-8pm Sun-Thu,
to 5pm Fri) A cooperative of 15 ceramic artists,
Chomer Tov (meaning 'good material') is
both a small gallery and a shop. A dynamic
space, it features both functional (eg bowls
and cups) and imaginative designs, as well
as modern Judaica.

Agas & Tamar   JEWELLERY
(Map p118; ☑03-516-8421; www.agasandtamar
design.com; 43 Shabazi St, Neve Tzedek; ☉10am-
7pm Sun-Thu, to 4pm Fri) Pass through an old
metal door to discover the workshop and
retail space of Einat Agassi and Tamar Harel-
Klein, who use gold and silver to create
'storytelling jewellery' inspired by a theme
or historical artefact (coin, nail, seal etc).

Orit Ivshin   JEWELLERY
(Map p118; ☑03 516-0811; www.oritivshin.com; 54
Shabazi St, Neve Tzedek; ☉10am-7pm Sun-Thu, to
3pm Fri) Jeweller Orit Ivshin makes delicate
handmade pieces in 19-carat gold at his
Neve Tzedek atelier, many of which he en-
crusts with diamonds. Gorgeous.

Ronit   JEWELLERY
(Map p118; ☑03-516-2721; http://ronitjewelry.com;
20 Shabazi St, Neve Tzedek; ☉10am-7pm Sun-Thu,
to 3pm Fri) Necklaces featuring leaf and boat
motifs are some of the many hand-crafted
pieces on offer at Ronit Cohen's atelier. Most
are plated with 24-carat gold rather than being solid, meaning that they fall within most
budgets.

🔒 Jaffa (Yafo)

Shelley Dahari   FASHION & ACCESSORIES
(Map p128; ☑03-620-8004; www.shelleydahari.
com; 14 Rabbi Yohanan St, Jaffa; ☉9.30am-8pm
Sun Thu, to 4pm Fri) Beach-loving fashionistas
should head to this boutique in Jaffa's flea
market to source a designer swimsuit by
the Israeli label Ugly Duckling and a stylish
galabiya (loose, full-length kaftan) by Karen
Shavit to wear over it.

Zielinski & Rozen   COSMETICS
(Map p128; ☑054-774-0566; 10 Rabbi Pinchas St;
☉10.30am-7pm Sun-Thu, 9.30am-4pm Fri; 🚌Dan
10, 18, 25, 41) Planters filled with sweetly
scented jasmine adorn the front of this chic

MARKETS & MALLS

Locals like to shop, and Tel Aviv has more than its fair share of street markets and shopping malls. Head to the Carmel Market (p117) for fresh produce and cheap clothing,
to Jaffa's Flea Market (p129) for Altezachen ('old things' in Yiddish) and antiques, and
to historic Sarona (p124), built by the German Templers, for international upmarket
shopping and chef-style street food. If you have any energy and credit left, consider the
following:

Gan Ha'ir Mall (Map p122; ☉8am-8pm Sun-Thu, 8am-4pm Fri) In a central location just
north of Rabin Sq, this upscale mall has brand-name boutiques and an organic market.
Has cooked-food stalls on Friday.

Ramat Aviv Mall (www.ramat-aviv-mall.co.il; 40 Einstein St, Ramat Aviv; ☉9.30am-9.30pm
Sun-Thu, to 3pm Fri) The city's biggest and swankiest mall, with a great selection of top-
end designers. Near Tel Aviv University.

Kikar HaMedina (HaMedina Sq) This wide, circular plaza is the place to fulfil all your
Gucci, Tag Heuer and Versace needs.

Dizengoff Centre (Map p118; ☑03-621-2400; cnr Dizengoff & King George Sts; ☉9am-
midnight Sun-Thu, to 4pm Fri, 8pm-midnight Sat; 🚻) Israel's first mall is filled with cafes,
fast-food joints, mobile-phone stands and high-street retail stores. A popular Israeli
cooked-food market is held every Friday before Shabbat from 9am.

Nahalat Binyamin Crafts Market (Map p118; www.nachlat-binyamin.com; ☉10am 5pm
Tue, to 6pm or 7pm summer, 10am to 4.30pm Fri) On Tuesday and Friday, arts-and-crafts
street stalls are set up in this pedestrianised street next to Carmel Market. A great place
to look for creative Judaica (Jewish ritual objects).

Old Port Farmers' Market (☑077-541-1393; http://shukhanamal.co.il/english; Hangar 12,
Old Port; ☉9am-4pm Sun, to 8pm Mon-Thu & Sat, 7am-5pm Fri) Set in a restored hangar, this
mostly organic food market is small but delicious.

perfumerie, which has the appearance and feel of an old-fashioned apothecary's shop. Bottles of perfume, hand wash, room scent and body wash are ready to buy, but it's also possible to book a consultation to have a personalised perfume created.

❶ Information

DANGERS & ANNOYANCES

Tel Aviv is a remarkably safe city. Despite the sometimes harrowing headlines, Tel Avivians are generally unperturbed by the threat of terrorism. The streets are safe to walk at all times of the day and night.

To report a bicycle theft or any other crime, go to **Dizengoff Police Station** (Map p122; ☑ 03-545-4444; 221 Dizengoff St). To avoid theft, bicycles should be locked with a heavy-duty chain and kept within eyesight where possible. Also, if taking a dip in the sea, don't leave your expensive belongings on the beach, or else ask someone to keep an eye on your bag.

INTERNET ACCESS

Tel Aviv is one of the most tech-savvy cities in the world, so it's not surprising that wi-fi is readily available in most cafes, restaurants and hotels, plus there are free hot spots on the main boulevards and along the shore.

MEDICAL SERVICES

Tel Aviv has top-quality medical services, and hotels can contact a doctor or hospital in case of emergency.

Ichilov Hospital (Tel Aviv Sourasky Medical Centre; Map p118; ☑ 03-697-4444; www.tasmc.org.il; 6 Weizmann St; ⊗ emergency 24hr) Near the city centre, Ichilov is the city's big central hospital, with a 24-hour emergency room and a travellers' clinic (the Malram Clinic) for immunisations.

Superpharm This handy pharmacy chain has a number of branches in town, including at 129 Dizengoff St (Map p122; ☑ 077-888-0730; ⊗ 8am-midnight Sat-Thu, to 6pm Fri),

62 Sheinkin St (Map p118; ☑ 077-888-0830; ⊗ 8am-11.30pm Sun-Thu, to 5.30pm Fri, 8pm-midnight Sat) and 4 Shaul HaMelech Blvd (Map p118; ☑ 077-888-0390; ⊗ 24hr Sun-Thu, closed 6pm Fri-8pm Sat). The Dizengoff St branch is open on Shabbat.

Tel Aviv Doctor (Map p122; ☑ 054-941-4243, toll-free 1-800-201-999; www.telaviv-doctor. com; 46 Basel St, near Basel Sq) A well-equipped medical clinic with multilingual doctors. It offers medical check-ups, lab tests and X-rays, and does emergency visits.

MONEY

If you're seeking exchange bureaux, you'll find no shortage on Allenby, Ibn Gabirol and Dizengoff Sts. Most are open from 9am to 9pm Sunday to Thursday, and until 2pm on Friday.

You'll have no problem finding ATMs, but as they aren't refilled on Friday night or on Saturday, they sometimes run out of cash at those times. Banks have sporadic opening hours and generally higher commission rates than the bureaux.

TOURIST INFORMATION

Tel Aviv's main **tourist information office** (Map p118; ☑ 03-516-6188; www.visit-tel-aviv.com; 46 Herbert Samuel Esplanade; ⊗ 9.30am-5.30pm Sun-Thu, to 1pm Fri Nov-Mar, to 6.30pm Sun-Thu, to 2pm Apr-Oct) has super-helpful staff and can provide maps, brochures and plenty of advice.

The friendly and helpful staff at the **Jaffa Tourist Information Office** (Map p128; ☑ 03-516-6188; www.visit-tel-aviv.com; 2 Marzuk Ve-Azar St, Jaffa; ⊗ 9.30am-5.30pm Sun-Thu, to 1pm Fri, 10am-4pm Sat Apr-Oct, 9.30am-5.30pm Sun-Thu, 9am-2pm Fri Nov-Mar) near the clock tower can provide recommendations and a free Jaffa map.

❶ Getting There & Away

BUS

Most intercity buses depart from the 6th floor of Tel Aviv's enormous, confusing and filthy Central Bus Station (Map p118), where there's also an

---

INTERNET RESOURCES

DIY Tel Aviv (www.diytelavivguide.com/blog) Alternative guide to food, drink, nightlife, shopping and culture.

Midnight East (www.midnighteast.com/mag) Interesting arts- and culture-focussed blog.

Secret Tel Aviv (www.secrettelaviv.com) Listings and advice from locals; check the Facebook group.

Time Out Israel (http://timeout.co.il/en) Plenty of Tel Aviv listings and features.

Tel Aviv Nonstop City (https://tel-aviv.gov.il/en) The municipality's excellent website.

Visit Tel Aviv (www.visit-tel-aviv.com) Official tourist website.

information desk. Suburban and city buses use the 4th and 7th floors. Tickets can be bought from the driver or from ticket booths. Note that during Shabbat you'll have to resort to sheruts (shared taxis).

Egged buses (www.egged.co.il) leave for Jerusalem (405; 16NIS, one hour, every 20 minutes); Haifa (921; 27NIS, 1½ hours, every 25 minutes); Tiberias (836; 37.50NIS, 2½ hours, every 30 minutes); Nazereth (826; 34NIS, 2¾ hours, every 45 minutes); and Eilat (393, 394 and 790; 70NIS, 5½ hours, hourly). You'll need to book tickets to Eilat in advance (call *2800 or go to www.egged.co.il), as these services are usually full. Metropoline buses travel to/from Be'er Sheva (353, 369 and 370; 15NIS, 1½ hours, every 30 minutes).

Tel Aviv's second bus station, the open-air Arlozorov Bus Terminal adjoins the Tel Aviv Savidor Merkaz train station northeast of the city centre. To get there, take bus 61 (6.90NIS), which goes along Allenby, King George, Dizengoff and Arlozorov Sts, or bus 10 which goes along Ben Yehuda St. If staying in the centre or the north, Egged bus 480 (16NIS, one hour, every 10 minutes) is the most convenient service to Jerusalem and leaves from the main station car park.

SHERUT

Sheruts (shared taxis, in most cases yellow minibuses) depart from Tsemach David St outside the Central Bus Station and head to Jerusalem (26NIS, on Shabbat 36NIS) and Haifa (30NIS, on Shabbat 45NIS).

From the Arlozorov Bus Terminal sheruts wait on Namir Rd and go north to Herzliya (15NIS) and Netanya (20NIS).

From Ben Gurion International Airport (www.iaa.gov.il) there are sheruts to Jerusalem (from 42NIS), Haifa (from 78NIS) and Akko (from 90NIS). The ticket price is the same on weekdays and Shabbat and includes up to two suitcases.

TRAIN

Tel Aviv has four train stations: Savidor (Arlozorov (Mercaz) Station), HaHagana, HaShalom and University.

From Savidor, you can travel by train to Haifa (27.50NIS, one hour) via Netanya (13.50NIS, 25 minutes) every 30 minutes and on to Akko (35.50NIS, 1½ hours) and Nahariya (39.50NIS, 1¾ hours). Trains run every 30 minutes from 6am to 8.30pm Sunday to Thursday and then hourly from 8.33pm to 11.33pm. Trains stop around 4pm on Friday and resume after 9pm on Saturday. The station is situated 2.7km east of the beach and 1.5km east of Ibn Gabirol St, at the eastern end of Arlozorov St. The station is sometimes also called Tel Aviv Merkaz (Central Tel Aviv), Tel Aviv Tzafon (North Tel Aviv) and Arlozorov.

Heading south, you can travel down the coast to Ashkelon (22NIS, one hour) and as far as Be'er Sheva (27NIS, 1¼ hours), both departing hourly.

ℹ MAPS OF TEL AVIV

The English-language Tel Aviv-Jaffa Tourist map is an excellent resource and is available from tourist information offices. Most hotels supply free tourist maps of the city. Abraham Hostel (p136) has a particularly good map with recommendations.

To reach Savidor from the city centre, take bus 61 north from Allenby or Dizengoff Sts to the Arlozorov Bus Terminal, which is a two-minute walk from the station.

ℹ Getting Around

TO/FROM THE AIRPORT

The most straightforward method of getting from Ben Gurion International Airport into Tel Aviv is by train – the station entrance is outside the international terminal building, to the left. Except on Shabbat and Jewish holidays, trains run every 30 minutes between 5.35am and 11.35pm, stopping at all four Tel Aviv stations, with extra services at 12.53am, 1.53am, 2.53am, 3.53am and 4.53am to Savidor station only. The fare is 14NIS. Check the Israel Railway website (www.rail.co.il/en) for more.

Prices for taxis are controlled, and either meters or pre-set official prices are used; there's an orderly taxi rank just outside the international terminal building. Depending on traffic, the ride into central Tel Aviv takes about 20 minutes and should cost 160NIS (day rate) and 200NIS (9pm to 5.30am). There's usually an extra charge of 5NIS per suitcase.

A taxi between Sde Dov airport and the city centre should cost less than 50NIS.

BICYCLE

The quickest and easiest way to travel around Tel Aviv is on a bicycle, thanks in part to 120km of dedicated bike paths along thoroughfares such as Rothschild Blvd, Chen Blvd, Ben-Gurion Blvd and Ibn Gabirol St. For epic rides, go to Park HaYarkon (p126) and head east, or pedal along the 10km coastal promenade. For rentals, try **O-Fun** (☑ 03-544-2292; http://ofun.co.il; 19/ Ben Yehuda St; per hr/24hr/weekend 25/75/130NIS; ⊗ 9.30am-7pm Sun-Thu, to 2pm Fri) on Ben Yehuda St or the other branch of **O-Fun** (Map p118; ☑ 03-522-0488; http://ofun.co.il; 32 Allenby St; ⊗ 10am-7pm Sun-Thu, to 2pm Fri) on Allenby St.

BUS & SHERUT

Tel Aviv city buses are operated by the Dan cooperative (www.dan.co.il) and follow an efficient network of routes, from 5.30am to midnight, except Shabbat.

BICYCLE BOOM

Being a compact city, there is no better way to see Tel Aviv than on two wheels. The city now has about 120km of dedicated bike paths running along many of the major thoroughfares, through Park HaYarkon and along the coastline from just north of Sde Dov airport southward, via Jaffa, to the suburb of Bat Yam. A free map of the bike-path network can be picked up at tourist information offices.

Be aware that cyclists should stay on the designated cycle paths where possible and can get fined if riding on pavements. The major boulevards of Ben-Gurion, Chen, Rothschild and the seafront promenade have connected bicycle lanes.

Not to be confused with O-Fun (which is a bicycle hire shop), the municipality-run **Tel-O-Fun** (www.tel-o-fun.co.il) is a citywide bike-rental scheme similar to Paris' or London's bicycle hire schemes.

Tel-O-Fun lets riders pick up and drop off the green bicycles at more than 75 docking stations. A daily access card costs 17NIS (23NIS between 2pm Friday and 7pm Saturday) and a weekly card costs 70NIS.

The first 30 minutes of usage are free; after that there are fees that get progressively higher, starting at 5NIS per 30 minutes and quickly rising to 20NIS, 40NIS, 80NIS and 100NIS an hour. To avoid fees, simply return your bike and, after waiting at least 10 minutes, take another one. Tourists don't need to open a account, instead they pay by credit card at any Tel-O-Fun station.

Electric bicycles are massively popular with young Tel Avivians and can obviously zoom by much faster. If hiring such a bike, riders must be over 16, wear a helmet and not exceed the legal speed limit of 25km an hour.

A ticket for a single ride costs 6.90NIS, a one-day pass *(hofshi yomi)* allowing unlimited bus travel around Tel Aviv and its suburbs costs 13.50NIS and a weekly card *(hofshi shavoui)* costs 64NIS.

You can buy one-day or weekly passes from bus drivers or get a Personal Rav Kav (top-up) travel card. These can be obtained at no charge from a Dan information counter at the Central Bus Station or the Arlozorov Bus Terminal from 8am to 6pm Sunday to Thursday or until 1pm on Friday. You'll need to fill out an application form and bring it, a passport photograph and your passport with you. It's easier to purchase an Anonymous Rav Kav card from any bus driver (no photograph or ID needed).

There are three major local bus terminals: the Central Bus Station (near HaHagana Train Station), the Arlozorov Bus Terminal (near the North Tel Aviv/Savidor Train station) and the Carmelit Terminal, at the lower end of the Carmel Market. At the Central Bus Station, local buses leave from the 4th and 7th floors, and also from Levinsky St.

Many bus stops now show waiting times and the very handy Moovit app (https://moovitapp.com) shows real-time updates of all routes.

Currently, these are the major Tel Aviv bus routes:

Bus 4 Central Bus Station via Allenby St and Ben Yehuda St to the Reading Terminal, north of the Yarkon River. Departs 4th floor.

Bus 5 Outside Central Bus Station (ground floor), along Allenby St, up Rothschild Blvd, along Dizengoff St, Nordau Ave, Ibn Gabirol St, Pinkas St, Weizmann St and HaMaccabi St and then back. Useful for the HI Hostel, the Egyptian Embassy, HaBima Sq and Dizengoff Sq.

Bus 10 Savidor train station via Arlozorov St, Ben Yehuda St, Allenby St, Herbert Samuel Esplanade, Yerushalayim Ave (Jaffa) and on to Bat Yam.

Bus 18 Savidor train station to Ichilov Hospital, Rabin Sq, King George St, Allenby St, Yerushalayim Ave (Jaffa) and on to Bat Yam.

Bus 25 Tel Aviv University to **Reading Terminal** then Rabin Sq, King George St, Allenby St and Carmel Market, then on to Jaffa and Bat Yam.

Sherut 4 Same route as bus 4; operates on Shabbat.

Sherut 5 Same route as bus 5; operates on Shabbat.

City Tour (Bus 100) Dan also runs a special tourist service in a panoramic open-top bus. It starts at the Old Port and includes stops at all the major museums and Old Jaffa. It runs hourly from 9am to 4pm, Sunday to Thursday, to 1pm on Friday.

CAR

Finding street parking in downtown Tel Aviv can be very difficult. Cars are only allowed to park in spaces with blue-and-white kerbs. Most streets require payment during the day (6.20NIS per hour), except on Shabbat (ie 1pm on Friday to 9am on Sunday), and are reserved for residents with local parking stickers from 5pm to 9am.

Among the complicating factors: the yellow signs that explain the rules that apply to the side of the street they're on may not be in English. Parking next to a red-and-white kerb is illegal – if you park in one of these spaces your car *will* be towed.

Privately owned parking lots and garages (often signposted with electronic information on whether they're full) charge upwards of 60NIS per 24 hours of parking. Public car parks charge considerably less (usually a flat rate of 20NIS from 7am to 7pm, or 8NIS to 10NIS per hour). There are conveniently located large public car parks in front of the Old Railway Station (p130) on Herbert Samuel Promenade and just south of Jaffa Port (p129).

The city's biggest parking lot is the Reading Terminal, on the outskirts of Tel Aviv near Park HaYarkon. Because of its location and good bus connections, it's often used as a 'park and ride' option.

Parking on Shabbat (Friday evening to Saturday afternoon) is usually easier as many Tel Avivians leave the city on day trips, and most parking lots are open. Useful parking lots are located on Ben Saruk St (near Arlozorov St), Sarona (Kaplan St), Basel St and HaBima (Rothschild Blvd).

Most of the main car-rental agencies have offices on HaYarkon St.

TAXI

Plan on 40NIS to 50NIS for most trips within the central city. The most popular taxi app in town is Gett Taxi (https://gett.com).

AROUND TEL AVIV

Gush Dan גוש דן غوش دان

POP 3.7 MILLION

Gush Dan, meaning 'Dan Bloc', is a large area of central Israel, best known for its long stretch of golden beaches between Tel Aviv and Netanya. Besides the beaches, it's also the nation's economic heart, bringing with it high-tech business parks, shopping malls and its fair share of road traffic.

Named after the biblical tribe of Dan – which is said to have resided in this coastal region – it comprises the greater Tel Aviv area and a web of suburbs and municipalities. The more affluent suburbs, such as Herzliya, are mainly to the north of Tel Aviv and not-so-affluent suburbs, such as Ramla, are to the south, though Rishon LeZion is an exception. Home to more than 40% of modern Israel's population, Gush Dan is at the core of modern Israeli life.

Herzliya הרצליה هرتسليا

📷 09 / POP 92,000

Herzliya, Tel Aviv's affluent northern neighbour, is popular because of its fine, clean beaches, marina and string of seafront cafes. Just 13km north of Tel Aviv, its shores are notably quieter, though the town itself offers less to travellers.

Named after Theodor Herzl, the founder of modern Zionism, Herzliya started as a small farming community in 1924 and now consists of two main areas separated by Hwy 2. Herzliya Pituach (west of the highway) is where most of the restaurants, shops and beaches are found, whereas central Herzliya, east of the highway, is mainly residential and commercial.

Herzliya Pituach is home to some of Israel's wealthiest residents and foreign ambassadors (evident in the villas), as well as being one of Israel's leading high-tech industry hubs, home to companies such as Apple, Microsoft and Amazon. *Pituach*, by the way, means 'development'.

☉ Sights

★ **Herzliya Beach** BEACH

(🅿) The long stretch of white sandy beaches from the marina to the Apollonia National Park is the main pull for people coming to Herzliya. Thanks to its sheer width, it offers more space than the sometimes crowded beaches of Tel Aviv, and it is still lined with seafront bars, hotels and the odd surf shack.

At the southern end of the beach is the marina with its slightly dated Arena shopping mall; to the north side are the stunning sand dunes and jagged cliffs of Apollonia. For those wanting to do more than sunbathing, there's beach volleyball, kayaking and surfing along the shore.

Apollonia National Park NATIONAL PARK

(📷 09-955-0929; adult/child 22/9NIS; ⊙8am-5pm Apr-Sep, to 4pm Oct-Mar, closes 1hr earlier Fri & holidays; 🅿) This picturesque coastal park contains the ruins of a Crusader castle that becomes the venue for open-air concerts during summer weekends. There are some stunning views out over the Mediterranean, and nearby you can see the remains of a Roman villa and the well-kept 13th-century Sidni Ali Mosque.

The park can be reached by a 3km walk up Wingate St or easily by car from Hwy 2 (Kfar Shemaryahu junction), just beyond

Around Tel Aviv

0 ——— 5 km
0 ——— 2.5 miles

Alexander Stream
National Park (8km);
Mikhmoret
Beach (9km);
Haifa (64km)

Netanya

Tulkarem

57

2 Separation Wall
Section

MEDITERRANEAN
SEA

4

6

Apollonia
National
Park

Rishpon

Ra'anana

Kfar
Sava

Herzliya
Pituach

Herzliya 531

20

Ramat
HaSharon

Tel Aviv
University

5

B'nei
Brak

Kafr
Qasim

Tel Aviv

Petah
Tikva

Jaffa

Ramat Gan

6

Bat
Yam

Holon

1

Ben Gurion
International
Airport

WEST
BANK

2

Rishon
LeZion

Lod

4311

Palmachim

Ramla

431

1

4

Rehovot

Jerusalem
(45km)

6

the small town of Nof Yam. There are also picnic grounds and grassy sand dunes in the adjacent Hof Hasharon National Park – great for a day out with children.

✖ Eating

There are many restaurants for all budgets around the marina, on the beach and further inland in the business district.

★ Zozobra

ASIAN $$

(✆ 09-957-7077; www.zozobra.co.il; 7 Shenkar St; mains 49-83NIS; ✆ noon-midnight) Much more than a noodle bar, Zozobra is based on the concept of top Israeli chef Avi Conforti and his love of Eastern cuisine. It offers the usual papaya salads and pad thai dishes, but there's also Korean, Indian and Japanese influences here. Diners sit at long communal tables.

Derby Bar

SEAFOOD $$$

(✆ 09-951-1818; http://derbybar.co.il; Arena Mall; pasta 69-89NIS, mains 99-135NIS; ✆ noon-midnight; 🐾) If you like looking at expensive yachts while eating your shrimp, then this restaurant is for you. Attached to the sometimes noisy Arena shopping mall, Derby has an expansive waterside terrace where it serves seafood, fish and pasta dishes. Beer is the usual accompaniment – there are six brands on tap.

🍸 Drinking & Nightlife

Yam Bar

BAR

(✆ 09-959-7102; www.facebook.com/YamBar Herzliya; 100 Ramat Yam St; ✆ 5pm-2am) At the northern end of Herzliya, Yam Bar is all about the beachfront location. Set on a wooden deck, just metres away from the sand, it's a relaxed place to watch the Mediterranean sunset with a cold beer. Happy hour is from 5pm to 8.30pm.

ℹ Getting There & Away

Metropoline bus 90 leaves from Tel Aviv's Carmelit Terminal and Arlozorov St every 20 minutes (9NIS, 30 minutes). Egged buses 501, 502, 524, 525 and 531 leave from Tel Aviv Central Bus Station (10.90NIS, 30 minutes). Trains run every 20 minutes (10NIS, 10 minutes). The train station is quite far from the beach, so take a taxi or bus 29 (7NIS) to the marina.

Holon

حولون   חולון

✆ 03 / POP 188,834

The working-class city of Holon, situated about 7km southeast of Jaffa, is working hard to transform itself into a national cultural hub, and the opening of the Design Museum and its surrounding cultural centre have certainly rejuvenated the city. With parks and a children's museum, Holon makes for a fun family day trip. Founded on sand dunes in the 1930s, Holon is home to 400 of the world's remaining 800 Samaritans (the rest live near Nablus, on the West Bank).

◉ Sights

★ Design Museum Holon

MUSEUM

(✆ 073 215-1500; www.dmh.org.il; 8 Pinhas Eilon St; adult/child 11-17yr/child 5-10yr 35/30/20NIS; ✆ 10am-4pm Mon & Wed, to 6pm Tue, Thu & Sat, to 2pm Fri; 🅿; 🚌 89, 71) Ron Arad's elongated and extremely elegant swirl of red concrete and steel is one of Greater Tel Aviv's most striking examples of contemporary architecture. Inside, the museum includes two spaces that house regularly refreshed temporary exhibitions showcasing fashion, furniture and other design. Collections cover contemporary and historical design from around the world. There's also a cafe and design store.

Israel Children's Museum

MUSEUM

(✆ 03-650-3000; www.childrensmuseum.org. il; Mifratz Shlomo St, Peres Park; per experience 50-65NIS; ✆ 9am-1pm Sun, Mon & Fri, 9am-1pm

& 4-8pm Tue, Wed & Thu, 10am-1.30pm Sat; ⓅⒶ; ⓆDan 89, 96, 163, 172, 201) An experiential, interactive and educational museum for children aged 2½ to 11, the children's museum includes a magic forest (which covers emotions), kingdom of time (looking at growth and change) and butterfly enclosure for toddlers, as well as a cool aliens experience (set in a space ship) for older children. Advance bookings are essential.

❶ Getting There & Away

A number of buses run from Tel Aviv to Holon, including Dan bus 3 from Allenby St, Dan bus 89 from Ibn Gabirol St or Tel Aviv Central Bus Station or Egged bus 71 from the Arlozorov Terminal. From Rishon LeZion, take bus 2. Alternatively, it's a 15-minute taxi ride from the centre of Tel Aviv, which costs around 70NIS. Unfortunately, Holon's Wolfson Train Station is a long way from the centre of town.

Netanya   נתניה   نتانيا

▶09 / POP 192,160

Netanya offers the widest, cleanest and best beaches in Israel. While the city itself – the self-titled 'Israeli Riviera' – may feel like an old European seaside resort, its seafront is much more peaceful than its southern counterparts. Once popular with elderly visitors (especially French, British and Russian), Netanya is now starting to lure younger crowds. The spacious promenade with its children's parks, flower beds and water features, plus live music shows in the town's square, and a few lively bars, are helping to give Netanya a new lease of life.

◉ Sights

Israelis come from all over to enjoy Netanya's expansive golden **beaches**. There are lifeguards on duty, plus changing rooms, showers, lounge chairs and umbrellas. HaRishonim Promenade, the cliff above the beach, is great for strolling and sea views.

★**Netanya Beach**   BEACH
One of Israel's best-kept and most beautiful beaches, Netanya is actually a string of 12km-long sandy shores. The further you walk away from the city centre, the less crowded the beaches become. During weekdays these beaches offer ample space, but expect more crowds on the weekends. The promenade is decorated with flower beds and water fountains and has a good bicycle path. There's an elevator down to the main beach at the end of Herzl St.

THE WEIZMANN INSTITUTE OF SCIENCE

The world-renowned **Weizmann Institute of Science** (▶08-934-4499; www.weizmann. ac.il; 234 Herzl St, Rehovot; visitor centre free, garden adult/child 30/20NIS; house 20/15NIS; ☺visitor centre 9am-4pm Sun-Thu, garden 10am-4pm Mon-Thu, to 1pm Fri) is an educational campus open to the public, comprising a visitors centre, ecological gardens and the Weizmann House. One of the highlights for visitors is the **Clore Garden of Science**, an outdoor science museum with a glass ecosphere. Its hands-on exhibits explore solar energy, water power and other natural phenomena. The **Levinson Visitors Centre** has a multimedia exhibition about the institute's work and offers free walking tours around the campus in English or Hebrew.

Named after the first president of Israel, Chaim Weizmann, a leading research chemist and statesman, it was established in 1934 on moshav (cooperative settlement) land. The institute now provides facilities for cutting-edge research in fields such as biology, chemistry, biochemistry, physics and computer science.

Also on the institute's grounds, next to the tombs of Chaim Weizmann and his wife, Vera, is Weizmann House. Designed by German architect Erich Mendelsohn, a refugee from Nazism, the house was built in 1936–37. There is a museum inside displaying his personal collection of photos, books and memorabilia, notably his passport (the first in Israel). During WWI, Weizmann's scientific research proved invaluable to the Allied war effort, and the goodwill he generated may have influenced Britain's granting of the Balfour Declaration in 1917.

It's best to call in advance if you want to visit any of the institute's attractions.

The campus is in Rehovot, 25km south of Tel Aviv. You can get there by train from any Tel Aviv station. From the train station it's a 10-minute walk to the institute. You can also catch an Egged bus 201 or 301 (12.40NIS, 45 minutes, frequent) from the Central Bus Station.

Mikhmoret Beach
BEACH

(ℙ) Mikhmoret is a spectacular beach, where acres of sand dunes run alongside the Mediterranean coast. Also a residential moshav (cooperative settlement), it's a calm spot to while away a day. The beach is well equipped with showers and a shack selling food. Thanks to its sea breezes, it's also popular with kite flyers. The beach is 9km north of Netanya.

Alexander Stream National Park
NATIONAL PARK

(☑ 09-866-6230; www.parks.org.il; ☉ 8am-5pm Apr & Oct, to 6pm May & Sep, to 7pm Jul & Aug; ℙ) **FREE** This nature reserve is located on the expansive white sand dunes where the Alexander stream meets the Mediterranean Sea. Believe it or not, these shallow streams are home to the largest population of soft-shell turtles in the country. The population of turtles is in decline, but you can still view these lovable creatures from 'Turtle Bridge', a definite hit with the kids.

The park also comprises the remains of a 19th-century Ottoman lookout on a hill and Beit Yanai beach, which has a campsite (48NIS per vehicle per night). Not accessible by public transport, the park is a 15-minute drive north of Netanya on Hwy 2.

🛏 Sleeping

Hotel Orit
HOTEL $$

(☑ 09-861-6818, 054 657-9212; www.hotelorit.com; 21 Sderot Chen St; s/d 300/370NIS) Unlike most of the other hotels in Netanya, Orit is a cute, homely place that's slightly out of the city centre in a peaceful, residential area. Run by a friendly Swedish family, Orit offers a delicious Scandinavian-Israeli breakfast – muesli, followed by eggs, cheeses, salads and hummus. The simple but comfortable rooms come with fridges, and some have small balconies.

The hotel has a nicely kept garden and is just a 400m walk from the city centre and a 50m walk to the beach.

🍴 Eating

The main strip that runs down to Ha'Atzmaut Sq and the seafront, Herzl St, is lined with cafes and restaurants.

Marrakesh
MOROCCAN $$

(☑ 09-833-4797; 5 David HaMelech St; mains 60-125NIS; ☉ noon-midnight Sun-Thu, noon-3.30pm Fri, 8pm-midnight Sat) Tuck into tasty tagines, couscous and meat dishes in this kosher Moroccan restaurant near the seafront. The building is a cross between a giant tagine pot and a Bedouin tent; inside it is decorated with exotic lanterns and comfy cushions.

ℹ Information

The helpful **tourist office** (☑ 09-882-7286; www.gonetanya.com; Ha'Atzmaut Sq 12; ☉ 8.30am-4pm Sun-Thu, 9am-noon Fri) is housed in a kiosk at the southwestern corner of Ha'Atzmaut Sq.

ℹ Getting There & Away

Nateev Express buses (600, 601 and 605, 11NIS, 30 minutes) run roughly every 15 minutes to and from Tel Aviv's Central Bus Station and up Namir Rd (Hwy 2). Trains to/from Tel Aviv run twice an hour (13.50NIS, 25 minutes) but stop at the **train station** 2.5km west of the city centre, on the western side of Hwy 2. One of the best ways to reach Netanya is to take a sherut (yellow minivan) from Arlozorov Bus Terminal on Namir Rd (20NIS, 25 minutes).

Ramla
רמלה الرملة

☑ 03 / POP 73,686

It's not quite as old as nearby Jaffa – history here stretches back 'only' 1300 years – but Ramla's bustling market, underground pools and crumbling Islamic architecture make it an interesting half-day trip. Try to visit on a Wednesday, when the market is at its busiest.

Established in 716 CE by the Umayyid caliph Suleiman, Ramla ('Spot of Sand') was a stopover on the road from Egypt to Damascus. Before the arrival of the Crusaders in the 11th century, it was Palestine's capital and maintained its importance in the Middle Ages as the first stop for the Jerusalem-bound pilgrims who came ashore at Jaffa. Following the 1948 Arab–Israeli War, the majority of the Arab population was expelled or fled and was replaced by poor Jewish immigrants, mainly from Asia and North Africa. The population is now a mix of Muslim Arabs (16%), Christian Arabs (4%) and Jews (80%).

◉ Sights

★ Pool of Al Anazia
HISTORIC SITE

(Breichat Hakeshatot; ☑ 08-921-6873; www.goramla.com; HaHaganah St; adult/concession 14/12NIS; ☉ 8am-4pm Sat-Thu, to 2pm Fri, also to 6pm Wed & Thu Jun-Aug; ℙ) Atmospheric and shaded by ancient stone structures, the 'Pool of Arches'

Ramla

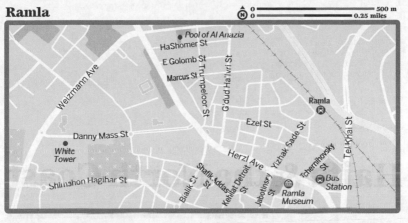

is an underground 8th-century reservoir. The most significant structure left from the Abbasid period, it is sometimes called the Pool of St Helena in reference to the Christian idea that the Empress Helena, mother of Constantine I, ordered its construction. Visitors explore the structure by rowboat, which is included in the price.

Ramla Museum   MUSEUM
(☑08-929-2650; 112 Herzl Ave; adult/concession 12/10NIS; ◷10am-4pm Sun-Thu, to 1pm Fri) Housed in a building dating from the British Mandate, this small museum provides an overview of the town's history. Exhibits include locally excavated gold coins from the 8th to 15th century, a collection of traditional products of Arab soap manufacture from the early 20th century and a display on the 1948 Arab–Israeli War in and around Ramla.

White Tower   HISTORIC SITE
(☑08-921-6873; Danny Mass St; adult/concession 10/9NIS; ◷8am-4pm Sat-Thu, to 2pm Fri; ℗) Experts can't agree whether this 14th-century tower was built as a minaret or a watchtower. One indisputable fact is that the 30m-high structure was built as an addition to the 8th-century White Mosque (Jamaa Al Abiad), of which only traces remain. The site includes three now-dry cisterns and the shrine of Nabi Salih, an ancient prophet mentioned in the Quran.

ⓘ Getting There & Away

Trains to Ramla (11NIS, 25 minutes) from Tel Aviv depart every 20 minutes throughout the day. Ramla Train Station is just a few minutes' walk from the Old City. Buses 450 and 451 depart from Tel Aviv's Central Bus Station every 20 minutes (15NIS, 40 minutes) and arrive at Ramla Bus Station on Herzl Ave.

Haifa & the North Coast

Best Places to Eat

➜ Uri Buri (p190)

➜ Ma'ayan HaBira (p171)

➜ Ein El Wadi (p172)

➜ Helena (p185)

➜ Nili Restaurant (p181)

Best Places to Stay

➜ Villa Carmel (p167)

➜ Bat Galim Hotel (p170)

➜ Port Inn (p170)

➜ Efendi Hotel (p190)

➜ Grushka Country Accommodation (p185)

Why Go?

On Israel's north coast, ancient history peeps out between the palm trees. Sandy beaches run parallel to the cobalt-blue Mediterranean, luring surfers and sunbathers to their breezy shores. But beach life is a blink of the eye in this historic area: in Caesarea, the well-conserved ruins of Herod's ambitious port stand proud against the sea, while life continues in the labyrinthine, centuries-old alleys in walled Akko.

The largest city is Haifa, a spirited port with a mixed Jewish and Arab population – and home to the region's star sight, the Baha'i Gardens. Sprawling across Mt Carmel, Haifa simmers with art, culture and fast-paced nightlife. Venture inland to the catacombs of Beit She'arim or biblical end-times location Megiddo. For art and wine, Ein Hod and Zichron Ya'akov deserve exploration. Spare time to ponder all you've seen within the luminous sea grottoes of Rosh HaNikra or by a golden beach in Akhziv.

When to Go

Haifa

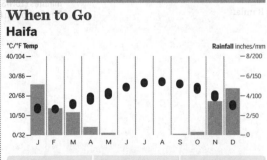

Apr & May Temperatures are pleasant and the Baha'i Gardens are in full bloom.

Jul & Aug Seek refuge from the summer heat in arty Ein Hod or Zichron Ya'akov's well-shaded bars.

Dec On weekends, join Haifa's carnival of united Jewish, Christian and Muslim celebration.

Haifa

חיפה, حيفا

📷 04 / POP 278,900

Haifa's neighbourhoods form an intriguing kaleidoscope: its smart German Colony, teeming Arab-Christian quarter and edgy Masada St each add their own verve to the port city.

Posing above roaring traffic and dockside bustle is Haifa's most celebrated sight, a Baha'i shrine and tropical gardens. Tumbling down the flanks of Mt Carmel (546m), the gardens bestow a radiant symmetry on this complex city, whose atmosphere can change from placid to fast-paced in the space of a few steps.

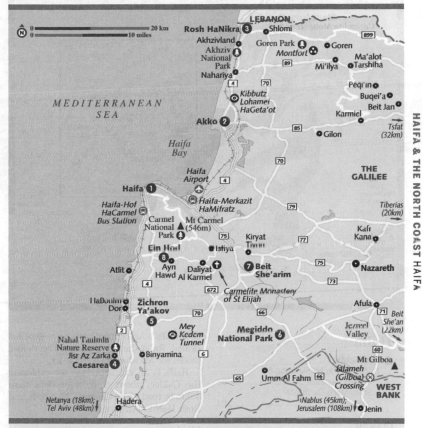

HAIFA & THE NORTH COAST HAIFA

Haifa & the North Coast Highlights

1 **Baha'i Gardens** (p159) Marvelling at perfectly groomed gardens that tumble down towards the Mediterranean.

2 **Akko** (p185) Exploring vaulted halls and hidden tunnels left by the Crusaders in this walled seaside city.

3 **Rosh HaNikra** (p193) Feeling lulled by the rise and fall of the sea within gleaming limestone grottoes.

4 **Caesarea** (p182) Imagining the roar of spectators as you stroll the amphitheatre of Herod's grandiose port city.

5 **Zichron Ya'akov** (p180) Clinking glasses of local wine in a chic 19th-century village on the flanks of Mt Carmel.

6 **Megiddo National Park** (p180) Scanning the horizon for signs of Armageddon at this atmospheric biblical site.

7 **Beit She'arim** (p177) Ducking into centuries-old burial caves, still daubed with mysterious inscriptions.

8 **Ein Hod** (p177) Getting eccentric with local artists in a village that doubles as an open-air gallery.

Haifa

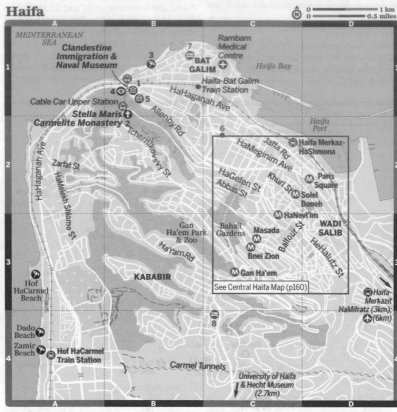

Haifa

◎ Top Sights

◎ Sights

◆ Activities, Courses & Tours

◉ Sleeping

British planners intended Haifa to serve as the Levant's main port and transport hub. That vision ended in 1948, when much of the city's Arab population were expelled or fled. Today the city is proud to serve as a model for Jewish-Arab coexistence.

Haifa is an excellent base for exploring the Galilee, about equidistant (less than 45km by road) from Caesarea, Nazareth, and Rosh HaNikra Grottoes.

History

There has been a port on the site of modern-day Haifa since at least as far back as the 14th century BC. During the Roman period, both before and after the destruction of the Second Temple (AD 70), Haifa was a mixed Jewish-Gentile town that garnered more than 100 mentions in the Talmud; because its residents did not pronounce the guttural Hebrew letters *het* and *'ayin* properly, they were not called upon to recite the Torah in public. Mt Carmel, whose name means 'vineyard of God', has been regarded as sacred since ancient times.

A thousand years ago, Haifa was a fortified, mainly Jewish town. In 1100, after it fell to the Crusaders, its Jewish and Egyptian defenders were put to the sword. Nearby Akko soon superseded Haifa in importance, and by the time of the Ottoman conquest of Palestine in the 1500s, Haifa was an insignificant village. The old city was destroyed and rebuilt by the bay, becoming 'new Haifa' (Haifa Al Jadida), growing into a major export centre for Palestine.

By the early 19th century, Haifa's industry had grown, along with its Sephardic Jewish community. In 1868 the German Templers moved in, and later that century the city became renowned as a Baha'i centre of faith when the remains of central figure the Báb were reinterred here. The city's modern revival really got under way in 1905 with the opening of a railway line linking Haifa with Damascus and, three years later, Medina. In September 1918, as British forces pushed north, three platoons of Indian horsemen, armed only with lances, overran Ottoman machine-gun positions.

During the British Mandate, Haifa rapidly became Palestine's main port, naval centre, rail-transport hub and oil terminal. The Technion-Israel Institute of Technology, whose graduates and professors would go on to win four Nobel Prizes in chemistry, opened its doors in 1924. From the 1920s to the 1950s, Haifa was the first sight of the Promised Land for many ship-borne Jewish refugees, who gradually transformed Haifa's population from majority Muslim to almost half Jewish. Arab-Israeli tensions brewed attacks from extremists on both sides. In April 1948, shortly before the British withdrawal, Haifa fell to Jewish forces and as many as 65,000 of the city's Arab residents fled or were forced to leave.

For the next three decades Haifa was a proletarian powerhouse though its socialist ideology had largely ebbed away by the 1980s. Today the focus has shifted from heavy industry to technology and electronics; an IT park near Haifa-Hof HaCarmel bus station is home to divisions of Google, Intel, IBM and other international high-tech heavyweights.

These days the mostly secular Jewish community enjoys a generally good relationship with the city's Arab population (10% of the total), which is mainly Christian.

⊙ Sights

⊙ Carmel Centre

The ridge line of Mt Carmel, with its exclusive residences and pine-shaded parks, overlooks the Mediterranean to the west and Haifa Bay to the northeast. The area's finest views are from Yefe Nof St, which roughly parallels HaNassi Ave and leads to the Baha'i Gardens.

The area's focal point – especially for dining, nightlife and commerce – is Carmel Centre (Merkaz HaCarmel), strung out along HaNassi Ave (Sderot HaNassi). The altitude ensures that it's always a few degrees cooler up here than down around the port.

Carmel Centre is linked to Hadar and Downtown (Paris Sq) by the Carmelit (under repairs at the time of research); the stop up here is called Gan HaEm. From the German colony, take buses 28, 37 or 37א.

★ **Baha'i Gardens** GARDENS
(Map p160; ☎04-831-3131; www.ganbahai.org.il; 45 Yefe Nof St, Panorama Tour; ⊙lower gardens 9am-5pm, closed Baha'i holidays & Yom Kippur; **P**) **FREE** These formal gardens flowing down 19 steep terraces to a resplendent domed shrine – the final resting place of the prophet-herald of the Baha'i faith – are Haifa's crowning attraction. There are bird's-eye views from the platform (Map p160; 61 Yefe Nof St; ⊙9am-5pm) at the top, but we highly recommend the free, 45-minute Panorama Tour. Tours begin daily (except Wednesday) at 11.30am in Hebrew and noon in English. Arrive half an hour ahead as it's first come, first served. Men and women must be covered from shoulders to knees.

The gardens are tended by the Baha'i World Centre, the religion's global headquarters. Emerald lawns and bright flower beds ripple down to the Shrine of the Báb (p161), which is even more dazzling against a backdrop of deep blue Haifa Bay. Completed in 1953, this glinting dome guards the mortal remains of the Báb, the spiritual predecessor to the Baha'i faith's main prophet Baha'ullah. After persecution and imprisonment, the Báb was executed in Persia in 1850 and his remains were secretly kept by his followers. They were brought to Haifa in 1909 and Baha'ullah chose this spot for the Báb's burial place. Combining the style and proportions of European architecture with motifs inspired by Eastern traditions, it was

HAIFA & THE NORTH COAST HAIFA

Central Haifa

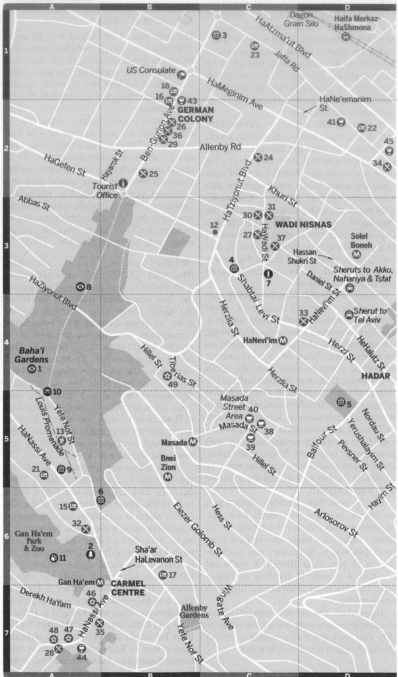

Central Haifa

- HaAtzma'ut Blvd
- Dagon Grain Silo
- Haifa Merkaz-HaShmona
- 3
- 23
- Jaffa Rd
- HaMeginim Ave
- US Consulate
- 18
- 16
- 43
- HaNe'emanim St
- 41
- 22
- 45
- GERMAN COLONY
- Ben-Gurion Ave
- 26
- 36
- 29
- Allenby Rd
- 24
- 34
- HaGefen St
- Hayarok St
- 25
- Tourist Office
- Abbas St
- HaTziyonut Blvd
- Khuri St
- 30
- 31
- WADI NISNAS
- 27
- 37
- HaWadi St
- Solel Boneh
- 12
- 4
- 7
- Hassan Shukri St
- Sheruts to Akko, Nahariya & Tsfat
- HaZiyonut Blvd
- 8
- Shabtai Levi St
- Herzlia St
- Daniel St
- 33
- HaNevi'im St
- Sherut to Tel Aviv
- Baha'i Gardens
- 1
- Hillel St
- Tiberias St
- HaNevi'im
- Herzl St
- Herzlia St
- Hetalutz St
- HADAR
- 10
- Louis Promenade
- Yefe Nof St
- 13
- 49
- Masada Street Area
- 40
- Masada St
- 38
- 5
- Nordau St
- Yerushalayim St
- HaNassi Ave
- 21
- 9
- Masada
- 39
- Hillel St
- Baltour St
- Pevsner St
- Bnei Zion
- 6
- 15
- 32
- Elezer Golomb St
- Hess St
- Arlosorov St
- Hayim St
- Gan Ha'em Park & Zoo
- 11
- 2
- Sha'ar HaLevanon St
- 17
- Gan Ha'em
- CARMEL CENTRE
- Derekh HaYam
- 46
- HaNassi Ave
- Allenby Gardens
- Wingate Ave
- Yefe Nof St
- 48
- 47
- 35
- 28
- 44

HAIFA & THE NORTH COAST HAIFA

designed by a Canadian architect, built with Italian stone and decorated with Portuguese fire-glazed tiles.

Framing the shrine, the gardens were laid out on the slopes of Mt Carmel between 1989 and 2001. They were given Unesco World Heritage status in 2008 along with Akko's Shrine of Baha'ullah (p189). Impressively symmetrical, the well-tended terraces have a regal feel: gurgling fountains, flower beds, stone eagles, hedges trimmed into eight-pointed stars, and lawns with barely a blade of grass out of place. (Suddenly, the stringent rules of conduct – no food, no smoking, no setting foot on the lawns – make a whole lot of sense.) The gardens are illuminated throughout the night, a spiritual solace for the Báb's years of imprisonment in near-darkness; you can enjoy this sparkling view from the German Colony.

Buildings (closed to the public) around the gardens include the **Universal House of Justice**, a domed neoclassical structure with Corinthian columns from which the Baha'is' spiritual and administrative affairs are governed; and the **Archives**, in a green-roofed structure that looks like the Parthenon, in which are kept more than 100 different translations of the Kitáb-I-Aqdas, the holy book of the Baha'i faith.

To get to the start of the Panorama Tour from Carmel Centre (the Carmelit's Gan HaEm stop), walk 1km north along Yefe Nof St, which affords the city's finest bay views. Alternatively, from Bat Galim Egged bus 136 zigzags via Ben Gurion Blvd up to HaNassi Ave (parallel to Yefe Nof). The tour finishes down on HaTziyonut Blvd – to get back up to Carmel Centre, there is usually a sherut (10NIS) waiting; count on paying about 30NIS for a taxi. Bus 115 links the lower entrance on HaTziyonut Blvd with Haifa-Hof HaCarmel bus station and Talpiot market.

Note that the line for the Panorama Tour can be long when there's a cruise liner or US Navy ship in port. Admission is limited to 60 people (120 if there are two guides available). See the website for a monthly schedule of less regular tours in Russian and Arabic.

Shrine of the Báb SHRINE
(Map p160; www.ganbahai.org.il; 80 HaTziyonut Blvd; ⊙9am-noon, closed Baha'i holidays & Yom Kippur) Though it's primarily a pilgrimage site, modestly dressed visitors are allowed to enter this domed shrine holding the remains of the Báb, spiritual predecessor to the Baha'i faith's main prophet Baha'ullah.

Central Haifa

Canadian architect William Sutherland Maxwell designed the shrine to unify Middle Eastern and European styles. It was built in 1953 with Italian stone and covered Portuguese glazed tiles.

After persecution and imprisonment, the Báb was executed in Persia in 1850 and his body kept by his followers until it was re-interred at this spot, chosen by Baha'ullah.

Louis Promenade   VIEWPOINT
(Map p160; Mt Carmel) A 15-minute walking path running parallel to Yefe Nof St, Louis Promenade offers lofty views over Haifa Bay and connects to other trails that thread their way around Haifa. A worthy photo op for aerial views; visit at sunset.

Tikotin Museum of Japanese Art   MUSEUM
(Map p160; ☎04-838-3554; www.tmja.org.il; 89 HaNassi Ave; adult/child 35/23NIS; ⊙10am-7pm Sat-Thu, to 1pm Fri) Founded in 1959 by art collector Felix Tikotin, this small, low-lit gallery immerses visitors in the sensory qualities of Japanese art. A visit here is best suited to Japanese art aficionados, though its 19th-century hanging scrolls, glazed bowls and calligraphy create a calming change of pace compared to Haifa's other major museums. The upper floor has a pleasant canteen selling homemade cakes.

Mané–Katz Museum   MUSEUM
(Map p160; www.mkm.org.il; 89 Yefe Nof St; adult/child 35/23NIS; ⊙10am-4pm Sun-Wed, to 1pm Fri, to 3pm Sat, 4-7pm Thu) Ukraine-born artist Emmanuel Mané-Katz (1894–1962) was an influential member of the early-20th-century School of Paris and is best known for his colourful depictions of the *shtetls* (ghettos) of Eastern Europe. In the late 1950s he was given this home by the Haifa city authorities in return for the bequest of his works. Hundreds of his paintings are displayed inside, alongside antiques and Judaica.

The museum closes down between temporary exhibitions, though its garden cafe remains open. Check the website for details before you go.

Gan Ha'Em
PARK

(Map p160; HaNassi Ave; ☉ 6am-9pm, all night Thu & Fri) Sculpted on the crest of Mt Carmel in 1913, this shady, kid-friendly public garden – whose name means 'Mother's Park' – has a zoo, a playground and an amphitheatre that hosts free concerts on some summer evenings. It's located across from the upper terminus of the Carmelit metro line.

Zoo
ZOO

(Haifa Educational Zoo; Map p160; www.haifa-zoo.co.il; HaNassi Ave; adult/student 38/25NIS; ☉ 9am-6pm Sat-Thu, to 2pm Sat Apr-Oct, 9am-4pm Sat-Thu, to 1pm Sat Nov-Mar; ℙ) The shaded slopes below Gan Ha'Em are home to a compact zoo with free-roaming peacocks, an aviary, a reptile house and habitats for monkeys, meerkats, ibexes, deer and more, though enclosures for larger animals like bears and Bengal tigers seem rather small.

◉ German Colony

Situated directly below – and in alignment with – the Baha'i Gardens, Ben-Gurion Ave is lined with handsome 19th-century houses with steep, red-shingled roofs and quotes from the Bible – in German – over the doors. This is the German Colony, established in 1868 by the Templers (not to be confused with the Crusader-era Knights Templar), a Pietist Protestant sect from southwestern Germany that sought to hasten the Second Coming by settling in the Holy Land. In the latter decades of the 1800s, the Templers built seven colonies in Palestine and are credited with introducing improved methods of transport, technology and agriculture.

The German Colony (Moshava Germanit in Hebrew) impressed Baha'ullah, the founder of the Baha'i faith, and was visited by Germany's Kaiser Wilhelm II in 1898. The Templers continued to live in the colony until 1939, when the British interned them as enemy aliens (many had joined the Nazi Party in the 1930s); most were later deported to Australia.

Today the German Colony is one of Haifa's premier dining areas. Look up the hill and you'll see the Baha'i Gardens (p159), down the hill and you can often see cargo ships docked in the port. Metronit bus lines 1 and 2 stop right nearby.

Haifa City Museum
MUSEUM

(Map p160; ☏ 04-911-5888; www.hcm.org.il; 11 Ben-Gurion Ave; adult/child 35/23NIS; ☉ 10am-4pm Sun-Wed, 4-7pm Thu, 10am-1pm Fri, to 3pm Sat) Split across two buildings, the City Museum examines Haifa's last century of history and features rotating exhibitions on contemporary life here. Most interesting are the displays characterising Haifa as the 'Red City' in the decades following the 1940s when Haifa had a strong socialist ideology.

◉ Wadi Nisnas

This village-like, mainly Christian Arab neighbourhood, in a little valley midway between Hadar and the German Colony, retains the feel of the old Middle East, with narrow lanes, stone buildings and a bustling food market.

Beit HaGefen Cultural Center
CULTURAL

(Map p160; ☏ 04-852-5252; www.beit-hagefen.com; 2 HaGefen St; tours from 40NIS; ☉ gallery 10am-3pm, to 2pm Fri & Sat) FREE In an old stone building across the street from the modern Beit HaGefen Arab–Jewish Center, this gallery-cum-social space sponsors interfaith social and cultural activities; call ahead to arrange two-hour tours of street art, neighbourhoods and spiritual sites.

The upstairs gallery puts on exhibitions related to intercultural coexistence and shared spaces and values.

Museum Without Walls
PUBLIC ART

(Map p160; www.mwwart.com; HaWadi St) FREE More than 60 open-air murals and sculptures form a route through the lanes and alleys of Wadi Nisnas, from superhero murals to mixed-media sculptures and pop art. Some are large and eye-catching, others so small you could walk right past them; find a map on the helpful website.

Haifa Museum of Art
MUSEUM

(Map p160; ☏ 04-911-5997; www.hms.org.il; 26 Shabtai Levi St; adult/child 45/30NIS; ☉ 10am-4pm Sun-Wed, to 1pm Fri, to 3pm Sat, 4-7pm Thu) Challenging and contemporary, the Museum of Art's three exhibition spaces showcase mixed media and photography by Israeli

❶ HAIFA MUSEUM TICKET

Museum aficionados can save some major money with a combo ticket (adult/student 60/30NIS) valid for a week at six Haifa exhibition spaces: the Mané-Katz Museum, the Tikotin Museum of Japanese Art, the Haifa Museum of Art, the Haifa City Museum, the National Maritime Museum (p165) and the Hermann Struck Museum. The pass is sold at each of the six museums.

THE BAHA'I FAITH

Founded in the middle of the 19th century, the Baha'i faith (www.bahai.org) believes that many prophets have appeared throughout history, including Abraham, Moses, Buddha, Krishna, Zoroaster, Jesus and Muhammad. Its central beliefs include the existence of one God, the unity of all religions, and the equality and unity of all human beings, including men and women (a truly revolutionary idea in Iran in the mid-1800s).

The origins of the Baha'i faith go back to Ali Muhammad (1819–50), a native of Shiraz, Iran. In 1844 he declared that he was 'the Báb' (Gate) through which prophecies would be revealed. The charismatic Ali was soon surrounded by followers, called Babis, but was eventually arrested for heresy against Islam and after years of imprisonment was executed by firing squad in Tabriz, Iran.

One of the Báb's prophecies concerned the coming of 'one whom God would make manifest'. In 1866, a Babi named Mirza Hussein Ali (1817–92) proclaimed that he was this prophetic figure and assumed the title of Baha'ullah, having received divine inspiration while imprisoned in Tehran's infamous Black Pit.

As with the Báb, Baha'ullah's declarations were unwelcome in Persia and he was expelled first to Baghdad, and then to Constantinople, Adrianople and finally the Ottoman penal colony of Akko. Sitting in his cell in Akko, he dedicated himself to laying down the tenets of a new faith, the Baha'i, whose name is derived from the Arabic word *baha* (glory).

Among his writings, Baha'ullah stated that one could not be born into the Baha'i faith; at the age of 15, a person chooses whether or not they want to take on the obligations of being Baha'i. He also spoke of gender equality, the oneness of humankind, world peace, the need for universal compulsory education, and harmony between religion and the sciences.

The Baha'i World Centre (the religion's global headquarters), famed for its gardens (p159), is on Haifa's Mt Carmel, while the holiest Baha'i site, the Shrine of Baha'ullah (p189), is near Akko; both are staffed by volunteers from around the world. Baha'is do not believe in proselytising their faith so they do not seek converts in Israel, nor is there any official Baha'i community in Israel.

The Baha'i faith now has an estimated five to six million followers worldwide. Tradition prescribes that a Baha'i who is able should make a pilgrimage to Akko and Haifa.

and international artists. If you enjoy confrontational artwork and lively debate, this airy gallery is well worth exploring (plus you can people-watch the local artistic community, who come here in droves to stroll and scratch their chins).

⊙ Hadar

Established as a 'garden city' in 1920, Hadar HaCarmel (Hadar for short) became Haifa's bustling commercial heart in the 1930s, when some superb Bauhaus buildings were constructed. Among the area's architectural gems is **Beit HaKranot**, on the northwestern corner of the intersection of Balfour and Herzl Sts – a grand office building dating to 1939. Nearby shops sell inexpensive and midrange clothing, accessories and shoes – and books in Russian.

Hadar is one of this diverse city's most diverse neighbourhoods. Over a third of the residents are immigrants from the former Soviet Union (especially Ukraine) and a quarter are Arabs; Hadar also has small ultra-Orthodox and Filipino communities.

The district occupies the lower slopes of Mt Carmel; Herzl St, the main drag, is about 1km south of Paris Sq and 1.6km northeast of Carmel Centre. The Carmelit's HaNevi'im stop is at the northwestern end of Herzl St, which – along with parallel HeHalutz St – is linked to both central bus stations by bus 115 and to Haifa-Hof HaCarmel by bus 112.

MadaTech MUSEUM
(National Museum of Science; Map p160; ☑04-861-4444; www.madatech.org.il; 25 Shemaryahu Levin St, Hadar; adult/child 75/65NIS; ☺10am-3pm Sun-Wed, to 5pm Thu & Sat, to 1pm Fri; P ♣) Kid-friendly science exhibits fill this elegant 1912 building, including hands-on displays in the astronomy rooms, optical illusions and a hall of mirrors (exhibits are labelled with the appropriate age group). The building was the first home of the Technion–Israel

Institute and its soaring arches and echoing hallways are a delight to wander. When Albert Einstein visited in 1923, he planted a palm tree that still stands out front.

◉ Stella Maris

★ **Stella Maris Carmelite Monastery**   CHURCH
(Map p158; ⊙6.30am-12.30pm & 3-6pm) The Carmelite Order was established in the late 12th century when Crusader-era pilgrims, inspired by the prophet Elijah, opted for a hermitic life on the slopes of Mt Carmel. Today the order lives on around the world and in the 'Star of the Sea' monastery, whose current building was constructed in 1836 at the northern tip of Mt Carmel. The sea views are magnificent. Wear clothing that covers your knees and shoulders; men should remove hats.

Inside the church, the beautifully painted ceiling and dome portray Elijah and the chariot of fire in which he is said to have ascended to heaven; King David with his harp; the saints of the order; the prophets Isaiah, Ezekiel and David; and the Holy Family with the four evangelists below.

On the path leading to the church entrance, a pyramid with a wrought-iron cross on top serves as a memorial for 200 sick and wounded French troops, hospitalised here, who were slaughtered by the Ottomans after Napoleon returned to Paris in 1799.

The monastery is accessible by cable car from Bat Galim's seafront promenade and by bus 115 from Hadar and Haifa-Hof HaCarmel; by buses 30 and 31 from Carmel Centre; and on foot from near Elijah's Cave.

◉ Maritime Museums & Elijah's Cave

This part of town is served by buses 111 and 112 from the German Colony, Wadi Nisnas and Hadar; bus 111 also goes to Haifa-Hof HaCarmel.

★ **Clandestine Immigration & Naval Museum**   MUSEUM
(Map p158; ☎04-853-6249; http://cng.shimur.org/clandestine-immigration; 204 Allenby Rd; adult/child 15/10NIS; ⊙10am-4pm Sun-Thu; ℗) Using a series of powerful video testimonials, this fascinating museum showcases the Zionist Movement's determined efforts to infiltrate Jewish refugees from Europe into British-blockaded Palestine from 1934

to 1948. The centrepiece is a WWII landing craft rechristened the *Af-Al-Pi-Chen* ('nevertheless' in Hebrew) that carried 434 refugees to Palestine in 1947; intercepted by the British, they were sent to internment camps on Cyprus. The museum is run by the Ministry of Defense, so you'll need your passport to get in.

Most compelling are the testimonials about life on board these surplus war ships; survivors describe gruelling conditions and overcrowding, but also an irrepressible optimism about their hopes of entering the Holy Land. Many never reached it, including the passengers on board the *Exodus:* this vastly overloaded steamer ship carried more than 4500 Holocaust survivors to Palestine in 1947 but was forced by the British to return to Europe.

National Maritime Museum   MUSEUM
(Map p158; ☎04-853-6622; www.nmm.org.il; 198 Allenby Rd; adult/child 35/23NIS; ⊙10am-4pm Sun-Wed, to 1pm Fri, to 3pm Sat, 4-7pm Thu; ℗) This museum, founded in 1953, covers five millennia of maritime history across its three floors, from barnacle-clung amphorae to Israel's recent naval history. Temporary exhibitions on themes from pirates to naval battles rotate on the ground floor, while the archaeological treasures – Egyptian canopic jars and Roman remnants recovered from Haifa Bay – are in the permanent collection above. Explanation is in English and Hebrew.

Elijah's Cave   RELIGIOUS SITE
(Map p158; Allenby Rd; ⊙8am-6pm, to 5pm winter Sun-Thu, to 1pm Fri, closed Sat & Jewish holidays) FREE Holy to Jews, Christians, Muslims and Druze, this cave is where the prophet Elijah is believed to have prayed before challenging the priests of Ba'al on Mt Carmel (1 Kings 18) and where he is said to have hidden from the wrath of Queen Jezebel afterwards (1 Kings 19:1–3). Upon entering, follow the signs to separate sections for men (to the right) and women (to the left); the cave is behind a velvet curtain. There's not much to see unless you're interested in Jewish pilgrimage sites. Dress modestly.

According to Christian tradition, Mary, Joseph and Jesus sheltered here on their return from Egypt. Muslims associate the site with Al Khidr (the Green Prophet), sometimes seen as an Islamic version of Elijah, or as his companion.

To get to Elijah's Cave from the National Maritime Museum, look for the asphalt path leading uphill from Allenby Rd. The path from Stella Maris down to the cave begins from the parking lot across the street from the church, along the fence of the Israeli navy base.

◉ University of Haifa

Perched high atop Mt Carmel, the University of Haifa is 6.5km southeast of Carmel Centre along the Mt Carmel Ridge. Arabs make up more than 30% of the student body, far more than at any other Israeli university.

From Sunday to Thursday when the university is in session, on-campus parking is limited to permit holders, but Hecht Museum visitors are usually waved inside for free.

To get to the university, take buses 37 or 37 from Hadar or Carmel Centre, bus 46 from Haifa-Hof HaCarmel, or buses 141 or 171 from Haifa-Merkazit HaMifratz.

★ Hecht Museum   MUSEUM
(📞04-825-7773; http://mushecht.haifa.ac.il; 199 Abba Hushi Blvd, Haifa University; ⊗10am-4pm Sun, Mon, Wed & Thu, to 7pm Tue, to 1pm Fri, to 2pm Sat; 🅿) FREE This university campus museum showcases engrossing archaeological finds such as well-restored mosaics and troves of ancient coins, but the pièce de résistance is the Ma'agan Mikhael Shipwreck, a 2400-year-old merchant vessel unearthed in 1985. Originally 12.5m long, the ship would have hauled 15 tons of cargo and has a rare one-armed wooden anchor.

Elsewhere, the art wing assembles mostly Impressionist and post-Impressionist works (part of founder Dr Reuben Hecht's own collection), including works by luminaries like Van Gogh and Modigliani.

The Oscar Ghez Collection is a poignant display of the works by 18 Paris-based artists who perished in the Holocaust. Meanwhile, temporary art exhibitions place the spotlight on young artists, portraiture, Israeli art colonies and a host of other themes.

The Hecht Museum is beneath the Eshkol Tower; follow signs to the building's lower floor and then continue along the corridor until you see amphorae.

Eshkol Tower   VIEWPOINT
(www.haifa.ac.il; 199 Abba Hushi Blvd, Haifa University; ⊗hours vary; 🅿) FREE A lift shudders its way up to the 30th-floor observation area of Eshkol Tower, the brazen high-rise topping Haifa University. Designed by renowned

Brazilian architect Oscar Niemeyer, the tower was completed in 1978. It has since been eclipsed as Haifa's tallest building, but the views remain exceptional – who would have thought that hulking Haifa could appear Lilliputian from above? A worthwhile photo op after visiting the Hecht Museum.

🏃 Activities

Bat Galim Beach   BEACH
(Map p158; www.batgalim.org.il; ⊗swimming 8am-6pm) Gentle waves lap the cove of this patrolled sandy beach in northern Haifa, a few blocks northeast of the lower cable-car station. It's small but popular with sunbathers and yogis and there are often enough waves to surf. There are snack stands and toilets.

It's located in the middle-class Bat Galim neighbourhood, the terminus of Metronit line 2, a few hundred metres from Rambam hospital.

Dado Beach   BEACH
(Map p158; off David Elzara St; 🚆Carmel Beach) Long, sandy and with plenty of surf, Dado is one of the great-quality beaches along the western edge of Haifa's headland, near Haifa-Hof HaCarmel station.

Zamir Beach   BEACH
(Map p158) This fine sandy beach on Haifa's western flank is close to several cafes and backed by a pretty promenade.

🍃 Courses

University of Haifa Ulpan   LANGUAGE
(📞04-824-0766; http://overseas.haifa.ac.il; University of Haifa) Some of Israel's most highly regarded university language programs are on offer here. Intensive Hebrew classes run for five or six hours a day Sunday to Thursday for summer courses in July and August (US$1400/2000 for one/two months) while a similarly intensive Arabic course is offered in August (US$1400).

It's possible to arrange dormitory accommodation on campus (from US$320 per month).

Ulpan Aba Hushi   LANGUAGE
(Map p158; 📞04-605-5149; 131 HaMeginim Ave) Intensive five-month, five-day-a-week Hebrew courses.

👉 Tours

Free Tours Haifa   WALKING
(📞058 604-8428; www.facebook.com/freetours haifa; ⊗10.30am most Wed) FREE Enjoy a live-

ly introduction to Haifa's main sights on a free three-hour walking tour led by an enthusiastic local guide. Tours take place most Wednesdays, but check ahead on the Facebook page or RSVP on the website.

✪ Festivals & Events

International Film Festival   FILM
(www.haifaff.co.il; 142 Hanassi Ave, box office; per screening 45NIS; ⊘mid-Oct) Israel's first international movie festival has been going strong since 1983. There are indoor and outdoor screenings at venues around town, plus the festival is an excellent excuse for craft fairs, food stalls, concerts and late-opening bars. Buy movie tickets at venues around town or from the box office.

Holiday of the Holidays   FAIR
(www.haifahag.com; ⊘Dec) A true coming together of Haifa's diverse communities, the Holiday of the Holidays features an outdoor carnival, fairs, food tastings and concerts in Wadi Nisnas and the German Colony, to celebrate the season's Jewish, Christian and Muslim festivals. It takes place on three Fridays and Saturdays in December.

🛏 Sleeping

🛏 Carmel Centre

★Molada Guesthouse   GUESTHOUSE $
(Map p160; ☏04-838-7958; http://molada.org.il; 82 HaNassi Ave; s/d/tr 200/350/525NIS; P🔊) Spartan but spotless, Molada attracts youthful guests who want a more sedate experience than a standard backpacker hostel. The college-dorm-style guesthouse has 16 double and triple rooms with spacious tiled bathrooms. Some overlook pine trees; the best peer towards the sea (ask for room 14 or 16). Reserve ahead by phone or online and arrange key pick-up in advance.

The guesthouse is situated down a driveway off HaNassi Ave. Reception (hours vary) is down the street at the Ruthenberg Institute for Youth Education (77 HaNassi Ave), where breakfast is also served. Ask in advance to gain access to the gated car park (free).

Beth Shalom Hotel   HOTEL $$
(Map p160; ☏04-837-7481; www.beth-shalom. co.il; 110 HaNassi Ave; s/d/tr US$85/110/140; P🔊) Run by a Swiss family, this great-value guesthouse feels a bit institutional but it's a well-oiled machine. Pine-accented, white-

walled rooms are compact but spotlessly clean, with adequate bathrooms and perks like safes and hairdryers. Family-friendly amenities include a small play area with ball pit, table tennis, a library and a lounge area with complimentary hot drinks.

Crowne Plaza   HOTEL $$
(Map p160; ☏04-835-0801; www.crowneplaza. com; 111 Yefe Nof St; d US$145-185; P@🔊▣) As swish and smooth-running as you'd expect of this hotel chain, the Crowne Plaza's rooms have large beds, polished wood floors and epic views of Haifa Bay. A business feel prevails, but it melts away after a stint in the sauna or indoor pool.

★Villa Carmel   BOUTIQUE HOTEL $$$
(Map p158; ☏04 837 5777; www.villacarmel. co.il; 30 Heinrich Heine St; r US$167-237; @🔊▣136) Gramophones and antiques set the nostalgic tone of this one-of-a-kind hotel. Rooms feature a tasteful mix of original art, dangling clocks, fleur-de-lis patterns and allusive murals. Walk-in showers and the rooftop Jacuzzi and sauna beckon to decadent weekenders, but it's the vintage feel of this 1942-built property (and appropriately genteel service) that lifts it above the competition.

🛏 German Colony

Colony Hotel Haifa   BOUTIQUE HOTEL $$
(Map p160; ☏04-851-3344; www.colonyhaifa.com; 28 Ben-Gurion Ave; d US$90-245; @🔊) This tastefully updated Templer building is the ideal spot to soak up the German Colony's history and atmosphere. Its 40 rooms have large windows, high ceilings, all-marble bathrooms and antique-themed furniture such as four-poster beds. Throw in a roof terrace, an excellent Mediterranean breakfast buffet and a Swedish massage (from 160NIS) and Colony Hotel is a winning package.

Haddad Guesthouse   GUESTHOUSE $$
(Map p160; ☏077 201-0618; www.haddad guesthouse.com; 26 Ben-Gurion Ave; d/tr from 360/460NIS; P🔊) In an enviable location in the middle of the German Colony, ensconced in a remodelled 19th-century house, this family-run hotel has four simple, pine-accented rooms on the ground floor and seven more – with kitchenettes – on the 2nd floor (with offices in between). Some of the bathrooms show signs of age but rooms are well equipped with hairdryers, kettles and TVs.

SHUJA_777 / SHUTTERSTOCK ©

1. Baha'i Gardens (p159), Haifa
Spectacular gardens lead to the exquisite gold-domed
Shrine of the Bab.

2. Rosh HaNikra Grottoes (p193)
Marvel at wave-sculpted cave mouths and the deep
blue sea at this geological wonder.

3. Hammam Al Pasha (p187), Akko
Built in 1780, this marble-adorned bathhouse is now an
evocative museum.

4. Caesarea National Park (p183)
Stroll around a vast Herodian amphitheatre and explore
Roman- and Crusader-era ruins.

Hadar

Loui Hotel
HOTEL $

(Map p160; ☑054 837-1342, 04-432-0149; www.louihotels.com; 35 HeHalutz St; d excl breakfast US$65-85; ☎) No-frills but very friendly, the Loui's 19 rooms are pleasant and practical, each with a kitchenette. The hotel has the feel of a creaky old joint that has been re-furbed repeatedly (since 1948, in fact). But these are minor complaints considering the bend-over-backward service and superb terrace area, where you can settle into a wicker chair and gaze out to sea.

Art Gallery Hotel
HOTEL $$

(Map p160; ☑04-861-6161; www.hotelgallery.co.il; 61 Herzl St; s/d 336/450NIS; ⓟ@☎) Original works by local artists adorn the public spaces and 40 mahogany-and-cream rooms of this hotel within a Bauhaus building. Some rooms feel a little poky but they are all kitted out with fridges, kettles and safes; opt for the 'Superior' rooms for bigger windows and more regal furnishings. Head up to the 5th-floor deck for port views.

The on-site gym is open 24 hours, plus you can treat yourself to a massage (from 200NIS). Situated near the Metronit's Talpiyot Market stop.

Hotel Theodor
HOTEL $$

(Map p160; ☑04-867-7111; www.theodorhotel.co.il; 63 Herzl St; s/d/tr US$125/155/215; @☎) Stacked inside a 23-storey tower above a shopping arcade, the 90-room Hotel Theodor feels more aimed at business than pleasure. Still, rooms are clean and modern, decorated in a neutral palette with tiled, monochrome bathrooms and large windows (most with bay views).

Walk through the chessboard-tiled arcade and climb one floor to reach the hotel's reception.

Downtown & Port Area

★ Port Inn
GUESTHOUSE $

(Map p160; ☑04-852-4401; www.portinn.co.il; 34 Jaffa Rd, Port Area; dm/s/d/tr/q 100/290/340/450/550NIS, d/tr with shared bathroom 260/300NIS; @☎) Budget travellers rightly flock to this charming guesthouse. A library and lounge are decked out with Turkish carpets, zany artwork and creeper plants, there's a garden out back offering journal-writing space on tiled tables, and the rooms are plain but perfectly clean.

Mixed dorm rooms have five or nine beds; single-sex dorms have nine.

Saint Charles Guesthouse
GUESTHOUSE $

(Map p160; ☑04-855-3705; https://saintcharlesguesthouse.wordpress.com; 105 Jaffa Rd, Port Area; s/d/f 180/300/390NIS; ☎) Slow-moving nuns, swishing their robes, are your hosts at the sedate, boarding-school-like Saint Charles. Operated by the Latin Patriarchate Rosary Sisters, the guesthouse offers high-ceilinged (if bare) rooms within an 1880 building. Antique tiles and an inner garden add to the contemplative feel, while the shared kitchen and port location round out a good-value package. Curfew is generally 10pm. Cash only. The gate is often locked – just ring the bell.

★ Bat Galim Hotel
BOUTIQUE HOTEL $$

(Map p158; ☑04-603-7800; www.batgalim-boutique-hotel.co.il; 10 Yonatan St, Bat Galim; d from US$114; ⓟ☎) Nestled in a snoozy residential part of northern Haifa, close to Bat Galim beach, is this immensely restful boutique hotel. The marine colour scheme, orthopaedic mattresses and in-room herbal teas lull guests to sleep, and a breakfast spread of poppy-seed yoghurt and fresh pastries awaits in the morning. Staff couldn't be friendlier.

Eating

German Colony

More than a dozen excellent restaurants, featuring Middle Eastern, European or a blend of both cuisines, line elegant Ben-Gurion Ave in the German Colony. Almost all are open seven days a week.

Al Diyar
MIDDLE EASTERN $$

(Map p160; ☑04-852-8939; 55 Ben-Gurion Ave; mains 55-98NIS; ⓧnoon-midnight; ✐) This large, family-focused restaurant is a hit with Haifa's Arab community. It serves a familiar range of Middle Eastern classics – huge spreads of Mediterranean vegetables, *fattoush* salad, grilled kebabs – along with pasta dishes and seafood such as garlic-drenched prawns.

Shtroudl
DESSERTS $$

(Map p160; ☑053 934-4986; www.shtroudl.rest.co.il; 39 Ben-Gurion Ave; mains 42-89NIS, desserts 25-39NIS; ⓧ8am-1am Sun-Fri) Shtroudl combines the sweet-toothed savvy of Germany and the Middle East, dishing up desserts in surrounds reminiscent of an eccentric aunt's summer house: ivy dangles, wind chimes rattle, and forks clash over cheesecake and apple strudel. Loosen your belt a notch if ordering the *kunafeh*, a formidable sweet cheese pastry lavished with syrup and a scoop of pistachio ice cream.

Douzan
MIDDLE EASTERN $$$

(Map p160; ☑04-852-5444; 35 Ben-Gurion Ave; mains 55-110NIS; ☺9am-11pm or later; 🐶🖼) Part Lebanese restaurant, part French-inspired coffee den with a hippie ethos, this eatery in the German Colony is original and genuinely friendly. Specialities range from *sfeeha* (pastries topped with minced beef, onions and pine nuts) to prawns in Mexican tomato sauce, and *rolettini* (cheese rolled in fried eggplant slices). Wash it down with ice-cold tamarind cordial, sipped to Douzan's guitar-driven soundtrack.

Reserve a little space for a Middle Eastern dessert, such as poached pears or rosewater-drenched milk pudding.

Faces
MEDITERRANEAN $$$

(Map p160; ☑04-855-2444; www.faces.rest-e. co.il; 37 Ben-Gurion Ave; mains 60-135NIS; ☺9am-midnight or later; 🐶🖼) Veal stroganoff, Cordon Bleu–style chicken medallions and mussels in Pernod form an eclectic menu that borrows from multiple Mediterranean cuisines. Flavour combinations sometimes miss the mark, though they're always fresh and served with flair either at tables on the outdoor terrace or in the sleek restaurant, with its brooding red-and-black colour scheme.

✖ Carmel Centre

Carmel Centre has a nice mix of upscale restaurants, sleek cafes and takeaway joints.

★ Gal's Bakery
CAFE $

(Map p160; ☑04-836-2928; http://galsbakery. rest.co.il; cnr HaNassi Ave & HaTishbi St; pastries 15-25NIS, mains 25-50NIS; ☺7am-10pm Sun-Thu, to 3pm Fri; 🐶🖼) Loyal to traditional recipes from around Europe, Gal's Bakery serves up poppyseed *babka*, *cremeschnitte* (custard slice), *chausson aux pommes* (apple pastry) and a medley of other sugar-dusted delights. The greenhouse-style dining area, with wicker chairs and cacti, is a soothing place to linger over coffee or brunches such as shakshuka (eggs baked in piquant tomato sauce). Kosher (dairy).

El Kheir
MIDDLE EASTERN $$

(Map p160; ☑04-850-0090; 139 HaNassi Ave; salads 40NIS, mains 59-98NIS; ☺noon-4pm & 6-10pm Sun-Thu, noon-10pm Fri & Sat; 🖼) This Druze-run family restaurant has kindly service and a broad selection of Lebanese and Syrian dishes: fried sea bream, paprika-dusted kebabs with bulgur wheat and speciality *shishbarak* (ground meat dumplings swimming in yoghurt). Vegetarians can fill themselves up with fried cauliflower with tahina, cheese and pomegranate pastries, and stuffed vine leaves.

Mandarin
CAFE $$

(Map p160; ☑04-836-3554; 129 HaNassi Ave; mains 45-74NIS; ☺8am-midnight, later Fri & Sat; 🐶🖼) Hidden away behind busy HaNassi Ave, this chain cafe serves a hotchpotch of East-meets-West recipes – with varying success. Offerings range from *pad ka pao* (Thai-style mincemeat with rice) to halloumi stir-fry, vegan burgers and goulash. The comfy cafe and its outdoor wooden deck are a restful place for a smoothie before a tour of the Baha'i Gardens.

✖ Downtown & Port Area

A few culinary gems shine brightly in this gradually reviving neighbourhood.

★ Ma'ayan HaBira
EASTERN EUROPEAN $$

(Map p160; ☑04-862-3193, www.facebook.com/ MaayaNHabira; 4 Nathanson St, Downtown; mains 30-120NIS; ☺10am-5pm Sun-Fri, to 11pm Tue, to 8pm Thu) Founded as a butcher's shop, a carnivorous theme endures in Ma'ayan HaBira's menu of Eastern European soul food. Lined with old photos and Bavarian beer tankards, the decor is as nostalgic as the recipes. *Kostiza* (pork slices glistening with fat) are served with vampire-extinguishing amounts of fresh garlic. Equally hearty are bowlfuls of smoky beans, jellied calf's foot and goulash.

Try to save room (it's not easy) for a dessert of chocolate-drizzled Bavarian cream.

There's live guitar music most Thursday nights.

✖ Wadi Nisnas

Rival falafel joints face each other across HaWadi St. Three blocks north, find shawarma shops around the intersection of Allenby Rd and HaZiyonut Blvd. Almost everything here is closed on Sunday.

HAIFA & THE NORTH COAST HAIFA

Felafel HaZkenim
FALAFEL $

(Map p160; 18 HaWadi St; falafel 15NIS; ⊗8am-7.30pm Mon-Sat; 🖋) Queues out the door lead the way to the best falafel in Haifa, served with a smile in unfussy surrounds. With the first bite of pita wrapped around hot, crunchy falafel – a recipe finessed since 1950 – with a small slick of tahina (sesame paste), you will forget the long wait.

Felafel Michelle
FALAFEL $

(Map p160; 21 HaWadi St; falafel 16NIS; ⊗8am-7.30pm Mon-Sat; 🖋) This hummus and falafel place is one of the most locally admired holes in the wall in Wadi Nisnas. Come hungry.

Abd Al Hadi
SWEETS $

(Map p160; 3 Sh'hadah Shalach St; sweets from 10NIS; ⊗9am-11pm) Tempting Middle Eastern pastries are piled high in the windows of this bakery, including *kunafeh* and numerous styles of flaky, nut-crammed baklava. Strong Turkish coffee offsets the post-sugar slump.

Souq
MARKET $

(Map p160; Yochanan HaKadosh St; ⊗6.30am-5pm Mon-Sat) The best place in Haifa for fresh fruit and veggies, along with picnic goodies like sweets, hummus and pastries.

★ Ein El Wadi
LEBANESE $$

(Map p160; ☎04-855-3353; 26 HaWadi St; mains 55-80NIS; ⊗10am-8pm Mon-Sat; 🖋) Dishes at this exemplary family restaurant are as authentic as its ancient stone arches. After a warm welcome, settle in for Lebanese and Palestinian specialities such as *fatayer* (spinach-stuffed pastry), *musakhan* (sumac chicken on bread) or, our favourite, *makloubeh* (layers of fragrant rice, stewed chicken and cauliflower).

Desserts are extremely rich and one portion of swimming-in-syrup *kunafeh* or rose-flavoured semolina is enough for two.

Vegetarian and gluten-free options are marked on the menu.

✖ Hadar

There are falafel, shawarma and other cheap eats along the northwestern part of Herzl St and edgy cafes on Masada St (great for brunch and light meals).

HaMis'ada Shel Ima
ETHIOPIAN $

(Mother's Restaurant; Map p160; 20 HaNevi'im St, cnr Shabtai Levi; mains 35-40NIS; ⊗noon-10pm Sun-Fri, sundown-10pm or 11pm Sat; 🖋) Stepping into this unpretentious eatery is like a quick trip to Addis Ababa, raucous soundtrack included. The satisfyingly spicy Ethiopian dishes are served on – and scooped up with – *injera* (spongy Ethiopian flatbread made with teff flour). Mains include *doro* (chicken prepared in chilli and onion), *kitfo* (raw or lightly cooked marinated beef) and, for vegetarians and vegans, *beyaynetu* (a combination platter with dollops of lentils, potatoes, carrots and spinach).

Look for the sign in the courtyard of the Amisragas building.

🍷 Drinking & Nightlife

A night out in Haifa can be as languid or off-the-wall as you choose. Carmel Centre has plenty of coffee houses and a few bars, but the best start to an evening is in the atmospheric German Colony, where many restaurants double as bars. A little louder are the hip, lefty cafes of the Masada St area; meanwhile, the pace picks up after 11pm at the live-music venues and pubs of the edgy Port Area (Downtown).

🍷 Downtown

Syncopa
BAR

(Map p160; 5 Khayat St; ⊗9pm-2am) A double-decker night spot with an oxblood-walled dive bar downstairs and a performance space upstairs. Expect soft rock, grunge and other guitar-driven styles, drum 'n' bass DJs, comedy or even spoken word; the events schedule is posted on the door. Some performances are free.

Eli's Pub
BAR

(Map p160; ☎054 635-4696; www.facebook.com/elis.pub; 35 Jaffa Rd; ⊗8pm-3am or later) Students mingle with seafarers at this casual pub where you can choose from 11 beers on tap (from 24NIS). A hammam in Ottoman times, this place really rocks from 10.30pm or 11pm on Monday (jam sessions), Wednesday (live jazz) and Saturday (local bands).

Libira
BEER HALL

(Map p160; ☎04-374-0251; www.libira.co.il; 26 HaNamal St; ⊗noon-1am) This feel-good beer hall with an industrial feel is a portside favourite. Top of the drinks menu are the homemade brews: weiss beer, bitter, double pils, smoked stout and strong ale. Owner Leonid Lipkin uses his own recipes to make nonfiltered, nonpasteurised beers, and also hosts occasional guest brews such as Palestinian Christmas ale. Libira is also suited to a blow-out feast, offering hearty Central European fillers like schnitzels and smoked goose breast, as well as mainstays like burgers (mains 28NIS to 90NIS).

Masada Street Area

Over the past several years, Masada St and its environs have firmly established a reputation as a bohemian enclave. This graffiti-daubed street is home to a growing number of alternative-clothing shops, tattoo parlours, and cafes that serve breakfasts and booze along with generous portions of left-wing politics. To get there from Herzl St in Hadar, walk about 500m up the hill (south-west), or take the Carmelit to the Masada stop and walk east.

Cafe Masada   CAFE
(Map p160; 16 Masada St; ⊙8am-2am, from 9am Sat; 🛜) Save the world over a coffee at this spirited hang-out, prowled by as many cats as art-lovers and activists. Eavesdrop the lively debate over shakshuka and sandwiches, or mingle with locals over a beer – it's an open-minded joint with a crowd that enjoys a good chinwag.

Café Puzzle   CAFE
(Map p160; 🗂04-866-0879; 21 Masada St; ⊙10am-midnight Sun-Fri, from 4pm Sat; 🛜) Popular with scenesters, students and young artists, Puzzle offers the holy trinity of great coffee, good vibes and decent wi-fi. Feeling peckish? Options include brunch (48NIS), soups and sandwiches (28NIS to 38NIS), or halva and homemade cakes (32NIS), served to the accompaniment of classic rock.

Elika   CAFE
(Map p160; 🗂052 443-3755; 24 Masada St; ⊙7am-1am) A beloved hang-out of Haifa's Arab community, in particular the arty set, Elika successfully muddles leftist nostalgia (old photos, Che Guevara prints) with sheer fun (occasional sports screenings and a well-stocked bar). Sup on tar-thick Turkish coffee or beer, line your stomach with mezze, and let the jazz and world-music soundtrack wash over you.

German Colony

Oak Bar   BAR
(Map p160; www.facebook.com/oakbarhaifa; 24 Ben-Gurion Ave; ⊙noon-late) Arabic pop music and the clickety-clack of board games provide the soundtrack at this easygoing bar on the German Colony's main drag. Prime location for beer-lubricated people-watching.

Carmel Centre

Pundak HaDov   BAR
(Bear Inn; Map p160; www.pundakhadov.rest-e.co.il; 135 HaNassi Ave; mains 55-90NIS; ⊙5pm-1am or later, from noon Fri) This loosely Irish-themed pub-restaurant pulls Staropramen and Guinness for an expat-heavy crowd, and serves satisfying pub food – chicken wings, hot dogs, sausage platters – that begs to be eaten by hand, in front of one of the regular sports screenings.

☆ Entertainment

A glut of events can be enjoyed during December's Holiday of the Holidays (p167) festival, but a creative, international student community also ensures a varied program of events year-round. For details on cultural events, see www.ethos.co.il, run by the Haifa municipality.

Beat Club   LIVE MUSIC
(Map p160; 🗂04-810-1961; www.ethos.co.il; 124 HaNassi Ave, Carmel Centre; admission 50-100NIS) Israeli and international bands rock out at this top performance venue, which is affiliated with the local music school and occasionally moonlights as a nightclub. Check the website for upcoming events.

Haifa Cinematheque   CINEMA
(Map p160; 🗂04-833-8888; www.haifacin.co.il; 142 HaNassi Ave, Carmel Centre; ticket 35NIS) Screens avant-garde, off-beat and art films in two halls. It's key venue for Haifa's film festival (p167).

Matnas Tverya 15   LIVE MUSIC
(Gould-Shenfeld Community Center; Map p160; 🗂04-850-7785; tveria15@hadarhaifa.org.il; 15 Tiberias St) A community centre with frequent amateur concerts, performances and classes (including yoga, Pilates and tango). Art exhibitions change on a monthly basis and it's a friendly, creative space to mingle with locals. Served by buses 115 and 133, or you can take the Carmelit to Masada. Call or email to find out what's on; the centre is lively, multilingual and welcoming to tourists.

Haifa Auditorium   CONCERT VENUE
(Map p160; 🗂04-835-3506; www.ethos.co.il; 140 HaNassi Ave, Carmel Centre) One of Haifa's principal venues for ballet, modern dance and music, the 1100-seat Haifa Auditorium

hosts performances by the Haifa Symphony Orchestra among other illustrious players.

🛍 Shopping

Flea Market
MARKET

(Shuk Pishpeshim; Map p160; www.facebook.com/shukpishpeshim.haifa; Kibbutz Galuyot St, Wadi Salib; ⊘9am-3pm) Amble past leather bags and picture frames, rifle through boxes of weathered postcards and sort treasure from trash at this flea market, 700m southeast of Paris Sq. It's excellent bargain-hunting terrain for collectors of curios; otherwise the area makes for an interesting stroll past antique shop fronts and sidewalk sellers.

The market is liveliest and has the most vendors on Saturday and Sunday, though you can enjoy a more subdued market experience all week long.

Turkish Market
MARKET

(HaShuk HaTurki; Map p160; Paris Sq, Downtown; ⊘10am-4pm Fri) Dock workers from Thessaloniki established this market back in the 1930s, though it eventually dwindled almost to nothing. The last decade of Downtown revival has brought it back to life as a small crafts fair, where local handicraft sellers ply their trade.

ℹ Orientation

Think vertically to get your bearings in Haifa: its neighbourhoods are stacked up the slopes of Mt Carmel, getting more stylish the higher you ascend. The city occupies a voluptuous bulge of coastal land; major roads follow the shore and cut east to west, but in between, steep streets transform road and bus journeys into a zigzag. Free street maps are available at most hotels and the Haifa tourist office.

The gritty Downtown (Ir Tachtit) and adjacent Port Area are on the flats adjacent to Haifa Port and the railway tracks. About 1km west of here, directly below the Baha'i Gardens, is Ben-Gurion Ave, the elegant main thoroughfare of the German Colony (p163). The mostly Arab neighbourhood of Wadi Nisnas (p163) is in a little valley midway between Paris Sq and the German Colony. To the northwest, across the train tracks, is Bat Galim, home of Rambam hospital and a beach. Stella Maris (p165) is accessible by aerial cable car from Bat Galim's seafront promenade. About 1km south (up the slope) from Paris Sq is Herzl St, the heart of Hadar HaCarmel, universally known as Hadar (p164).

Around the Carmelit metro upper terminus, Gan HaEm, is Carmel Centre (Merkaz HaCarmel; p159), the commercial heart of the affluent neighbourhoods that are strung out along the ridge of Mt Carmel.

ℹ Information

CONSULATES

US Consulate (Map p160; ☎04-853-1470; https://il.usembassy.gov; 26 Ben-Gurion Ave, German Colony)

MEDICAL SERVICES

Rambam Medical Centre (Rambam Health Care Campus; Map p158; ☎1-700-505-150, emergency room 04-777-3300; www.rambam.org.il; 8 HaAliya HaShniya St, Bat Galim; ⊘24hr) Northern Israel's largest hospital and one of the country's best equipped. Take a Bat Galim–bound bus (43 from Hof HaCarmel bus station, 16 or 136 from Lev HaMifratz, or 24 or 36 from the university) to get there.

MONEY

There are plenty of banks in Hadar, and more up around Carmel Centre.

TOURIST INFORMATION

Tourist Office (Haifa Tourist Board; Map p160; ☎04-853-5606; www.visit-haifa.org; 48 Ben-Gurion Ave, German Colony; ⊘8.30am-6pm Sun-Thu, to 1pm Fri) Situated near the top of Ben-Gurion Ave. Free maps offered.

ℹ Getting There & Away

AIR

Haifa Airport (HFA; ☎03-975-8337; www.iaa.gov.il; Derech Yigael Yadin), 7.5km southeast of Paris Sq, is connected by Arkia (www.arkia.com) flights to Eilat and charter flights to the Greek islands. Egged bus 58 from the central bus station reaches the airport.

BOAT

Ferries connect **Haifa port** (Map p160; www.haifaport.co.il; Kdoshei Bagdad St) with old Akko's marina twice daily on weekdays and three times on a Saturday; the journey takes 45 minutes, depending on sea conditions. Buy tickets up to an hour before departure time.

BUS

Haifa has two central bus stations. Haifa-Hof HaCarmel, used by buses heading south along the coast (ie towards Tel Aviv), is on the Mediterranean (western) side of Mt Carmel. It's 8km around the base of Mt Carmel from the German Colony, near the Haifa-Hof HaCarmel train station. The quickest way to get to Tel Aviv and other coastal cities is by train.

Other destinations include Atlit Detention Camp (bus 221, 25 minutes, two per hour), Jerusalem (Egged bus 940, 37.50NIS, two hours, every 30 to 90 minutes except Friday evening to sundown Saturday; Egged bus 947 takes an hour longer) and Zichron Ya'akov (Egged buses 202 and 921, 14.50NIS, one hour, at least hourly except Friday afternoon to Saturday night).

Haifa-Merkazit HaMifratz, on the Haifa Bay side of Mt Carmel, is used by most buses to destinations north and east of Haifa. It is 8km southeast of the German Colony, a few hundred metres – through the giant Lev HaMifratz shopping mall – from the Lev HaMifratz train station. Train is the fastest way to Akko and Nahariya. Destinations:

Afula (Nateev Express bus 301, 40 minutes, every 20 minutes except Friday afternoon to sundown Saturday) Frequent buses link Afula with Beit She'an.

Akko (Nateev Express buses 271 and 361, 16NIS, 35 to 45 minutes, every 10 minutes) Bus 271 continues north to the Baha'i Gardens, Kibbutz Lohamei HaGeta'ot and Nahariya.

Beit She'arim (HaShomrim Junction; Nateev Express bus 301, 13.50NIS, 15 minutes, three times a hour)

Jerusalem (Egged bus 960, 37.50NIS, two hours, one or two times an hour except Friday afternoon to sundown Saturday)

Kiryat Shmona (Egged buses 500 and 505, 37.50NIS to 44NIS, two hours, twice an hour except Friday afternoon to sundown Saturday)

Nazareth (Buses 331 and 332, shared between Nazareth Tourism & Transport and GB Tours; 19NIS to 26NIS, one hour, twice hourly Sunday to Friday, hourly all day Saturday)

Tiberias (Egged buses 430 and 434, 21.50NIS, 1¼ hours, three times per hour except Friday afternoon to sundown Saturday)

Tsfat (Nateev Express bus 361, 1¾ hours, twice an hour) via Akko (45 minutes).

Linking the two central bus stations is Metronit line 1 (30 minutes), which loops around via the German Colony and the Port Area; and bus 101 (20 minutes), which goes through the Carmel Tunnels, a toll-road tunnel under Mt Carmel.

All intercity bus tickets to Haifa include transport from one of the central bus stations into the city – provided you ask for a *kartis hemshech* (transfer ticket) when you buy your ticket (eg from the driver). The only catch is that you have to have a rechargeable Rav-Kav smartcard (sold by the driver).

SHERUT

Throughout the week sheruts (service or shared taxis) to **Akko** (Map p160; ☎ 04-862-2115), **Nahariya and Tsfat** (Map p160; ☎ 04-862-2115) and **Tel Aviv** (Map p160; ☎ 04-862-2115) depart from Hadar and various places around the intersection of Herzlia and HaNevi'im Sts (weekday/Shabbat 30/45NIS).

Book a day in advance for a **sherut to Ben Gurion airport** (Amal Taxi; ☎ 04-866-2324) from their central departure point (around the intersection of Herzlia and HaNevi'im Sts; 77NIS) or from your hotel (119NIS).

TRAIN

Haifa has four train stations:

Haifa-Hof HaCarmel Eight kilometres from the German Colony, west and then south around the base of Mt Carmel; near the Haifa-Hof HaCarmel bus station.

Haifa Merkaz-HaShmona (Haifa Center-HaShmona; Derech HaAtsmaut, Haifa port) In the city's Downtown (Port Area), 700m northwest of Paris Sq and 700m east of the German Colony.

Haifa-Bat Galim (Map p158; HaHayil St) In the seaside Bat Galim neighbourhood, near Rambam hospital and 1km southeast of the Stella Maris cable car.

Lev HaMifratz (HaHistadrut) Eight kilometres southeast of the German Colony and a few hundred metres – through the giant Lev HaMifratz shopping mall – from the Merkazit HaMifratz bus station.

Travel by train within Haifa, between any of these stations (every 10 to 20 minutes), costs 7.50NIS. Services leave from all four main train stations to Ben Gurion airport (35.50NIS, 1¼–1¾ hours, twice hourly), Akko (13.50NIS, 30 minutes, four times an hour), Nahariya (13.50NIS to 17.50NIS, 35 minutes to one hour, three an hour) and Tel Aviv (27.50NIS to 32.50NIS, one to 1¼ hours, two or three times an hour).

Trains do not run from Friday afternoon until sundown Saturday.

ⓘ Getting Around

BUS

The Carmelit metro is great for getting up and down the mountain, but for travel along Mt Carmel's flanks you'll need buses (run by Egged, Nateev Express and Omni Express). Much faster is Metronit, a three-line bus service inaugurated in 2013, that's as fast as light rail thanks to its dedicated lanes and synchronised traffic lights. Unlike standard buses, you must buy tickets (5.90NIS, valid for 90 minutes) before boarding; ticket machines are at each stop.

Metronit line 1 links the two central bus stations, Haifa-Merkazit HaMifratz and Haifa-Hof HaCarmel, via the Port Area and the German Colony at least twice an hour (every five minutes at peak times) 24 hours a day, seven days a week (yes, including Shabbat!). Line 2 links Bat Galim (Rambam hospital) with Haifa-Merkazit HaMifratz, also via the German Colony and the Port Area.

CAR

In Haifa, several major car-rental companies have agencies on side streets near Haifa-Merkazit HaMifratz bus terminal.

METRO

At the time of research, Haifa's six-station Carmelit (www.carmelithaifa.co.il) was out of action following a fire in February 2017. At the time of writing, repairs were ongoing to restore Israel's only metro (technically, a funicular railway), which connects Paris Sq (Kikar Pariz) in the Downtown (Port Area) with Hadar (HaNevi'im stop) and Carmel Centre (Gan HaEm stop). About 2km long, it whisks passengers up 268 vertical metres at a gradient of up to 17.5 degrees. Usual operating hours are between 6am and midnight from Sunday to Thursday, until 3pm on Friday and after 8pm on Saturday; check the website or ask locally.

Daliyat Al Karmel

دالية الكرمل   דלית אל כרמל

📞 04 / POP 16,780

Charmingly shabby and light on big attractions, Daliyat Al Karmel is nonetheless a fascinating place to glimpse the tight-knit Druze culture: an offshoot of Islam that draws inspiration from Islamic, Greek and other philosophies, and where intermarriage and conversion are forbidden. Established in the 17th century by Druze people from Lebanon, it's the world's southernmost Druze settlement and the largest in Israel.

Daliyat Al Karmel is a sprawling town on top of Mt Carmel, about 16km south of Haifa; years of growth have nearly fused it with the smaller Druze village of Isfiya (Usfiyeh), just to the north.

'Downtown' is a 200m stretch of the main street, Rte 672, through town. The town is at its busiest on Shabbat and Jewish holidays. Expect curious stares and friendly smiles when you pass through.

◎ Sights

Beit Oliphant   HISTORIC SITE
Signposted as Beit Druze, this was the home of the Christian and early Zionist Sir Laurence Oliphant and his wife Alice between 1882 and 1887. The Oliphants were among the few non-Druze to have a close relationship with the community and did much to help them. Oliphant's assistant at the time was Naphtali Herz Imber, author of the words to Israel's national anthem, 'HaTikva', first published in 1886.

The ancient Roman column out front is a memorial to Alice, who died at age 36 – and with whom Imber was said to have been madly in love. The house now serves as the **Druze Memorial Center**, which commemorates the 398 Druze who have died while serving in the Israel Defense Forces (IDF) since 1948. At the time of writing, it wasn't possible to go inside.

Shrine of Abu Ibrahim   ISLAMIC SHRINE
(⊙ hours vary) FREE This square little building is fronted with Jerusalem stone and topped with a small red dome. The shrine is dedicated to Abu Ibrahim, who the Druze believe the soul of Elijah was reincarnated in. Both men and women must be modestly dressed, including long sleeves, and must remove their shoes (place them on the shelf at the door). To get there, follow the signs to 'Holy Place'.

As you walk south along the main shopping street (Rte 672), the road does a 90-degree turn to the left, ie southeast); turn right (west) – the shrine is about 600m along.

✗ Eating

Andarin   MIDDLE EASTERN $$
(Rte 672; mains 55-120NIS; ⊙ 10am-10pm) Cordial service and truly satisfying shish kebabs make spotless Andarin the best pick on Daliyat's main road. Grills, including chicken and ground lamb, are served with a smorgasbord of salads, with some unexpected ingredients from kimchi to sweet-and-sour carrot.

Abu Anter   MIDDLE EASTERN $$
(📞 04-839-3537; Rte 672; mains 45-140NIS; ⊙ 10am-5pm) This welcoming restaurant favoured by locals offers standard Middle Eastern staples such as kebabs, falafel, stuffed grape leaves and *labneh* (thick yoghurt).

🛍 Shopping

In and among the restaurants, you'll find shops selling locally made Druze textiles, brightly coloured shawls and trousers, tabla drums, pottery and antiques – though be warned, the good stuff is muddled among made-abroad Tupperware and souvenirs of uncertain origin.

ℹ Getting There & Around

Bus 37 אlinks Daliyat Al Karmel and Isfiya with Haifa University, the German Colony, Baha'i Gardens and Bat Galim (5.90NIS, one to 1¼ hours,

BEIT SHE'ARIM

Nestled between Mt Carmel and Lower Galilee, spellbinding Beit She'arim National Park (☑ 04-983-1643; www.parks.org.il; adult/child 22/10NIS; ☺ 8am-5pm daylight-saving time, to 4pm winter time, closes 1hr earlier Fri, last entry 1hr before closing; ℗) is pitted with ancient catacombs, many of which you can enter. In the 2nd century AD, the town grew into a vibrant centre for Torah study, and spiritual luminaries were buried here. Walking paths link the beautifully restored cave tombs; most impressive is the triple-arched Tomb of Rabbi HaNassi, who handled political affairs between Jews and their Roman overlords. Pick up a trail map from the visitor centre.

For part of the late 2nd century AD, Beit She'arim was the meeting place of the Sanhedrin (the era's supreme council of rabbis), headed by Rabbi Yehuda HaNassi, who assembled Jewish scholars and compiled the Mishnah (the earliest codification of Jewish law) at Tzipori but asked to be buried here, inspiring others to do the same. During the 4th century the town was destroyed by the Romans, presumably in the process of suppressing a Jewish uprising. During the following 600 years the many tombs were looted and covered by rock falls. Archaeologists stumbled upon the remains of Beit She'arim in 1936.

As you drive towards the entrance of the park, the ruins of a 2nd-century synagogue are off to the left. Cave tombs are still being discovered at this vast site; the largest catacomb contains 24 separate chambers with more than 200 sarcophagi. Note the variety of symbols and inscriptions carved onto the coffins, including epithets written in Hebrew, Aramaic, Palmyran and Greek. Some of the people buried here, it is believed, came from as far away as Persia and Yemen.

An additional site in the national park, the six-chamber Menorah Caves Compound, can only be visited by guided tour with prior notice. It's worth it to see the elaborate stone carvings, including a menorah and Torah Ark.

Beit She'arim is about 23km southeast of Haifa, mostly along Rte 75. By bus, you can take Nateev Express bus 301 from Haifa-Merkazit HaMifratz (13.50NIS, 30 minutes, at least twice an hour); tell the driver you want to go to Beit She'arim and they will let you off at HaShomrim Junction, which is 1km north of the park along Rte 722.

two or three an hour); services don't run from Friday afternoon to sundown Saturday.

Parking can be hard to come by on Daliyat's jam-packed main street, but there's a privately run car park (off Rte 672; per car 15NIS) close to sights and restaurants. An attendant will appear to take your money.

Carmelite Monastery of St Elijah

دير المحرقة

מנזר כרמליתי של אליהו הקדוש

Carmelite Monastery of St Elijah MONASTERY

(Muhraqa; www.muhraqa.org; 4NIS; ☺ 9am-5pm summer, to 4.30pm winter; ℗) Spectacular views and surprising kitsch greet visitors to this lofty monastery. The Carmelite Monastery of St Elijah is known to Arab and Jewish Israelis as the Muhraqa ('it burns'), as it is believed to be where Elijah offered a sacrifice to God, answered by a fire from the heavens – while the competing offering from

450 prophets of Ba'al was ignored (1 Kings 18). The monastery garden is inhabited by quaint frog statues and garden gnomes, plus a fairy-light-strewn Virgin Mary. Also on the Catholic complex is a chapel (built 1883) and the lodgings of monks from the Discalced Carmelite Order ('discalced' is a fancy way of saying 'barefoot').

From the roof (access is via the shop), you can see the Mediterranean, Mt Hermon (when it's clear) and everything in between. Out front is a peaceful little garden with a statue of Elijah and a small walking trail.

The Muhraqa is 5km south of the centre of Daliyat Al Karmel; bear left at the signposted Y-junction.

Ein Hod & Ayn Hawd

عين هود وعين حوض عين הוד ועין חוד

Along Ein Hod's tangled lanes, bronze statues stare out from a giant sardine can and voluptuous stone sculptures beckon beneath flowering trees. This small community of artists is a scenic and surreal place to explore, and it's the best place to feel the pulse of contemporary Israeli art.

Behind the charming sandstone artists' studios is a dark past: residents of the former Arab village were driven out and re-established their community uphill in Ayn Hawd, which remains to this day. Whether as a day trip from Haifa or as a longer stay, a visit to Ein Hod and its surrounds is guaranteed to be thought-provoking.

◉ Sights

Several dozen artists live and work in Ein Hod. Many studios are closed to casual visitors, and debates simmer over whether tourists are a delight or a distraction to local creatives. You can increasingly visit various studios and galleries and, with advance reservations, attend workshops in fields such as ceramics, watercolour and oil painting, lithography and photography. For details, check out Ein Hod's official website, www.ein-hod.org, or the privately run www.ein-hod.info.

Janco–Dada Museum   MUSEUM
(☎ 04-984-2350; www.jancodada.co.il; adult/child 24/12NIS, incl Dada Lab 25/30NIS; ☉ 10am-3pm Sun-Thu, to 2pm Fri, to 3.30pm Sat, Dada Lab 11am-2pm Sat & holidays; 🚺) Glimpse into the creative mind of Marcel Janco at this 1983-built museum dedicated to his life and works. It was Janco's idea to establish this community of artists and you can see the art of Israel's most famous Dadaist in the permanent collection, as well as guest exhibitions by local artists. The wonderfully weird highlight is the downstairs Dada Lab, a surreal, hands-on space for kids to get creative, dress up and get a little bit messy.

The museum also serves as an occasional performance venue.

Ein Hod Gallery   GALLERY
(10am-4pm Sun & Tue-Thu, 10am-2pm Fri, 11am-4pm Sat) A good intro to Ein Hod's artistic community is this gallery of local sculptures and paintings. The exhibition space dates to 1953, when the creative community was in its infancy.

Studio Magal   GALLERY
(☎ 04-984-2313; ☉ 10am-5pm) Ceramics (including Judaica), mosaics and expressionist paintings (oil and watercolour), the latter by Ben-Tzion Magal (1908–99).

Nisco Museum   MUSEUM
(☎ 052 475-5313; adult/child 30/20NIS; ☉ 10am-5pm Mon-Sat) This offbeat collection of mechanical music instruments was assembled by New York–born Nisan Cohen, who's happy to play records from his Yiddish music archive on a vintage Victrola. Tours begin on the hour. It's situated a few hundred metres down the hill (towards Rte 4) from the gate to Ein Hod.

☞ Tours

Shuli Yarkony Tours   WALKING
(☎ 052 645-6072; shuliyarkony@gmail.com) Licensed guide Shuli Yarkony leads walking tours into Ein Hod artists' studios that are usually inaccessible, and her family connections to local artists often make for a lively experience. Rates vary by tour length and size of group, and Shuli can conduct tours in English or Hebrew. Reserve well ahead.

✖ Eating

Makolet   SUPERMARKET $
(☉ 9am-5pm or later) Ein Hod's only mini-mart with fresh produce.

★ HaBayit   MIDDLE EASTERN $$
(Al Beyt; ☎ 053 944-2990; http://albeet.rest.co.il; Ayn Hawd; set meals from 110NIS; ☉ noon-6pm; 🖉) Situated 4km up the hill from Ein Hod in Ayn Hawd, this family-run restaurant serves authentic Arab cuisine. Set meals include a huge variety of salads, soups, stuffed chicken, slow-roasted lamb, homemade breads and spiced okra, all flavoured with herbs plucked from the slopes of Mt Carmel. There's no menu; it's all at the chef's discretion – though they will cater for vegetarians.

Book ahead for Friday and Saturday.

Nof Hvade   MIDDLE EASTERN $$
(☎ 04-671-2560; http://nofmulhavadi.co.il; Ayn Hawd; mains 50-80NIS; ☉ 9am-last customer; 🖉) Enjoy spectacular hill views from this warm and welcoming family restaurant in lofty Ayn Hawd, 4km up the steep road from the artists' village. Great grills are accompanied by garnishes such as pickled cauliflower and tahini, while vegetarians can feast on stuffed vine leaves and *mujaddara* (lentils and rice with fried onions).

Follow the restaurant signs downhill towards the left after entering Ayn Hawd and look for the 'Ein Hood' mosaic with doves; the stairs here lead up to the restaurant.

NORTH COAST BEACHES

A string of fine-sand beaches stretches along Israel's northern Mediterranean coast. From south to north, these are some of the prettiest spots to sunbathe.

Beit Yanai (parking per car 24-33NIS) Equidistant between Tel Aviv and Haifa, this excellent beach has free showers and toilets, a patrolled swimming area and snack stands. There's plenty of space to stretch out and watch surfers challenge the waves.

Aqueduct (p185) Exactly as it sounds, a golden beach next to a section of Caesarea's Roman aqueduct. No admission fee. Situated 2.5km by road north of ancient Caesarea.

Dor A long fine-sand beach stretches south from Dor village, with patrolled zones for swimming, tidal pools and ruins to explore nearby. Ancient Dor was an important port city mentioned repeatedly in the Old Testament. Situated 10km northwest of Zichron Ya'akov.

Atlit With brown sugar sand and stiff breezes, Atlit is mostly unsupervised but good for sunbathing and kite-flying.

Hof HaCarmel beaches Fine-sand beaches Dado (p166) and Zamir (p166) extend along the western edge of Haifa's headland, near Haifa-Hof HaCarmel station.

Bat Galim (p166) Small, pleasant beach beloved of locals, a few blocks northeast of the lower cable-car station in Haifa (terminus of Metronit line 2).

Argaman (p189) Akko's municipal beach is 1.5km southeast of the old city.

Akhziv National Park (p193) About 4km north of Nahariya, Akhziv's two beaches are popular with families and picturesque.

HAIFA & THE NORTH COAST ATLIT

Doña Rosa   ARGENTINE $$$

(☑ 053 934 5520; www.donarosa.co.il; mains 56-88NIS, steaks 94-120NIS; ☺ noon-11pm Mon-Sat) Ein Hod's best spot for a slap-up feast, this Argentine steakhouse faithfully re-creates the flavours of the motherland, from meat and wine to the gaucho-inspired decor. Try to snag a balcony table. Reserve ahead for Thursday night, Friday and Saturday; there's live music on Saturday.

Atlit   עתלית عتليت

Atlit Detention Camp   HISTORIC SITE

(☑ 04-984-1980; http://eng.shimur.org/atlit; adult/child 32/27NIS; ☺ 9am-5pm Sun-Thu, to 1pm or 2pm Fri, tours by prior arrangement; ℗) In 1939, as the situation of the Jews of Europe became increasingly dire, the British government issued a white paper limiting Jewish immigration to Palestine to 10,000 to 15,000 'certificates' a year. If Jewish refugees could not come to Palestine legally, the leaders of the Zionist Movement decided, they would do so illegally. Thousands of Jews fleeing Nazism made it past the British blockade, but many more were captured and interned at the Atlit 'Illegal' Immigrant Detention Camp.

On 10 October 1945, the Palmach (the Special Forces unit of the Haganah) broke into the camp and released 208 prisoners. The daring infiltration, led by a young Yitzhak Rabin, caused the British to close the camp. Between 1946 and 1949, Holocaust survivors and other Jews arrested for illegally entering Palestine were sent to camps on Cyprus.

You can walk around the site on your own, but written explanation is scant; the best way to see the camp is on a 1½-hour guided tour (call ahead). Guides present the barracks (reconstructed); a dreadful wash house (largely original) where new arrivals were stripped of their clothing and disinfected with DDT; and a 34m-long ship very much like the ones used to ferry *ma'apilim* (clandestine immigrants) to pre-state Israel (the vessel here is actually the *Galina,* built in Latvia in the 1970s). A ship this size would have been packed with 600 to 800 refugees.

The Atlit camp is 16km south of Haifa and 20km north of Zichron Ya'akov. Bus 221 (every 30 minutes) links the camp with the Atlit train station (10 minutes), 3km to the south, and Haifa's Hof HaCarmel bus station (25 minutes).

Crusader Castle   RUINS

The wreck of a once-imposing Crusader castle, known in Latin as Castrum Pergrinorum and in French as Château Pèlerin (Pilgrims'

MEGIDDO (ARMAGEDDON)

St John predicted the last great battle on earth would take place at the sun-scorched hill at **Megiddo National Park** (Tel Megiddo; ☑04-659-0316; www.parks.org.il; Rte 66, Megiddo; adult/child 28/14NIS; ◷8am-5pm summer, to 4pm winter, closes 1hr earlier Fri), better known as Armageddon (Revelation 16:16). Aside from scuttling lizards, all's quiet today. Walking trails connect remnants from more than 25 distinct historical periods from 4000 BC to 400 BC. Only rubble remains of prayer structures and water cisterns, though a 15-minute introductory film and signposting offer tantalising historical details. There are expansive views, too: you'll see the Four Horsemen coming from miles away.

Megiddo has been the scene of many battles throughout the ages. Hieroglyphics on the wall of Karnak Temple in Luxor, Egypt, describe a battle in which Thutmose III quashed a rebellion at Megiddo in 1457 BC. Megiddo remained a prosperous Egyptian stronghold for at least 100 years and later on held out against the Israelites (Judges 1:27), probably only falling to David. Under his son Solomon, Megiddo was transformed into one of the jewels of the Israelite kingdom and became known as the Chariot City – excavations have revealed traces of stables extensive enough to have held thousands of horses.

For a while Megiddo was a strategic stronghold on the important trade route between Egypt and Assyria, but by the 4th century BC the town had inexplicably become uninhabited. However, its strategic importance remained, and among the armies that fought here were the British in WWI. On being awarded his peerage, General Edmund Allenby took the title Viscount Allenby of Megiddo. Jewish and Arab forces clashed here during the 1948 war.

The most tangible aspect of the excavations is the 9th-century-BC water system, which consists of a shaft sunk through solid rock down to a 70m tunnel. This hid the city's water source from invading forces, rather like Hezekiah's Tunnel (p75) in Jerusalem (though there is no water to slosh through here). Save the tunnel until last, as the 183-stair descent leads you out of the site, depositing you on a side road some 600m from the visitor centre.

Megiddo is 37km southeast of Haifa (along Rtes 75, 70 and 66), 45km east of Caesarea (via Rte 65) and 13km southwest of Afula (in the Jezreel Valley). Infrequent bus 300 from Haifa-Merkazit HaMifratz bus station takes 40 minutes to reach the intersection of Rte 66 and Tel Megiddo; it's a short walk to the site. By car it's an easy half-day trip from Haifa, Caesarea or Zichron Ya'akov (all less than one hour's drive).

Castle), sits on a promontory about 750m west of Atlit Beach. It's inside a military base used for training by Israel's marine commandos and so can't be visited, but you can see it from the beach.

Zichron Ya'akov

זכרון יעקב   زخرون يعقوب

☑04 / POP 22,500

Romantic though largely residential, Zichron Ya'akov exudes refinement from every sun-kissed stone wall. Established in 1882 by Jews from Romania, Zichron Ya'akov – near the southern end of the Mt Carmel massif – is best known for its pioneering role in Israel's wine industry and, more recently, for its attractive old town and upper-middle-class neighbourhoods. In its early years Zichron was endowed with riches by Baron Edmond de Rothschild

of the French banking family, who named it after his father James, aka Jacob (Ya'akov). Late-19th-century buildings still line its streets and many of them now harbour artists' studios, boutique shops and cafes, making the old town perfect for wandering. In the surrounding countryside wineries round out the relaxing air.

◉ Sights

The late-19th-century main street, HaMeyasdim, which is now (mostly) pedestrianised, is lined with restaurants, cafes and shops tucked away in restored stone buildings.

◉ Town Centre

Carmel Winery   WINERY
(☑04-629-1788; www.carmelwines.co.il; 2 Derech HaYekev; tasting/tour per person 25/30NIS; ◷wine shop 9am-5pm Mon-Thu, to 2pm Fri, cellar tours

10am & noon Fri) Sip dry reds, well-rounded rieslings and light, sparkling 'Buzz' wines at this winery founded in 1882. Reservations for tastings at the shop aren't necessary, but call ahead for Friday cellar tours (particularly if you want an explanation in English).

First Aliya Museum MUSEUM
(2 HaNadiv St; adult/student & child 20/15NIS; ⊙9am-4pm Mon-Thu, to 2pm Fri) Striking displays and short films relate the struggles of early Zionist pioneers: fleeing pogroms in their homelands, escaping Ottoman detection on their arrival in the Holy Land, and the difficulties of nurturing farms and vineyards in an inhospitable climate. With an injection of funds from Baron Edmond de Rothschild, agricultural communities like Zichron Ya'akov were born and soon thrived.

NILI Museum MUSEUM
(☑04-639-0120; www.nili-museum.org.il; 40 HaMeyasdim St, cnr Jabotinski St; adult/child 26/20NIS; ⊙9am-3pm Sun-Thu, to noon Fri) Guided tours lead visitors through the turbulent life of Aaron Aaronsohn (1876–1919), a noted agronomist and botanist who, along with his family, founded and led a pro-British WWI spy ring known as NILI. Tours of their former family home take place in Hebrew on the hour; tours in English are every 1½ hours (but it's best to call or email ahead to confirm times).

⊙ Around Zichron Ya'akov

★**Ramat HaNadiv Gardens** GARDENS
(☑04-629-8111; www.ramat-hanadiv.org.il; ⊙8am-4pm Sat-Thu, to 2pm Fri; P) **FREE** Walking trails weave among palm groves, rose beds and succulents at these expansive botanic gardens, 4km southwest of central Zichron Ya'akov. The gardens are a living memorial to Baron Edmond de Rothschild, who is credited with helping to establish agricultural communities during Israel's early years; he is buried in the crypt here.

★**Tishbi Winery** WINERY
(☑04-628-8195; www.tishbi.com; wine tasting with/without tour 40/35NIS; ⊙shop 8am-5pm Sun-Thu, to 1pm Fri, tours 10am, noon & 2pm Sun-Thu) Gastronomes won't want to miss swirling a wine glass or three at this atmospheric vineyard, 4km south of central Zichron Ya'akov. Tishbi was established in the late 19th century by Lithuanian immigrants and has been family-run ever since. A standard tasting session offers a primer from mal-

bec to chardonnay, but we love the wine and chocolate experience (45NIS to 55NIS), which pairs wines with gourmet chocolates. Book ahead.

There's a superb **kosher restaurant** attached to the winery or head to the affiliated **wine bar** (cnr HaMayesdim St & Sderot Nili; ⊙8am-10pm Sun-Thu, to 3pm Fri) in central Zichron Ya'akov.

🛏 Sleeping

Beit Maimon Hotel BOUTIQUE HOTEL $$
(☑04-629-0390; www.maimon.com; 4 Tzahal St; s/d from 480/600NIS; P ⊛ ⊚ ⊛) With hardwood furnishings, stone-tiled bathrooms, genuine service and Mediterranean views from the breakfast terrace, Beit Maimon balances cosiness with chic. For a hot tub and coastal views, spring for a romantic 'superior seaview' room (200NIS extra). From HaMeyasdim St, it's a 15-minute walk west through residential streets lined by peach trees. Minimum two-night stay on Shabbat.

Attached Casa Barone is one of the most popular restaurants in town.

My Place in the Colony GUESTHOUSE $$
(☑054 234-2947; Hanadiv St 32; r from 380NIS; P ⊡) An exuberant welcome sets the tone for this reassuringly old-fashioned guesthouse, set within a 19th-century stone building and with solid wood furnishings and grandmotherly floral patterns. Bathrooms aren't too spacious but the rooms themselves are ample and feature kitchenettes. The backyard turns into a bewitching den when illuminated at night.

🍴 Eating

Cucina ITALIAN $$
(☑053 427-2527; http://cucina.rest.co.il; 41 HaMeyasdim St; mains 50-95NIS; ⊙noon-10pm; ⊠⊛) Slick Italian restaurant serving a classy array of *aperitivi* and Mediterranean-style tapas alongside the usual favourites: beef carpaccio, ricotta-stuffed ravioli, as well as pizzas and fish dishes. There are a few options aimed at children, included kid-sized pizza.

★**Nili Restaurant** EUROPEAN, SEAFOOD $$$
(☑04-629-2899; www.nilirestaurant.com; 43 HaMeyasdim St; mains 60-110NIS; ⊙8am-11pm Sun-Thu) This well-run kosher restaurant offers almost every imaginable preparation of fish: homemade sushi, tangy ceviche, baked mullet and bream, or hunks of salmon swirled into tagliatelle. Everything

JISR AZ ZARKA

Most drivers along Rte 2 (the Tel Aviv–Haifa expressway) barely look as they zoom past Jisr Az Zarka, Israel's only remaining Mediterranean seaside Arab village. Social problems and crime have given Jisr a bad rep, but local activists and a modest guesthouse aim to change the fortunes of this former fishing town. Slowly but surely, backpackers are arriving to immerse themselves in local Arab culture and watch the sun set from the quiet beach.

Jisr was founded in the 1830s by families from Egypt who came to Palestine along with the forces of Egyptian ruler Muhammad Ali (1769–1849). It is named for a stone bridge over adjacent Al Wadi Az Zarka (the Blue River), constructed for the visit of Kaiser Wilhelm II in 1898. Thanks to a history of good relations with nearby Jewish villages, it emerged unharmed from the 1948 war.

Though rough around the edges, **Juha's Guesthouse** (☑052 862-2088, 058 588-5589; www.zarqabay.com; Markaz Al Qarya, Rte 6531; dm 85NIS, r 320NIS, with shared bathroom 250NIS; 🅿🛜) is becoming a surprise hit among backpackers detouring from Israel's tourist trail. Run by Jisr local Ahmed and Jewish Israeli Neta, the guesthouse has an eight-bed dorm, double rooms with shared and private bathrooms (the latter in a lonely separate annexe), and a cosy chill-out lounge with adjoining kitchen.

The road to Jisr Az Zarka, Rte 6531, is accessible from Rte 4 (the old Tel Aviv–Haifa Hwy) but not from Rte 2 (the new Tel Aviv–Haifa Hwy). Kavim bus 69 links Jisr Az Zarka with Binyamina's train station (12 minutes, four or five daily Sunday to Thursday, two Friday).

is beautifully prepared and plated and the warm service and menu of local wines invite lingering.

🛍 Shopping

Many of the stone buildings on HaMeyasdim St have been converted into boutiques and jewellery shops. The street is an excellent place to swoop down on unique women's clothing, accessories, handmade souvenirs and cosmetics. Duck into courtyards for some of the most interesting finds.

ℹ Getting There & Away

Buses stop on HaNadiv St between the First Aliya Museum and the HaMeyasdim St pedestrian zone. Egged bus 202 reaches Haifa-Hof HaCarmel (14.50NIS, 30 minutes, 13 daily Sunday to Thursday, six on Friday, one on Saturday night). For Tel Aviv, board Egged bus 872 (21.50NIS, 2¼ hours, eight daily Sunday to Thursday, five Friday, three Saturday night), which stops at the Central Bus Station and Arlozorov bus station.

Mey Kedem מי קדם مي كيدم

Mey Kedem Tunnel ARCHAEOLOGICAL SITE
(☑04-638-8622; www.meykedem.co.il; Moshav Amikam; adult/child 30/25NIS; ⊙9am-4pm Sat-Tue, to 1pm Fri Mar-Oct) To supply water to Caesarea, the Romans built an extraordi-

nary 23km-long system of canals, pipes and aqueducts and a 6km-long tunnel. A 300m section of the tunnel is now open for exploration, provided you don't mind wading through 70cm-deep H_2O. Bring a flashlight, a change of clothes and footwear suitable for getting wet. Admission includes a one-hour guided tour. This is a great activity if you've got kids, especially on a hot summer's day (but it's not for the claustrophobic).

By road, Mey Kedem, near the religious community of Moshav Amikam and part of the larger Alona Park, is 18km from Zichron Ya'akov.

Caesarea קיסריה قيصارية

☑04 / POP 4800
Time-worn ruins are strewn along the crystalline Mediterranean shore of Caesarea (Qeysarya; pronounced 'kay-*sar*-ee-ya' in Hebrew). Once a storied port city to rival Alexandria and Carthage, Caesarea is now split between old and new: the ancient city's remains form Caesarea National Park while chic residential neighbourhoods – and Israel's only international golf club – lie east.

Despite efforts by various conquerors to keep the port in service, time and warfare eventually had their way. By the 14th century most of Caesarea had disappeared under the shifting dunes. Archaeological excavations have revealed impressive Roman sites (rivalled, in Israel, only by Beit She'an). Shut your eyes and imagine chariots careening round the amphitheatre and murmured prayers in shadowy shrines to Mithras; then open them to see a slew of waterside cafes and restaurants where you can dine until late.

History

Ancient documents reveal that Caesarea first prospered as a Phoenician settlement during the Hellenistic period. In 30 BC Herod the Great was awarded the site and a few years later set about building the most grandiose port city imaginable, dedicating it to his patron, the Roman emperor Augustus Caesar. For 12 years, hundreds of builders and divers worked around the clock. To create the harbour's two breakwaters, stretching for 540m on the southern side and 270m on the north, vast quantities of stone were lowered into the open sea.

As he pursued his massive construction project, Herod became increasingly tyrannical, and those who disobeyed his orders were usually executed. Herod entered biblical infamy for the Massacre of the Innocents (Matthew 2:16–18), in which he is believed to have ordered the murder of all infant boys in Bethlehem to avoid losing his throne to a prophesied King of the Jews. Following Herod's death, Caesarea Maritima – which at its height had 50,000 residents – became the capital of the Roman province of Judea (Iudaea).

Pontius Pilate resided here as prefect from AD 26 to 36. His name appears on an inscription, found in the ruins of the theatre, that constitutes the only archaeological evidence that the man whom the Bible says ordered Jesus's crucifixion actually existed; the original is on display at the Israel Museum (p86) in Jerusalem. According to the New Testament (Acts 10), a Roman centurion named Cornelius, a member of the garrison here, was the first Gentile to be converted to Christianity, baptised by Peter himself.

Caesarea is believed to be the site of initial religious tensions that sparked riots that eventually led to the First Jewish–Roman War (AD 66 to 70), in which the Jews rose up against – and were crushed by – the Romans (and expelled from Jerusalem). Thousands of captives were executed in Caesarea's amphitheatre. Some 65 years later, after the Romans put down the Bar Kochba Revolt, the amphitheatre again became an arena of cruelty as 10 Jewish sages, including Rabbi Akiva (p215), were publicly tortured and executed.

The city was conquered by the Arabs in AD 640 and subsequently fell into disrepair. In 1101 the Crusaders under Baldwin I took Caesarea from the Muslims and discovered in the city the *Sacro Catino,* a hexagonal, green-glass bowl that they believed to be the Holy Grail (the vessel from which Jesus drank at the Last Supper). It is now kept at the Cathedral of St Lorenzo in Genoa. The Crusaders favoured Akko and Jaffa as their principal ports, so only part of Herodian Caesarea was rehabilitated.

The city changed hands between the Crusaders and the Muslims four times until King Louis IX of France captured it in 1251. That same year he added most of the fortifications visible today, but they proved totally inadequate against the onslaught of the Mamluk sultan Beybars, who in 1265 broke through the Crusader defences and devastated the city.

The ruins remained deserted and over time were swallowed by shifting, wind-blown sands. In 1878 Muslim refugees from Bosnia, fleeing the Austrian conquest of their homeland, were settled here by the Turks – the mosque and minaret by the harbour date from this period. Their descendants fled or were forced to leave during the 1948 war.

It was only with the establishment of Kibbutz S'dot Yam in 1940 that ancient Caesarea began to re-emerge. While tilling the land, farmers found bits and pieces of the old city and archaeologists soon followed. From the 1990s, archaeology teams from the US and across Israel arrived to undertake more thorough excavations, some of which continue today.

⊙ Sights

Caesarea National Park ARCHAEOLOGICAL SITE (www.parks.org.il; adult/child 39/24NIS, harbour only 14NIS; ⊘8am-5pm Sat-Thu, to 4pm Fri Apr-Oct, 8am-4pm Sat-Thu, to 3pm Fri Nov-Mar, last entry 1hr before closing) The wave-lashed location of this large archaeological site enhances the experience of exploring its Roman- and Crusader-era ruins. You'll duck through magnificent stone vaults, stroll around a vast Herodian amphitheatre and peer at ruins left by numerous conquerors.

A full-price ticket allows you into the Roman ruins and multimedia presentations; a

Ancient Caesarea

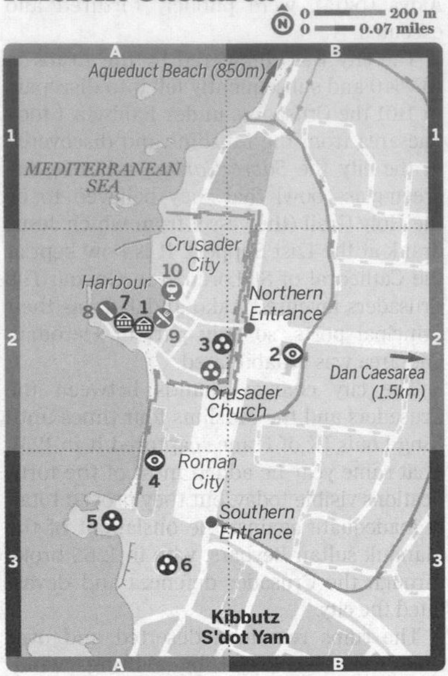

Ancient Caesarea

Aqueduct Beach (850m)
MEDITERRANEAN
SEA
Crusader
City
Harbour 10
Northern
Entrance
Crusader
Church
Dan Caesarea
(1.5km)
Roman
City
Southern
Entrance
Kibbutz
S'dot Yam

Ancient Caesarea

◎ Sights

◆ Activities, Courses & Tours

✖ Eating

◉ Drinking & Nightlife

harbour-only ticket, available at the northern entrance, buys access to the harbour area and the Crusader city. After closing time, entry to the harbour – including restaurants and bars – is free.

Entering through the northerly Crusader gate, you'll pass the **Cardo** (excavated Byzantine street) and the site of a Crusader City. Just south is the **temple platform**; during Herod's time this was a shrine to Roma and Augustus, though a succession of places of worship were constructed and demolished over the years: a Byzantine church, a mosque, and a Crusader-era church. On the pier visitors can pop into multimedia displays on ancient Caesarea including the **Time Tower** and **Caesarea Experience** (Time Trek; ⊙8am-5pm Sat-Thu, to 4pm Fri Apr-Oct, 8am-4pm Sat-Thu, to 3pm Fri Nov-Mar, last entry 1hr before closing).

Continuing south is the showpiece of the national park, the **Herodian Amphitheatre**, a 10,000-seat hippodrome where slaves and prisoners battled wild animals and chariots careened around a U-shaped track. Jutting out to sea after the southern end of the amphitheatre is the Roman-era **Promontory Palace**, while a **Roman theatre** – Israel's oldest – lies east.

Caesarea National Park has two entrances: the northern (Crusader gate) entrance, which takes you through the Crusader ramparts to the harbour and its restaurants; and, 600m to the south, the southern (Roman Theatre) entrance. Coach tours often drop visitors off at one and pick them up at the other, but if you'd like to circle back to your car, the northern entrance is a better bet.

Crusader City   ARCHAEOLOGICAL SITE
(Caesarea National Park) The original 9th-century walls enclosing this fortified Arab city were bulked out into a Crusader fortress by King Louis IX of France (St Louis), better known for building Ste-Chapelle in Paris. The ramparts, 900m long and 13m high, were made all the more impassable by a 9m-deep moat. To get an overview of the site, head up the slope from the minaret by the harbour. A path leads to the remains (three rounded apses) of a 13th-century **Crusader Church**, built over the site of an older Byzantine church.

The ruined city, situated between the national park's northern entrance and the harbour, is accessible whenever the park is open.

Caesarea Maritima Museum   MUSEUM
(☎04-636-4367; www.caesareamuseum.com; Kibbutz S'dot Yam; adult/child 18/12NIS; ⊙10am-4pm Sun-Thu) Coins, amphorae, jewellery and other relics of ancient Caesarea from Rome to the Crusader era are displayed in this museum in Kibbutz S'dot Yam, signposted around 600m south of the national park's southern entrance. You'll also find Jewish headstones and religious objects from Caesarea's old synagogue.

Aqueduct Beach BEACH
(Caesarea Beach) FREE Exactly as it sounds, a golden beach next to a section of Caesarea's Roman aqueduct. It's 2.5km by road north of ancient Caesarea.

🏃 Activities

Old Caesarea Diving Centre DIVING
(☑04-626-5898; www.caesarea-diving.com; Caesarea Harbour; gear rental per day 165NIS, intro dive incl gear 240NIS, open-water certification 1460NIS; ⊗9am-5pm Sun-Thu, 7am-5pm Fri & Sat Apr-Nov, 10am-4pm Sun-Thu, 7am-4pm Fri & Sat Dec-Mar) This fully certified and well-established dive centre offers half-hour introductory dives to a depth of up to 6m (no certification required) as well as beginner and advanced PADI courses so you can earn or renew your certification here before heading to Eilat.

🛏 Sleeping

★Grushka Country
Accommodation GUESTHOUSE $$
(☑04-638-9810; www.6389810.com; 28 HaMeyasdim St, Binyamina; d 385-540NIS, extra person 90NIS; P@🛜) An effusive Dutch owner sets the tone for this amiable four-room guesthouse. Wood ceilings, attic rooms and the occasional clog infuse it with Dutch flavour and there's a peaceful back garden with patio chairs. Breakfast costs extra. It's a 10-minute walk from Binyamina train station.

Dan Caesarea HOTEL $$$
(☑04-626-9111; www.danhotels.com; 1 Rothschild St; d US$260-350; P@🛝) This resort, 1.5km inland from the national park, is satisfyingly luxurious. Rooms feel a little beige but have huge beds and modern bathrooms; most have balconies, and the best are angled towards the sea. A classy, wood-floored gym adjoins saunas, Jacuzzi and massage rooms, there's a kids club, and the outdoor pool (April to October) is framed by lawn chairs and palms.

🍴 Eating

The harbour, home to half a dozen midrange and top-end restaurants, is a gorgeous spot for a seaside meal – worth a trip even if you're not in the mood for antiquities. Restaurants serve a range from Middle Eastern staples to seafood.

★Helena MEDITERRANEAN $$$
(☑04-610-1018; www.hellena.co.il; Caesarea Harbour; mains 70-120NIS; ⊗noon-11pm) The chefs at this chic, shoreside restaurant borrow from Italian and Greek cuisine. The menu roams from classic bistro meals (maple-glazed pork, grilled sea bream) to intriguing flavour pairings such as fennel and pomelo salad and mussels cooked in apple cider. Service manages to be personable yet slick, as does the stone-clad interior flecked with modern art.

🍷 Drinking & Nightlife

Beach Bar BAR
(☑04-636-3989; www.beach-bar.co.il; Caesarea Harbour; beer 28-32NIS; mains 50-100NIS; ⊗9am-late Mar-Oct, shorter hours winter) This bar is located on a protected little bay (where there is no lifeguard but access is free). Order a drink or something to eat (salad, schnitzel with chips, pizza, burger), and you can use the lounge chairs, umbrellas and changing rooms. Enjoy Greek music on Thursday from 9pm, jazz on Friday from 7pm and Brazilian music on Saturday from 9pm.

❶ Getting There & Away

Caesarea is 40km south of Haifa and 57km north of Tel Aviv. It's easily accessible from Zichron Ya'akov (14km northeast) and lies 10km (via Rte 4) south of Jisr Az Zarka.

Kavim bus 80 connects the national park with Caesarea–Pardes Hanna train station (30 minutes) every one to two hours; from there, trains go at least hourly to Tel Aviv (22NIS, one hour) and, via Binyamina, to Haifa (20.50NIS, 45 minutes). Alternatively, take Kavim bus 68 to Binyamina train station, from where trains connect to Tel Aviv (22NIS, one hour, four hourly) and Haifa (20.50NIS, 30 minutes, half-hourly).

A taxi to either Binyamina or Caesarea–Pardes Hanna train station costs about 50NIS.

Akko (Acre) עכו عكا
☑04 / POP 47,675

On a peninsula jutting into the Mediterranean, centuries of history are stacked within the Crusader walls of Akko (Acre). Pencil minarets and painted church domes strain above ramparts smoothed by sea winds. Its stone bastions and deep moats are the very same that greeted Marco Polo and countless pilgrims, mystics and scholars who passed through 750 years ago.

Awarded Unesco World Heritage status in 2001, Akko today has the feel of a Dubrovnik with rough edges. The scent of coffee, spice and frying fish waft through warren-like markets and the old city's alleys dart in a zig-zag, leading disoriented visitors ever deeper.

It's easy enough to tramp around old Akko on a day trip from Haifa, though sights are so numerous (and the dining scene so good) that it's worthwhile staying the night. Either way, spare a moment to fold away your map and surrender to Akko's bewitching jumble of streets.

History

Considered one of the Middle East's longest continually inhabited cities, Akko's archaeological remains date back to the early Bronze Age. In 333 BC Alexander the Great granted the city the right to mint coins, something it continued to do for six centuries. After Alexander's death, Akko was taken by the Egyptian Ptolemites. In 200 BC they lost it to the Syrian Seleucids, who struggled to keep it until the Romans, led by Pompey, began two centuries of rule.

The Arabs conquered Akko in AD 638. The city enjoyed fairly untroubled times until the arrival of the Crusaders, who seized the city in 1104 and established it as their principal port (and lifeline to Europe), with separate quarters for merchants from the rival Italian maritime cities of Genoa, Pisa and Venice. The city fell to Salah Ad Din (Saladin) in 1187, but four years later it was retaken during the Third Crusade by armies under the command of Richard I of England (Richard the Lionheart) and Philip II of France.

Under the Crusaders, Akko – a city of some 60,000 – was home to one of the most important Jewish communities in Palestine. The Spanish philosopher, scholar and physician Maimonides spent five months here in 1165, and the Catalan philosopher, Kabbalist and biblical commentator Nahmanides passed through Akko in 1267 on his way to Jerusalem.

In 1291 the Mamluks appeared with an army that outnumbered the defenders 10 to one. After a two-month siege, during which most of the city's inhabitants escaped to Cyprus, the city fell. To prevent Akko from being retaken by the forces of Christendom, the Mamluks reduced the city to rubble; it remained in ruins for the next 450 years.

The rebirth of Akko was the work of a Bosnian mercenary, Ahmed Pasha, better known as Al Jazzar (The Butcher) because of his ruthlessness in suppressing revolts. Taking advantage of the weak and corrupt Ottoman administration, Al Jazzar established a virtually independent fiefdom and bullied the port back into working order. By 1799 the city had become important enough for the 30-year-old Napoleon to attempt its capture, but he was repelled by Al Jazzar with some help from the English fleet; the defenders' resolve, it is said, was stiffened by reports of Napoleon's slaughter of Ottoman POWs after the fall of Jaffa. Among the more unlikely witnesses to Napoleon's efforts to capture the city was the Hasidic mystic and visionary Rabbi Nachman of Breslov (1772–1810), who at the end of a pilgrimage to the Holy Land spent a chaotic Shabbat here on his way back to Ukraine.

Akko remained in Ottoman hands until the British captured northern Palestine in September 1918. After they built modern port facilities in Haifa, Akko's importance declined, although its citadel was maintained as Palestine's main prison. During the 1930s, Akko was a hotbed of Arab hostility towards Jewish immigration, but Jewish forces captured the town fairly easily in 1948; three quarters of the Arab population of some 17,000 were expelled or fled.

Today Akko, like Haifa, is a mixed city: about 70% of the residents are Jews and 30% Arabs; the population of the old city is about 95% Arab. In recent years, Arab families from villages around the Galilee have been moving into the city's historically Jewish neighbourhoods.

◉ Sights

A self-guided tour of Akko's Crusader sites takes at least two hours. But there's no need to cram everything into one day: combined tickets (with Turkish bathhouse adult/child 62/54NIS, without bathhouse 40/36NIS) are valid for a year. Great deals are also available for combo tickets that include Rosh HaNikra Grottoes (adult/child 95/80NIS; p193) and/or the Holocaust museum (72/64NIS; p192) at Kibbutz Lohamei HaGeta'ot.

◉ Old City

City Walls   HISTORIC SITE
Fortified, wrecked and refortified by Muslims, Crusaders and Mamluks, old Akko is encircled by a sea wall to the west, south and southeast, and by ramparts (that you can walk on). A dry moat was dug to the north and northeast, mainly between 1750 and 1840.

In the old city's northeastern corner stands **Burj Al Kommander**, a bastion that affords great views over the skyline of Akko. From there, the **Land Wall Promenade** – accessible by stairways from the interior of the old city – heads south for 200m to the 12th-century **Land Gate**, once the city's only terrestrial entrance. Until 1910, the only other way in or out was via the **Sea Gate**, which these days faces the marina and its colourful fishing boats.

The old city's northwestern corner is anchored by **Burj Al Karim**, also known as the **English Fort**. From here, the 12th-century **sea wall** (refaced in the 18th century by Al Jazzar with stones scavenged from the Crusader castle at Atlit) runs due south (parallelled by HaHagana St) to the black-and-white-striped **lighthouse**, and then east – with the strollable **Sea Wall Promenade** on top – to the marina.

★ **Knights' Halls**   HISTORIC SITE
(Hospitaller Fortress; adult/child 25/22NIS; ☺8.30am-5pm Sat-Thu, to 4pm Fri) Akko's crowning attractions are the stone-vaulted Knights' Halls. Wandering these echoing chambers gives captivating insights into the medieval knights who once patrolled, dined and prayed here. An audio guide (included in the ticket price) evokes the sounds and smells of life in the citadel, built 800 years ago by the Hospitallers (a monastic military order). The Beautiful Hall, where pilgrims en route to the Holy Land were welcomed, is most impressively preserved.

Hammam Al Pasha   MUSEUM
(Turkish Bathhouse; adult/child 25/21NIS) Built in 1780 by Al Jazzar and in use until the 1940s, this richly ornamented marble and tile hammam now plays host to a 30-minute multimedia show about its last bathhouse attendant, sprinkled with insights into daily life in Ottoman Akko. The show is cheesy but raises a wry smile, leading headphone-clad visitors around various chambers while re-creating the sights and sounds of the hammam.

Templars' Tunnel   TUNNEL
(adult/child 15/12NIS; ☺9.30am-6.30pm Sat-Thu, to 5.30pm Fri, closes 1hr earlier in winter) This extraordinary underground passageway, 350m long, was built by the Knights Templar (a Christian military order) to connect their main fortress, just north of the black-and-white-striped lighthouse at old Akko's south-

western tip, with the marina (Khan Al Umdan). It was discovered by accident in 1994.

You can enter at either end; tickets to all the Crusaders sites are sold at both access points. Inside, buttons let you start films in either Hebrew or English.

Treasures in the Wall Museum   MUSEUM
(Burj Al Kommander; adult/child 15/12NIS; ☺10am-5pm) Stroll into the Galilee of a century ago at this museum of traditional crafts, wedged into the old city's far northeastern upper ramparts. The museum is laid out like a Galilee town souq (market) of the late Ottoman period, with blacksmith, tinsmith, potter, pharmacy, dentist, goldsmith and woodworking shops, along with Damascus furnishings inlaid with pearl and bone.

The entrance is up on the Land Wall Promenade, accessible from street level via a number of staircases.

Al Jazzar Mosque   MOSQUE
(☎04-991-3039; Al Jazzar St; 10NIS; ☺8-11am, 11.45am-3pm & 3.30-6pm winter, 8am-noon, 12.45-4pm & 4.45-7.30pm summer, longer prayer breaks Fri) The graceful silhouette of the green-domed Al Jazzar Mosque, with its slender, 124-stair minaret, dominates the northern end of Akko's old city. Al Jazzar himself designed the mosque in classic Ottoman Turkish style, and oversaw its construction in 1781. Inside are beautifully restored marble *minbar* (pulpit) and ornate *mihrab* (Mecca-facing niche), with delicate calligraphy soaring on the blue and green tiles above. Dress modestly (cover from shoulders to knees); women must cover their heads with a shawl.

The mosque stands on the site of a former Crusader cathedral, the cellars of which were put into use by the Turks as cisterns. The columns in the courtyard were 'adopted' from Roman Caesarea.

Around by the base of the minaret, the small twin-domed building contains the sarcophagi of Al Jazzar and his adopted son and successor, Süleyman.

Underground Prisoners Museum   MUSEUM
(☎04-991-1375; cnr HaHagana St & north wall of old city; adult/child 15/10NIS; ☺8.30am-4.30pm Sun-Thu) Dedicated to Jewish armed resistance during the British Mandate, this museum occupies a massive structure built by the Turks in the late 18th century on 13th-century Crusader foundations. It was used as a prison by both the Ottomans and the British. People jailed here included Revisionist Zionist leader Ze'ev Jabotinsky (from 1920 to 1921)

Akko (Acre)

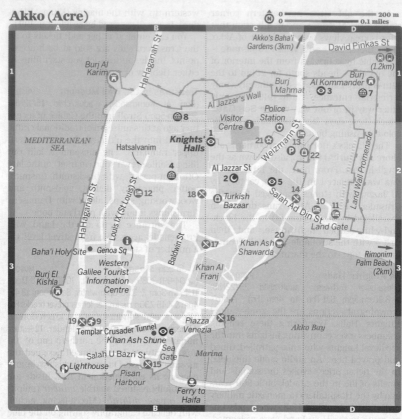

Akko (Acre)

and eight Jewish underground fighters who were executed by hanging. The museum is run by Israel's Ministry of Defense; show your passport to get in.

The museum is peopled with grey statues and has a soundtrack of clanking chains, adding to the bleak mood. A film features the Etzel's (Irgun's) daring mass breakout of 1947 (that scene in the movie version of *Exodus* was filmed here).

Baha'ullah, founder of the Baha'i faith, was imprisoned here by the Ottomans in the late 19th century. His cell, a holy place for the Baha'i, is open only to Baha'i pilgrims.

Souq Al Abiad MARKET
(White Market; Salah Ad Din St; ☺8am-late afternoon) The original Ottoman-era market on this spot was burned down within a year of being built; local legends blame a careless hookah smoker for the blaze. The market was hurriedly rebuilt and it brims with stalls to this day. Sugar cane is squeezed into juice, sacks of saffron seem full to bursting, *kunafeh* is sliced, and sellers holler about the peerless craftsmanship of sandals, lanterns and scarves.

⊙ Baha'i Sites

Akko's main Baha'i sites are 4.5km northeast of the old city, where Rte 4 meets Rte 8510. Buses that pass by this way include Nateev Express bus 271 (every 10 to 15 minutes Sunday to Friday afternoon, every 45 to 60 minutes Saturday evening), which serves Nahariya (one hour), Akko (25 minutes) and Haifa-Merkazit HaMifratz (50 minutes).

Baha'i Gardens GARDENS
(www.ganbahai.org.il; Rte 4; ☺9am-4pm Wed-Mon, noon-4pm Tue) FREE While they don't match the scale of Haifa's strikingly steep Baha'i Gardens (p159), these formal gardens are utterly picturesque, with meticulously tended flower beds, fountains and lawns trimmed with microscope accuracy. The gardens surround the **Shrine of Baha'u'llah** (www.bahaullah.com; ☺9am-noon Fri-Mon) FREE, where the founder of the Baha'i faith was interred.

Argaman Beach BEACH
A broad, sandy municipal beach with lifeguards. Though not one of Israel's best, it's makes for a pleasant break from exploring Akko's ancient sights. Situated about 1.5km southeast of the old city.

🏃 Activities

From the marina, boaters offer splashy thrill-rides (per person 20NIS) around the city walls to a soundtrack of high-energy Arabic pop music.

Ghattas Turkish Baths BATHHOUSE
(☎04-689-7462; www.ghattasbath.com; 11 HaHagana St; 2hr per person 300 400NIS, minimum 2 people; ☺9.30am-7.30pm) Reserve at least a few days ahead for olive-oil body scrubs and massages at this sumptuous Turkish bathhouse. Transforming this Ottoman building into a traditional bathhouse was a labour of love for Akko-born owner Emil Ghattas, and its marbled fittings truly conjure the spirit of a lost era. The spa has a hammam, dry sauna, hot tub and traditional treatments.

🎊 Festivals & Events

Alternative Theatre Festival THEATRE
(☎tickets 04-838-4777; www.accofestival.co.il) Akko's fringe festival brings performances to beaches, streets and ancient buildings in the old city, usually with plenty of events (tickets from 40NIS) that highlight the region's multicultural tapestry.

🛏 Sleeping

Travellers on all budgets can sleep within Akko's old city walls. At the cheaper end of the scale, historic guesthouses can be charming and inconvenient in equal measure (poor phone signal, variable levels of maintenance). Meanwhile, top-end hotels conjurer Ottoman luxury down to the last detail. Just southeast of the walled city, there are modern beach resorts.

Akko Gate Hostel HOSTEL $
(☎04-991-0410; www.akkogate.com; 13/14 Salah Ad Din St; dm/tr/q US$20/78/110/125; @🖀) Run by the friendly Walid, this long-running hostel has an enviable old-city location near the market and falafel joints on Salah Ad Din St. Wrought-iron bed frames and tiled floors characterise the well-worn rooms within this Ottoman-era building, each with mini-fridges and TVs.

HI Knights Hostel HOSTEL $$
(☎02-594-5711, reservations 1-599-510-511; www.iyha.org.il; 2 Weizmann St; dm 135-155NIS, d 380-500NIS; @🖀) Looking more like part of the old city walls than a modern hostel, this 76-room IYHA hostel runs like clockwork. The clean dorm and private rooms feel

institutional but the building has unique features, including an ancient aqueduct running through it and ruins in the courtyard. Book well ahead as it's popular with groups.

★ Efendi Hotel
HISTORIC HOTEL $$$

(📞074 729-9799; www.efendi-hotel.co.il; Louis IX St; d US$320-730; 🐾) With the same proprietor as world-famous Uri Buri restaurant, it's no surprise this boutique hotel is the ultimate in Ottoman luxury. The Efendi inhabits two Ottoman-era town houses, authentically restored under the supervision of antiquities experts. Its 12 rooms have marble fittings, Turkish rugs, pristine white walls and huge beds dressed in Egyptian cotton.

Amenities include a Turkish hammam, a rooftop patio with sea views, and a basement from the Crusader period, now used as a wine bar.

Akkotel
HOTEL $$$

(📞04-987-7100; www.akkotel.com; 1 Salah Ad Din St; s/d/tr/q US$165/200/250/290; 🅿😺🐾) Embedded in the old city ramparts, this family-run hotel has 16 individually decorated rooms (including five for families). Vaults and stone walls (some 1m thick) give common areas and many of the rooms a whisper of old-city atmosphere, and the rooftop terrace affords fantastic views of the city and bay. There's limited parking so ask ahead.

✗ Eating

Old Akko has some excellent dining options, particularly if you're in the mood for seafood. A number of restaurants and cafes shelter under the Turkish arches of Khan Ash Shawarda. For cheap eats, find several places selling hummus, falafel and shawarma along Salah Ad Din St. Hummus joints are generally open from morning until 3pm (earlier, if the hummus runs dry).

Hummus Said
MIDDLE EASTERN $

(📞04-991-3945; hummus 17NIS; 🕒6am-2.30pm Sun-Fri; 🖉) Cheap and immensely satisfying, Said's velvety hummus is the best in Akko and comes served with plenty of pickles, salads and pita, plus a bonus garnish of fava beans or garlic. Expect queues.

Abu Suheil
MIDDLE EASTERN $

(Hummus Suheila; 📞04-981-7318; 14/21 Salah Ad Din St; hummus 20NIS; 🕒9am-5pm Wed-Mon) A tiny and utterly unpretentious Middle Eastern joint where visitors are greeted with big smiles and even bigger heaps of creamy, pine-nut-clad hummus, plus hot fresh falafel and myriad salads. Look for a black sign with Hebrew lettering.

Kukushka
FAST FOOD $$

(📞04-901-9758; Turkish Bazaar; snacks 40NIS; 🕒11am-6pm or later) What's this? Pale ale, crab-meat falafel and skewered prawns at a hip hole in the wall in the Turkish Bazaar? Kukushka feels like a delicious secret. The moreish, tapas-style snacks are ideal to grab on the go.

Doniana
SEAFOOD $$

(📞04-991-0001; Pisan Harbour; mains 48-115NIS; 🕒noon-midnight; 🖉) Excellent grilled fish and seafood and stunning Mediterranean views make this restaurant a great option for a romantic meal. Meat lovers can order a tender steak, perhaps complemented by a red wine from the Golan. Dishes come with all-you-can-eat sides and salads (45NIS if you order them as a meal).

Its name, pronounced dun-ya-na in Arabic, means 'our world'. Find it up the stairs from the eastern end of the Pisan Port.

★ Uri Buri
SEAFOOD $$$

(📞04-955-2212; HaHaganah St; mains 82-134NIS, half portions 51-78NIS; 🕒noon-midnight; 🖉) Dining at Uri Buri is enough of a reason to place Akko on your travel itinerary. Lovers of seafood will quickly understand why chef Uri is so legendary. Start with wafer-thin salmon sashimi freshened by wasabi sorbet, followed by huge prawns and artichoke swirled into buttery, black-rice noodles, or sea bass simmered in coconut milk and apple.

Gourmands will be delighted to find that the restaurant encourages the ordering of two half portions, rather than a single main course (and they're sizeable, too).

Staff, who genuinely adore the menu, are happy to prepare dishes that cater to vegan, gluten-free, lactose-free or other dietary requirements. It's a good idea to call ahead, especially on Friday and Saturday; your best chance of an impromptu visit is on weekday lunch times.

El Marsa
MEDITERRANEAN $$$

(📞04-901-9281; www.elmarsa.co.il; Talmi St, Fisherman's Wharf; lunch menu 80-90NIS, evening mains 59-119NIS; 🕒noon-midnight; 🖉🐾) After stints in Michelin-starred restaurants, chef Alaa Musa returned to his home town Akko to open El Marsa, whose inventive, Galilee-sourced menu hits the spot. Ceviche, grilled barramundi and salads of local herbs are standouts, and there's a good wine list to go with it. The harbourside restaurant feels crisp and modern despite being set in a 13th-century building.

Drinking & Nightlife

El Bourj Cafe
COFFEE

(☑053 937-4925; Khan Ash Shawarda; ☺10am-midnight) El Bourj Cafe serves decent coffees within the charismatic confines of an 18th-century caravanserai.

☆ Entertainment

Akko Theatre Centre
THEATRE

(☑04-991-4222; www.acco-tc.com; 1 Weizmann St) Forging links between Jewish and Arab performers, Akko Theatre Centre is proud of its program of innovative multidisciplinary performances for adults and children, in particular the Alternative Theatre Festival (p189).

Shopping

Turkish Bazaar
MARKET

(☺8am-6pm) Built in the late 1700s as Akko's municipal market, this bazaar now hosts handicraft and souvenir sellers. Quality is variable but keen shoppers can rummage for jewellery, belly-dancing scarves, baskets, spices and more.

Kurdi Spice & Coffee
FOOD & DRINKS

(☑04-991-6188; Souq Al Abiad; ☺10am-6pm) Deep within the souq, this tourist-friendly shop ships herbs, spices and coffee worldwide.

Information

DANGERS & ANNOYANCES

Old Akko shuts down after dark, so exert normal safety precautions if walking around at night. **Police station** (☑04-987-6736, 04-987-6808; 1 Weizmann St) A community police station is located in the car park between the visitor centre and the HI youth hostel.

MONEY

The old city (eg around Al Jazzar St) has several licensed exchange bureaux. Banks with ATMs can be found in the new city.

TOURIST INFORMATION

Visitor Centre (☑04-995-6706; www.akko.org.il; ☺8.30am-6.30pm summer, to 4.30pm winter, closes 2hr earlier Fri; ☎) Get a free map, see a scale model of the city and watch an eight-minute introductory film (available in nine languages). Tickets are sold at a kiosk out front; pick up a free audio guide at a second kiosk, just after the entrance to the Knights' Halls (ID deposit required).

Western Galilee Tourist Information Centre (☑04-601-5533; www.westgalil.org.il; Genoa Sq; ☺9am-5pm Sun-Thu, to 2pm Fri, 10am-4pm Sat) A pamphlet-packed regional tourist centre with information covering Akko, day-trip ideas and beyond.

Getting There & Away

Train is the fastest and most scenic way to travel to/from Nahariya (7.50NIS, 10 minutes, three times per hour), Haifa Merkaz-HaShmona (13.50NIS, 30 minutes, three times per hour), Tel Aviv (35.50NIS, 1¾ hours, twice hourly) and Ben Gurion airport (44NIS, two hours, twice hourly).

Nateev Express buses 271 and 361 link Akko with Haifa-Merkazit HaMifratz (16NIS, 35 to 45 minutes, every 10 minutes); bus 271 continues north to Nahariya (8.50NIS, 35 minutes, every 10 to 15 minutes) via the Baha'i Gardens and Kibbutz Lohamei HaGeta'ot.

Ferries (☑052 888-8784; one-way/return 30/55NIS) connect old Akko's marina with Haifa port twice daily on weekdays and three times on Saturday; the journey takes 45 minutes, depending on sea conditions. Buy tickets up to an hour before departure time.

Sheruts (shared taxis) wait outside the Akko bus station and depart when full to Haifa (Hadar) and Nahariya.

Getting Around

To get from the **train station** (Rte 8510) and adjacent bus station to old Akko, it's a 1.5km walk (about 20 minutes) to the southwest, or you can take a **taxi** (☑04-955-5544) for 15NIS to 25NIS. Driving into narrow-laned old Akko is stressful and parking spaces are few. There are numerous paid spaces around the entrance to the walled city (some metered in two-hour slots, others around 20NIS to 25NIS for all day).

Kibbutz Lohamei HaGeta'ot
كيبوتز مقاتلون
קיבוץ לוחמי הגטאות

☑04

Kibbutz Lohamei HaGeta'ot (meaning Ghetto Fighters' Kibbutz) was established in 1949 by Jews who spent WWII fighting the Nazis in the Warsaw Ghetto and the forests of Poland and Lithuania. Today this tiny community, midway between Akko and Nahariya on the eastern side of Rte 4, has two museums bearing witness to incredible bravery: from daredevil escapes plotted in sewers to spiritual resistance through the clandestine cultivation of Jewish education and culture. It's a moving and educational half-day trip from Akko or Nahariya.

◉ Sights

Beit Lohamei HaGeta'ot　　MUSEUM
(Ghetto Fighters' House Museum; ☑04-995-8014; www.gfh.org.il; adult/child incl Yad Layeled 30/15NIS; ☺9am-4pm Sun-Thu; Ⓟ) Founded in 1949, the same year as the kibbutz, the world's first Holocaust museum focuses on the Warsaw Ghetto Uprising. The kibbutz founders considered it their duty to future generations to document the bravery of partisan fighters. The resulting museum provides an excellent account through dioramas, video testimonials and slideshows of artworks created by inhabitants of the Warsaw Ghetto, though its layout isn't always intuitive.

**Yad Layeled Children's
Memorial Museum**　　MUSEUM
(☑04-995-8044; www.gfh.org.il; adult/child incl Beit Lohamei HaGeta'ot 30/15NIS; ☺9am-4pm Sun-Thu; Ⓟ) This powerful memorial to the 1.5 million Jewish children killed in the Holocaust is housed in a circular building, intended to symbolically unify their stories. Appropriate for children aged 10 and above, the museum leads visitors through eyewitness accounts of Jewish children during WWII, including ones about hiding from the Nazis and living in concentration camps.

Aqueduct　　HISTORIC SITE
Built by Al Jazzar around 1780 and reconstructed in the early 19th century, this Ottoman aqueduct once supplied Akko with water from the Galilee uplands. Take in a great view of this sweeping structure from the entrance to Beit Lohamei HaGeta'ot.

✕ Eating

★ Alto Dairy　　CHEESE $$
(☑04-985-4802; http://altodairy.co.il; Kibbutz Shomrat; cheese/mains from 10/60NIS; ☺8.30am-5pm Sun-Thu) Creamy Tomme cheese, tangy blues and yoghurt thick enough to snap a plastic spoon are just a few of the delights of this all-goat-milk dairy, 1.5km south of Lohamei HaGeta'ot in little Shomrat. It's run by local farmer Ariel Mazan, who is passionate about high-quality, nutrient-packed goat milk – and it shows in the rich local cheeses and desserts on sale.

ⓘ Getting There & Away

The kibbutz is on Rte 4 about midway between Akko and Nahariya. The many buses that pass by this way, linking the two cities, include Nateev Express 271 (every 10 to 15 minutes Sunday to Friday afternoon, every 45 to 60 minutes

Saturday evening). The journey to either Akko or Nahariya takes 15 minutes and costs between 5NIS and 7NIS.

Nahariya　　נהריה نهريا
☑04 / POP 54,305
Twinned with Miami Beach, Florida, Nahariya may not gleam as brightly as its US counterpart, but it's enormously popular with sun-seekers. The town's focal point is 1km-long HaGa'aton Blvd, which runs along both banks of the eucalyptus-shaded Ga'aton River (actually a concrete canal) and is lined with cafes, ice-cream joints, flower shops and places to eat.

Founded by German-Jewish refugees in 1935, Nahariya still feels a bit like a Central European beach resort of the interwar era: a well-worn sunbather's retreat.

⏦ Sleeping

Amigo Hotel　　HOTEL $$
(☑04-992-2967; http://amigohotel-nahariya. weebly.com; 41 Kaplan St; d from US$90; Ⓟ☎) Rooms are somewhat spartan, but the beachside location of Amigo's is hard to beat; it's roughly 750m south of main drag HaGa'aton Blvd. Breakfast not included.

✕ Eating

HaGa'aton Blvd had a big choice of fast food, sushi, Middle Eastern fare and European-style coffee and gelato parlours. The pier-style entertainment area near the beach has snack stalls and frozen-yoghurt stands.

ⓘ Getting There & Away

Nahariya is 36km northeast of Haifa, 11km north of Akko and 10km south of Rosh HaNikra.

The best way to get here is by train. Two or three trains per hour head south from Nahariya's **train station** (cnr HaGa'aton Blvd & Rte 4) to Akko (7.50NIS, seven minutes) and Haifa Merkaz-HaShmona (17.50NIS, 35 minutes); half-hourly trains go to Tel Aviv (39.50NIS, 1¾ hours) and Ben Gurion airport (48.50NIS, two hours).

North of Nahariya

Montfort　　מונטפור مونفورت
Originally built by the noble De Milly family, what remains of **Montfort Castle** FREE is a striking ruin, reached by a pleasant hike. The castle's name was changed from

ROSH HANIKRA GROTTOES
··

Bone-white limestone cliffs seem to burst from the deep blue sea at **Rosh HaNikra Grottoes** (☑073 271-0100; www.rosh-hanikra.com; Rosh HaNikra; cable car adult/child 45/36NIS; ⊙cable car 9am-6pm Sun-Thu, to 4pm Fri), a geological beauty spot straddling the Israel–Lebanon border. A cable car descends steeply to the bottom, a journey of barely a minute; from here visitors step into wave-sculpted cave mouths, listening to water mercilessly lashing the rock. If you listen very carefully you might hear fruit bats nesting in the rock folds.

Behind the lower cable-car station, inside a naturally cool rail tunnel, you can watch a **film** on the area's geography and the history of the Haifa–Beirut railway, whose tunnels were excavated by British army engineering units from New Zealand and South Africa in 1941 and 1942. Unsurprisingly, the line has been out of commission since 1948.

At the ticket windows, it's possible to hire a **bike** (72NIS including the grottoes) for the 5km round-trip ride to **Betzet Beach**.

Up top, you can peer through a camouflaged border gate on the Israel–Lebanon border and pose for a picture next to a sign pointing to Beirut. A few kilometres north is the Naqoura base of the 12,000-member United Nations Interim Force in Lebanon (Unifil), which has been patrolling the border since 1978.

If you're hungry, there's a snack bar down below and a cafeteria and restaurant next to the border gate. The cable car is wheelchair accessible, but the caves are not. It's a good idea to wear shoes with grippy soles.

Nateev Exprees bus 31 links Rosh HaNikra with Nahariya (7.40NIS, 17 minutes, every 1½ to two hours except Shabbat).

Montfort ('strong mountain' in French) to Starkenberg ('strong mountain' in German) when the De Millys sold it to the Teutonic knights. In 1271 the Muslims, led by the Mamluk sultan Beybars, took the castle after a previous attempt, five years earlier, had failed. The Crusaders surrendered and retreated to Akko.

Dilapidated Montfort isn't quite as impressive as other Crusader castles in Israel. To the right of the entrance is the governor's residence, with the tower straight ahead. The two vaulted chambers to the right are the basement of the knights' hall; next to them is the chapel. Trails to Montfort can be picked up about 18km northeast of Nahariya from Goren Park, 9km east of the town of Shlomi (along Rte 899). A picnic area here, with benches, drinking water and plenty of shade, looks towards the castle. The hike to the castle from the trailhead takes about 45 minutes to one hour.

Akzhiv   אכזיב שאטئ الزيب

The stretch of coastline between Nahariya and Rosh HaNikra is known as Akhziv.

Akhziv National Park   BEACH
(www.park.org.il; adult/child 35/21NIS; ⊙8am-5pm Sep-Jun, to 7pm Jul & Aug; ℗) About 5km north of Nahariya, Akhziv National Park has broad lawns, traces of a Phoenician port, and a small, shallow, family-friendly beach. Changing rooms are situated on and around a little hill, formerly the site of an Arab village whose residents fled in 1948. A few hundred metres south is a much longer and wider beach with sunshades, showers and a snack bar.

It's possible to stay the night in a tent, campervan or simple en suite bungalow, at the attractive **campground** (☑04-982-3263; camping per adult/child 63/53NIS, bungalow from 450NIS; ⊙reception noon-7pm; ℗) overlooking the water.

Akhzivland   AREA
(☑054 467-9689; near Akhziv National Park; museum admission 20NIS; ⊙hours vary; ℗) So irresistible is the pull of this sparkling stretch of coast that nonconformist activist Eli Avivi declared it an independent state in 1971, irritating Israeli authorities as he drew the boundary lines of his own Elysian retreat. Avivi, now in his 80s, still welcomes visitors to his leafy compound. The centrepiece is a thrillingly odd **museum** of antiquities, costumed mannequins, animal skeletons, and newspaper clippings and video (Hebrew only) about Akhzivland. Follow 'Eli Avivi' signs near Akhziv National Park.

The former Arab village on this site, Az Zib, was left empty when residents fled in

1948. Eli Avivi decided to set up a kibbutz on this spot in 1952, which quickly gathered pace as a hippie retreat with utopian ideals, even attracting famous visitors such as Sophia Loren during the 1960s.

Avivi began to clash with Israeli authorities, who initially wanted to turn this strategic slip of coast into a military base. The defining moment came when the government decided to create Akhziv National Park. Avivi held firm, refusing to give up his land; and when the Israeli authorities fenced him off from his beloved beach, he renounced Israeli citizenship and Akhzivland was born – complete with mermaid flag and passport stamps.

Call ahead about staying in one of the on-site rooms (☑054 467-9689; r excl breakfast from 400NIS; ℗) or camping in the yard.

Lower Galilee & Sea of Galilee

בגליל התחתון ובכנרת

الجليل الاسفل بحيرة طبريا

Best Places to Eat

➜ Magdalena (p228)

➜ AlReda (p203)

➜ Abu Ashraf (p202)

➜ Tibi's Steakhouse & Bar (p228)

➜ Cafederatzia (p208)

Best Places to Stay

➜ Fauzi Azar Inn (p202)

➜ Arbel Guest House (p217)

➜ Pilgerhaus Tabgha (p227)

➜ Ein Harod Guest House (p212)

➜ Genghis Khan in the Golan (p229)

➜ Setai Sea of Galilee (p229)

Why Go?

Blessed with rugged hills cloaked in wildflowers in spring, archaeological sites from the early centuries of Christianity and ancient stone synagogues, the Lower Galilee – the part of northern Israel south of Rte 85 (linking Akko with the Sea of Galilee) – is hugely popular with hikers, cyclists, Israeli families (both Jewish and Arab) on holiday, Tel Aviv epicureans and, of course, Christian pilgrims.

Green, lush and chilly in winter (the perfect time for a hot-spring dip) and parched in summer (when you can beat the heat in the Sea of Galilee), this is where it's believed Jesus of Nazareth lived, preached and performed some of his most famous miracles. But these days even Nazareth is much more than a place of Christian pilgrimage – it now boasts one of Israel's most sophisticated dining scenes. The shimmering Sea of Galilee (in Hebrew, the Kinneret), too, juxtaposes holiday pleasures with archaeological sites linked to Jesus's ministry.

When to Go
Nazareth

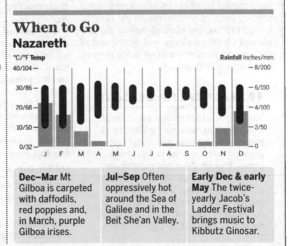

Dec–Mar Mt Gilboa is carpeted with daffodils, red poppies and, in March, purple Gilboa irises.

Jul–Sep Often oppressively hot around the Sea of Galilee and in the Beit She'an Valley.

Early Dec & early May The twice-yearly Jacob's Ladder Festival brings music to Kibbutz Ginosar.

Nazareth

الناصرة   נצרת

♫ 04 / POP 75,700

Nazareth has come a long way since its days as a quiet Jewish village in Roman-ruled Galilee, so if you're expecting bucolic rusticity, be prepared for a surprise. These days, Israel's largest Arab city is a bustling minimetropolis, with shop-lined thoroughfares, traffic jams and young men with a penchant for showing off at the wheel. The Old City, its stone-paved alleys lined with crumbling Ottoman-era mansions, is working to reinvent itself as a sophisticated culinary and cultural destination.

According to the New Testament, it was in Nazareth (Al Naasira in Arabic, Natzrat or Natzeret in Hebrew) that the Angel Gabriel appeared to Mary to inform her that she would conceive and give birth to the Son of God, an event known as the Annunciation (Luke 1:26–38).

Everything in Nazareth is open for business on the Jewish Sabbath (Friday night and Saturday). On Sunday, however, stores and most restaurants are closed.

History

In the 6th century, Christian interest in Nazareth was rekindled by reports of miracles, but a century later the Persian invasion brought massacres of Christians. After the arrival of Islam in 637 CE, many locals converted to Islam, though a significant Christian minority remained.

The Crusaders made Nazareth their Galilean capital in 1099 but were driven out a century later by Saladin (Salah Ad Din). In the mid-1200s, the Mamluk Sultan Baybars banned Christian clergy, and by the end of the century Nazareth was no more than an impoverished village.

ⓘ PRACTICAL TIP: GET LOST

You are going to get lost in the maze of alleyways that make up the Old City, so you may as well relax and enjoy! Complicating matters is the lack of street signs – though given that most street names are four-digit numbers, it should come as no surprise that locals don't use them. On the brighter side, free colour maps of Nazareth are usually available at all of the Old City's guesthouses.

Churches were re-established in Nazareth in the 17th and 18th centuries. Napoleon Bonaparte briefly captured the town in 1799. By the end of the Ottoman period, Nazareth had a sizeable Christian community and a growing array of churches and monasteries (there are now about 30).

Today about 30% of the population of Nazareth is Christian (the largest denominations are Greek Orthodox, Melkite Greek Catholic and Roman Catholic), down from about 60% in 1949. Tensions between Christians and Islamists occasionally flare up and have caused some Christians to move out of the city.

⊙ Sights & Activities

★ **Basilica of the Annunciation** CHURCH
(♫ 04-565-0001; www.nazareth-en.custodia.org; Al-Bishara St; ⊙ Upper Basilica 8am-6pm, Grotto of the Annunciation 5.45am-6pm, silent prayer 6-9pm) Dominating the Old City's skyline is the lantern-topped cupola of this Franciscan-run Roman Catholic basilica, an audacious modernist structure that's unlike any building you've ever seen. Constructed from 1960 to 1969, it's believed by many Christians to stand on the site of Mary's home, where many churches (but not the Greek Orthodox) believe the Annunciation took place.

The **Upper Basilica**, its soaring dome shaped like an inverted lily, 'glorifies Mary as the Mother of God'. With lovely mid-20th-century flair, the bare cast concrete is adorned with indented dots.

In the dimly lit lower church, a sunken enclosure shelters the **Grotto of the Annunciation**, the traditional site of Mary's house, and remnants of churches from the Byzantine (4th century) and Crusader (12th century) eras.

The walls of the courtyard and the upper church are decorated with a series of vivid **mosaic panels**, donated by Catholic communities around the world, depicting Mary and the infant Jesus in styles that boldly reflect the cultures of their countries of origin. A panel from Brazil was added in 2016.

Confessions can be made in a variety of languages from 8.30am to 11.30am and 3pm to 5pm. Regular events:

Angelus Prayer At noon daily, in the Grotto

Marian Prayer 8.30pm Tuesday

Eucharistic Adoration 8.30pm Thursday

Candlelight Procession 8.30pm Saturday

Live webcasts of some events can be seen via www.cmc-terrasanta.com.

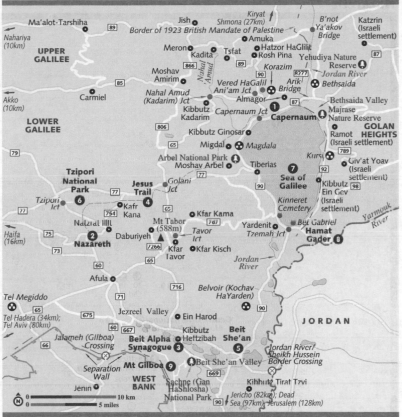

Lower Galilee & Sea of Galilee Highlights

① Capernaum (p221)
Visiting an area believed to be one of the focal points of Jesus's ministry.

② Nazareth (p196)
Dining in the Arab-fusion restaurants of the Galilee's culinary capital.

③ Beit Alpha Synagogue (p211) Identifying the Zodiac signs, Jewish symbols and biblical personages depicted on the mosaic floor.

④ Jesus Trail (p201)
Hiking from Nazareth to the Sea of Galilee.

⑤ Beit She'an (p209)
Imagining what Roman-era life was like as you explore ancient colonnaded streets.

⑥ Tzipori National Park (p205) Admiring the brilliant mosaics, including the 'Mona Lisa of the Galilee'.

⑦ Sea of Galilee (p219)
Taking a dip in the refreshing waters on a scorching summer's day.

⑧ Hamat Gader (p228)
Lolling about in steaming mineral-water pools on a chilly winter's day.

⑨ Mt Gilboa (p212)
Getting lost among the spring wildflowers.

Free brochures in a dozen languages – as well as shawls and skirts to cover exposed shoulders and knees (deposit of ID required) – are available at the Pilgrims Office (⊙9am-noon & 2-6pm Mon-Sat), 20m

to the left of the basilica's main gate. Inquiries can be sent in by email.

St Joseph's Church   CHURCH
(Al Bishara St; ⊙8am-6pm) Across the courtyard and a grassy park from the upper

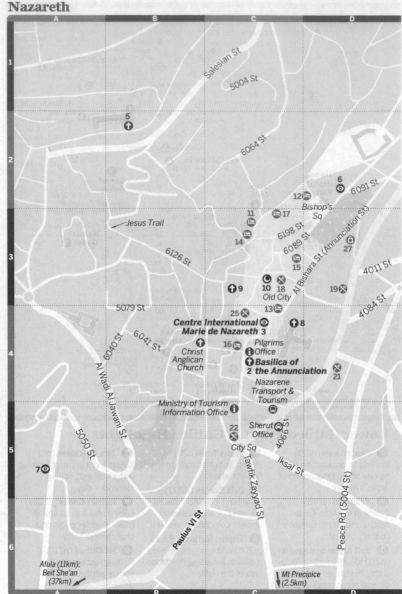

LOWER GALILEE & SEA OF GALILEE NAZARETH

level of the Basilica of the Annunciation, this neo-Romanesque Franciscan church, built in 1914, occupies a site believed by popular tradition to be that of Joseph's carpentry workshop. It was constructed on top of the remains of a Crusader church.

Down in the crypt, signs explain the in situ archaeological excavations.

★ **Centre International Marie de Nazareth** CULTURAL CENTRE
(📞 04-646-1266; www.cimdn.org; 15 Al Bishara St; recommended donation 50NIS; ⊙9.30am-

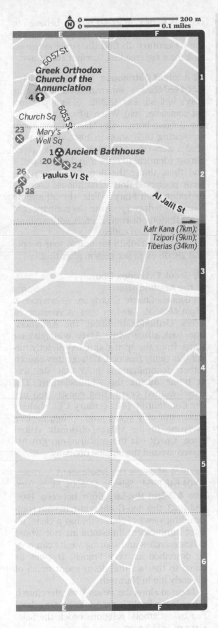

Nazareth

⊙ Top Sights
1 Ancient Bathhouse	E2
2 Basilica of the Annunciation	C4
3 Centre International Marie de Nazareth	C4
4 Greek Orthodox Church of the Annunciation	E1

⊙ Sights
5 Basilica of Jesus the Adolescent	B2
6 Cave of the 40 Holy Monks	D2
7 Nazareth Village	A5
8 St Joseph's Church	C4
9 Synagogue-Church	C3
10 White Mosque	C3

🛏 Sleeping
11 Abu Saeed Hostel	C3
12 Al Mutran Guest House	D2
13 AlReda Guesthouse	C4
14 Fauzi Azar Inn	C3
15 Simsim Backpackers	C3
16 Sisters of Nazareth Guest House	C4
17 Vitrage Guesthouse	C3

⊗ Eating
18 Abu Ashraf	C3
19 Al Taboun	D3
AlReda	(see 13)
20 Avra	F2
21 Elmokhtar Sweets	D4
22 Mahroum Sweets	C5
23 Mama Cafe	E2
24 Rose Mary	E2
25 Souq	C4
26 Tishreen	E2

⊙ Entertainment
Liwan Culture Cafe	(see 15)

🛍 Shopping
Cactus Gallery	(see 1)
27 Elbabour Galilee Mill	D3
28 Sport Al Ein	E2

LOWER GALILEE & SEA OF GALILEE NAZARETH

noon & 2.30-6pm Mon-Sat, last entry 5pm) Almost across the street from the Basilica of the Annunciation, this stunning complex is run by Chemin Neuf, a Roman Catholic community based in France, as a venue for ecumenical work among Christians and for inter-religious dialogue. The peaceful rooftop gardens, landscaped with plants mentioned in the Bible, afford 360-degree panoramas, while in the basement there are in situ ruins from as far back as the First Temple period.

A four-room multimedia presentation, available in 14 languages, illustrates biblical highlights (from Creation to the Resurrection), with an emphasis on the lives of Mary and Jesus. Films in 16 languages are shown; some can also be watched on www.netforgod.tv. Prayers (in French) are held at 6pm daily. Wheelchair accessible.

Christ Anglican Church   CHURCH

(☑04-655-4568; www.j-diocese.org) Consecrated in 1871, this solidly built stone church was only the second Anglican church to be constructed in the Holy Land (the first was in Jerusalem); the spire was finally completed in 2014. Inside, the austere, white-washed walls are softened by Gothic arches, with stained glass adding a dash of colour.

Synagogue-Church   CHURCH

(☺8am-noon & 3-7pm except during prayers, closed Sun morning) Hidden away in an alleyway off the souq, this humble Crusader-era structure, now a Catholic church, stands on the site of the synagogue where it is believed that the young Jesus quoted Isaiah (61:1–2 and 58:6) and revealed himself as the fulfilment of Isaiah's prophesy (Luke 4:15–30). The adjacent **Greek Catholic Church** (same hours), with its magnificent dome and two bell towers, was constructed in 1887 for the local Melkite Greek Catholic community.

White Mosque   MOSQUE

(Al Jaami Al Abyad; 6133 St; ☺9am-6.30pm or 7pm except during prayers) Built in the late 1700s by Sheikh Abdullah Al Fahum – his tomb can be seen through a glass door off the sanctuary – this mosque is known for its long-standing support of harmony between Nazareth's different faith communities. You can leave your shoes on, except on the rugs. The office, to the right of the door, has scarves for women to cover their heads, and information sheets in English. The interior and the courtyard, with a fountain for ablutions, are mostly modern. The colour white symbolises simplicity, purity, unity and peace.

Cave of the 40 Holy Monks   CAVE

(No 21 6198 St; donation requested; ☺tours 9am-1pm Mon-Sat) Under the compound of the Greek Orthodox Bishopric, this network of caves is named after 40 monks believed to have been martyred here by the Romans in the 1st century. To find the street entrance, look for a sign reading 'Ancient Holy Cave'.

★ Ancient Bathhouse   ARCHAEOLOGICAL SITE

(☑04-657-8539; www.nazarethbathhouse.com; Mary's Well Sq; tour 120NIS; ☺9am-7pm Mon-Sat, sometimes Sun) When Elias Shama and his Belgian-born wife Martina set about renovating their shop in 1993, they uncovered a network of 2000-year-old clay pipes almost identical to ones found in Pompeii – and then, under the floor, an almost perfectly preserved Roman bathhouse once fed by water from Mary's Well. The 30-minute tour, which draws you into the excitement of serendipitous discovery, ends with walnut-stuffed dates and coffee.

Tours cost 120NIS for one to four people and 28NIS extra per person after that.

★ Greek Orthodox Church of the Annunciation   CHURCH

(St Gabriel's Church; Church Sq; ☺7am-noon & 1-6pm Mon-Sat, 7am-1pm Sun) According to Greek Orthodox tradition, the Annunciation took place while Mary was fetching water from the spring situated directly under this richly frescoed, 17th-century church (other denominations hold that she was at home during the Annunciation). The barrel-vaulted **crypt**, first constructed under Constantine (4th century CE), shelters Nazareth's only year-round spring, a place everyone in the village obviously visited often. Check out the centuries-old **graffiti** carved around the outside doorway.

Basilica of Jesus the Adolescent   CHURCH

(☑04-646-8954; Salesian St/5004 St; ☺9am-noon & 3-6pm Mon-Sat) Built between 1906 and 1923, this neo-Gothic church, with commanding views of Nazareth, has a clean, almost luminescent limestone interior whose delicate arches and soaring vaults can only be described as 'very French'. It owes its name to the fact that Jesus spent much of his early life in Nazareth.

Located along the **Jesus Trail**, the church is inside the École Jésus Adolescent, a school run by a Catholic religious order, the Salesians of Don Bosco.

The church is a steep, 2km walk from the Old City, or you can take bus 15 from Paulus VI St. From the school's big, sliding steel gate, head left up the stairs and, at the top, enter the door to your right; the church is at the end of the long hallway.

THE GOSPEL TRAIL

The Gospel Trail, sponsored by Israel's Ministry of Tourism, goes from Nazareth (actually, from Mt Precipice) to Capernaum, passing through the landscapes where Jesus is said to have once walked. Marked by upright boulders bearing the trail's logo (an anchor) in mosaic, this 62km trail – intended for hikers, cyclists and horse riders – largely avoids built-up areas.

THE JESUS TRAIL

The 65km Jesus Trail (www.jesustrail.com) takes walkers from Nazareth's Church of the Annunciation to Tabgha and Capernaum on the Sea of Galilee. Along the way, it passes through Jewish, Christian, Muslim, Bedouin and Druze communities and a gorgeously varied landscape: rugged hills, olive groves, forests and clifftop lookouts. Highlights include Christian holy sites, ancient synagogues, a Crusader-era battlefield and Nebi Shu'eib, the Druze religion's most important shrine. If you enter nature reserves or national parks along the way (eg Tzipori and Arbel), you are subject to paying the entry fee.

Walking the entire trail, which is marked with orange blazes, usually takes four days, but shorter sections can be enjoyed as day hikes. Provided you have decent shoes and plenty of water, the route is suitable for all ages and abilities. Camping is an option, but there is plenty of accommodation along the way, ranging from B&Bs to top end hotels. The itinerary and GPS waypoints are available on the excellent website, or you can purchase two first-rate guides: *Hiking the Jesus Trail* by Anna Dintaman and David Landis, and *Jesus Trail and Jerusalem* by Jacob Saar.

Nazareth Village FARM
(☑ 04-645-6042; www.nazarethvillage.com; Al Wadi Al Jawani St/5079 St; adult/child 50/25NIS; ⊘ 9am-5pm, last tour 3.30pm Mon-Sat) If you've ever been curious about day-to-day life in Nazareth in the time of Jesus, consider stopping by this recreation of a 1st-century Galilean farmstead. The wine press, quarries and some of the vineyard terraces are authentically ancient, but everything else – the threshing floor, the burial cave, the olive press, the carpenter's and weaver's studios, the synagogue – are recreations that accurately portray life 2000 years ago. Crafts are demonstrated by actors and volunteers in period costume.

Call ahead to find out when guided tours (1¼ hours) in your language are scheduled. Run by the Nazareth Trust (www.nazareth-trust.org), the village is a circuitous 1km west of the Basilica of the Annunciation.

⌖ Tours

Daily at 9.30am, Fauzi Azar Inn (p202) offers two-hour cultural tours of the Old City (20NIS for nonguests) that focus on things you can't see on your own. They also have free Arabic lessons (Monday and Wednesday at 7pm), Arab cooking workshops (50NIS; Tuesday at 7pm) and Arabic music nights (Friday at 7pm).

⌸ Sleeping

Demand for accommodation from pilgrimage groups peaks in March, April, October, November and around Christmas and New Year, while backpackers tend to be most numerous from late June to October and around Christmas and New Year. At these times, it's sensible to reserve ahead.

All the small guesthouses in the Old City are well signposted along alley walls.

Vitrage Guesthouse B&B $
(☑ 052 525-8561, 04-657-5163; www.vitrage-guesthouse.com; No 4 6083 St; s/d/tr with shared bathroom 210/234/270NIS, small rooms 150/198/250NIS; ☎) More a homestay than a B&B, this simply furnished nine-room guesthouse is run by Bishara, a retired *vitrage* ('stained glass' in French) artisan, who grew up here (and was baptised in the garden pool), and his wife. He's happy to show visitors how stained glass is made and often invites guests to dine with the family. Excellent value.

Simsim Backpackers GUESTHOUSE $
(☑ 077 551-7275; www.simsim-guesthouse.com; 6132 St; dm excl breakfast 70NIS; ☎) Run by friendly Sami and Silke, this attractive guesthouse has 23 dorm beds (mostly bunks), seven of them in an all-female room. Amenities include kitchen facilities. Great value. Reception is inside the adjacent Liwan Cultural Cafe.

Abu Saeed Hostel GUESTHOUSE $
(☑ 04-646-2799; www.abusaeedhostel.com; 6097 St; dm excl breakfast 75NIS, d/tr 350/430NIS, with shared bathroom 230/300NIS; ☎) Staying here is like being the guest of a local family in the slightly chaotic 350-year-old house, equipped with two ancient cisterns, hand-me-down furniture, a family 'museum' and a plant-filled courtyard whose residents include land turtles, goldfish and lovebirds. Rooms

and showers are basic. Has a kitchen for self-catering and a chill-out area on the roof.

Sisters of Nazareth Guest House
GUESTHOUSE $

(☏04-655-4304; acceuilnasra@live.fr; 6167 St; dm/s/d/tr excl breakfast 85/250/300/430NIS) Set around a flowery courtyard with archaeological excavations underneath, this 61-room establishment, in a building that dates from 1855 (a new wing opened in 2017), is run by the Sisters of Nazareth, a French Catholic order. The spotless, barracks-like dorm rooms, with four to six beds each, are single-sex. Note that the gate is locked for the night at 10.30pm sharp.

Breakfast costs 25NIS. Reservations can be made by email or fax up to one or two weeks ahead; walk-ins are welcome.

★ Fauzi Azar Inn
GUESTHOUSE $$

(☏04-602-0469; www.abrahamhostels.com; dm 85-100NIS, d 335-385NIS, all excl breakfast; @🛜) Hidden away in a gorgeous, two-century-old stone house in the Old City, this place has oodles of charm – and so do the staff. The 14 rooms are simple but tasteful, though they're no match for the lounge's arched windows, marble floors and 5m-high frescoed ceiling. A great place to meet other travellers – or to volunteer (see website).

Anyone with a passport stamp from Lebanon, Iraqi Kurdistan or Iran gets the first night in a dorm bed free. Doing laundry costs 15NIS.

★ Al Mutran Guest House
GUESTHOUSE $$

(☏04-645-7947; www.al-mutran.com; Bishop's Sq; d US$110-140, q ste US$200; 🛜) Adjacent to the residence of Nazareth's Greek Orthodox *mutran* ('bishop' in Arabic), this family-run gem, with 11 rooms, occupies a gorgeous, 200-year-old mansion with 4.5m-high ceilings, Ottoman arches and antique floor tiles. Breakfast is served in the stylish lobby, decorated with embroidered pillows and Bedouin textiles.

AlReda Guesthouse
B&B $$$

(☏04-608-4404; alreda2000@hotmail.com; 21 Al Bishara St; d/tr/q 800/900/1000NIS) On the top floor of an Ottoman mansion, this vast, all-wood studio apartment affords breathtaking views. Unbelievably romantic.

✖ Eating

Foodies around Israel and beyond know that Nazareth's delicious dining scene is worth braving the traffic for. The buzzword is 'fusion', with European-inspired dishes blended with local seasonings and then served – with a generous helping of Arab hospitality – in atmospheric Old City mansions or at Mary's Well Sq.

Locals eat late, often beginning dinner at 9pm or even 10pm.

★ Abu Ashraf
MIDDLE EASTERN $

(Diwan Al Saraya; ☏04-657-8697; 6134 St; mains 20NIS; ⊗8am-8pm Mon-Sat; 🖊) This old-time coffeehouse is famous all over town for its *katayef* (sweet pancakes folded over goat's cheese or cinnamon walnuts and then doused with geranium syrup), coffee (a special mix of five kinds of bean plus cardamom) and collection of antiques. Ebullient owner Abu Ashraf loves to share stories about Nazareth.

It also has excellent vegetable salads, *freekeh* (roasted green wheat), *labneh* (thick yoghurt) and *kibbeh* (meat-filled cracked wheat croquettes). Built around 1730, this place is not to be confused with a modern copycat of the same name nearby.

Souq
MARKET $

(Market Sq & 6152 St; ⊗approx 8am-3pm Mon-Sat) Fruit, veggies, bread and even pita pizzas are on sale along the narrow, winding alleys of the Old City's market.

Al Taboun
MIDDLE EASTERN $

(Paulus VI St; mains 25-30NIS; ⊗9am-10pm Mon-Sat; 🖊) The decor is unspeakably tacky, but the shawarma, hummus plate and veggie salad-and-starter spread are tops.

Mama Cafe
CAFE $

(☏04-637-7807; 6089 St; cakes 12-30NIS; ⊗7.30am-7pm or 7.30pm Mon-Wed & Sat, to 11.30pm or later Thu & Fri; 🛜) Decorated with colourful photos by local artists, this mellow cafe and cake shop serves sandwiches, fresh-squeezed juices and homemade baked goods, including cheesecake. Salads cost 20NIS to 40NIS, while brunch is 28NIS.

Elmokhtar Sweets
PASTRIES $

(Paulus VI St; per kg 70-90NIS; ⊗9am-11.30pm or midnight) A brightly lit sweets emporium that could be at home in Beirut or Cairo. It has a selection of mouth-watering baklava, superb *kunafeh* (a hot, thin, syrupy cheesecake) and homemade halva.

Mahroum Sweets
PASTRIES $

(www.mahroum-baklawa.com; cnr Paulus VI & Al Bishara Sts; per kg 80NIS; ⊗8am-midnight) A family tradition since 1890, this pastry shop, which moved to a new location in 2017, is one of the best places in Israel for baklava and other syrup-soaked Arab pastries, as well as *kunafeh* and Turkish delight.

Avra
GREEK $$

(☏04-659-1547; Mary's Well Sq; mains 32-86NIS; ⏱8.30am-midnight or later Mon-Sat) 'Avra' means 'good atmosphere' in Greek, and that's exactly what this cafe-restaurant has, along with delicious Greek and Palestinian dishes and a soundtrack of traditional and modern Greek instrumental music. The speciality is the Ouzo Plate, which mixes Greek favourites such as meat-stuffed grape leaves, feta and kalamata olives with a local or Greek ouzo.

Also has pasta, sandwiches, authentic Greek salads and Greek-style iced coffee.

Rose Mary
CAFE $$

(☏04-647-1212; www.nrmary.com; mains 38-88NIS; ⏱9am 11.30pm Tue-Sat, from 6pm Mon, 10am-11.30pm Sun; 🎵) This convivial bistro-cafe serves French and Italian dishes prepared with top-quality ingredients and fresh Galilean spices. The house speciality is shrimp and calamari with garlic and arak sauce. Also serves locally made pork chorizo, an excellent chef's salad, pasta and sandwiches.

Tishreen
MEDITERRANEAN $$

(☏04-608-4666; www.tishreen.rest.co.il; 56 Al Bishara St; mains 52-129NIS; ⏱10am-11pm; 🎵) The wood-fired oven at this well-loved restaurant, adorned with antiques and wine bottles, turns out Arab- and Mediterranean-inspired dishes such as aubergine stuffed with pesto and cheese, as well as excellent *muhammar* (Arab pizza topped with chicken and onion), hearty meat dishes, pasta and meal-size salads. Also worth trying: a traditional Galilean dish called *freekeh*, made with cracked green wheat.

★ AlReda
FUSION $$$

(☏04-608-4404; 21 Al Bishara St; mains 50-100NIS; ⏱7pm-2am; 🎵) In a 200-year-old Ottoman-era mansion, this atmospheric restaurant – the songs of the legendary Egyptian singer Umm Kulthum are on high rotation – serves traditional Nazarene recipes with a Mediterranean twist. Specialities include seasonal dishes made with okra (*bamya*) and wild thistle (*akub*), and fresh artichoke hearts filled with chopped beef, almonds and pine nuts.

Owner Daher Zeidani encourages guests to share the generous portions to taste different dishes. It has a bar.

🍷 Drinking & Nightlife

Wine, beer and spirits are widely available in Christian areas. Many of Nazareth's trendiest spots for sipping can be found at or around Church Sq and Mary's Well Sq, focal point of the city's nightlife zone.

☆ Entertainment

Liwan Culture Cafe
ARTS CENTRE

(☏04-628-3511; 6132 St; ⏱8am-8pm or later) Founded to help bring cultural life back to the Old City, this cafe hosts exhibitions by Palestinian artists, most of them from the Galilee, and several free cultural events every week. A vegetarian *plat du jour*, cooked by local women, is available at lunchtime; beverages include Palestinian wines and two West Bank beers, Taybeh and Shepherd's.

Also serves as an information centre for tourists.

🛍 Shopping

★ Elbabour Galilee Mill
FOOD

(Galilee Mill; ☏04-645-5596; www.elbabour-shop.com; entrances on Al Bishara St & Paulus VI St; per 100g 25NIS; ⏱8.30am-7pm or 7.30pm Mon-Sat) The other-worldly aroma inside this spice emporium, run by the same family for four generations, has to be inhaled to be believed. Shelves, sacks, bins and bottles display more than 2600 products, from exotic spice mixtures (including Pierina's Spice, based on a secret recipe passed down by owner Tony's mother) to herbal teas, and from dried fruits to aromatic oils. The name is the local pronunciation of *al vapeur* ('the steam' in Arabicised French), the name given in the 1890s to the steam engine that once ran the company's infernally noisy, German-made flour mill. Products can be ordered online and shipped around the world.

Cactus Gallery
ARTS & CRAFTS

(www.nazarethcactus.com; Mary's Well Sq; ⏱9am-7pm Mon-Sat, sometimes Sun) The shop above Nazareth's sensational Roman-era ancient bathhouse (p200) sells creative modern jewellery and gorgeous Palestinian embroidery, made from old dresses in a convent in Jerusalem.

Sport Al Ein
SPORTS & OUTDOORS

(Sport HaMa'ayan; ☏052 353-5362; Paulus VI St; ⏱8.30am-8pm Mon-Sat) If you'll be camping along the Jesus Trail or on the shores of the Sea of Galilee, this fishing-supplies shop is a good place to buy inexpensive sleeping bags, tents and travel mattresses. Situated 150m down Paulus VI St from Mary's Well.

ℹ️ Information

Basilica of the Annunciation Pilgrims Office (p197) Has details on prayers and other activities at the basilica.

Ministry of Tourism Information Office (📞04-657-0555; www.goisrael.com; 58 Casanova St; ⊗8.30am-5pm Mon-Fri, 9am-2pm Sat) Has a free English map of Nazareth and brochures about Nazareth and the Galilee in a dozen languages.

Nazareth Cultural & Tourism Association (www.nazarethinfo.org) Has a useful website.

ℹ️ Getting There & Away

BUS

Nazareth does not have a proper bus station. Rather, intercity buses stop along traffic-plagued Paulus VI St between Mary's Well and the Basilica of the Annunciation – on the northbound side for Kafr Kana, Tiberias and Akko, on the southbound side for Haifa, Tel Aviv and Jerusalem. One intercity bus company, **Nazarene Transport & Tourism** (www.ntt-buses.com; Paulus VI St; ⊗5.30am-6pm), has a city-centre office that can supply timetables.

Akko (Nazareth Tourism & Transport bus 353 and Egged bus 343, 21.50NIS, 50 minutes, hourly except Friday evening and Saturday before sundown)

Haifa (Merkazit HaMifratz and/or Merkaz HaShmona Train Station, Nazareth Tourism & Transport buses 332 and 342 and GB Tours bus 331, 16NIS, 50 minutes, at least twice an hour except Friday evening)

Jerusalem (Egged bus 955, 37.50NIS, two hours, twice in the morning Sunday to Thursday, one Friday morning, two Saturday night)

Tel Aviv (Egged bus 826 and Nazareth Tourism & Transport bus 833, 34NIS, 2¾ hours, several times an hour) Stops on Rte 75.

Tiberias (Nazareth Tourism & Transport bus 431, 16NIS, one hour, hourly except Friday evening and Saturday before sundown) Some buses stop on Nazareth's ring road, Rte 75, instead of on Paulus VI St.

Buses to Amman, Jordan, are run by **Nazarene Tours** (📞04-601-0458; 3 Marj Ibn Amer St; 80NIS; ⊗departures 8.30am Tue, Thu & Sat).

SHERUT

Sheruts (shared taxis) leave from 4066 St, just off Paulus VI St (across the street from Nazarene Transport & Tourism) – look for a tiny **office** (📞04-657-1140; 4066 St) on the right with a faded red-on-white sign in Arabic and Hebrew. Destinations include the following:

Jenin (West Bank) (25NIS, 30 to 40 minutes, departure at 7.30am to Jenin, at 11am to the Jalameh/Gilboa crossing, 10km south of Afula)

Tel Aviv (Central Bus Station, 32NIS Sunday to Friday morning, 40NIS Friday afternoon and Saturday, 1½ to 1¾ hours, departures 8am to 3pm or 4pm)

TAXI

Cabs can be ordered from **Mary's Well Taxi** (📞04-655-5105, 04-656-0035).

Kafr Kana   כפר כנא كفر كنا

📞04 / POP 12,300

Site of two picturesque stone churches – one Greek Orthodox, the other Catholic – the Arab town of Kafr Kana (Cana) is believed to be the site of Jesus's first miracle (John 2:1–11), when he changed water into wine at a wedding reception. The town – about 10% of its population Christian – is situated about 8km northeast of central Nazareth on the road to Tiberias (and on the Jesus Trail).

👁️ Sights

Most of Kafr Kana's Christian sights are on or near souvenir shop–lined Churches St, which intersects the main road through town (Rte 754) at an oblique angle; the intersection – marked by a large white-on-black sign – is 200m north of the Rte 754 entrance to the Cana Greek Orthodox Wedding Church.

Cana Greek Orthodox Wedding Church & Monastery   CHURCH
(Greek Orthodox Church of St George; Rte 754; ⊗10am-3pm, closed on Greek Orthodox holidays) This richly decorated, late-19th-century church – topped by a round tower and a brown dome – shelters two ancient jars believed to have been used by Jesus to perform the wedding miracle and what is believed to be a relic of the Apostle Simon.

Cana Catholic Wedding Church   CHURCH
(Churches St; ⊗8am-5.30pm Mon-Sat, from noon Sun) This green-domed Franciscan church, built in the late 1800s, stands on the site where Catholics believe Jesus performed the wedding miracle. An ancient jar that may have been among the six used by Jesus when he turned water into wine can be seen in the basement (access is around the side of the church). Under the floor of the nave, through a glass tile, you can see a 4th-century Jewish inscription in Aramaic.

🛏 Sleeping

Cana Guest House　　　　GUESTHOUSE $
(☑04-651-7186, Salman 050 400-7637; www.cana
guesthouse.com; dm/d/tr with shared bathroom &
excl breakfast 120/350/480NIS; @ 🛜) The welcoming Billan family has turned four apartments into 18 comfortable, clean rooms,
many quite spacious; private bathrooms are
planned. Dorms have four beds. Guests can
use the kitchen and hang out in the lemon
tree–shaded courtyard. Situated behind the
Cana Catholic Wedding Church compound,
70m up an alley from Churches St.

Breakfast costs 35NIS, a packed lunch
35NIS and a hearty, home cooked dinner
75NIS.

❶ Getting There & Away

A slew of short-haul bus lines connect Kafr Kana
with Nazareth's Old City (Paulus VI St), 8km to
the southwest.

Nazareth Tourism & Transport's bus 431
(hourly except Friday evening and Saturday)
links Kafr Kana with Tiberias (12.50NIS, 27 minutes, hourly except Friday evening and Saturday
before sundown).

Tzipori　　　صفورية　ציפורי

Among the most impressive Roman-era
sites anywhere in Israel, Tzipori was once
a hugely important centre of post-Temple
Jewish life. Highlights include grand public
amenities, a synagogue and what may be the
country's most beautiful ancient mosaics.

👁 Sights

★ **Tzipori National Park**　ARCHAEOLOGICAL SITE
(Zippori, Sepphoris; ☑04-656-8272; www.parks.
org.il; adult/child 28/14NIS; ☒8am-4pm or 5pm,
closes 1hr earlier Fri, last entry 1hr before closing)
In ancient times, Tzipori was a prosperous
and well-endowed city with stone-paved
roadways (you can still see the ruts left by
Roman wagons), a sophisticated water-
supply system (you can walk through part of
the underground aqueduct), a marketplace,
bathhouses and a 4500-seat theatre. Today,
the star attraction is a mosaic portrait of a
contemplative young woman nicknamed
the Mona Lisa of the Galilee, discovered
inside the (now air-conditioned) remains of
a Roman villa.

Two seven-minute films provide fascinating background on the site: one at the park
entrance, the other in the 5th-to-7th-century
synagogue (air-conditioned), whose mosaic floor is decorated with a beautiful Zodiac circle. The whole site is wheelchair
accessible.

It was in Tzipori, in the 2nd and 3rd centuries CE – a generation or two after the Bar
Kochba Revolt (132–135 CE) against Rome –
that Rabbi Yehuda HaNassi is believed to
have redacted the Mishnah (the earliest codification of Jewish law). A bit later on, Tzipori scholars contributed to the Jerusalem
(Palestinian) Talmud.

🛏 Sleeping & Eating

There's a small grocery (tzarchaniya) in
Moshav Tzipori, situated just west of the national park.

Zippori Village　　　　　　B&B $$
(☑04-646-2647; www.zippori.com; Moshav Tzi-
pori; d excl breakfast from 400NIS; 🛜 📺) Run by
the friendly, knowledgeable Suzy and Mitch
(who grew up in Denver and New York City
respectively), the five two-room cottages
come with gorgeous Galilean views, cheerful
if old-fashioned decoration, a spa bath and a
children's sleeping area (reached via a steep
ladder). The fully equipped kitchenettes are
kosher dairy. Breakfast costs 100NIS for two.
To get here, count 20 speed bumps from the
moshav entrance and turn left.

🍷 Drinking & Nightlife

If you've come to Tzipori looking for night-
life, you're about 1700 years too late.

❶ Getting There & Away

The village of Tzipori and Tzipori National
Park are 11km northwest of Nazareth, a few
kilometres north of Rte 79. There's no public
transport.

Mt Tabor Area

Mt Tabor　　جبل الطور　הר תבור

Rising from the Jezreel Valley, remarkably
symmetrical Mt Tabor (588m) dominates
the landscape between Nazareth and the Sea
of Galilee, affording spectacular views, fine
hikes and, if you're into that sort of thing,
hang-gliding.

You don't have to be a Christian pilgrim
to enjoy the beauty of Mt Tabor, the biblical
site of the Transfiguration of Jesus (Mat-
thew 17:1–9, Mark 9:2–8 and Luke 9:28–36),

JEKLI / SHUTTERSTOCK ©

ALLA KHANANASHVILI / SHUTTERSTOCK ©

1. Sea of Galilee (p219)
Take in spectacular views across Israel's largest freshwater lake.

2. Tzipori National Park (p205)
Admire ancient mosaics – the star attraction – at this fascinating park.

3. Nazareth (p196)
Sample local produce at one of the city's markets.

4. Beit She'an National Park (p209)
Play archaeologist as you explore Roman Empire ruins at this extensive site.

in which 'his face became as dazzling as the sun; his clothes as radiant as light' and he is said to have spoken with the prophets Moses and Elijah. Two compounds crown the mountain, one Catholic (Franciscan), the other Greek Orthodox (closed to the public).

According to the Hebrew Bible, Mt Tabor was where the Israelites, led by the prophetess Deborah, defeated a Canaanite army under the command of Sisera (Judges 4). The mountain was much contested during the Crusader period.

◉ Sights & Activities

The **Israel National Trail** goes up and over Mt Tabor, intersecting two marked trails that circumnavigate the mountain: **Shvil HaYa'aranim** and, up near the summit, the **Sovev Har Tavor** (Mt Tabor Circuit). The topographical map to have is SPNI Map No 3 (*HaGalil HaTachton HaAmakim v'HaGilboa*).

Franciscan Monastery & Church CHURCH
(☉ 8am-5pm Mon-Sat, 8am-noon & 2-5pm Sun) An avenue of cypresses leads through this Catholic compound to a monastery, home to three Franciscan friars (helped by lay volunteers from Italy), a small garden of plants from around the world, the ruins of a Byzantine-era monastery, and the Roman–Syrian-style **Basilica of the Transfiguration**, one of the Holy Land's most beautiful churches.

Consecrated in 1924, it is decorated with lovely gold-flecked mosaics and has a crypt reached by 12 broad steps. Women are asked to dress modestly (no sleeveless shirts or miniskirts), men to take off their hats. Up to the right from the entrance to the church, a **viewing platform** offers spectacular panoramas of the Jezreel Valley's multihued patchwork of fields.

❶ Getting There & Away

Mt Tabor is about midway between Tiberias and Afula, just off Rte 65. From Rte 7266 – which goes all the way around the base of the mountain, connecting the Arab villages of Shibli and Daburiyeh with Rte 65 – it's a teeth-clenching 3km ride (with 16 hairpin turns) up to the summit.

Kfar Tavor   כפר תבור كفر تافور
☑ 04 / POP 3800
Founded in 1901, the Jewish village of Kfar Tavor is the main commercial and tourism hub for the Mt Tabor area, offering visitors places to eat and sample local wines.

◉ Sights & Activities

Kfar Tavor and nearby villages such as Kfar Kisch make a great base for hiking along the **Israel National Trail** and a spur of the **Jesus Trail** – for instance, northeast to the Yardenit baptism site on the Sea of Galilee, or west up Mt Tabor. Sections of both trails can be ridden by bicycle. For cyclists there's also a single track through **Beit Keshet Forest** (northwest of Kfar Tavor) and some fine routes on the **Sirrin Heights** (east of Kfar Tavor).

Tabor Winery   WINERY
(☑ 04-676-0444; www.twc.co.il; Kfar Tavor Industrial Zone; ☉ 9am-5pm Sun-Thu, to 2pm Fri winter, to 4pm Fri summer) Known for its reds (merlot, cabernet sauvignon, shiraz) and whites (chardonnay, sauvignon blanc, roussanne and gewurztztraminer), this well-regarded winery produces about two million bottles a year. Wines made from tannat and marcelin grapes were first marketed in 2017. Offers free tastings, sales and, for groups of 10 or more, tours.

✖ Eating

Cafederatzia   CAFE $$
(☑ 04-676-6233; cnr HaMeyasdim & Bar Giyyora Sts; mains 38-62NIS; ☉ 8.30am-11.30pm Sun-Thu, to 4.30pm Fri, 10am-11.30pm Sat; 🖥🖉) This friendly cafe, delightful in every way, serves generous salads, shakshuka, quiche, pasta, hamburgers and boutique hot dogs, as well as gluten-free bread, baked goods and Tavor wines by the glass. Breakfast for one/two costs 58/109NIS. In good weather you can eat outside in the olive garden.

❶ Getting There & Away

Kfar Tavor is a stop for most of the many buses travelling between Tiberias and Afula.

Kfar Kama   כפר כמא كفر كما
☑ 04 / POP 3200
Kfar Kama is an excellent place to encounter the Circassians, a Caucasian people of the Sunni Muslim faith who were forced out of their homes in the northern Caucasus – between the Black and Caspian Seas – as the Russian Empire expanded southward in the mid-1800s. A local museum features Circassian culture and history.

At least half a million Circassians found refuge in the Ottoman Empire. In 1876 some of them settled in Kfar Kama, one of only two Circassian villages in Israel (the other is Reyhaniye). The Circassians have always enjoyed good relations with their Jewish neighbours, and all Circassian men – long famed as fierce warriors – are drafted into the Israel Defence Forces (IDF). Signs around the spotless, well-off town are in Hebrew, Circassian (spoken at home and taught in school) and Arabic.

⊙ Sights

Circassian Heritage Center   MUSEUM
(✓050 585-7640; www.circassianmuseum.co.il; adult/child 25/20NIS; ⊙9am-5pm) Housed in a complex of century-old basalt houses, this museum offers a fascinating peek at the local Circassian community and their daily life during Ottoman times. Admission includes a 20-minute film (with English subtitles) and a one-hour tour that takes in traditional Circassian clothing, musical instruments, household objects and agricultural implements. Call ahead for English tour times.

✘ Eating

Laoz   CIRCASSIAN $$
(✓050 302-0992; Shahso St; mains 40-90NIS; ⊙noon-10pm or later; ✐) An informal restaurant featuring a 'Circassian meal' that includes *halozh* (pastry filled with Circassian cheese and deep-fried in olive oil) and *mataza* (dumplings filled with Circassian cheese and green onions, served with yoghurt), in addition to shakshuka and the usual selection of Middle Eastern grilled meats. Situated right at the western entrance to town.

❶ Getting There & Away

Superbus buses 30 and 33 link Kfar Kama with Tiberias (10NIS, 50 minutes) at least hourly.

Jezreel & Beit She'an Valleys   עמק יזרעאל ובית שאן
مرج ابن عامر مرج بيسان

The largely agricultural Jezreel Valley (Plain of Esdraelon) is home to a number of veteran kibbutzim and a spectacular Byzantine-era synagogue mosaic. Stretching for about 45km, from a bit west of Nazareth southeast to the Jordan River, it is bounded on the south by the partly forested slopes of Mt Gilboa.

At its eastern end, the Jezreel Valley merges into the Beit She'an Valley, site of

Israel's most impressive Roman ruins. This area forms part of both the Jordan Valley and the Great Rift Valley.

Beit She'an   بيسان   בית שאן
✓04 / POP 17,300

Founded sometime in the 5th millennium BCE, Beit She'an – strategically situated at the intersection of the Jezreel and Jordan Valleys – has the most extensive Roman-era ruins in Israel. The struggling modern town has little to offer the visitor except a youth hostel and some restaurants.

⊙ Sights

★ **Beit She'an
National Park**   ARCHAEOLOGICAL SITE
(✓04-658-7189; www.parks.org.il; Rte 90; adult/child 28/14NIS; ⊙8am-4pm Oct-Mar, to 5pm Apr-Sep, closes 1hr earlier Fri, last entry 30min before closing) Beit She'an's extraordinary Roman ruins are the best place in Israel to get a sense of what it was like to live, work and shop in the Roman Empire. Colonnaded streets, a 7000-seat **theatre** that looks much as it did 1800 years ago (the original **public bathrooms** are nearby), two **bathhouses** and huge stone columns that lie right where they fell during the 749 earthquake evoke the grandeur, self-confidence and decadence of ancient Roman provincial life.

The path to the theatre and the **Cardo**, the hugely impressive colonnaded main street, is wheelchair accessible.

Towering over the Roman city, known in Greek as Scythopolis, is **Tel Beit She'an**, created by at least 20 cities built and rebuilt one on top of the other. The viewpoint atop the tel offers near-aerial views of the Roman ruins.

On Monday to Thursday evenings from March to November, **She'an Nights**, an after-dark multimedia spectacular in English or Hebrew (adult/child 55/45NIS), brings alive the ruins with projected images but is not a satisfactory substitute for a daylight visit – it's too dark to read the signs and most of the site is off-limits. The show is cancelled if it rains. Call ahead for reservations on 04-648-1122 or 1222-3639. To get to the park entrance, head down the hill for a few hundred metres from the Bank Leumi branch at 81 Sha'ul HaMelech St.

🛏 Sleeping

Several kibbutzim near Beit She'an, such as Kibbutz Kfar Rupin, have guesthouses.

HI – Beit She'an Guest House   HOSTEL $$
(☎02-594-5644; www.iyha.org.il; 129 Menahem Begin Ave/Rte 90; s/d 400/530NIS, additional adult/child 160/125NIS; @🛏🖥) Within easy walking distance of Beit She'an's antiquities, this hostel has 80 rooms (18 of them added in 2017), attractive public areas, a great rooftop patio and a pool (open April to Sukkot). Rooms are practical and clean and have five beds; individual dorm beds are not available. Situated a bit south of the intercity bus stops. Wheelchair accessible.

🍴 Eating

Dining options in Beit She'an are pretty much limited to falafel, shawarma and grilled meats.

Shipudei HaKikar   MIDDLE EASTERN $$
(☎04-606-0198; www.shipudey-hakikar.co.il; 1 Shaul HaMelech St; mains 38-120NIS; ⊙11.30am-midnight Sun-Thu, from 30min after sundown-midnight Sat; 🖥) Widely acclaimed as Beit She'an's best place to eat. Excellent shish kebab is served with freshly baked *laffa* (flat pita) and is preceded by 18 super-fresh salads, including eggplant, hummus and tahina. If you're not ordering a main, the salads cost 36NIS – a superb veggie meal! Grilled meat in *laffa* or a baguette, without salads, costs 38NIS to 60NIS.

Situated 1km northwest of the Roman antiquities in a building with a clock tower on top (just past the police station).

ℹ Getting There & Away

BUS
Beit She'an does not have a proper bus station. Rather, buses stop along Menahem Begin Ave (Rte 90) about 100m north of the Beit She'an Guest House (youth hostel).

Afula (Superbus buses 411 and 412, 10NIS, 30 minutes, two or three times an hour except Friday evening and Saturday before sundown)

Jerusalem (Egged buses 943, 961 and 966, 37.50NIS, 2¼ hours, every 30 to 90 minutes Sunday to Friday afternoon and Saturday night) Via the Jordan Valley (West Bank).

Tel Aviv (Egged bus 843, 37.50NIS, three hours, three daily Sunday to Thursday, one Friday, two Saturday night)

Tiberias (Superbus bus 28, 14NIS, 35 minutes, every 45 minutes Sunday to Thursday, hourly until mid-afternoon Friday and after sundown Saturday) Has stops along the southwestern coast of the Sea of Galilee.

To get to Nazareth, change buses in Afula.

The legendary Rakevet HaEmek (Jezreel Valley rail line) reopened in 2016, linking Beit She'an's train station, situated 2.5km northwest of the national park, with **Haifa-Merkaz HaShmona** (20NIS, 45 minutes, hourly).

THE JEZREEL VALLEY RAILWAY, THEN & NOW

From shortly before WWI until 1951, you could hop on the legendarily slow **Jezreel Valley Railway** in Haifa at 8am and pull into Hamat Gader at 11.45am – or, until 1946, arrive in Damascus at 7.47pm. Or you could transfer to the Hejaz Railway in the Syrian town of Daraa, 60km east of Hamat Gader, and roll south. (Daraa is where the first confrontations of the Syrian civil war took place in 2011.) Until the Hejaz Railway was knocked out of commission during WWI by Lawrence of Arabia and his Bedouin fighters, you could take the train all the way to Medina, now in Saudi Arabia.

In the 1930s, the Jezreel Valley Railway helped transport construction materials for the 942km **Kirkuk-Haifa Pipeline** that, until 1948, carried crude oil from Iraq to the refineries of Haifa Bay. Remains of the pipeline can still be seen on the Golan Heights. Regional peace would make rebuilding the pipeline very attractive both economically and strategically – and turn Haifa into the major Mediterranean port the British intended it to be.

Proposals to place the Jezreel Valley Railway back into service have been mooted for decades, but in 2016 a standard-gauge line (the Ottoman tracks were narrow gauge) from Haifa to Beit She'an (covers 61km in 45 minutes) was finally inaugurated. At a later stage, there are plans to extend the line to Irbid, Jordan, allowing the Hashemite Kingdom to take advantage of Haifa's Mediterranean port facilities.

Travellers headed to Jordan can make use of the Jordan River/Sheikh Hussein border crossing, 8km east of town.

Belvoir   כוכב הלוא   בלוואר

Set on a hilltop 550m above the Jordan River, **Belvoir Crusader Fortress** (Kochav HaYarden National Park; ☑04-658-1766; www.parks.org.il; adult/child 22/9NIS; ☺8am-4pm or 5pm, closes 1hr earlier Fri, last entry 1hr before closing), measuring an impressive 110m by 110m, consists of concentric ramparts, gates, courtyards and towers that afford spectacular views of the Jordan and Jezreel Valleys and Jordan's Gilead Mountains. Highlights include a dining room topped by a Gothic vault, a huge stone cistern and, along the western side, a deep dry moat. It's noticeably cooler up here than in the valley below. There's excellent signage in English and Hebrew.

Built by the Knights Hospitaller starting in 1168, Belvoir ('beautiful view' in French; the Hebrew name, Kochav HaYarden, means 'star of the Jordan'; the Arabic name, Kawkab Al Hawa, means 'star of the wind') was forced to surrender to Muslim forces in 1189 after a 1½-year siege. The defenders were permitted to retreat to Tyre unharmed, in acknowledgement of their courage.

The panoramic, 1.2km-long **Wingate Trail**, outlined with rocks, goes along the slope below the ruins. Posted maps explain what you're seeing on both sides of the border, including details on local plate tectonics and the route of the pre-1948 oil pipeline from Kirkuk (Iraq) to Haifa.

Next to the ruins stands a **sculpture garden** of works – made of cut-out steel plates – by the award-winning Israeli artist Yigal (Igael) Tumarkin (b 1933), creator of the Holocaust memorial on Tel Aviv's Rabin Sq.

Belvoir is 20km north of Beit She'an and 20km south of the Sea of Galilee, 6km off Rte 90 along a one-lane road.

Beit Alpha Synagogue   כניס בيت الفا   בית הכנסת בית אלפא

No one was more surprised than the members of Kibbutz Heftzibah when they went out to dig an irrigation channel in 1928 and uncovered a stunning, Byzantine-era (6th-century) mosaic floor. Further excavation revealed the rest of the **Beit Alpha Synagogue** (☑04-653-2004; www.parks.org. il; Kibbutz Heftzibah; adult/child 22/9NIS; ☺8am-4pm or 5pm, closes 1hr earlier Fri, last entry 1hr before closing), whose extraordinarily mosaics are vividly evocative of ages past.

ⓘ VISITING JENIN

Travel to/from the Jenin area of the northern West Bank, through the Separation Barrier, is via the Israel Defense Forces' **Jalameh (Gilboa) crossing**, 10km south of Afula along Rte 60.

The three mosaic panels depict traditional Jewish symbols such as a Torah ark, two menorahs (seven-branched candelabras) and a shofar (ram's horn) alongside a spectacular, 12-panel Zodiac circle, a pagan element if there ever was one. At the bottom, above inscriptions in Aramaic and Hebrew, Jacob (holding a knife) is shown about to sacrifice his son Isaac, alongside the ram that God (represented by a hand from heaven) sent to be sacrificed in the boy's stead; each character is labelled in Hebrew. A 13-minute film (in six languages), projected above and onto the mosaic, provides an excellent introduction. Wheelchair accessible.

Kibbutz Heftzibah is 8km west of Beit She'an along Rte 669. Superbus bus 412 (twice hourly except Friday night and during the day Saturday) goes both to Beit She'an (3.80NIS, 11 minutes) and Afula (7.40NIS, 20 minutes).

Up the hill from the Beit Alfa Synagogue, deep inside Kibbutz Heftzibah, is something unexpected: a lovely little Shinto-style **Japanese garden** (☑Na'ama 054 663-4348; Kibbutz Heftzibah; tour adult/child 25/10NIS) with a serene koi pond, built by members of the Makoya, a Japanese Christian movement whose members have been studying Hebrew at the kibbutz since 1962. For a one-hour tour of this private garden, call Na'ama.

Gan-Garoo Australian Park   حديقة استرالية "جن جرو"   גן גארו האוסטרלי האוסטרלי

Kids will love **Gan-Garoo Australian Park** (☑04-648-8060; www.nirtours.co.il/gan_garoo; Rte 669, Kibbutz Nir David; adult/child under 2yr 48NIS/ free; ☺9am-4pm Sun-Thu, to 3pm Fri, to 5pm Sat Sep-Jun, 9am-8pm Sat-Thu, to 3pm Fri Jul & Aug), a delightful little corner of Australia, where – amid Aussie vegetation – they can pet and feed friendly, free-range kangaroos. Another hit: in the aviary (open for 20 or 30 minutes every hour or two) visitors can feed apple slivers to colourful **lorikeets** and **cockatiels**. Ever resourceful, the birds have developed a habit of hopping onto people's shirts and licking their neck sweat for its salt content.

Opened in 1996, this fully accredited zoo, run by Kibbutz Nir David, is also home to cassowaries, emus, flying foxes and Israel's only koala. Situated 6.5km west of Beit She'an, next to the entrance to Sachne (Gan HaShlosha) National Park.

Ein Harod עין חרוד عين حرود

Ein Harod is actually two kibbutzim, torn apart 65 years ago by their shared socialist ideology. One is home to a renowned art museum, while the other has a lovely hillside guesthouse.

◎ Sights

Museum of Art, Ein Harod MUSEUM
(Mishkan Le'Omanut; ☑04-648-6038; www.mu seumeinharod.org.il; Kibbutz Ein Harod Meuchad; adult/child 40/20NIS; ◷9am-4.30pm Sun-Thu, to 1.30pm Fri, 10am-4.30pm Sat) Almost as remarkable for its modernist building (inaugurated in 1948, with additions from the 1950s) as its outstanding art collection (mainly by Israeli and Jewish artists), this pioneering museum puts on highly regarded temporary exhibits (explanatory sheets available in English) in its 14 halls. Also has a permanent exhibition of Judaica. By car, take Rte 71 to Kibbutz Ein Harod Meuchad and follow the signs to 'Museums'.

🛌 Sleeping

★**Ein Harod Guest House** GUESTHOUSE $$
(☑04-648-6083; www.ein-harod.co.il; Kibbutz Ein Harod Ichud; d/chalet Sun-Wed from 500/990NIS, Thu-Sat from 600/1360NIS, additional child 160NIS; @🛜🐾) Perched on a hilltop with clear-day views of Mt Carmel, Mt Hermon and the mountains of Gilead in Jordan, this welcoming guesthouse has both traditional kibbutz rooms and romantic wooden 'Iris' chalets with 50 sq metres of luxury. By car, take Rte 716 to Kibbutz Ein Harod Ichud – the entrance is 1km north of Rte 71.

Facilities include 50 rooms (including eight set to open in 2018) and a 50m swimming pool (open May to October). Tours of the kibbutz's agricultural branches are available on request.

ℹ Getting There & Away

Superbus bus 41 links both Ein Harod kibbutzim with Afula (7.40NIS, 25 minutes).

Mt Gilboa הר גלבוע جبل فقوعة

The rugged, 18km-long ridge known as Mt Gilboa (highest point 536m), which runs along the southern side of the Jezreel Valley, makes for a great nature getaway. After the winter rains (December to March or

---

SOCIALIST PASSIONS

Life at Kibbutz Ein Harod, midway between Afula and Beit She'an (about 14km from each), carried on in relative tranquillity from its founding in 1921 until the very early 1950s. That was when an ideological dispute over Israeli Prime Minister David Ben-Gurion's strategic preference for the capitalist United States over the socialist Soviet Union flared into a full-fledged ideological conflagration. Complicating matters was the fact that, at the time, Stalin was staging anti-Semitic show trials in which prominent Jews were being accused of trumped-up counter-revolutionary crimes and then executed. Stalin's devotees at the kibbutz, who were of the 'you can't make an omelette without breaking a few eggs' school of hard-line socialism, stood by their man.

Passions flared – these were, after all, people who lived every minute of every day by their socialist ideals – and soon barricades went up in the dining hall, good friends stopped speaking to each other, fisticuffs were exchanged and couples broke up. Finally, Ein Harod split into two separate kibbutzim, Ein Harod Meuchad, run by the Stalin loyalists, and Ein Harod Ichud, under the control of the Ben-Gurionists (ironically, both *meuchad* and *ichud* mean 'united').

Resentments smouldered for decades, and even today some old-old-timers are angry about their rivals' craven betrayal. It was only 30 years ago that the first 'mixed' Ichud-Meuchad couple tied the knot, and just 20 years ago that agricultural and limited cultural cooperation between the two kibbutzim resumed. Today, Kibbutz Ein Harod Ichud – whose sources of income include wheat, cotton, milk from cows and sheep, fish ponds and the production of ultra-advanced miniature cryocoolers – is still a traditional 'collective' kibbutz, while Kibbutz Ein Harod Meuchad, controlled by the hard left six decades ago, has chosen the route of capitalist privatisation.

April), the area is carpeted with wildflowers, including the purple Gilboa iris (blooms in late February and early March). According to the Bible, this was where King Saul and his son Jonathan were supposedly slain in battle with the Philistines (I Samuel 31:1-13).

For a lovely hilltop drive with stupendous views of the Jezreel Valley (in the other direction, you can see the Palestinian villages around Jenin), take 28km-long Rte 667 (Gilboa Scenic Rd), which links Rte 675 (8km southeast of Afula via Rte 71) with the Jordan Valley's Rte 90.

◉ Sights

Nachmani Winery
WINERY

(☑ 053 772 0369; www.nachmaniwines.com; 329 HaRav David Nuri St, Gan Ner; tour 30NIS) UK-born Frances and her Moroccan-born husband David have turned a wine-making hobby into a micro-winery that produces just 2100 bottles a year. You can sample their prize-winning wines – made from grapes harvested by hand at dawn and in the crusher by 7am – on their lovely back patio, all the while enjoying splendid views of the Jezreel Valley. Call ahead to arrange a 45-minute tour or a cheese-and-wine spread (45NIS).

✖ Eating

Herb Farm on Mt Gilboa
BISTRO $$$

(☑ 04-653-1093; www.herb-farm.co.il; Rte 667; mains 85-139NIS; ⊙ noon-10pm Mon-Sat, plus 9-11am Fri; ☑) For a hearty, country-style meal in a rustic setting, head to this family-run restaurant, which has both meat (Cornish hen, steak, lamb chops) and veggie/vegan options – as well as lovely views of the Jezreel Valley. Reserve ahead on Friday and Saturday. Situated on Rte 667, 3.5km southeast of Rte 675; follow the yellow signs to 'Country Restaurant'.

Tiberias
טבריה طبريا

☑ 04 / POP 42,600

Tiberias is one of Judaism's four holy cities, the burial place of venerated Jewish sages and a very popular base for Christians visiting holy sites around the Sea of Galilee. It's also one of the most aesthetically challenged resort towns in Israel, its sunbaked lakeside strip marred by 1970s architectural monstrosities. So the sacred and the kitsch – plus beaches, hot springs and a growing ultra-Orthodox population – coexist side by side in a whirl of holiness, hawkers and hedonism.

Tiberias is often oppressively hot in July and August.

THE MONGOLS WERE HERE

The year was 1260, the place very near present-day Kibbutz Ein Harod. The belligerents were the mighty Mongol Empire and the Egyptian Mamluks. In a cataclysmic clash known to history as the **Battle of Ein Jalut**, the Mongols were decisively and enduringly defeated for the first time in their history, bringing their expansion into Southwest Asia to a screeching – and permanent – halt.

History

Tiberias' hot springs have been luring pleasure seekers since well before 20 CE, when Herod Antipas, son of Herod the Great, founded the town and named it in honour of the Roman emperor Tiberias (r 14–37 CE).

After the Judeans' disastrous Bar Kochba Revolt (132–135 CE), Tiberias became one of the most important centres of Jewish life in the Land of Israel, playing a key role in the redefinition of Judaism after Temple sacrifices in Jerusalem were halted by the Roman victory of 70 CE. Some of the greatest post-Second Temple sages, including Yehuda HaNassi, chief editor of the Mishnah, lived here, and much of the redacting of the Jerusalem (Palestinian) Talmud also seems to have taken place in Tiberias. From the late 2nd century, the Sanhedrin (ancient Israel's supreme court) was based in the town. The system still used today to indicate vowel sounds in written Hebrew was developed in – and named after – Tiberias.

The Crusaders took Tiberias in 1099, building a massive fortress a bit north of the town's Roman-Byzantine centre. In 1187 Saladin captured the town and shortly thereafter devastated Crusader forces at the Horns of Hattin, 8km due west of Tiberias.

In 1558, the newly arrived Ottomans granted tax-collecting rights in the Tiberias area to Dona Gracia (www.donagraciaproject.org), a Lisbon-born Conversa (outwardly Catholic but secretly Jewish) woman who had found refuge from the Inquisition in Istanbul.

In the early 1700s, a Bedouin sheikh named Daher Al Omar established an independent fiefdom in the Galilee, with Tiberias as its capital, and invited Jewish families to settle in the town. By the end of the Ottoman period, Jews constituted the great majority of Tiberias' 6500 residents.

Tiberias was almost completely demolished in the great earthquake of 1837.

Sights

Yigal Allon Promenade

Most of Tiberias' sights are along the boardwalk (of sorts) that runs along the lakefront. Parts are tacky, faded and/or for rent, and the area can feel forlorn in winter. But the views of the Sea of Galilee and the Golan never get old. Sites below are listed from north to south.

St Peter's Church CHURCH
(☎04-672-0516; www.saintpeterstiberias.org; Yigal Allon Promenade; ☺visits 8.30am-12.30pm & 2.30-5.30pm Mon-Sat, Mass in English 7pm Tue-Thu, 6.30pm Fri & Sat, 8.30am Sun) This rare Crusader church – administered by Koinonia Giovanni Battista, a Catholic community based in Italy – has a peaceful, grapevine-shaded courtyard and a ceiling shaped like an upturned boat, a nod to Peter, a Sea of Galilee fisherman. The interior paintings of Jesus on the Sea of Galilee date from 1902. There's a hostel for Catholic pilgrims here.

A replica of the Vatican's famous statue of St Peter stands in the courtyard near the carved-stone **Monument to the Virgin of Czestochowa**, erected in 1945 by Polish soldiers billeted here during WWII.

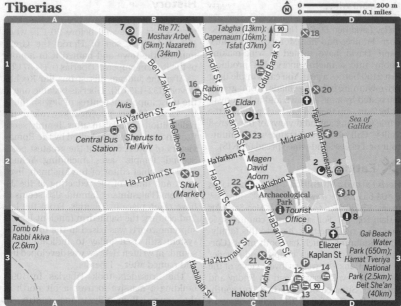

Tiberias

Galilee Experience   MUSEUM
(☑ 04-672-3620;   www.thegalileeexperience.com;
Yigal Allon Promenade; US$8;   ☺ 8.30am-10pm
Sun-Thu, to 5pm Fri, 5-10pm Sat) On the upper
floor of a 1970s eyesore, the Galilee Experience screens a Christian-oriented film (21
minutes in English and Chinese, 36 minutes
in 10 other languages) on the biblical history
of Galilee.

Al Bahr Mosque   MOSQUE
(Sea Mosque; Yigal Allon Promenade) Built of
basalt in the 18th century, the Sea Mosque
once had a special entrance for the faithful
who arrived by boat.

**Church & Monastery
of the Apostles**   CHURCH
(Yigal Allon Promenade;   ☺ 8am-4pm Mon-Sat)
From the serene, flowery courtyard, steps
lead down to a Greek Orthodox church, its
air of mystery enhanced by gilded icons,
brass lamps and elaborately carved wood.
The three chapels are dedicated to the 12
disciples, Sts Peter and Paul, and Mary Magdalene. To see if a monk is available to show
you around, ring the bell high up on the
right lintel of the red door situated 10m west
of the overhead pedestrian bridge.

⊙ Tombs of Jewish Sages

Many of Tiberias' Jewish visitors are drawn
to the city at least partly by the desire to
pray – and ask for divine intercession – at
grave markers believed to belong to some of
Judaism's most eminent sages. If you were
assembling an all-star team of the most influential Jewish thinkers of all time, these
four rabbis would certainly be on it.

**Tomb of Rabbi Meir
Ba'al HaNess**   RELIGIOUS SITE
(☺ 6am or 7am-10pm or later Sun-Thu, to 2hr before
sunset Fri) A complex of religious buildings
has grown around the reputed burial place
of Rabbi Meir Ba'al HaNess, a 2nd-century
sage often cited in the Mishnah (*ba'al haness* means 'master of miracles'). The tomb
itself, with separate, curtained entrances for
men and women, is inside a domed Sephardi synagogue, situated just down the slope
from its Ashkenazi counterpart, topped with
a taller dome. The complex is 2.5km south
of the city centre, 150m up an asphalt road
from Hamat Tveriya National Park.

Behind the Sephardi section, market
stalls sell holy amulets, including specially
blessed olive oil and arak (50NIS). Nearby,
personal blessings are available in exchange
for a charitable donation.

ⓘ ONLINE RESOURCES

**Jordan Valley Regional Council Tour-
ist Information** (www.ekinneret.co.il)

Galilee Development Authority (www.
gogalilee.org)

Travelujah (Christian Tourism) www.
travelujah.com

BibleWalks (www.biblewalks.com)

Rabbi Meir's *hilula* (a celebration held
by Hasidim on the anniversary of a sage's
death) is just three days before that of Shimon Bar Yochai, who's buried at Mt Meron,
so some pious Jews travel to the Galilee to
take in both hugely popular events.

Tomb of the Rambam   RELIGIOUS SITE
(Ben Zakkai St;   ☺ 24hr) Rabbi Moshe Ben
Maimon (1135–1204) – better known by his
acronym, the Rambam – was a Cordova-
born polymath famous for his rationalist
approach to religion and life (he was fond
of quoting Aristotle). The site where he is
believed to be buried was refurbished, and
had a shade roof added, in 2017.

The Rambam's most famous works are
the *Mishneh Torah*, the first systematic
codification of Jewish law; *Guide to the
Perplexed*, a work of theology, written in
Judeo-Arabic, that is still hugely influential
today; and various books on medicine (he
served as the personal physician of the sultan of Egypt, where he spent the last decades of his life).

**Tomb of Rabbi
Yohanan ben Zakkai**   RELIGIOUS SITE
(Ben Zakkai St;   ☺ 24hr) Rabbi Yohanan ben
Zakkai, Judaism's most eminent 1st-century
sage, played a central role in replacing an-
imal sacrifices – the raison d'être of the
Temple in Jerusalem, destroyed in 70 CE –
with prayer. His grave site is a just few
metres down the hill from the grave of
Cordova-born sage the Rambam.

Tomb of Rabbi Akiva   RELIGIOUS SITE
(HaGevura St;   ☺ 24hr) Rabbi Akiva, a leading Mishnaic sage (and teacher of Rabbi
Meir Ba'al HaNess), played a major role in
establishing rabbinic (ie post–Second Temple) Judaism. He was tortured to death by
the Romans because of his support for the
Bar Kochba Revolt – indeed, his enthusiasm
for resistance to the Romans was such that
he declared Bar Kochba to be the Messiah.
What is believed to be his dome-topped

tomb, offering breathtaking views, is on the hillside about 3km (by road) west of the town centre.

☉ Elsewhere in Town

Hamat Tveriya National Park NATIONAL PARK
(☑04-672-5287; www.parks.org.il; Eliezer Kaplan Ave/Rte 90; adult/child 15/7NIS; ☉8am-5pm daylight-saving time, to 4pm winter, closes 1hr earlier Fri, last entrance 1hr before closing) Back in Roman times, the fame of Tiberias' hot springs was such that in 110 CE the Emperor Trajan struck a coin dedicated to them – it depicted Hygeia (from which the word 'hygiene' is derived), the goddess of health, sitting on a rock and enjoying the waters. Today, the star attractions here are 17 small hot springs, a pool you can dip your toes into and a **4th-century synagogue** (now air-conditioned) that's decorated with a beautiful **Zodiac wheel** mosaic. Situated 2.5km south of the centre; served by local bus 5.

Al Amari Mosque MOSQUE
(HaBanim St) With its black basalt walls, white dome and striped minaret, this mosque looks a bit lost in the courtyard of a modern commercial centre. Built by Daher Al Omar in 1743, it has not been in use since Tiberias' Arab minority was evacuated by the British in April 1948.

🕏 Activities

Along the Yigal Allon Promenade, half-a-dozen operators, including **Tiberias Water Sports** (☑052 807-7740; Yigal Allon Promenade; ☉closed Sat) and **Water Sports Center** (☑052 349-1462; Yigal Allon Promenade; ☉closed Fri & Sat), offer motorboat rental (100NIS for 30 minutes), waterskiing (200NIS for 15

OFF THE BEATEN TRACK

THE SANHEDRIN TRAIL

Set to open in 2018 to celebrate Israel's 70th year of independence, the 70km-long Sanhedrin Trail will link sites across the Lower Galilee, from Tiberias to Beit She'arim, that are associated with the Great Sanhedrin, a Galilee-based court and council whose 70 or so sages made Jewish law in the centuries after the destruction of the Second Temple in 70 CE. Divided into five one-day segments, hikers will be able to connect with ancient times using an augmented reality app.

---

minutes) and banana-boat rides (40NIS for 15 minutes). Closed on rainy days, cold days, Shabbat and Jewish holidays.

Tiberias Hot Springs HOT SPRINGS
(Ma'ayanot Hammei Tveriya; ☑04-612-3600; www.hamei-tveria.co.il; Eliezer Kaplan Ave/Rte 90; adult/3-12yr 88/45NIS; ☉8am-6pm Sun, Mon & Wed, to 7pm Tue & Thu, to 3.45/5pm winter/summer Sat, closes 1hr earlier in winter) For the sort of relaxing soak and *shvitz* (steam bath) so appreciated by the Romans, head to this modern spa. Emerging from the ground at 52°C, the mineral water gets cooled a bit before it's piped here. Situated 2.5km south of the town centre, across the street from Hamat Tveriya National Park; served by bus 5.

The complex also has two saunas (one wet, one dry) and four mineral- and fresh-water pools for adults and kids (open year-round), or you can indulge yourself with a Swedish massage (210NIS for 30 minutes). Locker rental costs 15NIS; a towel is 10NIS. Has an on-site restaurant.

Gai Beach Water Park WATER PARK
(☑04-670-0713; www.gaibeach.com; over 3yr 90NIS, Jul & Aug 99NIS; ☉9.30am-5pm approx Passover-Sukkot) Has a fine, 50m-long Sea of Galilee beach, five water slides (including one at a terrifying 70-degree pitch), a wave machine and a special section for small kids. Situated about 1km south of the town centre. Locker rental is 15NIS.

🛌 Sleeping

Tiberias has some of the Galilee's cheapest dorm beds as well as one of northern Israel's most luxurious hotels. Boisterous domestic tourists take over in July and August, when the weather is too hot for all but the hardiest foreign visitors.

★Tiberias Hostel HOSTEL $
(Rabin Sq; dm 75-100NIS, s 180-250NIS, d 230-350NIS; @🛜) Yet another excellent ILH hostel, this place has a real backpacker vibe, a rooftop chill-out area with fairy lights, a full kitchen for guests and friendly staff who are happy to provide tips on local sights and activities. Breakfast costs just 15NIS; the non-meat Friday dinner is also a bargain (15NIS to 35NIS).

Aviv Hostel HOSTEL $
(☑04-672-0007; 66 HaGalil St; dm US$20-30, s/d/tr excl breakfast US$50/60/80; @🛜) Best thought of as a cheap hotel. Staff fail to create a backpacker vibe, the 26 rooms are

slightly scuffed and the sheets are polyester, but amenities include seaview balconies, proper spring mattresses and fridges. Dorm beds are all nonbunk; women-only dorms are available. Lift-equipped. A superb buffet breakfast costs US$12.

★ Arbel Guest House
GUESTHOUSE $$

(☑04-679-4919; www.4shavit.com; Moshav Arbel; dm/d excl breakfast US$30/110, Fri, Aug & holidays US$37.50/160, additional person US$33; ☎☀) Moshav Arbel is just 8km northwest of central Tiberias, but this tranquil B&B feels a world away when you're lazing in a hammock by the 12.5m pool or relaxing among bougainvillea, grape arbours and 60 kinds of fruit tree. The six two-room units, each with space for four or five, are eclectically decorated, and all have hot tub and kitchenette. Excellent value.

Superb breakfasts cost US$13.50. Arbel is 80m above sea level, so it's cooler than Tiberias in summer and warmer than the Golan in winter.

Aviv Holiday Flats
HOTEL $$

(☑04 671-2272; http://aviv-hotel.xwx.co.il; 2 HaNoter St; s/d/tr/q excl breakfast 300/400/500/600NIS; ☎) The 30 handsome, modern studio apartments have at least 30 sq metres of space, balconies, kitchenettes, comfy sheets and new mattresses in 2017. One of the best deals in town. A copious buffet breakfast costs 50NIS.

Rimonim Galei Kinnereth
HOTEL $$$

(☑04-672-8888; www.rimonim.com; 1 Eliezer Kaplan St; d Sat-Wed from US$280, Thu & Fri from US$400; ☎☀) A favourite of David Ben-Gurion back in the 1950s, the doyen of the Tiberias hotel scene – opened in 1946 – retains some of its late-Mandate-era charm. Amenities include a pebbly private beach, a spa and a kids club for children aged five to 10 (daily in July and August, on Friday and Saturday the rest of the year). See if you can identify some of the hotel's more famous guests in the mural behind reception.

There's a small exhibition on the hotel's storied history in the Hermon Room (2nd floor).

Scots Hotel
HOTEL $$$

(☑04-671-0710; www.scotshotels.co.il; 1 Gdud Barak St/Rte 90; d from US$390; @☎☀) Built in the 1890s as a hospital, this sumptuously restored complex – still owned by the Church of Scotland – is graced by meticulously tended gardens, breezy courtyards and a dazzling lake-view pool (open April to October). Has 69 rooms and a spa with Turkish hammam, hot tub and massage. Discounts are often available.

Nonguests can visit the gorgeous, tranquil gardens from about 10am to 4pm on Sunday to Wednesday.

Emily's Boutique Hotel
HOTEL $$$

(☑04-664-7500; www.emilys-hotel.com; 66 HaGalil St; d/tr US$167/230, additional child US$42; ☎) Run by a local family, this hotel is a good bet all around. The 48 rooms are spacious (28 sq metres) and come with parquet floors, high ceilings, sparkling tile-and-brass bathrooms and sea views. The atrium lobby has a koi pond, while the halls are decorated with historic B&W photos of Tiberias.

✕ Eating

Fruit and Vegetable Market
MARKET $

(HaPrachim St; ⊙6am-8pm Mon-Thu, to 1hr before sundown Fri, some shops also open Sun; ☝) Some of the stall owners may be a bit, shall we say, uncouth, but the produce is top quality and cheap.

Baguette Levin
FAST FOOD $

(☑04-857-7762; 32 HaGalil St; ⊙noon-4am Sun-Thu, noon-6am Fri, 10am-4am Sat) Specialises in shawarma and schnitzel on a baguette or in a pita. Open very late and on Shabbat.

Supersol Express
SUPERMARKET $

(HaBanim St; ⊙7.30am-8pm Sun-Thu, to 4.30pm Fri summer, to 2pm Fri winter) Small supermarket with picnic supplies and food for Shabbat.

Guy
ISRAELI $$

(☑04-672-3036; HaGalil St, cnr Achva St; mains 38-75NIS; ⊙noon-9pm or 10pm Sun-Thu, to 2.30pm Fri winter, to 4pm Fri summer; ☝) An unpretentious, old-time Mizrahi (Oriental-Jewish) restaurant featuring home-style grilled meats, soups (winter only) and a delicious array of stuffed vegetables, as well as Ashkenazi-style chopped liver, Iraqi-style *kibbeh* (spiced meat balls in tangy soup) and Lebanese-style *kibbeh* (a fried cracked-wheat dumpling stuffed with chopped meat). Cash only.

Little Tiberias
INTERNATIONAL $$

(☑04-679-2806; www.littletiberias.com; HaKishon St; mains 59-155NIS; ⊙noon-10.30pm Sat-Thu, to 11pm Fri; ☝) Serves fish (grilled, baked or fried), meat, seafood and pasta, on solid pine tables. Open Shabbat.

★ Yisrael's Kitchen
ISRAELI $$$

(☑04-679-4919; www.4shavit.com; Arbel Guest House, Moshav Arbel; mains 76-128NIS; ⊙breakfast begins 8-9.20am, dinner begins 6-7.30pm daily) An 8km drive from Tiberias (take Rte 77 to Rte 7717), this rustic, family-run restaurant features local produce and warm, from-the-heart country cooking. Specialities include huge (500g) portions of Galilee-raised steak and lamb served in terracotta casseroles, baked St Peter's fish and yummy desserts, including homemade ice cream. Call to reserve.

Has a good selection of wines from the Galilee and the Golan.

Decks
STEAK $$$

(☑04-671-0800; www.decks.co.il; Lido Beach, Gdud Barak St; mains 75-175NIS; ☉noon-11pm Sun-Thu, noon-1½hr before sundown Fri, opens after sundown Sat) Legendary for grilled meats – including filet mignon, baby lamb and goose liver (not force-fed) – that are prepared outdoors over a mixture of five kinds of wood: olive, citrus, cherry, walnut and eucalyptus. A wood taboun is used to bake focaccia fresh for each diner. Occupies a hangar-like space built out over the sea, offering gorgeous views. Has an excellent wine list. Kosher.

Galei Gil
SEAFOOD $$$

(☑04-672-0699; Yigal Allon Promenade; mains 68-105NIS; ☉10.30am-11pm daily; 🎗) Has tables on a romantic wooden deck overlooking the lake – the sea views are unbeatable. Eight varieties of fresh fish from the Sea of Galilee and the Mediterranean are available either grilled or fried, along with meat and soups. Open Shabbat.

❶ Information

Banks with ATMs can be found around the intersection of HaYarden and HaBanim St.

Magen David Adom (☑04-671-7611; cnr HaBanim & HaKishon Sts; ☉first aid 7pm-midnight Sun-Thu, 2pm-midnight Fri, 10am-midnight Sat, ambulance 24hr) Run by privately run Malram (www.mrlm.co.il), this after-hours clinic provides first aid and can arrange house (and hotel) calls by doctors.

Poriya Hospital (Baruch Padeh Medical Center; ☑04-665-2211; www.poria.health.gov.il; Rte 768; emergency room 24hr) Tiberias' government hospital is 8km southwest of the city centre. Linked to Tiberias by Superbus buses 37 and 39 (40 minutes, twice hourly except Friday afternoon and Saturday).

Tourist Office (☑04-672-5666; HaBanim St; ☉8am-4pm Sun-Thu, to noon Fri) Has loads of free brochures on the Sea of Galilee, including Christian sites, and worthwhile hiking and cycling maps (eg for the Kinneret Trail). Situated in an open-air archaeological park with the ruins of a 5th-century synagogue and mosaics depicting Jewish symbols such as a *lulav* (palm frond) and *etrog* (a kind of citrus fruit).

❶ Getting There & Away

BUS

Most intercity buses stop at the 1970-style **central bus station** (www.bus.co.il; HaYarden St); some short-haul lines also stop along HaGalil St. Destinations:

Beit She'an (Superbus bus 28; 14NIS, 35 minutes, every 45 minutes Sunday to Thursday, hourly until mid-afternoon Friday and after sundown Saturday) Has stops along the south-western coast of the Sea of Galilee.

Haifa-Merkazit HaMifratz (Egged buses 430 and 434; 21.50NIS, 1¼ hours, twice an hour except Friday afternoon to sundown Saturday)

Jerusalem (Egged buses 959, 961 and 962; 37.50NIS, 2¾ hours, every one or two hours except Friday evening to sundown Saturday)

CYCLING AROUND THE SEA OF GALILEE

Parts of the Sea of Galilee are great cycling territory. Completely circumnavigating the lake (about 65km) takes about six hours. For about 70% of the way around you can follow the **Kinneret Trail** (Shvil Sovev Kinneret), but the rest (including from Ein Gev on the east coast to Arik Bridge at the lake's northern tip) has to be done on highway shoulders for now. Make sure you have a good (eg 1:50,000-scale) map as the route is not well signposted.

For a nice half-day ride from Tiberias, you can head 8km south to **Yardenit**, from where an 8km circuit follows the Jordan River.

Start early to beat the heat and take plenty of water. When riding on roads, make sure you're highly visible and stay on the verge (shoulder), as far as possible from traffic. Do not ride after sundown.

Aviv Hostel Bike Rental (☑04-672-0007, Beni 050 728-2052; 66 HaGalil St; per day 70NIS; ☉6am-6pm winter, 7am-7pm summer) rents out 24-speed mountain bikes. Prices include helmet, lock and maps. Staff are happy to provide maps and information on itineraries and routes. If your bike has mechanical problems, they'll come out and do repairs.

Buses 959 and 962 take Rte 6, bus 961 goes via Beit She'an and the Jordan Valley.

Katzrin (Rama buses 52 and 57; 14.50NIS, 35 to 50 minutes, a dozen daily except mid-afternoon Friday to sundown Saturday) Bus 52 goes via the Sea of Galilee's northwestern shore, including Capernaum, while slower bus 57 follows the lake's southeastern and eastern shores, passing by Ein Gev and Kursi National Park.

Kiryat Shmona (Egged buses 541 and 840; 27NIS, one hour, hourly) Passes by Rosh Pina.

Nazareth (Nazareth Tourism & Transport bus 431; 16NIS, one hour, hourly except Friday evening and Saturday before sundown) In Nazareth, some buses stop on the ring road, Rte 75, instead of on Paulus VI St.

Tel Aviv (Egged buses 836 and 840; 37.50NIS, 2¾ hours, at least hourly except mid-afternoon Friday to mid-afternoon Saturday)

Tsfat (Superbus bus 450; 14NIS, 37 minutes, every 40 minutes Sunday to Friday afternoon, three Saturday night)

CAR

The Golan, the Galilee panhandle, Beit She'an, Nazareth and even Akko are an hour or less away. Tiberias is the best place in the Galilee to hire a car. Rental companies include **Avis** (☑ 04-672-2766; www.avis.co.il; 2 Ha-Amakim St, cnr HaYarden St) and **Eldan** (☑ 04-672-2831; www.eldan.co.il; 26 HaBanim St).

SHERUT

The fastest way to get to Tel Aviv is to take a **sherut** (☑ Moshe 050 755-9282; 40NIS; ☻5am-7pm or later Sun-Thu, to 2.30pm Fri) from the parking lot just below the central bus station.

TAXI

Tiberias' taxi services include **Moniyot Tveriya** (☑04-655-5550).

SEA OF GALILEE

بحيرة طبريا   ים כנרת

The shores of the Sea of Galilee (in Hebrew, Yam Kinneret or HaKinneret), by far Israel's largest freshwater lake, are lined with great places to relax: beaches, camping grounds, cycling trails and walking tracks.

Jesus is said to have spent most of his ministry around the Sea of Galilee. This is where he is believed to have performed some of his best-known miracles (the multiplication of the loaves and fishes, walking on water), and it was overlooking the Kinneret that he delivered the Sermon on the Mount.

The Jordan River flows into the Sea of Galilee near the ruins of the ancient city of Bethsaida, providing three-quarters of the

---

SEA OF GALILEE STATS
➡ Surface area when full: 170 sq km
➡ Length of shoreline: 53km
➡ Maximum depth: 44m
➡ Volume of water when full: 4.3 cu km
➡ Average surface water temperature in February: 14.7°C
➡ Average surface water temperature in August: 28.6°C

lake's annual intake. It exits the lake, on its way to the Dead Sea, next to the Yardenit baptism site, at the lake's far southern tip.

Camping is permitted at almost all Sea of Galilee beaches, including those that charge fees.

Rte 90 runs along the entire western edge of the Sea of Galilee, Rte 92 follows the eastern shore and Rte 87 connects the two, running along the lake's northwestern shore.

The entire shoreline is served by two Rama buses that link Tiberias with the Golan town of Katzrin. Bus 52 goes via the Sea of Galilee's western and northwestern shores, including Tabgha and Capernaum, while slower bus 57 follows the lake's southwestern and eastern shores, passing by Ein Gev and Kursi National Park.

Northwestern Shore

As Hwy 90 and the parallel Kinneret Trail (Shvil Sovev Kinneret) curve around the northwestern shore of the Sea of Galilee, they pass by some of Israel's most significant New Testament sites.

Two Catholic churches a few hundred metres apart occupy the stretch of Sea of Galilee lakefront known as **Tabgha** (an Arabic corruption of the Greek *hepta pega*, meaning 'seven springs'). An attractive walkway links Tabgha with Capernaum, a distance of about 3km.

Places in this section are listed more or less from southwest to northeast.

⊙ Sights

Arbel National Park   NATIONAL PARK
(☑04-673-2904; www.parks.org.il; adult/child 22/9NIS; ☻8am-4pm or 5pm, closes 1hr earlier Fri, last entry 1hr before closing) Towering over the Sea of Galilee and offering breathtaking views of the Golan Heights and Mt Hermon, Arbel Cliff is 181m above sea level, which

makes it 390m above the vast blue lake below. Great rambling territory, it is on both the Israel National Trail and the Jesus Trail (yes, hikers have to pay the entry fee).

The park is 11.5km northwest of Tiberias; take Rte 77, Rte 7717 and then the Moshav Arbel access road, whence a side road leads northeast for 3.5km.

For great views, you can walk to the **Carob Tree Lookout** (30 minutes return) and, a few minutes further along the ridge, the **Kinneret Lookout**. A moderately difficult, three-hour circuit (minimum age seven) that requires some cliff clambering with cables and hand-holds takes you past the **Cave Fortress** (restored in 2017), apparently built by a Druze chieftain in the 1600s. It's also possible to do a circuit (five to six hours) that heads down to the **Arbel Spring** and then back up to park HQ via Wadi Arbel and the ruins of a 6th-century **synagogue** (wheelchair accessible) – the latter is 800m towards Moshav Arbel along the park's sole access road.

In 1187 Saladin inflicted a definitive defeat on the Crusaders at the **Horns of Hattin**, the ridge a few kilometres west of Arbel Cliff. As you look west from park HQ, the ridge is directly behind Moshav Arbel.

Magdala ARCHAEOLOGICAL SITE
(☑04-620-9900; www.magdala.org; Migdal Junction, Rte 90; adult/child 15/10NIS; ◉8am-6pm) When the Legionnaires of Christ, a Catholic congregation based in Mexico, began building a spiritual retreat in 2009, they were astonished to discover a synagogue from the 1st century CE, dated to the time of Jesus by a local coin minted in 29 CE. The excavations – work continues every summer – are now an open-air museum. Situated 6km north of Tiberias on the site of the ancient town of Magdala (Migdal in Hebrew), home of Mary Magdalene.

Inside the synagogue, archaeologists found the **Magdala Stone**, a rectangular altar – discovered facing south towards Jerusalem – decorated with a seven-branched menorah that is unique because it was carved when the Temple in Jerusalem was still standing. The altar may have been used

> ### ❶ PRACTICAL TIP: MODEST DRESS
> ·······················
> The Christian sites along the Sea of Galilee's northern shore require that visitors dress modestly (no tank tops or shorts above the knee).

to read the Torah. The original is at the Israel Museum in Jerusalem (there's a copy here).

Visitors can also see the elegant **Worship Center** and its six mosaic-adorned chapels. Volunteers conduct free tours in English, Spanish and sometimes other languages. A 160-room guesthouse is under construction.

★ **Ancient Galilee Boat** HISTORIC SITE
(Jesus Boat; ☑04-911-9585; www.bet-alon.co.il; Kibbutz Ginosar, Rte 90; adult/child 20/15NIS; ◉8am-5pm Sat-Thu, to 4pm Fri) In 1986, when the level of the Sea of Galilee was particularly low, a local fisherman made an extraordinary discovery: the remains of a wooden boat later determined to have plied these waters in the time of Jesus's ministry. The 8.2m fishing vessel, made of 12 kinds of (apparently recycled) wood, can be seen inside Kibbutz Ginosar's **Yigal Alon Centre**. Wall panels and three short films tell the fascinating story of its discovery and preservation (so does the website).

Outside, the lovely shoreline is bordered by expanses of waving reeds and a garden of sculptures by Jewish and Arab artists.

Church of the Multiplication of the Loaves & Fishes CHURCH
(☑04-667-8100; www.dvhl.de; Tabgha; parking 10NIS; ◉8am-4.45pm Mon-Fri, to 2.45pm Sat, 11am-4.45pm Sun) This austere German Benedictine church was constructed in 1982 on the foundations of a 5th-century Byzantine church. The rock under the altar is believed by some to be the 'solitary place' where Jesus is said to have laid the five loaves and two fishes that multiplied to feed 5000 faithful listeners. In 2015, parts of the complex were badly damaged in an arson attack for which a right-wing Jewish extremist was convicted.

Church of the Primacy of St Peter CHURCH
(Tabgha; ◉8am-4.50pm) A shady, fragrant garden leads down to the lakeshore and to this Franciscan chapel (built 1933), lit by the vivid colours of abstract stained glass. The flat rock in front of the altar was known to Byzantine pilgrims as Mensa Christi (Christ's Table) because it was believed that Jesus and his disciples breakfasted on fish here (John 21:9).

On the side of the church facing the lake, a few steps cut out of the rock are said by some to be where Jesus stood when his disciples saw him, in the biblical account. (On the other hand, the steps may have been cut in the 2nd or 3rd century, when the area was quarried for limestone.) Just west of the church, a path leads to three serene outdoor

THE RED LINE

Israelis follow the water level of the Sea of Galilee – in newspapers, on the radio and on TV – at least as closely as they do stock-market indexes. As winter rains flow into the lake, news reports follow its progress towards full capacity (208.8m below sea level), while in summertime, the lake's descent towards (and sometimes even below) the 'red line' (213m below sea level) – beyond which pumping may adversely impact water quality – generates news flashes and, at times, screaming, doom-laden headlines. Recent dry winters have kept the lake well below capacity – in 2017, it lacked more than 4m of water – leading to an unprecedented rise in salinity. If not for the huge desalinisation plants along the Mediterranean coast and the fact that 85% of the country's waste water is reused for agriculture (by far the highest percentage in the world), Israel would have a national water crisis.

To find out the current state of the lake, stop by the Water Level Surveyor (Yigal Allon Promenade; ☺24hr), a 5m-high sculpture shaped like the land surrounding the Sea of Galilee.

chapels surrounded by the reeds and trees that grow along the lakeshore.

★ **Mount of the Beatitudes** CHURCH
(Har HaOsher; ☎04-671-1223; Rte 90; per car 10NIS; ☺gate & church 8-11.45am & 2-4.45pm) Since at least the 4th century, this landscaped hillside is believed to be where Jesus delivered his Sermon on the Mount (Matthew 5–7), whose opening lines – the eight Beatitudes – begin with the phrase 'Blessed are...'. The sermon also includes the Lord's Prayer and oft-quoted phrases such as 'salt of the earth', 'light of the world' and 'judge not, lest ye be judged'.

An octagonal Italianate Roman Catholic church, built between 1936 and 1938 with help from Mussolini, is looked after by Franciscan nuns. The Beatitudes are commemorated in stained glass just below the dome, while the seven virtues (justice, charity, prudence, faith, fortitude, hope and temperance) are represented around the altar. The balcony and tranquil gardens have breathtaking views of the Sea of Galilee. The pilgrims hostel (p227) is open to visitors of all faiths.

Monte delle Beatitudini (as it's known in Italian), situated on the Jesus Trail, is a 3.1km drive up the hill from Tabgha's Church of the Multiplication of the Loaves & Fishes. Walking is also an option – from just outside the mount's entrance booth, a 1km path leads down the hill to Tabgha, hitting Rte 87 at a point about 200m east of the Church of the Primacy of St Peter.

Capernaum ARCHAEOLOGICAL SITE
(Kfar Nachum, Kfar Nahum; 5NIS; ☺8am-5pm, last entry 4.30pm) The New Testament says that the prosperous lakeside village of Capernaum (estimated population 1500), on the imperial highway from Tiberias to Damascus, was Jesus's base during the most influential period of his Galilean ministry (Matthew 4:13, Mark 2:1, John 6:59). It is mentioned by name 16 times: this is where Jesus is believed to have preached at the synagogue (Mark 1:21), healed the sick and recruited his first disciples, fishers Peter, Andrew, James and John and Matthew the tax collector.

The Franciscan friars who run the site, dressed in brown cassocks with a white rope around the waist, are happy to answer questions. An explanatory sheet (1NIS) is available at the ticket window.

Capernaum's renowned synagogue, whose facade faces south towards Jerusalem, consists of two superimposed structures. The reconstructed building that can be seen today, known as the 'White Synagogue' because it's made of light-coloured limestone, was built in the late 4th century atop the dark basalt foundations of the 'Synagogue of Jesus', which – despite its name – appears to have been built at least a century after the Crucifixion.

On the other side of the tree-shaded benches from the synagogue, 10m to the right of the olive press, a menorah decorates the upper lip of a column. A nearby column bears a 5th-century inscription in Hebrew commemorating a donation made by someone named Alpheus, son of Zebidah.

A modern, glass-walled church (1991; now air-conditioned), used for frequent Masses in dozens of languages (ask the officiating priest if you'd like to join), is dramatically suspended over the ruins of an octagonal, 5th-century church that partly obscures St Peter's House, where Jesus is believed to have stayed.

LOWER GALILEE & SEA OF GALILEE NORTHWESTERN SHORE

1. Western Wall (p65), Jerusalem **2.** Via Dolorosa (p60), Jerusalem **3.** Dome of the Rock (p58), Jerusalem **4.** Qasr Al Yahud (p280), Jericho

LINGLING7788 / SHUTTERSTOCK ©

Religious Sites

Modern-day travellers can visit places of monumental importance to the three great Abrahamic religions: Judaism, Christianity and Islam. Both believers and the merely curious often find themselves surprised, inspired and moved by these time-honoured sites.

Via Dolorosa

Threading through Jerusalem's Old City, the 'Way of Sorrows' (p223) follows the path that Jesus, bearing the cross, is believed to have taken on the way to Calvary. The 14 Stations of the Cross commemorate important events along the way.

Dome of the Rock

Topped by a shimmering golden dome, this 7th-century Islamic shrine (p58) stands atop the massive stone from which the Prophet Mohammed is believed to have ascended to Heaven during his Night Journey.

Western Wall

Many visit Judaism's holiest site (p65) to press their hands against the wall and stuff a prayer into the cracks between the stones.

Mount of Olives

Jews come to the Mount of Olives (p77) to visit the world's oldest Jewish cemetery, while Christian pilgrims are drawn here by dome- and mosaic-adorned churches and the 2000-year-old olive trees of the Garden of Gethsemane.

Jericho

Possibly the world's oldest city, Jericho (p279) is best known in the Bible as the place where Joshua's trumpets brought down the walls and Jesus was both tempted by the Devil and baptised by John the Baptist.

Church of the Holy Sepulchre

Incense, candles, icons and the hushed prayers of pilgrims set the mood inside Christianity's holiest site (p60), believed since at least the 4th century to be the site of Jesus's crucifixion, burial and resurrection.

Mt Zion

A single structure on Mt Zion (p71) is believed to shelter both the Room of the Last Supper, one of Christianity's holiest sites, and King David's Tomb, sacred to Jews.

Tomb of the Patriarchs

According to both Genesis and the Quran, Abraham and his family are buried in the highly contested Tomb of the Patriarchs (p283), the Holy Land's second-most-sacred site for both Muslims and Jews.

Ashkenazi Ari Synagogue

This ancient synagogue (p235) stands on the spot where the great 16th-century Kabbalist Yizhak Luria (aka the Ari) used to greet the Shabbat.

Church of the Nativity, Bethlehem

Duck through the low stone entrance (p267), intended to inspire humility, and make your way down to the traditional site of Jesus's manger, marked by a silver star with 14 points.

Tabgha

Situated on the shores of the Sea of Galilee, Tabgha (p219) is where Jesus is believed to have miraculously multiplied five loaves of bread and two fishes to feed a congregation of 5000.

1. King David's Tomb (p71), Mt Zion, Jerusalem 2. Church of the Multiplication of the Loaves & Fishes (p220), Tabgha 3. Church of the Nativity (p267), Bethlehem

ⓘ PRACTICAL TIP:
ROUND-THE LAKE TRAIL

Part of an energetic campaign by environmentalists to ensure unrestricted, free public access to the entirety of the Sea of Galilee shoreline, this trail – known in Hebrew as **Shvil Sovev Kinneret** – will eventually make it possible to walk all the way around the lake, a distance of about 65km. For now, about 45km – including the southern half of the lake, from Tiberias to Ein Gev, and the northeastern coast – are trail marked (with blue, purple and white blazes) and ready for use.

Near the entrance to the site, there's a row of impressive stone lintels decorated with fruit and plant motifs but, in accordance with the Third Commandment (Exodus 20:4), no images of people or animals.

Capernaum is 16km northeast of Tiberias and 3km northeast of Tabgha. Hwy 87 has three signs indicating turn-offs to Capernaum – to get to the archaeological site, take the westernmost of the three.

Monastery of the Twelve Apostles　CHURCH
(Monastery of the Holy Apostles; ☑ 052 885-8421; ☉ approx 9am-4pm, to 6pm daylight-saving time) Peacocks strut around the serene, deeply shaded lakefront garden of this Greek Orthodox site, 200m as the crow flies (1.6km on foot or by car) northeast of the Capernaum synagogue, at the eastern edge of the ancient city. The chapel-sized church, its distinctive red domes visible from afar (including from the Mount of the Beatitudes), dates from 1925, but the whole complex – from the grape trellises to the rich interior iconography (redone for the millennium) – casts a very Byzantine spell. To get there, follow the signs on Rte 87 to 'Capernaum (Orthodox)' and turn right just before the entrance to Capernaum National Park.

Domus Galilaeae　CHRISTIAN SITE
(☑ 04-680-9100; www.domusgalilaeae.org; ☉ visits 9am-noon & 3-4.30pm Mon-Sat) Near the summit of the Mount of the Beatitudes, this exquisite modern complex serves as a venue in which Christians – especially Catholic seminarians – can get to know both modern-day Judaism and Christianity's Jewish roots to better understand Jesus and his message. Inaugurated by Pope John Paul II in 2000, the campus, including a striking modern cloister, can be visited on free half-hour tours.

Korazim National Park　ARCHAEOLOGICAL SITE
(☑ 04-693-4982; www.parks.org.il; Rte 8277; adult/child 22/9NIS; ☉ 8am-4pm or 5pm, closes 1hr earlier Fri, last entry 1hr before closing) On a hillside overlooking the Sea of Galilee, Korazim is a good place to get an idea of the layout of a prosperous, midsized Galilean town in the time of Jesus and the Talmud (3rd to 5th centuries CE). The synagogue is known for its extraordinary basalt carvings, which depict floral and geometric designs – permitted by Jewish law – as well as Hellenistic-style representations of animals, humans (eg people stomping on grapes) and mythological figures (Medusa!).

Two extraordinary objects were found inside the synagogue: a richly decorated column thought to have held up the table used to read the Torah; and an armchair bearing an inscription in Aramaic. The originals are now in the Israel Museum in Jerusalem (in situ you can see replicas). The people of Korazim – along with the inhabitants of Capernaum and Bethsaida – were denounced by Jesus for their lack of faith (Matthew 11:20–24).

The park, which is wheelchair accessible, is on Rte 8277, 2.5km east of Rte 90 (Korazim junction, ie Vered HaGalil), and 8km west of the ruins of Bethsaida (in Park HaYarden).

Bethsaida　ARCHAEOLOGICAL SITE
(Beit Tzayda; ☑ 04-692-3422; www.parkyarden. co.il; Rte 888 just north of Rte 87; per car to 7pm 60NIS, after 7pm or overnight 100NIS; ☉ 24hr) The ruins here, inside **HaYarden Park Nature Reserve** (Jordan River Park), are believed to be those of the ancient fishing village of Bethsaida, where Jesus is said to have fed 5000 people with just five loaves of bread and two fish (Luke 9:10–17), walked on water (Mark 6:45–51) and healed a blind man (Mark 8:22–26) – and where he also issued a stern rebuke to the town (Luke 10:13–15).

Two **walking circuits** are trail-marked in black: a 500m route around the basalt ruins, which don't look like much to the untrained eye (signs help visitors imagine the original structures); and a 1km route down to the spring and back. The site is surrounded by pre-1967 Syrian trenches and minefields.

The Bethsaida Excavations Project (www. unomaha.edu, search for 'Bethsaida'), which accepts volunteers for its summer digs, is based at the University of Nebraska at Omaha.

Bethsaida is in the far northeastern corner of the Sea of Galilee, about 6km from Capernaum. In ancient times the lake, now 2km away, probably came up to the base of the tel.

🏃 Activities

Vered HaGalil Stables
HORSE RIDING

(☑ guesthouse 04-693-5785, stables 050 238-2225; www.veredhagalil.com; cnr Rte 90 & Rte 8277; 1-/2hr ride 145/250NIS, sunset ride 160NIS, children's pony ride 10min 35NIS; ⊙ 9am-6pm) Stickers reading 'Shalom, y'all' greet visitors to this Western-style dude ranch, established in 1961 by an immigrant from Chicago. Offers horse riding (minimum age 10) and introductory rides for children (minimum age three). Call to reserve. Also has 30 guest rooms. Situated 6.7km (by road) up the hill from Tabgha.

🎉 Festivals & Events

Jacob's Ladder
MUSIC

(www.jlfestival.com; adult/child 5-12yr 455/290NIS, Fri only 245NIS, Sat only 240/140NIS; ⊙ Dec & May) Founded by a group of Anglo-Saxim (English-speaking immigrants) back in 1978, this twice-a-year festival features bluegrass, folk, country, blues, Irish jigs and world music. Performances by Israeli and international artists take place around the Nof Ginosar Hotel (10km north of Tiberias). Events are wheelchair accessible.

Winter Weekend takes place on a Friday night and Saturday in early December. The Spring Festival is staged over a long weekend (Thursday to Saturday) in early May.

🛏 Sleeping

Inbar Country Lodging
GUESTHOUSE $$

(☑ 04-698-7302; www.inbar.co.il; Kibbutz Inbar, Rte 806; dm excl breakfast 100NIS, d from 350NIS; 🛜) Israel's smallest kibbutz (just five families) runs a delightful hillside guesthouse, part of the ILH network, where hammocks swing amid tranquil, fragrant gardens of mint, rosemary and luisa. The 19 rooms are spacious, neat and comfortable, with all-tile bathrooms – great value. Situated 21km west-northwest of the Mount of the Beatitudes, 32km southwest of Tsfat and 38km east of Akko.

HI – Karei Deshe Guest House & Youth Hostel
HOSTEL $$

(Kare Deshe; ☑ 02-594-5633; www.iyha.org.il; dm 130NIS, d 430-530NIS; 🛜) This sparkling-white facility, right on the lakeshore, has 82 rooms (with 18 more set to come in 2018), a sandy beach and lots of trees and grass. Dorm beds are available, in rooms with four or six beds, *except* on Friday, Saturday and Jewish holidays and in July and August. These are also the times when the hostel is most often booked out. Hukuk Beach is next door.

The nearest bus stop, on Rte 90 next to the Sapir water-pumping station (3km south-

west of Capernaum Junction), is served by all buses heading north from Tiberias; from there it's a 1.2km walk to the hostel.

★ Pilgerhaus Tabgha
GUESTHOUSE $$$

(☑ 04-670-0100; www.dvhl.de; s/d Sat-Wed 500/680NIS, Thu & Fri 600/880NIS; 🅿🛜) Opened in 1889, this 72-room German Catholic guesthouse – geared to Christian pilgrims but open to all – is a tranquil place with glorious gardens, right on the shores of the Sea of Galilee. Renovated in 2016, it's ideal for meditation and reflection amid exemplary Germanic cleanliness and order. Wheelchair accessible. Reserve well in advance, especially in the spring and fall. Situated about 500m from Capernaum Junction.

Nof Ginosar Hotel
HOTEL $$$

(☑ 04-670-0300; www.ginosar.co.il; Kibbutz Ginosar, Rte 90; d/tr from US$180/250; 🅿🛜🏊) This kibbutz old-timer, founded in 1964, has 170 elegant hotel rooms, 75 'country lodging' rooms, a gym (opened in 2017), flowery grounds and its very own Sea of Galilee beach. The peanut-shaped pool is open from April to October. Situated 200m from the Ancient Galilee Boat and 8km north of Tiberias.

Mount of the Beatitudes Pilgrims Hostel
GUESTHOUSE $$$

(☑ 04-671-1200; ospbeat@netvision.net.il; s/d incl half-board US$155/220) Simple pilgrims accommodation, with spectacular views of the Sea of Galilee, at the lovely Mount of the Beatitudes.

🍴 Eating

A Dabbah supermarket (open daily) and fast-food joints can be found in the shopping mall at Migdal Junction (Rte 90).

Ein Camonim
CHEESE $$

(En Kammonim; ☑ 04-698-9680; www.eincam onim.rest-e.co.il; Rte 85; all-you-can-eat meal 97NIS, breakfast for 1/2 people 70/130NIS; ⊙ restaurant & shop 9am-5pm; 🅿) Surrounded by Galilean brushland, this family-run 'goat cheese restaurant' serves up a gourmet vegetarian feast that includes eight to 10 kinds of Israeli- and French-style goat cheese, freshly baked bread, salads and wine. Has a few kids (baby goats) for the kids (children) to pet. It's a good idea to reserve ahead on Friday and Saturday. Situated 20km northwest of Tabgha, just off Rte 85 at a point 4.8km west of Nahal Amud Junction.

Ktzeh HaNahal
LEBANESE $$

(☑ 04-671-7776; www.kazehanahal.rest.co.il; Rte 90; mains 70-115NIS, 4-course set meal 129NIS;

⊙noon-midnight; 🅿) From the outside you'd never guess that this unassuming restaurant serves up a sumac-accented Lebanese feast. After a parade of 11 mezze, you might want to try *shishbarak* (meat-stuffed dumplings cooked in tangy goat's milk) or Antabli kebab with roasted tomatoes.

Situated at the intersection of Rte 90 and the access road to the Ancient Galilee Boat, next to the Delek petrol station (look for a red, green and white sign).

★ **Magdalena**   ARABIC $$$
(📞04-673-0064; www.magdalena.co.il; shopping mall, Migdal Jct, Rte 90; mains 90-165NIS; ⊙noon-10pm) Subject of a glowing *New York Times* review in 2016, this 'chef's restaurant' features innovative 'Galilean Arab' cuisine that combines ingredients and recipes that chef Zuzu Hanna learned from his mother – in the Upper Galilee village of Rameh – with modern gourmet techniques such as *sous vide*.

The menu, based on herbs and vegetables that grow in the Galilee and beef, lamb, chicken, fish and seafood, changes with the seasons. Save room for the award-winning *halawet el jeben* (semolina dough filled with sweet Arab cheese and sprinkled with honey and pistachios). Incongruously situated above the Dabbah supermarket, with the entry around back.

Tibi's Steakhouse & Bar   STEAK $$$
(📞04-633-0885; www.tibis.rest.co.il; cnr Rte 90 & Rte 8277, Vered HaGalil Stables; steaks 135-160NIS, pasta 59-75NIS; ⊙8-10.30am & 12.30-10pm; 🅿) Run by renowned chef Chaim Tibi, this sleek restaurant – the architecture has an alpine-chalet vibe – specialises in steaks from the Golan but also has good options for vegetarians, such as salads and pasta. The excellent wine list includes quite a few boutique wines.

❶ Getting There & Away

All the buses (Egged and Superbus) that link Tiberias with points north via Rte 90, including Tsfat, Rosh Pina and Kiryat Shmona, pass by Magdala (Migdal Junction; 8.20NIS, 11 minutes), Ginosar (the Ancient Galilee Boat), Capernaum Junction (Tzomet Kfar Nahum, which is a short walk from Tabgha but about 4km west of Capernaum) and the Mount of the Beatitudes' 1km-long access road. Rama bus 52 (three or four daily Sunday to Friday), which links Tiberias with the Golan town of Katzrin (14.50NIS, 50 minutes), runs along the northwestern edge of the Sea of Galilee (Rte 87), passing by Capernaum (10.50NIS, 15 minutes).

Eastern Shore

The eastern shore of the Sea of Galilee, paralleled by Rte 92, offers access to the country's largest wetlands, a variety of beaches (both free and with amenities) and an important New Testament site. The hot springs of Hammat Gader are 10km east of the lake's southern tip.

◉ Sights

Majrase Nature Reserve   NATIONAL PARK
(📞04-679-3410; www.parks.org.il; adult/child 28/14NIS; ⊙8am-4pm or 5pm, closes 1hr earlier Fri, last entry 1hr before closing) Located in the northeastern corner of the Sea of Galilee, the spring-fed streams and jungle-like wetlands of this reserve are ideal for a refreshing 'water hike'. The **wet circuit** (there's also a 20-minute dry one) takes 40 to 60 minutes; be prepared for water that's up to neck height right after rains (60cm deep in summer). The lagoons near the lake are off-limits to allow fish and water turtles to breed.

Changing rooms are available; bring shoes suitable for walking in water. Some trails are wheelchair accessible. Situated 2km off Rte 92; follow the signs to 'Daliyyot Estuary' or 'Bethsaida Valley'.

Kursi National Park   ARCHAEOLOGICAL SITE
(📞04-673-1983; www.parks.org.il; cnr Rte 92 & Rte 789; adult/child 14/7NIS; ⊙8am-4pm Oct-Mar, to 5pm Apr-Sep, closes 1hr earlier Fri, last entry 30min before closing) Mentioned in the Talmud as a place of idol worship, this Gentile fishing village – discovered by chance in the early 1970s – is where Jesus is believed to have cast a contingent of demon spirits out of two men and into a herd of swine (Mark 5:1–13, Luke 8:26–39). The beautifully conserved ruins feature an impressive 5th-century Byzantine monastery.

Near the basalt gate to the antiquities, an audio guide provides excellent historical background in five languages. The site is fully wheelchair accessible. This is considered a Christian holy site, so dress modestly (no bathing suits). Situated 30km from Tiberias if you go around the southern side of the Sea of Galilee and 33km if you take the highway that parallels the lake's northern side.

🏃 Activities

Hamat Gader   HOT SPRINGS
(📞04-665-9999; www.hamat-gader.com; adult/child 107/80NIS; ⊙8.30am-10pm Mon-Fri, to 7pm Sat, to 5pm Sun Oct-late Apr, 8.30am-5pm Sun-Wed, to 10pm Thu & Fri, to 7pm Sat late Apr-Sep) A fa-

vourite of the Romans, whose impressive **2nd-century bath complex** can still be seen, this 42°C natural hot spring 150m below sea level is great for warming the bones on a chilly winter's day. It has picnic facilities, a restaurant and snack counters. You generally need to book ahead for spa treatments. Wheelchair accessible.

The temperature of the main open-air pool is about 37°C; staying in for more than 10 minutes is inadvisable.

Kids will love the free-range peacocks, the troupe of performing parrots and the **zoo**, which has baboons, ibexes, ostriches, alligators (feeding is usually at 1.30pm Monday to Friday) and, in the mist-cooled **petting corner**, cuddly rabbits. In the warm season, kids can also frolic in the water slide-equipped **splash pool** (open from about May to September).

Hamat Gader, part of British-mandated Palestine, was occupied by the Syrians in 1948, thoroughly enjoyed by Syrian army officers during the 1950s and 1960s despite being in the demilitarised zone, and recaptured by Israel in 1967.

The site is 9.5km southeast of Tzemah Junction along Rte 98, which affords fine views across the Yarmuk River (a major tributary of the Jordan) into the Hashemite Kingdom.

🛏 Sleeping

Leafy Moshav Ramot (www.ramot4u.co.il), 3km up the hill from Rte 92 and a favourite with domestic tourists, has several dozen upmarket *tzimmerim* (B&Bs); the website has details (in Hebrew). There are more B&Bs in nearby Golan villages, including Giv'at Yoav.

★ **Genghis Khan in the Golan**   HOSTEL **$$**
(☑ 052 371-5687; www.gkhan.co.il; Giv'at Yoav; dm/6-person tent 100/750NIS; linen & towel per stay 20NIS) Hosts Sara and Bentzi Zafrir offer the warmest of welcomes and a fantastic independent-travel vibe here. Inspired by the yurts (*gers*) used by the nomads of Mongolia, they designed and handmade five colour-coded yurts with space for up to 10 on comfortable foam mattresses. Powerful air-con units make sure you stay cool in summer and toasty warm in winter.

Private bathrooms are located right outside each yurt. In the kitchen, the pans, plates and fridge space are, like the tents, colour-coded, and guests can cook with fresh thyme, lemongrass and mint grown in the herb garden (a row of recycled tyres). A number of the hiking paths pass by here.

Situated on the western slopes of the Golan 13km southeast of Kursi (Kursy) Junction (the intersection of Rtes 92 and 789). Bus 51 links Giv'at Yoav with Tiberias (35 minutes, eight daily Sunday to Thursday, six on Friday, one on Saturday night); Sara is happy to pick up guests at the bus stop.

Ein Gev Holiday Resort   HOTEL **$$$**
(☑ 04-665-9800; www.eingev.com; Kibbutz Ein Gev, Rte 92; d US$185-200; @ 🏠) From 1948 to 1967, when most of the Sea of Galilee's eastern coast was under Syrian control, the only way to get to Kibbutz Ein Gev was by boat. Today, the seaside kibbutz owns banana, citrus, date, avocado, mango and lychee orchards, a cowshed and this delightful 178-room hotel, which boasts the Sea of Galilee's only natural sand beach. Options include sunny beachfront family units (US$268 to US$308) and romantic, couples-only 'Sea Rooms' (890NIS to 1330NIS); 30 rooms were totally renovated in 2017. Situated about 1.5km south along Rte 92 from the vehicle entrance to Kibbutz Ein Gev and its port area.

Setai Sea of Galilee   DESIGN HOTEL **$$$**
(☑ 04-843-2222; www.thesetaihotel.co.il; Tze'elon Beach, Rte 92; d from US$460; 🏠 🏊) Opened in 2017, this premium luxury hotel is gorgeously sited just metres from the seashore. When you're not relaxing in the infinity pool or being pampered in the spa, you can have a vegetarian lunch in the lounge restaurant or dinner in the chic, modern restaurant, which could be in Miami Beach (where the Setai chain is based). Has 110 huge rooms (at least 46 sq metres); 43 private villas, each with private pool, are under construction.

🍴 Eating

Moshav Ramot has several nice restaurants, and there are more places to eat, including a famous fish restaurant, at the Ein Gev port.

Moshbutz   STEAK **$$**
(☑ 04-679-5095; www.moshbutz.com; Dalyot St, Moshav Ramot; mains 68-159NIS, kids' menu 49NIS; ⏱ 1-9pm Sun-Wed, noon-10pm Thu-Sat) This homey meat restaurant is renowned for its fabulous Golan-raised steaks, juicy burgers and creative salads as well as starters such as grilled aubergine in tangy goat's-milk yoghurt and French onion soup. The food is complemented by boutique Golan wines and microbrews, charming service and great views down to the Sea of Galilee. Reservations are highly recommended.

To get here from the moshav's gate, take the third right.

LOWER GALILEE & SEA OF GALILEE EASTERN SHORE

❶ Getting There & Away

Rama Bus 52 connects Tiberias with Katzrin, passing by Ein Gev and Kursi National Park as it follows the lake's southwestern and eastern shores.

Southwestern Shore

The southwestern shore of the Sea of Galilee is blessed with free public beaches, a number of interesting sites associated with the early Zionist pioneers (this is where the kibbutz movement started) and the hugely popular Yardenit baptism site. Places in this section are listed from north to south.

◉ Sights

Kinneret Cemetery   CEMETERY

(Rte 90; ☉24hr) Shaded and serene, this luxuriantly leafy lakeside cemetery, established in 1911, is the final resting place of socialist Zionist pioneers such as **Berl Katznelson** (1887–1944), who lived at the centre of a celebrated love triangle (his grave is flanked by those of his first and second wives), and **Shmuel Yavnieli** (1884–1961), who worked to bring Yemenite Jews to Israel. It is 9km south of Tiberias and 300m south of Kinneret Junction.

Also buried here is the Hebrew poet **Rachel** (Rachel Bluwstein; 1890–1931). Books of her hugely popular poems, many of which have been set to music, can be found in a stainless-steel container attached to her grave. She appears on the Bank of Israel's 20NIS banknote.

In the spring of 1917, the Ottomans expelled the entire Jewish population of Tel Aviv and Jaffa. Of the 2000 refugees who fled to the Galilee, 430 died and 10 are buried here, commemorated by 10 anonymous gravestones and a stone plaque, erected in 2003, bearing their long-lost names.

Yardenit Baptismal Site   RELIGIOUS SITE

(☏04-675-9111; www.yardenit.com; Kibbutz Kinneret; ☉8am-6pm, to 5pm Dec-Feb, to 4pm Fri) FREE This hugely popular, eucalyptus-shaded baptism site, run by Kibbutz Kinneret, is on the Jordan River 100m south of where it flows out of the Sea of Galilee. Christian pilgrims flock here to be baptised in white robes (bring your own or rent/purchase for US$10/25, including towel and certificate). Changing rooms are provided (2NIS).

All around the site, panels made of Armenian tiles, sponsored by Christians from around the world, quote Mark 1:9–11 in 102 languages (and counting). Those furry ro-

dents paddling around the fish-filled Jordan are nutrias (coypus), natives of South America. The site has a restaurant (open daily).

Yardenit is 10km south of Tiberias and 200m west of Rte 90. It's 1km northwest of **Kibbutz Degania Alef** (http://degania.org.il), the world's first kibbutz, founded in 1910.

Bet Gabriel   NOTABLE BUILDING

(☏ext 3, 04-675-1175; www.betgabriel.co.il; Rte 92) FREE Opened in 1993, this lakeside cultural centre – one of Israel's most beautiful buildings – is known for its art exhibitions, first-run cinema (two screens, with two more set to open in 2019), pop and classical concerts, bagel cafe (closed Friday evening and Saturday) and inspiring sea views. In November 1994 it served as the venue for a ceremony reconfirming the peace treaty between Israel and Jordan. Situated at the southern tip of the Sea of Galilee, 300m east of Tzemah Junction.

King Hussein's red-and-white *keffiyeh* (chequered scarf worn by Arabs) and a sword given to Shimon Peres by Yasser Arafat can be seen in the **Peace Room** (call ahead to arrange a free tour).

🛏 Sleeping

HI – Poriya Sea of Galilee

Guesthouse & Hostel   HOSTEL $$

(☏02-594-5720; www.iyha.org.il; dm US$27, d 430-500NIS, additional adult/child 140/120NIS; @🛜) Perched on a hillside high above the Sea of Galilee, the lovely Poriya (Poria) campus boasts a glass-walled lobby with spectacular views, 58 rather spartan rooms, and proximity to the Switzerland Forest. Dorm rooms have six beds. Also offers tile-roofed wooden cabins. Serves dinner (adult/child 83/61NIS) on Friday and Saturday (and sometimes on other days). Situated 9km south of Tiberias, a steep 4km up Rte 7877 from Rte 90. No public transport.

🍴 Eating

There's a cluster of cafes and fast-food joints, some open on Shabbat, at the southern tip of the Sea of Galilee, in the shopping centre situated just southwest of the roundabout where Rte 90 meets Rte 92.

❶ Getting There & Away

Rte 90 between Tiberias and Tzemah Junction (at the Sea of Galilee's southern tip; 30 minutes) is served by Superbus buses 26 and 28, all Tiberias–Beit She'an buses, and Rama bus 57, which continues around to the lake's eastern shore and, finally, northeast to Katzrin (on the Golan).

Upper Galilee & Golan

הגליל העליון רמת הגולן
الجليل الاولى هضبة الجولان

Best Places to Eat

➡ Dag Al HaDan (p250)

➡ HaAri 8 (p241)

➡ Shiri Bistro & Wine Bar (p246)

➡ Lishansky Since 1936 (p251)

➡ Meatshos (p254)

Best Places to Stay

➡ Villa Tehila (p245)

➡ Lishansky Since 1936 (p251)

➡ Ohn–Bar Guesthouse (p243)

➡ Golan Heights Hostel (p257)

Why Go?

The rolling, green hills of the Upper Galilee (the area north of Rte 85) and the wild plateaus and peaks of the Golan Heights offer an incredible variety of activities to challenge the body and the soul and to nourish the stomach and the mind. Domestic tourists flock to the area – some are looking for luxurious tzimmerim (B&Bs), boutique wineries and gourmet country restaurants, while others come in search of superb hiking, cycling, white-water rafting, horse riding and even skiing. The region has even more attractions: dazzling carpets of spring wildflowers, some of the world's best birdwatching and the spiritual charms of Tsfat, the most important centre of Kabbalah (Jewish mysticism) for more than five centuries. The entire region, its summits mercifully temperate in summer, is just a short drive from the Christian sites and refreshing beaches of the Sea of Galilee.

When to Go
Tzfat

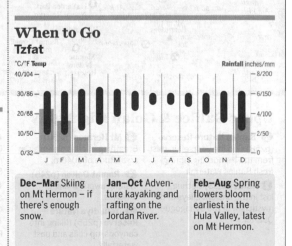

Dec–Mar Skiing on Mt Hermon – if there's enough snow.

Jan–Oct Adventure kayaking and rafting on the Jordan River.

Feb–Aug Spring flowers bloom earliest in the Hula Valley, latest on Mt Hermon.

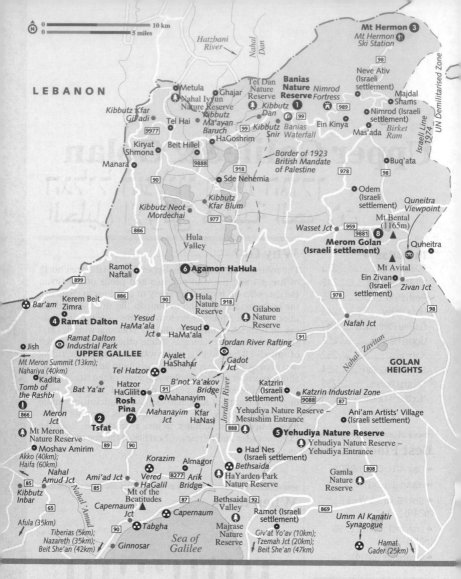

Upper Galilee & Golan Highlights

❶ Banias Nature Reserve
(p258) Cooling yourself in mist
from the thundering, spring-
fresh Banias Waterfall.

❷ Tsfat (p233) Getting
lost in the ancient alleys and
mysticism of the Synagogue
Quarter.

❸ Mt Hermon (p260)
Breathing in crisp alpine air at
an altitude of 2040m.

❹ Ramat Dalton (p245)
Visiting award-winning
wineries.

**❺ Yehudiya Nature
Reserve** (p255) Hiking into
canyons, up cliffs and past
waterfalls.

❻ Agamon HaHula (p247)
Getting a close-up view of
migrating cranes from the
Safari Wagon.

❼ Rosh Pina (p245) Staying
at a luxury B&B in a flowery,
old stone house.

❽ Merom Golan (p256)
Riding up a volcano with a
genuine Israeli cowboy.

❶ Getting There & Away

The best way to explore the region is by car: distances are relatively short, and buses to the many lovely villages and nature reserves run just a few times a day. There's a rental agency, **Eldan** (☑ 04-690-3186; www.eldan.co.il; 4 Sinai St), in Kiryat Shmona, but you'll be better off hiring a vehicle in Tiberias, Haifa, Tel Aviv or Jerusalem.

The main bus hub is Kiryat Shmona.

UPPER GALILEE

In the mountainous area north of Rte 85 you can meet Jewish mystics (in Tsfat), cheese- and wine-makers (on the Dalton Plateau), Tel Aviv hipsters (in Rosh Pina) and bird-watchers (in the Hula Valley). East–west Rte 85 can whisk you from Akko to the Sea of Galilee in just 50 minutes.

Tsfat

צפת صفد

☑ 04 / POP 33,350 / ELEV 900M

The mountain-top city of Tsfat is an ethereal place to get lost for a day or two. A centre of Kabbalah since the 16th century, it's home to an otherworldly mixture of Hasidic Jews, artists and devout-but-mellow former hippies, more than a few of them American immigrants who turned to mysticism in a 1960s-inspired search for spirituality and transcendental meaning.

In the old city's labyrinth of cobbled alleys and steep stone stairways, you'll come across ancient synagogues, crumbling stone houses with turquoise doorways, art galleries, artists' studios and Yiddish-speaking little boys in black kaftans and bowler hats. Parts of Tsfat look like a *shtetl* (ghetto) built of Jerusalem stone, but the presence of so many mystics and spiritual seekers creates a distinctly bohemian atmosphere.

History

Founded in the Roman period, Tsfat was fortified by Yosef ben Matityahu (later known as Josephus Flavius), commander of Jewish forces in the Galilee in the early years of the Great Jewish Revolt (66–70 CE). According to the Jerusalem Talmud, Tsfat was the site of one of the hilltop fire beacons used to convey news of the sighting of the new moon in Jerusalem.

The Crusaders, led by King Fulk of Anjou, built a vast citadel here to control the highway to Damascus. It was later captured by Saladin (1188), dismantled by the Ayyubids

(1220), rebuilt by the Knights Templar (1240) and expanded by the Mamluk Sultan Beybars (after 1266).

During the late 15th and 16th centuries, Tsfat's Jewish community increased in size and importance thanks to an influx of Sephardic Jews expelled from Spain in 1492. Among the new arrivals were some of the Jewish world's preeminent Kabbalists. During this period, Tsfat was an important stop on the trade route from Akko to Damascus and was known for its production of textiles. A Hebrew printing press – the first such device anywhere in the Middle East – was set up in Tsfat in 1576.

In the late 1700s, Tsfat saw an influx of Hasidim and their Lithuanian rivals from the Russian Empire.

Tsfat was decimated by the plague in 1742, 1812 and 1847, and devastated by earthquakes in 1759 and 1837. The latter disaster killed thousands and caused all but a handful of buildings to crumble.

In 1929, 18 Jews were killed in anti-Zionist rioting, causing many Jews to flee; those who remained organised self-defence units and fortified the Jewish quarter. In 1948, the departing British handed the town's strategic assets over to Arab forces, but after a pitched battle Jewish forces prevailed and the Arab population fled – among them, 13-year-old Mahmoud Abbas, who became president of the Palestinian Authority in 2005.

◉ Sights

◉ Synagogue Quarter

Tsfat's long-time Jewish neighbourhood spills down the hillside from HaMaginim Sq (Kikar HaMaginim; Defenders' Sq), which dates from 1777; all of Tsfat's historic Kabbalist synagogues are a quick (if often confusing) walk from here. If you're short on time, the two to visit are the Ashkenazi Ari and Caro Synagogues. Galleries filled with exuberant Jewish art line the main alleyway, known as Alkabetz St and Beit Yosef St.

Synagogue hours tend to be irregular, especially in winter, and unannounced closings (eg for Monday and Thursday morning bar mitzvahs) are common. Visitors should wear modest clothing (no shorts or bare shoulders); kippot/yarmulkes are provided for men (or you can wear any hat). Caretakers appreciate a small donation (5NIS). Synagogues are closed to tourists on Shabbat and Jewish holidays.

Tsfat

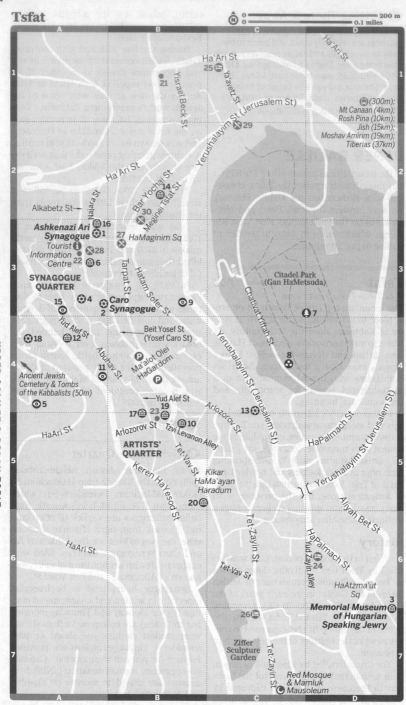

0 — 200 m
0 — 0.1 miles

Ha'Ari St

25 Ya'avetz St

21 Yisrael Beck St

Yerushalayim St (Jerusalem St)

29

(300m);
Mt Canaan (4km);
Rosh Pina (10km);
Jish (15km);
Moshav Amirim (19km);
Tiberias (37km)

Ha'Ari St

Bar Yochai St

14

Alkabetz St

30 Meginei Tsfat St

Ashkenazi Ari 16
Synagogue 1

27 HaMaginim Sq

Tourist
Information 28
Centre 22 6

**SYNAGOGUE
QUARTER**

Tarpat St

Hatam Sofer St

15 4

Caro 2
Synagogue

9

18 12

Yud Alef St

Abuhav St

Beit Yosef St
(Yosef Caro St)

11

Ma'alot Olei
HaGardom

**Ancient Jewish
Cemetery & Tombs
of the Kabbalists (50m)**

5

Yud Alef St

17 23 19

10

Arlozorov St

Tzvi Levanon Alley

**ARTISTS'
QUARTER**

Tet-Vav St

Kikar
HaMa'ayan
Haradum

20

Keren HaYesod St

HaAri St

HaAri St

Citadel Park
(Gan HaMetsuda)

Chativat Yiftah St

7

8

Yerushalayim St (Jerusalem St)

13

Arlozorov St

HaPalmach St

Yerushalayim St (Jerusalem St)

HaPalmach St

Aliyah Bet St

Tet-Vav St

Tet-Zayin St

Tet-Vav St

Yud Zayin Alley

24

HaAtzma'ut
Sq

3

**Memorial Museum
of Hungarian
Speaking Jewry**

26

Ziffer
Sculpture
Garden

Tet-Zayin St

Red Mosque
& Mamluk
Mausoleum

Tsfat

★**Ashkenazi Ari Synagogue** SYNAGOGUE
(Najara St; ⏰approx 9.30am-7pm Sun-Thu, to 1pm Fri, closed during prayers) Founded in the 16th century by Sephardic Jews from Greece, this venerable synagogue looks much as it did 150 years ago. It stands on the site where, according to tradition, the great Kabbalist Yitzhak Luria (Isaac Luria; 1534–72; often known as the Ari) used to greet the Sabbath. In the 18th century it came to serve Tsfat's Ashkenazi Hasidic community, hence the synagogue's name (the Jerusalem-born Ari himself had a Sephardic mother and an Ashkenazi father).

Destroyed in the 1837 earthquake, the structure was rebuilt in the 1850s. High atop the mid-19th-century holy ark (where the Torah scrolls are kept), carved and elaborately painted according to the traditions of Galicia (Poland), the lion has a human-like face that worshippers speculate may be that of the Ari (the Hebrew word *ari* means 'lion').

Safed Candles Gallery GALLERY
(☎04-682-2068; Najara St; ⏰9.30am-6.30pm Sun-Thu, to 12.30pm Fri, to 1.30pm Fri in summer) If you've ever wondered how Shabbat, Havdalah and Hanukkah candles are dipped, decorated and braided, drop by to watch an expert candlemaker at work – she's often here until 4pm from Sunday to Thursday. Other waxy highlights include the world's largest braided Havdalah candle (it's got 180 strands) and some masterworks of kitsch: David holding aloft the severed head of Go-

liath, Samson battling the Philistines and a chess set that pits a line-up of well-known Hasidim against equally famous Litvaks (Misnagdim). Situated 50m down an alley from the Ashkenazi Ari Synagogue.

★**Caro Synagogue** SYNAGOGUE
(☎04-692-3284, Eyal 050 855-0462; Beit Yosef St; donation 5NIS; ⏰9am-5pm or 6pm Sun-Thu, closes 1hr earlier in winter, 9am-noon Fri) Decorated with Middle Eastern arches, hanging lamps and bookshelves heavy with holy texts, this synagogue – like the street it's on – is named in honour of Toledo-born Rabbi Yosef Caro (1488–1575), author of the Shulchan Aruch (the most authoritative codification of Jewish law). It was founded as a house of study in the 1500s but was rebuilt after the earthquakes of 1759 and 1837 – and again in 1903.

In the 16th century, Caro, the head of Tsfat's rabbinical court, was the most respected rabbinical authority not only in Palestine but in many parts of the Jewish Diaspora. According to tradition, an angel revealed the secrets of Kabbalah to Caro in the house below the synagogue. To the right as you face the ark, hanging in one of the windows, you can see the twisted remains of a Katyusha rocket from Lebanon that landed just outside in 2006.

Abuhav Synagogue SYNAGOGUE
(☎04-692-3885; Abuhav St; ⏰usually 9am-5pm Sun-Thu, to noon Fri) Named after the 15th-century Spanish scholar Rabbi Yitzhak Abuhav, this synagogue was founded in the 16th

SHABBAT IN TSFAT

On Shabbat (Friday night and Saturday until sundown), commerce completely shuts down. While this may be inconvenient if you're looking for a bite to eat, the lack of traffic creates a meditative, spiritual atmosphere through which joyful Hasidic tunes waft from hidden synagogues and unseen family dining rooms. Do not photograph observant Jews on Shabbat and holidays.

The **House of Love & Prayer** (☑ 054 804-8602; www.carlebach.intzfat. info/en; 72 Yerushalayim St, under Bank HaPoalim) sings its prayers according to the mellow spiritual tradition of Rabbi Shlomo Carlebach (those seeking to pray on Shabbat are welcome), and some Hasidic groups hold *farbrengen* (joyous community gatherings).

century but moved to its present location after the 1759 earthquake. The ornately carved courtyard, restored in the late 20th century, is often used for weddings.

Inside, the four central pillars represent the four elements (earth, air, water and fire) that, according to Kabbalists (and ancient Greeks such as Aristotle), make up all of creation. The oval dome has 10 windows, one for each of the Ten Commandments; representations of the 12 Tribes of Israel; illustrations of musical instruments used in the Temple; pomegranates (said to have the same number of seeds as there are Jewish commandments, 613); and the Dome of the Rock, a reminder of the Temple in Jerusalem.

Kadosh Dairy   DAIRY

(Kadosh Cheese; ☑ 04-692-0326; 34 Yud Alef St; ⊙ 8am-8pm Sun-Thu, to 1hr before sundown Fri) Run by the Kadosh family for seven generations, this microdairy produces minuscule quantities of deliciously sharp, salty *gvina Tzfatit* (Tsfat-style cheese, aged for six months), as well as a variety of other cheeses, including blue cheese, *kashkaval* and pecorino, and homemade ice cream. You can usually watch cheese being made on Sunday, Tuesday and Thursday from 8am to 3pm. To get there from the Synagogue Quarter, follow the signs down the hill to 'Safed Cheeze' or 'Zefat Cheeze'.

The dairy also sells halva made with honey, stuffed grape leaves and local wines. A sampler plate with about 10 cheeses and bread – enough for a meal – costs 50NIS.

Sephardic Ari Synagogue   SYNAGOGUE

(Synagogue Ha'Ary Sefaradi; Ha'Ari St; ⊙ approx 12.15-5pm Sun-Wed, to 3pm or 4pm Thu, closed Fri) Tsfat's oldest synagogue – it's mentioned in documents from as far back as 1522 – was frequented by the Ari, the great 16th-century Kabbalist, who found inspiration in the panoramic views of Mt Meron and the tomb of Shimon bar Yochai. To the left of the raised *bimah* (platform) is a small room, glowing with candles, where he is said to have studied mystical texts with the prophet Elijah. The present structure is partly the result of rebuilding after the earthquake of 1837.

HaMeiri Museum   MUSEUM

(☑ 04-697-1307; 158 Keren Ha-Yesod St; adult/child 20/13NIS; ⊙ 8.30am-2.30pm Sun-Thu, to 1.30pm Fri) Housed in a 150-year-old building that once served as the seat of Tsfat's rabbinical court, this museum illustrates Jewish life in Tsfat during the 19th and early 20th centuries. Exhibits include unique household and Jewish ritual objects made by local tinsmiths using empty kerosene cans (some even incorporate the Shell logo into the design). To get there, go all the way to the bottom of the Ma'alot Olei HaGardom staircase and turn right.

Upstairs is a re-creation of a one-room apartment inhabited by a family with six children. The mother got to sleep in the one bed, and the shower consisted of a hanging bucket made of reused tin with a showerhead welded to the bottom.

Visitors are asked to check in their backpacks so they don't knock anything over. Signs are in English.

HaMeiri Dairy   DAIRY

(☑ 04-692-1431, Yaniv 052 372-1609; www.hameiri -cheese.co.il; Keren HaYesod St; ⊙ 11am-3pm Sun-Thu, to 1.30pm Fri) Run by the same family for six generations, this small dairy takes about 80,000 litres of sheep's milk a year and turns it into delicious cheeses, including soft, creamy Bulgarian cheese (aged for a full year) and a variety of *gvina Tzfatit* that's harder, saltier and sheepier than the supermarket variety – both can be purchased at the tiny deli counter.

⊙ Artists' Quarter

The neighbourhood south of the Ma'alot Olei HaGardom stairway used to be Tsfat's Arab quarter, as you can see from the minarets, but after the 1948 war the area was developed as an Israeli artists colony. To help things along, the government declared that any artist who was willing to live in Tsfat for at least 180 days a year would be given a free house and gallery.

In the '50s and '60s, some of the country's most celebrated painters (Moshe Castel, Yitzhak Frenkel, Shimshon Holtzman, Arieh Merzer and Menahem Shemi), inspired by Tsfat's stunning landscapes and mystical traditions, opened studios and held exhibitions in the town. Art lovers escaped the heat of Tel Aviv and spent their summers holidaying in the city's two dozen hotels.

Most of the galleries and studios around the quarter are open to visitors, with many artists happy to talk about their work and even happier to make a sale.

◉ Ancient Jewish Cemetery

The weed-covered, rock-strewn jumble of sun-baked graves below the Synagogue Quarter doesn't look like much, but for followers of Jewish mysticism, the spirits of the great 16th-century Kabbalists buried here make this hillside an exceptional place to connect with the divine spark through prayer and meditation. A wander through the area is a bit otherworldly at any time, but it's particularly magical in the early evening, when you can walk in the flickering glow of memorial candles, often to the haunting echoes of chanted prayers and psalms.

Any Kabbalist that was even slightly famous has had their gravestone painted 'Tsfat blue', a light hue that reminds passers-by that Kabbalah's spiritual role is to connect the heavens and the earth.

To avoid impure thoughts among the pious men who come to pray in Tsfat's ancient Jewish cemetery, in some places Hebrew signs direct women to separate prayer areas. As at any holy site, visitors should dress modestly.

Ari's Mikveh
RELIGIOUS SITE
(off Ha'Ari St; ◎24hr) A boldface Hebrew sign on the gate reads 'entry for men only'. The reason: not fear of women but rather the fact that inside naked men are taking ritually purifying dips in the cool, somewhat turgid waters of a natural spring. According to some traditions, the spring was once used by the Ari; these days the site is especially popular with Breslov (Bratzlav) Hasidim.

Tombs of the Kabbalists
CEMETERY
(off Ha'Ari St; ◎24hr) The graves of many of Tsfat's greatest sages and Kabbalists are about one-third of the way down the slope of the Ancient Jewish Cemetery, just below a solitary pine tree in an area where the con-

verging double walkways are covered with transparent roofing. If you can't read Hebrew, ask passersby for help in finding the tomb of **Yitzhak Luria** (Isaac Luria; born in Jerusalem in 1534, died in Tsfat in 1572), aka HaAri, the father of modern Jewish mysticism (Lurianic Kabbalah).

Near the tomb of Luria is that of **Shlomo Alkabetz** (born in Thessalonika c 1500, died in Tsfat in 1580), best known for composing the hymn 'Lecha Dodi'. **Yosef Caro** (born in Toledo in 1488, died in Tsfat in 1575), the most important codifier of Jewish law, is buried about 100m further down the hill. In 2017 a tomb believed to be that of the great Spanish poet, biblical commentator and philosopher **Abraham ibn Ezra** (1089–1167) was discovered.

◉ Elsewhere Around Town

Davidka Monument
MEMORIAL
(Yerushalayim St) This monument recalls the role played by the homemade Davidka mortar in securing the Jewish victory in the 1948 Battle of Tsfat. Its 40kg shells were notoriously ineffective, but their loud booms may have caused a rumour that Jewish forces had an atomic bomb, sowing panic among the Arab population. About 3m to the left, a free audio guide tells the dramatic tale of the battle for Tsfat in 1947 and 1948 – from the Israeli perspective, of course.

Directly across the street, a one-time Dritish police station – now the home of the Tsfat Academic College – is still riddled with bullet holes from 1948.

Citadel Park
PARK
(Gan HaMetsuda; Chativat Yiftach St; ◎24hr) The highest point in central Tsfat (834m), now a breeze-cooled park, was once part of the largest Crusader fortress in the Middle East. The size of eight football pitches, its outer walls followed the line now marked by Jerusalem St.

Citadel Ruins & Cistern
RUINS
(Chativat Yiftach St; ◎24hr) Near the southern tip of Citadel Park, the ruins of one of the citadel's inner walls can be seen along Chativat Yiftach St. From there, a path and stairs lead up the hill, between Crusader walls, to a viewpoint; walk under an old water pipe and you'll get to a dark, flat, 20m-long tunnel (watch your step) that takes you into an ancient stone cistern. Stand in the middle and see what happens when you clap. Other footpaths lead up to the ridge line, which affords panoramic views in all directions.

TSFAT'S GALLERY SCENE

A retreat and inspiration for Israeli artists since the 1950s, Tsfat is home to one of Israel's largest collections of artists' studios and art galleries, making it the best place in the country (along with Jerusalem) to shop for Judaica (Jewish ritual objects). You'll find compelling original art, commercial semi-kitsch and everything in between, and almost all the works – menorahs, *mezuzahs* (boxes containing Torah extracts), illuminated Hebrew manuscripts, jewellery, glasswork, sinuous modern sculpture, paintings – are imaginative, uplifting and colourful. Most, in the mystical Hasidic tradition, are also joyous.

In the Synagogue Quarter, dozens of galleries can be found along **Alkabetz St**, a stone-paved alleyway that stretches south from the Ashkenazi Ari Synagogue; further south it is known as **Beit Yosef St** (Yosef Caro St). More galleries, as well as artists' studios, are hidden away in the Artists' Quarter along the alleys around the General Exhibition, including Tet-Vav St.

The galleries mentioned below are listed from north to south.

Kabbalah Art (☑054 202-7832; www.kosmic-kabbalah.com; 38 Bar Yochai St, Synagogue Quarter; ⊘9am-7pm Sun-Thu, to 2hr before sundown Fri) Denver-born David Friedman uses the mysteries of the Hebrew alphabet, Kabbalistic symbols such as the Tree of Life, and the universal language of colour and geometry to create striking visual representations of Kabbalah, and is happy to give visitors a short introduction to Kabbalah. Situated about 150m northwest of HaMaginim Sq.

Fig Tree Courtyard (28 Alkabetz St, Synagogue Quarter; ⊘9am-6pm Sun-Thu, to 2pm Fri) Set around a centenarian fig tree and a 9m-deep cistern (visible through a glass floor panel), this collection of four galleries is one of Tsfat's classiest – highlights include hand-woven Judaica and exquisite silver jewellery. From the rooftop patio you can see half the Galilee, from Mt Meron all the way south to Mt Tabor, with the cliffs of Amud Stream (Nahal Amud) in the depths below. Restrooms available.

Canaan Gallery (☑04-697-4449; www.canaan-gallery.com; Fig Tree Courtyard, 28 Alkabetz St, Synagogue Quarter; ⊘9am-6pm Sun-Thu, to 2.30pm Fri) Continuing Tsfat's centuries-old textile tradition, begun by Jews fleeing the Inquisition, Orna and Yair Moore's studio produces richly textured tapestries, wall hangings and Jewish ritual objects (talitot, kippot, challah covers) as well as shawls and scarves made from cotton and chenille. You can see weavers at work one floor up from the shop.

General Safed Exhibition (Ta'arucha Klalit; ☑04-692-0087; 1 Tet-Vav St; ⊘10am-5pm, to 6pm summer Sun-Thu, 10am-2pm Fri & Sat) Opened in 1952, this group gallery – housed in the desanctified, Ottoman-era Market Mosque – displays, sells and ships works by about 50 painters and eight sculptors, including some very talented immigrants from the former Soviet Union. If you find yourself intrigued by a particular artist's work, ask for directions to their studio.

Safed Craft Pottery (HaAri Pottery; ☑054 434-5206; www.facebook.com/haaripottery; 63 Yud Alef St, Artists' Quarter; ⊘usually 10am-5pm Sun-Thu, to 3hr before sundown Fri) UK-born potter Daniel Flatauer works in the English studio pottery tradition, producing tableware, kitchenware and Judaica that is both functional and extraordinarily beautiful. He has one of the only salt kilns in Israel – if you're not sure what that means, ask him – and also works with fiendishly difficult crystalline glazes. If the door is locked, give him a ring.

Sheva Chaya Glassblowing Gallery (☑050 430-5107; www.shevachaya.com; 7 Tet-Vav St, Artists' Quarter; ⊘10am-5pm Sun-Thu, to 2pm Fri) Kabbalistic concepts and women's themes in Judaism are represented in the art of Denver-born painter and glass-blower Sheva Chaya Shaiman. She sometimes does glass-blowing demonstrations – call ahead for times.

Tzfat Gallery of Mystical Art (☑04-692-3051; www.kabbalahart.com; 35 Tet-Vav St, Artists' Quarter; ⊘usually 9am-5pm Sun-Thu, to noon Fri) Avraham Loewenthal, who hails from Detroit, is happy to explain the symbolism of his inspirational paintings and prints, whose abstract forms are rooted in Kabbalistic concepts. Situated across the street from HaMa'ayan HaRadum Sq.

★ **Memorial Museum**
of Hungarian Speaking Jewry   MUSEUM
(☎04-692-5881; www.hjm.org.il; HaAzma'ut Sq; admission 20NIS, incl tour 35NIS; ⊙9am-2pm Sun-Thu, to 1pm Fri) Evocative artefacts (including a synagogue ark from Tokaj), photographs and documents do a masterful job of recalling the lost world of pre-WWII Hungarian-speaking Jewry. A 17-minute film provides historical context. If you're interested, museum cofounder Chava Lustig may be willing tell you about life in the Budapest ghetto (1944–45), which she survived as a 14-year-old. The museum has extensive archives for those interested in doing family research. For a tour, call ahead.

Red Mosque
& Mamluk Mausoleum   MOSQUE
(Tet-Zayin St) Decorated with inscriptions glorifying the Mamluk Sultan Beybars (1223–77), the Red Mosque (interior closed to the public) was built at the very end of his reign. The mausoleum was constructed in 1372 as the final resting place of a local governor.

📖 Courses

A variety of organisations work to connect Jews – and, in some cases, non-Jewish travellers as well – with Jewish mysticism and traditional Hasidic life. For a list of options, see the 'Learning Centers' section of http://safed.co.il.

Note that some places have an ulterior agenda (turning secular Jews into Orthodox ones) that they're not necessarily aboveboard about, so while questioning may ostensibly be encouraged, those in search of truly open and intellectually honest give-and-take may come away disappointed.

Tzfat Kabbalah Center   RELIGIOUS
(International Center for Tzfat Kabbalah; ☎04-682-1771; www.tzfat-kabbalah.org; 1st fl, Fig Tree Courtyard, 28 Alkabetz St, Synagogue Quarter; ⊙9am-6pm Sun-Thu, to 1pm Fri) Adherents of all religions, or none at all, are welcome to drop by for an introduction to Jewish mysticism and on-the-spot meditation. Hour-long personalised workshops with Eyal Riess, who lectures around the world on the Tsfat Kabbalah tradition, cost 150NIS to 250NIS. The center screens films on the subject in Hebrew, English, Spanish and Russian and sells Kabbalah amulets and jewellery.

Livnot U'Lehibanot   RELIGIOUS
(☎04-697-0311; www.livnot.org; 17 Alkabetz St, Synagogue Quarter) Offers well-regarded, co-ed classes, hikes, inexpensive accommodation and community-service opportunities to Jewish adults aged 21 to 30. Founded in 1980, it's Orthodox-run but open and pluralistic. The name means 'to build and be built'.

Ascent Institute of Safed   RELIGIOUS
(☎077 360-1101; www.myascent.org; 2 Ha'Ari St; ⊙classes daily) Offers Jews interested in 'spiritual discovery' drop-in and weekend classes on the Torah and Jewish mysticism. Run by members of the Chabad Hasidic movement, some of whom believe that Menachem Mendel Schneerson (1902–94), aka the Lubavitcher Rebbe, is the Messiah.

For 200NIS, a rabbi will sit with you for an hour (also possible via phone and Skype) to find your Personal Torah Code, based on your birth date, which Ascent promises will reveal your true personality and your purpose in life and equip you for spiritual and material success. The real deal? You decide.

🧭 Tours

While it's easy to float around Tsfat on your own little trip, this is a town where stories and secrets run deep, so having a guide can help.

Path of the Heart   WALKING
(B'Shvil HaLev, Tzfat Experience; ☎04-682-6489, 050 750-5695; www.shvilhalev.co.il; 7 Tet-Vav St, Artists' Quarter; 2hr tour up to 10 people US$125) Runs experiential walking tours of the old city accompanied by Hasidic guitar melodies, tales of the Kabbalists and an exploration of their spiritual message.

Yossi Stepansky   WALKING
(☎052 458-9009; stepansky@bezeqint.net) An archaeologist, author and licensed tour guide, Yossi's walking tours focus on the city's history, archaeology and spiritual message.

✨ Festivals & Events

Tsfat International Klezmer Festival   MUSIC
(www.klezmerim.info; ⊙mid-Aug) Eastern European Jewish soul music fills the squares and alleys of the old city for three days in mid-August. All performances are free. Accommodation is in very short supply, so book far ahead.

🛏 Sleeping

Because most B&B and holiday apartment owners keep the Shabbat, it's not usually possible to check in on Saturday until after sundown, and some places have a two-night weekend minimum. Room prices rise precipitously during the Tsfat International Klezmer Festival (mid-August), around the Jewish holiday of Lag BaOmer (33 days after Passover) and during the three weeks following the fast of Tish'a b'Av (late July or early August). Reserve well ahead.

🛏 City Centre

Carmel Hotel
HOTEL $$

(☑050 242-1092, 04-692-0053; 8 Ha'Ari St, cnr Ya'avetz St; s/d/q excl breakfast 300/350/600NIS; @🖥) Thanks to owner Shlomo – who is likely to insist that you try his limoncello – staying here is like having the run of a big, old family house. Some of the 12 simply furnished rooms are romantic and some aren't, but they're all clean and practical and some have fantastic views.

Artist Quarter Guest House
B&B $$$

(☑054 776-4877, 077 524-0235; www.artistquarterguesthouse.com; 43 Yud Zayin Alley, Artists' Quarter; d 600-850NIS, additional person 200NIS; 🖥) Northern Californians Joy and Evan Yisrael warmly welcome guests to their two spacious, Ottoman-era rooms, both with high, vaulted stone ceilings and Moroccan-style furnishings. Swedish massage available for women and men.

Ruth Rimonim
HOTEL $$$

(☑04-699-4666, reservations 03-675-4594; www.rimonim.com; Tet-Zayin St, Artists' Quarter; d 700-800NIS; @🖥📶) Housed in part in a one-time Ottoman-era post house, this veteran hotel has stone-walled common areas with wrought-iron furnishings, expansive gardens that include a herb garden (you can pick your own herbal tea), a spa and 77 elegant, modern rooms with sparkling marble bathrooms. Nonguests can use the outdoor pool (open June to August; adults only) for 50NIS.

Beit Yosef Suites
B&B $$$

(☑04-692-2515, 054 247-2323; www.beityosef.co.il; d from US$170; 🖥) Rents out 13 one-, two- and three-bedroom apartments with cosy, eclectic decor, in old stone buildings in the Artists' Quarter. The same family, originally from Los Angeles, runs a cafe, which is where breakfast is served. Reserve by phone or online; when you arrive, someone will meet you with the key.

🛏 Mt Canaan

Back before air-conditioning, 950m-high Mt Canaan (Har Kna'an) – now a neighbourhood of Tsfat – offered a welcome 'hill station' escape from the summer heat. The area is about 4.5km northeast of the old city.

⭐ Safed Inn
GUESTHOUSE $$

(Ruckenstein B&B; ☑04-697-1007; www.safedinn.com; cnr HaGdud HaShlishi St & Merom Kna'an St; dm/d excl breakfast US$29/100, Sun-Wed US$29/87, additional person US$29; ⊙reception 8am-8pm; @🖥) Opened in 1936, this garden guesthouse has a sauna, an outdoor hot tub (open 8pm to 11pm), washing machines and 18 comfortable rooms (including one that's wheelchair accessible), all of them unaffected by interior-design theories. Dov and LA-raised Riki get rave reviews for their local knowledge and tasty continental/Israeli breakfasts (30/60NIS).

It's linked with Tsfat's central bus station by Nateev Express bus 3 (4.10NIS, 20 minutes, twice an hour until 9pm Sunday to Thursday and to 2.30pm Friday), or you can take a taxi (day/night 20/25NIS).

🍴 Eating

All along Yerushalayim St, more than a dozen small eateries sell falafel, *sabich* (a pita stuffed with deep-fried eggplant and egg), shawarma, pizza and baked goods. There are several more places to eat at around HaMaginim Sq, on the edge of the Synagogue Quarter.

Lahuhe Original Yemenite Food Bar
YEMENI $

(☑050 225-4148; 22 Alkabetz St, Synagogue Quarter; mains 25-35NIS; ⊙8.30am-7.30pm Sun-Thu, to 4pm Fri summer, 8.30am-6pm Sun-Thu, to 2pm Fri rest of year) Decked out in a gown and kaftan that Abraham might have worn, Ronen flips pan-fried 'Yemenite pizza' called *lachuch*. Also serves Yemenite soup and *qat (khat)* juice, which is illegal in many Western countries but not in Israel.

⭐ Elements Cafe
VEGETARIAN $$

(☑054 653-0668; www.elementscafe.co.il; 5 HaMaginim Sq, 3m down an alley; mains 25-55NIS; ⊙11am-6pm or later Sun-Thu year-round, 11.30am-2.30pm Fri summer; 🖥📶) 🌱 Serving wholesome food that nourishes both body and soul, this cafe offers a menu that's 100% vegan and gluten-free, a healthful, positive vibe and reasonable prices. Specialities include soup, pizza, homemade sauerkraut, stir-fried rice or quinoa (45NIS), and desserts such as coconut-chai ice cream and smoothies made with almond milk, dates, chia seeds and carob. Cincinnati-born owner Zev is happy to give tips on visiting Tsfat.

Gan Eden ITALIAN $$
(☑04-697-2434, 053 944-3471; www.seudabe
ganeden.rest.co.il; 33 HaGdud HaShlishi St, Mt Ca-
naan; mains 49-95NIS; ⏱9am-10.30pm Sun-Thu,
to 2.30pm Fri; ✐) Renowned for scrumptious
antipasti, super-fresh salads and oven-baked
fish, prepared under the supervision of
chef Rafi; and for fabulous desserts, many
of them chocolate-based, made by his wife,
pastry and bread chef Yael. In an early-20th-
century house with a lovely garden and
views to Mt Meron. Kosher dairy. Break-
fast (124NIS for two) is served from 9am to
12.30pm. It's well worth the 3km ride from
the town centre (day/night taxi 20/25NIS).

Tree of Life Vegetarian Cafe VEGETARIAN $$
(☑050 696-0239; HaMaginim Sq, Synagogue
Quarter; mains 38-53NIS; ⏱10am-8pm Sun-Thu,
9.30am-10pm or later Sun-Thu summer, 9.30am-2hr
before sundown Fri; ✐) If you're in the mood
for something healthy – chickpea flour and
vegetable quiche, for instance, or açai berries with fruit, granola and chia seeds – LA-
raised Feiga's tiny vegetarian eatery may be
the ideal destination. Lots of dishes (such as
pizza) are vegan and/or gluten-free.

Specialities include quesadillas (corn or
whole wheat), quinoa with sautéed veggies
and herbs, and vegan ice cream made with
coconut and almond milk.

★**HaAri 8** ISRAELI $$$
(☑04-692-0033; www.haari8.rest.co.il; 8 Ha'Ari
St; mains 68-134NIS; ⏱noon-10pm Sun-Thu;
✐⊞) When the mayor has VIP guests,
this is where he brings them. Specialities
include grilled meats, steak and Moroccan
pastry 'cigars', and fish. Vegetarian options
include fresh salads, soups, pasta, quiche
and grilled portobello mushrooms. Has a
playroom for kids.

ⓘ Orientation

Central Tsfat's main thoroughfare, lined with
shops and eateries, is north–south Yerusha-
layim St (Jerusalem St). West of here, a broad
staircase called Ma'alot Olei HaGardom divides
the Synagogue Quarter (to the north) from the
Artists' Quarter (to the south). The main alley
in the Synagogue Quarter, famous for its many
art galleries, is called Alkabetz St and Beit Yosef
St (Yosef Caro St). The Kabbalists' tombs are
further down the slope.

ⓘ Information

MEDICAL SERVICES

Founded in 1910, the 331-bed government **Rivka
Ziv Hospital** (Sieff Hospital, Ziv Medical Center;
☑04-682-8811; www.ziv.org.il; HaRambam St;

⏱emergency 24hr) is 3km southwest of the
central bus station. In recent years it has treated
thousands of Syrians wounded in the civil war.
Served by local buses 6 and 11.

TOURIST INFORMATION

For information on Tsfat's history, attractions,
accommodation and study options – and some
colourful local personalities – check out www.
safed.co.il. The English-speaking staff at the
Tourist Information Center (☑04-692-4427;
www.livnot.org; 17 Alkabetz St, Synagogue
Quarter; ⏱8.30am-5pm Sun-Thu, 9am-1pm or
2pm Fri) are happy to provide information on
visiting Tsfat and on local volunteering oppor-
tunities for both non-Jews and Jews. Run by
Livnot U'Lehibanot (p239).

ⓘ Getting There & Away

BUS

The **central bus station** (www.bus.co.il; HaAtz-
ma'ut St), situated about 700m east of the Syna-
gogue Quarter, has numerous services.

Haifa-Merkazit HaMifratz (Nateev Express
bus 361; 22.40NIS, 1½ hours, twice an hour)
Goes via Akko (one hour).

Jerusalem (Nateev Express bus 982; 37.50NIS,
3¼ hours, six to nine daily Sunday to Friday
afternoon and on Saturday night)

Kiryat Shmona (Nateev Express bus 511;
16NIS, one hour, hourly) Goes via Rosh Pina
(9.60NIS, 45 minutes) and the Hula Valley.

Tiberias (Superbus bus 450; 14NIS, 37
minutes, every 40 minutes Sunday to Friday
afternoon, three Saturday night)

The fastest way to get to Tel Aviv is to take Na-
teev Express bus 361 to Akko and then hop on
a train.

UPPER GALILEE & GOLAN TSFAT

Mt Meron Area

جبل الجرمق   הר מירון

The rolling hills of the northern Galilee, which are drawing increasing numbers of wine aficionados, are dominated by antenna-topped Mt Meron (1204m), the Galilee's highest peak. Originally much of the area was planted with deciduous fruit trees, such as pear and apple, but more and more land is being given over to vineyards, especially on and around Ramat Dalton (the Dalton Plateau). Visitors have also discovered the charms of dining in the Jewish, Arab and Druze villages scattered around the base of the mighty mountain.

◉ Sights

Bar'am National Park   ARCHAEOLOGICAL SITE
(☑04-698-9301; www.parks.org.il; Hwy 8967; adult/child 14/7NIS; ☉8am-4pm or 5pm Sat-Thu, to 3pm or 4pm Fri) Site of a well-to-do village from the 1st to the 7th centuries AD, Bar'am National Park is best known for its impressive Talmudic-period synagogue, solidly built of finely hewn limestone around 400 CE. At the top of the hill, surrounded by fields and a grove of cypress trees, stands a Maronite church that's still used by the former residents of the Christian-Arab village of Bir'am, evacuated by the Israeli army 'for two weeks' during the 1948 war.

Tomb of the Rashbi   JEWISH SITE
(Rte 866; ☉24hr) Authorship of the Zohar, the most important work of Kabbalah (Jewish mysticism), is traditionally credited to the 2nd-century-CE Jewish sage Rabbi Shimon bar Yochai, who is often known by his acronym, the Rashbi (Rashby). Scholars believe the work was compiled in Spain in the 13th century. By tradition, his tomb is on Mt Meron's slopes, 5km northwest of Tsfat, somewhere under a rigorously segregated complex (men to the left, women to the right) that appears to date, in part, from the Crusader period.

Since the Rashbi's precise burial place is unknown, there is no actual tomb, just a blue-velvet-covered *tziun* (marker) inside a multi-alcove synagogue. Above it, candles flicker behind smoke-darkened glass while all around ultra-Orthodox men pray fervently.

Other important sages who are believed by some to be buried in the immediate vicinity include the renowned 1st-century-BCE sage Hillel the Elder, who summed up Juda-

ism with the single commandment 'What is hateful to thee, do not unto thy fellow man'; and Hillel's great rival in legal disputations, Shammai.

On the eve of the holiday of Lag BaOmer, tens of thousands of mostly Haredi pilgrims flock to the tomb of the Rashbi, spending the whole night in passionate prayer, with singing and dancing around bonfires. Some pilgrims perform a ceremony, known as Upsherin in Yiddish and Halaaka in Judeo-Arabic, at which three-year-old boys are given their first haircut.

The Rashbi's blue-domed grave complex, situated on the hillside above Moshav Meron (gate locked from sundown on Shabbat and Jewish holidays), is run rather chaotically by quarrelling Haredi groups. Adding to the intense atmosphere is the fact that the complex serves as a place of refuge for homeless people, some with psychiatric issues, and for criminals recently released from prison. To get to the tomb, you may have to run a gauntlet of beggars.

⛏ Sleeping

Bikta BeKadita   B&B $$$
(☑04-692-1963; www.kadita.co.il; off Rte 89; cabin excl breakfast Sun-Wed 650NIS, Thu-Sat 850NIS; ☏☒) Perched on an isolated hilltop, artsy, rustic Bikta BeKadita – inspired by the American back-to-nature movement of the 1960s – has an ecological philosophy and a hippy vibe. The five eclectic and very creative cabins, surrounded by mulberry and other fruit trees, are built of sustainable materials; each has room for two to four people and comes with a kitchenette and a hammock.

Hosts Doron and Mika produce about 400 bottles of wine a year from their own vineyard. Situated 4.5km northeast of Meron Jct, 1km off Rte 89 along a one-lane part-gravel road.

Moshav Amirim   امیریم   מושב אמירים

♫04 / POP 800 / ELEV 600M

Founded in 1958 by pioneers of the Israeli vegetarian movement, Amirim is still 100% veggie or vegan – no one here cooks, eats or serves meat, fowl or fish. Set on the southeastern slopes of the Mt Meron massif, the moshav is known for its clean air (no chicken coops or cow sheds), excellent organic food, rustic guesthouses and spiritually oriented residents. It's a beautiful place to bliss out.

🏃 Activities

A 25m swimming pool (open July and August) lies in an enchanting canyon. Trails lead into the nearby Mt Meron Nature Reserve. Everything is well signposted.

Many locals are as passionate about alternative medicine as they are about vegetarianism, and yoga teachers, massage therapists, naturopaths and practitioners of shiatsu, reflexology and tai chi abound. For details, see http://amirim.com/health/en.

🛏 Sleeping

Amirim has an (over)supply of about 170 tzimmer (B&B) rooms. From about December to March, prices drop by as much as 30%.

★ Ohn–Bar Guesthouse GUESTHOUSE $$
(☎04-698-9803; www.amirim.com; Mitzpe Kinneret St; d/q excl breakfast from 585/795NIS, additional child 50NIS; @) 🏊 Perched on a terraced hillside, these 14 wooden units come with a balcony or yard, spa bath, fully equipped kitchen and cable internet (rather than microwave-emitting wi-fi). Outside, hammocks swing among the fruit trees, and there's an organic vegetable garden. In-room breakfast costs 120NIS per couple. Owners Ohn and Anva are excellent sources of information on the area.

Campbell Family Guest Rooms B&B $$
(☎04 608 9046, 054 532-2640; alitamirim@hot mail.com; HaOranim St; d 1/2 nights 400/700NIS; 🛜) Friendly British expat Phillip Campbell and his wife Alit rent out two unpretentious double rooms with a working fireplace, kitchenette, patio and jacuzzi. A great spot for some peace and quiet. Situated just up the block from the synagogue.

🍴 Eating

Having breakfast/dinner delivered to your B&B generally costs 120/200NIS per couple.

Bait 77 VEGETARIAN $
(Bayit 77; ☎04-698-0984; www.bait77.com; 77 Mitzpeh Menahem St; mains 24-38NIS; ⊗8.30am-6pm Fri-Sun, to 9pm Thu, open daily mid-Jul–Aug; 🍴) This cheerful little bakery and cafe, run by Melbourne-raised ex-hippie Joy and her son Ariel, specialises in light, healthy meals: soup, salad, quiche, pasta, pizza and focaccia, complemented with homemade cakes, pastries and gluten-free muffins. Breakfast, served all day, costs 55NIS. Thursday is pizza night in the garden. Also on offer: wholewheat bread and pitas – and, on Friday, sweet challah bread.

El Galil ARABIC $$
(☎052 517-7400; Mitzpe Kinneret St; 4-course meal 100NIS; ⊗9am-9pm) This restaurant – whose staff hails from the Arab village of Rama – specialises in veggie and vegan versions of Levantine culinary classics, including *siniya* (lentils baked with vegetables and tahini), *menazali* (eggplant in tomato sauce with whole chickpeas) and stuffed cabbage and grape leaves. Situated just up the hill from the swimming pool.

ℹ️ Getting There & Away

Nativ Express bus 361 (twice hourly) links Amirim Junction, 1km to 1.5km from the moshav, with Haifa's Merkazit HaMifratz bus station (22.40NIS, 1¼ hours) and Tsfat (11.50NIS, 20 minutes).

Jish   الجش   ג'יש

☎04 / POP 3080

The only village in Israel with a Maronite (Eastern Catholic) majority, serene hillside Jish is a relaxing spot to spend a few days, dining in the excellent local restaurants and exploring the nearby Dalton Plateau and its wineries.

Jish was settled by migrants from what is now Lebanon in the 18th and 19th centuries. Aramaic, the language of Jesus and an important source of identity for Maronites, is still used here in church liturgy.

During the Great Jewish Revolt (66–70 CE), Jish – then, as now, known in Hebrew as Gush Halav – was the last place in the Galilee to fall to the Romans, according to Josephus Flavius.

👁 Sights & Activities

Near the entrance to the village, you can visit a large, modern Maronite church and, across the street, the tombs of Shamaiya and Avtalion, Jewish sages who served on the Sanhedrin (ancient Israel's supreme court) in Jerusalem during the 1st century BCE. In a small valley 800m east of the entrance to Jish, hikers can explore the remains of an ancient synagogue (3rd or 4th century) amid gorgeous fig and olive groves.

A paved, 2.5km hiking and cycling path known as the Coexistence Trail (wheelchair accessible) heads east from Jish, leading to Moshav Dalton via the Dalton Reservoir.

At local farms you can pick your own cherries (May), peaches (starting in June), raspberries (summer), figs (from August) and apples (late August to October).

DON'T MISS

WINERY TOURS

Wines from this region are attracting growing attention on the world scene – and winning top international awards. Some 300 wineries of all sizes have set up shop, including about 30 on the Golan in Israeli settlements; 90 in the Upper Galilee; 30 in the Western Galilee; 30 in the Lower Galilee and on Mt Carmel; 70 in the Judean Hills; and 30 in the deserts of the Negev.

Quite a few wineries are happy to welcome visitors. To create your own 'wine route,' check out the following wineries:

➡ Adir Winery (p245)

➡ Bahat Winery (p256)

➡ Dalton Winery (p245)

➡ Golan Heights Winery (p252)

➡ Odem Mountain Winery (p257)

➡ Pelter Winery (p256)

Wine connoisseurs might want to look out for two excellent wine guides:

➡ *The Wine Route of Israel,* 4th edition (Eliezer Sacks, Yaron Goldfischer and Adam Montefiore, 2015)

➡ *The Ultimate Rogov's Guide to Israeli Wines* (Daniel Rogov, 2012) A comprehensive guide by Israel's premier wine critic, who died in 2011.

Useful websites covering the wine scene include www.winesisrael.com. Shiri Bistro & Wine Bar (p246) in Rosh Pina is a great place to taste hard-to-find boutique vintages.

Among kosher wines (not all Israeli wines are), the most nuanced are those that are not *mevushal* (flash pasteurised), a process connected to kosher certification that can degrade a wine's delicate flavours and aromas.

UPPER GALILEE & GOLAN MT MERON AREA

🛏 Sleeping

Ruah Glilit　　　　　　　　　B&B $$
(📞052 281-0433; swojish@yahoo.com; d 450NIS) George Samaan (Saman), an internationally known oud, *saz* and violin player (you can see him on YouTube), and his wife Eva offer guests a warm, musical welcome in a cosy sitting room outfitted with an upright piano, gramophone and wood-burning stove. The three upstairs rooms feature glass-enclosed wooden balconies and gorgeous views. Situated 600m up the main street from the town entrance.

🍴 Eating

★**Baladna**　　　　　　　　　ARABIC $$
(📞054 469-6610; mains 40-80NIS; ⊙3pm-3am, closed Mon) Ensconced in two 19th-century stone houses, this atmospheric restaurant specialises in authentic Galilee-style Arab cuisine, including dishes made with *freekeh* (roasted green wheat). Owner Tony's other offerings include delicious home-baked breads, pork loin, large salads, six beers on

tap and lots of cocktails. Situated 600m up the main street from the town entrance.

Sometimes has live music (Arabic, Hebrew, world music).

Misedet HaArazim　　　　　LEBANESE $$
(📞Wiam 054 552-5590; Rte 89; mains 50-110NIS, 4-course meal 85NIS; ⊙10am-10pm or 11pm; 📵) Authentic Lebanese offerings include eight kinds of hummus, stuffed grape leaves, grilled meats, *shishbarak* (meat dumplings in yoghurt sauce) and *sheikh al mahshi* (courgette stuffed with ground beef and lamb and cooked in yoghurt sauce). A selection of two-dozen different veggie salads costs 45NIS per person (35NIS if you also order a main dish; minimum two people), while *fattoush* salad costs 30NIS. For dessert, try the chocolate shawarma.

Situated at the entrance to Jish; the sign features a green cedar of Lebanon.

ℹ Getting There & Away

Jish is 13km northwest of Tsfat, right where Rte 89 does a 90-degree turn. It is linked to Tsfat

(11.50NIS, 20 minutes, every one or two hours) by Nateev Express buses 43 and 367; the latter also goes to Nahariya (16NIS, 50 minutes).

Ramat Dalton رمת دلتون هضبة دالتون

Sometimes called (with a bit of exaggeration) the 'Israeli Napa Valley' or 'Israel's Tuscany', Ramat Dalton (the Dalton Plateau) produces some truly excellent wines. Several wineries do their thing in and around the Ramat Dalton Industrial Park, 4km northeast of Jish on Rte 886.

◉ Sights

Adir Winery   WINERY
(☑04 699 1039; www.adir-visit.co.il; Rte 886, Ramat Dalton Industrial Park; ◷9am-5pm Sun-Thu, to 2pm or 3pm Fri) Adir has built a reputation for producing outstanding wines and equally good goat cheeses and for serving great dairy meals. Sampling three wines, four cheeses and the sublime goat's milk frozen yoghurt costs 35NIS. Serves breakfast (75/135NIS for one/two), brunch (150NIS for two) and lunch (quiche or a cheese platter) on a lovely patio until 2pm; reserve ahead. Adir produces about 200,000 bottles a year.

Dalton Winery   WINERY
(☑04-952-7107; www.dalton-winery.com; Rte 886, Ramat Dalton Industrial Park; ◷10am-5pm Sun-Thu, to 2pm or 3pm Fri) Dalton produces some excellent, award-winning wines. Three or four of them can be sampled for 20NIS in a log-cabin-style tasting centre (the modern production facilities are across the car park). Forty-minute tours start at 10.30am, noon and 2pm; call ahead if you can. Out back, each row of the tiny vineyard produces a different kind of grape.

✖ Eating

Pitputim   BAKERY $
(☑052 612-4962; www.pitputimbakery.com; Rte 886, Ramat Dalton Industrial Park; ◷9am-4pm Sun-Thu, to 2pm Fri) Israel's only 100% spelt bakery has delicious bread, crackers, cookies and snacks.

Nalchik   CIRCASSIAN $$
(☑04-699-0548; Nalchik St, Reyhaniye; mains 29-50NIS; ◷noon-9.30pm Mon-Sat; ✍) Circassian specialities at this family-run restaurant include *majmak* (cooked lentils, eaten with pita), *shush barak* (ground-veal-filled dumplings served in light tomato soup), *kulak* (chickpea-filled dumplings, served with yoghurt), *halozh* (pastry filled with Circassian cheese and deep-fried in olive oil) and *mataza* (dumplings filled with Circassian cheese and green onions, served with yoghurt). Situated 4.5km north of the Ramat Dalton Industrial Park.

Rosh Pina راش پینا روش بينا

☑04 / POP 2900

Rosh Pina's 19th-century stone houses, oozing with charm, were discovered years ago by Tel Aviv chicsters. The town now plays host to artists' studios and some of the more upscale sleeping and dining in the Upper Galilee.

◉ Sights

Old Town   HISTORIC SITE
(Pioneers Restoration Site; ☑04-693-6913; www.roshpina.org.il; ◷exhibits 9am-4pm Sun-Thu, 10am-2pm Fri & Sat, some galleries closed Sat) Rosh Pina was settled in the 1870s by Jews from Tsfat and, after 1882, by immigrants from Romania. The old town consists of just three short cobblestone streets, one of them, with Parisian pretension, called HaBoulevard. Visitors can explore the quiet lanes, lined with pretty, restored (and unrestored) stone houses; visit the **old synagogue** (1887), which still has its original wood furnishings; and pop into a dozen **galleries** (www.art.roshpina.co.il) where artists – some well known – sell jewellery, ceramics, sculpture and paintings.

Professor Mer's House (1887) has a small museum with exhibits on his anti-malaria work and Rosh Pina's early years; this is the place to come for visitors' information. **House of the Dignitaries** (Beit HaPkidut) has a new multimedia exhibit, also on Rosh Pina's storied history. Signs show the way to the shady, hillside **Baron's Garden** (founded 1885) and the **Old Cemetery** (via Ben Arieh St). At the very top of HaHalutzim St, next to a giant wind chime, the **Nimrod Lookout** memorial affords breathtaking views of the Hula Valley, the Golan and Mt Hermon; use of the binoculars is free.

⊨ Sleeping

Rosh Pina's many B&Bs, great for a romantic getaway, are most crowded – and priciest – on Thursday and Friday nights.

★ Villa Tehila   B&B $$$
(☑04-693-7788; www.villa-tehila.co.il; HaHalutzim St; d Sun-Wed 690NIS, Thu-Sat 890NIS; @🛜☒) At this fabulous B&B, 19th-century stone

UPPER GALILEE & GOLAN ROSH PINA

courtyards shelter bubbling fountains, glittering fairy lights, stained glass and a veritable menagerie – llamas and ponies live out back. During the British Mandate, the Lehi Jewish underground had a secret weapons cache here. These days, there's 11 rooms with jacuzzi, all of them exquisite. Book well ahead on Jewish holidays and in August.

Pina Barosh B&B $$$
(☑04-693-6582; www.pinabarosh.com; HaHalutzim St; d Sun-Wed from 600NIS, Thu-Sat from 750NIS; �) The seven atmospheric rooms (there's also a luxury villa), arrayed around the central courtyard of a one-time livestock yard, feature vaulted ceilings, spa bath and exposed brick- and stonework. Breakfast is served at Shiri Bistro until 1pm.

✖ Eating

Some of Rosh Pina's restaurants are up around the old town, while others – including shawarma joints – are 1.5km down the hill in and around the modern Centre HaGalil mall just off Rte 90.

★ Shiri Bistro & Wine Bar BISTRO $$$
(☑04-693-6582; www.pinabarosh.com; HaHalutzim St; mains 65-145NIS; ⊗8.30am-11pm or later; ✔) Fresh-cut flowers, flickering candles and spectacular views greet you at this Mediterranean-inflected French bistro, named after the chef, whose great-great-great-grandparents built the place in the late 1870s. It has one of the best wine lists in Israel, with about 250 Galilee and Golan wines – including rare boutique vintages – available by the glass.

▾ Drinking & Nightlife

Tangerine BAR, CAFE
(☑054 477-6361; HaBoulevard; ⊗9am-4pm Sun-Fri, 8pm-2am or 3am daily) A great spot to meet locals, this convivial, two-room pub serves brunch and great vegetarian sandwiches during the day and tasty 'Italo-Galilean' cuisine, including pizza and calzone, at night. Occasionally hosts live music. Situated on the ground floor of Professor Mer's House – the entrance is around back.

ℹ Getting There & Away

The old town is at the upper edge of Rosh Pina, at the top of HaHalutzim St, which heads 1.5km up the hill (west) from the roundabout next to the Centre HaGalil shopping mall on Rte 90.

All long-haul buses serving the Hula Valley and Kiryat Shmona (eg to/from Tiberias or Tel Aviv) pass the entrance to Rosh Pina on Rte 90.

Nateev Express bus 511 (hourly) links the outskirts of Rosh Pina's old town with Tsfat (via Rte 8900; 8.50NIS, 25 minutes) and Kiryat Shmona (15NIS, 30 minutes).

Hula Valley
وادي الحولة عמק החולה

The lush wetlands of the Hula Valley are a crucial stopping point for the half-a-billion migratory birds who pass through Israel each year on their way from Europe to Africa and back, making the area one of the best places in Asia for birdwatching.

The swamps of the Hula Valley were once notorious for malaria, but a massive drainage program completed in 1958 got rid of the anopheles mosquitoes – and destroyed one of the country's most important wetlands. In recent years about 10% of the old lake has been restored, in part to protect the water quality of the Sea of Galilee.

The Society for the Protection of Nature in Israel (SPNI) was founded in 1953 by people galvanised into action by the draining of the Hula.

◉ Sights

★ Hula Nature Reserve PARK
(☑04-693-7069; www.parks.org.il; adult/child 35/21NIS; ⊗8am-5pm Sun-Thu, to 4pm Fri, last entry 1hr before closing) Migrating birds flock to the wetlands of Israel's first nature reserve, founded in 1964. More than 200 species of waterfowl mingle happily with cormorants, herons, pelicans, storks and cranes, while water buffalo (*jamoose*) roam certain areas of the reserve, their grazing important to the preservation of open meadows. The circular, 1.5km-long Swamp Trail, which passes birdwatching hides and an observation tower, is wheelchair accessible.

The visitors centre screens an excellent, 40-minute 3D film (the English version lasts 15 minutes) on bird migration and has informative dioramas on Hula wildlife (Hebrew signage only). In the shallow lake, you may spot fur, shells and fins in addition to feathers – these will be attached to nutrias, otters, swamp turtles, and catfish weighting up to 20kg. Unlike the rest of Israel, the Hula's vegetation is at its greenest in the

UPPER GALILEE & GOLAN HULA VALLEY

summer. Around sunset in winter, you can see birds returning from their daytime feeding. Renting binoculars costs 10NIS.

★**Agamon HaHula**   PARK
(☏04-681-7137; www.agamon-hula.co.il; donation 5NIS; ⊗9am-5pm winter, to 6pm fall & spring, to 7pm summer, opens at 6.30am Fri & Sat, last entry 1hr before closing) These restored wetlands are one of the best places in Israel to see cranes, pelicans, storks and an incredible 400 other bird species. To cover the 8.5km path around the site, you can either walk or rent a mountain bike (50NIS), a four-wheeled pedal cart (185NIS for up to five people) or a golf cart (149/199/259NIS for two/four/six people). The entire site is wheelchair accessible.

In the 1980s, the Hula's cotton fields were converted to growing food crops, including peanuts, wheat, potatoes, carrots and peas. Unfortunately, cranes devour peanuts with as much gusto as Israeli kids snarf their favourite peanut-based junk food, Bamba, so conflict between the birds, protected by law, and local farmers was inevitable.

Happily, an elegant solution was found. It turns out that the best way to encourage the birds to continue on their way to Ethiopia and Sudan is to feed them – if they can't find nibbles, research shows, they stick around longer and end up munching through even more winter crops. Or they may stop migrating altogether: 40,000 cranes have already decided to become wintertime couch potatoes. From late November to late March, an entire field is now given over to supplying the migrating birds with six to eight tonnes of corn daily, delivered by tractor.

Seeing wild cranes up close is notoriously difficult because, under normal circumstances, the entire flock will take to the sky en masse if anyone comes near, landing in the safety of a neighbouring (peanut) field. A local farmer noticed that the one moving object that the cranes showed no fear of was their great benefactor, the corn tractor. So he had a brilliant idea: the corn tractor could be used to transport not only corn but also birdwatchers – without the cranes paying the least attention. That's how the 50-seat **Safari Wagon** (Aglat Mistor; adult/child 57/49NIS, at dawn 85/65NIS, at sunset 62/53NIS; ⊗hourly 9am-1hr before dark late Sep-Apr, often also 5.30am or 6am & 7.30pm in summer) was born. Camouflaged and pulled by an utterly unremarkable (from a crane's point of view) John Deere tractor, it offers visitors unparalleled crane-watching opportunities – you can see the birds without even having to crane your neck. It's a good idea to call ahead for times and reservations.

Other birds that can be seen here seasonally including pelicans (September, October and March to mid-April), 40,000 of whom fly between the Danube Delta in Romania and the Blue Nile and Lake Victoria in Africa; storks (August, September, April and May), at least 500,000 of whom pass by twice a year; and a wide variety of raptors. Don't expect to see many birds in the summer.

A new visitors centre, named for former Canadian Prime Minister Stephen J Harper, was due to open in 2018.

Tel Hatzor   ARCHAEOLOGICAL SITE
(Tel Hazor; ☏04-693-7290; www.parks.org.il; old Rte 90, near Kibbutz Ayalet HaShachar; adult/child 22/9NIS; ⊗8am-4pm or 5pm Sat-Thu, to 3pm or 4pm Fri, last entry 1hr before closing) At Tel Hatzor, archaeologists have uncovered no fewer than 21 layers of settlement from 3rd millennium BCE to 732 BCE, when the Israelite city that stood here – whose 10th-century-BCE gate may have been built by Solomon – was destroyed by the Assyrians. In times of siege, the supply of water was ensured by an extraordinary underground system whose 40m-deep shaft is now accessible via a spiral staircase. Tel Hatzor has been a Unesco World Heritage site since 2005.

Excavations, staffed by volunteers from around the world, continue every summer. In 2010 the foot of a stone statue of an Egyptian official (2nd millennium BCE) was found. The entry ticket is valid for the archaeological museum at nearby Ayalet HaShachar, open from 9am to 1pm on Friday and Saturday.

🛈 Getting There & Away

All buses travelling to/from Kiryat Shmona pass through the Hula Valley on Rte 90.

Galilee Panhandle

The northernmost sliver of the Galilee – bounded on the north and west by Lebanon, on the east by the Golan and on the south by the Hula Valley – is home to nature reserves, excellent museums, fine restaurants and villages with plenty of B&Bs. Many of the area's sites are along Rte 99, which runs more or less parallel to the Lebanese frontier on its way from Kiryat Shmona eastward to Mas'ada. The Golan's Banias Nature Reserve is 5km east of the Tel Dan Nature Reserve.

Known in Hebrew as Etzba HaGalil (literally 'the Galilee finger'), the Galilee Panhandle got its English name because the area's elongated shape reminded people of such American geographical features as the Texas Panhandle.

◉ Sights

★ Upper Galilee Museum of Prehistory

MUSEUM

(☏04-695-4628; www.ugmp.co.il; Kibbutz Ma'ayan Baruch; adult/child 25/20NIS; ◷10am-1.30pm, to 4pm on Passover, Sukkot & Aug) Israel is home to some of the world's most important prehistoric sites, several of them in the Hula Valley. This gem of a museum, which draws prehistorians from around the globe, displays objects made by human beings between 780,000 and 6000 years ago, including an unsurpassed collection of Palaeolithic hand axes and, incredibly, the skeleton of a woman buried alongside a dog 12,000 years ago. The entry fee includes a tour, usually available in English.

Tel Dan Nature Reserve

PARK

(☏04-695-1579; www.parks.org.il; adult/child 28/14NIS; ◷8am-4pm or 5pm Sat-Thu, to 3pm or 4pm Fri, last entry 1hr before closing) This half-square-kilometre reserve, 1.6km north of

---

RAFTING THE JORDAN

First-time visitors may be surprised at the Jordan's creek-size proportions, but first-time rafters are often bowled over – sometimes into the soup – by how powerful its flow can be. The wildest bit of the river, a 13km stretch known as the **Yarden Harari** (Mountainous Jordan), runs from B'not Ya'akov Bridge (on Rte 91) to Karkom (about 6km north of Rte 87's Arik Bridge, near the Sea of Galilee). You can run the rapids here as soon as the river's springtime flow isn't so powerful that it's dangerous.

All the outfits offering rafting trips have changing rooms (bring a bathing suit), showers and lockers for valuables (10NIS to 20NIS); some places will hold your car keys (and in some cases your mobile phone) for no charge. Unless you're told otherwise, assume that you'll get either wet or drenched.

Discounts of 20% are often available on the internet if you buy your ticket ahead of time (at least 24 hours ahead for some places), or take advantage of locally distributed coupon books.

Jordan River Rafting (☏04-900-7000; www.rafting.co.il; Rte 918; ◷trips begin 9.30am-3.30pm Sun-Fri, regular route Passover-October, Yarden Harari Dec or Jan-Apr) Taking on the wild, untamed Yarden Harari (16km in three to five hours; departs at 10am) costs 400NIS per person (minimum age 15). The company's Regular Route (one to 1½ hours; minimum age five) costs 93NIS per person in a two-person inflatable kayak or a raft with room for three to eight. Also offers a zipline (25NIS) and mountain biking (80NIS; not available when the 8km, 1½-hour riverside track is too muddy). Has a kosher restaurant that specialises in grilled meat and fish. Situated 11km northeast of Rosh Pina and 1.6km north of Gadot Junction on Rte 91; from the northeastern corner of the Sea of Galilee, take Rte 888.

Kfar Blum Kayaks (☏04-690-2616; www.kayaks.co.il; Beit Hillel; ◷trips begin 10am-3pm, open approx Passover-Sukkot) A refreshing 4km descent (1¼ hours; minimum age five) in an inflatable two-person kayak or a raft (for two to six) costs 97NIS, while a more challenging 8km route (2½ hours; minimum age 10) costs 129NIS. Both start on the Hatzbani River and end on the Jordan. Buses take you to your starting point, from where you float downriver on your own. Also has an Active Amusement Park for kids.

Ma'ayan-Hagoshrim Kayaks (☏077 271-7500; www.kayak.co.il; Kibbutz Ma'ayan Baruch; ◷trips begin 9am or 10am-3pm or 4pm Apr-Oct) Run by two neighbouring kibbutzim, this veteran outfit offers trips in inflatable kayaks (for two people) and rafts (for two to five or six). The 1½-hour Family Route (5km; minimum age five) costs 97NIS per person; the wilder, two-hour Challenge Route (6km; minimum age 10) is 117NIS. Has a campground (125NIS per person, including tent and mattress). Based up near the Lebanese border just off Rte 99; take the turn-off to Kibbutz Ma'ayan Baruch.

UPPER GALILEE & GOLAN GALILEE PANHANDLE

Rte 99, boasts two major attractions. The first, an area of lush forest, is fed by year-round **springs** that in normal years gush 8 cu metres of water per second into the Dan River (the most important tributary of the Jordan). The second is the remains of a grand **ancient city** inhabited by the Canaanites in the 18th century BCE and the Israelites during the First Temple period (from the 12th century BCE).

You can explore the reserve on three trails, sections of which are virtual tunnels through thick brambles and undergrowth: the **Short Trail** (45 minutes), the **Long Trail** (1½ hours) and the **Ancient Dan Trail** (two hours). Significant sections are wheelchair accessible. All pass a 40cm-deep wading pool, a great place to cool your feet (swimming is prohibited elsewhere in the reserve).

Because the reserve is a meeting place of three ecosystems, it supports a surprisingly varied selection of flora and fauna, including the Indian crested porcupine and the endangered fire salamander, a speckled orange-and-black critter with five toes on its back feet but only four on its front feet. Some of the reserve's non-native tree species, including eucalyptus (gum) and silver poplar, are being cut to make room for native species.

The **Tel Dan Stele** (House of David Stele), found by an archaeology team from Hebrew Union College in 1993, is a fragment of a 9th-century-BCE tablet in which the king of Damascus boasts, in Aramaic, of having defeated both the 'king of Israel' and the 'king of the House of David'. This is the earliest known reference to King David from a source outside the Bible; the original is at the Israel Museum in Jerusalem.

Galil Nature Center   MUSEUM
(Beit Ussishkin; ☑04-694-1704; http://museum.teva.org.il; Kibbutz Dan; adult/child 20/15NIS; ⊙9am-3pm Sun-Thu, to 2pm Fri, 10am-3pm Sat) This museum's **archaeology section** focuses on nearby Tel Dan Nature Reserve, while in the old-fashioned but informative (and, in its own way, beautiful) **natural history room**, you can get a close-up look at mounted mammals, birds and butterflies that you're not likely to encounter in the wild (this is the largest and most important taxidermy collection in Israel).

The museum screens a 17-minute **film** (in eight languages) on the geography, ecology and history of the Hula Valley and Mt Hermon; a partly animated, six-minute film for families was being prepared when we last

visited. The 1040km **Israel National Trail**, which goes all the way to the Red Sea, begins in the parking lot. The Syrian tank on the nearby lawn was knocked out by kibbutz members at the beginning of the 1967 Six Day War.

Situated 300m off the access road to Tel Dan Nature Reserve.

🏃 Activities

Mifgash HaOfanayim   CYCLING
(Bike Place; ☑04-689-0202, Asaf 050 757-8403; www.bikeplace.co.il; Rte 9888, Moshav Beit Hillel; 4hr/full day 55/90NIS; ⊙8am-6pm Sun-Thu, to 2.30pm Fri, 9am-2.30pm Sat) A Galilee cycling institution, this shop rents and repairs bikes and can supply you with route tips and cycling maps. The two brothers who run this place speak excellent English (their mother is from Detroit). Situated 2km south of Rte 99.

🍴 Eating

Most of the area's eateries are on or near Rte 99. At Gan HaTzafon (HaTzafon Garden) shopping mall, on Rte 99 4km east of Rte 90, you can find falafel, sushi and other fast food, and there are several well-regarded, seven-day-a-week restaurants. At proper restaurants, it's a good idea to reserve ahead on Friday night and Saturday.

Minimarket Nofit HaHermon   SUPERMARKET $
(Nofit HaHermon Mall, Rte 99; ⊙24hr) Sells picnic supplies and camping equipment 24/7.

Lechem'keh   BAKERY $
(Little Bakery; ☑04-644-1978; Nofit HaHermon Mall, Rte 99; sandwiches 18-45NIS, light meals 44-55NIS, breakfast 41-65NIS; ⊙8am-6pm Sun-Thu, to 2pm Fri) The area's finest micro-bakery has evolved into a cheery little gourmet cafe with scrumptious pastries. Situated in a rundown little strip mall, Nofit HaHermon Mall, on the south side of Rte 99, 1.5km east of the intersection of Rte 99 and Rte 90.

Thali   INDIAN $$
(☑04-607-7764; Nofit HaHermon Mall, Rte 99; mains 31-59NIS; ⊙noon-10pm Sun-Thu, to 4pm Fri; ☑) Opened in 2016, this Indian restaurant, decorated with embroideries from Rajasthan, is 100% vegetarian. Its lip-smacking signature dish, the Thali Platter, consists of dhal, *aloo gobi* and carrot *matar* served on a stainless-steel platter. Also has biryani and plenty of vegan and gluten-free options

Cheese ITALIAN $$
(☑04-690-4699; Rte 9888, Beit Hillel; mains 42-114NIS, breakfast 44-60NIS, set lunch 59-89NIS; ⊙9am or 9.30am-11pm; 🛜🍴) Run by two brothers, this airy eatery serves delicious 'Italo-Galilean' dishes, including a fine selection of pasta and pizza (including vegan and gluten-free versions), as well as shakshuka. Situated in Beit Hillel about 2.5km south of Rte 99.

★ **Dag Al HaDan** SEAFOOD $$$
(☑04-695-0225; www.dagaldan.co.il; off Rte 99; mains 52-135NIS; ⊙noon-10pm; 🍴) One of Israel's finest fish restaurants. Except when it's raining, diners sit outside under gorgeous fig trees with the cold, clear waters of the Dan burbling by – pure magic. Renowned for grilled trout and smoked trout, raised in ponds just 50m away (which you can visit), that are served with superb oven-roasted potatoes. Vegetarians can choose from goat-cheese-stuffed mushrooms, quiche and gnocchi.

Certified kosher from Sunday to Thursday. Reserve ahead for Saturday lunch from July through Sukkot. Situated 1km north of Rte 99, across the highway from Kibbutz HaGoshrim.

❶ Getting There & Away

Rama (☑04-373-2099; www.golanbus.co.il) bus 58 links Kiryat Shmona with Majdal Shams along Rte 99.

Kiryat Shmona & Tel Hai
קרית שמונה ותל חי كريات شمونة تل حاي
☑04 / POP 23,100

Kiryat Shmona is a sunbaked, hard-scrabble 'development town' (a town established in the 1950s to house Jewish refugees from the Arab countries) with little to offer the visitor except the promise of transport from the faded, grubby bus station. The town is almost completely shut on Shabbat.

The name, which means 'Town of the Eight', honours eight Zionist pioneers, including Josef Trumpeldor, killed in 1920 at Tel Hai, 3km to the north.

◉ Sights

Open Museum of Photography MUSEUM
(☑04-681-6700; www.omuseums.org.il; Tel Hai Industrial Park, east side of Rte 90; adult/child 3-18yr 22/18NIS; ⊙8am-4pm Mon-Thu, 11am-2pm Sat) Temporary exhibitions, by renowned Israeli and international photographers, change twice a year. An interactive section for kids explores the principles of photography and includes a walk-in camera obscura and a camera lucida. Signs are in Hebrew and Arabic but docents can explain in English. From central Kiryat Shmona, head north on Rte 90 for 3km and follow the signs to 'Photography'.

❶ Getting There & Away

BUS
Kiryat Shmona is the Galilee Panhandle's main bus hub. Destinations include the following:

Haifa-Merkazit (Egged buses 500 and 505; 37.50NIS, two hours, two or three times a hour)

Jerusalem (Egged bus 963; 42.50NIS, 3¼ hours, twice a day Sunday to Thursday, one Friday) Via Hwy 6.

Katzrin (Rama buses 54 and 59; 16NIS, 70 minutes, 10 daily Sunday to Thursday, four on Friday, one Saturday night) Goes via Merom Golan and Ein Zivan.

Majdal Shams (Rama bus 58; 14.15NIS, 30 minutes, seven daily Sunday to Thursday, three on Friday until early afternoon, one Saturday night) Stops along Rtes 99 and 989 include the Banias Nature Reserve, Nimrod Fortress and Neve Ativ.

Tel Aviv – Central Bus Station (Egged buses 840 and 845, 42.50NIS, 3¾ hours, at least hourly)

Tiberias (Egged buses 541 and 840; 27NIS, one hour, hourly) Passes by Rosh Pina.

Tsfat (Nateev Express bus 511; 16NIS, one hour, hourly) Travels via Rosh Pina's old town (15NIS, 40 minutes) and the turn-offs for Agamon HaHula (12.50NIS, nine minutes), the Hula Nature Reserve (12.50NIS, 12 minutes) and Tel Hatzor.

TAXI
For taxis based at the bus station, call 04-694-2333 or 04-694-2377.

Metula מטולה مطولة
☑04 / POP 1600 / ELEV 442M

Situated at the northernmost tip of the Galilee Panhandle, this picturesque, hilltop village – surrounded on three sides by Lebanon – is a lovely spot to enjoy international views and some excellent dining.

Metula was founded in 1896 with help from the French branch of the Rothschild family. In 1920 its location played a crucial role in the decision to include the Galilee Panhandle in the British mandate of Palestine rather than the French mandate of Lebanon. Today, the economy is based on tourists in the mood for a Swiss Alpine vibe, and on fruit orchards growing apples, cherries, pears, peaches, plums, nectarines, kiwi and lychees.

◎ Sights

Strolling up and down Metula's quaint main street, you'll pass solid stone houses built a century or more ago; ceramic panels explain their history.

★ Nahal Iyyun
Nature Reserve NATURE RESERVE
(☑ 04-695-1519; www.parks.org.il; adult/child 28/14NIS; ⊙ 8am-4pm or 5pm, closed 1hr earlier Fri) One of the Galilee's loveliest creek-side trails, about 3km long, follows the Iyyun (Ayun) Stream from its crossing from Lebanon into Israel, through a cliff-lined canyon, to four waterfalls, including the 31m-high Tanur (Chimney) Waterfall. The park has two entrances: one in Metula's northeastern corner, just 100m from the border fence (last entry 1½ hours before closing), the other – offering an easy round-trip circuit to the Tanur Waterfall – on Rte 90 3km south of town (last entry one hour before closing).

From the lower entrance, a short walk leads to three wading pools for kids (entering the water elsewhere in the reserve is forbidden), and there's a wheelchair-accessible trail.

Dado Lookout VIEWPOINT
(⊙ 24hr) Perched on the upper slopes of the hill southwest of HaRishonim St – the one with the red-and-white antenna tower on top – this lookout offers spectacular, often windy views. To the south you can see the Hula Valley, to the east the Golan (including Mt Hermon and the twin volcanoes of Avital and Bental), and to the north the fields and hills of Lebanon: the Ayoun Valley is in the foreground, while on the horizon it's easy to spot **Beaufort Castle**, a Crusader fortress.

🏃 Activities

Canada Centre ICE SKATING
(☑ 04-695-0370; www.canada-centre.co.il; 1 HaRishonim St; ice skating 1½hr 70NIS, pool 60NIS, bowling per game 30-33NIS, billiards 30min 10NIS, combo ticket 139NIS, incl trampolines 155NIS; ⊙ closed Sun except Jul & Aug) The facilities here are showing their age, but that doesn't preclude having lots of kid-friendly fun at the Olympic-sized ice rink (open 10am to 4pm or 5pm), indoor and outdoor swimming pools (open 10am to 8pm, to 6pm

Friday, to 7pm Saturday), 10-lane bowling alley (open 10am to 6pm), billiard tables and trampolines.

🛏 Sleeping & Eating

All five of the town's hotels are on HaRishonim St. The town has four excellent rustic restaurants, all of them in historic houses along HaRishonim St.

Travel Hotel Metulla HOTEL $$
(☑ 04-688-3040; www.travelhotels.co.il; 52 HaRishonim St; d/apt from 500/650NIS, Thu & Fri extra 100NIS, additional child 100NIS; ☜) Oriented towards lovers of the outdoors, this attractive and thoroughly modern place – right in the centre of the village – has 23 rooms and four apartments; the latter have space for four or five. Guests get free use of the Canada Centre swimming pools. Staff are happy to help guests plan outings and hikes. Wheelchair accessible.

★ Lishansky Since 1936 HISTORIC HOTEL $$$
(Villa Lishansky; ☑ 04-699-7184, Cléry 050 833-4552; 42 HaRishonim St; d 600-750NIS; ⊙ restaurant 8.30am-noon & 6.30-10pm or later Mon-Sat; ☜) Built in the Bauhaus style in 1936 by the family of a famous WWI spy, this place retains its original architecture, interior design and furnishings. The four spacious guest rooms connect to a sitting room that's so authentically 1930s that it feels like a British Mandate army officer in full dress uniform might walk in and click his heels.

The restaurant serves hearty beef, duck and fish dishes, homemade smoked trout, and mushroom soup prepared with Galilean herbs and spices. Main dishes cost 86NIS to 115NIS, breakfast is 60NIS.

HaTachanah STEAK $$$
(☑ 04-694-4810; www.hatachana.rest.co.il; 1 HaRishonim St; mains 65-215NIS; ⊙ 1-10pm or later Mon-Sat; ☜) Modern and airy, with Wild-West-meets-Swiss-chalet decor and panoramic views, this highly regarded restaurant serves first-rate steaks (from Kfar Szold) as well as hamburgers, soups, salads and lamb chops, which you can wash down with Golan beer. Kiddie portions are available (of the mains, not the beer). It's a good idea to reserve on Thursday night, Friday, Saturday, holidays and from mid-July to August.

❶ Getting There & Away

Egged buses 20 and 20 אlink Metula with Kiryat Shmona (10.50NIS, 24 minutes, eight daily Sunday to Thursday, five on Friday), via Tel Hai.

UPPER GALILEE & GOLAN GALILEE PANHANDLE

GOLAN HEIGHTS

هضبة الجولان   רמת הגולן

Offering commanding views of the Sea of Galilee and the Hula Valley, the volcanic Golan plateau is dry and tan in summer, and lush, green and carpeted with wildflowers in spring. Its fields of basalt boulders – and, on its western edge, deep canyons – are mixed with cattle ranches, orchards, vineyards and small, middle-class communities, both Israeli and Druze.

Israel's control of the Golan Heights has been a source of tension between Israel and Syria since 1967, when the area was captured from Syria. In the bitterly fought 1973 Yom Kippur War, Syrian forces briefly overtook much of the Golan before being pushed back. All around the Golan, you'll see evidence of these conflicts: abandoned Syrian bunkers along pre-1967 frontlines; old tanks left as memorials near the 1973 battlefields; and Israeli bunkers facing the disengagement 'buffer' zone between the two regions, staffed by the blue-helmeted soldiers of the UN Disengagement Observer Force. In 1981, Israel unilaterally annexed the area – a move which has not been recognised internationally or by the UN – and has developed settlements across it. Despite the ongoing political dispute, the Druze and Israeli communities exist in harmony here, and travellers shouldn't expect to experience any tension on the ground.

❶ Getting There & Around

Bus services around the Golan and to Kiryat Shmona, Rosh Pina and the entire shoreline of the Sea of Galilee (including Capernaum, Kursi and Tiberias) are run by **Rama** (p250), whose hub is in Katzrin. The main routes, some of them served by several lines with slightly different itineraries, run up to 10 times a day from Sunday to Thursday, up to five times on Friday until mid-afternoon, and once on Saturday afternoon or evening.

Although we do not recommended it, many Israelis hitchhike their way around the Golan.

Katzrin   كتسرين   קצרין

☑ 04 / POP 6900

Katzrin (Qazrin), 'capital of the Golan', makes an excellent base for exploring the central and southern Golan and stocking up on picnic supplies. Founded in 1977, this is by far the region's largest Israeli settlement.

The lively little commercial centre, **Merkaz Eitan**, is a classic 1970s complex that was spruced up considerably a few years

back. Among the additions: a tile-covered sculpture that is as whimsical as it is colourful. In addition to a bank, a pharmacy and some eateries, the complex has a first-rate museum. Except for one grocery, everything closes on Shabbat.

◉ Sights

★ **Golan Archaeological Museum**   MUSEUM
(☑ 04-696-1350; Merkaz Eitan; adult/child 19/16NIS, incl Ancient Katzrin Park 28/20NIS; ⊙ 9am-4pm Sun-Thu, to 2pm Fri) A real gem of a museum. Highlights include extraordinary basalt lintels and Aramaic inscriptions from 32 Byzantine-era Golan synagogues; coins minted during the Great Jewish Revolt; a model of Rujum Al Hiri, a mysterious Stone Age maze 156m across, built some 4500 years ago; and a film (available in nine languages) that brings to life the Roman siege of Gamla. Wheelchair accessible. Situated 100m west of the Merkaz Eitan commercial centre, next to the library.

Ancient Katzrin Park   ARCHAEOLOGICAL SITE
(Ancient Qazrin; ☑ 04-696-2412; adult/child 26/18NIS, incl Golan Archaeological Museum adult/child 28/20NIS; ⊙ 9am-4pm Sun-Thu, to 2pm Fri, 10am-4pm Sat, closes 1hr later in Aug) To get a sense of life during the Talmudic period (3rd to 6th centuries) when the Golan had dozens of Jewish villages, drop by this partly reconstructed Byzantine-era village. Highlights include a basalt synagogue, a working olive-oil press, an audiovisual presentation (with air-con!) on the deliberations of Talmudic luminaries (not shown on Saturday) and free-range peacocks.

In August and on Jewish holidays such as Passover and Sukkot, there are reenactments by actors in period costumes. Fresh pitas are often available at the *beit lehem* (bread house). Wheelchair accessible. Situated 1.6km east of the Merkaz Eitan commercial centre.

Golan Heights Winery   WINERY
(☑ 04-696-8435; www.golanwines.co.il; Katzrin Industrial Park; tasting 10NIS, incl tour 20NIS; ⊙ 8.30am-5.30pm Sun, to 6.30pm Mon-Thu, to 2pm or 3pm Fri, last tour 4.30pm Sun-Thu, 12.30 or 1pm Fri) Winner of many international awards, this highly regarded winery (total annual production: 5.5 million bottles) offers guided cellar tours (advance reservations recommended) and wine-tasting. The shop sells more than 50 wines bottled under its Yarden, Gamla (Gilgal in the US), Hermon and Galil Mountain labels. All wines are kosher but, happily, not *mevushal* (flash pasteurised).

Kesem Hagolan MUSEUM
(Golan Magic; ☑04-696-3625; www.magic-golan.
co.il; Hutzot HaGolan Mall, Katzrin Industrial Zone;
adult/child 26/21NIS; ⊘screenings 9am-5pm Sat-
Thu, to 4pm Fri) An excellent introduction to
the Golan, this centre takes you on a half-
hour virtual journey around the region, projected on a 180-degree panoramic screen (in
English hourly on the half hour). Also has
a 1:5000-scale topographic model of the Golan. Situated in the shopping mall 2km east
of Merkaz Eitan commercial centre, next to
the Industrial Zone.

🛏 Sleeping

Golan Garden Hostel HOSTEL $
(☑053 430-3677; www.golangarden.com; 12
Hukuk St; dm/d with shared bathroom 100/300NIS;
@🤶) This mellow 18-bed place – run by
super-friendly Alon and Daniel – has a chill-
out lounge with bean-bag chairs, a full kitch-
en for self-caterers, dorm rooms with four or
six beds, a hammock on the back patio, and
guitars and drums for guests to play. Rents
mountain bikes for 50NIS a day. A great
deal! Laundry costs 15NIS, including drying.
Rents out camping equipment (eg a sleeping
bag for 15NIS a day).

Blueberry Rooms GUESTHOUSE $$
(☑04-696-2103; blueberrygolan@gmail.com; Mer-
kaz Eitan; d excl breakfast 350NIS, additional child
50NIS; 🤶) Situated in Katzrin's main shopping
and dining precinct, this establishment –
the closest thing in town to a hotel – has 10
simple but spacious rooms with pine-wood
ceilings and parquet floors; amenities in-
clude fridges and microwaves. Reception is
in the Blueberry Cafe & Restaurant, which is
where breakfast (40NIS) is served.

SPNI Golan Field School HOSTEL $$
(☑04-696-5030; www.natureisrael.org; 2 Zavitan
St; d 375-503NIS, additional adult 127-157NIS, child
84-113NIS; 🤶) Housed in an unpretentious
1970s complex at the edge of town, the 33
simple rooms, all with fridges, can sleep
four to nine, making them a good option for
families and groups (individual dorm beds
not available). Wi-fi is restricted to the lobby
area. Situated 1km from Merkaz Eitan commercial centre – head down Daliyot St and
then turn left on Zavitan St.

Sometimes (eg on Jewish holidays and in
August) offers free group hikes.

✗ Eating

Fast food (hummus, shawarma, bad pizza,
hamburgers) is available in the Merkaz Eitan commercial centre – except on Shabbat,

---

> **ℹ HIKING SAFELY ON THE GOLAN**
>
> The Golan's most visited nature re-
> serves issue excellent trail maps when
> you pay your admission fee, but if you'll
> be hiking further afield, the map to
> get – if only to avoid minefields and
> Israel Defence Forces' firing zones –
> is the Hebrew-only **SPNI Map 1**, a
> 1:50,000-scale topographical trail map
> which covers Mt Hermon, the Golan and
> the Galilee Panhandle (ie the Hula Valley
> and surrounds). It is sold at most of the
> area's national parks.
>
> In nature reserves with entry fees, up-
> to-the-minute details on trail conditions
> are available from the friendly rangers
> who staff the information counters. For
> certain routes you'll be asked to register,
> possibly by leaving a card on your dash-
> board so if rangers find your car after
> dark, they'll know where to send the
> rescue teams.

when your eating options shrink to one grocery and, 2km or 3km east in the Industrial
Zone, two restaurants.

HaMakolet Shel HaRusim SUPERMARKET $
(Merkaz Eitan, facing Lev Katzrin Mall; ⊘9am-9pm
Sun-Thu, 8am-11pm Fri, 10am-10pm Sat) Run by
a couple from Uzbekistan, this seven-day-a-
week 'Russian' grocery sells bread, cheeses,
lox, matjes herring and wines, including
many products from the former USSR. The
beers on offer include Baltika (from Russia)
and Obolon (from the Ukraine). Does not
carry fruits and vegetables. Open Shabbat.

Co-op Shop SUPERMARKET $
(Lev Katzrin Mall; ⊘8am-9pm Sun-Tue, to 10pm
Wed & Thu, 7am-2.30pm or 4pm Fri) Picnic supplies for a hike or Shabbat. Situated 100m
east of Merkaz Eitan commercial centre.

Golan Brewhouse PUB FOOD $$
(☑04-696-1311; www.golanbeer.co.il; Hutzot HaGo-
lan Mall, Katzrin Industrial Zone; mains 52-139NIS;
⊘11am-10.30pm; ☝) Endowed with a circular
wooden bar and panoramic windows, this
popular pub-restaurant serves Golan-raised
steaks, hamburgers, chicken, fish, salads,
veggie mains, soups (winter only) and some
damn fine Bazelet microbrews.

The Brewhouse Beer Sampler (14NIS)
gets you a whisky tumbler of each of the Bre-
whouse's four beers (an amber ale, a pilsner,

a Doppelbock and a wheat beer), brewed in the copper vats in the corner. Most of the time a seasonal beer is also available. For 48NIS you can sample 200ml of each and munch on olives and sauerkraut.

★**Meatshos**   STEAK $$$
(☑04-696-3334; www.meatshos.co.il; Katzrin Industrial Zone; mains 59-159NIS; ⊙noon-6pm Mon-Thu, 1-10pm Fri, noon-7pm Sat) Renowned for its flavoursome steaks, chops and hamburgers (250g to 750g), made from Golan-raised, 1½-year-old calves and lambs. Also serves vegetarian lasagne and Salokiya boutique wine (red/white per glass 42/32NIS), made right on the premises. Situated at the far northern end of the Industrial Zone next to the fire station, 1km past the Golan Heights Winery.

❶ Information

Run by the regional council, the town's **information centre** (☑04-696-2885; www.tourgolan. org.il; Hutzot HaGolan Mall, Katzrin Industrial Zone; ⊙9am-4pm Sun-Thu) has brochures and free maps in Hebrew, English and Russian, and can supply details on accommodation, hiking and winery visits. Situated in the shopping centre 2km east of the town centre, behind the round fountain.

Get a free consultation with experienced SPNI guides about Golan hiking options at **SPNI Hiking Information** (Merkaz Hadracha; ☑04-770-9460; www.teva.org.il; SPNI Golan Field School, 2 Zavitan St; ⊙8.30am-5pm Sun-Thu). You can also phone with questions. Sells 1:50,000-scale hiking maps (90NIS).

❶ Getting There & Away

BUS

Katzrin is the Golan's only real bus hub. Rama buses (p250) head to virtually every part of the plateau (Ein Zivan has especially convenient services), as well as to Tiberias, Rosh Pina and Kiryat Shmona. Bus 57 follows the Sea of Galilee's eastern and southwestern coasts (including Kursi) on its way to Tiberias; bus 52 goes to Tiberias via the lake's northwestern coast (including Capernaum). To get to Neve Ativ, Majdal Shams and other places near Mt Hermon, you generally have to change in Kiryat Shmona (the only exception: twice-daily bus 87).

Long-haul Egged services include the following:
Haifa – Lev HaMifratz (bus 503; 37.50NIS, 2½ hours, four daily Sunday to Thursday, two on Friday)
Jerusalem (bus 966; 42.50NIS, four hours, one to three daily)

Tel Aviv – Central Bus Station (bus 843; 42.50NIS, 3½ hours, four or five daily Sunday to Thursday, one on Friday, one on Saturday)

Southern Golan

The area south of Katzrin overlooks the Sea of Galilee from the east, affording fine views of the lake, the sparkling lights of Tiberias and the hills of the Galilee. The area has some excellent hiking, especially in and around the Yehudiya and Gamla Nature Reserves, and several fascinating historical sites.

Yehudiya Nature Reserve
שמורת טבע יהודיה   محمية طبعية يهودية

Both casual strollers and experienced hikers – especially those who aren't averse to getting wet – will find plenty to engage and challenge them in the 66-sq-km **Yehudiya Nature Reserve** (☑Meshushim entrance 04-682-0238, Yehudiya entrance 04-696-2817; adult/child 22/9NIS; ⊙8am-4pm Sat-Thu, to 3pm Fri late Oct-late Mar, 7am-5pm Sat-Thu, to 4pm Fri late Mar-late Oct). Mammals you might encounter include gazelles and wild boar, while the cliffs are home to birds of prey as well as songbirds. Swimming is permitted in the reserve's natural pools – hugely refreshing on a hot day.

Most of the trails follow three cliff-lined wadis, with year-round water flow, that drain into the northeastern corner of the Sea of Galilee. **Wadi Yehudiya** and **Wadi Zavitan** are both easiest to access from the Yehudiya Parking Lot (Chenyon Yehudiya), which is on Rte 87 midway between Katzrin and the Sea of Galilee.

Wadi Meshushim, easiest to get to from the Meshushim Parking Lot, is situated 2.8km along a gravel road from Rte 888, which parallels the Jordan River. The parking lot is 8km northeast of the New Testament site of Bethsaida.

The rangers at both entrances to Yehudiya (pronounced yeh-hoo-*dee*-yah) are extremely knowledgeable and can point you in the right direction, as well as register you, for your own safety. The only map you'll need is the excellent colour-coded one provided at the ticket booths.

Stick to marked trails. People have fallen to their deaths while attempting to negotiate treacherous makeshift trails, and there's an army firing zone east of Wadi Yehudiya (across Rte 87).

Rama (p250) buses 52 and 57 (eight to 10 daily Sunday to Friday), which connect Katzrin with Tiberias, stop at the Yehudiya Parking Lot (4.40NIS, 20 minutes from Katzrin). Egged bus 843, linking Katzrin with Tel Aviv, also passes by here.

A bus schedule is usually posted at the Yehudiya Parking Lot information counter.

Gamla Nature Reserve

שמורת טבע גמלא   محمية طبيعية جملا

The site of a thriving Jewish village during the late Second Temple period, Gamla dared to defy the Romans during the Great Jewish Revolt and as a result was besieged by Vespasian's legions. Today, you can visit the ruins at **Gamla Nature Reserve** (☑04-682-2282; www.parks.org.il; Rte 808; adult/child 28/14NIS; ☺8am-4pm or 5pm Sat-Thu, closes 1hr earlier Fri, last entry 2hr before closing), which afford spectacular views of the surrounding countryside. From park HQ, walking down to, and around, ancient Gamla takes two to three hours.

Historian Josephus Flavius recorded the Romans' seven-month siege (67 CE), the defenders' valiant stand and the bloody final battle, and reported a Masada-like mass suicide of thousands of Jews (for which there's no archaeological evidence). After Gamla – perched atop a rocky ridge shaped like a camel's back (*gamla* is the Aramaic word for camel) – was identified in 1968 based on Flavius' precise descriptions, excavations unearthed an enormous quantity of Roman siege weaponry (some can be seen in Katzrin's Golan Archaeological Museum; p252) as well as one of the world's oldest synagogues, believed to date from the 1st century BCE (ie from the time of the Second Temple).

Gamla is known for the **Griffon vultures** (with an astonishing wingspan of 2.7m) that nest in the reserve's cliffs and soar majestically over the valley below. Sadly, they are becoming rarer, victims of high-voltage electrical lines, quadcopters and poisoned carrion that a tiny minority of ranchers set out – illegally – to kill wolves and jackals. Fifteen years ago there were some 200 on the Golan; today only about 15 survive. To help the local population recover, Griffon vultures from Spain have been brought here and released. Half-hour talks on the birds (in Hebrew) generally begin daily at 11am and 1pm at the **Vulture Lookout**.

A remarkable 51m-high waterfall can be seen from the **Waterfall Overlook** (Tatzpit HaMapal); the trail to get there (1½ hours return) passes a field dotted with **dolmens** (basalt grave markers) erected by nomads 4000 years ago.

On the plateau around the parking lot, the wheelchair-accessible **Vulture Path** (Shvil HaNesharim; 20 to 30 minutes) affords a fine panorama of the ancient city.

Gamla is 20km south of Katzrin.

Umm Al Kanatir Synagogue

בית הכנסת אום אל קנטיר   كنيس ام القناطر

What's truly extraordinary about the 6th-century **Umm Al Kanatir Synagogue** (Ein Kshatot Synagogue; off Rte 808, just west of Moshav Natur) is that after it was destroyed in the great earthquake of 749 CE, the site, because of its remoteness, remained almost completely undisturbed until the 21st century. Because none of the basalt blocks were carried away for reuse elsewhere, archaeologists have been able to reassemble the entire splendid structure using the original stones, with the help of 3D laser scanning, microchip labels and a yellow overhead crane.

The ark, oriented towards Jerusalem, is richly decorated with spread-winged eagles, grape bunches and Jewish symbols such as the menorah, *lulav* (palm frond) and *etrog* (a citrus fruit). An underground visitors centre, with spectacular views of the Sea of Galilee, was under construction at the time of research.

Ani'am Artists' Village

☑04 / POP 500

This quiet Israeli settlement is home to nine attractive studios and galleries arrayed along a brick-paved pedestrian street. The artists – including two ceramicists and a New York–born goldsmith, Joel Friedman of Golan Gold, who makes exquisite braided gold jewellery – are happy to tell visitors about their crafts. Most places are open Monday to Thursday from 11am to 4pm or 5pm (later in August); Friday and Saturday hours tend to be 11am to about 3pm (4pm in summer).

Ani'am has two kosher restaurants – one dairy, the other meat – that are closed on Friday night and Saturday.

Central Golan

Spread across the rocky, volcanic plateau that gives the Golan Heights their name, the sparsely populated Central Golan is home to cattle ranches, vineyards, wineries, a

ℹ SYRIAN CIVIL WAR SPILLOVER

Syria's brutal civil war has occasionally spilled over into this area, with a number of stray shells and rockets landing on the Israeli side of the disengagement lines. Such incidents seem to have stopped following a mid-2017 ceasefire, but check into local security conditions before you venture near the frontier, especially along Hwy 98 and around Mt Bental and the Quneitra Viewpoint.

boutique chocolate factory, farms where you can pick your own berries and fruits, and the twin volcanoes of Avital and Bental, which tower over the Syrian town of Quneitra and the UN-monitored disengagement zone. The area is bounded by Katzrin to the south, Odem to the north and, to the east, the 1974 disengagement line.

Ein Zivan עין זיוון עין זיון

▸ 04 / POP 280

Thanks to its two wineries and chocolate factory, Kibbutz Ein Zivan, an Israeli settlement established in 1968, makes a good place to spend an afternoon.

◉ Sights

Pelter Winery WINERY
(☑ 054 248-6663; www.pelter.co.il; ◷ 10am-4pm) In 2001, after studying wine-making in Australia, Tal Pelter founded a winery that now turns shiraz and chenin blanc grapes (among others) into 300,000 bottles of reds and whites a year. Free tours (15 to 30 minutes) end with a tasting. A platter with four Pelter goat cheeses (made by Tal's wife Inbar), bread and olive oil costs 25NIS; freshbaked focaccia (55NIS for two) is available on Fridays and Saturdays.

Bahat Winery WINERY
(☑ 04-699-3710; www.bahatwinery.co.il; tour adult/child 25/10NIS; ◷ 10am-6pm Sun-Thu, to 4pm Fri, closes 1hr earlier in winter) A true boutique operation, Bahat – housed in a one-time plasticsandal factory – produces just 20,000 bottles of wine a year, including port (first sold in 2017) and an interesting blend of cabernet sauvignon and shiraz. Short tours of the one-room production facilities, in Hebrew and English, leave every half-hour and end with a tasting session. Edibles on offer include

cheese platters, pizza and salads. Kids can make their own labelled bottle of professionally corked grape juice (25NIS).

ℹ Getting There & Away

Ein Zivan is 20km northeast of Katzrin. **Rama** (p250) buses 14, 59 and 87 link Ein Zivan with Katzrin every hour or two.

Quneitra Viewpoint

موقع المراقبة القنيطرة תצפית קוניטרה

From high atop Mt Avital, top-secret Israel Defence Forces' electronics peer deep into Syria, but the Quneitra Viewpoint (Rte 98; ◷ 24hr), on the volcano's lower flanks, also affords fine views into Israel's troubled northern neighbour. The site – at which an 'audio explanation station' describes the battles fought here in 1973 – overlooks the ruined town of Quneitra, one-time Syrian 'capital of the Golan', just 2km away.

At the end of the Six Day War, Quneitra, at the time a garrison town defending Damascus (60km to the northeast), was abandoned in chaos by the Syrian army after Syrian government radio mistakenly reported that the town had fallen. It changed hands twice during the 1973 Yom Kippur War, which Israel began with just 177 tanks against the attacking Syrians' 1500. Inside the UN buffer zone since 1974, the town has been under the control of Syrian rebel forces since 2014.

About 150m north along Rte 98, a Yom Kippur War memorial is marked by the turret of a US-built Israeli tank and an 'audio explanation station'. A path leads down the slope from the viewpoint to the Golan Volcanic Park–Avital (HaPark HavVolkani; Rte 98; ◷ 10am-4pm), situated in an old quarry whose excavations exposed many layers of the Golan's eventful geological history. Signs are in Hebrew, Arabic and English.

The viewpoint and park are on the eastern side of Rte 98, 1.3km north of Zivan Jct.

Merom Golan מרום גולן مروم جولان

▸ 04 / POP 675 / ELEV 977M

Nestled at the base of the western slopes of Mt Bental, this Israeli settlement is known for its horse riding and steak restaurant – and for the cafe it runs atop Mt Bental.

🏃 Activities

Havat HaBokrim HORSE RIDING
(☑ 052 851-4434; www.meromgolantourism.co.il; 1½hr ride 150NIS, 5min child ride 30NIS; ◷ rides approx every 2hr 10am-4pm Sun-Thu, at 10am, noon

& 3pm Fri & Sat) Head into them thar (volcanic) hills with the *bokrim* (cowboys) of Havat HaBokrim, a Golan-style dude ranch that offers horse riding. Reserve ahead by phone.

🛏 Sleeping & Eating

Merom Golan Resort Village GUESTHOUSE $$$
(📞04-696-0267; www.meromgolantourism.co.il; d US$159-196; 🖥🏊) Rest your saddle-weary body at this attractive and very comfortable resort village, which has 46 wood-and-basalt, spa-equipped chalets and 32 guestrooms surrounded by lovely gardens. Another 38 boutique-hotel-style rooms were set to open in 2018. Wheelchair accessible.

★**HaBokrim Restaurant** STEAK $$$
(📞04-696-0206; www.meromgolantourism.co.il, mains 66-142NIS; Fri buffet adult/child 125/60NIS; ⏰noon-10pm Sun-Thu, noon to 3pm & 7-9pm Fri) Opened in 1989, this veteran meatery is famed for its mouth-watering Golan-raised steaks (sirloin and entrecôte) and hamburgers, and also serves fish, vegetarian gnocchi, Bazelet beer on tap and a good selection of children's meals. Golan wines cost 25NIS per glass. Kosher, so Friday dinner is a buffet.

ℹ Getting There & Away

Rama (p250) buses 14, 59 and 87 link Merom Golan with Katzrin (10.50NIS, 30 minutes, hourly).

Mt Bental   הר בנטל   جبل بنطل
ELEV 1165M

Part of a nature reserve, the summit of this volcanic ash cone affords fantastic panoramas. From old Israeli trenches and bunkers, you can see the Hula Valley, Lebanon, Mt Hermon, the Syrian-controlled part of the Golan and Mt Bental's volcanic twin, Mt Avital. The clearest views of the Quneitra area are in the late afternoon. UN troops have turned one corner of the site into an observation post to keep an eye on the Syrian civil war; at the time of research, visitors had reported hearing distant artillery fire. It's open 24 hours a day, except when there's snow.

The somewhat smelly underground section of the trench system, last used in the Yom Kippur War, can be explored. Above ground, two 'audio explanation stations' provide historical information in Hebrew and English, and signposts – some faded – point the way to Damascus (60km), Haifa (85km), Amman (135km), Jerusalem (240km), Baghdad (800km) and Washington, DC (11,800km).

🍴 Eating

Coffee Anan SANDWICHES $$
(📞04-682-0664; www.meromgolantourism.co.il; sandwiches 35-39NIS; ⏰9am-5pm, closed when snowy) This mountain-top eatery serves sandwiches, salads, homemade cakes, *bourekas*, shakshuka and ice cream. Named in honour of former UN Secretary General Kofi Annan, once in charge of the UN troops on patrol down below; in Hebrew, the name also means 'cafe in the clouds'.

Odem   אודם اودم
📞04 / POP 150 / ELEV 1050M

This small Israeli settlement is a great place to sample local wines, pick summer fruits and berries, and meet other travellers.

◎ Sights

Odem Mountain Winery WINERY
(📞04-687-1122; www.harodem.co.il; ⏰9am-5pm Sun-Thu, to 4pm Fri) Keep an eye out for this family-run boutique winery's light, summery rosé (made with cabernet sauvignon and syrah), their cabernet franc red and Gewürztraminer. Sampling two wines is free, while four/six costs 20/35NIS (free if you buy a bottle). Tours cost 20NIS and include a tasting session. The winery has an annual production of 105,000 bottles.

Ya'ar HaAyalim ZOO
(📞050 522-9450; www.yayalim.co.il; child 2-12yr/accompanying adult 60/35NIS; ⏰9am-5pm, to 7pm Jul & Aug; 🖱) Kids will love this gravelly tree-shaded hillside, home to three species of deer (from Northern Europe, the Himalayas and Japan), ibexes, 85cm-high miniponies that children can ride on, a petting zoo, pedal cars, five trampolines and a rope park with a 15m zipline.

🛏 Sleeping

★**Golan Heights Hostel** HOSTEL $
(📞054 260-0334; www.thegolanheightshostel.com; dm 100NIS, d 350NIS, with shared bathroom 270NIS; @🖥) This is what a hostel is supposed to be. Amenities include great chill-out spaces for socialising, a spacious kitchen, a library of English books, laundry facilities and cheerful wall murals. Heating is underfloor, a blessing in winter. There are nine rooms, three of them dorms with six or eight bunk beds. Liad, the enthusiastic and welcoming owner, has prepared a guide with details on local hikes and activities, available for download from the website.

Northern Golan

The northernmost section of the Golan cascades down the flanks of towering Mt Hermon, from the Mt Hermon Ski Station to the Druze villages of Majdal Shams, Mas'ada and Ein Kinya. Many of the area's most picturesque sites, including the mighty, Crusader-era Nimrod Fortress and Banias Nature Reserve, are on or near Rte 99, which continues west through the Galilee Panhandle to Kiryat Shmona.

Nimrod Fortress

מבצר נמרוד ‎ قلعة الصبيبة

Built by Muslims in the 13th century to protect the road from Tyre to Damascus, **Nimrod Fortress** (☑ 04-694-9277; www.parks.org.il; Rte 989; adult/child 22/9NIS; ⊙ 8am-4pm or 5pm Sat-Thu, closes 1hr earlier Fri, last entry 1hr before closing) rises fairy-tale-like on a long, narrow ridge (altitude 815m) on the southwestern slopes of Mt Hermon. The work that went into building such a massive fortification – 420m long and up to 150m wide – on the top of a remote mountain ridge boggles the mind. If you're going to visit just one Crusader-era fortress during your trip, this should be it.

Background on the fortress' colourful medieval history, including its destruction by the Mongols, can be found in the excellent English map-brochure given out at the ticket booth. Highlights include an intact 13th-century hall, complete with angled archers' slits, in the **Northern Tower**.

The castle, visible from all over the Hula Valley, is protected by near-vertical cliffs and vertiginous canyons on all sides but one. South of Nimrod is Wadi Sa'ar, which divides the Golan's basalt plateau (to the south) from

the limestone flanks of Mt Hermon (to the north). The fortress is served by Rama bus 58 from Kiryat Shmona to Majdal Shams.

Banias Nature Reserve

שמורת טבע הבניאס ‎ محمية طبيعية بنياس

The gushing springs, waterfalls and lushly shaded streams of **Banias Nature Reserve** (☑ Banias Springs entrance 04-690-2577, Banias Waterfall entrance 04-695-0272; www.parks.org.il; Rte 99; adult/child 28/14NIS; ⊙ 8am-4pm or 5pm Sat-Thu, to 3pm or 4pm Fri, last entry 1hr before closing) form one of the most beautiful – and popular – nature spots in the country. The park has two entrances on Rte 99 that are about 3.5km (1½ hours on foot) apart. The name 'Banias' derives from Pan, Greek god of the countryside, to whom a temple here was dedicated back in Roman times.

Many sections of the park's four trails (visitors receive a map) are shaded by oak, plane, fig and carob trees. The **Suspended Trail**, a boardwalk cantilevered out over the rushing, crystal-clear Banias (Hermon) Stream, gives a pretty good idea of how the ancients might have imagined the Garden of Eden. A 15-minute walk upstream is the 10m **Banias Waterfall**, with its sheer, thundering drop into a deep pool; tempting as it may look, swimming is prohibited here and throughout the reserve. Both sites can be visited on a 45-minute circuit from the Banias Waterfall entrance, which before 1967 was in a demilitarized zone.

Near the reserve's Banias Springs entrance, the excavated ruins of a **palace complex** built by Herod's grandson, Agrippa II, can be seen on a 45-minute walking circuit.

Delicious Druze pitas are usually available at or near both of the reserves' two entrances, which are also both served by Rama bus 58, which links Kiryat Shmona with Majdal Shams.

Nimrod

נמרוד ‎ نمرود

☑ 04 / POP 20

This isolated hilltop Israeli settlement off Rte 98 (and on the Golan Trail), with its staggering views and winter snows, is a great place to bliss out. Also known as Nahal Nimrod, the total population is only five families.

🛌 Sleeping

Ohel Avraham   TENTED CAMP $
(Abraham's Tent; ☑ 052 282-1141, 04-698-3215; tepee 100NIS plus per person 60NIS, camping per person 60NIS, d prefab cabins 400NIS; ⊙ approx

---

DON'T MISS

SPRING WILDFLOWERS

The fields, hills and wadis of the Golan plateau burst into bloom from about February to April (the exact dates depend on the rains). The higher up Mt Hermon you go, the later the wildflowers bloom (until August). The area's nature reserves offer excellent trails to hillsides carpeted with flowers. To find out where to go to find the blooms at their peak, ask the rangers at any of the nature reserves.

Passover-Sukkot, prefab units year-round) The year could be 1969 at this hippy-ish hillside encampment, which has four tepees, four Mongolian-style tents, a large Bedouin-style tent and some shacks – a great spot to chill out. Except in the cabins, bathrooms and cooking facilities are shared. Bring a sleeping bag; mattresses are supplied. Very basic.

Bikta BaArafel   GUESTHOUSE **$$**
(📱 052 269-7718; www.bikta.net; d excl breakfast 500NIS, additional person 100NIS, camping per person 50NIS; 🛜) Built mostly of recycled wood, the 10 rustic rooms – all with kitchenettes, spa baths and balconies – are surrounded by organic cherry, apple and apricot trees. Breakfast costs 60NIS; for dinner you can order meat or veggie stew (70NIS). To camp, bring your own tent and sleeping bag; renting a mattress costs 15NIS.

Majdal Shams مجدل شمس מג'דל שמס

📱 04 / POP 10,640

The largest of Golan's four Druze towns, Majdal Shams is the commercial and cultural focal point of the area's Druze community. Druze flags (with five horizontal stripes) flutter in the wind, and you often see men with elaborate moustaches sporting traditional Druze attire, including a black *shirwal* (baggy trousers) and a white fez. That said, the town is considerably less conservative than many Druze villages in the area: young people dress like their secular Israeli counterparts, and alcohol is available in several pubs.

In the centre of town, in the middle of a traffic circle, stands a heroic **equestrian statue** of Sultan Pasha Al Atrash, Druze hero of the 1925 uprising against French colonial rule in Syria.

Higher education is hugely important here. Before civil war engulfed Syria, some 400 Golan Druze studied at Syrian universities. Now most young locals choose to pursue university studies in either Israel or Germany.

🛏 Sleeping

Narjis Hotel   HOTEL **$$**
(Malon Butik Narkis; 📱 04-698-2961; www.narjishotel.com; Rte 98; d in summer/winter 500/680NIS; ⏰ reception 9am-6pm; 🛜) This stylish hotel, owned by a Majdal Shams family, has 18 huge, romantic rooms with modern decor, jacuzzis, balconies and fridges. Reserve ahead. Situated 200m towards Mt Hermon from Hermon Junction, the roundabout at the intersection of Rte 989 and Rte 98.

SWEET RIVALRY

In Majdal Shams, two rival places selling scrumptious baklava and soft, warm *kunafeh* (a syrupy cheese-based pastry) can be found a few hundred metres down Rte 989 from its intersection with Rte 98: **Abu Jabal** (📱 04-687-1515; Rte 989; baklava/kunafeh per kg 65/50NIS; ⏰ 8am-9pm), which has red-and-white sign with Hebrew and Russian lettering; and, 250m further down the hill, **Abu Zeid** (📱 04-698-4846; Rte 989; baklava/kunafeh per kg 65/50NIS; ⏰ 8am-9pm), which has a sign with pink Hebrew lettering).

Sanabl Druze Hospitality   B&B **$$$**
(📱 050 577-8850; sanabl.tal@gmail.com; Ein Kinya; d 650-850NIS, additional adult/child 300/200NIS; 🛜) Situated in the Druze village of Ein Kinya, 9km southwest of Majdal Shams, this family-friendly B&B has three doubles and two spacious apartments with fine views of Nimrod Fortress and Hula Valley. It occupies a chocolate-brown house with Jerusalem-stone trim on the northern side of town, uphill from the main street – look for signs with a green, red and white logo.

🍴 Eating

At the western entrance to Majdal Shams, near the intersection of Rte 98 and Rte 989, there's a row of eateries selling falafel, hummus, shawarma, Druze pita *(pita Druzit)* – pita filled with *labneh* (thick yoghurt), and *sahlab* (a hot drink made with ground orchid bulbs). Two pubs serve Western style food.

🍺 Drinking & Nightlife

Why?   PUB
(📱 054 793-7187; Rte 98; ⏰ 11am-late) A simpatico spot for a beer (there are six on tap) or a bite (grilled meats, hummus, ravioli) to a soundtrack that is often mellow blues. Situated 50m east of the Narjis Hotel.

Green Apple Bar & Cafe   PUB
(📱 04-687-1400; www.046871400.com; Rte 98; ⏰ 11am-11pm, to 2am or 3am Thu & Fri) This Irish-style pub-restaurant, which could easily be in Chicago, has five beers, including Guinness, available on tap. Sometimes has live music on Thursday from 9pm. Situated next to the Narjis Hotel.

❶ Getting There & Away

Majdal Shams is 30km east of Kiryat Shmona. It is served by Rama (p250) bus 58 from Kiryat Shmona; its other stops include Neve Ativ, Nimrod Fortress and Banias Nature Reserve.

Mt Hermon خبل الشيخ הר החרמון

Massive Mt Hermon is known for its crisp mountain air (even in summer), delicate alpine plants and unpredictable snowfall. The mountain's 2814m summit is in Syrian territory; the highest point controlled by Israel is 2236m.

🏃 Activities

Skiing

Hitting the slopes of Mt Hermon can be pricey – but for locals it's a lot cheaper than flying to Austria (before 1948, Palestinian Jews with a passion for winter sports used to head to Lebanon).

In winter, there's usually 3m or 4m of snow at the top of Mt Hermon; the record, set in 1992, was 10m. Details on snow conditions are available by phone or online through the ski station.

If you decide to ski, make sure your travel insurance covers 'high-risk' sports and includes evacuation.

Mt Hermon Ski Station SKIING
(📞1-599-550-560; www.skihermon.co.il; Rte 98; winter adult/child 39/34NIS, summer free; ⊙8am–4pm, last entry 3pm or sometimes later) The facilities at Mt Hermon look like a low-altitude, low-budget ski station in the Alps circa 1975, so be prepared to be greeted by cheesy, giant snowmen made of styrofoam. In good years, there are 30 to 40 ski days between December and March, not enough to meet demand,

so the pistes are often crowded. In bad years, the pistes may hardly open at all.

The site has three blue (easy) runs, seven red (difficult) runs and two runs rated black (very difficult). The longest is 1248m, with a vertical drop of 376m; the highest begins at 2036m. To get you uphill, there are 11 lifts, including five chairlifts and five T-bars.

In addition to winter entry fees (paid at toll booths on the road up), costs include a ski pass (all day/afternoon 250/200NIS) and equipment rental, which can include skis (adult/child 140/120NIS), a snowboard (140NIS) and/or ski trousers or jacket (60NIS each).

Year round, once you're inside the site, you can generally stay until sundown.

Summertime Activities

In the warm season, there's access to a 2040m-high ridge – and its riot of alpine wildflowers – by **chairlift** (adult/child three to 12 years 49/42NIS; first ascent 8am, last descent 3.30pm). The ride is a blast, with great mountain views, but there's not much to see up top except Israeli bunkers in the distance, so it's worth timing your ascent to coincide with a free, 1½-hour **guided walk** (11am and 1pm on Friday and Saturday in June and July, daily in August and during the Passover and Sukkot holidays). Led by an SPNI guide, the stroll takes a look at plants, flowers and local military history; get to the lift a half hour ahead. The blooming season up here lasts from late May to August, which is three or four months later than on the coast.

❶ Getting There & Away

The ski station is 9km up the hill from Majdal Shams along Rte 98.

West Bank

الضفة الغربية   הגדה המערבית

Best Places to Eat

➜ Fadwa Cafe & Restaurant (p273)

➜ Hosh Al Jasmine (p273)

➜ Abu Omar (p281)

➜ La Vie Cafe (p277)

➜ Al Aqsa (p289)

Best Places to Stay

➜ Hosh Al Syrian Guesthouse (p272)

➜ Area D Hostel (p275)

➜ Walled Off Hotel (p111)

➜ Khan Al Wakalah (p289)

➜ Sami Youth Hostel (p281)

Why Go?

You hear the word 'welcome' a lot in the West Bank. Whether it is shouted by a vendor in a bustling souq, said with a smile over a plate of falafel or roared over Arabic music blasting from a taxi, Palestinians always want to make tourists feel appreciated.

Given its association with political strife and violence, this can come as a surprise to first-time visitors. But while the West Bank is a political tinderbox, it is something else too: an addictive tapestry of bustling souqs and chaotic streets, of rolling hills and chalky desertscapes, of thick, black coffee served in porcelain cups and of cities so steeped in history that it is humbling.

It is that magic, at times elusive and at others effervescent, that allows the West Bank to cast its spell on travellers – to inspire, challenge, entice and defy – now, as it has done for millennia.

When to Go
Bethlehem

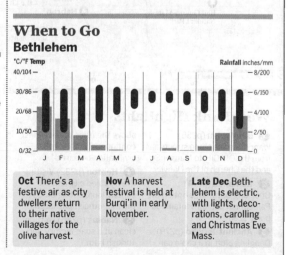

Oct There's a festive air as city dwellers return to their native villages for the olive harvest.

Nov A harvest festival is held at Burqi'in in early November.

Late Dec Bethlehem is electric, with lights, decorations, carolling and Christmas Eve Mass.

West Bank Highlights

1 Bethlehem (p266)
Wandering the stone streets from the Old City to Manger Sq and the Church of the Nativity.

2 Ramallah (p274)
Checking out what's hot on the Palestinian capital's infamous party scene.

3 Ancient Jericho (p279)
Dangling aloft in a cable car

above the ruins of the oldest continuously inhabited civilisation on earth.

4 Hebron (p282) Visiting the troubled city and its contentious resting place of the monotheist patriarchs.

5 Nablus (p286) Getting clean at a soap factory and Turkish bath.

6 Freedom Theatre (p290)
Meeting the inspiring actors at this world-renowned theatre.

7 Mt Gerizim (p287)
Clambering up to the platform on the mountain, believed by Samaritans to be God's first creation on Earth.

History

As a geographical designation, the West Bank was a creation of the 1948 Arab–Israeli War, which resulted in areas north, east and south of Jerusalem – the 22% of Mandatory Palestine now known as the West Bank – falling under Jordanian control. The name is derived from the area's position on the western bank of the Jordan River.

Historically, Jews have called the area Judea (Yehuda) and Samaria (Shomron), in reference to the West Bank's southern and northern lobes, respectively. Contemporary use of this expression – the preferred nomenclature among Jewish settlers and right-wing Israelis – is contentious since it suggests a belief that contemporary Israeli policy should be based on the biblical boundaries of the Land of Israel. You may also hear the terms 'the Occupied Palestinian Territories' or 'the Territories'.

West Bank Palestinian culture still bears the stamp of 400 years of Ottoman Turkish rule, during which the area was part of the Ottoman province of Syria. Shorter occupations, such as the post-WWI British Mandate (1917–48), have also left their mark (English is still taught widely in Palestinian schools).

Although few in number, Jews maintained a presence in the West Bank (particularly in Hebron) throughout the Ottoman period. In the late 19th and 20th centuries large numbers of Jews immigrated from Russia, Yemen and other countries, but few settled in the mountainous regions that would later become the West Bank.

During the 1948 Arab–Israeli War, Jordan captured (and later annexed) the West Bank, only to lose control of the area to Israel in the 1967 Six Day War. During the 1970s and 1980s, Jordan sought to reunify with the West Bank but relinquished all claims to the Palestine Liberation Organisation (PLO) in 1988.

In the wake of the First Intifada (Arabic for 'uprising' or 'shaking off'), from 1987 to 1993, the Oslo Accords were set. These interim agreements between the Israeli government and the PLO gave control of some areas (such as Jericho, Ramallah and Jenin) to the newly created Palestinian Authority, and implied the possibility of a future Palestinian state.

Both sides were unhappy with the accords and their aftermath. Violence continued, with both Israeli and Palestinian deaths. The failure of US-sponsored peace talks at Camp David in 2000 paved the way for the outbreak of the Second Intifada that year.

The Second Intifada (2000–05) brought the worst violence in a generation. High-profile killings shocked both sides. Bloody battles and military attacks caused thousands of casualties, and there were scores of suicide bombings in Israel. In response, Israel constructed a separation wall (p271), sealing off the West Bank from Israel. After Yasser Arafat's death in 2004, Mahmoud Abbas became Palestinian leader in 2005.

In 2006, Hamas, a militant Islamic group, won parliamentary elections, causing the prompt scale-back of international aid (because many countries consider it a terrorist organisation). A civil war broke out between Hamas and Fatah a year later, leaving the former in charge of Gaza and the latter the West Bank.

Demonstrations across the West Bank intensified during the 2014 war in Gaza, which lasted 60 days and resulted in 1200 Palestinian and 73 Israeli casualties. Violence continued into 2015, with a spate of stabbings by Palestinian attackers in Jerusalem and the West Bank.

At the time of writing, hopes of peace talks were derailed after US President Donald Trump declared Jerusalem to be the

CHECKPOINTS

Checkpoints (in Hebrew, *machsomim*) control the flow of travellers between the West Bank and Israel. There are also some checkpoints inside the West Bank, although these tend to be less stable, shifting locations, shutting down altogether or popping up in new locations.

Most checkpoints are run by the Israel Defence Forces (IDF), although some have been outsourced to private contractors. The latter tend to be more troublesome and more likely to question foreigners and search their bags.

Operating hours of checkpoints vary, but most of the major ways in and out of the West Bank are now open 24 hours: these include Checkpoint 300 in Bethlehem and Qalandia, near Ramallah. Jalameh, north of Jenin, is only open 8am to 7pm.

In general, travellers are not checked when going into the West Bank, only when travelling from the West Bank back into Israel.

Foreign-passport holders are allowed to travel through IDF checkpoints into areas under the control of the Palestinian Authority, but by military order, Israeli citizens are forbidden from doing so.

There is no cost involved with crossing a checkpoint, and foreign-passport holders do not need any special documentation. Just show your passport and visa and put your bags through an X-ray machine. The procedure is generally fast, but with waiting time you can expect to be at a checkpoint for 15 to 20 minutes (or longer if lines have formed).

Try to avoid passing through a checkpoint in the early morning (7am to 9am) or on Muslim or Jewish holidays because of long lines.

Foreigners can take a vehicle into and out of the West Bank (if you've got a rental car, make sure your insurance policy covers travel to the Palestinian Territories – most don't), but there can sometimes be delays upon your return to Israel because the soldiers may inspect the vehicle for explosives.

The following are some of the main checkpoints into and out of the West Bank:

Qalandia Between Jerusalem and Ramallah. Use this checkpoint for Ramallah, Nablus and Jenin. Qalandia is one of the busiest checkpoints, and it sports some grim metal corrals and locking turnstiles of the sort you'd expect to see at a maximum-security prison. Be aware that Qalandia is occasionally the scene of violence between Israeli soldiers and stone-throwing Palestinian youths, particularly on Fridays or when political tension is high.

Checkpoint 300 Located south of Jerusalem at the entrance to Rachel's Tomb. One road leads to the checkpoint for cars and one for pedestrians. This is an indoor checkpoint, and the conditions are better than at Qalandia. It is open 24/7.

Bethlehem (highway) You will go through this checkpoint if you take bus 231 from Bethlehem. It resembles a toll gate, and security is very light. Tourists may remain on the bus during the passport check (Palestinian passengers are asked to line up outside the bus). It's open 24/7.

Jalameh Located 10km south of Afula, this checkpoint is one of the best in terms of ease and accessibility. However, long lines have been reported, and it is only open between 8am and 7pm.

Abu Dis This checkpoint connects East Jerusalem to Abu Dis, from where travellers can connect to Jericho. It is a pedestrian-only checkpoint and is usually closed at night.

For more details on the conditions at individual checkpoints, visit the website of the left-wing Israeli group Machsom Watch (www.machsomwatch.org).

capital of Israel, much to the anger and dismay of the Palestinians. Speculation is also swirling about a successor to Mahmoud Abbas – in his 80s – as Palestinian leader.

Across the cities of the Fatah-ruled Palestinian Authority, you'll spot big banners proclaiming the Palestinians' right to a seat at the United Nations as well as calls for Palestinian rights to return to land lost in 1948.

At the same time, Palestinian discontent simmers as the Israeli government continues to expand Israeli settlements in the region. In the meantime, Palestinians maintain efforts to build their institutions and economy – and to push for an independent homeland.

Climate

Bethlehem, like Jerusalem, can be snowy in winter and enjoys cooler climes in the midst of the otherwise sweltering summer. If you're seeking Yuletide spirit, bring your woolly jumper and don't miss out on a crisp, cold Bethlehem Christmas.

Balmier Jericho is the place to escape chillier winter days and can be oppressively hot during the summer months. If you're considering doing some hiking around Wadi Qelt or elsewhere, spring and autumn are the best times.

Tours

Backpacker hostels, including those in Jenin, Nablus, Ramallah and Bethlehem, are excellent places to ask about tours, and for those travelling solo they provide good opportunities to meet others and share costs.

Those who want to set up a tour before they leave should contact one of a number of organisations that offer tours; **Green Olive Tours** (www.greenolivetours. com) is particularly recommended. The Beit Sahour based **Siraj Center for Holy Land Studies** (www.sirajcenter.org) runs cycling and walking trips. **Bike Palestine** (www.bikepalestine.com) runs a seven-day bike tour from Jenin to Jerusalem. **Walk Palestine** (www.walkpalestine.com) brings tourists on walking tours that last three to 14 days, staying with locals in villages on a route that makes up part of the **Abraham Path** (www.abrahampath.org).

Getting There & Away

Entering the West Bank always involves passing through an Israeli checkpoint, either on a bus, by car or on foot. Israeli taxis and buses cannot cross into Area A (marked by the large red signs warning Israelis not to pass), so you either need to take an Arab bus (such as from East Jerusalem), or you can take an Israeli bus or taxi to the checkpoint, cross on foot and pick up a Palestinian taxi or bus on the other side.

If you're considering driving yourself, bear in mind that most Israeli rental-car agencies won't allow you to take their cars into Palestinian areas. **Dallah** (☑ 02-627-9725, 057-756-9405; www.dallahrentacar.com) and Goodluck (www.goodluckcars.com) are notable exceptions; both are based close to Jerusalem's American Colony Hotel.

Ben Gurion Airport to Damascus Gate (Jerusalem) Outside the arrivals hall, yellow and white sheruts wait (24 hours) to take passengers from the airport (near Tel Aviv) to Jerusalem. Drivers will want to know either a hotel or a drop-off point. If you are going straight to the West Bank, ask for Damascus Gate.

Damascus Gate (Jerusalem) to Ramallah From Damascus Gate, cross the road and walk up Nablus St (opposite) until you reach the Arab bus station (on your left). There, either the 218 or 219 bus will take you to Ramallah, via Qalandia Checkpoint. You will not need to get off at the checkpoint. In summer, the buses run to Ramallah until 9.30pm – in winter, only until 6pm or 7pm at the latest. The final stop is the city's main bus station, directly opposite Area D Hostel (7NIS).

Damascus Gate (Jerusalem) to Bethlehem Directly opposite the Old City is another bus station, this time with buses to Bethlehem. Bus 231 takes you directly to the city without stopping and bus 234 takes you via Checkpoint 300, where you will need to get off the bus and pass through on foot. For the Walled Off Hotel, it is best to take bus 234 and walk to the hotel from the checkpoint (15 minutes) or take a taxi (no more than 10NIS). For everywhere else take bus 231 and then a taxi into town (no more than 20NIS).

King Hussein Bridge (Jordan) to Damascus Gate (Jerusalem) Outside the arrivals hall, sheruts wait to take passengers to Jerusalem. Once you arrive at Damascus Gate, take buses either to Ramallah or Bethlehem.

Nazareth/Afula to Jenin Take a shared taxi to the Jalameh Checkpoint, where you can cross on foot and pick up a Palestinian bus or taxi on the other side for the 25-minute drive to Jenin.

Note that once buses have stopped running between Jerusalem, Ramallah and Bethlehem it is possible to take an Israeli taxi to Qalandia or Checkpoint 300 and then a Palestinian taxi to your destination. In both cases you will need to bargain hard with the driver.

ⓘ MEDIA IN ENGLISH

This Week in Palestine (www.thisweekinpalestine.com) is a free monthly booklet with listings, articles, events and maps related to the West Bank.

POST-OSLO GEOGRAPHY: AREAS A, B & C

The West Bank is divided into three areas, designating the amount of civil and military power exercised by Israelis and Palestinians respectively.

Area A (around 17%): under full Palestinian civil and military control; you'll see red signs forbidding Israelis from entering. Includes the cities of Ramallah, Nablus, Tulkarem, Jenin, Qalqilya, Bethlehem, Jericho, parts of Hebron and some other small towns and villages.

Area B (around 24%): under Palestinian civil control but Israeli military control. Includes many rural Palestinian areas.

Area C (about 59%): under full Israeli control. Includes many sparsely populated areas, outskirts of towns and villages, the West Bank's highway network and most of the Jordan Valley.

🛈 Getting Around

The West Bank is served by an excellent and easy-to-use public transport network, and buses and shared taxis called servees (pronounced ser-vees) run from the major cities to most – if not all – sites and cities you will want to visit. Most signs are in Arabic, but as long as you know the name of where you are going, it is relatively easy to get on the right bus or shared taxi, and it will set you back a fraction of the cost of a private taxi.

Most buses, even between cities, will cost between 5NIS and 20NIS.

Since distances are short (and local knowledge of roads essential), many tourists choose to hire a taxi by the hour or for the day. Ask a tour operator to set you up with a reliable driver.

Most taxi drivers in Bethlehem are used to the needs of tourists and can run ad hoc day trips all over the West Bank. They hang around Bab Iz Qaq (where the Jerusalem bus stops) or the entrance to the Bethlehem checkpoint. Prepare to haggle hard.

Palestinian Territory roads are a mixed bag; potholes and bad signage can be a problem, but it is the quirks of Palestinian driving that may prove the biggest challenge, especially for first-time Middle East drivers. A general rule is every man or woman for him/herself.

Israeli licence plates are yellow, while Palestinian plates are green and white. Yellow-plated cars, while fine to drive throughout most of the West Bank – especially in more peaceful times – might cause you to be mistaken for an Israeli or Jewish settler and treated with hostility. Some tourists place a keffiyeh (a chequered scarf worn by Arabs) on the dashboard to avoid trouble in the more fraught areas. Be particularly careful if driving in Hebron or in some of the refugee camps.

Since roadblocks, Israeli settlement construction and separation-wall building work are all ongoing, accessibility and roads can change quickly. It pays to buy an up-to-date road map (maps bought in Israel cover the West Bank, too). GPS is useless on the Palestinian side of the Green Line, and the best way to find your destination is to roll down the window and ask someone.

Bethlehem   בית לחם بيت لحم
🎵 02 / POP 47,000

Bethlehem may no longer be the 'little town' of Christmas carols, but you don't have to go far in what is now a pulsing city to see the stories of Mary and Joseph, stars, mangers and a saviour hardwired into every paving stone, street and church.

Like Jerusalem, every Christian denomination – Lutheran, Syriac, Catholic, Orthodox – is present here and the city positively hums with activity, its winding streets congested with traffic and its main square filled with snap-happy pilgrims scrambling to keep up with their guides.

But there is plenty to see and do for even for the nonreligious. There's a lively Old City and bazaar and numerous sites around town, including the epic Mar Saba Monastery. Many tourists also come for the street art – particularly several stencils by British street artist Banksy – that have turned the Israeli Separation Wall that now divides Bethlehem from Jerusalem into a vast canvas.

History

Built along ancient footpaths, the town where Mary and Joseph went for a census and returned with a son has had residents since as far back as the Palaeolithic era. It is thought to have first developed in the 14th century BCE as a city state named Beit Lahmu (after Lahmu, goddess of protection), and later took the Hebrew Bible name, Ephrata.

In 313 CE, three centuries after the birth of Jesus, the Roman Emperor Constantine made Christianity the official state religion. Bethlehem soon became a popular, well-to-do pilgrimage town, with flourishing monasteries and churches. Even after the Muslim conquest of the city in 638, a treaty was signed guaranteeing Christians property rights and religious freedom, and Bethlehem continued to prosper for the next millennium or so.

Bethlehem's numbers swelled after the 1948 Arab–Israeli War, when Palestinian refugees from the newly created State of Israel poured into town. Many continue to live, along with their descendants, in the refugee camps of Aida, Dheisheh and Al Azzah on the edges of town.

Today Bethlehem continues to rely – as it has for the last 1700 years or so – on the tourist and pilgrim trade. It is easily the most visited city in the West Bank, especially around Christian holidays, with crowds flocking here for Easter and for the traditional Christmas Eve midnight Mass.

◉ Sights

The narrow limestone streets and exotic shopfronts of Manger Sq and the Old City are a scene from another age, particularly Pope Paul VI St, Star St and the narrow alleys connecting the two. Visit on a Sunday to experience some church services. Most in attendance will be Palestinians and resident monks and nuns, but visitors are welcome to attend or stop in for a few moments of contemplation.

Opening hours of churches and other sites in (and outside) Bethlehem can change without notice, but a general rule in the West Bank is to start early and expect most sites to close their doors at sunset or an hour before.

Most of the city's sights are within walking distance of the town centre; pick up a taxi on Manger St or on Manger Sq to venture to Shepherds' Field, Mar Saba Monastery or Herodium.

From Bab iz-Zqaq (where bus 231 from Jerusalem stops), walk up Pope Paul VI St for five minutes to Cinema Sq, from where it's a 10-minute walk to Manger Sq. For those who took the bus to the checkpoint, taxi drivers wait to bring travellers into the city for around 20NIS.

If you get a taxi to Manger Sq, walk from here along bustling Pope Paul VI St (taking in the souq to the left) and then take a right to loop around and return down charming Star St for an atmospheric taste of the Old City.

◉ Old City

Church of the Nativity CHURCH
(◷ 6.30am-7.30pm spring-autumn, to 6pm winter) **FREE** For the millions of pilgrims who descend on the Holy Land every year, the Church of the Nativity is the main reason for visiting Bethlehem. The church, believed to be built on the spot where Jesus was born, was originally commissioned in 326 CE by Emperor Constantine and has seen innumerable transformations since. A restoration project is underway to preserve the building.

To really get the most out of a visit, negotiate a price from one of the handful of tour guides you'll find milling about outside.

You'll have to duck to get through the tiny Ottoman-era door into the church, aptly

---

INSIDE THE WEST BANK

To make the West Bank all the more accessible, explore the work of some of the following organisations:

Alternative Tourism Group (www.patg.org) Offers plenty of information, and recommended day tours of Hebron and Bethlehem.

Palestine Fair Trade Association (www.palestinefairtrade.org) Organises homestays and voluntary work placements in Palestinian homes and farms, particularly during the annual olive harvest.

Palestinian Association for Cultural Exchange (www.pace.ps) Offers one-day and longer tours of Nablus, Hebron, Qalqilya and around. Supports local cooperatives and can arrange lecture programs.

Siraj Center for Holy Land Studies (www.sirajcenter.org) Organises and coordinates plenty of activities and encounters throughout the West Bank.

Bethlehem

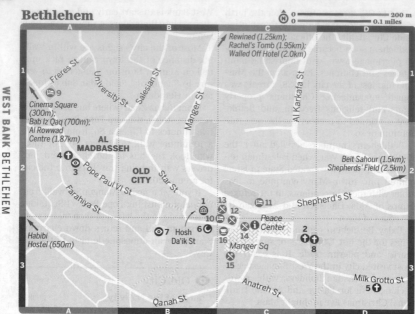

Bethlehem

◉ Sights
1 Bethlehem Museum	B2
2 Church of the Nativity	C3
3 International Center of Bethlehem	A2
4 Lutheran Christmas Church	A2
5 Milk Grotto Chapel	D3
6 Mosque of Omar	B3
7 Souq	B3
8 St Catherine's Church	C3

🛏 Sleeping
Dar Annadwa	(see 3)
9 Grand Hotel Bethlehem	A1
10 Hosh Al Syrian Guesthouse	C3
11 Manger Square Hotel	C2

✴ Eating
12 Afteem	C3
13 Fadwa Cafe & Restaurant	C2
14 Peace Center Restaurant	C3
15 Square	C3

🍷 Drinking & Nightlife
16 Star Bucks	C3

named the **Door of Humility**. Originally the entrance was much larger, but the Crusaders reduced its size to prevent attackers from riding in on horseback. Later, either during the Mamluk or Ottoman periods, it was made even smaller, and you can still see the outline of the original 6th-century doorway and, within it, the Crusader-era arch.

Walking from the door towards the nave, it is possible to look through wooden trapdoors at Constantine's original 4th-century mosaic floor, rediscovered in 1934.

In the 6th century, the church was rebuilt almost entirely by Emperor Justinian, after the majority of it was destroyed in a Samaritan revolt. The mammoth red-and-white limestone columns that still grace the nave are probably the only surviving remnants of the original structure. Some of them are decorated with frescoes of saints, painted by Crusaders in the 12th century. To the right of the Door of Humility, a doorway leads to the Armenian Monastery, these days housing just six monks to service the needs of Bethlehem's 300-strong Armenian congregation. The Armenians flourished during the 1600s, when they were noted for their transcribed and illuminated versions of the Bible.

At the front of the nave, descend the stairs to enter the **Grotto of the Nativity**. It's popular with tour groups, but if you time your visit over lunchtime midweek, you'll likely have the grotto entirely to yourself (on a weekend you may have to stand in line for an hour or more). There is a rather zealous security guard who has been known to physically remove pilgrims whom he thinks are staying too long.

Atmospherically lantern-lit and redolent with mystery, a **14-pointed silver star** marks the spot where Jesus is said to have been born. The **Chapel of the Manger** ('the Crib') to one side of the grotto represents the scene of the nativity, while the chapel facing it houses the Altar of the Adoration of the Magi, which commemorates the visit of Caspar, Balthazar and Melchior. The Persians spared the church and grotto when they sacked Palestine in 614 CE, ostensibly because they saw a depiction of the magi in their own native costume.

Though all might seem serene down here, conflict has actually rocked this cradle for ages. The 14-pointed star was stolen in 1847, each of the three Christian communities in residence (Greek Orthodox, Armenians and Catholics, who have bitterly and ceaselessly fought for custodianship of the grotto) blaming the others. A copy was subsequently supplied to replace it, but the fights didn't end there, and administrative domination of the church changed hands repeatedly between the Orthodox and Catholics.

To this day, management of the church is divvied up metre by metre between the Orthodox, Catholic and Armenian clerics (this system of management for holy places is known as the 'status quo'). Take the grotto lanterns, for example: six belong to the Greek Orthodox, five to the Armenians and four to the Catholics.

St Catherine's Church CHURCH
(Manger Sq; ⊙6.30am-7.30pm spring-autumn, to 6pm winter) **FREE** Midnight Mass at this pink-toned church, next door to the Church of the Nativity, is broadcast across the world on Christmas Eve, but there's nothing like being there in person for an atmospheric – if rather lengthy – Christmas experience.

To access the church via the Church of the Nativity, you need to wander through the Crusader-era Franciscan cloister with a statue of St Jerome.

Milk Grotto Chapel CHURCH
(Milk Grotto St; ⊙8am-6pm summer, to 5pm winter) **FREE** A short walk from Manger Sq is the lesser-known Milk Grotto Chapel.

Legend has it that Mary and Joseph stopped here to feed the baby during their flight to Egypt; a drop of milk touched the red rock, turning it white.

Mosque of Omar MOSQUE
(Manger Sq; ⊙10-11am, 1.30-2pm & 5-7pm) **FREE** Opposite the Church of the Nativity and named after the second Muslim caliph, Omar Ibn Al Khattab, this is the only mosque in Bethlehem's Old City. It was built in 1860 on land granted by the Greek Orthodox Church in honour of Omar, the Prophet Muhammad's father-in-law, who in 637 took Jerusalem from the flagging Byzantines and then stopped for prayer at the Christian Church of the Nativity.

He declared, in his Pact of Omar, that the basilica would remain a Christian shrine, and that Christians, even under Muslim rule, would remain free to practise their faith.

Bethlehem Museum MUSEUM
(☑02-274-2589; www.arabwomenunion.org; Star St; 10NIS; ⊙8am-1pm & 2-5pm Mon-Sat) The museum, housed in a typical 19th-century Palestinian home, is made up of three rooms recreated as a traditional Bethlehem family abode, with many exhibits dating back more than 200 years. Your entrance fee gets you a rather cursory tour by one of the staff, as well access to the gift shop, where you can buy embroidery produced by the Bethlehem Arab Women's Union.

Souq MARKET
FREE Has a range of fruit and vegetables, meat and fish, junk, shoes and some mighty tasty snacks. Known to locals as the Green Market, the souq was established in 1929.

International Center of Bethlehem CULTURAL CENTRE
(Dar Annadwa; ☑02-277-0047; www.annadwa.org; Pope Paul VI St, Madbasseh Sq) This Lutheran-run centre puts on concerts, plays, films, English-language documentaries, workshops and lectures. There's also a coffee shop, guesthouse, art gallery and gift shop, known as the Cave, where local artists show off their work. It is often closed for private events.

Lutheran Christmas Church CHURCH
(☑02-274-2312; www.bethlehemchristmasluther an.org; Pope Paul VI St, Madbasseh Sq; ⊙9.30am-3pm Mon-Fri, 10.30am-noon Sun) Built in the 19th-century church, the Lutheran Christmas Church is linked to the International

Center of Bethlehem (p269) and was inaugurated by Kaiser Wilhelm II in 1898 during his visit to the Holy Land. Visitors can see the stained-glass windows commissioned and donated by the kaiser himself. Lutheran services are held on Sunday at 10.30am. Visitors should contact the church (via its website) ahead of a visit.

☉ Outskirts of Town

Rachel's Tomb   RELIGIOUS SITE
(www.rachelstomb.org; ⊘12.30am-10.30pm Sun-Wed, 24hr Thu) **FREE** In a desolate corridor created by Israel's separation wall and near the main checkpoint into town on the Israeli side, stands Rachel's Tomb. Rachel is said to have died here while in childbirth after which her husband, Jacob, 'set a pillar upon her grave'.

Visiting the tomb is difficult. Although the gate is only a few metres from the entrance to Checkpoint 300, it is not possible to go through on foot. You will either need your own car or an Israeli taxi. Alternatively Egged bus 163 from Jerusalem's Central Bus Station goes all the way to the tomb.

Once at the tomb, there are separate sides for men and women (kippas for men are available at the door).

Revered by followers of all three Abrahamic religions – Jews and Muslims in particular – it has been enshrined and guarded for centuries, from the Byzantine and Islamic eras through to the Crusaders, and during the epochs of the Ottomans and Israelis.

Shepherds' Field   PARK
(⊘9am-3pm Mon-Sat) **FREE** If you've always wondered where exactly 'shepherds watched their flocks by night', drop into Shepherds' Field, a parklike area just outside Beit Sa-

hour. As well as the strollable grounds, you'll find a Byzantine cave housing a chapel and the 1953 Italian-designed Church of the Angels.

To reach Shepherds' Field, take a private taxi from Bethlehem (20NIS).

Solomon's Pools   PARK
(10NIS; ⊘8am-midnight) During Roman times, a series of natural springs filled three mammoth rectangular reservoirs supplying water via aqueducts to Jerusalem and Herodium. King Solomon enjoyed respite beside their serene shimmer, where he is said to have written the Song of Solomon. The springs were used into the 20th century for irrigating crops in the surrounding fertile valley, while successive armies have also set up camp here. An Ottoman fortress is still evident, the historic last stop for pilgrims on their way to Jerusalem.

Unfortunately, the pools are now fenced off and the water largely drained, but the park that surrounds them is a popular barbecuing spot with locals on the weekends.

A taxi to Solomon's Pools from Bethlehem will cost 20NIS to 30NIS.

Museum of Palestinian Heritage   MUSEUM
(⊘8am-4pm Sat-Thu) **FREE** This impressive museum in the new complex of buildings opposite Soloman's Pools is the personal collection of one man, Ishaq al Hroub, who gathered this remarkable selection of traditional Palestinian exhibits over five decades in his basement in Dura, near Hebron. Ishaq, whose collection includes everything from Ottoman-era pottery to traditional Bedouin wedding garb, is happy to guide tourists around the exhibits between 8am and 4pm.

VISITING A REFUGEE CAMP

The term 'refugee camp' often brings to mind crowded tents, abject poverty and disease, but as many of the West Bank's camps have existed since 1948, many look like established albeit ramshackle neighbourhoods of existing cities, with shops, restaurants and cafes.

Developed and still operated by the United Nations Relief and Works Agency, the camps are generally safe and in some cases (Dheisheh in Bethlehem and Aqbat Jabr in Jericho) have tourist infrastructure, including hostels and visitor centres.

But with a few exceptions, most camps should not be visited without a local guide who can explain the context and is aware of the security situation. One minute it can seem peaceful but the next violence might break out between demonstrators and Israeli soldiers, filling the air with tear gas, hurled stones and rubber bullets.

The best way to visit a refugee camp – as with all politically sensitive areas in the West Bank – is on an organised tour. Those arranged by the Walled Off Hotel (p111) in Bethlehem to nearby Aida camp are particularly recommended.

ISRAEL'S SEPARATION WALL

From 1967 until the Second Intifada (2000–05), most Palestinians were still able to cross into Israel from the West Bank with relative ease, many commuting on a daily basis.

But in the mid-1990s and even more so during the Second Intifada, scores of suicide bombers crossed into Israel from the West Bank, killing hundreds of Israeli civilians. Israel responded with military incursions into areas controlled by the Palestinian Authority, and both security experts and the Israeli public called on the government to build a security barrier.

From the point of view of the Israeli left, a barrier would only further the Oslo Accords process (which had as its goal the establishment of two separate states), along the lines of 'good fences make good neighbours'. But there was opposition, from Jewish settlers not wanting to find themselves on the West Bank side of the wall, and from West Bank Palestinians, whose villages and fields were bisected by the wall, and whose access to Jerusalem the borders made difficult or impossible.

Except in Jerusalem, most of the barrier (about 5% of which is a concrete antisniper wall up to 8m high) matches the Green Line (the 1949 armistice between Israel and Jordan) – but only roughly. Quite a few sections loop and scoop around Israeli settlements, separating Palestinians from their communities, businesses, schools and crops. Palestinians call the separation wall the 'Apartheid Wall' and see it as part of a concerted campaign to grab land wherever possible. Israel – where the barrier is seen as a security success – says that the route of the wall can always be modified, for example, if there is a final status accord on borders.

Demonstrations are periodically held in parts of the West Bank where the wall cuts through villages. The Israel Defence Forces (IDF) regularly disperse the crowds with tear gas and rubber bullets – as well as live ammunition, according to both local and international NGOs. Protestors have frequently been injured and some killed.

Al Rowwad Centre CULTURAL CENTRE
(☏ 02-275-0030; www.alrowwad.org; ⊙ 9am-5pm Thu-Tue) FREE Al Rowwad is buried in the narrow streets of Aida refugee camp and is best visited as part of an organised tour. The centre is a wealth of information on the history of the camp and the Palestinian refugee issue more generally. Solo travellers should email ahead.

Al Rowwad offers drama, music, computer and arts training, as well as arranging special classes and workshops for women, the blind and residents with disabilities.

⊙ Around Bethlehem

★Mar Saba Monastery MONASTERY
(⊙ 8am-5pm Sat-Tue & Thu) A must-see on any journey through the Holy Land is Mar Saba Monastery, a bleak and beautiful 20km drive east of Bethlehem (beyond Beit Sahour).

Women must view the phenomenal cliff-clinging copper-domed hermitage, founded in 439 CE, from the opposite slope, but men are permitted inside, where tours are available with one of the 15 monks in residence.

Also residing here (rather more eternally) are the remains of 5th-century ascetic St Saba, whose body lies in the church's second chapel, and the skulls of some 120 monks massacred here in 614 CE.

If you're driving, the monastery is well signposted from Beit Sahour. Otherwise, you'll need to take a private taxi out to Mar Saba from Bethlehem; plan on around a three-hour journey, costing 120NIS to 150NIS.

Be aware that the monastery closes between noon and 1pm for the monks to have lunch.

Herodium PALACE
(Herodion; adult/child 29/15NIS; ⊙ 8am-5pm Apr-Sep, 8am-4pm Oct-Mar) King Herod's spectacular fortress-palace, Herodium, built between 23 and 15 BCE, was known through the centuries to Arab inhabitants as the Mountain of Paradise. It rises from the Judean Desert like a flat-topped caricature of a volcano (the top is actually an extension of the natural hill, hollowed out to hold Herod's palace), 9km south of Beit Sahour.

The complex features a series of stunning remains of Herod's own personal 'country club' (which included a bathhouse and

DON'T MISS

WALLED-OFF HOTEL

For 10 years British street artist Banksy has been stencilling his work on and around the wall that separates Bethlehem from Jerusalem. Now he's opened **Walled Off Hotel** (☎02-277-1322; www.walledoffhotel.com; 182 Caritas St; dm US$30, d US$215-265, ste US$965; 🅿🛜), opposite the wall, which promises 'the worst view in the world'. The view may be unconventional, but the hotel itself is slick and stylish – and surreal (one suite has a tiki bar).

Home to a museum, a piano bar and an art gallery, Walled Off also boasts some of the most high-end dorms in the Middle East, if not the world, with fresh towels, mini-fridges and in-room music.

The hotel was built in secret and was only due to stay open for a year, but in September 2017 began taking bookings for the winter season, suggesting that it will remain. The hotel offers useful and informative tours to nearby Aida refugee camp as well as to other nearby cities, such as Jericho and Hebron.

rooftop pool) and also includes King Herod's own tomb, discovered in 2007.

Though it was sacked by the Romans in 71 CE, much remains at the site, with still more awaiting further excavation – including a network of tunnels used by Jewish rebels during their uprising against Rome. You can clamber through many of the tunnels today.

Herodium falls under 'Area C' and is thus under full Israeli control (you'll see the military base at the foot of the hill); the site itself is administered by the Israeli Parks and Nature Authority. This means it is possible to access from Jerusalem without passing through Checkpoint 300, either with your own car (it is signposted from Rte 60) or via a taxi, although Israeli taxis are significantly more expensive.

To get here, take a private taxi from Bethlehem and negotiate at least an hour's waiting time. Try to avoid Fridays, when Herodium fills with tour buses.

🛏 Sleeping

Bethlehem has a huge amount of accommodation for tourists, although traditionally it has been pretty basic, catering mostly to a pilgrim crowd. That is starting to change, and at the budget and midrange level, there are a number of good options.

Ibdaa Cultural Centre
Guesthouse   GUESTHOUSE $

(☎02-277-6444; www.ibdaa48.org; Dheisheh Refugee Camp; dm/d 50/100NIS; @🛜) A great little hostel in the cultural centre of the same name, Ibdaa is located in the narrow streets of Dheisheh refugee camp, a 20-minute drive out of town toward Hebron. Facilities are ba-

sic, but as a window into Palestinian life away from the tourist hordes, it is unparalleled.

The Ibdaa Centre is just off the Jerusalem–Hebron Rd, next to the taxi stand.

Habibi Hostel   HOSTEL $

(www.bethlehemyhostel.com; Palestine St; dm 75NIS, d 150-250NIS; 🛜) A basic but homely hostel on the 2nd floor of an apartment building 15 minutes downhill from Manger Sq, Habibi Hostel is popular with volunteers, backpackers and activists and is Bethlehem's only real budget stay. Habibi has single-sex dorms and at least one private room.

Dar Al Balad   HOTEL $

(info@daralbalad.ps; Beit Sahour; s/d 150/250NIS; 🛜) A quiet and cosy option in nearby Beit Sahour, Dar Al Balad has a dozen rooms arranged around a shaded courtyard in a restored family-run hotel. Many of the rooms have windows onto the streets of the recently restored Beit Sahour old town.

★Hosh Al Syrian
Guesthouse   BOUTIQUE HOTEL $$

(☎02-274-7529; www.hoshalsyrian.com; d $70-140; 🛜) Every now and then a hotel comes along and raises the game, and Fadi Kattan's beautiful Hosh Al Syrian Guesthouse has done just that. Tucked away in the Syrian quarter, a two-minute walk from Manger Sq, some rooms have terraces overlooking the roofs of the Old City.

Wi-fi is only accessible in shared areas; as Kattan says, 'You come here to relax'.

Manger Square Hotel   HOTEL $$

(www.mangersquarehotel.com; Manger St; s/d/tr US$90/130/150; ♿) This four-star hotel over the road from Manger Sq was built in 2012 and is excellent value considering the location. Some rooms have views over the valley behind Bethlehem, others over the Old City. Staff are polite and helpful and in summer there is a rooftop pool.

Grand Hotel Bethlehem
HOTEL $$
(📞02-274-1440; www.grandhotelbethlehem.com; Pope Paul VI St; s/d US$55/85; 📶) Neat, clean, efficient and in the middle of the action, the Grand Hotel might not have bags of character, but rooms are comfy and central.

Breakfast is served at the hotel's Mariachi Bar, and the coffee shop serves Mexican dishes and seafood daily until midnight.

Dar Annadwa
GUESTHOUSE $$
(Abu Gubran; 📞02-277-0047; www.diyar.ps; 109 Pope Paul VI St; s/d US$72/102; 📶) This comfortable Lutheran-sponsored hotel is in the same building as the International Center of Bethlehem (p269) with 13 rooms each named after a village in the Palestinian Territories. It is a quiet, if a little dated, spot in a great location, but it's pricey given other options nearby.

Book ahead because reception is often closed.

✖ Eating

For fast food, stroll along Manger St or head up to the small souq just off Pope Paul VI St. Here you'll find fist-size falafel, sizzling shawarma and lots of tempting produce for picnics or self-catering.

Afteem
MIDDLE EASTERN $
(Manger Sq; mains 6-35NIS) A Bethlehem institution for decades, top-notch hummus and *masabacha* (warm hummus with whole chickpeas) are just two of the dishes on the menu at this popular eatery close to Manger Sq.

Peace Center Restaurant
SANDWICHES, ITALIAN $
(Manger Sq; mains 20-45NIS; ⊙9am-11pm Mon-Sat) This Manger Sq eatery is the place to go for traditional Palestinian food downtown, with a range of dishes including *makloubeh* ('upside down' chicken, under rice cooked with nuts and spices) and *mansaf* (chicken or lamb over rice with a thick, meaty broth) on its varied and reasonable menu.

Staff are friendly and helpful, and even if you're not hungry, the terrace is a nice place for a mint lemonade and shisha.

Square
MIDDLE EASTERN, WESTERN $
(Manger Sq; mains from 35NIS; ⊙9am-midnight; 📶) A lounge-style place on the opposite side of the square to Peace Center, Square is a good spot for an early evening beer with a view of the Church of the Nativity. It has a range of Arabic and Western dishes, including the Palestinian Temptation Platter, a mixture of local and Levantine mezze.

★Hosh Al Jasmine
MIDDLE EASTERN $$
(Beit Jala: mains 30-55NIS) This local restaurant on a hillside in Beit Jala serves homely Palestinian food, beers and wine on the grounds of an organic farm, with hens clucking, birds singing and fantastic views over the hills of the southern West Bank. Lunch and dinner are served on rickety wooden tables perched on the very edge of the valley, while couches and treehouse-like raised platforms are a great place to relax and enjoy a shisha. The best time to come is at sunset.

Hosh Al Jasmine can be tricky to find, so make sure the taxi driver knows it before you set off.

Fadwa Cafe & Restaurant
ARABIC $$
(www.hoshalsyrian.com/fawda-cafe-restaurant; Hosh Al Syrian Guesthouse; mains 30-70NIS; ⊙by appointment only, lunch 12:30-2pm, dinner 6.30-8.30pm) Set in the grounds of the Hosh Al Syrian Guesthouse, the Fadwa Cafe & Restaurant is where chef Fadi Kattan cooks up sensational Franco-Palestinian fusion dishes. Kattan uses only fresh ingredients, so meals must be booked 24 hours ahead. The cafe is open for drinks 8am to 10pm daily.

Kattan serves up a different menu depending on what meat and vegetables are available from local farmers but has some signature dishes, including a deconstruction of the Palestinian desert *kunafeh* that is a cooked peach inside a nest of shredded wheat.

🍷 Drinking & Nightlife

Alcohol is widely available in Bethlehem's restaurants, and there are even a few bars, although mostly located downhill from the Old City, which shuts down after dark.

★Rewined
BAR
(⊙7pm-late Thu-Sun) This uber-trendy haunt 15 minutes' walk downhill from the Old City serves a variety of local beers and wine, as well as cocktails and shisha, to a mostly local crowd relaxing on couches on a terrace overlooking Manger St.

WEST BANK BETHLEHEM

Central West Bank

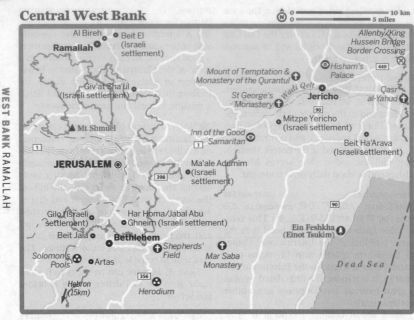

Star Bucks CAFE
(Manger Sq; ⊙8am-11pm) No relation to
Ramallah's famous Starbucks copycat, Star
Bucks Bethlehem is a small coffee kiosk with
great views across Manger Sq to the Church
of the Nativity. Its frappachinos are a god-
send on a hot afternoon.

❶ Information

Peace Center (☑02-276-6677; ⊙8am-3pm
Mon-Thu & Sat; ☎) This information desk gives
away city maps and provides helpful hints on
accommodation and transport. It often holds
art and photography exhibitions.

❶ Getting There & Away

Bus 231 from Jerusalem to Bethlehem (30
minutes) departs every 15 minutes between
6am and 9pm (until 6.30pm in winter) from the
Damascus Gate bus station, via Beit Jala.

Alternatively, take bus 234 from Jerusalem
to the main Bethlehem checkpoint (Checkpoint
300) and get a taxi into Bethlehem (20NIS).

The best way to get from Bethlehem to the
sites that surround it is by taxi, and drivers will
clamour to offer visits to multiple sites for a
fixed price (something around 50NIS an hour is
standard, but you'll need to haggle). It is actually
pretty good value, especially if you are in a small
group, and many drivers speak good English and
can answer your questions. Drivers generally

congregate outside Checkpoint 300, Manger Sq
or the 231 bus stop to Jerusalem.

Alternatively, it's possible to get shared
taxis from the main bus station to Jericho and
Hebron.

Ramallah
رام الله رمאללה

☑02 / POP 65,000
In a region where the lives of cities can
often be measured in terms of millennia,
Ramallah – little more than a hamlet until
the late 19th century – is a veritable new kid
on the block. But the de facto capital of the
Palestinian Territories has made up for lost
time: today it is a vibrant, bustling and cosmopolitan city that is the West Bank's political and economic heart.

Although Ramallah lacks the religious
fervour of Hebron or Nablus, the flags and
graffiti that adorn every wall leave you in
no doubt where you are. But the city is not
all about politics. The tiny shops, cafes and
eateries that line the arteries that lead off
Al Manara Sq – with its iconic four lions –
are fascinating places to wander, and the
nearby Al Masyoun is the centre of Ramallah's famous – some argue infamous –
nightlife.

◉ Sights

Most tourists begin their exploration of Ramallah in Al Manara Sq, which is a short walk from where buses arrive from Jerusalem.

The streets that branch off Al Manara lead to the city's other neighbourhoods. Al Raeesy St (also known as Main St) and Palestine St (directly opposite) lead to the Old City and the entrance to the street market respectively, and are packed with coffee shops and kebab houses.

Set on a steep hill, Ramallah can be a disorientating and tiring place to get lost, but locals can generally point you in the right direction. Taxis are also relatively cheap; a journey within the city should cost 10NIS to 20NIS.

★ Yasser Arafat Museum   MUSEUM
(Muqata'a; Al Itha'a St; 5NIS; ⊙10am-6pm Tue-Sun) Next to the ornate tomb of the late Palestinian leader Yasser Arafat is a new museum that bears his name. Divided into two parts, the first half traces Arafat's life alongside that of his Fatah movement and other Palestinian factions.

Those less interested in Palestinian politics may prefer the second section, where Arafat spent his final years under Israeli siege from 2001 to 2004. The restored facility includes his bedroom, where khaki green uniforms still hang in the wardrobe.

A final exhibit shows the various toxicology reports that claim that Arafat may have been poisoned before he died in a Paris hospital in 2004, reminding visitors of the role he still plays in Palestinian politics even after his death.

On the way into the museum lies Arafat's mausoleum, cast in Jerusalem stone and guarded by two stern-looking Palestinian soldiers (who nonetheless do not object to photos).

The Muqata'a complex is a government building, so security is tight: expect to be trailed by museum 'staff' and bring ID or you won't be allowed in.

It is around 1km from Al Manara on the road to Birzeit and Nablus, an easy walk from downtown.

Dar Zahran Heritage Building   GALLERY
(www.darzahran.org; ⊙11am-7pm Mon-Sat) FREE
One of Ramallah's oldest buildings, Dar Zahran was restored and converted into a gallery-cum-museum in 1990, and plans are now underway for a coffee shop on the upper floor. Built 250 years ago when Ramallah was little more than a hamlet, the building has photographs from as far back as 1850 and exhibitions of contemporary Palestinian art.

Nelson Mandela Square   MONUMENT
It appears that a visit to Ramallah is no longer complete without a stop at this towering statue of the late Nelson Mandela for a selfie. Unveiled in 2016, the 20ft statue was a gift from Johannesburg, which is twinned with the Palestinian capital.

Madiba stands, fist forever raised, on a roundabout some 15 minutes outside of the city. Either catch a service on Al Tira St away from town or take a taxi.

Mahmoud Darwish Museum   MUSEUM
(☎02-295-2809; www.darwishfoundation.org; 5NIS; ⊙10am-6pm) Palestinian poet Mahmoud Darwish was buried on this hilltop in Al Masyoun after his death in 2008, and this recently completed complex in his honour is certainly a grand tribute. The museum itself is a little underwhelming (exhibits include Darwish's final boarding pass, briefcase and desk) but the gardens and outdoor theatre with views across the city is a pleasant enough spot.

A taxi from downtown will cost 15NIS to 20NIS, but if you can find a sherut going this way, it is just 3NIS.

🛏 Sleeping

Ramallah has an excellent range of accommodation, with at least two good youth hostels, a decent number of midrange options and one top-end hotel, the Millennium (formerly the Mövenpick). Stay as close as possible to Al Manara or Arafat Sq if you can.

★ Area D Hostel   HOSTEL $
(☎056 934-9042; http://ramallahhostel.com; Vegetable Market St; dm/d/apt 70/200/250NIS; P❋@☎) Area D is one of only a handful of international standard hostels in the West Bank and by far the best for visitors to Ramallah. Its spotless dorms and double rooms are basic, but the shared lounge is a great place to relax, meet other travellers and plan excursions.

The hostel is located above Ramallah's service taxi garage, opposite the bus station for Jerusalem. Area D is a reliable place to organise tours to other cities, including Hebron, and staff are a wealth of information about travel inside the West Bank and beyond.

Ramallah

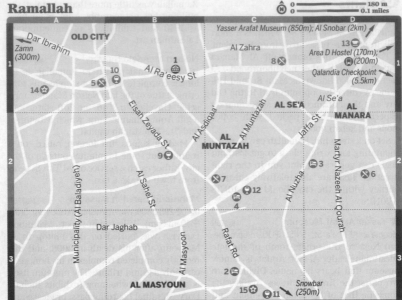

WEST BANK RAMALLAH

Ramallah

Hostel in Ramallah   HOSTEL **$**

(☑02-296-3555; www.hostelinramallah.com; Al Nuzha St; dm/s/d 50/105/130NIS; 🛜) This quirky hostel a five-minute walk from Yasser Arafat Sq is spread over three floors of an apartment building, with a half-dozen dorms and a range of single and double rooms. Staffed by a rotating cast of international volunteers, it has one of the best roof terraces in the city.

Beauty Inn   HOTEL **$$**

(☑02-246-4040; www.beautyinn.ps; Al Muntazah; s/d/ste US$90/120/180; 🅿@🛜🏊) Tucked away on a quiet street close to the Khalil Sakakini Cultural Centre, this is a smart, clean midrange option with a pool, a gym and corridors lined with pictures of the Palestinian Territories. Some rooms are better than others so ask to see a couple when you check in.

Royal Court Suites Hotel   HOTEL **$$**

(☑02-296-4040; www.rcshotel.com; Jaffa St; s/d 280/370NIS; @🛜) This is a reliable midrange option 15 minutes' walk downhill from the centre of town and next to Sangria's. Many of the rooms come with kitchen facilities and balconies and all have wi-fi. Consider asking for a room at the back of the hotel where it is much quieter.

Millennium Ramallah   HOTEL **$$$**

(☑02-298-5888; Emil Habibi St; s/d US$185/200; 🅿🛜🏊) Formerly the Mövenpick (and still referred to as such by taxi drivers), the

Millennium is probably Ramallah's smartest hotel and the go-to place for business travellers. It has huge rooms, excellent staff and great facilities, including a gym and pool (summer only). The pool is open to nonguests (100NIS) between 9am and 6pm.

Eating

From Italian to Mexican to sushi, Ramallah is home to an ever-changing roster of restaurants that cater to locals and tourists alike. But by far the best and cheapest way to eat in Ramallah is to visit the local restaurants around Al Manara Sq. The Al Muntazah neighbourhood has a host of chic cafes, bars and dining destinations.

Boaz   ARABIC $
(mains 6-20NIS; ⊙10am-late) Across the road from La Grotta, close to the Old City and down the hill from Al Manara, Boaz is a hole-in-the-wall kebab house with a few plastic tables outside opposite a popular shisha spot. Boaz, the owner, or one of his staff will ask whether you want lamb or chicken along with spicy *moutabel* (eggplant-based dip), hummus and Arabic salad.

Rukap's Ice Cream   ICE CREAM $
(ice cream 10-24NIS; ⊙8am-late) Renowned on both sides of the Green Line, Rukap's is to Ramallah what *kunafeh* (warm, syrupy cheese pastry) is to Nablus. Choose between a small cone (10NIS) up to a large (16NIS) and bowls large enough to feed an army. Flavours range from the usual stalwarts to local favourites, such as Arabic gum, lemon and tutti frutti.

★ La Vie Cafe   INTERNATIONAL $$
(📋02-296-4115; Castel St; mains 35-70NIS; ⊙10am-midnight Sat-Thu, 4pm-midnight Fri) Tucked away on a quiet street just 10 minutes' walk from Al Manara, this place has a diverse menu of pasta, pizza and sandwiches, with much of its produce grown in owners Saleh and Morgan's roof garden. On weekends, La Vie is a popular nightspot, serving a range of beers, wines and cocktails.

It is open for breakfast and lunch but doesn't really get going until late afternoon.

Pronto Resto-Café   ITALIAN $$
(Al Muntazah; mains 45-75NIS; ⊙7am-11pm) It's no longer the only place to get pizza in Ramallah, but it is easy to see how Pronto has survived since 1997 in a city where many restaurants barely last a year. From the fish (from Jaffa) to the wine (from Bethlehem), Bassem Khoury and family prioritise local ingredients and Pronto remains the only place for real Italian food in Ramallah.

Drinking & Nightlife

Ramallah is the only party spot in the West Bank (although Bethlehem has a couple of good bars). Whether you prefer uber-trendy cocktail lounges or dive bars, you are unlikely to go thirsty. Both Area D (p275) and Hostel in Ramallah (p276) organise weekly pub crawls, usually on Thursday (the Friday night equivalent in the West Bank).

★ Birzeit Brewery   BREWERY
(⊙9am-5pm) Since it opened in 2015, Birzeit Brewery's Shepherds beer has taken the West Bank by storm, challenging years of domination of the Palestinian Territories' beer market by Taybeh. Visitors to its hub of operations in the Christian village of Birzeit are given a tour by one of the three brothers who run the brewery as well as a pint of beer to enjoy at their leisure. It also has an excellent gift shop.

★ Snowbar   BAR
(📋02-296-5571; www.al-snowbar.com; ⊙noon-late May-Oct) For two decades, Snowbar has been the place to see and be seen in Ramallah. Although it has an often deserved reputation as a late-night party spot, on weeknights Snowbar has a chilled-out vibe with a mostly local crowd lounging over cocktails, beers and shisha. It's a 20NIS ride from downtown Ramallah; all the taxi drivers know it. Snowbar has a pool (open 10am to 5pm) and hosts regular events and party nights, particularly on the weekends.

★ Berlin Pub   COCKTAIL BAR
(⊙5pm-late; 📶) Berlin is the latest hip spot on Ramallah's ever-changing nightlife scene. The barman trained in Germany before opening this tiny cocktail bar and pub and prides himself on the lack of a menu, preferring punters to just tell him what they like.

Radio   BAR
(⊙noon-late; 📶) Ramallah veterans who remember the infamous Beit Aneeseh can rest assured that Radio, located in the same building, is filling the gap that the late-night party spot left when it was shut down in 2014. Radio has a similar grungy vibe, with live music, shisha and cheap beers either inside or in the garden. The entrance is around the back of the building rather than through the front gate, which is usually locked.

La Grotta   BAR

(Old City; ⊙ 6pm-late) A tiny, alternative hang-out close to the Old City, La Grotta is run by a local musician and is a popular late-night spot. There are a few tables outside, but the main bar is up the steps on the 1st floor of a traditional Palestinian house. It can be tricky to find: walk down Main St and turn left at the garage.

Sangria's   BAR

(📞 02-295-6808; Jaffa St; ⊙ noon-midnight; 🛜) A veteran Ramallah hang-out, Sangria's beer garden is the place to be on Thursday and Saturday nights. The Mexican and international menu is ambitious, but you are here for the drinks – arguably some of the best in the city, with everything from local Taybeh beer to a range of cocktails and sangria, of course.

Stars & Bucks   CAFE

(Al Manara; ⊙ 8am-late) A Ramallah institution and not just because of its mischievous take on the logo – or indeed, the entire concept – of the US coffee giant. Stars & Bucks is a great place to hang out with coffee or mocktails overlooking the bustle of Al Manara Sq.

☆ Entertainment

There is a lot going on in Ramallah, but you tend to need to be in the know to find out what is on when. Ask at your hotel, check online or pick up the entertainment listing *This Week in Palestine*.

Al Kamandjati   ARTS CENTRE

(📞 02-297-3101; www.alkamandjati.com; Old City) This small conservatory, which features an ancient arch with an edgy, modern copper entryway, offers intimate concerts and recitals. Outside of official performances, there is little going on at Al Kamandjati so be sure to check the program online before you go.

Khalil Sakakini Centre   CULTURAL CENTRE

(📞 02-298-7374; www.sakakini.org; Al Muntazah) Hosts art exhibitions by the locally and internationally renowned, along with a whole host of other cultural pursuits. Check the website for upcoming events.

ℹ Getting There & Away

From the old Arab bus station in East Jerusalem, take bus 218 or 219 to Ramallah (30 minutes).

As a rule of thumb, the smaller the bus, the faster the journey. Buses to/from Ramallah operate from 6am to 9.30pm or 10pm in summer or until 7pm in winter, after which you can take a service taxi from Ramallah to Qalandia and then a taxi to Jerusalem, or vice versa.

You will not need to get off the bus on the way into the West Bank, but on the way out, all passengers disembark and go through airport-style security. Have your passport and Israeli visa ready to show the soldiers behind the bulletproof glass. Also hold onto your ticket to show to the driver once you're on the other side of the checkpoint.

The bus station in Ramallah is a five-minute walk from Al Manara Sq and a two-minute walk from the service garage, where shared taxis leave to destinations throughout the West Bank.

Ramallah's location in the centre of the West Bank and excellent bus links both north (to Nablus and Jenin) and south, to Jericho, make it a great base for travellers.

ℹ Getting Around

Everything within the Ramallah area is 10 minutes or less by private taxi and should cost 15NIS to 20NIS, but agree on the price with the driver before setting off.

A cheaper way of getting around during the day is by service taxi. You can hail them on any street and ask for your destination. Most will drop you off at Al Manara for 3NIS.

Taybeh الطيبة   טייבה

📞 02 / POP 1400

Taybeh, on a remote hillside 15km outside of Ramallah, was just another West Bank village until local lad Nadim Khoury returned from university in the US and decided to start brewing beer.

Now Taybeh beer has become an empire, sold throughout the West Bank (and increasingly even over the Green Line in Israel) as well as in Germany, Sweden and the US.

Taybeh's annual Octoberfest attracts thousands of locals, expatriates and tourists and with its new winery and hotel, the Khoury family are hoping to encourage visitors to spend a little longer in the village, believed to be the place Jesus and his disciples stayed in the hours before his death.

Taybeh is home to a number of interesting churches and chapels as well as fascinating Byzantine ruins. Take a shared taxi from the service taxi garage below Area D Hostel in Ramallah.

◉ Sights

Taybeh Winery   WINERY

(📞 02-289-9440; www.taybehwinery.com; 100 Main St; ⊙ 8am-4pm; 🅿) Canaan, the son of Taybeh Brewery founder Nadim Khoury, began making wine in this modern facility below the Taybeh Golden Hotel in 2013 and now produces five wines, three red and two white. Guests are given a tour of the winery and can choose to sample either three (50NIS) or five (80NIS) wines, alongside food. It is best to email ahead.

☞ Tours

★ **Taybeh Brewing Company** BREWERY
(📞02-289-8868; www.taybehbeer.net; ⊗8am-4pm) FREE An essential stop on any West Bank itinerary, Taybeh Beer Brewery offers free tours daily, often given by master-brewer Madees Khoury herself. Visitors can observe the beer making – and occasionally bottling – process and learn about how this tiny Christian village ended up exporting beer across the West Bank, Israel and the wider world.

Founded in 1994 by Madees' father, Nadim Khoury, Taybeh now produces half a dozen beers, with plans afoot to launch a much-anticipated IPA alongside its pilsner, amber and dark ales.

🛏 Sleeping

Taybeh Golden Hotel HOTEL $$
(📞02-289-9440; www.taybehgoldenhotel.com; 100 Main St; d/ste US$110/160; 🅿@🔊) Situated above Taybeh Winery (p278), Taybeh Golden Hotel is an uber-modern family-run place just a few minutes' walk from centre of the village. Some of the rooms have epic views across the surrounding mountains and olive groves. Built in 2015, the hotel has two restaurants and a choice of 80 rooms, primarily doubles and suites.

❶ Getting There & Away

Service taxis to Taybeh go from the 2nd floor of the multistorey car park beneath Area D Hostel, Ramallah, directly opposite the bus station where buses arrive and depart from Jerusalem.

When returning, it is possible to flag a service from Taybeh's Main St to either Ramallah or Qalandia Checkpoint should you want to go to Jerusalem.

Jericho יריחו اريحا
📞02 / POP 20,300

Whether you are walking around ancient ruins or observing epic monasteries carved into the Judean mountains, it is impossible not to feel a sense of history in Jericho, which is proudly dubbed the 'world's oldest continuously inhabited city' by the local authorities.

It is no idle boast: archaeological evidence traces settlement here back more than 10,000 years, and the ashes of the empires that have fought and conquered Jericho over the millennia can be seen throughout the city.

Jericho may have modernised since then, but small-scale farming is still a way of life for many of its inhabitants, and the city can feel a bit scruffy and unkempt. But, with its palm trees, date plantations and smiley demeanour, it also feels very different to the rest of the West Bank and makes a great stop for a day or two.

History

Settled history in Jericho dates to around 10,000 BCE when hunter-gatherer groups settled here around a spring. Mudbrick buildings were erected at the site, and by 9400 BCE it's believed that some 1000 people lived here.

For the biblically astute, Jericho is known as the first city the Israelites captured after wandering for 40 years in the desert: shaken by horn blasts and the Israelites' shouts, the city walls came crashing down (Joshua 6). Following Alexander the Great's conquest of the region in the 4th century BCE, Jericho became his personal fiefdom.

Further waves of occupiers arrived and departed until Jericho fell into the hands of Mark Antony, who gave it to Cleopatra as a wedding gift. Herod later leased it from Cleopatra and improved its infrastructure with aqueducts and a hippodrome. The 1st-century aristocracy of Jerusalem used the city as a winter getaway.

Christians celebrate Jericho as the place where John the Baptist received his own baptism in the Jordan River and where the temptation of Jesus took place on the mountain.

After the signing of the 1993 Oslo Accords, Jericho was the first city to be handed over to Palestinian Authority control.

◉ Sights

Tel Al Sultan RUINS
(Ancient Jericho; adult/student/child 10/7/5NIS; ⊗8am-5pm) It is impossible not feel a sense of history strolling around the mounds and ruins at Tel Al Sultan, where remains of dwellings and fortifications dating back some 10,000 years have been unearthed. You will see what look like sand dunes and stairways (the oldest known stairways in the

world); underneath, the layers of civilisation beneath go back even further into the mists of history.

The remains of a round tower, thought to date from 8000 BCE, indicates that Jericho was possibly the world's first fortified city; legend has it that the tower withstood seven earthquakes.

Though a large portion of ancient Jericho remains unexcavated, Tel Al Sultan is an essential part of any trip to the city. What has already been identified here is very well explained on signposts throughout the site.

Mount of Temptation & Monastery of the Qurantul RELIGIOUS SITE

(⊘8am-4pm Mon-Fri, to 2pm Sat & Sun) FREE One of Jericho's – indeed, the entire West Bank's – most impressive sights is the Monastery of the Qurantul, built on the spot where the Bible says Jesus resisted Satan after his 40-day fast in the desert.

It is an incredible feat of engineering, cut into the cliff face with dramatic views over the Dead Sea to Jordan.

Opening times for the monastery are sporadic, but as with all tourist attractions in the Palestinian Territories, it is best to go early – or at least a couple of hours before sunset. Note that the caretaker may lock the door if he is showing big groups around, so it is worth hanging around a few minutes if you find it closed.

Cable cars stop just before the monastery, and even the short climb up the stairs to the front gate can be a struggle in the midday heat. The juice sellers and a couple of restaurants provide a good spot to catch your breath.

★ Hisham's Palace RUINS

(Khirbet Al Mafjar; 10NIS; ⊘8am-6pm) A short drive north of Tel Al Sultan, this is a spot not to be missed. The sprawling winter hunting retreat of Caliph Hisham Ibn Abd al Malik must have been magnificent on its creation in the 8th century, with its baths, mosaic floors and pillars – so much so that archaeologists have labelled it the 'Versailles of the Middle East'. It was not fated to last, however – it was destroyed by an earthquake soon after its creation.

The caretaker will direct you to a cinema, where you will be shown a 20-minute video on the history of the site, which gives much-needed perspective for a walk around the ruins. A high point is an amazingly well-preserved 'tree of life' mosaic in the entertaining room of the bathhouse. On one

side of the tree, two deer graze peacefully, while on the other a deer is attacked by a lion. There are various interpretations of the mosaic, including the struggle between good and evil, peace and war, and good versus bad governance.

Russian Museum & Tree of Zacchaeus MUSEUM

(adult/child 20/10NIS; ⊘9am-5pm) A short walk from the town centre, the Russian Museum traces the history of the Russian Orthodox Church in the Holy Land and has an interesting collection of archaeological finds, including an impressive mosaic, coins and religious artefacts. Its garden is home to the Tree of Zacchaeus, a sycamore believed to be more than 2000 years old that's mentioned in the Bible.

The story goes that a wealthy tax collector who was too short to see Jesus amid the crowds climbed this very tree to get a better view. Seeing this, Jesus asked the tax collector if he could visit his home, a gesture that so moved Zacchaeus that he decided to dedicate himself to a life of charitable deeds.

Visitors who don't want to visit the Russian Museum but still want a glimpse of the tree can do so from a little further up Ein Al Sultan St, albeit only through the railings.

Qasr Al Yahud RELIGIOUS SITE

(⊘9am-4pm) FREE At an isolated spot on the Jordan River, on the border between Jordan and the West Bank, stands the reputed spot of Jesus's baptism by John, which began his ministry. John is said to have chosen the site because it was an important crossroads for passing traders and soldiers, but the same cannot be said today. Guarded by an Israeli checkpoint, the access road passes through minefields before reaching a car park, from which it is a short walk to the river.

At the river, expect to see dozens of pilgrims, most in white T-shirts or smocks, taking turns walking to the water and submerging themselves. On the Israeli side, the edge of the caged-off area denotes the border and prevents over-excited pilgrims from wading into Jordan.

Just metres away, armed Jordanian soldiers loll on a bench, facing their Israeli counterparts.

Whether you are religious or not, it is a beautiful and fascinating spot, and the site has been fully renovated with changing facilities, a gift shop, a food and drink outlet and shaded areas where you can sit and admire the view.

Nabi Musa
MOSQUE

(⊙8am-sunset) **FREE** About 10km north of the Dead Sea, Nabi Musa is where Muslims believe Moses (Musa in Arabic, Moshe in Hebrew) was buried. A mosque was built on the site in 1269, under Mamluk Sultan Baybar (it was expanded two centuries later), and annual week-long pilgrimages set out from Jerusalem to Nabi Musa – which continue today.

St George's Monastery
MONASTERY

(⊙9am-1pm) **FREE** The spectacular St George's Monastery is a must-see in Wadi Qelt, built into the cliff face in the 5th century. The paintings inside the main chapel are worth the walk, and parts of the original mosaic floors are visible below perspex screens. Up another flight of stairs there is a beautiful cave chapel.

From the car park, it is a gruelling 10-minute hike to the monastery – expect to be hassled by donkey-taxi vendors the entire way.

Drinking water is available at the monastery. You'll see signposts along the way for the three main springs (Ein Qelt, Ein Farah and Ein Fawwar).

The only way to visit the monastery, like many other sites in and around Jericho, is by taxi (usually arranged in Bethlehem) or ideally with your own car. It is an easy drive from Jerusalem.

Inn of the Good Samaritan
HISTORIC SITE

(adult/child 22/10NIS; ⊙8am-5pm) Located just off the main road from Jerusalem to Jericho, this site is associated with the popular biblical story about the Good Samaritan who, according to the parable, stopped to help a stricken traveller, dressed his wounds and took him to a nearby inn.

Archaeologists have unearthed a Herod-era palace on the site, as well as a church built by the Byzantines and an inn constructed during the Crusader period. The site is well orientated and interesting, and audio guides are included in the entrance fee.

🏃 Activities

Jericho Cable Car
CABLE CAR

(www.jericho-cablecar.com; 60NIS; ⊙8am-7pm Mon-Thu, to 10pm Fri) The Swiss-made red cable cars that ply the route between Tel Al Sultan and the Mount of Temptation are visible throughout Jericho. The cable cars look dated, but the 20-minute ride is a great way to see the city and the farms that dominate

its outskirts. Even when the site is quiet, cars leave fairly regularly.

🛏 Sleeping

★ Sami Youth Hostel
GUESTHOUSE $

(📞02-232 4220; eyad_alalem@live.com; r 120-150NIS; 🛜) One of the West Bank's best budget stays, Sami Youth Hostel is nestled deep in the refugee camp on the outskirts of Jericho with a dozen clean and quiet rooms in an enigmatically furnished two-storey building. By far the best thing about Sami Youth Hostel is Sami himself, who speaks fluent English and treats his guests more like family members than customers.

Coming into Jericho from Hwy 90, take a left at the first roundabout and then continue straight – the guesthouse will be on your right. Failing that, ask locals for 'Hotel Sami', and they will point the way.

Oasis Hotel
HOTEL $$$

(📞02-231-1200; www.oasis-jericho.ps; s 450-550NIS, d 550-650NIS; ❀🛜🏊) Formerly the Intercontinental (the logo of which is still visible on the side of the building), the Oasis Hotel is expensive, but its clean modern rooms, helpful staff and choice of two swimming pools make it a popular high-end choice. Its location, just off the Jerusalem-Jericho road, make it a great hub for exploring not only Jericho but also the Dead Sea and beyond.

🍴 Eating

The roads surrounding Jericho's central square are packed with kebab and falafel stands, as well as small coffee shops. A kebab or sandwich is unlikely to cost more than 10NIS, and the park in the centre of the roundabout is a lovely spot to sit, eat and watch the locals playing cards and smoking shisha.

★ Abu Omar
MIDDLE EASTERN $

(Ein Al Sultan St; mains 20-50NIS; ⊙6am-midnight) Next to the main square, this local favourite serves the best roast chicken in the West Bank, period. It is double the price for a sit-down meal versus taking away, but grabbing a table is well worth it.

Al Essawe
MIDDLE EASTERN $

(Main Sq; mains 15-45NIS; ⊙6am-11pm) On a corner overlooking Jericho's main square, Al Essawe's lovely 2nd-floor terrace is an excellent place to watch the world go by. The owner speaks English, and the restaurant serves the usual Arabic fare, kebabs, falafel and mezze. Don't miss the fresh lemonade.

ℹ️ Information

Tourist Information Centre (📞 02-231-2607; Main Sq; ⊗ 8am-5pm; 🐦) An essential first stop for independent travellers. The staff at this excellent booth in the city's main square speak perfect English and are a wealth of information on what to see and how to get there. It can arrange tours, recommend hotels and help travellers plan their day, or longer stay, in Jericho.

ℹ️ Getting There & Around

Service taxis from Jerusalem to Jericho go from the Abu Dis checkpoint (12NIS) but are awkward to catch and travellers often opt to go via Ramallah (18NIS) or Bethlehem (21NIS).

Alternatively, you can hire a cab driver in Bethlehem or Ramallah for a day trip to Jericho and its surroundings. Most drivers will ask for at least 200NIS to 250NIS a day. If you hire a taxi in Jerusalem, it can be double that.

Jericho is not a very walkable city away from downtown: it is dusty and humid and many of its sights are on opposite sides of the city. Service taxis (about 3NIS) serve many of the sights, but it is quicker and easier to negotiate a rate with a local driver (20NIS to 30NIS an hour is fair).

Even if you only visit Jericho for the day, do not forget your passport as Israeli checkpoints on the road out of the city are common.

Hebron חברון الخليل

📶 02 / POP 183,000

Believed to be the final resting place of Abraham (Ibrahim to Muslims), his sons and their wives, Hebron is of intense importance to all three monotheistic faiths: Christianity, Judaism and Islam.

Sadly, the common thread of belief has done little to improve relations between Muslims and Jews in Hebron (Al Khalil in Arabic), and the city has frequently been marred by religious violence.

Today, Hebron is unique in the West Bank in that Israeli settlers live in the very heart of the city, rather than on its outskirts, metres away from Palestinian homes and behind blast walls, barbed wire and thousands of heavily armed Israeli soldiers.

Hebron has been famous since antiquity for the leather, blown glass and hand-painted pottery made by its craftsmen.

Most visitors come to Hebron on a guided tour, but travellers wanting to explore on their own will find it an easy day trip from Bethlehem.

History

According to the Hebrew Bible, Hebron was founded around 1730 BCE. Its biblical name, Kiryat Arba (the Village of Four), perhaps refers to its position on four hills on which four Canaanite tribes settled.

For the few centuries before 1900, Hebron was home to a small Jewish community, but in 1929, Arab nationalists attacked the city's Jews – all of them non-Zionist ultra-Orthodox – and killed 67 of them. The rest of the community fled.

After 1967, Orthodox Jews returned to the city, and a prominent feature of today's Hebron is the presence of Israeli soldiers guarding Jewish enclaves – populated by some of the West Bank's most hardline settlers – in the town centre. The suburb of Kiryat Arba, now home to more than 7000 Jews, was established nearby.

In 1994, during the Muslim holy month of Ramadan and on the Jewish holiday of Purim, Brooklyn-born physician Baruch Goldstein opened fire on Palestinians while they prayed in the Ibrahimi Mosque, killing 29 men and boys and injuring a further 200.

Moderate settlers view Goldstein as a cold-blooded killer. However, extremist Jewish settlers, who see local Palestinians as foreign interlopers in the Land of Israel, consider him a hero, and his gravesite remains a popular place of pilgrimage.

Many streets in Hebron are barricaded and completely off-limits to Palestinians, and the doors of many of the shops in its souq were welded shut in the late 1990s, turning the historic neighbourhood into a ghost town.

It is still common to see Israeli military patrols in the Old City, and there are regular flare-ups between stone-throwing Palestinian youths and soldiers, especially on Fridays.

In 2017, Unesco recognised both Hebron's Old City and the Ibrahimi Mosque/Tomb of the Patriarchs as Palestinian World Heritage sites, placing both on its 'in danger' list. The move provoked fury from Israel, which accused the UN of denying the centuries-old Jewish links to the city.

👁️ Sights

For most travellers, there are three main parts to Hebron. The first is Ras Al Jora (Jerusalem Sq), set on Hebron Rd (also known as Shari'a Al Quds) as it comes in from Bethlehem. The area is a commercial hub with plenty of restaurants and workshops that produce glass and ceramics.

About 3km south, Hebron Rd becomes Ein Sarah St, which eventually runs into Al Manara Sq (really just a junction). From Al Manara Sq, turn right and walk for about 200m to reach the bus station, or turn left and walk for 10 minutes to reach Bab Al Zawieh, the entrance to the Old City souq and further to the Ibrahimi Mosque.

The Jewish section of town lies south of the Old City, beyond high walls and barbed-wire fences. You can easily walk there from the Ibrahimi Mosque/Tomb of the Patriarchs. You can also cross at the checkpoint at Al Manara Sq. Have your passport handy to cross through checkpoints between the Arab and Jewish parts of town.

◉ Old City

The Old City's stunning yet often crumbling Mamluk-style Ottoman architecture includes a souq, but merchants have been moved to an outdoor area because of friction with Jewish settlers.

When walking through the town, look out for the nets hung over the narrow streets to catch trash thrown from the upstairs windows (home to settlers) at the Palestinian shops below.

You can also peer through the barbed wire at the gold souq, once renowned throughout the region but now completely off limits.

Ibrahimi Mosque/Tomb of the Patriarchs   MOSQUE, SYNAGOGUE
(⊙8am-4pm Sun-Thu, except during prayers) The focal point of Hebron for most visitors is the Tomb of the Patriarchs (Cave of Machpelah), known to Muslims as Ibrahimi Mosque (Ibrahim is the Muslim name for Abraham). The site is sacred to both Muslims and Jews – be aware of the strict security and separate prayer spaces for each. When coming from the Old City, you will need to pass through an Israeli checkpoint and show your passport.

Looking rather like decorated tents, the mostly Mamluk-era cenotaphs commemorate the patriarchs Abraham, Isaac and Jacob, and their wives, but it's the cave below that both Jews and Muslims believe was chosen by Abraham as the actual final resting place of his family.

You can peer into the cave through a metal grate in the corner of the mosque. As you walk into the room that allows viewing of the cenotaph of Abraham, note the small niche near the door where you can see a footprint. The Muslims believe this to be Muhammad's footprint, while Jews believe it was created by Adam.

Built by Herod (notice the Herodian stones at the base of the walls), the complex was altered by the Byzantines in the 6th century – they added a church, beside which a synagogue was built. When the Arabs conquered the area in the following century, the church was converted to a mosque, but the synagogue remained intact. After the Crusaders left the scene, the Mamluks built another mosque.

When entering the mosque, you will be asked to remove your shoes, and women will be handed a head covering. When entering the synagogue, men will be offered kippas and women a scarf to cover their shoulders.

◉ Outskirts of Town

Hebron Glass and Ceramics Factory   WORKSHOP
(Natsheh Brothers; ☑02-222-8502; hebronglass@yahoo.com; Ras Al Jora, ⊙8am-6pm, closed Fri mornings) FREE This factory on the outskirts of Hebron, on the main road into the city from the north, has been in the Natsheh family for 350 years. Visitors can observe glassmakers fire and blow everything from wine glasses to ornate coloured bottles in the ceramic kiln, and buy souvenirs at the attached shop for a fraction of the prices in Bethlehem and Jerusalem.

🛏 Sleeping

If you are interested in a homestay, it is always best to organise it in advance, either through your hostel or hotel in Bethlehem, Ramallah or Jerusalem or through organisations such as France's Association d'Échanges Culturels Hebron-France (www.hebron-france.org).

✕ Eating

Abu Salah   MIDDLE EASTERN $
(Bab-e-Zawi; mains 10-35NIS; ⊙7am-10pm) Perched on the edge of Hebron's Old City, this busy restaurant is one of the best for shawarma. It has a handful of chairs where locals perch to chomp down on their pitas, either chicken or lamb.

1. Mar Saba Monastery (p271)
This dramatic cliff-clinging hermitage was founded over 1500 years ago.

2. Crafts in Hebron (p282)
Shop for souvenirs in this West Bank city, famed for its hand-painted pottery.

3. Jericho (p279)
Take a cable-car trip for sweeping views of the 'world's oldest continuously inhabited city'.

4. Ibrahimi Mosque/Tomb of the Patriarchs (p283)
This complex is sacred to both Muslims and Jews as the resting place of Abraham's family.

ISRAELI SETTLEMENTS

Israeli colonies set up in the Palestinian Territories are most often referred to as 'settlements'. There are approximately 350,000 Israeli settlers in the West Bank, living in more than 100 settlements, with hundreds of thousands more living in parts of Jerusalem captured by Israel in7 1967.

Settlements range in size from a collection of caravans on a remote hilltop to large urban areas, such as Ma'ale Adumim near Jerusalem, home to tens of thousands of Israelis and now effectively a suburb of Jerusalem. There are a variety of reasons cited by settlers for why they live on the West Bank: most commonly, cheaper housing prices than in Israel and, among the religious, the fulfilment of biblical prophecy and an extension of the will of God.

Under almost all interpretations of international law, which forbids the transfer of civilians to land under military occupation, Israeli settlements in the West Bank and in East Jerusalem are illegal. The Israeli right disputes this interpretation of international law. Key complaints against Israeli settlements are that they often occupy private Palestinian land (as opposed to state-owned land), divert precious water resources from surrounding Palestinian cities, towns and villages and, most significantly, fragment the territory of the West Bank, making the establishment of a coherent, contiguous and viable Palestinian state impossible.

The US and European Union have declared the settlements an obstacle to peace, but Israeli Prime Minister Benjamin Netanyahu's right-wing coalition government has continued to construct housing in Israeli settlements in the West Bank and in East Jerusalem.

To find out more, visit the websites of Palestinian NGO Al Haq (http://alhaq.mits.ps) or left-wing Israeli organisation B'Tselem (www.btselem.org). For a settler perspective, the Israeli settlement of Gush Etzion, near Bethlehem, has a visitor centre and museum (www.gush-etzion.org.il).

❶ Getting There & Away

The best way to reach Hebron from Jerusalem is to go via Bethlehem in one of the regular service taxis. From the bus station in Hebron, it's possible to catch service taxis to Jericho, Bethlehem and Ramallah between 5am and 6pm. Vehicles leave when full.

For a very different perspective – that of Hebron's Jewish settlers – take Egged bus 160 from Jerusalem's Central Bus Station. It stops right by the Ibrahimi Mosque/Tomb of the Patriarchs, from where you can walk into the Arab side of the city.

By the far the best way to see Hebron is on an organised tour via hostels and hotels in Bethlehem, Jerusalem or Ramallah, many of which take groups to the city at least twice a week. Tours organised by **Area D Hostel** (p275) in Ramallah are particularly recommended.

Nablus شكم نابلس

📱 09 / POP 126,000

Located on an important trade route between Damascus and Jerusalem, Nablus has been settled since before the Roman era, and the land beneath the modern city –

set in a valley – is layered with millennia of plunder and glory.

Set between Mt Gerizim and Mt Ebal, Nablus (Shechem in Hebrew) has historically been an exporter of olive oil, cotton and carob but is best known these days for its soap factories, olive-wood carving and *kunafeh*, a syrupy wheat and cheese pastry famous throughout the Middle East.

Nablus today is a bustling, exciting and vibrant metropolis, with a stunningly beautiful Old City that rivals Jerusalem's – not least because of the lack of tour groups clogging its narrow alleyways. The city is also a hotbed of Palestinian activism, and more often than not its central square is covered in flags, banners and posters of martyrs, those killed in the decades-long struggle with Israel.

History

After the 12 tribes of Israel split into two rival kingdoms in the 10th century BCE, Shechem was briefly the capital of the northern faction, that is, of the 10 tribes that would eventually be lost to history.

In 70 CE, the Romans obliterated ancient Shechem and set up Flavia Neapolis (New City), whose name the Arabs would later pronounce as Nablus.

Graeco-Roman cults developed, only to be destroyed in 636 CE when the city was conquered by Arab forces. Christian shrines were converted to Muslim mosques, and Nablus developed the character it still displays today. The Old City dates back to Ottoman times, though relics from as long ago as the Roman occupation can still be spotted.

Some of the West Bank's most hard-line Israeli settlers live in settlements surrounding Nablus. On nearby hilltops, you'll see Bracha, Itamar, Yitzhar and Elon Moreh, often in the news because local Jewish extremists have clashed either with Palestinians or with Israeli soldiers.

◉ Sights

The focal point for visitors to Nablus is Al Qasaba (Casbah or Old City), where you'll find an Ottoman-era rabbit warren of shops, stalls and pastry stands, spice sacks and vegetable mounds. Amid the clamour, you'll find dozens of contemplative mosques, including the Al Kebir Mosque (⊘7am-10pm, closed during prayers).

For more information on things to do and see, go to www.nablusguide.com.

Touqan Soap Factory   FACTORY
(Martyrs Sq; ⊘6am-3pm Sat-Thu) FREE One of a number of soap factories open to visitors in Nablus, Touqan opened in 1872, and the techniques of soap making here have not changed much since. You can buy soap for 7NIS, and tours are free.

On the ground floor, visitors can observe soap being mixed in huge, steaming stone vats before it is spread on the floor upstairs and cut into cubes by barefoot workers with extended metal sickles. In the next room, the soap is piled in head-height cairns before being wrapped by hand by workers who go through a staggering 1000 pieces an hour.

Tell Balata Archaeological Park   RUINS
(adult/student/child 10/7/5NIS; ⊘8am-5pm Sun-Thu, from 10am Fri & Sat) Tell Balata is the remains of what is believed to be the first settlement in Nablus, the Canaanite town of Shechem, dating from the first and second centuries BCE. Shechem was orientated around a spring in the valley between two mountains, Gerizim and Ebal. Close to Jacob's Well, Tell Balata boasts some interesting ruins and an excellent – albeit tiny – museum.

The archaeological park is relatively new, having been developed with support from Unesco. As a result, ruins are still being discovered. By far the most impressive is the remains of a fortress temple that archaeologists believe was used as a public place of worship. A path around the edge of the site also allows visitors to trace the old city walls.

Tell Balata is well signposted from the road from Ramallah and, more often than not, deserted. On the upside, this means you often have it to yourself; on the downside it means you may only be able to get into the museum (well worth a visit) by hammering on the door to rouse the sleeping porter.

Jacob's Well   CHURCH
(donations appreciated; ⊘8am-noon & 2-4pm) Near the entrance to Balata, the largest refugee camp in the West Bank, is the spot where Christians believe a Samaritan woman offered Jesus a drink of water, before he revealed to her that he was the Messiah (John 4:13–14). A Byzantine church destroyed in the Samaritan revolt of 529 CE was replaced by a Crusader church, which itself fell into ruins in the Middle Ages. The current church, St Photina the Samaritan, was built in the 1860s by the Greek Orthodox Patriarchate.

The church grounds are a stunningly beautiful spot, the immaculate chapel set in lush, quiet gardens filled with neighbourhood cats. Go down the steps close to the altar to see the well itself.

About 300m southeast, a compound known as Joseph's Tomb in recent years been a source of considerable friction between Jews, who come here to pray under IDF escort (in coordination with the Palestinian Authority), and local Arabs.

Samaritan Ruins   HISTORIC SITE
(adult/child 22/10NIS; ⊘8am-4pm Sat-Thu, to 3pm Fri) The ancient site of the Samaritan Temple is a 10-minute walk uphill from the village, via a locked gate: ring the intercom and a guard will let you through.

Once you pay at the desk, you are free to wander around the site at your leisure. You'll see the lowered floor that Samaritans say was the foundation of their temple, which was built in the 5th century BCE and only survived 200 years before being destroyed by the Maccabees (a Jewish rebel army) in 128 BCE.

Nablus

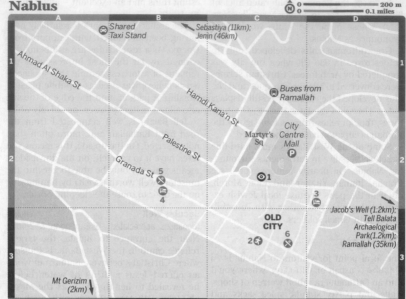

Nablus

Also on the site is the rock that Samaritans believe was where Abraham was about to sacrifice his son, Isaac, and dozens of temple buildings connected via shaded wooden pathways. The remains of a church, first constructed in 475 CE, have also been found on the mountain. You can rent binoculars for an extra 10NIS.

From the centre of Nablus, Mt Gerizim can be reached by taxi in around 10 minutes. It's a 50NIS to 70NIS journey including wait time.

If driving from Ramallah, turn left at Tapuah Junction to avoid driving through Nablus; the site is well signposted. Taxis have to wait outside the village at a military checkpoint, so be prepared to pay your driver in advance.

Samaritan Museum   MUSEUM
(⌨ 02-237-0249; 15NIS; ⊙ 9am-3pm Sun-Fri) Members of an ancient religion closely related to Judaism, the Samaritans believe that Mt Gerizim was not only the first piece of land ever created but also that it's the location chosen by God for his Temple (while Jews believe this is Temple Mount in Jerusalem). Learn more about the Samaritan community at this excellent museum, where an English-speaking guide will show you a video and answer any questions you have about the site or the faith.

Sebastia   RUINS
FREE Sebastia is a collection of ruins above a village of the same name that is believed to be one of the oldest continuously inhabited places in the West Bank.

A prominent settlement during Hellenistic and Roman eras, Christians and Muslims believe Sebastia to be the burial site of St John the Baptist. Situated on a hill with panoramic views across the West Bank, the site includes an amphitheatre (which once held 7000 people) and the remains of a Byzantine church.

St John's grave was desecrated in the mid-4th century and his bones partly burned, with surviving portions taken to Jerusalem and later to Alexandria, Egypt, where they were interred at a Coptic monastery. A mosque complex in the village of Sebastia contains a **shrine** to St John and a small **museum** (8am to 3pm Sunday to Thursday).

Despite obvious neglect (many of the ruins are strewn with trash and some are daubed with graffiti), Sebastia is an essential stop on a West Bank itinerary for history buffs. For the less archaeologically inclined, it is a peaceful place to walk among the olive groves and take in sensational views.

Sebastia is 11km from Nablus; a taxi with waiting time will cost around 150NIS. Alternatively, take a shared taxi from Nablus.

🏃 Activities

★ Hammam Al Shifa   BATHHOUSE
(35NIS; ⊙ men 8am-10pm, women 8am-5pm Sun & Tue only) Hand over your valuables before changing into a towel (or swimming costume, if you have one). The hammam has a hot room (a heated platform for lying on), a sauna and steam room. Massages are not for the faint-hearted. This hammam can be hard to find, but locals will point the way.

Founded in the 13th century, Hammam Al Shifa is one of the oldest in Nablus. It is very much a male-oriented place, but is open twice weekly to women.

🛏 Sleeping

★ Khan Al Wakalah   HOTEL $$
(s/d 180/250NIS, d without air-con 100NIS) Set in a beautifully restored Mamluk-Ottoman-era currency exchange in the Old City, Khan Al Wakalah has been a pit stop for travellers between Damascus and Jerusalem (as well as religious pilgrims on their way to Mecca and Medina) for centuries. Its 24 rooms are set around a shaded courtyard with big comfy beds and stunning interiors of wood and traditional Nablus stone.

The restoration of Khan Al Wakalah, aided by a €2.5 million donation from the European Union, was completed in 2008 after the building was all but destroyed during the Second Intifada. It was used as an events venue until the hotel opened in 2017. The hotel's sole single room, on the 2nd floor, is one of its best.

Al Yasmeen Hotel   HOTEL $$
(☑ 09-233-3555; www.alyasmeen.com; s/d/tr US$60/75/90; @ 🖥) Al Yasmeen's location in the heart of the Old City makes it a perennially popular choice with both local and international tourists visiting Nablus. Staff are polite and helpful, and although many of the rooms are in dire need of refurbishment (ask to see a few), they are clean, quiet and affordable.

🍴 Eating

In addition to confectioners selling Turkish delight, halva (squares of fruit and nuts covered with a sweet sesame paste) and syrupy pastries, Nablus is full of cafes for sipping and puffing. An essential part of any trip to Nablus is trying *kunafeh*, a Palestinian dessert famous throughout the Middle East.

★ Al Aqsa   ARABIC $
(Old City; kunafeh 6NIS; ⊙ 1-7.30pm Sat-Thu) This tiny eatery next door to the Al Kebir Mosque in the Casbah is unanimously considered to produce the finest *kunafeh* in the Palestinian Territories. Every day the warm, elastic cheese and syrup-soaked wheat shreds (it works, trust us) is divvied up from huge circular trays and dispensed to a throng of hungry customers. Do as the locals do and eat standing in the street outside.

Al Aqqad   ARABIC $
(Hitten St, mains 10-30NIS; ⊙ 8am late Sat-Thu) This is a classic sawdust-on-the-floor Nablusi eatery just a short walk from the main gate into the Old City. Staff speak little English but will happily serve you a delicious shawarma pita packed with chicken or lamb, pickles and fiery chilli.

Zeit ou Zaatar   ARABIC $$
(mains 35-70NIS; ⊙ noon-10pm) Situated in the lobby of the Al Yasmeen Hotel, Zeit ou Zaatar is worth noting because of its excellent range of both Palestinian and Levantine dishes, including *mansaf* (lamb cooked in yoghurt over rice). The restaurant is one of only a handful open on a Friday. Be warned: portions are enormous.

❶ Information

Good Samaritan Center (⊙ 9am-4pm Sun-Fri) An excellent place for information about Mt Gerizim.

❶ Getting There & Away

There is no direct bus service to Nablus from Jerusalem. The best way to reach the city is from **Ramallah**, where buses leave from the central bus station throughout the day. A taxi from Qalandia checkpoint will cost around 100NIS. There is a **shared taxi stand** to the north of Martyrs Sq, where you can take service taxis to Ramallah and Jenin.

To get to the Samaritans, take a taxi from downtown. It should cost 50NIS to 70NIS, including waiting time, but you'll have to negotiate.

Jenin جنين גׄנׄין

✈ 04 / POP 40,000

Jenin may lack the jaw-dropping historical sites of Nablus and Bethlehem, the nightlife of Ramallah or the religious significance (and tension) of Hebron and Jerusalem, but for those who make it this far north the city possesses a raffish, ramshackle sort of charm.

Jenin struggled to recover from the violence of the Second Intifada and today it still feels like a city down on its luck. The Jenin Cinema reopened in 2010 with German funding but struggled to make ends meet and was recently demolished, bringing an end to a project that had once heralded the city's rebirth.

But whether you are getting lost in the alleys of its packed souq for an hour, checking out the world-famous Freedom Theatre or spending a night or two staying with olive-oil farmers in nearby villages, Jenin feels very much off the traditional tourist trail.

◉ Sights

Cross the street from **Masjid Jenin Al Kabir** and enter a dense network of alleys that form the **Old City**, today largely occupied by furniture makers, barbers and machinists. Two blocks south of the mosque is King Talal St, which leads to Jerusalem Sq, the main bus station and the Cinema Guesthouse. It's fun to wander into the souq, north of King Talal St, which is absolutely bursting with activity.

The Christian village of Burqi'in – home to the fourth oldest church in the world – is a 20-minute drive outside of town. Service taxis leave from the station close to Cinema Guesthouse.

★ **Freedom Theatre**　　　　　THEATRE
(✆ 04-250-3345; www.thefreedomtheatre.org; ⏰ 9am-5pm) FREE Set in Jenin's refugee camp, the Freedom Theatre has persevered in the face of unimaginable odds, including the assassination of its founder, Juliano Mar Khamis, by masked gunmen in 2011. Palestinian filmmakers, actors and directors who worked in the theatre since it was established have also had to put up with significant Israeli restrictions on movement. Despite this, the theatre holds regular performances and visitors are always warmly received. Drop them an email to let them know you are coming.

As well as performances, which are publicised on the website, the theatre holds photography exhibitions as well as filmmaking workshops. Plans are afoot to launch a theatre school for Palestinian children in 2018. They are often looking for volunteers.

The Freedom Theatre, Jenin's main 'sight' since the demolition of the Jenin Cinema, is a 25-minute walk south of Jerusalem Sq.

Greek Orthodox
Church of St George　　　　　CHURCH
(⏰ 8am-6pm, closed 1-3pm Sun) FREE On the periphery of Burqi'in, the Greek Orthodox Church of St George is built on the site where Jesus is said to have healed 10 lepers. Believed to be one of the world's oldest surviving churches (dating to the 4th or 5th century CE), it is built around the cave where the lepers were living when Jesus passed through the village.

Service taxis (3NIS) go here from a station about 300m west of the Masjid Jenin, close to Cinema Guesthouse.

In the courtyard are several shafts that lead to a cave beneath the church where persecuted Christians would hide in Roman times. Ask staff to unlock the hatch and let you descend the ladder and have a nose around.

Canaan Fair Trade　　　　　FACTORY
(✆ 04-243-1991; www.canaanfairtrade.com; ⏰ 8am-5pm Sun-Thu) ✐ Located around 2km beyond Buqi'in, this olive-oil factory practises fair-trade policy with its farmers. A tour of the factory includes a tasting, and if you want to get to know the olive farmers, they can set you up with a homestay. A good time to visit is the first Friday of November, when the factory holds its annual harvest festival. It is best to call or email to let them know you are coming, especially for homestays.

🛌 Sleeping & Eating

★ Cinema Guesthouse   GUESTHOUSE $

(📞 059 931-7968; www.cinemajenin.org; 1 Azzaytoon St; dm/s/d 75/125/250NIS; 🌐🛜) A quiet spot in the heart of chaotic Jenin, this is a great place to meet other travellers (or NGO workers, journalists, activists and the like) and unwind for a day or two. It has three spacious dorm rooms, a couple of tiny private rooms and a nice kitchen for cooking communal meals. Breakfast is an extra 10NIS. The English-speaking manager is a font of information on the area. It's opposite the central bus station.

Aawtar   INTERNATIONAL, MIDDLE EASTERN $

(Cinema Circle; mains 20-60NIS; ⊙ 8am-midnight) Head up to Aawtar's spacious roof garden for a choice of Arabic and Western dishes under the stars. Even on cool evenings, the terrace is packed with groups drinking, eating and chatting over shisha. Downstairs, the restaurant has bay windows overlooking the street and serves Arab staples as well as pizza, burgers and enormous salads.

ℹ Information

Don't be put off by the rather ramshackle tower block that houses the **Jenin Tourism Office** (⊙ 10am-2pm Sat-Thu), opened in 2013 with the aid of funding from the Spanish government. The centre has a number of interesting rooms, which include a timeline of Jenin's history from 7000 BCE to 2002, touch-screen photography exhibitions and examples of handicrafts. English-speaking staff give useful advice on what to do in Jenin and the surrounding area.

ℹ Getting There & Away

There are frequent buses between Nablus and Jenin (15NIS) and between Jenin and the northern checkpoint of Jalameh (4NIS to 5NIS) for travellers heading to Afula, Haifa or Nazareth.

Note that unlike other West Bank checkpoints, which operate 24 hours, Jalameh is open only from 8am to 7pm. Expect long delays and heavy security when leaving the West Bank in your own car, especially on weekends.

The Gaza Strip

قطاع غزة

רצועת עזה

Gaza in Numbers

→ Total population: 1.81 million

→ Estimated refugees in Gaza: 1.1 million

→ Total area: 360 sq km

→ Average age: 18 years

→ Unemployment: 45%

Gaza Throughout History

→ 1516–1917: Ottoman Empire

→ 1917–48: British Mandate

→ 1948–67: Egyptian occupation

→ 1967–2005: Israeli occupation

→ 2006–present: Hamas control

Introduction

Gaza has been off limits to travellers since 2007, when Islamist party Hamas seized control of the strip and Israel responded by sealing its 1.8 million people off by land, air and sea. Even if it were possible for tourists to enter Gaza, it would not be advisable: Hamas fought three wars with Israel between 2006 and 2014, and the strip remains an unstable and dangerous place.

Gaza is one of the most densely populated places in the world – and one of the poorest, where hundreds of thousands of people live either in ramshackle refugee camps or in bombed-out buildings. Sealed off in their slither of land, surrounded by heavily fortified Israeli walls on three sides and a closed border with Egypt in the south, ordinary Gazans can only wait and hope that their leaders, their enemies and their international allies can finally find a way to end the stalemate.

Further Reading

→ *Gaza, a History,* by Jean Piere-Filiu (2014)

→ *Footnotes in Gaza: a Graphic Novel,* by Joe Sacco (2010)

→ *Gaza Writes Back: Short Stories from Young Writers in Gaza,* edited by Rafeet Alareer (2014)

→ *The Book of Gaza: a City in Short Fiction (Reading the City),* edited by Atef Abu Saif (2014)

History

Commerce & Conquerers

Settlement in Gaza is thought to date back to the Bronze Age, when it was used by the ancient Egyptians as a centre of trade. As far back into antiquity as 1500 BCE, an inscription on the Temple of Amun at Karnak in Egypt noted that Gaza was 'flourishing'.

By the time Alexander the Great arrived, in 332 BCE, the land had already passed through the hands of the Philistines, the Israelites (under King David and King Solomon), the Assyrians and the Persians. In 63 BCE, Gaza became part of the Roman province of Judea (later named Syria Palaestina) and was governed by a diverse 500-man senate. In the late 4th century, the Bishop Porphyrius forced Gazans to convert to Christianity and burned down the pagan Temple of Marna to replace it with a church.

Islam arrived in 635 CE, turning churches into mosques, a process that was briefly reversed in 1100 by the Crusaders, who built a cathedral that now forms part of the Great Mosque. During the 14th century, Mamluk rule came to Gaza, but the population dwindled because of a deadly plague in the 1340s. In 1516 Ottoman Empire rule began, lasting until the British arrived in 1917.

Withdrawal & War

During WWI, the British air force under General Edmund Allenby pounded Gaza while taking Palestine from the Turks, reducing much of the city to rubble. In 1927, a huge earthquake finished off much of what was left standing after the war.

Gaza was under British Mandate administration until 1948 when, with the creation of the State of Israel, Palestinian refugees flooded into the area, swelling its population from 35,000 to 170,000 in a matter of months. Egypt immediately responded to the declaration of Israel's independence in 1948 by occupying Gaza. During the occupation, housing projects were expanded, but after President Nasser closed the Straits of Tiran in 1967, the Six Day War began and Israel took control of Gaza.

Israeli settlers arrived in the 1970s, and growing tensions ignited Palestinian activism and riots. The radical Islamic organisation Hamas was formed in 1987, and the First Intifada began. A brief period of calm followed the Oslo Peace Accords, and win 1994 the Palestinian Authority (PA) assumed administrative control of parts of Gaza. But talks to transfer permanent control to the PA failed, and a Second Intifada began in September 2000, causing a series of Hamas suicide bombings and Israeli Air Force strikes.

THE GAZA STRIP HISTORY

DANGERS & ANNOYANCES

Gaza is inaccessible to all but a tiny minority of journalists and aid workers. Governments of most countries advise against all travel to the strip.

Both Israel and Hamas – or, often, more extreme elements in Gaza – routinely break ceasefire agreements, the former with its controversial targeted assassinations of senior militants and the latter through rocket attacks, which often provoke Israeli air strikes.

Foreign journalists and aid workers have been killed in recent years while working in Gaza, including an Italian activist who was kidnapped and murdered by an Islamist group in 2011 and an Associated Press cameraman who was killed by unexploded Israeli ordinance while reporting on the aftermath of the 2014 war.

The Israeli authorities have made it clear that they will prevent any vessels from breaching the naval blockade, so participating in any sort of protest flotilla is not advised. In 2010, an Israeli commando raid on a Turkish protest ship aiming to land in Gaza left nine dead, with a 10th activist dying in hospital four years later after a protracted coma.

International journalists and aid workers who want to enter Gaza not only need to gain permission from Israel but also from Hamas, who control the entry and exit of reporters on the other side of the formidable Erez crossing. On the occasions when the border at Rafah from Egypt is open, this crossing is a long, complicated and often dangerous process, not least because of the ongoing instability in North Sinai.

GAZA IN PEACETIME

Gaza does not feel like the rest of the Palestinian Territories – the traffic-snarled streets and general aura of chaos are more reminiscent of Cairo than Ramallah – but even in peacetime the strip is an intensely political place. It is not unusual to see armed militants at pro-Hamas rallies, while the first rocket Hamas fired at Tel Aviv in 2012 is memorialised in a monument on one of Gaza City's main thoroughfares. Many homes are riddled with shrapnel and bullet holes, and posters of 'martyrs' killed in the fighting with Israel are ubiquitous.

Gaza has an incredibly young population: more than 43% are under 14, and the whole population has a median age of 18 (compared to 40 in most European nations). While much attention is paid to their attendance at the infamous 'Hamas summer camps' (where children barely out of nappies pose with machine guns and go through military drills), most young Gazans dream of being entrepreneurs, business people and journalists rather than militants.

The strip is football-mad, home to some 30 domestic clubs and dozens of beachfront shisha bars that show European games late into the night. Like many other Arab countries, and Israel, most Gazans are either die-hard fans of Real Madrid or Barcelona, and when the two clubs meet the atmosphere is electric.

Gaza's tragedy is that life needn't be as bad as it is. Literacy levels in the strip are upwards of 97% and its seas hold untapped natural gas reserves worth up to US$7 billion. Gaza's historic sites go back three millennia, and it is home to one of the most beautiful coastlines in the Mediterranean.

Even in its current state, it is at the beach where Gaza really comes to life in peacetime. In the evenings, mothers clad in long black robes bathe toddlers in the shallows, families huddle in tents and the local kids scream and play in the booming surf.

At these moments, Gazans can get a glimpse of what life was like before the wars, the hatred and the violence, and what, *insh'allah* (God willing), it will one day be again.

Under international pressure and in a bid to improve Israel's home security, Prime Minister Ariel Sharon ordered Israel's disengagement from Gaza and removed all of the strip's 21 Israeli settlements, with their 8000 inhabitants, in August 2005. Afterwards, a power struggle within Palestinian ranks began, culminating in the victory of Hamas in the January 2006 PA elections and the subsequent withdrawal of much international aid.

In June 2006, Israel Defence Forces soldier Gilad Shalit was kidnapped at the Gaza–Israel border. Several days afterwards, Israel launched 'Operation Summer Rains', a series of attacks that killed some 280 Palestinian militants and more than 100 Palestinian civilians. In 2007 violent clashes broke out within Palestinian ranks as Hamas took control from Fatah.

Meanwhile, from 2005 to 2008, thousands of Kassam and Grad rockets and mortars were fired on southern Israel from within Gaza, culminating in 87 rockets in just 24 hours on 24 December 2008. In response,

Israeli forces launched 'Operation Cast Lead' by air and then by land. The Gaza War resulted in the deaths of more than 1400 Palestinians, with thousands made homeless. Israel lost 10 soldiers and three civilians. Many NGOs declared a humanitarian crisis, and Israel declared a ceasefire after three weeks of fighting.

Gaza under Hamas

In 2011, kidnapped soldier Shalit was handed over as part of a prisoner swap that saw 1027 Palestinians released from Israeli jails. The deal was a major coup for Hamas, increasingly unpopular in Gaza because of ongoing economic malaise.

The Islamist party got a further boost in June 2012 with the election of Muslim Brotherhood leader Mohamed Morsi in Egypt. As the flow of goods through tunnels that linked the strip with Sinai surged, Gaza experienced a rare period of economic growth.

But the boom, like Morsi's government, was to be short-lived.

On 10 November 2012, a mortar fired from Gaza hit an Israeli military jeep, wounding four soldiers, and a retaliatory Israeli air strike killed four Palestinian teenagers while they played football. The killings provoked dozens of rockets which, in turn, led to Israel's assassination of Hamas military commander Ahmed Jabari. By the time Egypt was able to negotiate a ceasefire on 21 November, more than 100 Gazans had been killed and almost 1000 wounded.

Rebuilding Gaza's shattered infrastructure in the wake of the war was easier than in 2009 because of Hamas' Egyptian allies, as well as significant financial aid from Qatar. But the coup that overthrew Morsi and installed the Egyptian military in Cairo in July 2013 was a hammer blow for Hamas, as the tunnels were gradually dismantled and the Rafah border once again slammed shut. As the year rumbled on, Hamas' popularity in Gaza once again began to wane.

In early 2014, with both Hamas and Fatah in the West Bank facing rising anger for their failure to improve the lives of Palestinians in either territory, the two parties signed a unity deal ending their seven-year split. Although welcomed internationally, the deal was greeted with horror by Israeli Prime Minister Benjamin Netanyahu, who accused Mahmoud Abbas, president of the Palestinian Authority, of choosing Hamas over peace with Israel.

At the end of April, peace negotiations between Israel and the PA – doomed for some time – finally broke down. By the time war broke out between Israel and Hamas in June 2014, relations between Israelis and Palestinians were at their lowest since the Second Intifada (2001–05). Over the next 50 days, 73 Israelis and more than 2100 Palestinians would be killed and tens of thousands made homeless, while the limited infrastructure that Gaza had been able to develop was severely damaged by Israeli air strikes.

In 2017, Hamas elected hardliner Yahya Sinwar to replace Ismail Haniyeh, who had served as prime minister in Gaza since the takeover in 2007. Sinwar, who rejects negotiations with the Israelis (and even opposed his own release in the 2011 prisoner swap), was formerly head of Hamas' military wing, Al Qassam Brigades, raising fears of a new conflict with Israel.

At the same time, Hamas – itself designated a terrorist association by the US and European nations – was increasingly being challenged by more radical groups in Gaza that drew inspiration from Isis, which has a prominent affiliate in Sinai to the south.

Gaza Today

Life in Gaza over the past decade has gone from bad to worse to worse still. After the 2014 war with Israel, the United Nations estimated that 100,000 more Gazans were left homeless as Israeli bombs levelled entire neighbourhoods in Beit Lahia and Shejaiya, in Gaza City.

The 2014 war was a watershed for Gaza and Israel. Even veteran Gaza-watchers were shocked at the range and ferocity of the rockets that Hamas and other Palestinian militants had stockpiled and fired at Israeli cities as far north as Netanya and Jerusalem.

By the time the conflict was over, 2100 Palestinians and 73 Israelis were dead. During peace talks in Cairo, Hamas demanded an

RECONSTRUCTION EFFORTS

At a summit in Cairo in October 2014, international donors promised US$5.4 billion for rebuilding Gaza following the war, with Qatar alone promising US$1 billion and the US offering US$212 million. The EU put forward US$568 million. The United Nations Relief and Work Agency had called for donations of US$1.6 billion – the biggest sum it had ever sought to raise, claiming that even before the war Gaza had a shortage of 75,000 homes, as well as deficient water, sewage and power infrastructure.

Of course, the commitment of funds was only the beginning of a long and uncertain process of reconstruction. Israel has restricted the importation of construction materials to Gaza since Hamas took power, arguing that they are used to construct tunnels and weapons depots. Reconstruction will also rely on renewed cooperation between Hamas and Fatah, which controls the Palestinian Authority. Improved relations with Egypt will also be crucial to allow import of materials through the Egypt–Gaza border. As of 2017, this remained elusive.

end to the blockade and permission to build a port and airport, but three years later, it had only managed to secure a meagre extension of the fishing zone off Gaza's coast – quite a price, many Palestinians argued, for the number of dead.

In the wake of the war, Israel accused Hamas of using concrete brought in to rebuild infrastructure to instead build tunnels under the border, with the intention of attacking Israeli towns and cities. Hamas meanwhile faced an increasingly vocal – and violent – jihadist movement in the strip.

Estranged from Fatah and the Palestinian Authority, internationally isolated and losing support from moderates and radicals alike, Hamas – and the 1.8 million Gazans it governs – looks increasingly forced into a corner since the 2014 war. Given that, the fear is that another conflict with Israel is not just likely – but inevitable.

The Dead Sea
البحر الميت

ים המלח

Best Places to Stay

➜ Shkedi's Camplodge (p314)

➜ Ein Gedi Kibbutz Hotel (p303)

➜ Hod HaMidbar (p311)

Best Family Hikes

➜ Wadi David (p302)

➜ Wadi Arugot (p302)

➜ Wadi Bokek (p311)

Why Go?

The lowest place on the face of the earth, the Dead Sea brings together breathtaking natural beauty, compelling ancient history and modern mineral spas that soothe and pamper every fibre of your body. The jagged bluffs of the Judean Desert, cleft by dry canyons that turn into raging tan torrents after a cloudburst, rise from the cobalt-blue waters of the Dead Sea, heavy with salt and oily with minerals. In oases such as Ein Gedi, year-round springs nourish vegetation so lush it's often been compared to the Garden of Eden. Atop the bluffs lies the arid moonscape of the Judean Desert; in the valley, human beings have been hard at work for millennia, building Masada and Qumran (where the Dead Sea Scrolls were found) in ancient times and, more recently creating kibbutzim, luxury hotels, hiking trails, bike paths and even a world-famous botanic garden.

When to Go
Ein Gedi

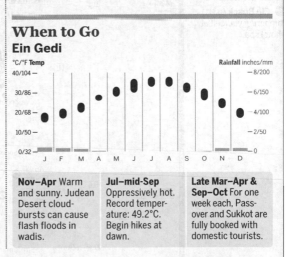

Nov–Apr Warm and sunny. Judean Desert cloudbursts can cause flash floods in wadis.

Jul–mid-Sep Oppressively hot. Record temperature: 49.2°C. Begin hikes at dawn.

Late Mar–Apr & Sep–Oct For one week each, Passover and Sukkot are fully booked with domestic tourists.

The Dead Sea Highlights

1 Ein Bokek Beach (p311) Floating in the briny, soothing waters of the Dead Sea.

2 Snake Path (p309) Ascending Masada's trail before dawn and watching sunrise from the top.

3 Ein Gedi Nature Reserve (p301) Taking a refreshing dip in waterfall-fed plunge pools.

4 Masada Museum (p308) Imagining life among the defenders of Roman-besieged Masada.

5 Neot HaKikar (p313) Cycling one of the wide wadis.

6 Qumran National Park (p306) Envisioning the daily routine of the ancient Essenes, who wrote and hid the Dead Sea Scrolls.

7 Shkedi's Camplodge (p314) Shooting the breeze around the campfire.

8 Ein Bokek (p311) Pampering yourself at a hotel spa.

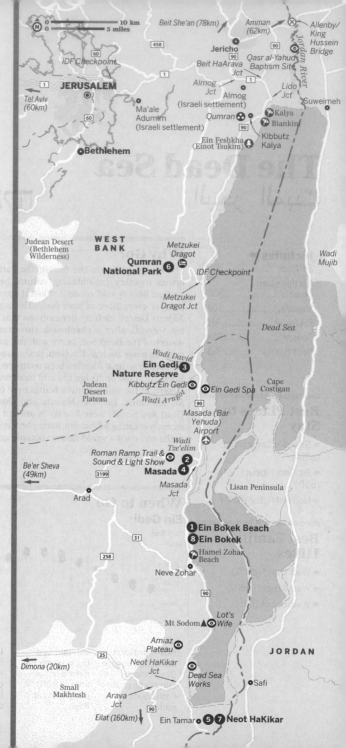

History

Awareness of the Dead Sea's unique qualities goes back to at least the 4th century BCE; luminaries such as Aristotle, Pliny and Galen all made mention of the sea's physical properties. The Nabataeans collected bitumen from the surface of the water and sold it to the Egyptians, who used it for embalming.

For most of history, though, the Dead Sea – today shared by Israel, the West Bank and Jordan – has been regarded as unhealthy and hence shunned; popular lore had it that no bird could fly over its waters without dropping from the sky. This made the area a favoured retreat of religious ascetics and political fugitives: the future King David, King Herod, Jesus and John the Baptist are all said to have taken refuge along its shoreline or in nearby mountains and caves.

Because it was seen as the 'Sea of the Devil', the area remained uncharted until it was finally explored in 1848 by a team from, of all places, the United States Navy. The Palestine Potash Company (now the Dead Sea Works) was established in 1930 by Moshe Novomeysky, a Siberian-born engineer and Zionist pioneer. The 1948 war left Israel with a quarter of the Dead Sea's shoreline and Jordan with the rest. Israel captured the lake's northwestern shore in 1967.

Geography

The Dead Sea (Yam HaMelach, meaning the Salt Sea, in Hebrew; Al Bahr Al Mayit, meaning the Dead Sea, in Arabic), whose surface is now about 431m below sea level, is the lowest point on the face of the earth. Connected to the Mediterranean Sea via the Jezreel Valley until about two million years ago, it forms part of the 6000km-long Great Rift Valley (Syrian-African Rift), which stretches from Lebanon's Bekaa Valley south to Mozambique and includes the Sea of Galilee and the Red Sea.

About 65km long and 18km across at its widest point, the Dead Sea is fed mainly by the Jordan River, supplemented by springs, seasonal wadis and flash floods. With no outlet, the in-flow has historically been balanced, more or less, by evaporation of about 1 cubic km a year. Water arrives with normal concentrations of minerals (mainly magnesium, sodium, calcium and potassium chlorides) – but, over the millennia, evaporation has removed vast quantities of water while leaving behind everything else, causing mineral concentrations in the lake to rise dramatically. The Dead Sea's salt concentration is about 34%, making it 10 times more saline than the ocean.

Because more than 90% of the water from the Jordan River basin is now diverted to agriculture and other uses in Lebanon, Syria, Israel, the West Bank and Jordan, the Dead Sea is drying up. Every year the water level drops by 1m to 1.2m, and the shore, depending on its gradient, recedes by up to 5m. Since the 1930s, the sea's surface area has shrunk by more than one-third.

The Med-Dead Project, a plan to refill the Dead Sea by reconnecting it with the Mediterranean, generating electricity by taking advantage of the 400m drop, was proposed in the 1980s but was eventually shelved because of the high cost. In 2013 an agreement was signed by Israel, Jordan and the Palestinian Authority to build a 180km-long 'Red-Dead Canal' through Jordan that would pump brine left over from a seawater desalination plant in Aqaba into the Dead Sea. Many environmentalists – including Friends of the Earth Middle East (EcoPeace Middle East; www.ecopeaceme.org) – are opposed to the plan, but construction is supposed to begin in 2018.

The Dead Sea's shores are dotted with springs and oases that provide water for 90 species of birds, 25 species of reptiles and amphibians, and 24 species of mammals, as well as more than 400 species of plants, some of them at the extreme northern or southern edge of their natural distribution.

These days the Dead Sea is in fact two separate lakes connected by an artificial channel. The larger northern basin is a proper, if shrinking, lake whose deepest point is about 300m below the surface. The shallow southern section (fronting Ein Bokek) – actually an expanse of artificial evaporation pools – would be completely dry if not for the water pumped in by the Dead Sea Works. Whereas the level of the northern lake is dropping, that of the southern section is actually rising due to the accumulation of salt deposits on the bottom of the evaporation pools. The two lakes are separated by a peninsula that juts from the Dead Sea's eastern shore and is known as Al Lisaan in Arabic and HaLashon in Hebrew (both names mean 'the Tongue').

Eating

Most people who stay at the Dead Sea eat breakfast and dinner at their hotels or hostels. As a result, the area has only a handful of restaurants – most are at Ein Bokek, plus there's one at Kibbutz Ein Gedi and another at Qumran National Park. Masada has a food court. Self-caterers can find food shops at Kibbutz Ein Gedi and Neot HaKikar.

❶ Getting There & Away

BUS

It's possible, though a bit fiddly, to explore the Dead Sea by public bus. To avoid hanging around wilting under the sun, plan your itinerary in advance.

Egged buses (www.egged.co.il) link sites along Rte 90 (including, from north to south, Qumran, Ein Feshkha Nature Reserve, Ein Gedi Nature Reserve, Kibbutz Ein Gedi, Ein Gedi Spa, Masada, Ein Bokek and Hamei Zohar) with the following destinations:

Be'er Sheva Egged bus 384 (27NIS, 1½ hours to Ein Bokek, five per day Sunday to Thursday, three on Friday)

Eilat Egged bus 444 (42.50NIS, 2¾ hours to Ein Bokek, eight per day Sunday to Thursday, three on Friday, three Saturday afternoon and evening)

Jerusalem Egged buses 444 and 486 (34NIS, one hour to Ein Gedi, about hourly 6.30am to 4.45pm Sunday to Thursday, until 2pm Friday, at least one Saturday night)

Tel Aviv Egged bus 421 (48.40NIS, 2½ hours to Ein Bokek, three daily Sunday to Thursday, one on Friday). In Tel Aviv departs from the Central (Arlozoroff/Savidor) train station; goes via Hwy 6.

All of these lines can be used for local travel north and south along Rte 90, eg from Masada to Ein Bokek or the Ein Gedi Nature Reserve.

Abraham Hostels (https://abrahamtours.com) offers one-day excursions to the Dead Sea for 150NIS to 280NIS from Jerusalem and Tel Aviv.

CAR

The Dead Sea's western coast is served by Rte 90. Israel's longest highway, it continues north to the Lebanese border and south to the Egyptian frontier at Taba. There's an army roadblock about 14km north of Ein Gedi.

The Dead Sea is served by three east–west highways:

Rte 1 Thanks to this modern, divided highway (and a stretch of Rte 90), Ein Gedi is only 75km from Jerusalem. Rte 1 passes through the West Bank but seldom has security issues. For Jerusalem-bound traffic, there's an army roadblock between the large Israeli settlement of Ma'ale Adumim and Jerusalem.

Rte 31 Connects Arad with Rte 90 at a point a few kilometres south of Ein Bokek. To get to the western, Roman ramp, side of Masada, take Rte 3199 from Arad.

Rte 25 Passes through Be'er Sheva and Dimona on its way to the Dead Sea's southern tip, near Neot HaKikar.

From Tel Aviv, the fastest way to drive to Ein Bokek is to take Hwy 6, but to get to Ein Gedi it's generally slightly quicker to go via Jerusalem.

Locals recommend that you arrive at the Dead Sea area with a full tank as the only petrol stations are (from north to south) at Lido junction (40km north of Ein Gedi near Jericho), Neve Zohar Junction (8km south of Ein Bokek) and Arava junction (33km south of Ein Bokek).

Most hikes are circuits so you end up where you began. For one-way hikes, you can arrange (for a fee) to be dropped off and picked up, eg by the kind folks at the B&Bs in Neot HaKikar.

Only one car-rental company (Hertz) has an office at the Dead Sea (at Ein Bokek).

Ein Gedi   עין גדי   عين جدي

Nestled in two dramatic canyons that plunge from the arid moonscape of the Judean Desert to the shores of the Dead Sea, Ein Gedi Nature Reserve is one of Israel's most magical desert oases. Its freshwater pools, cool streams, Eden-like waterfalls and luxuriant vegetation, fed by four year-round springs, are a haven for wildlife such as the majestic Nubian ibex (*ya'el* in Hebrew) and the boulder-dwelling hyrax (dassie or rock rabbit; *shafan sela* in Hebrew), both of which you're very likely to encounter (the ibex is easiest to spot during the first and last hours that the reserve is open). Ein Gedi is the northernmost natural habitat of a number of plants that are more usually found on the savannahs of East Africa, thousands of kilometres south along the Great Rift Valley.

Kibbutz Ein Gedi is on a low hill 3km south of Ein Gedi Nature Reserve.

History

Ein Gedi (literally 'Spring of the Kid', as in 'young goat') was first settled during the Chalcolithic Age (5000 years ago), when people just out of the Stone Age built a temple here. In the Bible, David fled to Ein Gedi to escape the wrath of Saul (I Samuel 23:29), and the oasis has a cameo role in the love poetry of the Song of Songs (1:14): 'My beloved is to me as a cluster of henna blossoms in the vineyards of Ein Gedi'. More recently, the erotic waterfall scene in one of Brooke Shields' worst movies, *Sahara* (1983), was filmed at Ein Gedi.

Sights & Activities

The plateau above Ein Gedi Nature Reserve – in fact, the eastern edge of the Judean Desert – is about 200m above sea level, 630m above the Dead Sea. Five trails head from the Ein Gedi area up to the plateau and its spectacular panoramas, taking you well away from the madding crowds.

The reserve's most difficult hike (six to eight hours) links Wadi Arugot with Wadi David via the Desert Plateau, **Ein Gedi Lookout** (Mitzpeh Ein Gedi) and Ein Gedi Spring. Marked by black blazes, it should only be attempted by very experienced hikers.

From north to south, the five challenging trails that lead up to the plateau are the **Yishay Ascent** (Ma'aleh Yishai), which climbs Mt Yishai (begins at the Ein Gedi Field School); the **Ein Gedi Ascent** (from Ein Gedi Spring, on the hillside between Wadi David and Wadi Arugot); **Bnei HaMoshavim Ascent** (an especially difficult route that begins at the upper section of Wadi Arugot); **Ha'Isiyyim Ascent** (from near the top of Wadi Arugot); and the **Tzruya (Zeruya) Ascent** (from near Kibbutz Ein Gedi).

A 1:50,000-scale SPNI trail map, sold at the entrance to Wadi Arugot, is a must for all these routes, which are closed in extreme heat and when there's a danger of flash floods. Park staff are happy to help with planning; before heading out, it's a good idea to let them know your route and phone number.

★ **Ein Gedi Nature Reserve**   NATURE RESERVE
(☑08-658-4285; www.parks.org.il; ⊙8am-4pm or 5pm) This reserve consists of two roughly parallel canyons, Wadi David and Wadi Arugot, each of which has its own entrance complex and ticket office. It is also home to an ancient synagogue.

When you buy your ticket you receive a colour-coded map brochure that has invaluable details on the area's trails (indicated using the same colours as the trail markings), how long each route takes, and the times by which you need to begin each circuit to finish by closing time.

Park rangers make sure that visitors do not enter the park before it opens or stick around after closing time (they can fine violators 365NIS). The reason: desert animals such as the wolf, jackal and fox need some people-less peace and quiet to search

THE DEAD SEA EIN GEDI

ℹ SAFE HIKING

A few tips on staying safe and healthy while hoofing it in the Dead Sea's unique geography and climate:

➡ Don't hike without a 1:50,000-scale SPNI topographical trail map (85NIS; not necessary at Ein Gedi unless you climb up to the plateau). The maps to have – available only in Hebrew – are No 11 *(Ein Gedi v'Daroma)* for Ein Gedi and places south of there; and No 8 *(Tzfon Midbar Yehuda v'Yam HaMelach)* for Ein Gedi and points north. Both can be purchased at the Ein Gedi Field School and the Wadi Arugot entrance to Ein Gedi Nature Reserve (p301).

➡ Bring along *lots* of water – at least 5L per person per day.

➡ To beat the heat of summer, hit the trail shortly after dawn (or as early as the nature reserve opens). On exceptionally hot days, the only safe trails are those along Wadi David.

➡ Flash floods can turn the dry canyons above the Dead Sea into raging torrents. In late autumn, winter and spring, keep an eye on weather reports and stay well away from narrow channels if there's any chance of a cloudburst up in the Judean Desert.

➡ In winter, temperatures can drop precipitously at night so bring along an insulated jacket to avoid hypothermia in case you get stuck.

➡ Keep out of areas where signs warn of sinkholes *(bol'anim)*, also called 'open pits'. These can open under your feet with no warning and swallow you alive – yes, this has happened to people!

➡ Stay out of the area's caves, such as those on Mt Sodom. All of them, including the famous Flour Cave, are closed to the public because various geological factors, including high salt content, make them susceptible to sudden collapse.

for food and drink (the reserve has the only year-round water sources in the entire area).

The last time a critically endangered Arabian leopard *(Panthera pardus nimr)* was spotted in the Ein Gedi area – carrying off Kibbutz Ein Gedi house pets for dinner – was in 2006. The species is now presumed to be extinct here.

Eating, smoking and pets are not allowed in the reserve.

Wadi David   HIKING
(Nahal David; Ein Gedi Nature Reserve; adult/child incl ancient synagogue 28/14NIS; ☺8am-4pm or 5pm, last entry 1hr before closing) Ein Gedi Nature Reserve's most accessible – and popular – pools and waterfalls are situated along **Lower Wadi David** (Nahal David Tachton), ie the area downstream from **David's Waterfall** (Mapal David; one hour return). The entrance pavilion has bathrooms where you can change into your bathing suit, free lockers (ask staff for a key) and free cooled drinking water.

The refreshments counter and adjacent shop sell sandwiches, ice cream, snacks and drinks, including espresso. If you don't have an empty bottle for water, ask staff for one that's on the way to being recycled.

To get to **Upper Wadi David** (Nahal David Elyon), which is significantly less

FESTIVALS

The Dead Sea's spectacular desert scenery and predictably dry weather make it an excellent venue for outdoor events.

Tamar Festival (☏03-723-0883; www. tamarfestival.com; ☺during Sukkot) Four-day festival of Israeli music, in late September or October, held atop and around Masada, at Kibbutz Ein Gedi and at Neot HaKikar.

Veredis Desert Challenge Festival (www.desertchallenge.co.il; ☺mid-Dec) Three days of mountain-bike races in the Mt Sodom area, including events that bring together Israelis and Palestinians.

Ein Gedi International Half Marathon (Ein Gedi Experience; www.eingedi -run.co.il; ☺late Jan) A half-marathon founded in 1983. Also has a 10km run and, for kids, a 2km route.

crowded, head up the trail that climbs the south wall of the canyon. A bit past tiny **Shulamit's Spring** (Ma'ayan Shulamit) is a T-junction: go right and you'll head down the slope to the section of Wadi David above David's Waterfall, including **Dodim Cave** (Lovers' Cave); hanging a left takes you to a **Chalcolithic Temple** (3000 BCE), the pools of **Ein Gedi Spring** (most of whose mineral water is diverted and bottled by Kibbutz Ein Gedi) and, near the base of Wadi Arugot, an archaeological site known as **Tel Goren** (7th to 8th century BCE).

Wadi David can get crowded, especially on Jewish holidays and on days when raucous coach loads of schoolkids are around. The first 400m of the trail, to the first waterfall, are fully accessible to wheelchairs.

Wadi Arugot   NATURE RESERVE
(Nahal Arugot; Ein Gedi Nature Reserve; adult/child incl ancient synagogue 28/14NIS; ☺8am-4pm or 5pm, last entry 2hr before closing) Generally less crowded but no less lovely than Wadi David, Wadi Arugot has a variety of streamside trails, rich in vegetation, that afford hikers an excellent introduction to the oasis' geography and ecosystems. Some routes are quite challenging.

Hikers must leave the upper reaches of Wadi Arugot (Nahal Arugot), ie the area above the Hidden Waterfall (HaMapal HaNistar), including the Upper Pools (HaBreichot HaElyonot), by 2pm (3pm during daylight savings time) in order to exit the reserve by closing time. The Wadi Arugot ticket office complex, a 20- to 30-minute walk (or a five-minute drive) from the Wadi David car park, has free lockers, a small refreshment counter with ice cream and cold drinks, and a shop that sells SPNI 1:50,000-scale trail maps.

Ancient Synagogue   ARCHAEOLOGICAL SITE
(Ein Gedi Nature Reserve; adult/child 14/7NIS, incl nature reserve 28/14NIS; ☺8am-4pm or 5pm) Situated about midway between the Wadi David and Wadi Arugot ticket offices, this 5th-century-CE synagogue sports a superb mosaic floor decorated with the 12 signs of the Zodiac and three Aramaic inscriptions, one of which calls down a curse on anyone who is quarrelsome, slanderous or larcenous. A model of the synagogue as it looked 1600 years ago was added in 2016.

Ein Gedi Botanical Garden   GARDENS
(☏08-659-4726; Kibbutz Ein Gedi; adult/child 20/15NIS; ☺9am or 9.30am-3.30pm or 4pm Sat-Thu, to 2pm Fri) These famous botanic gardens,

DANGER: SINKHOLES!

In 1990, the Geographical Survey of Israel counted fewer than 100 sinkholes around the shores of the Dead Sea's northern basin. Today, there are over 6000, with more than 500 opening up each year. Some are the size of a hot tub, while others are 30m deep and 50m across – together they are creating an environmental crisis.

The sinkholes are the result of the Dead Sea's ever-dropping water level. As the shoreline recedes, underground fresh water dissolves salt deposits located between 5m and 60m below ground. This creates cavities that rise to the surface a bit like like an air bubble in honey. Eventually, the loosely consolidated land above caves in.

Over the last few years, Ein Gedi Beach, Mineral Beach and a length of Hwy 90 near Ein Gedi have been closed after sections were swallowed up without warning. No one knows where the next gaping crater will suddenly appear, so the only access to the Dead Sea shoreline between the lake's northern tip (Kalya and Biankini Beaches in the West Bank) and Ein Bokek, is at Ein Gedi Spa – and even there, continued access is far from a sure thing.

For stunning aerial views of the sinkholes, check out videos on YouTube.

near the entrance to the kibbutz, are home to about a thousand species of indigenous and exotic plants, from near-mythological biblical species such as frankincense and myrrh to the highly poisonous Sodom apple, and from gargantuan baobab trees to tiny plants that can survive with minuscule quantities of water.

Ein Gedi Spa SPA
(☑08-620 1030; www.eingediseaofspa.co.il; Rte 90; adult without/with lunch 95/155NIS, child 5-12yr 56/110NIS; ☉9am-5pm Sat-Thu, 8am-4.30pm Fri) Situated 3km south of Kibbutz Ein Gedi, this spa – owned by the kibbutz – is a popular place to catch a float and coat yourself with invigorating natural black mud. The shoreline has receded 1.3km since the spa opened in 1984 so beach-goers take a little train (every 20 minutes) to the water's edge. Wheelchair accessible.

The spa has six sulphur pools and a freshwater pool, and offers a range of natural beauty and massage treatments. There's also a coffee shop and a restaurant. Lockers cost 18NIS, as does buying a towel.

🛏 Sleeping

Ein Gedi Youth Hostel HOSTEL $
(Beit Sarah; ☑02-594-5600; www.iyha.org.il; near Ein Gedi Nature Reserve; dm/s/d 132/321/410NIS, additional adult/child 120/94NIS; @�"") The sensational setting and simple but contemporary rooms, with three to five beds, make this 87-room hostel madly popular. Dinner is often available for 62NIS (71NIS on Friday). Offers discounts of 15% to 20% on various area attractions. Situated 200m up the slope from the Rte 90 turn-off to Ein Gedi Nature Reserve. Reserve well ahead.

Khan Ein Gedi HUT $
(Ein Gedi Camp Lodge; ☑Avi 052 606-3666, Ben 052 933-1019; www.facebook.com/eingedicamp lodge; Kibbutz Ein Gedi; dm in a hut 120NIS; ☉year-round; �"") Situated just outside the gate to Kibbutz Ein Gedi, this mellow, hillside operation has eight basic huts, each with five mattresses on the floor. Bathroom and kitchen facilities are shared. There's wi-fi in the chill-out area, whose wooden bar, open 24/7, sells pizzas.

SPNI Ein Gedi Field School HOSTEL $$
(☑08-658-4288, www.natureisrael.org/EinGedi; near Ein Gedi Nature Reserve; dm/s/d 132/329/379NIS, additional adult/child 7-14yr from 123/84NIS; �"") The 46 rooms, each with five or six beds, are not as swish as at the youth hostel, but this is an excellent launching point for hikes. Dinner (57NIS, on Friday 71NIS) is available most nights. Reception sells SPNI hiking maps. There's wi-fi at reception. Situated 800m up the hill from the Rte 90 turn-off to Ein Gedi Nature Reserve.

★ Ein Gedi Kibbutz Hotel HOTEL $$$
(☑08-659-4220; www.ein-gedi.co.il; Kibbutz Ein Gedi; d from US$200-245; @�"🏊") This delightful, low-rise campus, lushly planted with exotic trees and plants (including two immense baobab trees), offers a luxurious on-site spa and a deliciously cooling pool. There are four categories of very satisfying rooms (160 of them), some with space for two adults and two children. Deluxe rooms include free admission to Ein Gedi Spa. Kibbutz Ein Gedi was founded in the early 1950s; for years, the only access road was a dirt track to Arad.

1. Floating in the Dead Sea (p297)

With high levels of magnesium, iodine and bromine, the briny waters will calm your nerves and pamper your skin.

2. Ein Gedi Nature Reserve (p301)

One of Israel's most magical desert oases, with freshwater pools, Eden-like waterfalls and lush vegetation.

3. The Dead Sea (p297)

Stunning vistas abound at the lowest place on earth.

✗ Eating

This area has very few dining options, so arrive with picnic supplies or consider having dinner at your hotel or hostel. Lunch is available at Ein Gedi Spa (p303).

At the Ein Gedi Kibbutz Hotel (p303), the cafe (dairy; open daily) attracts a mix of tourists and kibbutzniks (kibbutz members). A copious, kosher meat buffet dinner costs 110NIS (140NIS Friday); nonguests are welcome if there's room (there usually is, except on Jewish holidays).

Kolbo Grocery SUPERMARKET $
(Kibbutz Ein Gedi; ⊙ 7.30am-8pm Sun-Thu, to 2pm Fri, 11am-2pm Sat) The only proper food shop in the area. Situated next to Kibbutz Ein Gedi's dining hall.

❶ Information

There's an ATM inside the Ein Gedi Kibbutz Hotel.

SPNI Ein Gedi Field School Information Office (☑ 08-658-4288; www.natureisrael. org/EinGedi; near Ein Gedi Nature Reserve; ⊙ 8.30am-4pm Sun-Thu) Free consultations by expert staff (when available) on area hikes, including family-friendly Wadi Mishmar and Wadi Tze'elim. Sells 1:50,000-scale SPNI topographical trail maps (87NIS). Situated 800m up the hill from the Rte 90 turn-off to the Ein Gedi Nature Reserve.

❶ Getting There & Away

Bus schedules are posted at both entrances to the Ein Gedi Nature Reserve (p301) and at the SPNI Ein Gedi Field School Information Office, the SPNI Ein Gedi Field School (p303) youth hostel (next to the lobby computers) and Ein Gedi Kibbutz Hotel (p303).

Northwestern Coast

Highlights along the Dead Sea's northwestern coast include the Qumran Caves, where the Dead Sea Scrolls were discovered, and some wild, unspoilt nature sites. Captured by Israel from Jordan in 1967, this almost uninhabited corner of the West Bank is just a short drive from Jericho.

◉ Sights

Qumran National Park ARCHAEOLOGICAL SITE
(☑ 02-994-2235; www.parks.org.il; Rte 90 near Kalya; adult/child 29/15NIS; ⊙ 8am-4pm or 5pm Sat-Thu, to 3pm or 4pm Fri, last entry 1hr before closing) World-famous for having hidden the **Dead Sea Scrolls** for almost 2000 years, Qumran was the site of a small Essene settlement around the time of Jesus – specifically, from the late 1st century BCE until 68 CE, when it was destroyed by the Romans. From an elevated wooden walkway, you can see the aqueduct, channels and cisterns that ensured the community's water supply.

Elsewhere are ritual baths (the Essenes were zealous about ritual purity); the refectory, in which communal meals were eaten; and the scriptorium, where some of the Dead Sea Scrolls may have been written. The ruins have undergone conservation but nothing has been added.

The small museum, which provides background on the people of ancient Qumran and their beliefs, has a seven-minute multimedia program (in 16 languages) and displays a few ancient items, including a sandal fragment. An audio guide is available in Hebrew and English. The site is wheelchair accessible and has a restaurant.

Qumran is a safe vantage point for watching wintertime flash floods.

Qumran is 35km east of Jerusalem and 35km north of Ein Gedi. All Jerusalem–Dead Sea buses pass here.

Ein Feshkha NATURE RESERVE
(Einot Tsukim; ☑ 02-994-2355; www.parks.org. il; Rte 90; ⊙ 8am-4pm or 5pm, to 7pm Jul & Aug, last entry 1hr before closing) Fed by crystal-clear springs, this lush oasis stretches for 6.5km along the base of the escarpment that forms the western edge of the Dead Sea valley. Shaded paths take you to several slightly brackish wading pools (open Friday and Saturday late March to November, daily July and August), including the lovely **Poplar Pool**, surrounded by salt-resistant vegetation, including tamarisks.

There's no access to the rapidly receding Dead Sea shoreline – some 2km from the water's edge a sign reads 'The sea was here in 1967'. However, you can see a **farm** from the Second Temple period where the Essenes of Qumran may have produced date wine and afarsimon oil, and raised sheep and goats.

The vast majority of the reserve – its 'biological core' – is closed to the public for reasons of conservation, but one section of the southern **Hidden Reserve** can be visited on a one-hour **guided tour** (in English at 11am and 1pm on Friday and Sunday from mid-September to June).

Ein Feshkha is 3km south of Qumran.

THE DEAD SEA SCROLLS

Few discoveries in the history of archaeology have elicited as much enduring world-wide fascination as the Dead Sea Scrolls, accidentally found at Qumran in 1947 inside earthenware jars by a Bedouin shepherd boy searching for a stray goat. Eventually about 950 different parchment and papyrus documents written during the Second Temple period and the earliest years of Christianity (200 BCE to 68 CE) were found in 11 caves. Most of the documents, which include the oldest known manuscripts of the Hebrew Bible, texts that didn't make it into the Bible and descriptions of life in Judea around the time of Jesus, are in Hebrew, some are in Aramaic and a few are in Greek. Many are in tiny fragments, making the process of reassembling and deciphering them long and arduous.

The scrolls are believed to have belonged to the Essenes, a separatist, ascetic Jewish sect – mentioned by Josephus Flavius – that moved to the desert to escape the decadence they believed was corrupting their fellow Jews.

The Israel Museum in Jerusalem, where some of the scrolls are on display, runs, with some help from Google, the Dead Sea Scrolls Digital Project (http://dss.collections.imj.org.il), which makes searchable, high-resolution digitised images of the scrolls available to the general public.

For some interesting facts on the scrolls, see www.centuryone.com/25dssfacts.html.

🛏 Sleeping

Metzukei Dragot   GUESTHOUSE $$
(☑ 052 247 4378, reservations 1-700-707-180; www.metzoke.co.il; d from 350NIS, dm in a huge tent excl breakfast US$27; ☺ reception 8am-8pm; 🛜) Perched on a cliff about 600m above the Dead Sea – the views are truly spectacular – this no-frills, hippyish holiday village hosts festivals, cultural events and New Agey conferences. The 53 simple, clean rooms have been recently renovated, and there are hundreds of sleeping spots in large Bedouin-style tents.

ℹ Getting There & Away

All the Egged buses that link Jerusalem to the Dead Sea pass through this area.

Masada   מצדה مسعدة

No place in Israel is as evocative of life in 1st-century Roman Judea as Masada, an isolated desert mesa where the last Jewish resistance to Roman rule was crushed in 73 CE after a dramatic, bloody siege. Today, visitors to the complex, declared a Unesco World Heritage site in 2001, can see palaces built by King Herod, structures used by the Jewish Zealots and, far below, the remains of the 10th Legion's siege bases. For a supremely romantic experience, climb to the top at dawn to watch the sunrise.

👁 Sights

⭐ **Masada**
National Park   ARCHAEOLOGICAL SITE
(Metzada; ☑ 08-658-4207, 08-658 4208; www.parks.org.il; adult/child 28/14NIS; ☺ 8am-4pm or 5pm Sat-Thu, to 3pm or 4pm Fri, last entry 1hr before closing) The plateau atop Masada, which measures about 550m by 270m, is some 60m above sea level – that is, about 490m above the surface of the Dead Sea. The easiest way up is by **cable car** (return/one way 74/56NIS, child 43/28NIS; ☺ every 15 minutes 8am-4pm or 5pm Sat-Thu, 8am-3pm or 4pm Fri), though you can also hoof it – up the Roman siege ramp (p309) from the western side or up the Snake Path (p309) from the eastern side. On the ruins, black painted lines divide reconstructed parts (above) from the original remains (below).

Visitors are given an excellent mapbrochure of the ruins, and historical background can also be gleaned from an audio guide (20NIS, including admission to the Masada Museum; p308). Both are available – in eight languages – at ticket windows, atop Masada and at the museum. On the eastern side, between the ticket windows and the cable car, an eight-minute film uses dramatic clips from an American miniseries (1981) starring Peter O'Toole to introduce Masada's bloody last stand.

Drinking water is available so bring a bottle to refill. Eating atop Masada is forbidden, as is carrying large backpacks – these can be

HISTORIC EVENTS ATOP MASADA

After the Romans conquered Jerusalem in 70 CE, almost a thousand Jews – men, women and children – made a desperate last stand atop Masada, a desert mesa surrounded by sheer cliffs and, from 72 CE, the might of the Roman Empire's Tenth Legion. As a Roman battering ram was about to breach their walls, Masada's defenders chose suicide over enslavement. When Roman soldiers swarmed onto the top of the flat-topped mountain, they were met with silence.

Until archaeological excavations began in 1963, the only source of information about Masada's heroic resistance and bloody end was Josephus Flavius, a Jewish commander during the Great Jewish Revolt (66–70 CE) who, after being captured, reinvented himself as a Roman historian. He writes that as the Roman siege ramp inched towards the summit, the defenders – Zealots known as Sicarii (Sikrikin in Hebrew) because of their habit of assassinating their (Jewish) rivals using a curved dagger (sica in Greek) hidden under their cloaks – began to set fire to their homes and possessions to prevent them falling into Roman hands. Ten men, who would have the task of killing everyone else, were then chosen by lot. Nine of the 10 were executed by one of their number before the last man alive committed suicide. When the Romans broke through everyone was dead – except for two women and five children, who had survived by hiding.

stored in lockers (10NIS) near the ticket windows on the eastern side.

Look down in any direction and chances are you'll be able to spot at least one of the Romans' eight military camps and their siege wall. The effort put into the siege by the Roman Legions is mind-boggling – no surprise, then, that they commemorated their victories over the rebels of Judea by erecting a monumental victory arch in the centre of imperial Rome, the **Arch of Titus**, whose design would later inspire Paris' Arc de Triomphe.

Masada has been a Unesco World Heritage site since 2001. The entire site, except the Northern Palace, is wheelchair accessible.

★**Masada Museum**　　　　　MUSEUM
(Visitors Centre; incl audio guide atop Masada 20NIS; ⊗8.30am-4pm or 5pm Sat-Thu, to 3pm or 4pm Fri, last entry 30min before closing) An outstanding and remarkably vivid introduction to Masada's archaeology and history, this museum combines 500 evocative artefacts unearthed by archaeologists (one coin and four papyri are replicas). There are presentations on key Masada personalities – Herod the Great, who built a palace here in the 1st century BCE, turncoat historian Josephus Flavius and Jewish commander Eliezer ben Yair –, to make the dramatic events of 73 CE seem close enough to touch. Visitors receive an audio headset, available in eight languages.

Objects on display include Roman arrowheads; a leather sandal once worn by a woman rebel; the remains of Roman-era dates, wheat, barley and olives; and 11 pot

shards, each inscribed with a name, that – as the Romans were about to breach the ramparts – may have been used to choose the 10 men assigned the task of killing everyone else.

Unless you're doing a sunrise climb, this museum makes an excellent first stop at Masada.

🏃 Activities

Paths link the remains of the eight **Roman military encampments** that still encircle Masada, making it possible to circumnavigate the mesa in part or in full. To get a sense of the area's geography, check out the 3D relief map facing the Visitors Centre ticket windows.

From the Visitors Centre, a challenging trail heads west up Mt Eleazar to **Camp H** (one hour one way). From here, Roman legionnaires could peer down at Masada, gathering aerial intelligence on the Zealots' activities. The path continues to the bottom of the siege ramp on Masada's western side.

Alternatively, you can walk north from the Visitors Centre, following the siege wall on a trail known as **Shvil HaRatz** (the Runner's Trail). It takes about three hours to get to the siege ramp on the western side.

Another trail links **Camp D** (north of Masada) with the eminently hikeable **Wadi Tze'elim**, 4km to the north.

These hikes should not be attempted without a 1:50,000-scale SPNI hiking map, on sale next to the eastern entrance ticket counters in the Visitor Centre.

Snake Path HIKING

(Masada National Park) This famously serpentine footpath winds its way up Masada's eastern flank, starting from near the Visitors Centre. Walking up takes 45 to 60 minutes; count on spending 30 minutes to get back down. To watch the sunrise from the summit, be at the trailhead an hour before the sun comes up – sometime between 4.30am (in June) and 5.30am (in December).

Before 8am, access (and ticket purchase) is from the security barrier near the youth hostel.

On particularly hot days and in inclement weather (a rainstorm or strong winds), park authorities close the trail. In July and August, ascending is permitted only until 8am, descending until 9am.

Siege Ramp Trail HIKING

(Masada National Park) The Romans wimped out and so can you – the path up the spine of their siege ramp takes only 10 to 15 minutes to climb. The catch is that the ramp (on the western side of the mountain) is accessible only from the town of Arad, a 68km drive from the Visitors Centre via Rte 31 and then Rte 3199.

If you'd like to watch sunrise from the summit, get to the base of the ramp half an hour before the sun comes up.

★ Festivals & Events

Sound & Light Show LIGHT SHOW

(☑08-995-9333; adult/child 45/35NIS; ☺9pm Tue & Thu Mar-Oct) This dramatic, open-air recounting of the history of Masada should be watched from the base of the Roman siege ramp on Masada's western side. The narration is in Hebrew but you can rent earphones (15NIS) for simultaneous translation into five languages. Access is via Arad and then Rte 3199; from the Visitors Centre, it's a 68km drive. Get there by 8.30pm.

🛏 Sleeping

There's a modern youth hostel at Masada's eastern entrance, or you can stay 16km south at Ein Bokek. If you'll be accessing Masada via the western side's Siege Ramp Trail (Roman Ramp), you might want to stay up in Arad.

Dead Sea Adventure Hostel HOSTEL $

(☑058-496-0748; www.deadseaadventurehostel. com; 68 Odem St, Arad; dm 85-115NIS; d 380NIS; ☎) This welcoming, all-vegetarian 'adventure hostel' has an old-time backpackers vibe and great chill-out areas. Furnishings are simple, but bunks are comfortable. Breakfast is pancakes. Runs well-regarded adventure tours to Masada and other area sites; see www.wild-trails.com for details.

Situated on the northern edge of Arad, 2.5km from the bus station; served by local buses 1 and 11.

Chenyon Layla
Metzada Ma'arav CAMPGROUND $

(Campsite Masada West; ☑08-628-0116, ext 1 08-628-0404; www.parks.org.il; western entrance, Masada National Park; camping adult/child 53/42NIS, mattress in large tent 75/65NIS, 5-person room with bathroom 450NIS; ☺office open 8am-4pm Sun-Thu) A modern, well equipped camping area on Masada's western side, near the base of the Roman siege ramp. Prices include the use of kitchen facilities and admission to Masada. Sleeping bags and mattresses can be rented for 10NIS per night. Check-in is from 4pm to 10.30pm; check-out is until 11am. Road access is via Arad.

HI – Masada Guest House HOSTEL $$

(☑02-594-5623; www.iyha.org.il; dm/s/d 170/400/530NIS; ☎❄⛱) This 89-room hostel is ideal if you'd like to climb the Snake Path to see sunrise from atop Masada. The five- or six-bed, single-sex dorm rooms border on luxurious. The swimming pool (8am to 5.45pm) is open from Passover to Sukkot. Dinner is served most nights and always on Friday.

Staff do their best to separate travellers from the packs of noisy schoolkids. Frequently booked out, especially on Friday, so reserving is a must. Situated a few hundred

---

THE MODERN MEANING OF MASADA

Over the past century, Masada has become Israeli shorthand for the attitude that 'they'll never take us alive'. During WWII, before the British stopped Rommel's German divisions at El Alamein (Egypt) in 1942, some Palestinian Jews made plans for a Masada-style last stand atop Mt Carmel, and a number of Israeli army units hold their swearing-in ceremonies here, vowing that 'Masada shall not fall again'. (Less apocalyptically, the Israeli air force has been known to send groups of officers up to do yoga at sunrise.)

ℹ PRACTICAL TIP: SWIMMING SAFELY & COMFORTABLY IN THE DEAD SEA

The waters of the Dead Sea have some fantastic healing powers, but unless you respect their bromines and chlorides you may find yourself significantly inconvenienced – or even biting your lip in pain. As a result, a few preparations are in order before you slip into the slimy brine:

➡ Don't shave your legs the day before you swim or you may find out more than you'd like to know about the meaning of the phrase 'to have salt rubbed into your wounds'. Other nicks and cuts – whether you realised you had them or not – are also likely to call attention to themselves.

➡ Do not wear jewellery – silver will turn jet black (don't worry, it can be cleaned) and other metals (including gold that isn't 24 carat) may also be affected.

➡ Wear waterproof sandals to protect your feet from the sun-scorched sand and, in some places, from sharp stones, both on shore and in the water.

➡ It's always a good idea to put on sunscreen. That said, the Dead Sea's dense, ultra-low-elevation air naturally filters the sun's harmful ultraviolet rays, making it much harder to get sunburnt than at sea level, despite scorching temperatures.

Staying safe while bobbing, paddling and drifting requires a bit more caution than at the sea shore.

➡ Do not under any circumstances dunk your head! If water gets in your eyes, it will sting horribly and temporarily blind you. Do not thrash around – calmly get out of the water and ask someone to help you rinse your eyes under a shower or tap (the Ein Bokek beaches have special eyewash stations).

➡ Swallowing just a few gulps of sea water – or inhaling it – is extremely dangerous and can even be fatal. Seek immediate medical attention (eg from lifeguards) if this happens.

➡ Drink *lots* of potable water – not only will the heat dry you out, but the water of the Dead Sea is so saturated with minerals that it will suck out your body's fluids like a thousand leeches. Remember what happened in high school physics class when you learnt about osmosis by putting a slice of fresh potato in saltwater?

➡ The Dead Sea can be so relaxing that some people don't notice when westerly winds gently blow them out towards the middle of the lake (ie towards Jordan). Broadsheet readers are in special danger – a newspaper makes an excellent sail!

---

metres below Masada's Visitors Centre (on the site's eastern side). Wheelchair accessible.

HI – Arad Youth Hostel
HOSTEL $$

(Blau Weiss Youth Hostel; ☑ 02-594-5599; www.iyha. org.il; 34 Atad St, Arad; dm/s/d 150/355/450NIS; ☎) Just five minutes' walk from Arad's bus station, this low-rise hostel has helpful staff and 53 clean and comfortable rooms surrounded by grass and attractive gardens. All have fridge, kettle and cable TV. The delicious buffet breakfast is a typically Israeli combination of vegetables, olives and cheeses. Makes a good base for travel to Masada's western (Roman siege ramp) entrance.

Yehelim
BOUTIQUE HOTEL $$$

(☑ 077 563-2806; www.yehelim.com; 72 Moav St, Arad; d/ste from 800/1300NIS; ☎) Nothing else in Arad even comes close in terms of comfort and style. In a lovely spot on the edge of town, this boutique gem offers glorious desert views, incredible breakfasts and a dozen spacious rooms – each one different – with tasteful furnishings, balcony and spa bath; the suites also have an espresso machine. Gets rave reviews.

🍴 Eating

Visitors Centre Food Court
FOOD HALL $

(eastern entrance, Masada National Park; mains from 25NIS; ⊙8am-4pm or 4.30pm; ☑) Stalls serve falafel, shawarma, sandwiches, salads and cold beer. At the cafeteria a meal costs 65NIS (55NIS for vegetarian), including a drink. Situated one floor below the ticket windows.

ⓘ Getting There & Away

Masada's Visitors Centre, on the eastern side of the mountain, is 21km south of the Ein Gedi Nature Reserve; the access road from Rte 90 is 3km long. All intercity buses serving the Dead Sea stop a few hundred metres from the Visitors Centre. Bus times are posted at Visitors Centre ticket windows.

The Roman siege ramp, on Masada's western side, is accessible from Arad (via Rte 3199). As the crow flies, the Visitors Centre is a bit over 1km from the siege ramp; by road the distance is 68km! There's no public transport so the only way to get there from Arad is by **taxi** (☑ 08-997-4444; day/night one-way 150/200NIS).

Ein Bokek   עין בוקק   عين بوقيق
☑ 08

Sandwiched between the turquoise waters of the southern Dead Sea and a dramatic tan bluff, Ein Bokek's strip of luxury hotels is the region's main tourist zone. Ein Bokek (also spelled En Boqeq) has the area's nicest free beaches and is the Dead Sea's main centre for treating ailments such as psoriasis, arthritis and respiratory conditions with naturally occurring minerals and compounds.

The three most commonly heard languages here are Hebrew, Arabic and Russian – the area is hugely popular not only with locals (Jews, Arabs and Druze) but also with immigrants and tourists from the former Soviet Union.

Unlike the beaches along the lake's northern basin, Ein Bokek fronts evaporation pools (kept full by Dead Sea Works pumps) rather than the open sea. That's why its lakeshore is not receding and sinkholes are not a problem here.

◉ Sights

A 3km-long **pedestrian promenade** (and bike path) and occasional buses (8.20NIS) link Ein Bokek's two beachside hotel zones, Ein Bokek (the main, northern one) and **Hamei Zohar.**

★ Ein Bokek Beach   BEACH
(☺ 24hr) FREE Running the length of the Ein Bokek hotel zone, this broad, clean beach – recently refurbished as a free, fully public amenity – is gloriously sandy. The best Dead Sea beach in Israel, it has an attractive promenade, lifeguards (7am to 6pm, 4pm in winter), shade shelters, open-air showers, gym equipment, changing rooms, bathrooms and night-time lighting. Facilities such as beach chairs are reserved for hotel guests.

🏃 Activities

Almost every Ein Bokek hotel boasts a spa with swimming pools, saunas, mineral baths, a long menu of health treatments and an army of predominantly Russian therapists. Most places charge nonguests 140NIS to 220NIS to use their facilities for the day, including beach chairs but not including special treatments. Some deals include lunch.

Wadi Bokek   HIKING
(Nahal Bokek) One of just three wadis on the Dead Sea's western shore that are fed by year-round springs (the other two are at Ein Gedi), Wadi Bokek has narrow gorges, lush vegetation and waterholes – perfect for an easy and refreshing hour-long hike. Access is through a pedestrian tunnel under Rte 90, located between the David Dead Sea Resort and Leonardo Inn Hotels, or you can park at the trailhead.

🛏 Sleeping

There's no budget or even midrange accommodation in the area's two hotel zones, lively Ein Bokek and smaller, quieter Hamei Zohar, but if you're up for a splurge there are loads of options: a dozen hotels offer air-conditioned facilities, gorgeous swimming pools, state-of-the-art spas and buffet bonanzas. A handful – those on the eastern side of the access road – offer direct beach access.

Ein Bokek's hotels tend to charge high-season prices from April to mid-June and from September to mid-November. Significant discounts are often available on the web, especially in the low season.

About 1.5m south of Hamei Zohar, Ein Bokek's southern hotel zone, beachless Neve Zohar (Newe Zohar) has some of the Dead Sea's cheapest B&Bs – we're talking 350NIS to 500NIS per room. Charm is lacking. For details, see www.sdom-deadsea.co.il.

Overnight camping (free) is allowed on two sections of Ein Bokek Beach: at the northern end of the new promenade, opposite the David Dead Sea Resort; and midway between Ein Bokek and Hamei Zohar. Look for signs indicating that camping is permitted.

Hod HaMidbar   HOTEL $$$
(☑ 08-668-8222; www.hodhotel.co.il; d incl half-board 1000-1800NIS; @🅿🛜❄) Right on the beachfront promenade, this 203-room hotel is known for its above-average service. The swimming pool overlooks the sea, while

THE DEAD SEA SODOM

SOOTHING & HEALTHFUL

The waters of the Dead Sea contain 20 times as much bromine, 15 times more magnesium and 10 times as much iodine as the ocean. Bromine, a component of many sedatives, relaxes the nerves; magnesium counteracts skin allergies and clears the bronchial passages; and iodine has a beneficial effect on certain glandular functions – or so it's claimed.

If this were not enough, the Dead Sea's extremely dense air – the area has the world's highest barometric pressure – has 10% more oxygen than sea-level air. Other healthful properties, especially for people with breathing problems, include high temperatures, low rainfall, low humidity and pollen-free air.

downstairs the glass-enclosed spa has sulphur pools and saunas. Offers free use of bicycles and free international phone calls.

Oasis Dead Sea Hotel HOTEL $$$
(☑08-668-8000; www.prima.co.il; d from 650NIS; @🛜🏊) With a small but sparkling lobby, this well-run hotel has 142 rooms, neatly tended gardens and two outdoor pools, one for adults, the other for kids. Shares a spa with the adjacent Oasis Spa Club Hotel, whose 98 rooms are adults-only. There's often live music in the lobby from 9pm. Situated across the road from the beach.

✖ Eating

Most of Ein Bokek's restaurants belong to hotels, and their lavish buffets cannot be described as inexpensive, even if you snag a half-board deal. If you're on a budget, options include cafes that serve sandwiches and, in the Petra Shopping Center, a McDonald's. Both Sky Blue Mall and Petra Shopping Center have mini-markets selling a small selection of picnic supplies.

Taj Mahal MIDDLE EASTERN $$
(☑053 650-6502; www.taj-mahal.co.il; mains 59-119NIS; ⊙noon-midnight; 🛜🍴) In a Bedouin tent (no air-con!) outfitted with rugs, pillows and low couches, Ein Bokek's best restaurant serves Middle Eastern grilled meats (kosher), hummus, shakshuka, East Jerusalem baklava, nargilehs (water pipes) and six

beers on tap. Situated on the grounds of the Leonardo Inn Hotel, facing Isrotel Ganim.

A belly dancer gyrates on Friday from 10pm.

Tapuah S'dom ISRAELI $$
(☑08-995-6128; mains 59-110NIS; ⊙9am-9pm or 10pm) Just south of Sky Blue Mall, this small restaurant offers sea views from some of its tables. Main dishes include beef, kebab, chicken, fish and pasta, and the menu also features large salads and yummy desserts. Breakfast costs 50NIS to 90NIS.

🛍 Shopping

Sky Blue Mall MALL
(Kanyonit Ein HaT'chelet) This mall, in the middle of the hotel zone, is the best place in Israel to buy Dead Sea beauty products. Shops also sell beach supplies, including thongs (flip-flops). A new, much larger mall, Kanyon Yam HaMelach, is being built next door.

ℹ Information

ATMs can be found in the Sky Blue Mall and the Petra Shopping Center (across the corridor from McDonald's). The malls also have exchange bureaux, but the rates are not great.

Dead Sea Tourist Information (☑08-997-5010; www.sdom-deadsea.co.il; Solarium -400; ⊙8am-5.30pm Sun-Thu, 9am-1pm Fri; 🛜) An excellent source of maps and details on hotels, B&Bs, restaurants, outdoor activities and bus schedules in the area stretching from Neot HaKikar to Ein Gedi (the area north of there, in the West Bank, belongs to a different regional council). Sells SPNI 1:50,000-scale hiking maps for 110NIS (SPNI field school at Ein Gedi has them for 87NIS). Situated across the street from the Daniel Hotel, inside the Solarium -400 complex.

ℹ Getting There & Away

Street parking in the Ein Bokek hotel zone, marked with kerbs painted blue and white, costs 5NIS per hour from 8am to 7pm (6pm on Friday) or 25NIS per day; paying ahead for more than one day is possible. Hotels have limited free parking. There are no left-luggage facilities at Ein Bokek.

Sodom סדום سدوم

By tradition, this area is the site of Sodom and Gomorrah, the biblical cities that were destroyed in a storm of fire and brimstone, punishment from God because of their people's depravity (Genesis 18–19). These days, Sodom is much better known for its desert hiking and cycling trails.

By day, the rusty (from the salt air) smokestacks, pipes and holding tanks of the Dead Sea Works (DSW) complex, a few kilometres south of Mt Sodom, look like a mid-20th-century industrial dystopia, but by night, when the sprawling facilities are lit by thousands of yellowish lights, the site has a mysterious, other-worldly beauty. Products made by the DSW from the waters of the Dead Sea – Israel's only major natural resource other than sunlight and the gas fields off the Mediterranean coast – range from magnesium chloride, anhydrous aluminium chloride and potash (for fertilisers) to table salt and inputs for cosmetics.

◉ Sights

Lot's Wife
LANDMARK

About 11km south of the southern end of Ein Bokek, high above the west side of Rte 90, a column of salt-rich rock leans precariously away from the rest of the Mt Sodom cliff face. It is popularly known as Lot's Wife because, according to the Bible, Lot's wife was turned into a pillar of salt as punishment for looking back to see Sodom as it burned (Genesis 19:17 and 19:26).

The Human Condition
SCULPTURE

(Matzav HaAdam; Rte 90; ⊙24hr) Atop a bluff overlooking the Dead Sea Works stands this modern sculpture, a rusted-steel column with old steel railway ties striving to climb it like desperate worms.

Next to the sculpture, a **viewpoint** looks out over a crazy juxtaposition of smoke-spewing heavy industry, electric-blue evaporation pools, green farm fields (over in Jordan) and the wild, tawny beauty of the desert. Views are best in the late afternoon, when the setting sun turns Jordan's Moab Mountains a reddish gold.

The 600m-long access road intersects Rte 90 250m north of the main entrance to the Dead Sea Works. Turn off at the white-on-brown sign reading 'Plant Viewing Point' (ignore the yellow 'no trespassing' sign, which refers to off-road areas) and follow the green signs marked (in Hebrew) 'LaMitzpeh' ('to the scenic lookout'). Beyond the sculpture, a 4WD road continues to the **Amiaz Plateau**.

🏃 Activities

Mt Sodom
HIKING, CYCLING

One of the world's stranger geological formations, Mt Sodom (summit elevation: 176m below sea level) is made almost entirely of rock salt, a highly soluble material that in any other climate would have melted away. Two trails head down Mt Sodom's steep flanks from a lookout point, reachable by 4WD, whose views are at their best in the late afternoon.

Mt Sodom is 250m high, 11km long and up to 2km wide. **Ma'aleh HaSulamot** (Ladders Ascent; 1½ hours to walk down), named after its many stairs, connects with Rte 90 across the highway from the sun-blasted huts of the Dead Sea Works' first workers' camp, built in 1934. Another descent to Rte 90 is **Shvil HaDagim** (Fishes Trail; 1½ hours down), so named because of the many fossilised fish you can see in the rocks.

Over the millennia the area's rare rainfalls have dissolved some of Mt Sodom's salt content, creating deep in the bowels of the mountain a maze of **caves** (closed to the public) up to 5.5km long, some of them filled with delicate, eerie salt stalactites. Many are connected to the surface by shafts that hikers need to be careful they don't fall into.

West of Mt Sodom, **Wadi Sodom** is ideal for mountain biking. If you start at the top (accessible by 4WD), it's about two hours, mostly downhill, to the Neve Zohar area. A round-trip circuit that connects with beautiful **Wadi Pratzim** (Wadi Perazim), whose upper reaches pass the famous **Flour Cave** (closed to the public), is another option.

❶ Getting There & Away

To explore this area you need your own wheels, preferably 4WD. Four-wheel-drive tour operators in Neot HaKikar and elsewhere can organise pick-up/drop-off and excursions.

Neot HaKikar

ناؤت هاكيكار ناות הכיכר

☑08 / POP 900

Snuggled up against the Jordanian border in one of Israel's most remote corners, this agricultural moshav (cooperative village) is the perfect base for exploring the wadis, plateaus and bluffs around the southern Dead Sea. Tranquil and laid-back, Neot HaKikar and its sister moshav, Ein Tamar, have some mellow B&Bs and all sorts of options for mountain biking, hiking, birdwatching and exploring the desert by 4WD. The nearest beach is 30 minutes away at Ein Bokek. Because of the intense summer heat, some places close from July to mid-September.

🏃 Activities

Hikeable and cyclable wadis *(nechalim)* within a 20-minute 4WD drive of here include Arava, Tzin (Zin), Amatzya (Amazyahu), Peres, Tamar, Tzafit and Ashalim. Other great places to pedal or hoof it include Mt Sodom and the Amiaz Plateau (Mishor Amiaz).

A wide variety of off-road cycling circuits, including one called HeCharitz ('the slit') and another that follows Wadi Sodom to Wadi Pratzim, can be found within a 30-minute drive of Neot HaKikar. From June to mid-September, say locals, it's simply too hot to hike or cycle safely.

The Small Makhtesh (HaMakhtesh HaKatan) – the smallest of Israel's three great erosion craters – is a 30-minute drive west. Your place of lodging can arrange to have someone take you out to the trailhead by 4WD (for a fee). Vehicles are not allowed inside the *makhtesh*.

The moshav has tennis and basketball courts, a children's playground and a public swimming pool (open from Passover to Sukkot).

A number of farmers offer tours of their fields that include an introduction to desert agriculture. Local artisans produce jewellery, pottery and metal sculptures.

Cycle Inn   CYCLING
(📞 052 899-1146; uzicycleinn@gmail.com; 5hr rental 75NIS; ⊘ mid-Sep–May) Rents mountain bikes; prices include helmets. Owners Uzi and Barak are happy to supply you with maps and the low-down on area trails.

☞ Tours

Barak Horwitz   ADVENTURE
(📞 052 866-6062; barakhorwitz@gmail.com; 2hr tour in 8-person 4WD 800NIS) A licensed tour guide, Neot HaKikar–based Barak Horwitz is intimately familiar with the Dead Sea area. He runs 4WD tours but is happy to provide tips on other outdoor activities (no charge), including hiking – feel free to contact him by phone or email. Also does guided tours of Masada and other Dead Sea sites.

🛏 Sleeping

Neot HaKikar has about 50 B&B units, none of which offer breakfast unless you special-order it (60/100NIS per adult/couple).

★ Shkedi's Camplodge   LODGE $
(Khan Shkedi; 📞 052 231-7371; www.shkedig.com; dm/d/q with shared bathroom & excl breakfast 100/350/450NIS; ⊘ closed Jul–mid-Sep; 🛜) A wonderful place to linger for a couple of days, this desert retreat is especially enchanting at night, when owner Gil Shkedi and his guests hang out around the campfire or sip beers in the chill-out tent. On hot days you can mist yourself while relaxing on a hammock.

Dorm beds, often booked out on Friday and Saturday, are inside cosy, spacious, wood-built dorm lodges; mattresses are on the floor. The clean, modern bathroom block looks vaguely Mexican. Has a fully equipped kitchen for self-caterers.

Melach HaAretz   B&B $$
(📞 08-655-1875, 050 759-4828; http://madmonynh.com; d excl breakfast 450-500NIS; 🛜) Has two studio apartments off a garden (great for kids) decorated with garrulous owner Asaf Madmony's extraordinary stone, wood and metal sculptures.

Korin's Home   B&B $$$
(HaBayit Shel Korin; 📞 050 680-0545; www.korins.co.il; d excl breakfast 700NIS, additional person 100NIS; 🛜) Like having your own spa-equipped three-room apartment. Each of the three units sleeps up to six.

🍴 Eating

Neot HaKikar and Ein Tamar each have an ATM-equipped grocery that's open for a while on Saturday night.

Lunch and dinner can be ordered a day ahead from local families; mains cost 70NIS to 100NIS.

❶ Getting There & Away

Neot HaKikar is 8km southeast of Rte 90's Neot HaKikar Jct and 11km southeast of Arava Jct, where Rte 25 from Dimona and Be'er Sheva intersects Rte 90.

All the buses that link Eilat with Be'er Sheva, Tel Aviv, the Dead Sea and Jerusalem stop at Arava Junction; accommodation owners are usually happy to pick you up.

The only bus that goes all the way into Neot HaKikar is bus 321, which does two circuits a day – one in the early morning, the other in the mid- to late afternoon – linking Neot HaKikar with Dimona (16NIS, 40 minutes) and Ein Bokek (16NIS, 45 minutes).

The Negev

النقب הנגב

Best Places to Eat

➡ Fish Market (p338)

➡ InnSense Bistro (p328)

➡ Kornmehl Farm (p322)

➡ Pastory (p338)

➡ Lasha Bakery (p328)

Best Places to Stay

➡ Midbara (p331)

➡ Carmey Avdat Winery (p323)

➡ iBex Hotel (p327)

➡ Kibbutz Lotan Guesthouse (p331)

➡ Khan Be'erotayim (p321)

➡ Shivta National Park (p320)

Why Go?

The Negev is the only part of Israel that feels vast and boundless. Stretching from the Red Sea north for 250km, the region's rocky, treeless hills and dry gullies have been attracting travellers, traders and nomads since the time of Abraham (Genesis 12:9 and 20:1). These days, sun-seekers, scuba divers, birdwatchers and hikers flock to the resort city of Eilat, where the sun shines 360 days a year. North of there, the kibbutzim of the Arava – part of the Great Rift Valley – attract environmentalists and visitors interested in sustainable desert development. Other tourists follow in the footsteps of the Nabataeans, who established impressive cities not only at Petra (which can easily be visited from Eilat) but also at Avdat, Shivta and Mamshit, now Unesco World Heritage sites. Perched on the rim of Israel's multi-hued 'grand canyon', hip Mitzpe Ramon is a magnet for creative minds, quirky entrepreneurs and serenity seekers.

When to Go
Eilat

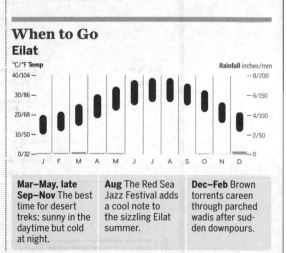

Mar–May, late Sep–Nov The best time for desert treks; sunny in the daytime but cold at night.

Aug The Red Sea Jazz Festival adds a cool note to the sizzling Eilat summer.

Dec–Feb Brown torrents careen through parched wadis after sudden downpours.

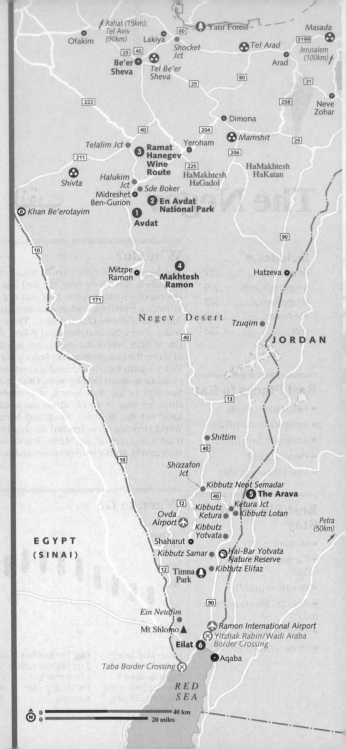

The Negev Highlights

1 **Avdat** (p320)
Exploring the ruins of a Nabataean Incense Route city.

2 **En Avdat National Park** (p321)
Hiking through a desert wadi to natural springs, pools and waterfalls.

3 **Ramat Hanegev Wine Route** (p323)
Sampling boutique wines grown in the Negev Highlands.

4 **Makhtesh Ramon** (p324)
Hiking through the vast, multi-coloured landscape of the world's largest 'erosion cirque'.

5 **The Arava** (p328) Visiting kibbutzim dedicated to living in harmony with the desert.

6 **Eilat** (p332)
Snorkelling and diving at truly magnificent coral reefs.

Be'er Sheva

بئر السبع   באר שבע

☑ 08 / POP 203,600

Long neglected as a tourist destination, the 'capital of the Negev' is starting to draw visitors thanks to the revitalisation of its old city, whose narrow side streets, grungy and completely ungentrified, are sprinkled with museums and Ottoman-era architecture. Sadly, in 2017 the city's famous Bedouin market closed after 112 years.

Be'er Sheva is southern Israel's principal commercial, industrial, health care, transport and academic hub. Jobs, shops, Soroka Hospital and the famously student-friendly Ben-Gurion University of the Negev are a huge draw for both Jewish and Bedouin Israelis.

History

Mentioned three dozen times in the Hebrew Bible, Be'er Sheva – the name might mean 'well of the oath', ' well of the seven' or 'well seven' – was an important urban centre during the Israelite period. Modern Be'er Sheva was founded by the Ottomans in the very early 1900s, in part to counter expanding British influence in the Sinai. The Turks were right to be concerned: by the end of 1917 the dusty outpost was under British control, having been captured by Australian regiments in, believe it or not, an old-fashioned cavalry charge. After the 1948 war, during which Egyptian forces briefly held the city, Be'er Sheva expanded rapidly, populated mainly by Jewish refugees and immigrants from Arab countries.

◉ Sights

Be'er Sheva's historic sights are clustered in the old city, a grungy, working-class area situated a walkable 1km southwest of the train and bus stations. The main drag is HaAtzma'ut St; part of parallel Kakal St has been turned into a modest pedestrian mall.

Negev Museum of Art & Museum of Islamic & Near Eastern Cultures   MUSEUM
(☑ 08-699-3535; www.negev-museum.org.il; 60 Ha'Atzmaut St; art museum adult/child 20/10NIS; both museums 35/20NIS; ⊙ 10am-4pm Mon, Tue & Thu, noon-7pm Wed, 10am-2pm Fri & Sat) Housed in the elegant Ottoman governor's mansion (1906), the art museum hosts temporary exhibitions that change three times a year (see the website for details). Nearby, an elegantly proportioned Ottoman mosque (1906), its arches inspired in part by the architecture of Germany (the Turks' allies at the time), puts on year-long exhibitions focussing on Islamic cultures.

Turkish Railway Station   HISTORIC BUILDING
(Engine 70414 Compound; ☑ ext 2, 08-623-4613; cnr Eli David & David Tuvyahu Sts; mini-museum & lounge car adult/concession 30/20NIS; ⊙ 9am-5pm Sun-Thu, to 1pm Fri) Built in 1915, the train station compound now houses a fascinating photo exhibit on Ottoman- and Mandate-era Be'er Sheva, including the town's capture by Anzac cavalry during WWI. You can also see a steam engine of the type that operated on the Be'er Sheva line until 1958 and visit an interactive mini-museum, a luxurious lounge car from 1922 and a Turkish WWI memorial built in 2002. The ticket counter can supply maps and visitors information on Be'er Sheva.

Commonwealth War Cemetery   CEMETERY
(www.cwgc.org; cnr HaAtzma'ut St & Hartzfeld St; ⊙ 24hr) This dignified WWI cemetery, its gardens and grave markers neatly tended, is the final resting place of 1241 Commonwealth soldiers, including 174 Australians, 31 New Zealanders and 67 men whose remains were never identified.

Negev Artists' House   GALLERY
(☑ 08-627-3828; 55 Ha'Avot St; ⊙ 10am-1.30pm Mon-Fri, 4-7.30pm Mon-Thu, 11am-2pm Sat) FREE This grand Mandate-era villa (1933) is now a four-room gallery featuring compelling works by artists from the Negev.

Tel Be'er Sheva   ARCHAEOLOGICAL SITE
(☑ 08-646-7286; www.parks.org.il; adult/child 14/7NIS; ⊙ 8am-4pm or 5pm, closes 1hr earlier Fri, last entry 1hr before closing) Declared a Unesco World Heritage site in 2005 (along with two other ancient cities in the Galilee, Hatzor and Megiddo), Tel Be'er Sheva was an important fortified city during the early Israelite period (10th century BCE). A superb example of biblical-era urban planning, it had a sophisticated water-collecting system that included a five-chamber cistern hewn into the bedrock, for use in times of siege. The site is 7km east of Be'er Sheva, next to the Bedouin town of Tel Sheva (turn off just before the welcome arch).

During WWI, British forces captured a Turkish artillery position atop Tel Be'er Sheva thanks to the bravery of the 11th North Auckland Mounted Rifles.

THE NEGEV BE'ER SHEVA

Be'er Sheva

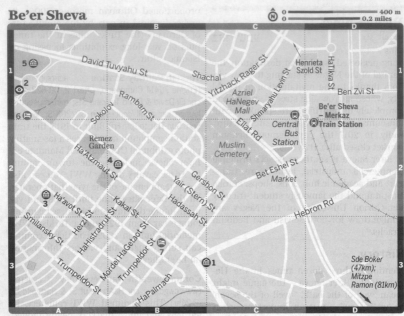

THE NEGEV BE'ER SHEVA

Be'er Sheva

◉ Sights

◉ Sleeping

The site is linked to Be'er Sheva's central bus station by Metropoline buses 10 and 15 (4.80NIS, 30 minutes, once or twice an hour).

Be'er Avraham　　　　　　MUSEUM
(Abraham's Well International Visitors Center; ☑08-623-4613; www.abraham.org.il; 2 Hebron Rd; tour adult/concession 34/20NIS; ◷8.30am-5pm Sun-Thu, 9am-1pm Fri, last tour 1hr before closing) According to the Bible, Be'er Sheva is where God appeared to Abraham (Genesis 26:23–25) and where Abraham made his covenant with Avimelech (Genesis 21:25–34) – that's why this visitors centre focuses on the life and times of the patriarch of the three Abrahamic religions.

There is no evidence that Abraham ever visited the courtyard's well, restored in the Ottoman era, but he is very present in the 45- to 60-minute tour, which includes a 15-minute audiovisual presentation (available in Hebrew and English, with subtitles in seven languages). Situated at the southeastern edge of the old city.

Israeli Air Force Museum　　MUSEUM
(☑08-990-6888; Hatzerim; adult/child incl tour 30/20NIS; ◷8am-4.30pm Sun-Thu) Parked on the tarmac, about 120 historic aircraft – including a Spitfire used in the 1948 war, captured Syrian and Iraqi MiGs, fighter jets and attack helicopters – illustrate the history of Israel's legendary air force. During the intermediate days of the Passover and Sukkot holidays, historic planes take to the skies and aircraft currently in Israel Defence Forces service are put on display. A much larger museum is in the planning stages. Bring your passport.

Situated 10km west of Be'er Sheva, on the edge of Hatzerim (Khatserim) air base. From the central bus station, take Dan BaDarom buses 40 or 41 (return 9.50NIS, 10 minutes, twice an hour).

📖 Sleeping

Hotel Aladdin
HOTEL $$

(☑ 08-866-0828; www.aladdin-negev.com; 1st floor, 25 Ha'Atzmaut St; s/d 300/400NIS; 🖥) A fine option if you'd like to stay in the old city, near attractions and restaurants. Run by a family from the former USSR, this place has 19 gleaming, spotless rooms – don't let the unpromising surroundings put you off.

Beit Yatziv
HOTEL $$

(☑ 08-627 7444; www.beityatziv.co.il; 79 Ha'Atzmaut St, Old City; s/d 300/400NIS, deluxe r 450NIS; ⊗ reception 7am-7pm Sun-Thu, to 11am Fri; P 🖥 ✉) Part of an educational and cultural centre, this youth hostel has 76 standard rooms, which are small and come with two twin beds, a fridge, a TV and a kettle; 24 deluxe rooms, which are newer and larger and have a desk; and a swimming pool (open to guests in July and August). Reserve by phone or email. If you'll be arriving when reception is closed, staff can leave a key with the guard. Served by bus 13. Reception is closed on Saturdays.

ℹ Getting There & Away

BUS

Be'er Sheva's central bus station is the Negev's most important bus hub. Destinations include the following:

Tel Aviv Central Bus Station (Metropoline buses 369 and 370; 18.50NIS, 1¾ hours, several times hourly)

Jerusalem (Egged bus 470; 34NIS, 1¾ hours, three times an hour)

Mitzpe Ramon (Metropoline buses 60, 64 and 65; 15NIS, 1¼ hours, two to four times an hour) Via Sde Boker and En Avdat.

Dead Sea (Egged bus 384; 27NIS, 1½ hours to Ein Bokek, five per day Sunday to Thursday, three on Friday) Via Arad.

Eilat (Egged buses 392, 393 and 397; 42.50NIS, 3½ hours, every hour or two) Operates until late afternoon on Friday and in the early afternoon on Saturday.

TRAIN

Direct trains link **Be'er Sheva – Merkaz Train Station** (Be'er Sheva – Center; www.rail.co.il) with Tel Aviv (27NIS, 1¼ hours, twice an hour) as well as Haifa (53NIS, 2¼ hours, hourly), Akko and Nahariya. The last train on Friday leaves at 1.16pm in winter, 3.16pm in summer; the first on Saturday is after sundown.

Negev Highlands
هضبة النقب   הר הנגב

The Negev Highlands (Ramat HaNegev), which cover some 20% of Israel, encompass dramatic desert landscapes, remote

---

OFF THE BEATEN TRACK

DAY TRIPS FROM BE'ER SHEVA

Be'er Sheva makes a good base for exploring the northern Negev. Highlights include sites that spotlight the region's Bedouin and their culture.

Museum of Bedouin Culture (☑ 08-991-3322; www.joealon.org.il; 15NIS; ⊗ 8am-4pm Sun-Thu) A good introduction to Bedouin life in the Negev. Exhibits include traditional clothes, household utensils, carpets, tools and jewellery as well as photographs. There's also a hospitality tent where visitors can sit with a local Bedouin, drink coffee and talk. Situated in the Joe Alon Center, which is 27km northeast of Be'er Sheva, behind (ie just west of) Kibbutz Lahav; entry includes an audio guide.

Sidreh – Lakiya Negev Weaving (☑ 08-651-9883; www.sidreh.org; House 92, Neighbourhood 3, Lakiya; tour 20NIS; ⊗ 9am-4pm Sun-Thu) Established in 1991 to provide income for Bedouin women and to preserve traditional wool spinning and hand-loom weaving techniques, this social enterprise conducts tours (reserve in advance) and sells the beautiful carpets, cushions and accessories that are produced by its members. Situated 18km northeast of Be'er Sheva, in the Bedouin village of Lakiya (Laqya). Follow the signs to 'Negev Weaving'; the site is behind the yellow-domed Abu Bakr Mosque.

Tel Arad National Park (☑ 08-699-2444; www.parks.org.il; adult/child 14/7NIS; ⊗ 8am-4pm or 5pm, closes 1hr earlier Fri, last entry 1hr before closing) In the Early Bronze Age (3100–2650 BCE), Tel Arad was the site of an Early Canaanite walled city whose remains can still be seen. After being uninhabited for some 1500 years, this spot was resettled by the Israelites starting in the 11th century BCE. The city was again destroyed in the early 6th century BCE, this time by the Babylonians. Highlights include the remains of an Israelite temple. Situated 39km east of Be'er Sheva.

THE INCENSE ROUTE

For centuries, the Nabataeans controlled the highly profitable desert caravan routes between Arabia and the empires of Greece and Rome. A nomadic people from the northern Arabian Peninsula, they arrived in the Negev around the 4th century BCE.

After the lands of the Nabataeans – masters of survival in even the harshest desert conditions – came under Roman control around the year 100 CE, they began culturally assimilating, adopting the Gregorian calendar, building permanent settlements and, eventually, adopting Christianity. They spoke a form of Aramaic, the lingua franca of the region, and were innovative engineers – because of the hostile desert environment, they developed sophisticated irrigation methods that are again being used today. To show off, their kings lavishly wasted water in front of guests.

At one point, the Nabataens' incense and spice trade route stretched from Yemen and Oman to the Mediterranean, passing through what is now Saudi Arabia, Jordan (Petra), Israel and Gaza. As a result, the Negev cities of Avdat, Mamshit, Shivta and Haluza became prosperous, while around them, in dry river beds, desert agriculture flourished. The remote ruins of three of these settlements were declared a Unesco World Heritage site in 2005 under the collective designation of the 'Incense Route – Desert Cities in the Negev'.

Avdat

Beautifully preserved, this ancient city 650m above sea level dominates the surrounding desert. Named after the Nabataean monarch Obada, it was built in the 3rd century BCE as a caravan stop on the road from Petra to the Mediterranean. Prosperous throughout the Byzantine period, the city was deserted following an earthquake in 630 CE and the Muslim takeover of the Negev six years later.

Buy your tickets at the **visitor centre** (☑08-655-1511; www.parks.org.il; adult/child 18/14NIS; ☺8am-4pm or 5pm, closes 1hr earlier Fri, last entry 1hr before closing) next to the petrol station, where you can watch a 10-minute film (in 10 languages) about the Incense Route. Next, visit the nearby Byzantine-era bathhouse before driving up the hill (or walking on a steep path) to the ruins of the city. Highlights include a Roman bathhouse, catacombs, several 4th-century churches, a pottery workshop and a Byzantine winepress.

Situated on Rte 40, Avdat lies 10km south of Sde Boker (Midreshet Ben-Gurion) and 23km north of Mitzpe Ramon. Metropoline buses 64 and 65, ply the route between Be'er Sheva (15NIS, 45 minutes) and Mitzpe Ramon (11.50NIS, 12 minutes), passing by twice hourly from Sunday to Thursday and hourly on Friday until the late afternoon.

Mamshit

The smallest but best-preserved Nabataean city in Israel, **Mamshit** (☑08-655-6478; www.parks.org.il; adult/child 22/9NIS; ☺8am-4pm or 5pm, closes 1hr earlier Fri, last entry 1hr before closing) was established in the 1st century BCE; in the 4th century, it became the Negev's only fully walled city. The excavations include ancient reservoirs, watchtowers, two 4th-century churches, and Roman and Byzantine cemeteries. A highlight is the large mosaic floor in the courtyard of the Church of St Nilus. Mamshit is on Rte 25, about 8km southeast of Dimona. Any bus heading from Be'er Sheva to Eilat via Dimona (eg bus 397) can drop you at the site's 1km-long access road (21.50NIS, 30 minutes).

Shivta

One of the most gloriously isolated spots in Israel, **Shivta** (☑050 738-3802; www.parks.org.il; ☺sunrise-nightfall) FREE was founded during the early Roman period (1st century BCE). Its well-preserved ruins – including three churches, houses, tiled streets and an impressive irrigation system – date from the Byzantine period (5th to 7th centuries CE), when it was an important stop on the caravan route between Egypt and Anatolia. Shivta is 60km southwest of Be'er Sheva, 8km south off Rte 211.

To fully enjoy Shivta's splendid desert isolation, stay overnight in a **B&B** (www.nabato.co.il; d incl breakfast Sep-May 420-550NIS, Jun-Aug 380-480NIS) in a stone building constructed in the 1930s by an Anglo–American archaeological research team.

The Israel Defence Forces' Shivta artillery base, 5km north, is linked to Be'er Sheva (13NIS, three to five times daily Sunday to Friday) by Metropoline bus 44. Inn owner Ami is happy to pick up his B&B guests at the bus stop.

kibbutzim, boutique vineyards and several important Nabataean sites. The nearby hip town of Mitzpe Ramon, high enough to get the occasional snowfall, is on the rim of Makhtesh Ramon.

Rte 10, which runs along the Egyptian border, is closed to civilian traffic for security reasons, but may open up during Passover, Sukkot and Hanukah.

Sleeping

Khan Be'erotayim BUNGALOW $$
(Be'erotayim Desert Lodge; 08-655-5788; www.beerotayim.co.il; 2km northwest of Ezuz; adult/child 3-13yr incl half-board 295/165NIS) In the middle of nowhere not far from the Egyptian frontier, this ecofriendly encampment (elevation 360m) is an excellent spot to enjoy the quiet of the desert wilderness, chill out around the campfire (always burning so the herbal tea and Arab coffee stay hot), and, at night, stargaze. Situated 85km southwest of Be'er Sheva and 14km south of Nitzana.

Accommodation is in basic adobe bungalows with mats on the floor and woodburning stoves; the chairs and tables were made by Sinai Bedouin. Bathrooms are shared. Meals are sourced locally as much as possible, and all electricity is solar. Offers guided camel rides (one hour for an adult/child costs 80/60NIS).

Getting There & Away

Metropoline buses 60 and 64, linking Be'er Sheva with Mitzpe Ramon, stop at sites all along Rte 40, including at Kibbutz Sde Boker, Midreshet Ben-Gurion and Avdat National Park.

Sde Boker שדה בוקר سديه بوكير
08 / POP 2230

Kibbutz Sde Boker achieved fame as the late-in-life home of Israel's first prime minister, David Ben-Gurion, whose modest home has become a pilgrimage destination for Israeli schoolchildren. It was established in 1952 by young pioneers who planned to breed cattle in the desert – that's why they named the kibbutz 'cowboy's field'.

Midreshet Ben-Gurion, 5km southwest (by road) of the kibbutz, is known for its spectacular desert setting – Wadi Tzin and En Avdat National Park are next door – and for cutting-edge research into desert ecology, arid-land agriculture and solar energy. Created as a regional academic centre, this attractive village is home to a satellite campus of Be'er Sheva's Ben-Gurion University of the Negev.

Sights

Ben-Gurion's Desert Home MUSEUM
(08-656-0469; www.bgh.org.il; Kibbutz Sde Boker; adult/concession 20/15NIS; 8.30am-4pm Sun-Thu, to 2pm Fri, 10am-4pm Sat) In his will, Israel's founding father asked that the unassuming kibbutz quarters where he lived with his wife Paula remain exactly as he left them, and that's what you see when you visit this museum: modest furnishings from the 1950s and 1960s, a library packed with books, and a 1952 wall map showing Israel's post-1948 borders. Situated on the southern edge of Kibbutz Sde Boker; turn off Rte 40 at the Delek petrol station.

Two films illustrate Ben-Gurion's life. One looks at his fierce determination to bring about Jewish national self-determination, narrated in a pretty good imitation of the great man's distinctive voice (12 minutes), while the other focusses on the challenges he faced as a leader (15 minutes).

Ben-Gurion Graves MEMORIAL
(Midreshet Ben-Gurion; 24hr) The graves of David (1886–1973) and Paula (1892–1968) Ben-Gurion lie in a spectacular clifftop setting overlooking sublimely beautiful Wadi Tzin (Zin) and the Avdat plain. A desert flora park has been planted next to the tombs, and wild ibexes often wander by.

En Avdat National Park NATIONAL PARK
(08-655-5684; www.parks.org.il; adult/child 28/14NIS; 8am-4pm winter, to 5pm summer, closes 1hr earlier Fri) En (Ein) Avdat comes as a huge surprise in this otherwise bone-dry desert: a year-round, freshwater spring that miraculously flows over a waterfall and through a narrow, winding ravine with steep sides of soft white chalk. Caves along the trail were inhabited by monks during the Byzantine period. To protect habitat for fauna such as the ibex, swimming and wading are prohibited.

The park has two entrances. The northern one, Zinim (Tzinim) Cliff, is just outside Midreshet Ben-Gurion's big yellow gate, while the southern one – which offers panoramas but no trails down into the wadi – is on Rte 40, 4km north of the Nabataean ruins of Avdat National Park. Except in designated picnic areas, eating in the park is not allowed; the only toilet facilities are at the entrances and at the Lower Parking Lot.

The two most popular trails begin at the Lower Parking Lot, a 3km drive from the northern entrance. The **Short Route** (start

WORTH A TRIP

GOURMET GOATS

The Negev Highlands have been supporting goats for thousands of years, so it should come as no surprise that gourmet goat farms have been appearing in recent years, often on or near the wine route. The following farms are 12km to 15km north of Sde Boker.

Naot Farm (📞054 421-8789; www.naotfarm.co.il; Rte 40; ☉sunrise-sunset) Has 50 goats, a dairy (visitors are free to walk around; milking is at 6am and 3pm) and a shop selling homemade goat *labneh* (thick yoghurt), *dulce de leche* and French-style cheeses (180NIS to 200NIS per kg). Also sells local wines. The five cabins afford gorgeous desert views. Situated 3km south of Tlalim Junction, 400m west of Rte 40.

Kornmehl Farm (📞08-655-5140; www.kornmehl.co.il; Rte 40; mains 44-66NIS; ☉10am-6pm Tue-Sun; 🖋) Has a 60-goat dairy and a train carriage–shaped shack where you can admire the desert landscape while dining on a cheese platter, goat's-cheese pizzas and calzones, and a refreshing homemade yoghurt drink. Situated 2.5km south of Tlalim Junction, on the east side of Rte 40.

THE NEGEV NEGEV HIGHLANDS

at least 1½ hours before the park closes) is a 1.6km circuit that takes you to En Avdat pool and the waterfall and back. The one-way **Long Route** (start at least 2½ hours before the park closes) goes to the park's southern entrance; because one section involves ladders that you can climb but not descend, this route cannot be done in the other direction. From near the southern entrance, it's easy to catch buses going north or south. A longer trail (15km) leads to **En Akev**, a freshwater spring (swimming permitted) further down Wadi Zin; count on this route taking six to seven hours.

The best times to visit are in the spring and fall. Park staff can provide you with a map and details on hiking options.

🏃 Activities

Geofun Desert Cycling　　　　CYCLING
(📞08-655-3350; www.geofun.co.il; Midreshet Ben-Gurion; mountain bike per day adult/youth 80/60NIS; ☉9am-6pm Mon-Thu, to 2pm Fri, closed Sat & Sun) Based in Midreshet Ben-Gurion's small shopping centre, Geofun rents and repairs bikes and sells cycling gear. Staff can supply cycling maps and are happy to help with trip planning.

🛌 Sleeping

Sde Boker Field School　　　HOSTEL $
(📞08-653-2016; http://sdeboker.co.il; Midreshet Ben-Gurion; hostel s/d from 240/290NIS, guesthouse from 320/420NIS, additional child 110NIS; 🖥) Sde Boker's 68-room field school, overlooking Wadi Tzin, has two sections. In the hostel, often filled with noisy school groups, the clean but small, basic rooms come with six beds and a kettle. In the Hamburg House

Guesthouse, rooms are spartan but more comfortable, with foam mattresses, cable TV, kettle and fridge.

Wi-fi is available in the office foyer. From mid-May to September, guests have use of the local swimming pools. If you'll be hiking, staff can arrange packed lunches. Reserve by phone or email.

Krivine Guesthouse　　　B&B $$
(📞052 271-2304; www.krivine-guesthouse.com; No 15, Neve Tzin Neighbourhood, Midreshet Ben-Gurion; d/q 550/750NIS, weekends & holidays extra per person 50NIS) At the end of a quiet residential alley, this guesthouse – run by Marion and John, who hail from France and England respectively – has a new common area, three suites, each with private patio, and one room; all come with colourful sheets and original artwork on the walls.

🍴 Eating

Midreshet Ben-Gurion's 1970s-style commercial centre has an upmarket deli-cafe (Knaaniya), a pizzeria (Domino), a falafel joint, a bakery (a branch of the renowned Lasha, based in Mitzpe Ramon) and a supermarket. There's nowhere to eat on Friday night, Saturday and Jewish holidays.

ℹ Information

Sde Boker Field School Field Study Center (📞08-653-2016; http://sdeboker.co.il; Midreshet Ben-Gurion; ☉8am-4.30pm Sun-Thu) The guides here are extremely knowledgeable about local mammals, reptiles and birds of prey and can supply information about hiking routes. Visiting the serpentarium costs 10/7NIS for an adult/child (call ahead).

❶ Getting There & Away

Metropoline buses 60 and 64, which link Be'er Sheva (13NIS, 40 to 50 minutes) with Mitzpe Ramon (13NIS, 40 minutes) once or twice an hour, stop at Kibbutz Sde Boker, Ben-Gurion's Desert Home, the main gate to Midreshet Ben-Gurion and the petrol station below the Avdat ruins. Bus 65 is twice as fast but stops only along the main roads. Inform the driver in advance where you want to get off. None of these services operate on Shabbat.

Mitzpe Ramon

متسبي رسون   מצפה רמון

📱 08 / POP 5000

In Hebrew, the word *mitzpe* means 'lookout', and Mitzpe Ramon, spectacularly sited on the northern edge of Israel's 'grand canyon', well and truly lives up to its name. Views are of the take-your-breath-away variety and help draw artists and visionary people look-ing for a less pressured and more creative lifestyle. As a result, the town – especially the Spice Route Quarter – positively pulses with innovative energy.

The wide, open spaces that surround Mitzpe, far from crowds and city lights (the stargazing here is superb), are equally suited to those seeking solitude and visitors look-ing for an activity-triggered adrenalin rush.

Despite being in the heart of the desert, Mitzpe (as it's often called) is also one of the coldest places in Israel because of its elevation (900m above sea level), so pack appropriately.

◉ Sights

Mitzpe Ramon's most dynamic neigh-bourhood, the Spice Route Quarter, is a cluster of hangars and warehouses built decades ago as an industrial zone. These days, this is the best place in town to feel Mitzpe's tremendous creative energy –

WORTH A TRIP

RAMAT HANEGEV WINE ROUTE

In recent years the number of wineries in the valleys and hills between Mitzpe Ramon and Be'er Sheva has grown tremendously. These vineyards mark the first attempts to nurture grapes in the Negev Highlands since the ancient Nabataeans made wine at Shivta and Avdat. Using both Nabataean technology and computerised watering systems, today's winegrowers have managed to turn some of Israel's most arid land into lush vineyards.

Located on the kibbutz of the same name, the **Sde Boker Winery** (Kibbutz Sde Boker; ⊘ 8.30am-4pm Sun-Thu, to 2pm Fri, 10am-4pm Sat) was established in 1999, in association with the Hebrew University's School of Agriculture in Rehovot, to test the possibility of growing wine grapes with brackish water. Winemaker Zvi Remak, who hails from San Francisco, concentrates on making handcrafted, barrel-aged red wines from cabernet sauvignon and merlot grapes. You can taste his wines at a stand in the visitor centre next to the Ben-Gurion Desert Home.

Nestled in a valley richly planted with olive and other fruit trees, surrounded by stony Negev slopes, the family run **Carmey Avdat Winery** (📞 08-653-5177; www.carmey-avdat. co.il; Rte 40, near Avdat National Park) was built on the ruins of an ancient agricultural settlement. Founded in 1998, it now produces rosé, merlot, cabernet sauvignon and a cabernet sauvignon/merlot blend. Cheeses and other local products can be purchased in the shop. This is also a lovely spot to spend a few nights (double US$156 to US$237). The six rustic cabins – four with gravel floors – come with fine desert views, a kitchen and a private dipping pool. Breakfast is delivered to guests.

At the the **Boker Valley Vineyards Farm** (📞 052 862-2930, 052 578-6863; www.boker farm.com; Rte 40), run by a friendly Israeli-Dutch family, the heady aromas of red wine permeate the cooperative wine cellar, where you can taste seven local wines for 25NIS (free if you purchase a bottle). They also grow wine grapes, olives and fruit (for jams) and sell local products, including cheese. Five rustic but comfortable wooden cabins (doubles US$165) are scattered on a rocky hillside, each with space for two to five, a hammock, a small kitchenette and an outdoor barbecue area. Guests love the spa-bath hut and the lavish home-cooked breakfasts. Situated 5km north of Kibbutz Sde Boker on Rte 40, on the west side of the highway between the Telalim and Halukim Junctions.

Other local wines to sample include those produced by Ashba, Derech Eretz, Nana (try its impressive chardonnay), Ramat Negev, Rota and Rujum. For more information about visiting the Ramat Hanegev region, go to www.negevtour.co.il.

Mitzpe Ramon

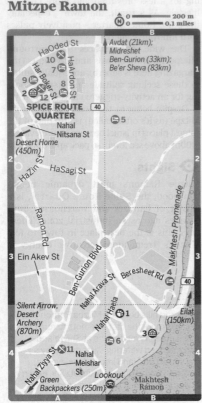

check out the artisanal factories, artists' studios, tiny boutique hotels, yoga studios, cafes and pubs as well as a weaving museum, a superb bakery and even a nationally prominent jazz club.

★ **Makhtesh Ramon**
Nature Reserve   NATURE RESERVE
(www.parks.org.il; ⊘24hr) FREE Sometimes described as Israel's very own grand canyon, Makhtesh Ramon is the largest protected area in Israel and is home to a huge number of hiking, cycling and horse-riding trails, as well as cliffs offering rappelling opportunities. About 300m deep, 9km wide and 40km long, it features multicoloured sandstone, volcanic rock and fossils.

Makhtesh Ramon Visitors Center MUSEUM
(☏08-658-8691; www.parks.org.il; adult/child 28/14NIS; ⊘8am-4pm or 5pm, closes 1hr earlier Fri, last entry 1hr before closing) Perched on the *makhtesh* rim, this visitor centre has

extremely helpful staff who are willing and able to answer questions about the Makhtesh Ramon Nature Reserve, its habitats and its outdoor activities. Most of the museum – *not* a must-see destination by any means – serves as a memorial for Israeli astronaut Ilan Ramon, who died in the Space Shuttle Columbia disaster, though the last section and several films focus on the *makhtesh's* geography and natural history. One-hour tours, some in English, begin every 15 minutes.

Lookout   VIEWPOINT
(Nahal Grofit St; ⊘24hr) Affords spectacular views of Makhtesh Ramon. Ibexes often wander along the cliff rim around here

Bio-Ramon   WILDLIFE RESERVE
(Hai Ramon Living Desert Museum; www.parks. org.il; adult/child 22/9NIS; ⊘8am-4pm or 5pm, closes 1hr earlier Fri) This pocket-sized wildlife park is an excellent place to see desert creatures you're unlikely to encounter in the wild because they are either nocturnal, endangered or both. The animals who live here – all of them rescues – include snakes (most of them venomous), scorpions, tortoises, rodents (eg the fat sand rat), lizards (eg spiny-tail), hedgehogs, porcupines and owls. A short film (in four languages) looks

at how nature finds ways to survive even in the harshest conditions. Bring your Ramon Visitors Center ticket to get a 25% discount.

EthnoCenter MUSEUM
(☐052 882-3895; www.ethnocenter.co.il; Spice Route Quarter; adult/child incl tour 25/15NIS; ☻10am-10pm Mon-Sat) Run by a friendly family from Dagestan, this one-room museum has exhibits and demonstrations on the weaving and tying techniques used to make the traditional rugs of the Caucasus.

🏃 Activities

Some of the best hiking trails in the country, including a section of the Israel Trail, can be picked up in and around Mitzpe. Choose from the easy **Green Trail** descent into the *makhtesh* (5.5km and 2½ hours one way), which takes you by the only spot where collecting coloured sand is permitted; a medium-to-difficult hike to an ancient **ammonite wall** (fossil bed; five to six hours one way); and a highly recommended hike from Mitzpe to the **Hemet Cistern** (16km and five hours one way). The latter follows a trail along the cliff edge, down into a lush

canyon and on to a 4000-year-old cistern. Before you head out, drop by the Makhtesh Ramon Visitors Center for hiking information and trail tips.

Other walks in the area include a 3.5km loop to **Wadi Ardon**; a 7km loop to Wadi Ardon and the **Nekarot Horseshoe**; and a hardcore five-to-six-hour climb up and down **Mt Ardon**.

Shvil Net (www.shvilnet.net) publishes a handy 1:40,000 map covering the Makhtesh Ramon area for cyclists and hikers, available at the Ramon Visitors Centre.

Alpaca Farm HORSE RIDING
(☐052 897-7010; www.alpaca.co.il; admission over age 3yr 30NIS, 1½hr horse ride 175-195NIS; 🚹) It's crazy enough to be genius: in 1988, 170 alpacas were flown from Peru, in a plane with the seats removed, to Mitzpe Ramon, whose climate is similar to the Andes, for the purpose of producing wool (just a few months later, Chile, Peru and Bolivia banned the export of alpacas). Wool production didn't turn out to be very profitable, but today you can pet and feed the alpacas and tour of the old wool-production facilities.

HIKING IN THE NEGEV

The Negev's trails take in a surprisingly wide variety of desert landscapes. Particularly recommended are those around Sde Boker, Mitzpe Ramon, Timna Park and Eilat.

The Society for the Protection of Nature in Israel (SPNI) has field schools with lodging at Mitzpe Ramon, Eilat and the northern Arava settlement of Hatzeva. Although they serve mainly school groups, staff are usually able to provide up-to-date information about local hiking trails and sell 1:50,000-scale hiking maps. Another good bet is to chat with staff at hostels – the people at Green Backpackers (p327) in Mitzpe Ramon and the Sde Boker Field School (p322) are particularly helpful. The Israel Nature and Parks Authority staff at the Makhtesh Ramon Visitors Centre in Mitzpe Ramon are a great source of information and maps.

The Negev environment can be unforgiving; follow these safety guidelines:

➡ Bring a 1:50,000-scale SPNI hiking map.

➡ Walk only on marked trails.

➡ Bring (and drink) plenty of water.

➡ Use sunscreen.

➡ Cover your head.

➡ Don't hike in high summer or in the middle of the day (noon to 3pm).

➡ Avoid the Israel–Egypt border area.

In winter, check the weather forecast to make sure you don't get caught in a flash flood.

Don't hike by yourself and be sure to inform someone of where you are going so that they can sound the alarm if you don't return from your hike as scheduled.

If you get lost in an area with phone reception, call the Israel Nature & Parks Authority hotline on *3639 to find out if a ranger is nearby. If you need to be rescued, dial 100 (Israel Police).

WHAT EXACTLY IS A MAKHTESH?

Usually translated as 'crater' and occasionally as 'canyon', a more accurate definition of a *makhtesh* is an 'erosion cirque' – a large, asymmetrical hole formed by erosion as the Negev made the transition from ocean to desert. Providing a peep into the Earth's crust, the *makhteshim* found in the Negev and Sinai (Egypt) are thought to be a unique geological phenomenon because each is drained by a wadi (valley).

Israel has three large *makhteshim*:

Makhtesh Ramon The world's largest *makhtesh* (40km by 9km). The town of Mitzpe Ramon is perched on its rim.

HaMakhtesh HaGadol The entrance to the 'Big Makhtesh' is about 6km southeast of the sleepy town of Yeroham. There's a beautiful drive right through the crater on Rte 225; look out for the coloured sands.

HaMakhtesh HaKatan The 'Small Makhtesh', nearly circular, is off the highway linking Dimona with the Dead Sea (Rte 25). Vehicles are not allowed to enter the *makhtesh* itself.

Also offers horse riding, for beginners and experienced riders, across the *makhtesh* floor and along its rim. Double saddles are available for parents with kids up to age six. Children under 25kg can take lama rides at the farm (20NIS).

Desert Archery ADVENTURE SPORTS
(☎050 534-4598, 08-658-7274; www.desertarchery.co.il; per person 50NIS, minimum 4) Imagine a game of golf in which you carry a bow and arrow instead of a club, and aim at balloons rather than a hole – that's desert archery. Reserve ahead. Situated next to Silent Arrow hostel.

iBex Excursions OUTDOORS
(☎052 436-7878, 052 361-1115; www.ibexhotel.co.il; 4 Har Ardon St, Spice Route Quarter) Aviva and Menachem can provide information about, and organise, cycling, horse, camel and tours of the *makhtesh* and the Negev Highlands, including the transportation of cyclists and their gear.

☞ Tours

★**Astronomy Israel** TOURS
(☎052 544-9789; www.astronomyisrael.com; adult/child 150/75NIS; ⊗nights Sat-Thu) Ira Machefsky, the self-proclaimed 'Starman of Mitzpe Ramon', runs nightly two-hour group tours to peer into Israel's clearest and darkest skies using both the naked eye and telescopes. Ira has a great sense of humour, and his well-honed and dramatic presentations include plenty of jokes, fascinating information and musical vignettes.

Yoash Limon OUTDOORS
(☎054 533-0948; www.4xdesert.com; jeep tour per person 120-150NIS) One of the most en-

thusiastic and experienced outdoors guides in the Negev, Yoash Limon has worked as a ranger at Bandelier National Monument in New Mexico. A hiking and rappelling enthusiast, he leads jeep tours, guided hikes and rappelling adventures around the region.

Ramon Desert Tours OUTDOORS
(☎052 396-2715; www.ramontours.com; 2-/4hr jeep tour per jeep 850/1200NIS) An experienced jeep tour operator, this local outfit can organise everything from a short tour of the *makhtesh* or Wadi Zin to multiday desert journeys.

Adam Sela ADVENTURE
(☎050 530-8272; www.adamsela.com) Specialising in desert adventure tours, Adam Sela's company offers jeep tours, trekking, canyoning, rappelling and mountain-bike rides. A two-/four-hour jeep tour for eight costs 850/1200NIS.

🛏 Sleeping

There are a lots of accommodation options in and around Mitzpe, ranging from boutique hotels to mud-built desert encampments.

Backpackers can sometimes take up 'volunteering' stints where they barter work for accommodation and meals at budget lodges or hostels.

Me'ever HOSTEL $
(☎08-949-5967; www.meeverland.com; 4 Har Boker St, Spice Route Quarter; dm excl breakfast 90NIS, d excl breakfast 250-360NIS; 🖻) Run mainly by volunteers, this 'creative space' – in a 1000-sq-metre hangar – hosts alternative festivals, events and workshops for up to 600 people and has studio space for dancing

and movement classes. Part of the facility is given over to very basic accommodation – you can sleep in a 24-bed dormitory, an indoor teepee or an adobe hut. Bathrooms are shared.

Green Backpackers HOSTEL $

(☑08-653-2319; www.thegreenbackpackers.com; 2/2 Nahal Sirpad St; dm 88-100NIS, d 385NIS, d with shared bathroom 285NIS; @🛜) Run with enthusiasm by keen hikers Lee and Yoash, this home-style hostel on the edge of town, with 24 beds, is the local backpacker hub. There's a tiny lounge with DVD library, a book exchange, communal kitchen and laundry facilities (25NIS per load). Tea and coffee are free; but a basic breakfast costs 10NIS.

If you're arriving by bus, ask to get off at the Nahal Sirpad/Har Gamal stop, which is in front of the hostel.

Silent Arrow LODGE $

(Hetz BaSheket; ☑052 661-1561; http://silentarrow.com; Mitzpe HaKochavim St; dm/s/d/q with shared bathroom & excl breakfast 90/170/270/470NIS) Seeking the tranquillity and simplicity of the desert? This encampment may fit the bill. A 20-minute (1.5km) walk from town, it offers basic accommodation, a spotless bathroom block, a chill-out courtyard, a fully equipped communal kitchen and a herb garden. Choose a mattress in a 30-bed communal tent or a private dome tent. All electricity is solar.

Desert Shade Eco-Camp LODGE $

(☑08-653-8229, 054 627-7413; www.desert-shade.com; dm 90NIS, s/d/tr/q tent 180/280/360/445NIS, cheaper weekdays; 🛜) Right on the edge of the *makhtesh*, with extraordinary views (especially at sunrise), this place has a Bedouin-style tent sleeping 20, smaller dorms and private 'ecotents' made of mud-covered canvas. Showers and toilets are in a clean barracks-like block off to the side. Communal areas include an attractive lounge-bar, a kitchen block and a campfire area on the crater's edge.

A light breakfast costs 30NIS. This must be the only hostel we've encountered with an on-site winery – be sure to sample its Rujum red blend.

★ iBex Hotel HOTEL $$

(☑052 436-7878, 052 361-1115; www.ibexhotel.co.il; 4 Har Ardon St, Spice Route Quarter; s/d/ste 477/530/665NIS; 🛜) The iBex's slogan is 'selling the experience, not just the room' and this convivial place does just that. Hosts and keen cyclists Aviva and Menachem offer seven small, desert-toned rooms, three garden suites with kitchenette, an airy lounge area, and a communal dining table at which they dispense homemade breakfasts, excellent coffee and advice on outdoor activities. Rates rise on weekends.

InnSense Suites BOUTIQUE HOTEL $$

(☑08-653-9595; www.innsense.co.il; 8 Har Ardon St, Spice Route Quarter; d Sun-Wed 500-650NIS, Thu-Sat 600-780NIS, additional child US$37; 🛜) Mitzpe's first boutique hostelry makes innovative use of one of the Spice Route Quarter's cavernous industrial buildings. The six suites here are huge, with soaring ceilings and sleekly modern decor; three are bi-level. The excellent on-site restaurant is a definite plus.

HI – Mitzpe Ramon Youth Hostel HOSTEL $$

(☑02-594-5566; www.iyha.org.il; 4 Nahal HaEla St; dm 145NIS, s 326-375NIS, d 430-480NIS; 🛜) Just 200m from the Makhtesh Ramon Visitors Center, this large hostel is near the edge of the crater but only some rooms offer views. Like all IHYA hostels, it is mainly geared towards groups, and breakfasts are excellent. The 47 rooms are clean and come with satellite TV, kettle and fridge.

Beresheet RESORT $$$

(☑08-569-8000, reservations 08-638-7799; www.isrotel.com; 1 Beresheet Rd; d US$350-510, villa from US$700; 🛜🏊) Perched right on the edge of the *makhtesh*, this luxury resort hotel has one of the most spectacularly sited infinity pools you're ever likely to dive into (there's also an indoor pool), two restaurants and a busy activities program. The breakfast buffet is renowned (nonguests can partake for 150NIS). It's worth paying extra for a room with crater view – enjoying a sunset drink from your private balcony is really very special.

A two- or three-night minimum sometimes applies on weekends, on holidays and in summer.

Desert Home B&B $$$

(Bait BaMidbar; ☑052 322-9496; www.baitbamidbar.com; 70 Ein Shaviv St; d Sun-Wed US$160, Thu & Sat US$170, Fri US$205; 🛜) On the edge of a quiet residential neighbourhood, this place is for travellers who enjoy their creature comforts. Each of the five units has a kitchenette and is decorated in a minimalist style with locally produced arts and crafts. Top marks for the desert view, the hot tub and the Israeli breakfast.

THE NEGEV MITZPE RAMON

Alpaca Farm B&B   B&B $$$

(☑052 897-7010, 08-658-8047; www.alpacas-farm.
com; d 650-750NIS; 🐾) The four B&B rooms,
set on a hillside, are spacious and comfort-
able, with wooden floors, satellite TV, kitch-
enette and a terrace with hammock. Kids
will love the on-site animals, which include
llamas, alpacas, camels and horses. Two-
night minimum on weekends.

✕ Eating

Almost all of the city's restaurants are in the
Spice Route Quarter.

★Lasha Bakery   BAKERY $

(☑08-865-0111; www.lashabakery.com; off Har
Boker St, Spice Route Quarter; ⊙9am-7pm Sun-
Thu, 8am-about 3pm Fri) Famed throughout
the Negev Highlands for its scrumptious ar-
tisanal breads, made with full-grain wheat,
rye and spelt and without preservatives, this
superb bakery also makes pastries and chal-
lah for Shabbat.

InnSense Bistro   BISTRO $$

(MaMitzpa'it;   ☑08-653-9595;   www.innsense.
co.il; 8 Har Ardon St, Spice Route Quarter; mains
55-70NIS; ⊙8.30am-10.30pm Tue-Thu, Sat & Sun,
8.30am-noon & 5.30-10.30pm Fri, 8.30am-noon
Mon; 🐾🌿) InnSense's bright, good-value
restaurant serves Mediterranean-inflected
dishes. The menu is seasonal but mains
range from pasta to chicken liver, and car-
amelised squash to beef-in-beer. Has a cute,
little, Alice in Wonderland–themed tea room
upstairs. One of the few places in town open
on Shabbat; reserve ahead for Friday night.

HaKatze   ISRAELI $$

(☑08-659-5273; 2 Har Ardon St, Spice Route Quar-
ter; mains 50-65NIS; ⊙noon-8pm or 9pm Wed-
Mon; 🌿) Locals rate this simple place highly.
The menu is home-style, featuring home-
made *labneh* (thick yoghurt flavoured with
garlic and mint) and hummus, salads, and
curried or stewed meats served with rice or
couscous. Has a shaded rear patio.

HeHavit   INTERNATIONAL $$

(☑053 944-1856; www.hahavit.rest.co.il; Nahal
Tziya St; meat mains 60-130NIS, pasta 45-55NIS,
salads 48-58NIS; ⊙noon-midnight Sun-Thu, noon-
3pm Fri, also open after sundown Sat; 🐾🌿) 'The
Barrel' serves hefty portions of fresh salad
(10 kinds), steak, burgers, schnitzel, sandwiches and pasta dishes in a pub-like atmosphere and is the only decent eatery in the
town centre. Has a good range of beers on
tap and a predilection for loud rock music
later in the evening.

☆ Entertainment

The Spice Route Quarter is home to several
pubs.

★Mitzpe Ramon Jazz Club   JAZZ

(☑050 526-5628;   https://jazzramon.wordpress.
com; HaBoker St, Spice Route Quarter; 30-40NIS;
⊙9.30pm-about 2am Wed, Thu & Fri) A respected stop on the Israeli live music circuit, this
intimate venue hosts major Israeli stars as
well as local artists. For details on concerts
(usually jazz, blues, reggae, African or rock),
see the website or Facebook page. There's a
free jam session starting at 11pm or midnight
every Thursday. This place is also a bar.

❶ Information

Before you head out to hike, it's a good idea to
stop by the Makhtesh Ramon Visitors Center
(p324), whose knowledgeable staff can provide
tips and insights as well as hiking maps.

❶ Getting There & Away

Metropoline buses 60 and 64 travel between
Mitzpe and Be'er Sheva (15NIS, 1¾ hours, at
least hourly) from 5am to 9.30pm via Avdat
National Park and Midreshet Sde Boker. Bus 65
(1¼ hours to Be'er Sheva) goes faster because
it only stops along the highway. None of these
services operate on Shabbat.

To get to Eilat (39.50NIS, 2¼ hours, four to
six daily Sunday to Thursday, one Friday), take
Egged bus 392, which starts its run in Be'er
Sheva. In Mitzpe, it stops along Rte 40.

The Arava

وادي عربة   הערבה

Stretching from the Red Sea to the Dead
Sea, the austerely beautiful and sparsely
populated Arava Valley has some of Israel's
most sublime desert scenery, especially at
Timna Park and around Kibbutz Lotan. In
recent years the area has become a hotbed of
research into ecologically sound desert development. To experience sustainable desert
living, head to Kibbutz Lotan.

The Arava has a great deal to offer outdoor enthusiasts. For desert hiking, Timna
Park is the best place to go. A popular 33km
bike trail runs along a wadi between Tzofar
and Paran (Faran) – it forms part of the Israel National Bike Trail.

The Arava is part of the Great Rift Valley (Syrian-African Rift), which runs for
some 6000km from Lebanon's Bekaa Valley to central Mozambique. To the east is

the majestic, multi-hued Jordanian mountain range known in Israel as the Edom Mountains.

◉ Sights

★ Hai-Bar Yotvata Nature Reserve
WILDLIFE RESERVE

(☑08-637-3057; www.parks.org.il; Rte 90; adult/child 29/14NIS; ⊗8.30am-4pm or 5pm, closes 1hr earlier Fri, last entry 1hr before closing) Established in 1968 to reintroduce animals that had died out in Israel, this 32-sq-km reserve on the Yotvata salt flats is home to a wide variety of desert creatures. You can drive through, safari-style, but only if you have your own car; count on spending about two hours. Herbivores you're likely to see include the Dorcas gazelle, Nubian ibex, Somali wild ass, scimitar-horned oryx and addax (white antelope).

Drive slowly, don't get out of the car, and of course don't feed the animals. You can open the car windows, but watch out for the ostriches, who sometimes poke their heads in looking for a handout. The facilities for rehabilitating injured animals and reptiles are no longer open to the public. Staff can provide information on hiking in the Arava and the Eilat Mountains and sell 1:50,000-scale hiking maps. The entrance is 35km north of Eilat, across Rte 90 from Kibbutz Samar.

Timna Park
PARK

(☑08-631-6756; www.parktimna.co.il; adult/child 49/39NIS, valid 3 days; ⊗8am-4pm Sat-Thu, to 3pm Fri Sep-Jun, to 1pm daily Jul & Aug) The site of some of the world's earliest copper mines (c 5000 BCE), the Timna Valley offers an awe-inspiring desert landscape of cliffs and rock formations in contrasting shades of burnt red, pink and tan. Its scenery and archaeological sites can be explored on over 20 hiking trails – many of them circuits – that take between one and 12 hours. Once you're inside the park, you can stay until sundown.

The new visitors centre screens short films on Timna's geography and ancient methods of copper production; it's well worth spending 10NIS for a guide booklet. Bicycles (20/60NIS per hour/day) can be rented at the visitors centre and the artificial lake, where there's a restaurant and paddle-boating. Historic sites include ancient mining shafts and the remains of smelting furnaces, temples and rock drawings (depicting ostriches, ibex and chariots) dating back to ancient imperial Egypt.

You could easily spend a whole day hiking here, but the park, 30km north of Eilat, is so spread out that you'll need a car.

☞ Tours

Kibbutz Lotan
ECOTOUR

(☑054 979-9030; www.kibbutzlotan.com; tour 30NIS) ⌖ Kibbutz Lotan has established an international reputation as an innovator in the quest for low-tech ways to provide food and shelter sustainably and affordably. An eye-opening guided tour (1½ hours, daily at 9.30am) takes you to the prototype EcoCampus, where you can try out a bicycle-powered washing machine, and the Eco-Park, where ideas for sustainable desert living – some of them pretty far-out – are given a trial run.

Tour participants see houses built of mud-covered hay bales, composting toilets and their by-products, a parabolic solar cooker that can set a palm frond alight in seconds, and playful sculptures made of painted mud.

Lotan's Center for Creative Ecology offers educational programs that teach participants hands-on skills in fields such as permaculture farming, ecofriendly waste treatment and the design of regenerative systems. The Eco-Experience (US$65 per day, minimum four days) mixes work on sustainable projects with classes and demonstrations. Graduates of the four-week Green Apprenticeship (US$2030) have established dozens of mud construction companies around the world. Both programs include lodging (in mud-covered geodesic domes) and full board.

Regional bus 20 from Eilat stops at the kibbutz, and Egged buses to/from Eilat stop on Hwy 90, 1.5km from the kibbutz.

Kibbutz Neot Semadar
ECOTOUR

(☑054 979-8966; www.neot semadar.com; Shizafon Junction, Rte 40; tour adult/child under 12yr 25NIS/free; ⊗gallery & tour 10am-1pm Sun-Fri) ⌖ This vegetarian kibbutz (population 200), on the plateau above the Arava (elevation 420m), is known around Israel for its organic agriculture, line of organic juices and Art Center, an extraordinary complex – Gaudí would have recognised the designers as kindred spirits – that took 15 years to build. The best way to see Neot Semadar is on a self-guided tour; no need to reserve ahead – just call from the entrance gate during opening hours.

ISRAEL'S KIBBUTZIM

Back in 1910, when the first kibbutz was established on the shores of the Sea of Galilee, the idea was both practical – growing crops in a harsh climate required collective action – and utopian. The word 'kibbutz' means gathering or clustering, and the original kibbutzniks (members of a kibbutz) were driven by equally weighted beliefs in socialism and Zionism. Committed to achieving Jewish national self-determination, they believed that farming collectively owned land would provide a sound economic and political underpinning for an eventual Jewish state.

At the outbreak of WWII, there were 79 kibbutzim in Palestine, all of which relied on agriculture for their livelihoods. The movement reached its apogee in the 1950s and 1960s, when many new kibbutzim were established by Nahal, an Israel Defense Forces program that combined military service with the establishment of new agricultural settlements.

In the 1980s, as a more individualist ethos gained currency, increasing numbers of residents started to leave their kibbutz homes and forge new lives and careers in Israel's rapidly expanding cities. A number of kibbutzim ended up in debt and, eventually, were forced to privatise. The others had no choice but to reinvent themselves by adopting new ways of structuring the kibbutz economy and finding new sources of income. Many diversified into non-agricultural endeavours, including manufacturing, artisanal industries, tourism and innovative, environmentally sustainable businesses.

Today, there are approximately 270 kibbutzim in Israel. Of these, about three-quarters function according to an economic model known somewhat euphemistically as 'renewing' (mitchadesh), under which kibbutzniks generate and keep their own income. The remaining quarter are run according to the traditional collective model (kibbutz shitufi), whereby members are compensated equally, regardless of what work each member does. Four of these collective kibbitzim are located in the Arava, and most have adopted a business plan that includes sustainable agriculture and tourism.

The tour starts with an 18-minute film on the history and philosophy of the Neot Semadar community and then takes you up the cooling tower, past the goat dairy and to the winery (free tasting), which produces just 10,000 bottles a year. Pay in the **gallery**, where you can admire and purchase gorgeous handmade jewellery, ceramics, weaving, metalwork and wood carving (available online through www.etsy.com).

The Art Center's pink, 36m tower is not just decorative: air flows into the top of the tower and, after being cooled by artificial rain, flows into the artisans' workshops at the base. See the website for details on volunteering (one-month minimum).

Neot Semadar is 60km north of Eilat and 90km south of Mitzpe Ramon (and 12km northwest of Kibbutz Lotan). It is served by all Eilat–Mitzpe Ramon buses.

Kibbutz Ketura   ECOTOUR
(☑08-635-6658; www.ketura.org.il; Rte 90) 🌱
Situated 50km north of Eilat, Ketura is exceptional in two ways: it has transformed itself from a purely agricultural kibbutz into a leader in innovative eco-technology, and it has a pluralistic approach to Judaism. It is home to the internationally renowned **Arava Institute for Environmental Studies** (http://arava.org), which conducts research into desert biodiversity, renewable energy, sustainable agriculture and trans-boundary water management. Tours (1½ hours) are free if you're staying in the guesthouse or 250NIS per group otherwise.

The Arava Institute runs semester-long environmental-studies programs, accredited through Ben-Gurion University, that bring together students from around the world. The kibbutz, founded in 1973, also has a date plantation, Israel's first photovoltaic solar field and an algae factory producing the powerful antioxidant Astaxanthin.

Samar Bike   CYCLING
(☑Yaron 052 304-0640, Yoni 054 496-4777; www.samarbike.com; Kibbutz Samar) Based at Kibbutz Samar, 34km north of Eilat, this outfit runs bike tours in the Arava and can supply pick-up, drop-off and logistics for cyclists following the Israel National Bike Trail. It works with the excellent guesthouse at Kibbutz Elifaz, which is tailored specifically towards bike tourism.

🛌 Sleeping

Six kibbutzim in the southern Arava have guesthouses: Eilot, Elifaz, Ketura, Lotan, Neot Smadar, and Yahel. In the northern Arava, a number of moshavim (cooperative settlements) have B&Bs, some of them quite stylish.

Kibbutz Lotan Guesthouse GUESTHOUSE $$

(🖉054 979-9030; www.kibbutzlotan.com; s 350-420NIS, d 430-510NIS, eco-dome d/tr 260/360NIS; 🕃🖥) 🖉 This pioneering eco-community offers two types of accommodation: traditional guesthouse rooms (26 of them) that are simple but comfortable; and 10 'eco-domes', adobe-covered geodesic domes with shared composting toilets. Facilities include a swimming pool, shady gardens, a children's playground, a basketball court and Frisbee golf. Breakfast, which makes the most of homegrown vegetables and dates, is served in the Tea House.

Egged buses travelling to/from Eilat (45 minutes) can drop passengers on Hwy 90 at the 1.5km-long access road to the kibbutz. Regional Council bus 20 comes into the kibbutz itself.

Kibbutz Ketura Guesthouse KIBBUTZ $$

(🖉08-735-6658; www.keren-kolot.co.il; Kibbutz Ketura; s 350-400NIS, d 420-530NIS; 🅿@🕃🖥) Ketura's guesthouse is comfortable and extremely well maintained. Facilities include bicycle hire and an on-site coffee shop (open 8am to 11pm except Shabbat). Guests receive a free tour of the kibbutz and, on Shabbat, are welcome to join members in the communal dining hall for a dairy Friday night dinner (adult/child 50/45NIS) and a meat Saturday lunch (45/40NIS). The synagogue holds pluralistic Shabbat services.

Egged buses travelling along Hwy 90 will drop passengers here (be sure to specify Kibbutz Ketura, not Ketura Junction). From Eilat, Regional Council bus 20 also stops here.

Desert Days CABIN $$

(Y'mei Midbar; 🖉052 617-0028; www.desert-days.com; Tzukim; d/tr 570/770NIS; 🅿🕃🖥) 🖉 Fourteen cabins made of straw bales and mud provide a base for city dwellers seeking a tranquil desert escape. The surrounds are stony and stark, but three wading pools soften the overall effect. The cabins, most with outdoor kitchens, can sleep up to six; green features include composting toilets, recycled grey water and solar electricity. Situated 114km north of Eilat, 1km off Rte 90.

Neot Semadar Guesthouse GUESTHOUSE $$

(🖉054 979-8957, 054 979-8433; www.neot-semadar.com; Kibbutz Neot Smadar; d excl breakfast 420-450NIS) A minimalist aesthetic is the hallmark of these 12 attractive, sustainably built cabins, which are set in a garden on an quiet hillock 1.5km east of the kibbutz. Each is equipped with a fridge and kettle. Meals, including breakfast, are available at Neot Semadar Inn.

★ Midbara BOUTIQUE HOTEL $$$

(🖉052 426-0320; www.midbara.co.il; Tzukim; d 650 1000NIS, Thu Sat 800 1200NIS; 🅿🕃🖥) Midbara offers 13 stylish, comfortable and well spaced mud cabins scattered along a small wadi planted with fruit trees. All have kitchens, a few have indoor fireplaces and most have a private relaxation pool (wood-heated in winter) and hammock. Children love the free bikes and animals (chickens, a camel, a peacock) – great for a family holiday. Situated 1.5km off Rte 90 at a point 114km north of Eilat.

Desert Routes Inn HOSTEL $$$

(Shvilim BaMidbar; 🖉03-500-4266, 052 366-5927; www.shvilimbamidbar.co.il; Hatzeva; d weekday/weekend excl breakfast 488/650NIS, from 400NIS summer; 🅿🕃🖥) The owners of this 14-room desert inn, close to the Jordanian border in the Northern Arava, are a goldmine of information about the area and can organise jeep, hiking and rappelling tours. They offer private and dorm rooms, and also operate a nearby camping ground. There's a hospitality tent and communal kitchen, making it a great option for self-caterers.

Situated 150km north of Eilat and 65km south of Ein Bokek (Dead Sea).

🍴 Eating

Restaurants can be found near Kibbutz Neot Smadar, and there are several roadside diners along Rte 90 in the northern Arava.

Neot Semadar Inn CAFE $$

(Pundak Neot Semadar; 🖉054 979-8908, 08-635-8180; www.neot-semadar.com; Shizafon Jct, Rte 40; cheese platter 48NIS, labneh 26NIS, mains 45NIS; ⊗7am-7pm Sun-Thu, to 3pm Fri, noon-6pm Sat; 🖉) 🖉 Run by vegetarian Kibbutz Neot Semadar, this all-organic place, with a lush rear garden, serves kibbutz-made goat's-milk cheese, ice cream and *labneh* (thick yoghurt), as well as a range of salads, egg dishes, hummus, pasta and cakes. Be sure to try one of the homemade fruit juices.

ℹ️ Getting There & Away

Almost all of the Egged buses linking Eilat with central and northern Israel travel through the Arava. If you're going to Tel Aviv or Jerusalem, reserving a seat ahead of time is highly recommended.

Eilat

אילת ايلات

🔲 08 / POP 49,700

Hugely popular with Israeli families looking for a beach break and Europeans taking refuge from bone-chilling winters back home, the Red Sea resort of Eilat is brash, ugly and almost inevitably crowded, a place where being scantily clad and sunburned is the rule rather than the exception.

However – and it's a big however – Eilat is also a place where visitors seem to have a great time and where children in particular seem blissfully happy. The turquoise waters of the Red Sea, home to some of the world's most spectacular coral reefs, offer snorkelling, scuba diving and swimming opportunities galore, and there are plenty of other attractions on offer, including (in no particular order) hiking amid spectacular desert scenery, VAT-free shopping and an aquarium. So far, the Red Sea's reefs have suffered almost no bleaching, perhaps because the kinds of coral found here are already used to elevated water temperatures.

◉ Sights

Eilat's beach stretches for 14km from the Jordanian border to the Egyptian frontier. East–west North Beach is fronted by high-rise hotels, while north–south South Beach runs from Mall HaYam (the shopping mall just south of the old airport) to the Taba border crossing.

Two sections of South Beach (the port and the navy base) are off-limits, and two beaches (Dolphin Reef and Coral Beach Nature Reserve) have entry fees. The rest – whose segments go by a plethora of largely unofficial names – are open to the public. Some of the South Beach beaches have cafes, deck chairs and other amenities.

North Beach BEACH
(Map p336; ⊙24hr) Pebbly North Beach and its promenade are often very crowded – for some people, that's one of the main draws. This is by far the most popular place in Eilat to see and be seen. The promenade's restaurants, cafes and bars are another enticement and ensure that the area is full of action until the wee hours. Public showers, bathrooms and a few changing booths can be found at the edge of the beach.

★**Coral Beach Nature Reserve** DIVE SITE
(Map p334; 🔲08-632-6422; www.parks.org.il; adult/child 35/21NIS; ⊙9am-5pm or 6pm, closes 1hr earlier Fri, last entrance 1hr before closing; 🔲15) The crystal-clear waters of this 1km-long reserve are the best place on the Israeli Red Sea coast for snorkelling. Access to the reef wall is by two wooden footbridges and one swim lane; snorkelling areas are marked off by buoys. Snorkelling kit can be rented for 23NIS (100NIS deposit). For picnic supplies, head to the supermarket across the street.

Underwater Observatory Marine Park AQUARIUM
(Map p334; 🔲08-636-4200; www.coralworld.co.il; Coral Beach; adult/child 109/89NIS; ⊙ticket sales 8.30am-4pm, site open to 6pm summer, to sundown rest of year; 🔲15) The stand-out feature of this aquarium complex, hugely popular with families, is the **observatory**, which takes you 12m below the surface of the Red Sea into the living reef for a scuba diver's view of the fish and corals. Other highlights include **Shark World**, a 7m-deep tank that's home to sharks and stingrays, and the excellent **Rare Fish Aquarium**. Tickets are valid for three days, but to come back, you need to get a photo re-entry ticket (free).

Every half-hour you can watch staff feed the fish and sea turtles (green and hawksbill), some of them enormous. Cruises on the park's **Coral 2000** glass-bottomed, deep-hulled boat leave hourly between 10.25am and 1.25pm (adult/child 28/22NIS). Guides, wearing turquoise-coloured shirts, are happy to answer questions. Situated at the southern tip of the Coral Beach Nature Reserve; a taxi from town costs about 40NIS.

Dolphin Reef Eilat BEACH
(Map p334; 🔲08-630-0111; www.dolphinreef.co.il; South Beach; adult/concession 67/46NIS; ⊙9am-5pm, to 6pm or later in summer; 🔲15) This privately run beach is famous for its abundant shade trees, free-range peacocks and resident pod of semi-wild bottlenose dolphins. Originally from the Black Sea, the dolphins can be observed from floating piers – great for lounging – and may sidle up to check you out during a guided snorkelling session (adult/child 290/260NIS; minimum age 10) or guided introductory scuba dive (adult/

SCUBA DIVING & SNORKELLING
....

The Red Sea's coral reefs offer some of the world's most thrilling scuba diving. All you need to do is pop your head underwater to see all sorts of extraordinary fish and coral (the area is thought to have 1200 species of fish and 250 of coral), making Eilat a great place for kids as well as for adult beginners looking to do a PADI scuba course. The best dive sites are Coral Beach Nature Reserve, Lighthouse Reef, Neptune's Tables (aka Veronica's Reef), the Caves and two offshore shipwrecks. For snorkelling, head to Coral Beach Nature Reserve (equipment available for rent), the public beach near the Princess Hotel (a bit north of Taba) and Lighthouse Beach (equipment rental available).

Prices vary but average around 230NIS for an introductory dive and 550NIS for a half-day PADI Discover Scuba Diving session, including equipment hire. To dive or snorkel independently, count on paying around 40NIS to rent a snorkel, mask and fins (a wetsuit costs an additional 40NIS to 60NIS), and 155NIS for a full scuba set; a tank refill is 25NIS.

Eilat has more than a dozen dive centres offering courses and equipment rental, almost all of them along South Beach. Most are open daily from 8am or 8.30am to 5pm or 5.30pm.

Aqua Sport International (Map p334; ☐08-633-4404; www.aqua-sport.com; northern end of Coral Beach; ☺8.30am-5.30pm) Founded in 1962, this respected, British-owned company offers all the PADI diving courses (including introductory courses) and a full-day snorkelling cruise (250NIS). Situated just south of the Coral Beach Club's pedestrian bridge. Has a branch just across the border in Taba, from where the two-hour sunset cruise departs.

Deep Siam (Map p334; ☐08-632-3636; www.deepdivers.co.il; Coral Beach; ☺8am-5pm) This highly regarded outfit offers introductory dives and a wide variety of scuba courses.

Manta Isrotel Diving Center (Map p334; ☐08-633-3666; www.divemanta.com; just north of Coral Beach; ☺8.30am-5pm, to 6pm summer) This veteran outfit offers introductory dives (220/360NIS for 25/40 minutes; minimum age eight), guided snorkelling (225NIS to 270NIS for up to three people) and SDI-TDI courses. Operates out of the Isrotel Yam Suf Hotel so it can offer services such as babysitting.

Reef Diving Group (☐08-630-0111; www.reefdivinggroup.co.il) A respected outfit with two Eilat branches and one in Tel Aviv.

Snuba (Map p334; ☐08-637-2722; www.snuba.co.il; South Beach 1km north of Taba) Especially popular with Russian tourists, Snuba offers PADI courses, introductory dives (220NIS) to the adjacent Caves Reef and a one-hour 'Snuba Adventure' for novices (200NIS; minimum age eight). Snuba diving (the name is a contraction of 'snorkel' and 'scuba'), in which air is supplied from the surface, does not require certification.

child 339/309NIS; minimum age eight). Physical contact with the dolphins is forbidden. Reserve ahead for both. Has two restaurants, one of them with a beach bar. Situated just south of the port.

Dekel Beach　　　　　　　　　BEACH
(Palm Beach; Map p334) Wedged between the port and the naval base about 1.5km south of the city centre, Dekel is less crowded than North Beach and is a popular snorkelling spot.

Village Beach　　　　　　　　BEACH
(Map p334) Situated just north of Coral Beach, this section of South Beach has free umbrellas, clean water for snorkelling and a bar hosting loud parties during summer.

Eilat Museum　　　　　　　　MUSEUM
(Map p336; ☐08-634-0754; www.eilat-history.org.il; adult/child 10/5NIS; ☺10am-8pm Mon-Thu, 10am-2pm Fri, noon-8pm Sat, to 10pm Mon-Thu & Sat Jun-Sep) Tells the fascinating history of Israel's Red Sea outpost. Exhibits cover the capture of Eilat in 1949 and include some great photos of the city's pioneers in the 1940s, 1950s and 1960s. Shows several films, most in English.

**International Birding
& Research Center in Eilat**　WILDLIFE RESERVE
(IBRCE; Eilat Birding Center; Map p334; ☐050 767-1290; www.eilatbirds.com; ☺park 24hr, office 8am-4pm Sun-Thu) FREE Hundreds of millions of migrating birds pass through Eilat twice a year as they fly between Europe and

Eilat

Email or call ahead for details on 1½-hour guided tours (35NIS if you join an already scheduled group). A ringing (banding) station operates during the first four hours of daylight from 15 February to 15 May and from 15 August to 31 November – visitors are welcome to stop by to see how birds are tagged and released for research purposes.

Botanical Garden of Eilat GARDENS (Map p334; ☎08-631-8788; www.botanicgarden. co.il; Carmel St, Industrial Zone; adult/child 28/22NIS; ⊗8.30am-7pm summer, to 5pm winter Sun-Thu, 8.30am-3pm Fri, from 9.30am Sat; ▣5 & 6) Planted with more than 1000 different types of tropical trees, plants and bushes from around the world, this lovely, privately run botanical garden (it began as a plant nursery) features a stream, waterfalls, walking tracks and – a lush surprise in this arid landscape – a misty rainforest. A taxi from the centre of town costs about 22NIS.

🕺 Activities

Eilat offers activities along, in, on and above the water for every age and level of expertise. You can also head for the (reddish) hills along trails that range from easy-peasy to very challenging.

Africa. The best place to spot them is this lakeside centre, situated 6km northeast of town; from the Yitzhak Rabin–Wadi Araba Border Crossing, go south for 400m (follow the signs). The staff are friendly and very knowledgeable.

The main months of migration are March to May and September to November. The best times of day to spot birds are the first four hours after daybreak and the last three hours of sunlight. During office hours, the IBRCE serves as a free information centre for birdwatchers, answering questions such as, 'Where can I find a little green bee eater?'.

A variety of companies offer one-day tours to Petra. Expect to pay about US$315 (which includes US$130 in border fees).

Camel Ranch   CAMEL RIDING

(Map p334; ☑08-637-0022; www.camel-ranch.co.il; Nachal Shlomo; camel safaris adult 150-245NIS, child 7-12yr 110-180NIS, Rope Park adult/child under 12yr 106/96NIS; ⊗4-8pm Mon-Sat Passover-Rosh HaShana, from 10am Mon-Sat Rosh HaShana-Passover) For a bit of desert adventure, head to the Camel Ranch. Camel safaris last 1½ to four hours; various versions, one of them at sunset, include a Bedouin tea break, supper and/or a campfire. Children under seven ride with their parents. It's a good idea to reserve ahead by phone or via the website (15% discount).

To explore the Rope Park (ropes course) you must wear covered shoes, be at least 1.2m tall and weigh less than 120kg. Situated 1.7km off Mitzrayim Rd/Rte 90; turn off the highway about 600m south of Dolphin Reef.

Alaemon Birding   BIRDWATCHING

(☑052 368-9773; http://eilatbirding.blogspot.co.il; full-day tour 1400NIS) Until 2014, keen birder Itai Shanni was the Eilat and Arava regional coordinator for the Israel Ornithological Centre. Now he operates ecotours focussing on birds and birding in the Arava. Advance bookings are essential – at least three weeks ahead from February to May, one week the rest of the year. Active Facebook pages include 'Alaemon Birding' and 'Eilat & Arava Birders'.

Ice Park Mall   ICE SKATING

(Map p336; cnr Kampen & Piestany Sts; incl skate rental 76NIS; ⊗11am-11pm, to midnight Jul & Aug) The featured attraction and namesake – of this shopping complex is Israel's largest ice-skating rink, the perfect place to relax and cool off on a scorching summer's day.

☞ Tours

Desert Eco Tours   ADVENTURE

(☑08-632-6477, 052 276-5753; www.deserteco tours.com) Offers jeep tours in the Eilat area (eg to the Red Canyon; 158NIS per person) and around the Negev, including Makhtesh Ramon. Also has popular tours to Petra and Wadi Rum in Jordan.

✴ Festivals & Events

★ Red Sea Jazz Festival   MUSIC

(☑tickets 03-511-1777; https://redseajazz.co.il; ⊗Jan & Aug) Going strong since 1987, the renowned Red Sea Jazz Festival takes place each year during the last week of August. Outdoor performances are staged around the Eilat Sea Port. The festival's legendary all-night jam sessions are free. Also stages a winter event in January.

Eilat Chamber Music Festival   MUSIC

(www.eilat-festival.co.il; ⊗Feb) Held over four days in early February, this international festival hosts chamber music ensembles, new productions, renowned soloists and masterclasses.

🛏 Sleeping

Eilat has about 50 hotels with 15,000 hotel rooms. Some of the most comfortable are along North Beach Promenade; prices tend to drop as you move inland. Inexpensive but decent places can be found on the side streets around the central bus station, 1.5km northwest of North Beach. Prices rise by about 25% at weekends and 50% (or more) during Israeli school holidays and in July and August.

Motel Aviv   HOTEL $

(Map p336; ☑08-637-4660; www.avivhostel.co.il; 126 Ofarim St; d excl breakfast 170-210NIS, ste excl breakfast 300-350NIS; 📶🛈) This five-story place, in proud possession of a mini swimming pool, is most definitely not a motel, but it's an excellent budget option nevertheless. Family-run, it has 40 rooms. Standard

---

WATER SPORTS

Companies operating from half-a-dozen beach docks along the North Beach Promenade, in front of the Royal Beach Hotel, offer a wide variety of activities that take place on – or in some cases above – the water. All are open from 9am until sundown.

In addition to two-hour boat excursions, perhaps in a glass-bottom boat (adult/child 80/50NIS), and motor-boat rental (150/250NIS for 30/60 minutes tooling around in a five-person boat), you can ride on a banana boat (45NIS per person), hire a jet ski (150NIS for 15 minutes, accompanied by an instructor), parasail, waterski (180NIS for 15 minutes, 250NIS including a lesson) and fly around on a flyboard (a platform that shoots into the air thanks to water jets powered by a jet ski; 390NIS for 20 minutes, including a lesson).

Eilat Town Centre

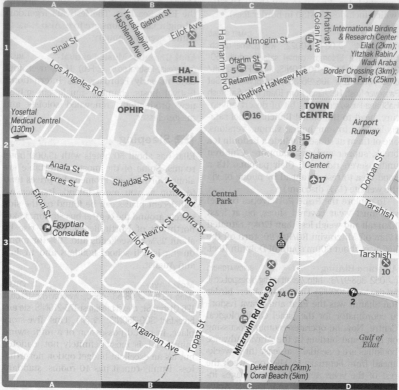

THE NEGEV EILAT

rooms are small with tiny windows, while suites are larger and some have sea views.

Arava Hostel   HOSTEL $
(Map p336; ☎08-637-4687; www.aravahostel.
com; 106 Almogim St; dm/s/d 80/200/240NIS;
@ ☎) The only place in Eilat with an authentic backpacker vibe, the ILH-affiliated, 100-bed Arava won't win any awards for its spartan rooms and dark, cramped dorms, or for its location. There are compensations, though: a date-palm-shaded front garden that's perfect for sunset beers, a communal kitchen, laundry facilities (20NIS per load) and free parking. Luggage lockers cost 10NIS.

Blue Hotel   HOTEL $$
(Map p336; ☎08-632-6601; www.bluehotel.co.il;
123 Ofarim St; s 216-342NIS, d 240-380NIS; @ ☎)
Run by a friendly Israeli-Irish couple, this place has 34 well-priced rooms – reached via open-air hallways – that are nothing to write

home about but do have useful amenities (fridge, cable TV, kettle). There are bicycles for hire and guests receive discounts on diving packages with the Reef Diving Group.

**Eilat Youth Hostel
& Guest House**   HOSTEL $$
(Map p336; ☎02-594-5605; www.iyha.org.il;
18 Mitzrayim Rd/Rte 90; dm 126-155NIS, s 300-376NIS, d 380-500NIS; @ ☎) This recently renovated 107-room hostel is an extremely attractive option, thanks to its location and its modern, clean and comfortable rooms and dorms. Often hosts school groups. There are plans to add a pool.

Orchid Reef Hotel   HOTEL $$$
(Map p334; ☎08-636-4444; www.orchidhotels.
com; Coral Beach; d standard/sea view 675/
800NIS, Thu & Fri 1250NIS; ☎ ☒) The Orchid Reef overlooks a lovely stretch of sand very near the Coral Reef Nature Reserve. It has a 10m pool, fitness room, spa and restaurant.

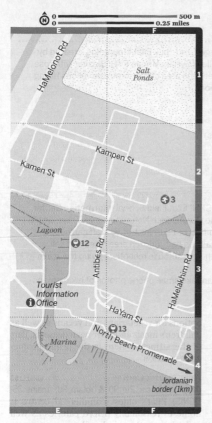

0 —— 500 m
0 —— 0.25 miles

Eilat Town Centre

THE NEGEV EILAT

all-Hebrew sign includes the number '1978' (the year HaLev HaRachav was founded) and the English word 'kosher'.

Uga Chaga
PASTRIES $

(Map p336; ☑ 050 996-7100; 173 Eilot Ave; mains 32-45NIS; ⊘ 8am-8pm Sun-Thu, to 3pm or 4pm Fri; 🛜📶) A long-time local favourite, this pleasant pocket cafe, filled with red couches and little white tables, serves French-style pastries and cakes, sandwiches, salads, shakshuka and pasta. It's perfect for breakfast or a light lunch.

The Brewery
PUB FOOD $$

(HaMavshela; Map p334; ☑ 08-935-0550; www. soof.co.il; 2 HaOrgim St, Industrial Zone; mains 58-125NIS; ⊘ 5pm-2am Sun-Thu, from 1pm Fri & Sat; 🛜) Founded in 2015, this convivial microbrewery – Eilat's first – has quickly established itself among locals as a favourite spot for a drink and/or a meal. If you're hungry, options include quite decent salads, pasta, fish, seafood and steak. If you're thirsty, try one of Soof Craft Brewery's six tasty brews.

Beach activities include snorkelling, windsurfing and sea kayaking, and bike use is free. The 79 comfortable rooms, decorated in desert tones, are spacious and most have a terrace with sea view.

✖ Eating

Visitor-oriented restaurants, cafes and pubs can be found on the North Beach Promenade and on the streets around the lagoons. The New Tourist Center (p338) is home to a number of reasonably priced eateries. For self-caterers, a number of little supermarkets can be found a block inland from North Beach and at various points along South Beach (Mitzrayim Rd/Rte 90).

HaLev HaRachav
FALAFEL $

(Map p334; HaTemarim Blvd; falafel 19NIS; shawarma 32NIS; ⊘ 11am-11pm Sun-Thu, to 3pm or 4pm Fri) Many locals swear that this eatery serves the best falafel and shawarma in town. The

DON'T MISS

DESERT HIKES

Towering over Eilat from the west are the jagged, red-rock Eilat Mountains, created by the tectonic movements of the Great Rift Valley (Syrian-African Rift). Blazing with rose and maroon (especially at sunrise and sunset), the area offers some marvellous hiking opportunities. Among the more popular options:

Red Canyon (easy; 2km, two hours)

Mt Tzfachot (easy; 4km, 2½ hours)

Sh'choret Canyon (easy; 3km, three hours)

Ein Netfim (medium; 2.5km, three hours)

Wadi Gishron (easy; 3km, three hours)

Mt Shlomo (difficult; 8km, six hours)

Hiking maps and advice are available at the SPNI Eilat Field School Information Center (p339), across Mitzrayim Rd/Rte90 from the Coral Beach Nature Reserve. There won't necessarily be an experienced guide in the office, but administrative staff can supply you with excellent sheets in English with details on half-a-dozen area hikes and sell 1:50,000-scale hiking maps (85NIS). From the guesthouse reception, go up the stairs and to the end of the hall.

At Eilat's Tourist Information Office you can take smartphone photos of hiking maps and information.

★**Pastory**　　　　　　　ITALIAN **$$**
(Map p336; ☎08-634-5111; http://pastory.co.il; 7 Tarshish St; mains 48-158NIS; ☺1-11pm) *Mamma mia!* Who would have thought that an authentic Italian-style trattoria serving *molto delizioso* cuisine would be found in a North Beach back street? This family-friendly place behind the Leonardo Plaza Hotel serves antipasti platters packed with flavourful morsels, al dente pasta with rustic sauces, piping-hot pizza with quality toppings and an irresistible array of homemade desserts and gelato.

Campania　　　　　　　ISRAELI **$$**
(Colonia; ☎08-933-4993; www.colonia.co.il; 160 Mitzrayim Rd/Rte 90; mains 44-98NIS; ☺9am-late; ☎✔) Just 300m north of the Taba border crossing, this outdoor eatery has great sea views to accompany the delicious, Mediterranean-inspired food. The homemade focaccia is heavenly, and the shakshuka and pizza are also very good. Everything is made with first-quality ingredients. It's possible to overnight here in eight deluxe tents.

Giraffe　　　　　　　　ASIAN **$$**
(Map p336; ☎08-631-6583; www.giraffe.co.il; Herods Promenade; sushi 16-45NIS; noodles 53-62NIS; mains 54-69NIS; ☺noon-11pm) The Eilat branch of this popular, nine-restaurant chain of pan-Asian noodleries offers great

options for vegetarians and vegans as well as children's meals and European desserts. Part of the attraction here is the prime promenade location.

New Tourist Center　　　　ISRAELI **$$**
(Map p336; cnr Rte 90 & Yotam Rd; mains 35-110NIS) Eilat's oldest commercial centre is home to reasonably priced eateries as well as Irish and other kinds of bars.

★**Fish Market**　　　　　SEAFOOD **$$$**
(Shuk HaDagim; Map p334; ☎08-637-9830; http://shokdagim.rest.co.il; Almog Beach, Rte 90; mains incl salads 79-119NIS; ☺12.30-11pm; ☎) Fresh fish from the Red Sea, the Mediterranean and Egypt's Nile Delta and beef from the Golan are the stars at this fish restaurant – some say it's Eilat's best. Specialities include barramundi. Every meal begins with a selection of Mediterranean salads. Has a Greek ambience, with blue and white banquettes, chequered table cloths and Greek music on the sound system.

Last Refuge　　　　　　SEAFOOD **$$$**
(Map p334; ☎08-637-3627; www.rol.co.il/sites/hamiflat; north end of Coral Beach; mains 92-140NIS; ☺12.30-10.30pm) Run aground in a 1970s time warp (fishing nets dangle from the ceiling, French chansons pine for Paris and garlic butter figures heavily on the menu), this place promises little on first in-

spection but confounds the sceptic with its delicious catch of the day (when available), grilled over coals, and fish such as locally caught swordfish.

Drinking & Nightlife

The drinking scene in Eilat is largely confined to raucous pubs on and around North Beach and in the New Tourist Center. The club scene is healthy, but venues have short lifespans and hot spots change every season – staff at your hotel should be able to give you the low-down.

Mike's Place
PUB

(Map p336; ☑08-864-9550; www.mikesplace bars.com; HaMayim St; ⊗noon-2am or later; ☜) At the southern branch of Mike's five-pub empire, Monday is open-mic night (from 10pm), Tuesday is for jam sessions (from 10pm), Wednesday is women's night, and there's live music on Thursday, Friday and Saturday starting at 10pm or 10.30pm. See the website for performance schedules

Three Monkeys Pub
PUB

(Map p336; ☑08-636-8888; North Beach Promenade; ⊗8.30pm-2am) Inevitably packed with sunburnt tourists, this place – run by Isrotel's Royal Beach Hotel – owes its popularity to its boardwalk location and the fact that it hosts live bands most nights from 9.30pm to 12.30am. Be warned that drinks are expensive and service can be both slow and abrupt.

Shopping

Eilat is a VAT-free city (that's why there are so many computer stores), so prices should be 17% lower than elsewhere in the country. Alas, this is not necessarily the case. Shopping malls make a good refuge from the midday heat, especially for kids.

Mall HaYam
MALL

(Map p336; 1 HaPalmach St; ⊗9am-11pm Sat-Wed, to midnight Thu, to 6pm Fri) Right on the seafront, this hugely popular mall is where locals and tourists go to buy up big in high-street stores including Zara, Mango and the local equivalent, Castro.

❶ Information

To change money, your best bet is one of the exchange bureaux near the central bus station (HaTemarim Blvd). The post office offers good rates, but be prepared for a wait.

Egyptian Consulate (Map p336; ☑08-637-6882; www.egyptembassy.net; 68 Efroni St; ⊗9.30-noon Sun-Thu)

Tourist Information Office (Map p336; ☑08-630-9111; www.goisrael.com; Bridge House, North Beach Promenade; ⊗8.30am-5pm Sun-Thu, 8am-1pm Fri; ☜) Run by the Ministry of Tourism, this extremely helpful office answers questions (in person, by phone and by email), supplies free maps and brochures, and gives away second-hand books in English, French, German and other languages. You can use your smartphone to (legally) photograph walking guides to eight area hikes. Has free wi-fi and sockets to charge smartphones and tablets.

SPNI Eilat Field School Information Center (Map p334; ☑08-632-6468; www.spni.org.il; across Mitzrayim Rd/Rte 90 from Coral Beach Nature Reserve; ⊗8am-3pm Sun-Thu) Don't count on there being an experienced guide in the office, but administrative staff can supply you with excellent sheets in English that have details on half-a-dozen area hikes, and sell you 1:50,000-scale hiking maps (85NIS). You can take smartphone photos of some materials. From the guesthouse reception, go up the stairs and to the end of the hall.

Yoseftal Medical Center (Map p334; ☑08-635-8015; Yotam Rd, just west of Argaman Ave; ⊗24hr emergency dept) Eilat's hospital has 68 beds.

❶ Getting There & Away

AIR

Ramon International Airport (www.iaa.gov.il), in the Arava Valley 18km north of Eilat, will replace Eilat's city centre **airport** (Map p336; ☑08-637-1515; www.iaa.gov.il) and **Ovda Airport** (☑08-367-5387; www.iaa.gov.il), long used by charter carriers from Europe. It will also serve as Israel's second full-service international airport. The new facility is named for Ilan Ramon, the Israeli astronaut who died in the Space Shuttle Columbia disaster, and his son Assaf, an Israel Air Force pilot who was killed when his F-16 crashed.

Both Arkia (www.arkia.com) and Israir (www.israirairlines.com) link Eilat with Ben Gurion Airport (35 minutes) and Tel Aviv's Sde Dov several times a day. Arkia also goes to Haifa. Prices vary depending on demand, ranging from as low as 86NIS to 420NIS one way to/from Tel Aviv.

Low-cost airlines such as Finnair, Ryanair, Scandinavian, Transavia and Wizz offer nonstop services to Eilat from a wide variety of European cities. Many services are seasonal (winter and spring).

BORDER CROSSINGS

The Yitzhak Rabin–Wadi Araba border crossing between Israel and Jordan is about 5km northeast of Eilat, while the Taba border crossing with Egypt is about 9km southwest.

ℹ️ EILAT'S CLIMATE

In July and August, daily highs average 40°C, though because humidity levels are extremely low (10% to 15%), you don't feel sweaty. In December and January, daily highs average 20°C. The city averages just 18 days of rain a year.

BUS

Eilat's **central bus station** (Map p336; www.bus.co.il; HaTemarim Blvd), about 1.5km northwest of North Beach, has excellent bus connections to the rest of Israel.

Be'er Sheva (Egged buses 392, 393 and 397; 42.50NIS, 3½ hours, every hour or two) Operates until late afternoon on Friday; service resumes in the early afternoon on Saturday.

Dead Sea (Egged bus 444; 42.50NIS, 2¾ hours to Ein Bokek, eight per day Sunday to Thursday, three on Friday, three Saturday afternoon and evening)

Jerusalem (Egged buses 444 and 445; 70NIS, 4¼ to five hours, 10 on Sunday, four daily Monday to Wednesday, seven on Thursday, three on Friday, three Saturday afternoon and evening) Bus 445 is an express service.

Mitzpe Ramon (Egged bus 392; 39.50NIS, 2¼ hours, four to six daily Sunday to Thursday, one Friday)

Tel Aviv (Egged buses 390, 393, 394 and 790; 70NIS, five to 5¾ hours, every hour or two) From Sunday to Thursday, there are departures from 4am or 5am to 7pm or 8pm, with a red-eye at 1am. On Friday, the last bus leaves around 3pm; service resumes on Saturday at 11am. To reserve a seat (highly recommended), go to www.egged.co.il (click 'Book Tickets Online') or call *2800; reservations can be made up to 14 days ahead.

ℹ️ Getting Around

The town centre is walkable, but you'll need a car, bus or taxi to get to South Beach and other places along Mitzrayim Rd/Rte 90 (the road to the Egyptian border at Taba).

BUS

Egged bus 15 leaves from the central bus station and travels via the North Beach hotels and the South Beach beaches to the Taba border crossing (4.20NIS, 36 minutes) every hour from about 8am to 9pm Sunday to Thursday, 8am to 3pm or 4pm Friday and 9am to 7pm Saturday. Travelling north from Taba, the bus changes its number to 16.

CAR

At least until Ramon Airport comes online, car-rental agencies are clustered in the Shalom Center, across from the old airport. Most are along Rte 90 facing the Paz petrol station; **Hertz** (Map p336; ☎ 08-637-5050; www.hertz.co.il; 8 HaTemarim Blvd, Shalom Center) is around the corner, a bit up HaTemarim Blvd. Other agencies include **Budget** (Map p336; ☎ 03-935-0016; www.budget.co.il; 2 HaTemarim Blvd, Shalom Center) and **Eldan** (Map p336; ☎ 08-637-4027; www.eldan.co.il; 2 HaTemarim Blvd, Shalom Center).

Parking in most parts of Eilat costs 5NIS per hour or 25NIS per day. Meters only take coins. A day ticket is valid all over the city.

TAXI

To reach the Yitzhak Rabin–Wadi Arava border crossing into Jordan, you'll have to take a taxi (50NIS). Although distances in Eilat are short, the heat means that taking a cab is sometimes a lifesaver. A taxi from the (old) airport to most parts of the city centre or North Beach costs around 15NIS to 20NIS; to Coral Beach you'll be looking at 35NIS.

Petra

البتراء

Best Places to Eat

➜ Al Saraya Restaurant (p352)

➜ Petra Kitchen (p347)

➜ Oriental Restaurant (p352)

➜ Basin Restaurant (p346)

Best Places to Stay

➜ Mövenpick Hotel (p352)

➜ Rocky Mountain Hotel (p349)

➜ Cleopatra Hotel (p349)

➜ Peace Way Hotel (p349)

➜ Petra Guest House Hotel (p352)

Why Go?

Petra, the great Ancient City that lies half-hidden in the wind-blown landscape in southern Jordan, is one of the world's most treasured Unesco heritage sites. Voted by popular ballot in 2007 as one of the 'New Seven Wonders of the World', it has retained its magnetism even through times of strife in the wider region.

A visit to Petra when it was rediscovered for the wider world by Burckhardt in the 19th century meant going in disguise, speaking in local dialect and engaging the trust of surrounding tribespeople. Today visitors are welcomed both by the Bedouin who still relate to the Ancient City as home, and by the townspeople of neighbouring Wadi Musa whose facilities make a several-day visit to the Ancient City a pleasure. With nearby Nabataean attractions at so-called Little Petra, desert camping and numerous hiking opportunities, at least two days should be allowed to do Petra justice.

When to Go
Wadi Musa

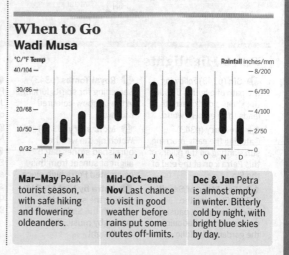

| | Mar–May Peak tourist season, with safe hiking and flowering oldeanders. | Mid-Oct–end Nov Last chance to visit in good weather before rains put some routes off-limits. | Dec & Jan Petra is almost empty in winter. Bitterly cold by night, with bright blue skies by day. |

History

Petra was established in the 4th century BCE by the Nabataeans, a nomadic tribe from Arabia. In its heyday, the city was home to around 30,000 people, including scribes and engineers who built a city of sophisticated culture with an emphasis on the afterlife. Around 100 CE the Romans assumed control, leaving trademark features such as the colonnaded street.

Earthquakes in 363 and 551 ruined much of Petra and it became a forgotten outpost, known only to local Bedouin who preferred keeping its whereabouts secret. In 1812 a young Swiss explorer, JL Burckhardt, ended Petra's splendid isolation, riding into the city disguised as a Muslim holy man.

During the 1950s, Petra achieved near-mythological status in Israel, and a number of young Israelis risked – and in some cases lost – their lives trying to visit the site surreptitiously. Israelis – and tourists visiting Israel – have been able to visit the site legally since the 1994 peace treaty between Jordan and Israel.

❶ Getting There & Away

Petra is a two-hour drive from Aqaba (120km) and the nearby Wadi Araba/Yitzhak Rabin border crossing with Israel. For a one-day tour from Eilat, expect to pay about US$315, including US$130 in border fees. By public transport, minibuses to Wadi Musa leave Aqaba between 6.30am and 8.30am, with one final run in the mid-afternoon.

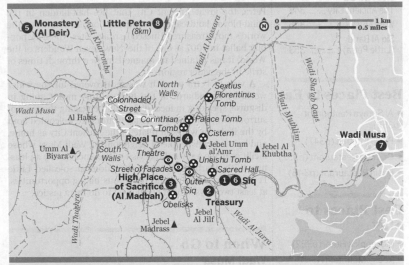

Petra Highlights

❶ **Siq** (p343) Following the path of pilgrims through the sheer-sided chasm that leads to an ancient world.

❷ **Treasury** (p343) Catching the early-morning sun slanting off the pillars of this Petra icon at the end of the Siq.

❸ **High Place of Sacrifice** (p343) Climbing the processional way, pausing for tea with the Bedouin in the gardens of wildflowers.

❹ **Royal Tombs** (p343) Searching for spirits lurking in the rainbow-coloured hollows.

❺ **Monastery** (p346) Watching the weather-burnished stones catch alight at sunset from this celebrated Petra high place.

❻ **Petra by Night** (p347) Letting the soul glide through the Siq's shadows, guided by music and candlelight.

❼ **Petra Kitchen** (p347) Preparing a traditional Jordanian supper in the company of fellow travellers, guided by experts, in Wadi Musa.

❽ **Little Petra** (p353) Enjoying Nabataean tombs and temples in a miniature siq outside the Ancient City often overlooked by tour groups.

If you cross from the West Bank into Jordan at King Hussein/Allenby Bridge, you can catch a minibus to Wadi Musa between 6am and noon at Amman's south bus station (Wahadat).

The Ancient City
◉ Sights

There are more than 800 registered sites in Petra, including some 500 tombs, but the best things to see are easy to find and easy to reach. From the main gate, a path winds 800m downhill through an area called **Bab As Siq** (Gateway to the Siq), punctuated with the first signs of the old city.

Start your visit to Petra at the Petra Visitor Centre (p347) plaza in Wadi Musa, across from the Mövenpick Hotel. This is where you buy tickets, get leaflets and a map, and use the toilets (although there are several inside the Ancient City).

Hikes you might want to consider include **Wadi Muthlim to the Royal Tombs** (1½ hours; guide mandatory), **Umm Al Bayara** (three hours one way) and **Jebel Haroun** (six hours return).

★ Siq
CANYON

The 1.2km Siq, or canyon, with its narrow, vertical walls, is undeniably one of the highlights of Petra. The walk through this magical corridor, as it snakes its way towards the hidden city, is one full of anticipation for the wonders ahead – a point not wasted on the Nabataeans who made the passage into a sacred way, punctuated with sites of spiritual significance.

★ Treasury
TOMB

(Al Khazneh) Known locally as the Treasury, this tomb is where most visitors fall in love with Petra. The Hellenistic facade is an astonishing piece of craftsmanship. Although carved out of iron-laden sandstone to serve as a tomb for the Nabataean King Aretas III (c 100 BCE–CE 200), the Treasury derives its name from the story that an Egyptian pharaoh hid his treasure here (in the facade urn) while pursuing the Israelites.

Street of Facades
RUINS

From the Treasury, the passage broadens into what is commonly referred to as the Outer Siq. Riddling the walls of the Outer Siq are more than 40 tombs and houses built by the Nabataeans in a 'crow step' style reminiscent of Assyrian architecture. Colloquially known as the Street of Facades, they are easily accessible, unlike many tombs in Petra.

ⓘ CAUTION: NO RAILINGS
....

The Ancient City is strewn with 'high places', once used for sacrifice or other rituals. These locations, all of which afford magnificent views and are a highlight of a visit, usually involve a steep hike up steps to a hilltop where there is no railing or other safety features.

★ High Place of Sacrifice
VIEWPOINT

(Al Madbah) The most accessible of Petra's 'High Places', this well-preserved site was built atop Jebel Madbah with drains to channel the blood of sacrificial animals. A flight of steps signposted just before the Theatre leads to the site: turn right at the obelisks to reach the sacrificial platform. You can ascend by donkey (about JD10 one way), but you'll sacrifice both the sense of achievement on reaching the summit and the good humour of your poor old transport.

★ Theatre
THEATRE

Originally built by the Nabataeans (not the Romans) more than 2000 years ago, the Theatre was chiselled out of rock, slicing through many caves and tombs in the process. It was enlarged by the Romans to hold about 8500 (around 30% of the population of Petra) soon after they arrived in 106 CE. Badly damaged by an earthquake in 363 CE, the Theatre was partially dismantled to build other structures but it remains a Petra highlight.

★ Royal Tombs
TOMB

Downhill from the Theatre, the wadi widens to create a larger thoroughfare. To the right, the great massif of Jebel Al Khubtha looms over the valley. Within its west-facing cliffs are burrowed some of the most impressive burial places in Petra, known collectively as the 'Royal Tombs'. They look particularly stunning bathed in the golden light of sunset.

Colonnaded Street
ARCHAEOLOGICAL SITE

Downhill from the Theatre, the Colonnaded Street marks the centre of the Ancient City. The street was built around AD 106 and follows the standard Roman pattern of an east–west *decumanus,* but without the normal *cardo maximus* (north–south axis). Columns of marble-clad sandstone originally lined the 6m-wide carriageway, and covered porticoes gave access to shops.

PETRA THE ANCIENT CITY

Petra

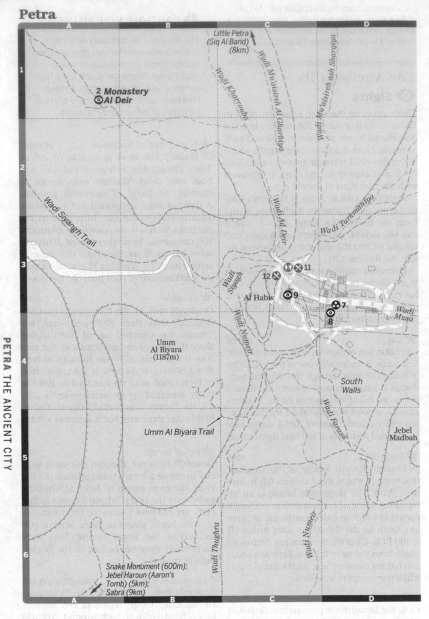

Little Petra
(Siq Al Barid)
(8km)

Wadi Mu'aisireh Al Gharbiya

Wadi Mu'aisireh ash Sharqiya

Wadi Kharrouba

2 Monastery
Al Deir

Wadi Siyagh Trail

Wadi Ad Deir

Wadi Turkmaniya

Wadi Siyagh

11

12

9

Al Habis

7

8

Wadi Musa

Wadi Numeir

Umm
Al Biyara
(1187m)

South
Walls

Umm Al Biyara Trail

Wadi Farasa

Jebel
Madbah

Wadi Thughra

Wadi Numeir

Snake Monument (600m);
Jebel Haroun (Aaron's
Tomb) (5km);
Sabra (9km)

PETRA THE ANCIENT CITY

Great Temple TEMPLE
A major Nabataean temple of the 1st century BCE, this structure was badly damaged by an earthquake not long after it was built, but it remained in use (albeit in different forms) until the late Byzantine period. A *theatron* (miniature theatre) stands in the centre. The temple was once 18m high, and the enclosure was 40m by 28m. The interior was originally covered with striking red-and-white stucco.

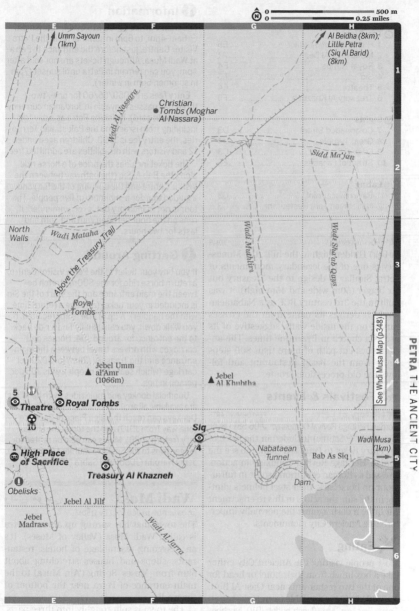

PETRA THE ANCIENT CITY

Qasr Al Bint   TEMPLE

One of the few free-standing structures in Petra, Qasr Al Bint was built in around 30 BCE by the Nabataeans. It was later adapted to the cult of Roman emperors and destroyed around the 3rd century CE.

Despite the name given to it by the local Bedouin – Castle of the Pharaoh's Daughter – the temple was originally built as a dedication to Nabataean gods and was one of the most important temples in Petra.

Petra

★**Monastery**   TOMB
(Al Deir) Hidden high in the hills, the Monastery is one of the legendary monuments of Petra. Similar in design to the Treasury but far bigger (50m wide and 45m high), it was built in the 3rd century BCE as a Nabataean tomb. It derives its name from the crosses carved on the inside walls, suggestive of its use as a church in Byzantine times. The ancient rock-cut path of more than 800 steps starts from the Basin Restaurant and follows the old processional route.

★✦ Festivals & Events

★**History of Petra**   PERFORMING ARTS
(Jordan Heritage Revival Company; ☑06 581 0808; www.jhrc.jo; ⊘Sat-Thu) Included in the price of the entry ticket to Petra is a chance to see the Jordan Heritage Revival Company in action. Dressed as Roman centurions, some in full armour on horseback, their steel helmets glinting in the sun, the actors in this re-enactment cut quite a dash against the normally imperturbable Ancient City monuments.

✗ Eating

Most people visiting the Ancient City either take a box lunch from their hotel or head for one of the two restaurants near Qasr Al Bint. A simple buffet is available from **Nabataean Tent Restaurant** (lunch buffet JD10, lunchbox JD7; ⊘10am-3.30pm), or a more lavish lunch is served outdoors or in an air-conditioned dining room at the **Basin Restaurant** (lunch buffet JD16, fresh orange juice JD4; ⊘noon-4pm; ☑). Water, tea and snacks are sold at kiosks with outside seating throughout the main parts of the site.

ℹ Information

The **ticket office** (☑03 215 6044; Tourism St; ⊘6am-4pm, to 6pm in summer) is in the Petra Visitor Centre, just before the entrance to Petra at Wadi Musa. Although tickets are not sold after 4pm, you can remain in Petra until sunset (7pm in summer, 5pm in winter).

Entry fees are JD50/55/60 for one-/two-/ three-day passes (payable in Jordanian currency or by credit card). If visiting Petra as a day trip, including from Israel and the Palestinian Territories, the entry fee is JD90. Children aged under 12 and visitors with disabilities are admitted free.

The ticket includes the price of a horse ride along the Bab Al Siq (the pathway between the Visitor Centre and the opening of the Siq) and a guided tour for a minimum of five people. The tour is not mandatory but is recommended; it runs on the hour between 7am and 3pm and lasts for two hours.

ℹ Getting Around

If you buy your ticket at the Petra Visitor Centre, a return horse ride for the 800m stretch between the main entrance and the start of the Siq is included in your ticket (arrange a return time with the handler). A tip of JD4 is appreciated. If you walk down, you can usually find a ride back to the entrance for around JD4. Horses and carriages with drivers travel between the main entrance and the Treasury (2km) for JD20 per carriage (which seats two people), plus JD5 per person in tips.

Unofficial donkey and mule rides (with handlers) are available all around Petra for negotiable prices. Donkeys can reach the High Place of Sacrifice (one way from JD10) and the top of the Monastery (return JD20). Mules can also be rented for longer trips to the Snake Monument (from JD25), Jebel Haroun (JD50) and Sabra (JD100).

Wadi Musa   وادي موسى
☑03 / POP 18,000 / ELEV 1150M
The town that has sprung up around Petra is called Wadi Musa (Valley of Moses). It's an easygoing assemblage of hotels, restaurants, shops and houses stretching about 5km from Moses' Spring ('Ain Musa) to the main entrance of Petra near the bottom of the wadi.

The town is split roughly into three parts. The upper part comprises a few top-end hotels lining the main road, each of which has spectacular views of the weathered sandstone landscape (although not of Petra itself). The town centre is where most of the cheaper hotels, the bus station and shops are located. The lower part of town, a 10-minute walk from the town centre, is where most of the top-end and midrange hotels, together with souvenir shops, tourist restaurants and the famed Cave Bar, are located.

Activities

A Turkish bath is the perfect way to ease aching muscles after a long day's walk in Petra. This time-honoured bathing experience is enjoying a current resurgence of popularity and many new baths have appeared in Wadi Musa, most attached to hotels.

The service on offer at a hammam (bathhouse) typically includes steam bath, massage, hot stones, scrubbing and 'body conditioning'. It's best to book ahead, especially if requesting a female attendant (women only). Prices are typically JD15 to JD30, depending on the combination of services on offer.

Salome Turkish Bath   HAMMAM
(☑03 215 7342; opppsite Al Anbat II Hotel; bath, body scrub & massage JD24; ☺3-10pm) Entered via a grotto displaying old farming implements, this bathhouse has an atmospheric sitting area for relaxing with herbal tea. Offering mixed bathing with body scrub and massage, this traditional little hammam makes a virtue out of staying the same while the rest of the town celebrates change.

Sella Turkish Bath   HAMMAM
(☑03 215 7170; www.sellahotel.com; King's Highway; ☺5.30-10pm) The Sella bathhouse has a comprehensive list of services, including sauna, and separate baths for men and women. Dead Sea products are on sale here.

Courses

★ **Petra Kitchen**   COOKING
(☑03 215 5900; www.petrakitchen.com; Tourism St; cookery course per person JD35; ☺6-9pm) For those wanting to know how to prepare wonderful hummus or bake the perfect baklava, Petra Kitchen offers a practical course, delivered in a single evening. Located 100m up the main road from the Mövenpick Hotel, it offers nightly cookery courses for those wanting to learn from locals how to cook Jordanian mezze, soup and main dishes in a relaxed family-style atmosphere.

Tours

Most hotels offer some kind of guided tour, either within Petra or more often in the local vicinity. Rocky Mountain Hotel (p349), for example, arranges a back trail entrance to Petra while Cleopatra Hotel (p349) takes residents further afield on overnight trips to Wadi Rum. There are also many excellent local guides working independently in the Petra area, but it's best to book these through the Petra Visitor Centre (☑03 215 6044; www.visitpetra.jo; Tourism St; ☺6am-6pm May-Sep, to 4pm Oct-Apr) FREE.

★ **Petra by Night**   TOURS
(Petra Visitor Centre, Tourism St; adult/child under 10yr JD17/free; ☺8.30-10.30pm Mon, Wed & Thu) The extremely popular Petra by Night Tour was introduced in response to numerous requests from visitors wanting to see the Siq and Treasury by moonlight. The 'tour' starts from the Petra Visitor Centre (cancelled if raining) and lasts two hours.

PETRA WADI MUSA

WALKING TIMES

To make the most of Petra you need to walk. The good news is that you don't have to be a serious hiker to have a 'Burckhardt moment' – you just need to know where to go and when. Times in the following table indicate one-way walks (unless stated otherwise) at a leisurely pace. At a faster pace without stopping, you can hike from the Petra Visitor Centre to the Treasury in 20 minutes and the Basin Restaurant in 40 minutes along the main thoroughfare. Don't forget to double the time for the uphill return journey.

DIRECT ROUTE	TIME (MIN)	DIFFICULTY
Visitor Centre to Siq Entrance	15	Easy
Siq Entrance to Treasury	20	Easy
Treasury to Royal Tombs	20	Easy
Treasury to Obelisk at High Place of Sacrifice	45	Moderate
Obelisk to Basin Restaurant (via main thoroughfare)	45	Easy
Treasury to Basin Restaurant	30	Easy
Basin Restaurant to Monastery	40	Moderate

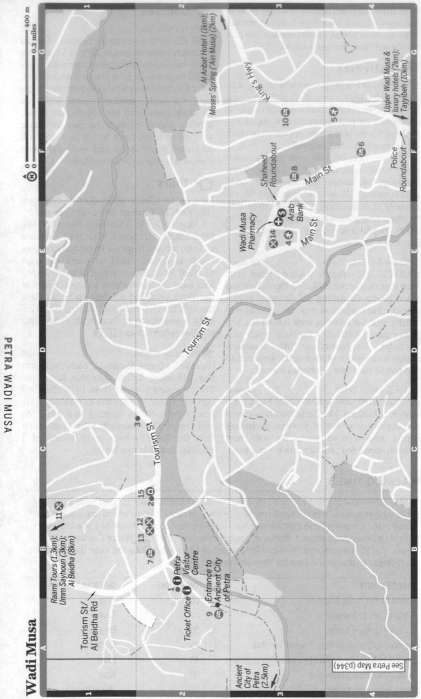

PETRA WADI MUSA

Wadi Musa

See Petra Map (p344)

Tourism St/
Al Beidha Rd

Raami Tours (1.3km);
Umm Sayhoun (3km);
Al Beidha (8km)

Tourism St

Tourism St

Petra
Visitor
Centre

Ticket Office

Entrance to
Ancient City
of Petra

Ancient
City of
Petra (2.5km)

Al Anbat Hotel I (1km);
Moses' Spring (Ain Musa) (2km)

King's Hwy

Upper Wadi Musa (2km) &
luxury hotels (10km);
Taayibeh (10km)

Police
Roundabout

Shaheed
Roundabout

Main St

Wadi Musa
Pharmacy

Arab
Bank

Main St

400 m
0.2 miles

Wadi Musa

Raami Tours TOURS

(☑07 9620 3790, 03 215 4551; www.raamitours.
com; Umm Sayoun Rd) This tour company, based
on the main road in the Bedouin village of
Umm Sayoun, designs tailor-made tours to
fit all schedules, special interests and budgets
(email at least three days ahead of arrival).

Petra Moon Tourism Services TOURS

(☑07 9617 0666; www.petramoon.com; Tourism
St; all-day horse rides to Jebel Haroun US$100, min
3 people) Petra Moon is the most professional
agency in Wadi Musa for arranging trips inside Petra and around Jordan (including Wadi
Rum and Aqaba). It can arrange horse riding,
fully supported treks to Dana (three nights),
hikes from Tayyibeh to Petra, and camel treks
in Wadi Rum. It also runs a popular 14-day
tour around Jordan for 10 to 26 people.

◎ Sleeping

Visitors have a choice of more than 70 hotels (none of which are inside the Ancient
City itself) catering to most budgets. Outside
high season (April to mid-May and October
to November) prices drop substantially from
official rates, especially for stays of three
nights or more.

◎ Wadi Musa Town Centre

The hotels in the town centre are most
convenient for the bus station, cheaper cafes and supermarkets. It's possible to walk
downhill to the Petra Visitor Centre from
here, but it won't leave as much energy for
exploring the Ancient City itself.

★ Peace Way Hotel BOUTIQUE HOTEL $

(☑03 215 6963; peaceway_petra@yahoo.com;
Main St; s/d/tr JD16/22/35; ☎⊛) This hotel
has undergone the most remarkable trans-
formation from budget to boutique. The

impressive makeover includes blue-lit ceilings, carved wooden doors and a handsome
chocolate brown theme to the corridors
and rooms, contrasted with cream-coloured
marble. Even more remarkable is that the
hotel has kept its budget prices, making this
central option very good value. Unusually,
it's pet-friendly too.

★ Rocky Mountain Hotel HOTEL $

(☑07 9694 1865, 03 215 5100; www.rocky
mountainhotel.com; King's Highway, s/d/tr/q
JD26/39/50/60; ⊛☎) This backpacker-
friendly hotel has caught just the right vibe
to make it Petra's most successful travellers'
lodge. There's a cosy communal area with
free tea and coffee and the *majlis*-style roof
terrace makes the most of the impressive
sweeping views. A free shuttle service to the
Petra entrance leaves at 7.30am and 8.30am,
returning at 4pm and 5pm.

★ Cleopatra Hotel HOTEL $

(☑03 215 7090; www.cleopetrahotel.com; Main St;
s/d/tr JD18/25/32; ⊛☎) One of the friendliest and most efficiently run budget hotels
in town, Cleopatra has bright, fresh rooms.
There's a communal sitting area in the lobby
where wi-fi is available for JD2. The hotel
can arrange overnight 4WD trips to Wadi
Rum (JD50 per person for a minimum of
three) and the ever-helpful Mosleh can organise other transport.

◎ Lower Wadi Musa

Most top-end and midrange hotels are located at the bottom end of town, within walking distance to the entrance to Petra and
well supplied with restaurants and souvenir
shops. Their proximity to the Petra Visitor
Centre can be a boon after a long day's hiking in the Ancient City.

Petra

A WALKING TOUR

Splendid though it is, the Treasury is not the full stop of a visit to Petra that many people may imagine. In some ways, it's just the semicolon – a place to pause after the exertions of the Siq, before exploring the other remarkable sights and wonders just around the corner.

Even if you're on a tight schedule or worried the bus won't wait, try to find another two hours in your itinerary to complete this walking tour. Our illustration shows the key highlights of the route, as you wind through Wadi Musa from the **1 Siq**, pause at the **2 Treasury** and pass the tombs of the broader **3 Outer Siq**. With energy and a stout pair of shoes, climb to the **4 High Place of Sacrifice** for a magnificent eagle's-eye view of Petra. Return to the **5 Street of Facades** and the **6 Theatre**. Climb the steps opposite to the **7 Urn Tomb** and neighbouring **8 Silk Tomb**: these Royal Tombs are particularly magnificent in the golden light of sunset.

Is the thought of all that walking putting you off? Don't let it! There are donkeys to help you with the steep ascents and Bedouin stalls for a reviving herb tea. If you run out of steam, camels are on standby for a ride back to the Treasury.

TOP TIPS

➡ From around 7am in summer and 8am in winter, watch the early morning sun slide down the Treasury facade.

➡ Stand opposite the Royal Tombs at sunset (around 4pm in winter and 5pm in summer) to learn how Petra earned its nickname, Pink City.

➡ Petra's oleanders flower in May.

Treasury
As you watch the sun cut across the facade, notice how it lights up the ladders on either side of Petra's most iconic building. These stone indents were most probably used for scaffolding.

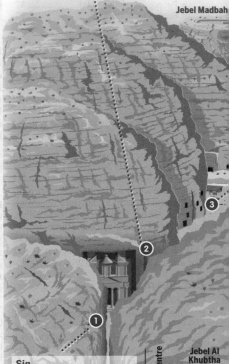

Jebel Madbah

Jebel Al Khubtha

To Petra Visitor Centre

Siq
This narrow cleft in the land forms the sublime approach to the ancient city of Petra. Most people walk through the corridor of stone but horse carts are available for those who need them.

ANOTHER WAY DOWN

A superb walk leads from the High Place of Sacrifice, past the Garden Tomb to Petra City Centre.

High Place of Sacrifice

Imagine the ancients treading the stone steps and it'll take your mind off the steep ascent. The hilltop platform was used for incense-burning and libation-pouring in honour of forgotten gods.

Outer Siq

Take time to inspect the tombs just past the Treasury. Some appear to have a basement but, in fact, they show how the floor of the wadi has risen over the centuries.

Street of Facades

Cast an eye at the upper storeys of some of these tombs and you'll see a small aperture. Burying the dead in attics was meant to deter robbers – the plan didn't work.

Stairs to High Place

5

6

Souvenir shops, teashops & toilets

Wadi Musa

Wadi Musa

To Ancient City Centre →

7

8

Royal Tombs

Jebel Umm al'Amr (1066m)

Royal Tombs

Royal Tombs

HEAD FOR HEIGHTS

For a regal view of Petra, head for the heights above the Royal Tombs, via the staircase.

Urn Tomb

Earning its name from the urn-shaped finial crowning the pediment, this grand edifice with supporting arched vaults was perhaps built for the man represented by the toga-wearing bust in the central aperture.

Silk Tomb

Perhaps Nabataean builders were attracted to Wadi Musa because of the colourful beauty of the raw materials. Nowhere is this more apparent than in the weather-eroded, striated sandstone of the Silk Tomb.

Theatre

Most stone amphitheatres are freestanding, but this one is carved almost entirely from the solid rock. Above the back row are the remains of earlier tombs, their facades sacrificed in the name of entertainment.

★ **Petra Guest House Hotel** HOTEL **$$**
(☎03 215 6266; www.guesthouse-petra.com; off Tourism St; r from JD75; P🅿🛜) Guests can't get closer to the entrance to Petra without sleeping in a tomb – and indeed the hotel's bar (the famous Cave Bar) is located in one. Accommodation ranges from spacious, motel-like chalets or sunny (if cramped) rooms in the main building. The staff are unfailingly delightful and the breakfast buffet is superior to most. Offers excellent value for money.

★ **Mövenpick Hotel** HOTEL **$$$**
(☎03 215 7111; www.moevenpick.com; Tourism St; r from JD500; P@🛜🏊) This beautifully crafted Arabian-style hotel, 100m from the entrance to Petra, is worth a visit simply to admire the inlaid furniture, marble fountains, wooden screens and brass salvers. As the hotel is in the bottom of the valley there are no views, but the large and super-luxurious rooms all have huge windows regardless. The buffet breakfast and dinner are exceptional.

🍴 Eating

The cheapest eating options are around Shaheed roundabout and Sanabel bakery. Most offer similar menus with falafel and shawarma as staples. Midrange options with a wider selection of Jordanian dishes are near the Petra entrance. International dining with alcohol is largely confined to five-star hotels. Wadi Musa has many grocery stores for picnic supplies and most hotels arrange snack boxes.

Sanabel Bakery BAKERY **$**
(off Main St; ⏱5am-midnight) Good for putting together a picnic, the Sanabel Bakery sells a delicious range of Arab sweets.

ⓘ DANGERS & ANNOYANCES

➡ Women travelling alone need to be more on their guard in budget hotels in Wadi Musa than in other towns in Jordan. It's worth making sure doors lock properly, and there are no peepholes.

➡ Attempts to befriend lone travellers are generally good-natured, but promises of undying love and affection should be treated with the suspicion they deserve.

➡ Alighting from the minibus in Wadi Musa with a backpack is likely to result in being cajoled into a particular hotel by persuasive touts. Deciding on a choice of hotel in advance helps.

★ **Oriental Restaurant** JORDANIAN **$$**
(☎03 215 7087; Tourism St; mains JD6; ⏱11am-9.30pm) This main-street favourite offers tasty grills and Jordanian fare, such as *mensaf* (lamb and rice dish). The outdoor terrace, bedecked with Doric columns, makes a sociable hang-out after the long hike back from Petra.

Red Cave Restaurant JORDANIAN **$$**
(☎03 215 7799; Tourism St; mains from JD5; ⏱9am-10pm) Cavernous and friendly, this restaurant serves local Bedouin specialities, including *mensaf* and *maqlubbeh* (steamed rice with meat, grilled tomato and pine nuts). It's a popular travellers' meeting point and a cosy place to come on a chilly evening or to catch the breeze on a hot summer's day.

★ **Al Qantarah** JORDANIAN **$$$**
(☎03 215 5535; www.al-qantarah.com; Lower Wadi Musa; lunch/dinner JD10/12; ⏱lunch 11.30am-4.30pm, dinner 7-10pm; P🍷) Wadi Musa's best restaurant specialises in Jordanian food and serves up to 500 people in one lunch sitting. There is no menu – lunch and dinner are buffet style with 15 kinds of salads and mezze, eight meat and soup dishes and eight kinds of dessert. There's a cooking station and live music every day in the delightful, traditional dining rooms.

★ **Al Saraya Restaurant** INTERNATIONAL **$$$**
(☎03 215 7111; www.moevenpick.com; Mövenpick Hotel, Tourism St; buffet dinner JD20; ⏱lunch 11am-3pm, dinner 7-10pm; P🍷) Serving a top-notch international buffet in an elegant banquet hall, this fine-dining restaurant offers a quality of dishes that matches the general opulence of the Mövenpick Hotel in which it is located. It's worth leaving time for a nightcap in the grand, wood-panelled bar afterwards, which sports a roaring fire in the hearth in winter or a rooftop cocktail in summer.

🍷 Drinking & Nightlife

★ **Cave Bar** BAR
(☎03 215 6266; www.guesthouse-petra.com; Petra Guesthouse, near Petra Visitor Centre; ⏱3-11pm) It's almost a crime to visit Petra and miss the oldest bar in the world. Occupying a 2000-year-old Nabataean rock tomb, this atmospheric Petra hot spot has been known to stay open until 4am on busy summer nights. Sitting among the spirits, alcoholic or otherwise, gives a flavour of Petra that's in animated contrast to the bar's ancient origins.

ℹ FINDING YOUR OWN PACE IN PETRA

Instead of trying to 'see it all' (the quickest way to 'monument fatigue'), make Petra your own by sparing time to amble among unnamed tombs or sip tea at a Bedouin stall.

Half Day (five hours) Amble through the Siq, absorbing its special atmosphere and savouring the moment of revelation at the Treasury. Resist the temptation to head for the Theatre; instead, climb the steps to the High Place of Sacrifice, passing a paintbox of rock formations.

One Day (eight hours) Complete the half-day itinerary, but pack a picnic. Visit the Royal Tombs, walk along to Qasr Al Bint and hike along the broad wadi that leads to Jebel Haroun as far as the Snake Monument – an ideal perch for a snack and a snooze. Save some energy for the climb to the Monastery, a fitting finale for any Petra visit.

Two Days Spend the second day scrambling through exciting Wadi Muthlim (if open) and restore energies over a barbecue in the Basin Restaurant. Explore the hidden beauty of Wadi Siyagh with its pools of water before strolling back along the Street of Facades. Sit near the Theatre to watch the sun go down on the Royal Tombs opposite – the best spectacle in Petra.

Al Maqa'ad Bar   BAR

(☑ 03 215 7111; www.moevenpickhotels.com; Mövenpick Hotel, Tourism St; ⏱ 4-11pm) The Mövenpick Hotel bar has a superb Moroccan-style interior with carved wooden grills and a grand chandelier. It's worth having a cocktail or an ice-cream special just to enjoy the ambience. A 26% tax and service charge is applied. There's another bar called the Roof Garden in the same hotel if weather allows.

🛍 Shopping

There are many souvenir shops near the entrance to Petra selling scarves, hats and fridge magnets. Throughout Wadi Musa, craftsmen patiently pour coloured sand into glass bottles; they will write a name in the sand if given enough time. Books on Petra can be found in the shops at the visitor centre and along Tourism St in lower Wadi Musa.

Made in Jordan   ARTS & CRAFTS

(☑ 03 215 5900; Tourism St; ⏱ 8.30am-11pm) This shop sells quality crafts from local enterprises. Products include olive oil, soap, paper, ceramics, table runners, nature products from Wild Jordan in Amman, jewellery from Wadi Musa, embroidery from Safi, camel-hair shawls, and bags from Aqaba as well as Jordan River Foundation goods. The fixed prices reflect the quality and uniqueness of each piece; credit cards are accepted.

ℹ Information

There are several ATMs dotted around town, including at the **Arab Bank** (Main St) in central Wadi Musa and at the Mövenpick Hotel near the Petra Visitor Centre. Many hotels will change money, albeit at a poor rate. The banks are open from about 8am to 2pm Sunday to Thursday and (sometimes) 9am to 11am on Friday.

The **Queen Rania Hospital** (☑ 03 215 0635; off King's Highway) offers high-standard health care and is open for emergencies without referral. It's located 5km from the police roundabout on the road to Tayyibeh.

The **Wadi Musa Pharmacy** (Main St; ⏱ 24hr), located near the Shaheed roundabout, has a wide range of medications and toiletries.

ℹ Getting Around

Wadi Musa bus station is in the town centre, a 10-minute walk uphill from the entrance to Petra. Yellow taxis with green places shuttle between the two (around JD4). Within Petra, the only way to reach most sites is by walking (strong, comfortable shoes are essential!) or by taking a camel, donkey or mule to more distant and uphill sites.

Siq Al Barid (Little Petra)
البتراء الصغيرة (السيق البارد)

Siq Al Barid (Cold Canyon) is colloquially known as Little Petra and is well worth a visit. It was thought to have served as an agricultural centre, trading suburb and resupply post for camel caravans visiting Petra. The surrounding area is picturesque and fun to explore, and is home to some of the oldest settlements in the world, including Al Beidha.

◉ Sights

⭐ **Little Petra Siq**   RUINS

(Siq Al Barid; ⏱ daylight hours) **FREE** An obvious path leads through the 400m-long Siq Al Barid, opening out into flat, sandy areas. The first open area boasts a **temple** while

ANIMAL WELFARE

If there's one area of complaint that understandably upsets visitors more than others in the Ancient City, it's the mistreatment of animals. Indeed, many visitors are now quick to admonish any incidents of animal mishandling, particularly from the younger boys, some of whom mete out the kind of treatment to animals that a harsh environment often delivers to them. This, of course, is no excuse, and the local community, together with the Petra administration, have come together over recent years to try to improve the welfare of the animals who form an essential part of the Bedouin family livelihood. These efforts are beginning to bear fruit, and animals appear generally in better condition, are better nourished and are on the whole better treated than in former times.

While most owners take responsibility for their animals very seriously, incidents of ill treatment still occur. Some visitors have suggested a ban on animal use, but this is more likely to encourage neglect of the family assets as Bedouin incomes are extremely limited and don't stretch to supporting a redundant 'family member'. While some Bedouin animal handlers resent tourists interfering in the way they treat their animals, most are now sensitive to the fact that their actions are under scrutiny. A word of encouragement to the animal handler about an alternative way of cajoling their charges into action is appreciated more than a diatribe against animal cruelty. All ill treatment should be reported to the tourist police at the Petra Visitor Centre, preferably with photographic or video evidence.

Tourists should ensure they are not too heavy for their mount, and should also pay the appropriate fare (as given at the Petra Visitor Centre) for the services they commission. It is largely as a result of cut-price fares that handlers feel pressured to return more quickly to base (thereby putting their animals at risk) to recoup the loss with an additional fare.

four **triclinia** – one on the left and three on the right – are in the second open area. These were probably used as dining rooms to feed hungry merchants and travellers. About 50m further along the siq is the **Painted House**, another small dining room reached by some exterior steps.

Al Beidha
RUINS

(☉ daylight hours) FREE The neolithic ruins of Al Beidha date back 9000 years and, along with Jericho, constitute one of the oldest archaeological sites in the Middle East. The remains of around 65 round (and later rectangular) structures are especially significant because they pinpoint the physical transition from hunter-gatherer to settled herder-agriculturalist communities. The settlement was abandoned around 6000 BCE, keeping the site intact. A 15-minute walking trail, starting to the left of the entrance to Little Petra, leads to the site.

🛏 Sleeping

There are several simple camps in the area that make a delightful rural retreat from the slightly claustrophobic atmosphere of Wadi Musa. If travelling with family, ask about discounts for children – some camps offer half-price for kids aged under 12.

Seven Wonders Bedouin Camp
CAMPGROUND $

(✆07 9795 8641; www.sevenwondersbedouin camp.com; off Al Beidah Rd; tent incl half-board per person JD30, B&B JD20) Signposted along a track off the road to Little Petra and tucked discreetly into a hillside, this relaxed and good-value camp looks particularly magical at night when the open fires are burning and the rocks behind the camp are illuminated. Accommodation is in simple but cosy tents with electric light, carpets and mosquito nets. Hot water and towels are available.

Ammarin Bedouin Camp
CAMPGROUND $$

(✆07 9975 5551; www.bedouincamp.net; half board per person in tent JD52) A 10-minute walk from Little Petra (signposted off the approach road), this camp is in Siq Al Amti, hidden in a spectacular amphitheatre of sand and hills, and run by the local Ammarin tribe. Accommodation comprises mattress and blankets in a sectioned Bedouin tent with concrete floors, with a clean shower and toilet block. Reservations (booked by email) are essential.

ⓘ Getting There & Away

From Wadi Musa, private taxis cost JD10 in one direction and between JD20 and JD25 return, including an hour's wait. Alternatively, it's a pleasant 8km walk following the road.

Understand Israel & the Palestinian Territories

Israel & the Palestinian Territories Today

A month rarely goes by without a reminder that Israel and the Palestinian Territories are at the centre of the most entrenched conflict in the Middle East. But in Jerusalem, Tel Aviv, Haifa, Ramallah and Nablus, life goes on for Israelis and Palestinians alike. When streets are abuzz with sounds, smells and soul, it is possible to see the region as something other than the poster child for division and strife. To see it how those who live here do: as home.

POPULATION ISRAEL:
8.2 MILLION (INCLUDING 550,000 JEWS WHO LIVE IN THE WEST BANK AND EAST JERUSALEM)

POPULATION PALESTINIAN TERRITORIES: 4.5 MILLION

••••••••••••••••••••••••••••••••

population per sq km

Israel   West Bank   Gaza

$\dagger$ ≈ 400 people

Prospects for Peace

The Hamas–Israel War of 2014 ended with few real gains for either side. Although both parties claimed victory, the open-ended, Egyptian-sponsored ceasefire did little to solve the underlying causes of the conflict, including the partial Israeli and Egyptian blockade of Gaza, the continuing occupation, the statelessness of Palestinians and Hamas' implacable opposition to peace with Israel. Israel's economy suffered from the direct costs of the conflict and a significant drop in tourism, while Gazans' dire economic situation and living conditions were made worse than ever; they have many years of rebuilding ahead of them.

With Israelis now feeling more vulnerable both militarily and in the court of world public opinion (and possibly, along with Hamas, in the International Criminal Court in the Hague), and Palestinian Islamists further radicalised by the death and destruction, moderates are facing an uphill battle.

Optimism about peace was widespread among both Israelis and Palestinians in the heyday of the Oslo peace process, back in the mid-1990s. But these days, after years of suicide bombings, rocket attacks and infiltration tunnels from Hamas-controlled Gaza, and continued Islamist calls for Israel's destruction, many Israelis are pessimistic about the chances for real peace and are wary of new, potentially risky initiatives. A 2016 poll found that almost 60% felt that the two-state solution for Israel and Palestine was dead.

A variety of factors have had a similar effect on the assessments by many Palestinians in the wake of the Hamas–Israel War, including continuing settlement construction, incidents of Israeli army brutality, daily humiliation at checkpoints and the right-wing, populist drift of Israeli politics. One thing has become clear: public optimism for a compromise peace, once extinguished, is very hard to rekindle.

Israeli Prime Minister Benjamin Netanyahu publicly abandoned what had already been a questionable commitment to a two-state solution to the conflict during his most recent election campaign. His statements ruling out an eventual Palestinian state put him further at odds with the US and much of the international community. Netanyahu, who won his fourth consecutive term in March 2015, also declared that his latest right-wing coalition government will continue to expand Israeli settlements.

The leadership of the Palestinian Authority, President Mahmoud Abbas and Prime Minister Rami Hamdallah, have a long record of support for a two-state solution, but have seemed reluctant to make any bold moves. Abbas has been putting his efforts into having the Palestinian Territories recognised by international bodies such as the United Nations, and has demanded that the international community set a date for an end to Israel's occupation.

If anything, the antipathy felt by Israelis and Palestinians towards each other is deeper than it has ever been, with mutual hatred translating into acts of sporadic violence with alarming regularity. Right-wing parties are more popular than ever, while in Gaza, the West Bank and in Israel itself, Palestinians are angered by what they see as the complicity of their leaders in the Israeli occupation, which marked its 50th anniversary in 2017.

'Price Tag' Attacks

Hard-line Jewish settlers in the West Bank see the outcome of the 1967 Six Day War as a miracle that proves we are living in the messianic age and view the 1993 Oslo Accords and the 2005 Gaza withdrawal as nothing short of apostasy. Since 2008, some of them have been employing violence to deter the Israeli government from implementing certain policies – for instance, against settlement outposts deemed illegal by the Israeli courts. These 'price tag' *(tag mechir)* attacks, as they are known, involve defacing mosques, smashing Palestinians' car windscreens, setting fire to Palestinian fields and cutting down olive trees, and – more recently – vandalising churches and harassing Christian clergy in Jerusalem.

Price-tag activists do not shy away from using threats and violence against their fellow Israeli Jews, and on several occasions have defaced the homes of left-wing activists, stoned the Israeli police and vandalised Israel Defense Forces vehicles and equipment.

The source of the price-tag ideology is the Hilltop Youth, second-generation settlers who believe that Halacha (Jewish law) takes precedence over laws enacted by the Knesset (Israeli Parliament) or decisions by Israeli courts and see themselves as uncompromising patriots and self-sacrificing heroes.

Best on Film

Sallah Shabbati (1964) Satire about immigrant life in a 1950s transit camp.
Yossi & Jagger (2002) Secret love between two buff Israel Defense Forces officers.
Omar (2013) Oscar-nominated thriller and love story set in the West Bank.
The Flat (2011) A filmmaker looks at his German-Jewish roots.
Strangers No More (2010) A South Tel Aviv elementary school takes in refugee children.
Precious Life (2010) Parents in Gaza fight for medical treatment in Israel for their baby.

Best in Print

My Promised Land: The Triumph and Tragedy of Israel (Ari Shavit; 2013) A penetrating personal look at Israel's existential fears.
The Iron Cage: The Story of the Palestinian Struggle for Statehood (Rashid Khalidi; 2007) Delves into Palestinian attempts to achieve independence.
To The End of The Land (David Grossman; 2008) A heartfelt novel on the emotional strains of a family whose son is a soldier in the Israel Defense Forces.
The Last Palestinian: The Rise and Reign of Mahmoud Abbas (Grant Rumley, Amir Tibon; 2017) Well-paced unauthorised biography of the Palestinian leader.
Judas (Amos Oz; 2014) A coming-of-age tale that unfolds in a divided Jerusalem of 1959–60.

History

The land that holds Israel and the Palestinian Territories has been inhabited – and contested – since the dawn of civilisation. A litany of the empires and kingdoms that have ruled the country reads like a Who's Who of Western and Middle Eastern history: there are Egyptians and Canaanites, Israelites and Philistines, Greeks and Judeans, Romans and Byzantines, Arabs and Crusaders (and, briefly, Mongols), Ottomans and British. Each left behind fascinating evidence of their aspirations and follies for modern-day travellers to explore.

Ancient Times

The land now occupied by Israel and the Palestinian Territories has been inhabited by human beings and their forebears for some two million years. Between 10,000 and 8000 BCE – a little later than in nearby Mesopotamia – people in places such as Jericho switched from hunting to the production of grain and the domestication of animals.

During the 3rd millennium BCE, the area was occupied by seminomadic tribes of pastoralists. By the late 2nd millennium BCE urban centres had emerged, and it is clear from Egyptian documents that the pharaohs had significant interests and influence in the area. Around 1800 BCE, Abraham is believed to have led his nomadic tribe from Mesopotamia to a land the Bible calls Canaan, after the local Canaanite tribes. His descendants were forced to relocate to Egypt because of drought and crop failure, but according to the Bible Moses led them out of slavery and back to the Land of Israel in about 1250 BCE. Conflicts with the Canaanites and Philistines pushed the Israelites to abandon their loose tribal system and unify under King Saul (1050–1010 BCE) and his successors, King David and King Solomon.

Myth and history intersect on the large, flat rock that now lies beneath Jerusalem's golden Dome of the Rock. Originally an altar to Baal or some other pagan deity, the rock is known to Jews as the Stone of Foundation, the place where the universe began and Adam was created out of dust. It's also said to be where Abraham bound his son Isaac in preparation to sacrifice him, as a sign of obedience to God. King Solomon built the First

TIMELINE	2 million BCE	9000 BCE	4500–3500 BCE
	Hominids inhabit Tel Ovadia, 3km south of the Sea of Galilee. Around 780,000 BCE their successors set up camp on the Jordan River 13km north of the Sea of Galilee.	Abundant water and a good climate attract early Neolithic people to Jericho, where they establish a permanent settlement surrounded by a mudbrick wall, grow food crops and flax, and raise goats.	Chalcolithic (pre-Bronze Age) people inhabit small villages in Jordan Valley and on the Golan, producing pottery and stone tools. Food sources include agriculture and domesticated goats and sheep.

Temple (Solomon's Temple) here in the 10th century BCE to serve as the centre of Jewish sacrificial worship.

After Solomon's reign (965–928 BCE), the Jews entered a period of division and periodic subjugation. Two rival entities came into being: the Kingdom of Israel, in what is now the northern West Bank and the Galilee; and the southern Kingdom of Judah, with its capital at Jerusalem. After Sargon II of Assyria (r 722–705 BCE) destroyed the Kingdom of Israel in 720 BCE, the 10 northern tribes disappeared from the historical record (even today, groups around the world claim descent from the 'Ten Lost Tribes').

The Babylonians captured Jerusalem in 586 BCE, destroying the First Temple and exiling the people of Judah to Babylonia (now Iraq). Fifty years later Cyrus II, king of Persia, defeated Babylon and allowed the Jews to return to the Land of Israel. The returning Jews immediately set about constructing the Second Temple, consecrated in 516 BCE.

> The earliest extra-biblical mention of Israel is on the Egyptian Museum's Israel Stela (1230 BCE), inscribed with the victory hymn of the Pharaoh Merneptah: 'Plundered is Canaan, carried is Ashkelon, Israel is laid waste.'

Greeks & Maccabees, Romans & Christians

When Alexander the Great died in 323 BCE, Ptolemy, one of his generals, claimed Egypt as his own, founding a line of which Cleopatra would be the last. He also took control of the Land of Israel, but in 200 BCE the Seleucids, another dynasty descended from one of Alexander's generals, captured it.

The 'Hellenistic' period – so called because of the Greek origin of the Seleucids and the Olympian cults they promoted – was marked by conflict between the Sadducees (mostly urban, upper-class Jews who were open to Greek culture and the refined Greek lifestyle) and the Pharisees, who resisted Hellenisation. When the Seleucid king Antiochus IV Epiphanes banned Temple sacrifices, Shabbat and circumcision, the Jews, led by Judah Maccabee, revolted. Using guerrilla tactics, they captured Jerusalem and rededicated the Temple.

1250 BCE	10th century BCE	late 10th century BCE	586 BCE
Estimated date of the Israelites' biblical exodus from Egypt. Archaeologists have found no evidence of Egyptian slavery, desert wandering or military conquest and posit that the Israelites originated in Canaan.	King Solomon, legendary for his wisdom, rules Israel and builds the First Temple in Jerusalem to house the Ark of the Covenant, containing the original Ten Commandments tablets.	The northern Kingdom of Israel splits from the southern, Jerusalem-based Kingdom of Judea. The 10 northern tribes are eventually lost to history; today's Jews are descended from the Judeans.	Nebuchadnezzar, King of Babylon, destroys the First Temple and exiles the Jews to Babylonia. Cyrus II, King of Persia, allows them to return to Judea 48 years later.

ARCH OF TITUS

In 82 CE the Romans celebrated Titus' hard-fought victory over Judea by constructing an impressive triumphal arch just off the Roman Forum in Rome. Still standing today, its friezes depict a procession of Roman legionnaires carrying off the contents of the Temple in Jerusalem, including a seven-branched menorah (candelabra). Over 17 centuries later, the Arch of Titus inspired the design of the Arc de Triomphe in Paris.

The Hasmoneans – as the dynasty founded by the Maccabees is known – became a useful buffer for the Roman Empire against the marauding Parthians, whose empire was based in what is now Iran. But the Hasmoneans fought among themselves and in 63 BCE Rome stepped in. The Romans sometimes ruled the area – which became the Roman province of Judea (also spelled Judaea or Iudaea) – directly through a procurator, the most famous of whom was Pontius Pilate, but preferred a strong client ruler such as Herod the Great (r 37–4 BCE), whose major construction projects included expanding the Temple.

The 1st century CE was a time of tremendous upheaval in the Roman province of Judea, not least between approximately 26 and 29 CE, when it is believed that Jesus of Nazareth carried out his ministry. The tension exploded in 66 CE, when the Jews launched the Great Jewish Revolt against the Romans, also known as the First Jewish–Roman War. Four years later, Titus, the future emperor, crushed the rebels and destroyed the Second Temple, leaving only one outer wall standing, now known as the Western Wall. Masada fell in 73 CE, putting an end to even nominal Jewish sovereignty for almost two millennia. However, although the Jews were expelled from Jerusalem, a large Jewish population remained in other parts of the Land of Israel.

Israelis call immigration to Israel *aliyah*, from a Hebrew root meaning 'to ascend'. Moving from Israel to another country is sometimes derisively called *yeridah* ('going down').

Just 60 years after Josephus Flavius wrote *The Jewish War,* his firsthand, decidedly pro-Roman account of the Great Jewish Revolt, another insurrection broke out. The Bar Kochba Rebellion (132–35 CE) was led by Simon Bar Kochba, whose guerrillas lived in caves near the Dead Sea; some Jews even considered him to be the Messiah. The Romans, under Hadrian, suppressed the rebellion with difficulty – and with great ferocity, essentially wiping out the Jewish population of Judea.

After his victory, Hadrian sought to erase both Judaism and any traces of Jewish independence: statues of Jupiter and of Hadrian himself were placed on the site of the Temple, Jews were barred from living in Aelia Capitolina (his new name for Jerusalem), and the Roman province of Judea was renamed Syria Palaestina after the Philistines, a coastal people of Mycenaean Greek origin who had been arch-enemies of the Jews for a millennium.

516 BCE	4th century BCE	167–161 BCE	63 BCE
The Second Temple is consecrated in Jerusalem. Though without the Ark of the Covenant, lost to Nebuchadnezzar, it serves as the focus of Jewish worship through animal sacrifices.	Nabataeans, a nomadic tribe from Arabia, establish Petra, now in Jordan. They wax wealthy from the incense trade between Yemen and the Horn of Africa and Greece and Rome.	Outraged by Seleucid king Antiochus' imposition of pagan sacrifices, the Jews, led by Judah Maccabee, revolt. Their victory, celebrated by the holiday of Hanukkah, establishes the Hasmonean dynasty.	The independent Kingdom of Judea becomes a Roman client state after Pompey captures Jerusalem. Roman proconsuls rule Judea but Temple sacrifices continue.

With the Temple destroyed and the elaborate animal sacrifices prescribed in the Torah suspended, Jewish religious life was thrown into a state of limbo. In an effort to adapt to the new circumstances, Jewish sages established academies around Roman Palestine and Galilee and set about reorienting Judaism towards prayer and synagogue worship, though the direction of Jewish prayer remained (as it does today) towards Jerusalem. The 'Rabbinic Judaism' practised today is almost entirely a product of the principles, precepts and precedents laid down by sages and rabbis after the destruction of the Second Temple.

In the years following Jesus's crucifixion, which some experts believe took place in 33 CE, Jews who believed him to be the Messiah and those who didn't often worshipped side by side, observing Jewish rituals with equal meticulousness. But around the time the Gospels were being written (late 1st century CE), theological and political disagreements emerged and the two communities diverged. Christian polemical tracts against the Jewish faith from this period, delivered from a position of weakness – at this time Christianity, unlike Judaism, was treated as an illegal sect by the Romans – would be used to justify anti-Semitism in subsequent centuries.

Christianity was generally suppressed by the Romans until 313 CE, when the Roman Empire's Edict of Milan granted tolerance to all previously persecuted religions, including Christianity. Shortly thereafter, Constantine the Great's mother, Helena, set about identifying and consecrating sites associated with Jesus's life. Many of the most important Christian sites, including the Church of the Holy Sepulchre in Jerusalem, date from this period.

The Byzantine Empire – the Christian successor to the eastern part of the Roman Empire – ruled Palestine from the 4th to the early 7th centuries CE. During this time, there were three revolts – one by the Jews of Galilee and two by the Samaritans – but as can be seen from the opulent ruins of Beit She'an and the Galilee's many beautiful Byzantine-era synagogues, the country was quite prosperous and, for the most part, at peace.

In 611 CE the Persians invaded, capturing Jerusalem, destroying churches and seizing the True Cross. Byzantine rule was restored in 628 CE – but it didn't last long.

Muslims & Crusaders

Islam and Arab civilisation came to Palestine between 636 and 638 CE, when Caliph Omar (Umar), the second of the Prophet's successors, accepted the surrender of Jerusalem from the Byzantines. This was just six years after the death of the Prophet Muhammad, whose followers had initially been told to pray facing Jerusalem; in 624 they were instructed to face Mecca.

> The Temple in Jerusalem was so central to Jewish life that some scholars estimate only 270 of the 613 Commandments that religious Jews are obligated to perform can actually be carried out in the absence of the Temple's priesthood and animal sacrifices

37 BCE	c 4 BCE	66–70 CE	67
The Roman Senate appoints Herod the Great as king of Judea. To win popular support, he rebuilds the Second Temple, including the Western Wall. He also constructs palaces atop Masada and at Herodium.	A Jew known to history as Jesus is born in Bethlehem. He grows up in Nazareth, preaches in Galilee and is tried and crucified in Jerusalem by Pontius Pilate.	Jewish anger at Roman oppression sparks the Great Jewish Revolt, crushed by Roman legions under Vespasian and Titus. Jerusalem and the Second Temple are destroyed, ending sacrifices.	Yosef ben Matityahu, commander of the Great Jewish Revolt in Galilee, is captured by the Romans and reinvents himself as the great Roman historian Josephus Flavius.

Al Haram Ash Sharif/Temple Mount was holy to the newly arrived Muslims because they believed it to be the site of Muhammad's Night Journey (Mi'raj) to behold the celestial glories of heaven. In the Quran, the ascension is described as happening in a 'faraway place', which Muslims interpret as meaning Jerusalem. It is for this reason that Jerusalem is considered to be Sunni Islam's third-holiest city (after Mecca and Medina).

Omar's successors built the Dome of the Rock and Al Aqsa Mosque on Al Haram Ash Sharif/Temple Mount, which had been a derelict trash dump during Byzantine times. Jews were again permitted to settle in Jerusalem. With Christianity respected as a precursor of Islam, the shrines of previous generations were preserved, though over time many Christians converted to Islam and began speaking Arabic.

Omar issued a famous promise to the Christians of Jerusalem that 'the security of their persons, their goods, their churches, their crosses' would be guaranteed. This promise was largely kept until 1009, when the

MYSTICAL JUDAISM

The leading thinkers of Spain's illustrious medieval Jewish community were rational philosophers whose interests encompassed both science and medicine. In 1492 Spain's Christian rulers expelled all the country's Jews, causing a crisis of faith to which the rationalists had no answer. (The expulsion, after all, seemed deeply irrational, unless you were the Spanish king and queen, who confiscated considerable property from departing Jews.) As a result, some Jews developed a new, mystical understanding of why bad things happened to them. The centre of this new mysticism was the hilltop Galilee town of Tsfat, where a number of eminent Spanish rabbis found a home. Its greatest figure was Jerusalem-born Yitzhak Luria (1534–72), who expanded an old form of mysticism called Kabbalah (pronounced kah-bah-*lah*) so that it could provide answers to the vexing spiritual questions haunting Jews after the Expulsion.

Lurianic Kabbalah (the word means 'receiving') was inspired by earlier texts such as the 13th-century *Zohar*, but Luria's adaptations and innovations had such an impact that many are now part of mainstream Jewish observance. Luria left no writings, but his assistant recorded the essence of his teachings. Luria asserted that in order to create the world, the Infinite (the Eyn-Sof) was damaged – to make a space in which to fit Creation. As a result, sparks from the Divine Light fell from their original position and were at risk of being used for evil purposes. Jews, he argued, could restore the Divine Light and repair the Infinite by performing the 613 Commandments (the 10 on Moses' tablets plus 603 others). This mystical approach gave Jews a way to understand the horror of the Expulsion from Spain and the Inquisition – as well as later persecution – because it asserted that evil was inherent in the world. It also directed them to look inward to build a higher degree of spiritual awareness and, in so doing, to 'repair the world'.

73	132–35	2nd century	313
Three years after the fall of Jerusalem, the desert stronghold of Masada succumbs to the might of the Roman legions, marking the end to all Jewish resistance in Judea.	After Hadrian bans circumcision, Bar Kochba leads the catastrophic Bar Kochba Rebellion, leading to a crushing Roman victory and the near-annihilation of the Jewish communities of Judea.	With Jerusalem in ruins and sacrifices halted, centres of Jewish learning are established in Yavneh, Tzipori and Beit She'arim. Oral traditions are written down in the Mishnah and, later, Talmud.	Constantine the Great, the Roman Empire's first Christian emperor, issues the Edict of Milan, granting freedom to all religions, including Christianity.

mentally disturbed Fatimid Caliph Al Haakim destroyed many churches and persecuted Christians and Jews.

Christian pilgrimage to the holy sites in Jerusalem was possible until 1071, when the Seljuk Turks captured the city and travel became difficult and often dangerous because of political turmoil. In 1095 Pope Urban II issued a call for a crusade to restore to Christianity the site of Jesus's Passion. By the time the Crusades began, the Seljuks had been displaced by the Fatimid dynasty, which was quite happy to allow the old pilgrimage routes to reopen – but it was too late for the Christian armies to turn back. In 1099 the Crusaders overwhelmed Jerusalem's defences and massacred the city's Muslims and Jews. It would be 200 years before the bloodshed came to a halt.

When the Crusaders took Jerusalem, they founded what even Arab chroniclers acknowledged was a prosperous state with an effective administration, based on the feudal system in force in Europe. The first King of Jerusalem was Baldwin I (r 1100–18), who saw himself as restoring the kingdom of the biblical David and who had himself crowned on Christmas Day in David's hometown of Bethlehem.

In 1187 the celebrated Kurdish-Muslim general Saladin (Salah ad Din) defeated a Crusader army at the Horns of Hattin in Galilee (near Arbel) and captured Jerusalem. Even Saladin's enemies acknowledged his decent treatment of prisoners and the honour with which he observed truces – not something that could be said for the Crusader chiefs.

The final Crusader left the Middle East with the fall of Akko in 1291, but the bloody symbolism of the Crusades lived on. When Britain's General Edmund Allenby entered Jerusalem in 1917 to become its first Christian ruler since Saladin's victory, he declared: 'now the Crusades are over'.

For a highly readable account of what the Arabs thought of the Crusaders, try *The Crusades Through Arab Eyes*, by Lebanese writer Amin Maalouf.

Ottomans, Zionists & British

The Ottoman Turks captured Constantinople in 1453 and built an empire that extended to the Balkans, the Middle East and North Africa. In 1516 Palestine was added to their territory, and two decades later Sultan Süleyman the Magnificent (r 1520–66) built the present massive walls around Jerusalem's Old City. For most of the 400 years of Ottoman rule, Palestine was a backwater run by pashas more concerned with tax collection than good governance.

The lack of effective administration in Palestine reflected the gradual decline of the Ottoman Empire, which would cease to exist at the end of WWI. But the final decades of the empire saw other forces taking shape in Palestine that remain strong today. Zionism arose largely in response to post-Napoleonic nationalism in Western Europe and waves of pogroms in Eastern Europe. At least small numbers of Jews had remained in Palestine continuously since Roman times (eg in the Galilee

HISTORY OTTOMANS, ZIONISTS & BRITISH

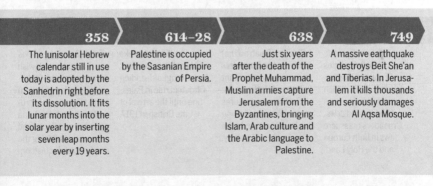

358
The lunisolar Hebrew calendar still in use today is adopted by the Sanhedrin right before its dissolution. It fits lunar months into the solar year by inserting seven leap months every 19 years.

614–28
Palestine is occupied by the Sasanian Empire of Persia.

638
Just six years after the death of the Prophet Muhammad, Muslim armies capture Jerusalem from the Byzantines, bringing Islam, Arab culture and the Arabic language to Palestine.

749
A massive earthquake destroys Beit She'an and Tiberias. In Jerusalem it kills thousands and seriously damages Al Aqsa Mosque.

town of Peki'in) and pious Jews had been immigrating whenever political conditions permitted, but organised Zionist immigration to agricultural settlements began in 1882 – for slightly different reasons, Jews from Yemen began arriving the same year. Known as the First Aliya (the Hebrew word for emigrating to the Land of Israel, *aliya* literally means 'going up'), this group was joined from 1903 by the Second Aliya, made up largely of young, secular-minded socialists. But until after WWI, the vast majority of Palestine's Jews belonged to the old-line Orthodox community, most of it uninterested in Zionism, and lived in Judaism's four holy cities: Hebron, Tsfat (Safed), Tiberias and Jerusalem, which had a Jewish majority since about 1850.

In 1896 a Budapest-born Jewish journalist named Theodor Herzl, convinced by the degrading treatment of Captain Alfred Dreyfus (court-martialled in Paris on trumped-up treason charges) that Jews would never achieve equality and civil rights without self-determination, formulated his ideas in *The Jewish State*. The next year, he opened the first World Zionist Congress in Basel, Switzerland. Inspired by political Zionism, young Jews – many of them secular and socialist – began emigrating to Palestine, mostly from Poland and Russia.

In November 1917 the British government issued the Balfour Declaration, which stated that 'His Majesty's Government view with favour the establishment in Palestine of a National Home for the Jewish People'. The next month, British forces under General Edmund Allenby captured Jerusalem.

Immediately after the end of WWI, Jews resumed immigration to Palestine, this time to territory controlled by a British-run mandatory government – approved by the League of Nations – that was friendly, modernising and competent. The Third Aliya (1919–23) was made up mostly of young, idealistic socialists, many of whom established kibbutzim (communal settlements) on marginal land purchased from absentee Arab landlords, deals that sometimes resulted in the displacement of Arab peasant farmers. But the Fourth Aliya (1924–29) was made up largely of middle-class merchants and tradespeople – not exactly the committed pioneers that the Zionist leadership had hoped for. In the 1930s they were joined by the Fifth Aliya, made up largely of refugees from Nazi Germany, many of them from comfortable bourgeois backgrounds.

The rise in Jewish immigration angered Palestinian Arabs, who were beginning to see themselves in Arab nationalist terms and to see Palestine's growing Jewish population as a threat to Arab interests. Anti-Zionist riots rocked the country in 1921 and 1929, but Jews continued to arrive, especially after Hitler's rise to power in 1933. In 1931 Palestine's 174,000 Jews constituted 17% of the total population; by 1941, there were 474,000 Jews, 30% of the total.

Baptist lay preacher Thomas Cook led a party of middle-class English tourists to Jerusalem in 1869. At the time, criminals were still being publicly decapitated by sword at Jaffa Gate.

1095–99	1187	1291	16th century
The First Crusade brings Christian armies from Europe to Muslim-ruled Jerusalem, which is defended by both Muslims and Jews. Crusaders massacre Jews in both Europe and the Holy Land.	Saladin (Salah ad Din) defeats the Crusaders at the hugely important Battle of Hattin, in the Galilee, and captures Jerusalem, allowing Jews to return to the city.	The Mamluks take Akko, the Crusaders' last stronghold, ending Christian rule in Palestine until the arrival of the British in 1917.	Tsfat (Safed) becomes a centre of Jewish scholarship and Kabbalah (Jewish mysticism) with the arrival of Jerusalem-born Isaac Luria (the Ari) and Sephardic rabbis fleeing the Spanish Inquisition.

ZIONISM

The Jewish Virtual Library (www.jewishvirtuallibrary.org) defines Zionism as 'the national movement for the return of the Jewish people to their homeland and the resumption of Jewish sovereignty in the Land of Israel'. The biblical word 'Zion' (Tziyon) refers both to Jerusalem, towards which Jews have prayed since the time of the Temple, and to the Land of Israel.

According to the historian Binyamin Neuberger, 'political Zionism, the national liberation movement of the Jewish people, emerged in the 19th century within the context of the liberal nationalism then sweeping through Europe. Central to Zionist thought is the concept of the Land of Israel as the historical birthplace of the Jewish people, and the belief that Jewish life elsewhere is a life of exile'.

This theme also appears in Israel's Declaration of Independence (1948), which states:

'The Land of Israel was the birthplace of the Jewish people. Here their spiritual, religious and political identity was shaped. Here they first attained to statehood, created cultural values of national and universal significance and gave to the world the eternal Book of Books. After being forcibly exiled from their land, the people kept faith with it throughout their dispersion and never ceased to pray and hope for their return to it and for the restoration in it of their political freedom.'

Among Zionism's practical goals: to provide the Jewish people – seen by Zionists as no less a nation than the Czechs, the Hungarians or the French – with national self-determination in a world made up of nation-states; and to offer individual Jews a place of refuge from anti-Semitic discrimination and persecution.

Growing Palestinian Arab opposition to Zionism and the policies of the British Mandate, especially regarding Jewish immigration, led to the Arab Revolt (1936–39), in which about 400 Jewish civilians and 200 British soldiers were killed. The Mandatory government suppressed the uprising with considerable violence, killing some 5000 Palestinian Arabs. Palestinian Jews took advantage of the Arab economic boycott to increase their economic autonomy – for instance, by establishing an independent port in Tel Aviv. However, the Arab Revolt succeeded in convincing the British – who, in case of war with Germany, would surely need Arab oil and political goodwill – to severely limit Jewish immigration to Palestine. Just as the Jews of Europe were becoming increasingly desperate to flee Hitler (the Nazis allowed Jews to leave Germany until late 1941 provided they could find a country to take them), the doors of Palestine slammed shut. Even after WWII, the British prevented Holocaust survivors from reaching Palestine, outraging Jewish public opinion in Palestine and the United States; refugees who tried to run the blockade were imprisoned on Cyprus.

1536	1799	1882	1909
Ottoman Sultan Suleiman the Magnificent begins building the present-day walls of Jerusalem's Old City.	Napoleon captures Gaza, Jaffa (where he massacres thousands of POWs) and Haifa but fails to take Akko and doesn't get anywhere near Jerusalem. Abruptly leaves his army and returns to France.	Pogroms in Russia spark the First Aliya, the first organised Zionist immigration to Palestine. Agricultural settlements such as Metula, Rosh Pina, Zichron Ya'akov and Rishon LeZion are soon established.	Led by Meir Dizengoff, 66 families found Tel Aviv on sand dunes north of Jaffa. The 5 hectares purchased by the group are parcelled out by lottery.

By 1947 the British government, exhausted by WWII and tired of both Arab and Jewish violence in Palestine, turned the problem over to the two-year-old United Nations. In November 1947, in a moment of rare agreement between the United States and the Soviet Union, the UN General Assembly voted in favour of partitioning Palestine into two independent states, one Jewish, the other Arab, with Jerusalem under a 'special international regime'. Palestinian Jews accepted the plan in principle, but Palestinian Arabs and nearby Arab countries rejected it. Arab bands immediately began attacking Jewish targets. The protection of Palestinian Jewish communities, economic interests and transport was led by the Haganah, an underground military organisation that would soon become the Israel Defence Forces (IDF).

As soon as the British left, at midnight on 14 May 1948, the Jews proclaimed the establishment of an independent Jewish state, and the armies of Egypt, Syria, Jordan, Lebanon and Iraq invaded Palestine. British Field Marshall Bernard Montgomery, who won fame for his North African desert campaigns during WWII, commented that Israel would survive no longer than three weeks. But to the Arab states' – and the world's – surprise the 650,000 Palestinian Jews were not defeated but rather took control of 77% of Mandatory Palestine (the Partition Plan offered them 56%). Jordan occupied (and annexed) the West Bank and East Jerusalem, expelling the residents of the Old City's Jewish quarter; Egypt took control of an area that came to be known as the Gaza Strip.

Independence & Catastrophe

The history of Palestine during the British Mandate comes alive through individual stories in the excellent *One Palestine, Complete* (2001), by Tom Segev, Israel's leading popular historian.

The 1948 Arab–Israeli War brought independence for Israel, a place of refuge for Holocaust survivors and Jewish refugees from the Arab countries, and a guarantee that Jews fleeing persecution would always have a country that would take them in. But for the Palestinian Arabs the 1948 war is remembered as Al Nakba, the Catastrophe.

Approximately 700,000 of the Arabs living in what was to become Israel fled or were expelled by the end of the year. The impact of this pivotal point in the conflict cannot be underestimated, resulting as it did in humanitarian disaster and the unresolved issue of Palestinian refugees today.

Numerous causes have been attributed to the mass exodus. Jewish military assaults on towns and villages, mortar shelling and sniper attacks forced Arabs from their homes in many cases. Reports spread fast of fallen towns and atrocities, such as the Deir Yassin massacre, in which more than 200 villagers were killed by Zionist militia. Intimidation and widespread fear of a similar fate led others to leave, in the belief they could return at a later date. At the close of 1948, over 80% of Palestinians had become refugees. Shortly after the exodus, a series of laws were passed by the Israeli government that prevented both displaced Arabs within Palestine and abroad from returning to their homes.

1910	1916	1917	1918
The first kibbutz, Degania, is established by socialist 'pioneers' from Russia at the southern end of the Sea of Galilee, on land purchased in 1904.	The secret Sykes-Picot Agreement divvies up the Ottoman Empire into spheres of influence. Palestine, Trans-Jordan and southern Iraq are earmarked for Britain; France gets Lebanon and Syria.	In the Balfour Declaration, the British government expresses support for a 'Jewish national home' in Palestine. British forces under General Allenby capture Jerusalem from the Ottomans.	British forces take northern Palestine from the Ottomans. In one of the world's last cavalry charges, an Indian cavalry brigade captures Haifa.

After Israel became independent, impoverished Jewish refugees began flooding in – from British internment camps on Cyprus (set up by the British to hold Jews intercepted on the way to Palestine), from 'displaced persons' camps in postwar Europe (including hundreds of thousands of Holocaust survivors), from countries soon to be locked tight behind the Iron Curtain (eg Bulgaria), and from Arab countries whose ancient Jewish communities became targets of anti-Jewish violence (eg Iraq, Yemen and Syria). Within three years, Israel's Jewish population more than doubled.

War & Terrorism

In the spring of 1967 Arab capitals, especially Cairo, were seething with calls to liberate all of historic Palestine – in the name of pan-Arab nationalism – from what was seen as an illegitimate occupation by Israel. Egyptian President Gamal Abdel Nasser closed the Straits of Tiran to Israeli shipping (including oil shipments from Iran, at the time an ally of Israel), ordered UN peacekeeping forces to withdraw from Sinai, and made rousing speeches listened to with rapt attention by tens of millions across the Arab world. Jordan and Syria massed troops on their borders with Israel. Terrified Israelis took Nasser at his word – on 3 May he declared, 'our basic objective will be the destruction of Israel' – and wondered if their fate would be similar to that of the Jews of Europe during WWII.

On 6 June Israel launched a pre-emptive attack on its Arab neighbours, devastating their air forces and then, in a three-front land war, the armies of Syria, Egypt and Jordan. In less than a week – that's why the conflict came to be known as the Six Day War (for an Israeli perspective, see www.sixdaywar.co.uk) – Israel captured Sinai and Gaza from Egypt, the West Bank and East Jerusalem from Jordan, and the Golan Heights from Syria.

Israelis reacted to the victory with nothing less than euphoria, and many could find no other explanation for their astounding victory than divine intervention. Some saw the triumph as proof that the messianic process was well and truly underway and sought to settle the newly captured lands. At the time, few Israelis were able to see the demographic, political and moral difficulties that Israeli control of the Palestinian Territories would entail.

In 1973 Egypt and Syria launched a surprise, two-front attack on Israel on Yom Kippur, the holiest day of the Jewish calendar. Unprepared because of intelligence failures born of post-1967 hubris, Israel was initially forced to withdraw but soon rallied and, with enormous casualties on both sides, pushed the Arab armies back. However, initial Egyptian battlefield successes made it possible for Egyptian President Anwar Sadat to portray the Yom Kippur War as a victory; and although in tactical and strategic terms it was Israel that had won on the battlefield, Israelis never saw the war as a victory.

Zionism struck a heroic chord in 1960s Hollywood. Paul Newman starred in *Exodus* (1960), based on Leon Uris' bestseller about a boat carrying illegal Jewish immigrants; and Kirk Douglas played an American war hero who joined the war for Israel's Independence in *Cast a Giant Shadow* (1966).

1929	1939–45	1946	1947
Arab-Jewish riots erupt because of a disagreement over Jewish access to the Western Wall. Many of Hebron's Jews are sheltered by Muslim neighbours, but 67 are killed by mobs.	Six million European Jews are murdered by the Nazis. Many Palestinian Jews volunteer for service in the British Army. Zionists smuggle Jewish refugees into Palestine.	Etzel (Irgun) underground paramilitary fighters under Menahem Begin blow up the south wing of Jerusalem's King David Hotel, a British military command centre, killing 91.	The UN General Assembly votes to partition Palestine into Jewish and Arab states, a plan accepted in principle by the Zionists but rejected by the Arabs. Fighting engulfs Palestine.

Thoroughly discredited by both the failures of the Yom Kippur War and the Labor Party's perceived corruption and lassitude, Prime Minister Golda Meir ended her political career in 1974. Three years later, the Labor Party, which had been at the head of every government since 1948, was voted out of office, in part by Mizrahi (Asian and North African) Jews angry at their economic and political marginalisation. Likud Party leader Menahem Begin, a right-wing former underground fighter (some would say terrorist because of his organisation's attacks on Arab civilians and symbols of the British occupation), became prime minister. But when Egyptian President Anwar Sadat stunned the world by travelling to Jerusalem (1977) and offering to make peace with Israel in return for an Israeli withdrawal from Sinai and promises (never fulfilled) of progress towards Palestinian autonomy, Begin accepted. With a beaming US President Jimmy Carter looking on, Begin and Sadat signed the Camp David Accords in 1978.

Israel completed its evacuation of Sinai, including 7000 settlers, in spring 1982 – just six weeks before simmering tensions between Lebanon-based Palestine Liberation Organisation (PLO) forces and Israel, and the attempted assassination of the Israeli ambassador to the UK by an anti-PLO Palestinian faction, were used by Israel's defence minister Ariel Sharon to justify launching a full-scale invasion of Lebanon. His objective was to drive the PLO out of Lebanon and install a pro-Israel Christian government. The war divided Israelis to an unprecedented degree as it dragged on and on, until 1985 (Israeli forces occupied a 'security zone' on Lebanese territory until May 2000). Many Israelis believed that the war was launched without proper government approval, and even more felt that their country was tainted when IDF soldiers failed to stop their Christian Lebanese allies from massacring Palestinians in the Beirut refugee camps of Sabra and Shatila in September 1982. A mass demonstration against the war and the massacre attracted 400,000 people in Tel Aviv, the largest civil demonstration in Israel's history. (Israel's ongoing trauma from the First Lebanon War was the subject of the 2008 Oscar-nominated animated film *Waltz with Bashir*.)

Meanwhile, Palestinian refugees waited in the West Bank and Gaza, in refugee camps in neighbouring countries, and across the Arab world and beyond for a solution to their plight. The PLO was set up in 1964 by the Arab League, made up of representatives of 22 Arabic-speaking nations. But it wasn't until after the Arab defeat in the 1967 Six Day War that a Palestinian leader willing to defy the Arab League won control of the PLO.

Born in Cairo in 1929, Yasser Arafat was in Kuwait working as an engineer in the late 1950s when he founded Fatah, a reverse Arabic acronym for 'Palestine Liberation Movement' and also the word for 'victory'. It was through the Fatah faction that he took over the PLO in 1969. From exile

Israel's Arab citizens – Palestinian Arabs who remained in their homes in 1948 and their descendants – lived under military law until 1966. They now number some 1.6 million; most live in the Galilee. Arabs living in East Jerusalem have blue Israeli ID cards, but most have not taken up Israel's offer of citizenship.

1948	1948–70s	1950	1951
The British leave Palestine; Zionist forces hold five Arab armies and local militias at bay; 700,000 Palestinian Arabs become refugees; the State of Israel is declared.	Some 600,000 Jews leave, flee or are expelled from Arab countries such as Yemen, Syria, Iraq, Egypt, Libya and Morocco and find refuge in Israel; many endure years in transit camps.	Jordan annexes the West Bank and East Jerusalem, captured in the 1948 war. The Hashemite Kingdom renounces its claims to the territory in 1988.	Jordan's King Abdullah I is assassinated on Temple Mount/Al Haram Ash Sharif in Jerusalem by a Palestinian nationalist. His grandson becomes King Hussein and rules until 1999.

THE JEWISH DIASPORA

During the 3300 or so years since the Children of Israel entered Canaan – according to the Bible after the Exodus from Egypt – there have always been Jews in the Land of Israel. But for about two-thirds of that time, most Jews lived outside the Holy Land, dispersed among other nations in communities collectively known as the Jewish Diaspora (from the Greek word for 'dispersion' or 'scattering').

The first major Diaspora community was established in Babylonia (now Iraq) after Nebuchadnezzar destroyed the First Temple and exiled the Jews in 586 BCE. When Cyrus II of Persia allowed them to return to Judea 48 years later, many stayed in Babylonia.

From the 3rd to the 6th centuries CE, Jewish sages in Palestine and Babylonia vied for supremacy in establishing Jewish law. Babylonia eventually won out.

In the 11th century, the seat of the Jewish world's greatest legal authorities shifted to North Africa (Cairo and Kairouan, Tunisia) and, more improbably, to the Rhineland, in a faraway land that the Jews called Ashkenaz. From the 13th to 15th centuries, many of the greatest sages lived in Spain, known in Hebrew as Sfarad.

Persecuted in Western Europe, Ashkenazi Jews began moving eastward into the Slavic lands from the 14th century, bringing with them a German-Hebrew patois known as Yiddish. By the 17th century the world's main centre of Jewish scholarship was in Lithuania and Poland. In the 18th century, for the first time in Jewish history, more Jews lived in Europe than in North Africa and Asia.

The Jews of Eastern Europe were again dispersed in the late 19th century when czarist pogroms forced many of them to flee. The expulsion of the Jews from Spain in 1492 scattered Sephardic Jews to the lands of the Ottomans (who welcomed the exiles) as well as the Netherlands, from where some eventually went to England. Of the Jews who remained in Europe and found themselves under Nazi occupation during WWII, the vast majority died in the Holocaust; most were either shot, their bodies dumped in mass graves, or killed in the gas chambers.

A few Sephardic Jews lived in colonial America before 1776, but most of the American Jewish community is descended from 19th-century Ashkenazi immigrants. Today, the United States and Israel, each with about six million Jews, vie for Jewish cultural and religious pre-eminence, just as Babylonia and the Land of Israel did 17 centuries ago.

in Jordan and later in Lebanon and Tunisia, he launched a campaign of hijackings, bombings and attacks against civilian targets designed to weaken Israel (which responded with a determined campaign that included cross-border commando operations and assassinations) and keep the Palestinian problem in the international headlines.

In 1987 a popular uprising against Israeli rule broke out in the West Bank and Gaza. Known as the First Intifada (Arabic for 'shaking off'), it was a spontaneous eruption of strikes, stones and Molotov cocktails.

1956	1964	1967	1972
After Egypt closes off the Red Sea to Israeli shipping, Israel captures Sinai. Britain and France try to use the conflict as a pretext to retake control of the Suez Canal.	The Arab League, meeting in Cairo, founds the Palestinian Liberation Organisation (PLO). Israel and Syria clash over water rights in the Jordan River basin.	In six days, Israel defeats Egypt, Jordan and Syria, more than tripling its territory. Israelis can pray at the Western Wall for the first time since 1948.	Palestinian terrorists belonging to Yasser Arafat's Fatah kill 11 Israeli athletes and coaches at the Munich Olympics. Golda Meir, prime minister of Israel, gives the order to hunt down the killers and assassinate them.

Arafat, based in Tunis, was at first out of touch with grassroots events in the Palestinian Territories but he soon took control, garnering worldwide sympathy for the Palestinian cause.

In 1988 Arafat publicly renounced terrorism and effectively recognised Israel. Five years later, Israel (under Yitzhak Rabin) and the PLO signed the Oslo Accords, so named because secret negotiations in the Norwegian capital laid the basis for an agreement under which Israel would hand over control of territory to the Palestinians in stages, beginning with the major towns of the West Bank and Gaza. The toughest issues – the future of Jerusalem and Palestinian refugees' right of return – were to be negotiated at the end of a five-year interim period. The Oslo formula was, essentially, 'land for peace' based on the two-state solution proposed by the UN in 1947.

The Oslo Era

Yasser Arafat arrived in Gaza to head the new Palestinian Authority (PA) in July 1994. Over the next few years, Israel handed over most of Gaza and the major West Bank towns to Palestinian control. But the Oslo Accords didn't bring real peace. Rather, they drove those on both sides who opposed the compromises to greater acts of violence. Hamas and Islamic Jihad took their terrorism to new heights with suicide bombings against Israeli civilians. Israel hit back by assassinating Hamas and Islamic Jihad leaders, using tactics that often resulted in civilian casualties. Military incursions and settler violence against local Palestinians increased and their expectations of an improved economy and freedom of movement were not fulfilled.

Perhaps the greatest single blow to the peace process came in November 1995, when a right-wing Orthodox Israeli shot Prime Minister Yitzhak Rabin after a Tel Aviv peace rally. The assassination was the culmination of several years of incitement from nationalist Israelis (especially Jewish settlers) bitterly opposed to Rabin's agreement to give up part of the historic 'Land of Israel'. Many Orthodox Jews (though not the ultra-Orthodox, who are non- or anti-Zionist) believe that the biblical lands they call Judea and Samaria (ie the West Bank) and Gaza came under Israeli control as part of a divinely ordained process heralding the beginning of the messianic era. Relinquishing control of land they see as Israel's God-given birthright would do no less than put an end to the messianic process. For messianists there can be no greater crime.

For most Israelis Rabin's killing was nothing less than a national nightmare, but in the end it accomplished much of what the assassin had hoped by robbing the peace process of an advocate whose military background – as a brigade commander in 1948 and later as chief of staff in the 1967 war – inspired Israelis to trust him on security issues.

Arab men are often referred to as Abu (meaning 'father of') followed by the name of their eldest son. Arafat was known popularly as Abu Ammar, but not because he had a son. He chose the name of a follower of the Prophet Muhammad as his nom de guerre.

1973	1978	1982	1987–93
Egypt and Syria launch a surprise attack against Israel on Yom Kippur, the holiest Jewish holiday.	Israel and Egypt sign the Camp David Accords. Israel opens an embassy in Cairo, Egypt establishes one in Tel Aviv, and Sinai is returned to Egypt.	Israel invades Lebanon, besieging Beirut. Lebanese Phalangists massacre Palestinians at Sabra and Shatila camps. Yasser Arafat and PLO fighters leave Beirut by sea, transferring their headquarters to Tunis.	Palestinian frustration with occupation explodes in the First Intifada. The Israel Defense Forces, trained to fight standing armies, responds ineffectively; Palestinian casualties generate international condemnation.

Rabin's death was followed by a string of Hamas suicide bombings that helped bring a right-wing coalition led by Benjamin Netanyahu to power. But in 1999 a centre-left coalition government led by former chief of staff Ehud Barak took office. Barak and Arafat agreed to a summit with US president Bill Clinton at Camp David, with the aim of striking a final peace deal. Negotiations, held against the backdrop of discontent since the Oslo Accords, failed. Widespread violence broke out, sparked by a controversial visit of Israel's Likud Party leader Ariel Sharon to Jerusalem's Temple Mount/Al Haram Ash Sharif. Both Sharon and Arafat were accused of stoking the unrest.

At first Arafat considered unleashing violence as a way to pressure Israel into making concessions, but he quickly lost control of the situation to young local Fatah leaders who felt he hadn't given them enough power since his return from exile – they accused him of giving all the top military and political jobs to corrupt, old party hacks who'd been with him in Beirut and Tunis. The young Fatah leaders quickly allied with Hamas and Islamic Jihad, eventually launching a wave of suicide bombings.

Israeli public opinion hardened, and in 2001 Ariel Sharon, a tough-talking former general who spoke privately of the Intifada as an 'existential danger' to Israel, and who had opposed Barak's efforts to reach a deal with Arafat, was elected prime minister. Sharon sent tanks to occupy West Bank towns previously ceded to Arafat, made frequent, bloody incursions into Gaza, and carried out 'targeted assassinations' of presumed terrorist leaders. He confined Arafat to his Ramallah compound by surrounding it with tanks. Depressed and sick, Arafat's command of events and – according to some aides – reality weakened until he was airlifted to France for treatment and died in November 2004. Over the course of the Second Intifada (2000–05), more than 1000 Israelis, 70% of them civilians, were killed by Palestinians, and approximately 4700 Palestinians, more than 2000 of them civilians, were killed by Israelis, according to the Israeli human rights group B'Tselem (www.btselem.org).

With his old enemy out of the way, Sharon – contradicting his reputation as an incorrigible hardliner – forged ahead with a radical plan to 'disengage' from the Palestinians, building the Separation Fence around most of the West Bank (despite furious opposition from Jewish settlers) and pulling out of isolated settlements. In August 2005 he completed the hugely controversial evacuation of all 8600 Israeli settlers from the Gaza Strip and four settlements in the northern West Bank. In January 2006 Sharon suffered a massive stroke; many Jewish settlers saw it as divine punishment for his betrayal of the Land of Israel. Sharon remained in a coma until his death in 2014.

Yasser Arafat made the chequered *keffiyeh* (chequered scarf worn by Arabs) famous around the world. His was black and white, the colours favoured by Fatah, and he arranged the folds to form an elongated triangle shaped like Palestine. Red-and-white *keffiyeh* are often worn by Jordanian Bedouin, leftist Palestinian groups and Hamas.

1988	1991	1993	1994
Arafat renounces terrorism in a speech to the United Nations General Assembly in Geneva.	Israel is hit by 39 Iraqi Scud missiles. Arafat supports Saddam Hussein's invasion and annexation of Kuwait; in response, Kuwait and other Gulf nations cut off PLO funding and expel Palestinians.	Israeli Prime Minister Yitzhak Rabin and PLO Chairperson Yasser Arafat, sworn enemies for decades, sign the Oslo Accords at the White House with an uneasy handshake.	Israel and Jordan sign a peace treaty, delimiting their long border and guaranteeing Jordan a share of Jordan River water. Embassies are opened in Amman and Ramat Gan.

A New Millennium

Ehud Olmert, Sharon's deputy, was elected as Israel's 12th prime minister in March 2006 on a platform that promised a further pull-back from much of the West Bank, but his plans were never implemented. A few months earlier, Hamas had won the Palestinian parliamentary elections, and the following year Hamas gunners took over the Gaza Strip by force; Fatah officials who didn't make it out were tortured and some killed – a few were thrown to their deaths from tall buildings. Since then the US and EU have continued to send significant aid to the Fatah-led Palestinian Authority in the West Bank, while Iran, despite disagreements over the civil war in Syria, has supplied weapons and money to Hamas in Gaza. Olmert was convicted of corruption and sentenced to six years in prison in 2014.

In summer 2006, Hezbollah guerrillas kidnapped two Israeli soldiers patrolling on the Israeli side of the Israel–Lebanon border. Israel entered a brief war with the Iranian-backed Lebanese militia, during which the latter launched thousands of rockets at Israeli cities, towns and villages, bringing northern Israel to a halt and killing 43 civilians. The scale of Israel's bombing attacks on Lebanese towns in return was widely condemned, and the war was a diplomatic disaster for Israel, but over a decade later the ceasefire agreed to at war's end was still holding.

In 2001 Hamas and Islamic Jihad began launching missiles from Gaza into nearby parts of Israel. These attacks escalated after Israel's 2006 withdrawal from Gaza, and over time homemade Qassam rockets were upgraded and supplemented by Iranian-supplied 122mm Grads capable of hitting Be'er Sheva, Rishon LeZion and perhaps Tel Aviv. However, the people of Sderot and nearby kibbutzim bore the brunt of the attacks. At the end of 2008 Israel launched a major offensive, dubbed Operation Cast Lead, aimed at halting the missile attacks. Battles raged for three weeks and, by the end, much of Gaza's infrastructure lay in ruins and thousands were homeless. According to the Israeli human rights organisation B'Tselem, during the operation 1397 Palestinians were killed by Israelis (Israel claims a large majority were militants) and five Israeli soldiers were killed by Palestinians. But Hamas remained in control and dug new smuggling tunnels to circumvent Israel's much-criticised blockade of Gaza (significantly eased for civilian goods in 2010). Egypt sealed the Gaza–Sinai border; in 2013 and 2014 the Egyptian army destroyed some 1200 smuggling tunnels, cutting off a significant source of revenue for Hamas.

Israel's 2013 general elections brought to power another coalition government headed by Benjamin Netanyahu; initially it focused on trying to force the men of Israel's growing ultra-Orthodox community to serve

---

Considered by many to be the Palestinian national poet, Mahmoud Darwish (1941–2008) wrote works expressing Palestinian anguish at their dispossession and exile. He was active in the PLO from 1973 to the 1990s. In one of his best-known poems, he wrote, 'We have a country of words.'

There are 20 refugee camps administered by the UN Relief and Works Agency (UNRWA) in the West Bank. The Gaza Strip has eight, and there's one in East Jerusalem. More than 50% of Palestinians are listed by the UN as refugees.

---

in the IDF and integrate into the workforce. Following the collapse of US-sponsored Israeli-Palestinian peace talks, in part because of continued settlement construction by the Netanyahu government, the PA applied for full membership as an independent state in a variety of international organisations, angering Israel. In 2014 Israeli president Shimon Peres (at age 90, the world's oldest head of state) was replaced in the largely ceremonial post by Reuven 'Ruby' Rivlin, a right-winger with a strong civil rights record.

In 2014 Fatah, which governs much of the West Bank, and Hamas, which controls Gaza, established a government of national unity, but differences and mistrust between the groups remain deep. Egypt, under President Abdel Fattah Al Sisi, is implacably hostile to Hamas, in part because of the Egyptian military's historic opposition to the Muslim Brotherhood.

Three Israeli teenagers were kidnapped and murdered by Palestinians in June 2014, after which violence swiftly escalated. Israel launched a major crackdown on Hamas in the West Bank in response to the kidnappings, killing 10 Palestinians in raids and arresting hundreds more. Rockets were fired into Gaza, and from Gaza into Israel.

The resulting 50-day Hamas–Israel War left more than 2100 Palestinians (69% of them civilians, according to a UN estimate) and 73 Israelis (67 of them soldiers) dead, large parts of the Gaza Strip (including 17,200 homes) in ruins, and hundreds of thousands of civilians – especially children – traumatised. Israel's Iron Dome anti-missile system virtually neutralised the threat to the Israeli population posed by Hamas.

The war did little to improve relations either between Israel and the Palestinians or between Fatah and Hamas. In 2015, Netanyahu was re-elected as prime minister and assembled a coalition of right-wing parties, including pro-settlement and ultra-orthodox groups. That year also saw a spate of killings in Israel and the West Bank, mostly by 'lone wolf' Palestinian attackers.

In response to an attack at the Al Aqsa Mosque compound by three Palestinian brothers on Israeli soldiers in 2017, Israel installed metal detectors at the gates of the site. The move resulted in weeks of protests by Palestinians outside the Old City, which eventually forced Israel to remove the metal detectors.

Some Jews believe that when the Messiah comes, the Temple will be rebuilt on Jerusalem's Temple Mount/Al Haram Ash Sharif. In the Old City's Jewish Quarter, you can find artists' renderings of the 'Third Temple'. Muslims, of course, prefer to keep the Dome of the Rock right where it is.

2006	2008–14	2015	2017
Attacks on the Galilee by Iranian-backed Hezbollah lead to Israel's Second Lebanon War. The hardline Islamist movement Hamas defeats pro-two-state Fatah in Palestinian parliamentary elections.	Radical Jewish settlers carry out 'price tag' attacks on Palestinians and the IDF in an effort to deter the Israeli government from policies detrimental to Israeli settlements in the West Bank.	Prime Minister Benjamin Netanyahu wins elections and assembles a coalition of right-wing parties, including ultra-Orthodox and pro-settlement groups.	US president Donald Trump declares Jerusalem the capital of Israel and promises to move the embassy, igniting protests across the Arab world.

People of Israel & the Palestinian Territories

Almost 13 million people live in Israel and the Palestinian Territories. Israel's population is 75% Jewish, 17.6% Muslim Arab, 1.7% Christian Arab and 5.7% other. The West Bank population is made up of about 83% Sunni Muslims, 13% Jews, perhaps 2% Christians, and 2% other. The population of the Gaza Strip is almost all Sunni Muslims. According to the Palestinian Central Bureau of Statistics, there are about 11 million Palestinians worldwide, of which the United Nations classifies five million as refugees.

Jews

Since 1948 Israel has absorbed more immigrants than any country on earth relative to its population. About 900,000 Jews from the former Soviet Union arrived in the 1990s; recent arrivals include thousands of Jews concerned about anti-Semitism in France.

During the Ottoman period, most Palestinian Jews lived in the holy cities of Jerusalem, Hebron, Tiberias and Tsfat (Safed), but starting in the 1880s Jews began immigrating to Palestine, not only for religious and spiritual reasons but also to further Jewish national self-determination – and to live and raise their children without fear of anti-Semitism.

Jews born in Israel are known as Sabras, after the prickly pear, a tenacious type of cactus *(Opuntia ficus-indica)* native to Mexico, whose fruit is prickly on the outside but soft and sweet inside.

Sepharadim

In 1492, the Jews of Sefarad (the Hebrew name for Spain) were given the choice of conversion, death or expulsion. Some Sephardic Jews (Sephardim) fled to North Africa, while others found refuge in the Ottoman Empire, whose sultan welcomed them with open arms.

Until the late 19th century, the majority of the Jews of Ottoman Palestine were Sephardim, defined not only by their origins in Spain but also by their religious liturgy, rites and melodies. Many of the leading Kabbalists (Jewish mystics) in 16th-century Tsfat (Safed) were Sephardic.

Much has been written about the condescension of some Ashkenazi Jews towards their non-European brethren, but one group has long looked out on the rest of the Jewish world with supreme confidence in its innate cultural superiority: the 'pure' Sephardim who can trace their lineage back to medieval Spain.

Judaism has three main liturgical and ritual traditions, Ashkenazi, Sephardic and Edot HaMizrah (Mizrahi), as well as a number of distinct local traditions from places such as Rome and Alsace (France).

For five centuries, the language of the old-line Sephardim in places such as Turkey, Greece, Bosnia and Bulgaria has been Ladino (Djudeo-Espanyol), which is essentially medieval Spanish (Castilian) mixed with words from Hebrew and – depending on where the exiles settled – elements of Turkish, Greek, Arabic and French.

For more information on Sephardic history and culture, see www.sephardicstudies.org. A site in Ladino (readable if you know Spanish), www.aki-yerushalayim.co.il/ay, has useful links.

Ashkenazim

The ancestors of today's Ashkenazim arrived in Ashkenaz (the old Hebrew name for Germany) in the 10th century. As successive expulsions forced the Jews of Ashkenaz to flee eastward, they were welcomed into what later became the Russian and Austro-Hungarian Empires. A thousand years ago just 3% of the world's Jews were Ashkenazim; by the 1930s that number had risen to 92%. Today about half of Israeli Jews (and three-quarters of Jews worldwide) trace their ancestry – either directly or via North and South America – to Central and Eastern Europe, especially Russia, Poland, the Ukraine, Belarus, Lithuania, Hungary, Romania and, of course, Germany and Austria.

Starting in 1882, pogroms and other forms of persecution led millions of Ashkenazi Jews to emigrate from Eastern Europe to the Americas and Western Europe, but small groups of Jews from countries such as Romania and Russia chose instead to move to Ottoman Palestine to establish agricultural settlements (eg Zichron Ya'akov). Friction soon developed between these Zionists, some of them socialists, and the traditionalist, ultra-Orthodox communities of Palestine, a conflict that continues to this day.

One of the cultural markers of the Ashkenazim is Yiddish, a mixture of medieval German, Hebrew and words of Slavic origin that is written in Hebrew characters. Yiddish words that have made their way into English (thanks in part to *Seinfeld*) include bagel, blintz, chutzpah, dyubbuk, glitch, klutz, lox, maven, mensch, noodge, nosh, oy vey, putz, shlemazel, shlemiel, schlep, schlock, schmaltz, schmooze, schmuck, shpiel, shpritz, shtetl, shtik, shvitz and tush.

In 1939, 11 to 13 million Jews spoke Yiddish; today, as a result of the Holocaust and linguistic assimilation in countries such as Israel, the USA, the Soviet Union and Argentina, only perhaps one million do. Visitors to Israel can hear Yiddish being spoken in places such as Jerusalem's ultra-Orthodox Mea She'arim neighbourhood.

> Because Mizrahi and Sephardi liturgy and ritual are similar in some ways, Mizrahim are sometimes subsumed under the umbrella term Sephardim despite the fact that the Jews of Baghdad, Damascus, Sanaa and Bukhara never got anywhere near the Iberian Peninsula.

Mizrahim

Jews whose families came to Israel from North Africa (Morocco, Algeria, Tunisia and Libya), the Middle East (eg Iraq, Syria, Yemen, Iran and Afghanistan) and Central Asia (eg Uzbekistan, Azerbaijan and Georgia), as well as India, are known as Edot HaMizrah ('communities of the East') or Mizrahim ('easterners'). This definition reflects common liturgical traditions as well as geography.

Yemenite Jews began emigrating to Ottoman Palestine in 1881. The number of Mizrahim swelled after 1948 as some 600,000 Jews immigrated to Israel from the Arab countries, many to escape violence and anti-Jewish decrees. In recent years, Mizrahi groups have begun demanding reparations for lost personal and communal property.

Mizrahim in Israel have long suffered discrimination at the hands of the Ashkenazim, and after 1948 many spent years in resettlement camps

---

THE LAW OF RETURN

Passed by the Knesset (Israeli Parliament) in 1950, Israel's Law of Return grants Israeli citizenship to any Jew – defined as anyone with at least one Jewish grandparent or who has converted to Judaism – and their legally married spouse (heterosexual or, as of 2014, same-sex) who requests it. Because the law guarantees that all Jews, anywhere in the world, who are faced with persecution always have a place of refuge – something that was emphatically not the case in the 1930s – the law is seen as one of the bedrocks of Israel's mission as a Jewish homeland.

In 2013 and 2014, Portugal and Spain passed their own 'laws of return' offering citizenship to the descendants of Sephardic Jews expelled from the Iberian Peninsula 500 years ago.

A variety of countries, including Armenia, China, Greece and Germany, have laws conferring citizenship or residency rights on the descendants of émigrés.

BLACK HEBREWS

Also known as the African Hebrew Israelites of Jerusalem (www.africanhebrewisraelites ofjerusalem.com), the Black Hebrews are African Americans who claim descent from the ancient Israelite tribe of Judah and see Israel as their ancestral homeland. After spending time in Liberia, they began settling in Israel in 1969 under the leadership of Ben Carter, also known as Ben Ammi Ben-Israel. Although not recognised as Jews by any stream of Judaism (their traditions include a vegan diet, fasting on the Sabbath and polygamy), they were granted permanent residency in 2004 and a path to citizenship in 2009; many volunteer for service in the army.

About 2500 Black Hebrews live communally in the Negev town of Dimona. The community is known for its gospel choir and for singer Eddie Butler, who represented Israel in the Eurovision song contest in 1999 and 2006.

and/or were sent to live in remote 'development towns' in the Negev or Galilee. In recent years, intermarriage between Mizrahim, Sephardim and Ashkenazim has become common, and while Mizrahim – especially the descendants of immigrants from Morocco – are still underrepresented in universities and overrepresented in prisons, Israeli popular culture is now much more inclusive. The ultra-Orthodox Shas political party draws almost all of its support from religiously traditionalist Mizrahim.

For centuries Mizrahi Jews spoke a number of distinctive dialects and languages, including Maghrebi Judeo-Arabic, Iraqi Judeo-Arabic (Yahudi) and Judeo-Tat (Juhuri), a Persian language spoken by the Mountain Jews of Azerbaijan.

> Although Jews make up just 0.2% of the world population, they have been awarded 27% of the Nobel prizes for chemistry, physics, medicine and economics.

Ethiopian Jews

Also known as Beta Israel (House of Israel) and, somewhat derogatorily, Falashas ('exiles' or 'strangers'), the Jews of Ethiopia trace their origins back to King Solomon and the Queen of Sheba (I Kings 10:1–13), though other traditions suggest that they may have been converted to Judaism almost two millennia ago by Yemenite-Jewish traders. But no one is quite sure how, or when, Jews got to Ethiopia.

The first Ethiopian Jews arrived in Israel in the 1960s, but it wasn't until two airlifts, Operation Moses (1984–85) and Operation Solomon (1991), that large-scale immigration began. Today, there are about 121,000 Jews of Ethiopian descent in Israel, 2% of Israel's Jewish population.

The transition to life in Israel has proved difficult for many of the Beta Israel and collectively they are among the poorest people in the country, with educational achievements that are well below average. Well-known Ethiopian-Israelis include the model Esti Mamo, who has appeared in *Elle* and *Vogue*, and Miss Israel 2013, Yityish Titi Aynaw. Six Ethiopian Jews have served in the Knesset (Israeli Parliament).

> Almost all Israeli and Palestinian Arabs are Sunnis, but Israel has one Alawite (Alawi) village: Ghajar, 4km due east (by air) from Metula, which is half in Lebanon and half in a sliver of land captured by Israel, along with the adjacent Golan, in 1967.

Muslims

Sunni Muslims make up 17.4% of the population of Israel, about 97% of the Arab population of the West Bank and more than 99% of the population of Gaza. About 90% of Israeli Arabs are Muslim; Muslims constitute 38% of the population of the Galilee. The largest Muslim-majority city in Israel is Nazareth (population 66,000). About a third of the residents of Jerusalem are Muslims.

Traditionally, Palestinian Muslims have been moderate in their beliefs and practices. The rise of Muslim fundamentalism among Palestinians since the 1970s, especially in evidence in Gaza and some parts of the West Bank (eg Hebron), has been attributed to a number of factors, including the 1979 Islamic Revolution in Iran; disillusionment with secular

Palestinian groups such as Yasser Arafat's Fatah, in part because of corruption; and the increasing influence of Islamist groups across the Arab and Muslim worlds. Hamas, the Islamist movement that controls Gaza, is the Palestinian branch of the Egyptian Muslim Brotherhood. In Israel, the Muslim Brotherhood gave rise to the Islamic Movement, which has a hard-line 'northern' branch and a moderate 'southern' branch that supported the Oslo Accords and has representatives in the Knesset.

Palestinian Muslims, both in Israel and the Palestinian Territories, see themselves as the guardians of Islam's third-holiest site, Al Aqsa Mosque in Jerusalem, and of sites such as the Ibrahimi Mosque (Cave of the Patriarchs) in Hebron. Muslim holy sites, including Jerusalem's Al Haram Ash Sharif (Temple Mount), are run autonomously by Muslim religious trusts known as *waqfs*.

Islam and Judaism have much more in common – in rituals, liturgy and jurisprudence – than either does with Christianity:

➡ Muslims pray five times a day, while Jews traditionally have three services a day.

➡ Muslim halal laws concerning which animals may be eaten and how they are to be slaughtered are very similar to Judaism's kosher laws (many Muslims consider kosher meat to be halal).

➡ The first part of the Shahada (Islamic creed), 'There is no God but Allah', is very similar to the Jewish Shema, 'Hear O Israel, the Lord is your God, the Lord is One' – both emphasise the absolute oneness and unity of God.

➡ The Arabic and Hebrew words for God, Allah and Elohim, derive from the same Semitic root.

Bedouin

About one in six Israeli Arabs is a Bedouin – that is, a descendant of one of the Arabic-speaking, Sunni Muslim nomadic groups that historically have raised sheep and goats in desert areas all over Arabia. About 220,000 Bedouin live in the Negev, in seven government-built townships and some 45 unrecognised villages; another 60,000 Bedouin live in villages in the Galilee. Although Bedouin are not drafted into the Israel Defense Forces (IDF), many volunteer, often serving as trackers.

There has long been tension between Negev Bedouin and the Israeli government as the latter, like its British and Ottoman predecessors, has tried to end the Bedouin's nomadic ways by moving them to permanent settlements.

Some Bedouin men still practice polygamy although it is forbidden under Israeli law.

Circassians

As the Russian Empire expanded into the northern Caucasus (the area between the Black and Caspian Seas) in the mid-1800s, hundreds of thousands of Circassians, a Caucasian people of Sunni Muslim faith, were forced from their homes. Many found refuge in the Ottoman Empire, some in what is now Israel.

Today about 4000 Circassians live in two Galilee villages, Kfar Kama and Rehaniye. Male Circassians are the only Muslims for whom service in the Israeli army is obligatory.

Christians

In 1920, about one in 10 people in what is now Israel and the Palestinian Territories was Christian; today Christians make up about 2% of the population of Israel and 0.8% of the population of the Palestinian Territories. Part of the reason for this precipitous drop is the growth in the number of Jews and Muslims, but emigration to the majority-Christian

---

PEOPLE OF ISRAEL & THE PALESTINIAN TERRITORIES CHRISTIANS

About 2000 Ahmadiyya Muslims, members of a famously tolerant community founded in India in the late 1800s, live in the Haifa neighbourhood of Kababir on Mt Carmel. To improve relations with their Jewish neighbours, they published a Yiddish translation of the Quran in 1987.

Israel's Vietnamese community of about 200 was established in 1977 when Prime Minister Menahem Begin welcomed Vietnamese boat people rescued in the South China Sea by Israeli merchant ships.

countries of Europe and North and South America has played a significant role. In recent years, a major impetus for emigration by Christians from the West Bank and Gaza has been the rise in Islamic fundamentalism.

In Israel, 80% of the Christians are Arabs; most of the rest are immigrants from the former Soviet Union. The largest Christian denominations in Israel are Eastern-Rite (Melkite) Catholics (53%), Greek Orthodox (27%), Latin-Rite Catholic (10%) and Maronite Catholics (7.5%). Christians have the highest rates of high-school graduation and eligibility for university study of any religious group in Israel, including Jews. Over the last few years, an increasing number of Israeli Christian Arabs have been volunteering to serve in the IDF.

Major Christian centres include Nazareth, whose Christian population has dropped from 60% in 1949 to less than 30% today, and Bethlehem, which was 80% Christian in the 1940s but is now less than a quarter Christian. Other cities with sizeable Christian communities include Jerusalem, Haifa and Nazareth.

Some 60,000 Africans, most from Eritrea and Sudan, have sought asylum in Israel after crossing the border from Egypt. In 2014, Israel began transferring Eritrean and Sudanese nationals to a desert prison, Holot, and in some cases paying them to relocate to Uganda or Rwanda.

Druze

The Druze speak Arabic but most don't consider themselves to be Arabs, and they believe in a strictly unitary God and accept many of the same prophets as Islam, but they are not Muslims – in fact, Orthodox Muslims have sometimes persecuted them as heretics – ever since their religion, an offshoot of Islam, was founded in Cairo in the early 11th century.

It was to escape persecution that the Druze established themselves in the remote mountains of southern Lebanon about a thousand years ago, and it is to prevent accusations of heresy that they keep the principles (eg reincarnation) and texts of their religion secret not only from outsiders but also from Druze laypeople (*juhhal*), revealing them fully only to the community's *uqqal* (wise men and women). Only the *uqqal* attend Thursday-night religious ceremonies. The Druze religion has forbidden conversion, either in or out, since the mid-11th century.

Israeli Druze live mainly on Mt Carmel (eg in Daliyat Al Karmel), in various Galilee villages and on the Golan Heights, whose largest Druze village – most of whose residents identify at least nominally as Syrian – is Majdal Shams. Tradition dictates that the Druze be loyal to their country of residence so Israeli Druze men are drafted into the IDF, and many make careers in the army and the Border Police. During the 2014 Hamas–Israel War, a Druze colonel commanded the IDF's elite Golani infantry brigade.

Often seen in Druze villages, the horizontally striped Druze flag – like the Druze star – has five colours: green (the mind), red (the soul), yellow (the word, mediator between the divine and the material), blue (the will and the realm of possibility) and white (the manifested will).

Samaritans

The Samaritan religion can probably best be described as an offshoot of Israelite-era Judaism. The Samaritans have a five-book Torah, written in Hebrew, but it differs in a number of significant ways from the Jewish Torah; for instance, regarding the place where God commanded that an altar for sacrifices be built – ancient Judaism established the Temple in Jerusalem, whereas the Samaritans built their Temple on Mt Gerizim, overlooking Nablus.

In Roman times, the Samaritans were powerful religious and political rivals of the Jews, which is why the New Testament's Parable of the Good Samaritan (Luke 10:25–37) is such a stinging rebuke of Judaism's Jerusalem-based priestly elite.

Today the Samaritans, who number just 760, are not considered Jews, but they are not exactly non-Jews either. Their religion and history are so closely tied to Judaism that they are eligible to receive Israeli citizenship based on the Law of Return, but in Israel they are considered – by themselves and by the Chief Rabbinate – to be a separate religious community.

Modern-day Samaritans (see www.thesamaritanupdate.com) live in two communities: one, Kiryat Luza, is on Mt Gerizim, near the West Bank city of Nablus; the other is in Israel, in the Tel Aviv suburb of Holon. While Israeli Samaritans are drafted into the IDF, their brethren in Kiryat Luza are Palestinian citizens. But every year the entire community joins together on Mt Gerizim to sacrifice sheep for Passover – so it was before 1967, when the two centres of Samaritan life were ruled by Jordan and Israel, and so it is today despite the complicated relationship between Israelis and Palestinians.

Regional Food

From traditional Middle Eastern and Mediterranean food to Franco-Israeli fusion, Israel is a food-lovers delight, with tiny hole-in-the-wall eateries, trendy bistros and high-end restaurants that would give any European city a run for its money. Restaurants offer a vast smorgasbord of delicious dishes, some of them hard to find outside the region, many of them vegetarian and all of them – including innovative fusion variants – likely to intrigue your taste buds.

What to Eat

Heavenly Hummus

....

Ali Caravan
(Tel Aviv)

....

Hummus Said
(Akko)

....

Abu Shukri
(Jerusalem)

....

Felafel HaZkenim
(Haifa)

➡ **Hummus** Made of cooked chickpeas, this creamy paste is beloved across religious, political and cultural boundaries. Made to be dipped or scooped up with fresh pita bread, it is often served with warm *fuul* (fava beans), whole boiled chickpeas or tahini (sesame seed paste); Arabs sometimes serve it with ground meat. One difference: while Jews eat hummus all day long, Arabs traditionally take their (warm) hummus in the morning or early afternoon.

➡ **Olives** Especially popular for breakfast and dinner, olives come in a wide variety of styles very different than their Greek, Italian or Spanish cousins. Sold from vats in both markets and supermarkets, one particularly tasty variety to look for is *surim d'fukim* (cracked Tyre olives).

➡ **Falafel** Deep-fried balls made of ground chickpeas, best when piping hot. They are typically served inside a pita or wrapped in a *laffa* (flat pita) along with hummus and/or tahina, tomato, cucumber, pickle slices, a hot condiment such as Yemenite *s'chug* and, sometimes, sauerkraut.

➡ **Sabich** Falafel's upstart rival consists of deep-fried eggplant, egg, boiled potato, cucumber, tomato, chopped parsley and tahina tucked into a pita; traditionally eaten by the Jews of Iraq on Shabbat morning.

➡ **Shawarma** Chicken, turkey or lamb grilled on a giant spit and sliced in layers before being stuffed into a pita – the ultimate street food.

A question you're likely to hear at breakfast time: would you like *betzei ayin* (sunny-side-up eggs), *beitzim mekushkashot* (scrambled), a *chavita* (omelette) or just a plain *beitza kasha* (hard-boiled egg)?

➡ **Grilled meats** On sunny weekends you're likely to see families in parks gathered around a *mangal* (portable brazier) chargrilling red meat, served with pita and hummus. Many Jewish- and Arab-run restaurants specialise in grilled meats – keep an eye out for kebab (ground meat balls on a skewer), *shishlik* (lamb or chicken chunks on a skewer), *me'urav yerushalmi* ('Jerusalem mixed grill': heart, liver, spleen and other chicken bits grilled on a *plancha*) and goose liver.

➡ **Labneh** A creamy, sour, yoghurt-type cheese, eaten with pita or *laffa,* that's smothered in olive oil and sprinkled with *zaatar* (a blend of local spices that includes hyssop, sumac and sesame).

➡ **Bourekas** Savoury, flaky Balkan pastries, often triangular, filled with salty Bulgarian cheese, mashed potatoes, mushrooms or spinach.

➡ **Shakshuka** A spicy egg and tomato stew, usually eaten for breakfast.

➡ **Kibbeh** Minced lamb or beef encased in bulgur wheat to create a dumpling shaped like an American football. Iraqi and Kurdish Jews eat *kibbeh* made with semolina in a tangy soup.

> ### VEGETARIAN BONANZA
> ....
> Few countries offer a better selection of vegetarian options than Israel. Street food includes falafel, *sabich* and *boureka;* almost all restaurants serve giant – and often creative – salads; and even in grilled-meat joints and meat-heavy Arab and Levantine eateries, the mezze-style appetisers can serve as a remarkably inexpensive vegetarian meal.

➜ **Jachnun** Rolled-up, buttery dough slow baked in a pot and served with grated tomatoes and *s'chug* hot paste; traditionally eaten by the Jews of Yemen on Shabbat morning.

➜ **Dates** Varieties include the yellowish, translucent *dekel nur (deglet nur)* and the giant *medjoul.* In the fall you'll see plump, unripe yellow dates for sale – freezing them shortly before consumption takes away the pucker effect.

Kosher & Halal

Traditionally, Jews and Muslims observe strikingly similar sets of dietary laws, the former known as kosher *(kasher)*, the latter as halal. Both religions allow only certain species of animal to be eaten, with pigs considered to be the most unclean of all the beasts, and have the same basic rules for slaughter: a blessing is recited and animals are killed while fully conscious, their throats slit with a sharp, non-serrated blade.

In addition, keeping kosher involves:

➜ Refraining from the consumption of mammals that do not both have cloven hoofs and chew their cud (cattle, sheep and goats are fine); seafood (shrimp, lobster, squid etc); amphibians, reptiles and insects (except locusts); most birds that aren't ducks or geese; and those few types of fish that lack fins and/or scales (eg eels and catfish).

➜ Not mixing meat and dairy products (yes, cheeseburgers and pepperoni pizza are out).

Food that is neither milk nor meat, such as vegetables and fish, is called *parveh* (parve) and can be eaten with either milk or meat dishes. Foods to which especially strict standards have been applied are called *kasher l'mehadrin.* Meat labelled 'glatt kosher' comes from mammals whose lungs have been certified to be 'smooth', ie free of adhesions.

Israeli law does not require restaurants to be kosher – it's up to the owner to arrange (and pay for) kosher certification by the local Rabbinate branch. Kosher restaurants, which must close on Shabbat and Jewish holidays, are almost always either *basari (fleyshig* in Yiddish; 'meat') or *chalavi (milchig* in Yiddish; 'dairy', ie vegetarian plus fish). In Tel Aviv, kosher restaurants are the exception rather than the rule, whereas in West Jerusalem it can be hard to find a place to eat on Shabbat.

Unlike Judaism, Islam strictly prohibits alcohol. Even foods with trace amounts of alcohol, or whose preparation involves alcohol (eg vanilla extract), are *haram* (forbidden).

Shabbat Foods

Israeli families from across the religious spectrum keep the ancient tradition of dining together on Erev Shabbat (Sabbath eve). On Friday evening, parents, children and grandchildren gather for a festive dinner, often after a battle of wills between in-laws over who gets to host the

'Im hareef v'amba?' the busy falafel guy asks. What he wants to know is whether you'd like *s'chug* (fiery Yemenite hot pepper paste) and *amba* (Iraqi-style mango chutney) shmeared inside or dripped on your falafel. Unless you're an old hand or a masochist, the prudent answer is *'ktzat'* (a bit).

Favourite cheeses in Israel include *gvina Bulgarit* (Bulgarian cheese, similar to feta), *gvina Tsfatit* (a soft, set cheese, originally from Tsfat), *gvinat emek* (a yellow cheese) and deliciously creamy cottage cheese, so popular that price rises set off a consumer boycott and Knesset inquiries a few years back.

BREAKFAST IN ISRAEL

Hotels, guesthouses and even hostels really shine come breakfast time. Most serve generous smorgasbords that include eggs, matjes herring, pickled herring, soft and hard cheeses, vegetable salads, green olives, jams, breads, breakfast cereals and hot drinks.

Based on the dining traditions of the kibbutzim, whose members often worked in the still-cool fields for several hours before breakfast, the 'Israeli breakfast' has become a much loved feature of the local hotel scene; variants are on offer in cafes and restaurants.

married children. In many homes, even secular ones, the lighting of the Shabbat candles is followed by Kiddush, the blessing over the wine. Traditional main dishes among Ashkenazim include chicken, or couscous for families with roots in North Africa.

Cooking is forbidden on Shabbat so the only hot foods that could traditionally be eaten for Saturday lunch – we're talking about the time before the invention of the electric hot plate – were slow-cooked dishes put on the fire the night before. That's how Jews in different communities around the world came up with *hamin* (*tsholent* in Yiddish), a rich, stick-to-your-ribs stew usually made with potatoes, meat, beans, barley, chickpeas and hard-boiled eggs.

> Palestinian Arabs, Bedouin and Druze often bake their breads in a *taboun* (clay oven), also used for pizzas and *bourekas* (stuffed, flaky Balkan pastries).

Festivals & Celebrations

Jewish

Food is a central feature of all Jewish festivals and celebrations, notable either for its omnipresence (eg on Passover and at weddings) or its absence (during fasts such as Yom Kippur, the Day of Atonement).

A few weeks before each Jewish holiday, you'll start seeing special foods and dishes in shops and markets.

➜ **Rosh HaShanah** The Jewish New Year begins sweetly with apples dipped in honey, honey cake, sweet round *challah* bread and pomegranates. Followers of Sephardi and Mizrahi traditions also eat foods such as leek, squash, beet, fritters and a fish head, each punningly associated with a blessing.

➜ **Yom Kippur** The menu consists of...nothing at all. About two-thirds of Israeli Jews, both religious and secular, refrain from eating or drinking for 25 hours and then dine in gatherings for a break-the-fast meal.

➜ **Sukkot** Commemorating the Israelites' 40 years of desert wandering after the Exodus, the eight-day holiday of Sukkot is noteworthy less for what is eaten than where: weather permitting, observant Jews take their meals in a *sukkah* (a rectangular hut with a flat roof made of branches); to find one, head to a kosher hotel or restaurant.

➜ **Hanukkah** Stuff yourself with *levivot* (*latkes* in Yiddish; fried potato pancakes) topped with sour cream or apple sauce and *sufganiot* (jelly-filled doughnuts).

➜ **Tu B'Shevat** On the New Year of the Trees, kids and adults eat dried fruits and nuts and plant trees.

➜ **Purim** *Oznei haman* ('Haman's ears'; *hamantashen* in Yiddish) are triangular pastries with a poppy-seed, prune or date filling; they are named after the archvillain of the Purim story, Haman.

➜ **Passover (Pesach)** Parsley, salt water, bitter herbs (usually horseradish or romaine lettuce), *charoset* (a sweet paste of grated apple, grated walnuts, sweet wine and chopped dates), a lamb shank bone and a roasted hard-boiled egg

> ### Local Brews
>
> *Goldstar, dark lager*
>
> *Maccabee, pale lager*
>
> *Taybeh, Palestinian beer*
>
> *Bazelet Amber Ale, from the Golan*
>
> *Alexander, boutique ale*
>
> *Dancing Camel, microbrews from Tel Aviv*
>
> *Shapiro, ales and stouts from Beit Shemesh*
>
> *Negev, brewed in the south*

symbolise aspects of the Exodus story. Instead of bread, which – along with all leavened foods – is forbidden, there's *matzah*, unleavened crackers made of just two ingredients: flour and water. (During Passover, Israeli law forbids the sale of bread in Jewish areas.) In Ashkenazi communities, other festive treats include chicken soup with *matzah* balls (*kneydlakh* in Yiddish; dumplings made of ground matzah, eggs and oil or chicken fat) and gefilte fish (poached cod or carp balls).

➜ **Shavuot** Judaism's most vegetarian major holiday is a time to dine on dairy. Popular cheese-based dishes include *blintzes* (stuffed, folded-over crêpes), often topped with sour cream.

Muslim

During the month of Ramadan, observant Muslims refrain from eating or drinking (or smoking or having sex) during daylight hours, but it's what happens before and, especially, after the fast that turns Ramadan into a culinary festival – and a time when many Muslims actually gain weight! Fasters generally awaken before sunrise to eat because they won't take food or drink again until the *iftar*, the festive, break-the-fast family feast at dusk. (In some places, such as the Israeli seaside town of Jisr Az Zarka, organised programs invite paying, non-Muslim guests to the *iftar* meal.) The best-known Ramadan treat is *qatayif*, a pancake folded over a cluster of crushed nuts or small mound of cheese and drizzled with sugar syrup.

On Eid Al Adha (Feast of the Sacrifice), Muslims traditionally sacrifice an animal, often a lamb or sheep, as an act of thanksgiving for God's mercy. Not surprisingly, lamb or mutton are often on the menu.

When a baby is born, relatives might prepare *mughly*, a spice-laden rice pudding said to aid lactation. During periods of mourning, bitter Arab coffee replaces the sugared variety.

On major holidays and celebrations, sweet pastries are everywhere. Keep an eye out for *maamoul* (grainy cookies made of buttery semolina and stuffed with dates or nuts) and a host of honeyed pastries and sweets, including baklava, that are carried to the homes of relatives and friends in wrapped bakery trays.

Lebanese and Palestinian specialities include the 'three Ms': *majadra* (rice and lentils garnished with fried onions), *mansaf* (lamb cooked in sour yoghurt and served atop rice) and *makloubeh* (layers of stewed chicken or lamb, rice and vegetables, turned 'upside down' before serving).

Where to Eat & Drink

Tel Aviv and neighbouring Jaffa have become international-calibre dining destinations, with food options for every budget, including a bumper crop of high-end brasseries and *mis'adot shef* (restaurants whose decor and dishes reflect the chef's larger-than-life personality). Jerusalem, too, has plenty of dining choices but, with a few exceptions, the standard is far below that of Tel Aviv. In other parts of the country, dining experiences well worth trying include seafood in Akko, traditional Arab cuisine in Haifa and the Galilee, locally raised steak on the Golan and meat-free meals in vegetarian Moshav Amirim in the Upper Galilee.

Most Jewish restaurants in Jerusalem are kosher, which means that, except for those in hotels, they're closed on Shabbat. Elsewhere in Israel, the vast majority of establishments offering fine dining are not kosher and so stay open seven days a week – and may serve milk and meat together, seafood and even 'white meat' (the Israeli euphemism for pork).

Most budget and midrange sit-down restaurants in the West Bank serve mainly Levantine Arabic fare such as *shish tawooq* (marinated chicken grilled on skewers) and kofta (lamb kebab), as well as a huge range of delicious mezze: hummus and *muttabal* (purée of aubergine

REGIONAL FOOD WHERE TO EAT & DRINK

Restaurant & Bar Listings

www.restaurants
-in-israel.co.il

www.restaurants.
co.il

mixed with tahini, yoghurt and olive oil), salads, *kibbeh* (meat-filled cracked-wheat croquettes) and fried cheese.

In the West Bank (particularly in Bethlehem), a number of restaurants offer traditional Palestinian dishes such as *mansaf* (literally 'exploded' chicken or lamb over rice with a thick, meaty broth) and *makloubeh* ('upside down' chicken, under rice cooked with nuts and spices). Meanwhile, no trip to the West Bank is complete without trying *kunafeh*, the sweet wheat-and-cheese-based desert that is native to the northern city of Nablus.

Daily Life

While you can learn quite a bit about a country by visiting historical sites, national parks and museums, the only way to get a sense of what really makes a place tick is to connect with the locals and their values, priorities and lifestyles.

Israelis

Although Israel is a Western-oriented liberal democracy with a booming high-tech economy, the country's incredible patchwork of ethnic groups, belief systems, languages and family stories make for a wide array of world views, personal priorities and lifestyles.

Values & Lifestyle

Israeli society was founded a century ago on socialist principles, exemplified by the shared communal life of the kibbutz (though even at the height of the kibbutz movement, only 3% of the Jewish population lived in one). These days, the vast majority of Israelis have shifted to a decidedly bourgeois and individualistic outlook, creating aspirations – including international travel – whose fulfilment depends in large part on finding good jobs with middle-class paychecks.

In the bubble of Tel Aviv, secular Jews – alongside smaller numbers of Modern Orthodox Jews and Israeli Arabs – work, shop, eat, play and create art with an intensity and panache that has a lot in common with Silicon Valley, Berlin and the booming cities of East Asia. Meanwhile, in Haredi (ultra-Orthodox) neighbourhoods such as Jerusalem's Mea She'arim, residents strive to preserve (or re-create) the lifestyle of 18th-century Eastern Europe. And although most kibbutzim have been 'privatised', with member-owned apartments and income determined by an individual's earning power, the residents of the country's 70 or so remaining 'communal' kibbutz im still live lives of 1950s-style socialist equality.

Hebrew culture and the arts are immensely important, so reading literature and going out to concerts, the theatre and films are an integral part of life for many Israeli Jews. A long-standing love of the outdoors has helped make Israelis an active lot: hiking, cycling, windsurfing, backpacking, camping and other leisure activities are hugely popular.

Family is hugely important for virtually all Israelis. Young Jews may leave the nest at 18 to serve in the army and then backpack through Southeast Asia but even among the most secular there is, for men as well as women, constant – some would say unrelenting – pressure to find a partner and bring children into the world.

Gays and lesbians can pursue an open and, if they choose, flamboyant lifestyle in Tel Aviv, but the smaller gay scene in more conservative Jerusalem is low-key and circumspect.

Military Service

Israel's military has been part of daily life since the country's birth, and for most young Israeli Jews being drafted – three years for men, two for women – is a rite of passage. Israel Defence Forces (IDF) service is also compulsory for Druze and Circassian men, and some Bedouin and Christian Arab men volunteer to serve. To the chagrin of many, draft

THE ROLE OF JUDAISM

Judaism – as a religion, a national identity and a civilisation – has a significant impact on the daily lives of all Israeli Jews. For the Orthodox and especially the ultra-Orthodox (Haredim), virtually every action and decision is governed by Halacha (Jewish law), as interpreted by more than 2000 years of legal precedent. Secular Jews pay little attention to the daily discipline of Jewish observance, but their lives are still defined by the weekly rhythm of Shabbat and the annual cycle of Jewish holidays. Many Jewish Israelis define themselves not as 'secular' (ie ideologically secularist) but as 'traditional' (*masorti*) – for instance, young people may have Shabbat (Saturday) lunch with their family before heading out to a football match.

The exponential growth of the Haredi community is creating all sorts of frictions, for example, in formerly secular neighbourhoods in which new Haredi residents demand that roads be closed on the Sabbath and swimming pools be segregated by sex.

Most schools run by the ultra-Orthodox teach only religious subjects, providing virtually no education in science, mathematics, history, literature or English and producing generations of young people with few job skills. A significant majority of ultra-Orthodox men never work; instead they are supported by government subsidies while studying in *yeshivot* (religious seminaries) and *kollelim* (seminaries for married men). Haredi women, who are not bound by the Halachic command to spend every waking moment on religious study, are entering the workforce in increasing numbers, often as their family's sole breadwinner – despite also having to look after six, eight or more children.

exemptions are granted to the vast majority of ultra-Orthodox Jewish men and to most Orthodox and all ultra-Orthodox Jewish women.

Reservists can be called up (though most aren't) for training every year or two, generally until age 40 for men and until age 24 (or until the birth of their first child) for women.

When asked about the presence of so many soldiers with automatic weapons in public spaces, some Israelis answer that while being armed to the teeth is hardly ideal, it sure beats what their grandparents had to go through, hiding from Cossacks in Russia or anti-Jewish mobs in Iraq.

Women

Israeli women have personal freedom, social status and professional opportunities on a par with their European counterparts and have played significant roles in the economy and politics (eg Golda Meir). However, as in Ottoman times, marriage and divorce for Jews remain in the hands of the Orthodox-dominated Chief Rabbinate, whose all-male religious judges favour traditional male prerogatives over women's rights.

In recent years, some of Israel's ultra-Orthodox communities have become noticeably more concerned (some would say obsessed) with 'modesty', attempting to enforce ever-stricter rules aimed at separating men and women. Attempts to gender-segregate public transport (women are sent to the back of the bus) and even sidewalks, and to ban images of women from advertising billboards, have been met with protests – and legislation forbidding the exclusion of women and images of women from the public sphere.

And then there is the ongoing debate about the separation of men and women at the Western Wall in Jerusalem, which has been segregated since 1967 (but before 1948 had always been a mixed prayer area). Since 1988, feminist group Women of the Wall have lobbied for an end to restrictions on female prayer at the site (women are forbidden from reading the Torah aloud and wearing prayer shawls). In 2017, Netanyahu scrapped a 2016 deal that would have created a mixed prayer area at the wall due to protests from ultra-Orthodox parties in his coalition.

Among Israeli Jews, 42% define themselves as 'secular', 38% as 'traditional' to one degree or another, 12% as modern Orthodox and 8% as ultra-Orthodox (Haredi). Source: a 2009 survey by Israel's Central Bureau of Statistics.

Palestinians

Daily life in the Palestinian Territories varies widely, from city to city and even street to street. But whether it's the conservative Muslim district of Hebron or a Christian neighbourhood in free-wheeling Ramallah, Palestinian cities are typically defined by their packed pavements, bustling markets and traffic-snarled streets. In the countryside, the pace of life among the rolling hills and olive groves is slower.

Values & Lifestyle

The ebb and flow of daily life in the Palestinian Territories depends largely on the security and economic situation. Gaza is in particularly dire straits as a result of the Israeli and Egyptian blockades, Egypt's sealing of hundreds of smuggling tunnels (2013–14) and Hamas' periodic confrontations with Israel.

In the West Bank, Israel has removed most internal checkpoints in recent years, making it easier for Palestinians to travel between home and work or school, but day-to-day life can be profoundly frustrating, and residents never know when they may find themselves in a humiliating – or at least time-wasting – confrontation with the Israeli security forces or settlers.

Despite everything, the Palestinians are determined to make the best of their tenuous situation. Family bonds are unbreakable and are often made stronger by intra-family business partnerships. Many extended families pool their income to build a large home so everyone can live under one roof, with separate units for each nuclear family. Palestinian men often spend their leisure time in the local coffeehouse, where old-timers play backgammon.

Life in Gaza is tightly controlled by the precepts of fundamentalist Islam but much of the West Bank retains a moderate outlook, and Ramallah in particular exhibits the trappings of modern Western living, including fancy cars, health clubs and late-night bars. Football and basketball are both popular sports, played by young Palestinians on makeshift fields and courts across the West Bank and Gaza.

Palestinians are steadfastly attached to their land, especially their olive groves, and many urban Palestinians return to their home villages to help with the harvest in October and November.

Employment & Income

Palestinians still earn far less than Israelis (average annual income is just US$3200 in the Palestinian Territories, compared to US$36,190 in Israel), and the lack of economic opportunity, especially for young people, has done much to keep Palestinians frustrated with their lot. With unemployment rates of 27% in the West Bank and 42% in Gaza and one of the highest birth rates in the world (Muslim Palestinian women have an average of seven children each, as do ultra-Orthodox Jewish women in Israel), the average Palestinian home is both overcrowded and poor.

Women

Palestinian women have traditionally played the role of home-based caregiver, but recent years have seen more women entering higher education and working outside the home. Except in fundamentalist areas, women have slowly made their mark on Palestinian politics – Ramallah, for instance, had a female mayor, Janet Michael, from 2005 to 2012, and Hannan Ashrawi is well known as an eloquent spokesperson for Palestinian rights.

Hundreds of thousands of ultra-Orthodox Israelis use 'kosher' mobile phones that block access to 'inappropriate' content and lack cameras and text messaging, potentially tools for illicit flirting. Some models come with a Yiddish interface and Hassidic ringtones.

According to the United Nations Development Programme, Israel ranks 19 (out of 187 countries) on its 2016 Human Development Index; the State of Palestine is ranked 114.

DAILY LIFE PALESTINIANS

Government & Politics

Politics looms especially large in the lives of Israelis and Palestinians, whose century-old confrontation periodically sweeps everyone up in unpredictable and sometimes violent events.

Israel's System of Government

Golda Meir (1898–1978), the world's third female prime minister (1969–74), was born in Kiev, grew up in Milwaukee and Denver, where she became a socialist Zionist, and moved to Palestine in 1921.

Because of long-standing disagreements over the most basic aspects of Israel's identity, including the role of religion, Israelis have been unable to agree on a constitution. Instead, the Knesset (Israeli Parliament) has cobbled together a set of laws with constitutional force, known as the Basic Law, that includes a partial Bill of Rights. The High Court of Justice has the power to judicially review laws passed by the Knesset, determining their constitutionality based on their compatibility with the Basic Law.

Legislative Branch & President

Israel is a parliamentary democracy whose unicameral legislature, the Knesset, has 120 members (MKs). It is elected by national proportional representation for a four-year term, though elections can be called early if the coalition loses a vote of no confidence (on average, Israeli governments last a bit over two years).

Because of the fragmented nature of Israeli society – religiously, ideologically, ethnically and linguistically – and the fact that any party that receives a mere 3.25% of the vote wins parliamentary seats, the Knesset typically includes a dozen or more parties. Achieving a 61-vote majority requires forming a coalition, which means that smaller parties often wield significant power.

All Israeli citizens aged 18 or over can vote. There is no absentee voting (except for diplomatic staff and members of the merchant marine) so Israelis living abroad cannot cast ballots unless they are physically present in Israel on election day. Voters vote for political parties, not specific candidates; if a party gets, say, 10% of the national vote, the first 12 candidates on its ranked election slate enter the Knesset.

Israel's head of state is the president, whose role is largely ceremonial except that after elections he or she decides which party leader will be given the opportunity to form a coalition and must also consent to the dissolution of parliament. Another presidential prerogative: issuing pardons. The Knesset elects the president for a single term of seven years.

Executive Branch

The prime minister presides over the cabinet (government), whose members (ministers) are chosen by the prime minister based, in part, on the electoral power of their respective parties; their appointment must be approved by the Knesset. Most cabinet members also serve as the executive heads of government ministries, though some serve as 'ministers-without-portfolio'.

The cabinet votes on the prime minister's security, foreign and domestic policies. Under the principle of 'ministerial responsibility', ministers must support policies endorsed by the cabinet even if they voted against them. The weekly cabinet meeting – often featured in the news – is held every Sunday.

Some members of the cabinet also serve in the powerful Security Cabinet, led by the prime minister. Its members – including the ministers of defence, foreign affairs, internal security, interior and treasury – make decisions about urgent defence and foreign-policy issues.

Judicial System

Israel has an independent judiciary with three tiers of courts: the Magistrates Courts, for ordinary criminal and civil trials; the District Courts, for appeals; and the Supreme Court, which serves as the highest court of appeal and, sitting as the High Court of Justice (known by its acronym, Bagatz), makes decisions concerning the legality of actions by government authorities.

Israel also has a system of religious courts – Jewish, Muslim and Christian – with jurisdiction over matters of personal status (mainly marriage and divorce). There is no provision in Israeli law for civil (ie secular) marriage and as none of the religious courts perform intermarriages, couples of mixed religious background wishing to wed can do so only outside Israel (eg in Cyprus). Civil marriages abroad, including homosexual marriages, are recognised in Israel.

Israeli Political Parties: An Introduction

Can't keep all the Israeli political parties mentioned in the news straight? Here's a rundown of the 10 parties represented in the 20th Knesset, elected in 2015:

Likud The centre-right party of Prime Minister Netanyahu includes far-right, populist elements. The 2015 election was viewed largely as a referendum on the leadership of Netanyahu, a divisive figure both at home and internationally. After a tight race, Likud won the 2015 elections with a decisive margin. The party takes a hard line on security issues and concessions to the Palestinians.

Labor Party A surprise win in the 2017 leadership elections by businessman Avi Gabbay has got supporters of the Labor Party wondering whether the party that once dominated Israeli politics can finally emerge from the shadow of Likud

Israeli President Reuven (Ruby) Rivlin of the right wing Likud, inaugurated in 2014 to succeed Shimon Peres, op poses territorial compromise – but also has a strong civil rights record. As president he has spoken out forcefully against discrimination and political incitement against Israel's Arab citizens.

GOVERNMENT & POLITICS ISRAEL'S SYSTEM OF GOVERNMENT

WHO'S WHO IN PALESTINIAN POLITICS

Palestine Liberation Organisation (PLO) Founded in 1964, the PLO is a coalition of Palestinian factions. The UN General Assembly recognised the organisation as the 'representative of the Palestinian people' in 1974 and gave it the status of a 'non-member observer state' in 2012.

Fatah Long the dominant political party in the PLO, Fatah ('conquest') – secular and nationalist in orientation – was founded by Yasser Arafat (1929–2004) and several young Palestinian refugees in 1959. During the 1970s and 1980s it engaged in international terrorism, but renounced violence in 1988 and recognised the 'right of the State of Israel to exist in peace and security' in 1993. After the Oslo Accords, Fatah, under Arafat, gained a reputation for corruption and undemocratic, untransparent ways.

Hamas Both a militant movement and a political party, Hamas currently rules Gaza. The Hamas charter calls for the destruction of the State of Israel through 'armed struggle' and the establishment of a Palestinian Islamic state in what is now the territory of Israel, the Gaza Strip and the West Bank.

Islamic Jihad An armed Islamist movement in Gaza and a rival to Hamas. Considered a terrorist organisation by Israel and most Western countries.

(Israel's last Labor leader was Ehud Barak in 2001). Key issues include negotiating with the Palestinians and addressing Israel's economic inequalities.

Joint Arab List The alliance of Hadash, Balad, United Arab List and Ta'al became the third-largest party in the Knesset after the elections, promising to represent the interests of the Arab minority. The party encompasses diverse ideologies.

Yesh Atid A centrist, free-market party founded in 2012 to represent the secular middle class; led by Yair Lapid.

Kulanu Influential right-leaning centre party led by Moshe Kahlon. The party's key issue is tackling the high cost of living in Israel.

Jewish Home Far-right party representing the national-religious Orthodox Zionists and the West Bank settlers. Led by software entrepreneur Naftali Bennet.

Shas A Mizrahi/Sephardi ultra-Orthodox party founded to fight discrimination against non-Ashkenazi Jews; supported by many 'traditional' Jews from North Africa.

Yisra'el Beitenu A secular, nationalist, right-wing party led by Soviet-born Avigdor Lieberman. Supported by many Russian-speaking immigrants.

United Torah Judaism An alliance of two rival Ashkenazi-ultra-Orthodox parties, Degel HaTorah, which is Litvak ('Lithuanian'), and Agudat Yisrael, which is Hasidic. Focuses on securing funding for the ultra-Orthodox sector.

Meretz A left-wing party with strong social-democratic credentials and an upper-middle-class Ashkenazi base of support.

Palestinian Authority

The Palestinian Authority (Palestinian National Authority; PA or PNA) is an interim administrative body set up in 1994 under the Oslo Accords to rule parts of the West Bank and Gaza for five years, until the establishment of a Palestinian state. Final-status negotiations have dragged on – and so has the PA.

As part of the Oslo peace process, the PA assumed control of civil and security affairs in the major cities of the West Bank; known collectively as Area A, this covers about 3% of the land area of the West Bank. A further 25% of the West Bank (most built-up villages), known as Area B, is under PA civil control; Israel retains responsibility for security affairs. The rest of the West Bank (some 72% of the land area) is designated as Area C, under full Israeli civil and security control. About 300,000 West Bank Palestinians live in Area C, whose Israeli settlements, military bases and bypass roads fragment PA-controlled areas into dozens of tiny enclaves.

Hamas: From Resistance to Government (2012), by Paola Caridi, looks at the complexities of the organisation's history.

Since Hamas' violent takeover of Gaza in 2007, the West Bank and Gaza have been governed by separate governments. The internationally recognised and funded Fatah-controlled PA government continues to exercise authority in much of the West Bank, while Gaza is under the rule of a Hamas government that Israel, Egypt, the US and many Arab and European governments have sought to isolate.

The Palestinian Legislative Council (PLC), also known as the Palestinian parliament, has 132 members elected from 16 districts in the West Bank and Gaza. The last elections, won by Hamas, took place in 2006.

The PA is headed by an executive president, directly elected – at least in theory – once every four years. Yasser Arafat held the post from 1994 until his death in 2004. In January 2005 Mahmoud Abbas (also known as Abu Mazen) was elected and has served as PA president ever since – there has been an absence of subsequent elections. The president nominates the PA's prime minister, who must be confirmed by the PLC.

The PLC has had difficulty functioning, in part because of Israeli restrictions on its members (especially those from Hamas) and in part because of the Fatah-Hamas split of 2007.

FATAH-HAMAS RECONCILIATION

After the 2006 Palestinian legislative elections, which Hamas won with 76 seats to Fatah's 43, Fatah military commanders refused to take orders from their rivals, and Hamas and Fatah were unable to reach an agreement on sharing power. The two sides were soon engaging in mutual kidnappings, attacks and assassinations. In 2007 Hamas forces ejected Fatah from Gaza in a bloody takeover that saw pitched street battles and party loyalists from both sides executed by their opponents. Fatah responded by cracking down on Hamas activities in the West Bank. Since then, the two discontiguous regions that make up the Palestinian Territories have been ruled by rival governments.

A new bid for reconciliation started at the end of 2017, but several previous attempts have foundered because of ideological differences, bitterness over past violence and deep mistrust. In their negotiations with Israel, the Palestinians are stuck between a rock and a hard place. On the one hand, Israel argues that it cannot negotiate a peace deal until there is a united Palestinian position; on the other, Israel refuses to deal with Hamas (and vice versa), ruling out having the Islamist group as part of a negotiating team.

But whatever happens, support for Hamas in both the West Bank and Gaza cannot be ignored. The group won elections in 2006 because it represented an alternative to Fatah, considered both corrupt and ineffectual by some Palestinians. That support is waning in Gaza as the humanitarian situation there worsens (its last power plant closed down in 2017, plunging the territory into darkness), but that is only bolstering more extreme Islamist elements in both the strip and the West Bank.

What is Hamas?

In 1987 Islamist leaders in Gaza set up the Palestinian wing of Egypt's Muslim Brotherhood, calling it Harakat Al Muqawama Al Islamiya (Islamic Resistance Movement). Better known by its acronym, Hamas, this Islamist organisation seeks to establish a Palestinian Islamic state in all of what is now Israel, the West Bank and Gaza. Because it has refused to renounce violence against Israeli civilians (eg suicide bombings and rocket attacks), Hamas is classified as a terrorist group by some countries, including Israel, the US, the UK and the EU.

By the early 1990s, Hamas – funded by Gulf countries and, later, Iran – was gaining status among Palestinians, not only for its uncompromising opposition to Israel but also for running youth clubs, medical clinics and schools in poor neighbourhoods. Whereas Arafat's Fatah Party was seen as corrupt to the core, Hamas was considered both pious and honest.

In 2005 the group agreed with Arafat's successor, Mahmoud Abbas, to accept a role in Palestinian parliamentary politics. In the Palestinian Authority elections of January 2006, Hamas won a surprise majority in the Palestinian Legislative Council (the PA parliament), in large part because voters were sick of Fatah's corruption and failure to deliver on Palestinian national aspirations.

The new Hamas government refused to recognise Israel, renounce violence or accept agreements with Israel signed by the PA – as demanded by Western countries – and found itself shunned. It also faced internal opposition from Fatah members loath to give up their non-Islamist nationalism, and their prerogatives and power. In 2007, in a bloody coup, Hamas forced Fatah out of Gaza and clamped down on dissent and launched a campaign of missile attacks against Israeli towns and villages. In response, Israel instituted a partial blockade of Gaza (for its own reasons, so did Egypt). In the following years, Hamas and Israel had three bloody confrontations: around New Year 2009, in late 2012 and during the summer of 2014.

Hamas leadership in Gaza faces challenges to its authority from radical Al Qaida and Isis-inspired groups, as well as more extreme parties such as Islamic Jihad.

Religion

Israel and the Palestinian Territories are the birthplace of two of the three great mono-theistic faiths, Judaism and Christianity. The third, Islam, considers Jerusalem to be its third-holiest city. Another world religion, the Baha'i faith, has its holiest sites in Haifa and Akko. Religion is as ubiquitous in Israel and the Palestinian Territories as politics, and visitors who do not come here explicitly for religious purposes will find that it still plays a significant role in their visit.

Judaism

One of the oldest religions still practised, Judaism is based on a covenantal relationship between the Jewish people and God. The most succinct summary of Jewish theology and Judaism's strict monotheism is to be found in the Shema prayer, which reads, 'Hear O Israel, the Lord is your God, the Lord is One'.

Before the Holo-caust, there were about 18 million Jews worldwide. Today, there are estimated to be about 13 million Jews, including about six million each in Israel and the US.

According to the Torah (the first five books of the Hebrew Bible), the covenant between God and the Jewish people began with the first monotheist, Abraham (19th century BCE), forefather of both Jews and Muslims. It was later confirmed and elaborated at Mt Sinai (13th century BCE), where the Israelites – in addition to receiving the Ten Commandments – were transformed from a tribal grouping into a people. The Jewish people are eternally bound by this covenant – this is the meaning of being 'chosen' – and are required not only to obey God's *mitzvot* (commandments) but also to demonstrate, through exemplary conduct, the truth of God's oneness to all the nations of the world.

Judaism holds that God is present in history and in the actions of human beings. Evil occurs when human beings wilfully and deliberately ignore God's will, good happens when they follow the rules he has laid down. Humans have both free will and moral agency: they can choose to follow either their evil impulses or their better natures.

Jewish history can be divided into two periods: before and after the destruction of the Second Temple in Jerusalem in 70 CE. Before that momentous year, Jewish ritual and service to God were focused on animal sacrifices carried out in the Temple in Jerusalem by the *kohanim* (members of the priestly class, from whom Jews with the family name of Cohen are descended). After the destruction of Jerusalem, sacrifices ceased and Judaism turned to prayer, meditation and study as the main methods of communication with the Divine. Over the next few centuries, Judaism's Oral Law was put into writing in the Mishna and further elaborated in the Talmud; much of the latter, written in Aramaic, reads like a shorthand protocol of legal deliberations.

Over the next 1500 years, generation after generation of sages – issuing legal rulings and teaching in places such as Babylonia (Iraq), Egypt, Spain, Tsfat (in the Galilee) and Lithuania – debated and refined both Jewish theology and the 613 commandments of Halacha (Jewish law). Orthodox Judaism (the most conservative of the religion's streams) holds that the Oral Law, in its entirely, was given at Mt Sinai, while the Reform, Conservative and Reconstructionist Movements believe that Judaism has always been dynamic and proactive, changing and developing over the generations as it has had to deal with new ideas and new circumstances.

JEWISH MENS' HEADCOVERINGS

If you see a man wearing a small, round, convex skullcap, chances are he is a religious Jew (unless he's the Pope).

There is no commandment specifying that Jewish men cover their heads. Rather, wearing a kippa (yarmulke in Yiddish, skullcap in English) is merely a tradition, albeit one that is well entrenched. All male visitors to Jewish holy sites are asked to cover their heads – either with a kippa or any kind of hat.

It is often possible to infer a Jewish man's background, religious orientation and even political beliefs by the type of kippa he wears. Zionist Orthodox Jews, including West Bank settlers, usually go for crocheted kippot with designs around the edges, while ultra-Orthodox (Haredi) men, of both the Hasidic and Litvak streams, generally wear black velvet or cloth kippot of medium size. The Bukharian Jews of Central Asia wear pillbox caps decorated with embroidery. An extra-large crocheted kippa is a sign that the wearer is probably either a follower of the Braslav Hassidic movement or a messianic Jewish West Bank settler. (Don't confuse such kippot with the white, crocheted skullcaps worn by Hajjis, ie Muslims who have made the pilgrimage to Mecca.)

Today, ultra-Orthodox (Haredi) rabbis – many of whom are non-Zionist (ie are at best ambivalent about the role of the State of Israel in Jewish history) – have exclusive control of state-supported Jewish religious practice in Israel through the Chief Rabbinate, despite the fact that their followers constitute only a small minority of the country's Jewish population. In the Diaspora, the vast majority of Jews belong to the liberal (progressive) movements or are not affiliated with any movement.

Jerusalem, Zion and Israel have played a central role in Judaism ever since God promised the Land of Israel to the Children of Israel in the Torah. When praying, Jews face Jerusalem, and virtually all synagogues are built with the Torah ark facing the Holy City.

Christianity

Christianity is based on the life and teachings of Jesus of Nazareth, a Jew who lived in Judea and Galilee during the 1st century CE; on his crucifixion by the Romans, and on his resurrection three days later, as related in the New Testament.

Christianity started out as a movement within Judaism, and most of Jesus's followers, known as the Apostles, were Jews. Like many Jews of his time, Jesus was critical of the decadence and materialism of Jerusalem's ruling class and contemptuous of Roman authority. But after his death, the insistence of Jesus's followers that he was the Messiah caused Christianity to become increasingly distinct from Judaism. The anti-Jewish polemics of some early Christians, written at a time when Christianity was a beleaguered sect persecuted by the Romans, would have serious implications in later centuries, when Christianity became all-powerful in Europe.

According to the New Testament, the Angel Gabriel – in an event known as the Annunciation – appeared to Mary in Nazareth and informed her that she would conceive and give birth to the son of God. Jesus was born in Bethlehem (in Christian terminology and art, his birth is known as the Nativity) but grew up back in Nazareth, where he later preached. Much of his ministry – and many of his best-known biblical miracles – took place around the Sea of Galilee, in places such as Capernaum, Korazim, Bethsaida and Kursi. The Sermon on the Mount was delivered just up the hill from Capernaum on the Mount of the Beatitudes, while the Transfiguration took place on Mt Tabor. Places believed to correspond to all these venues can be visited.

In 1920, one in 10 Palestinian Arabs was Christian; today, just one in 75 residents of the Palestinian Territories is. Bethlehem, which in 1948 was 85% Christian, is now more than three-quarters Muslim.

At the age of 33 or so Jesus, whose growing influence had caused alarm among Jewish and Roman authorities alike, was accused of sedition and condemned to death by the Roman prefect of Judea, Pontius Pilate. Christians believe that his suffering was foretold in the Hebrew Bible. According to the New Testament, after the Last Supper Jesus was arrested in Gethsemane; put on trial before the Sanhedrin (Jewish supreme court), Pontius Pilate and even Herod Antipas (the Roman-appointed king of Judea) himself; condemned to death; and mocked by Roman soldiers as he was led to Golgotha (Calvary), where he was crucified. Three days after his burial (Entombment), the New Testament says, his tomb was found to be empty, evidence of his resurrection.

The followers of Jesus came to be known as Christians (Christ is a Greek-derived title meaning 'Anointed One'), believing him to be the son of God and the messiah (the English word 'messiah' comes from the Hebrew *mashiach,* which also means 'anointed one'). Jews did not (and do not) accept Jesus as the messiah or as the son of God – this difference is the defining theological disagreement between the two faiths. Muslims consider Jesus to be a messenger of God and a prophet but do not believe that he was crucified or that he atoned for humankind's sins.

In about 325 CE, St Helena (Constantine the Great's mother) identified what she believed to be the location of Jesus's crucifixion and burial, marking the site with a predecessor of today's Church of the Holy Sepulchre. The First Crusade (1095–99) was launched in part to ensure Christian access to this site.

The ownership of holy sites in Israel and the Palestinian Territories has long been a subject of contention among the country's various Christian denominations. At a number of sites in Jerusalem and Bethlehem, relations are still governed by a 'status quo' agreement drawn up in Ottoman times. The Holy Land's largest denomination, the Greek Orthodox Church – almost all of whose local members are Arabic-speaking Palestinians – has jurisdiction over more than half of Jerusalem's Church of the Holy Sepulchre and a large portion of Bethlehem's Church of the Nativity.

> Only about 1400 Christians still live in Gaza. Since the Hamas takeover, Islamist hardliners have killed the owner of a Gaza City Christian bookshop for alleged proselytising (2007), bombed the Gaza City YMCA (2008) and attacked several churches.

Islam

Founded by the Prophet Muhammad (570–632 CE), who lived in what is now Saudi Arabia, Islam is based on belief in the absolute oneness of God (Allah) and in the revelations of his final prophet, Muhammad. The Arabic word *islam* means 'absolute submission' to God and his word.

Muhammad began preaching to the people of Mecca in about 610 CE, calling on them to renounce idolatry, believe in one God and prepare themselves for the Day of Judgement, when all humans would be held accountable for their actions.

Islam's sacred scripture is the Quran, which was revealed to Muhammad over the course of two decades. Believed by Muslims to be God's infallible word, it consists of 114 *suras* (chapters) written in highly complex – and often poetic – classical Arabic. The Quran presents God as the omnipresent creator and sustainer of the world, infinite in his wisdom and power. Sayings and acts attributed to the Prophet, believed to illustrate correct Islamic behaviour and beliefs, are known as *hadith.*

Islam and Judaism share common roots, and Muslims consider Adam, Noah, Abraham, Isaac, Jacob, Joseph and Moses to be prophets. As a result, Jews and Muslims share a number of holy sites, including Al Haram Ash Sharif/Temple Mount in Jerusalem and the Ibrahimi Mosque/Cave of Machpelah (Tomb of the Patriarchs) in Hebron.

> Excellent primers on the Muslim faith include *Inside Islam* (2002), edited by John Miller and Aaron Kenedi, and *Islam: A Short History* (2000), by Karen Armstrong. *No God But God: The Origins, Evolution, and Future of Islam* (2005) by Reza Aslan received critical acclaim for its liberal interpretation of Islam.

THE FIVE PILLARS OF ISLAM

➜ **Shahadah** Islam's confession of faith, the Shahadah sums up the Islamic belief in the absolute oneness of God and the finality of Muhammad's prophecy: 'There is no God but Allah, and Muhammad is the messenger of Allah'. Anyone who recites the Shahadah – which appears on the flag of Saudi Arabia – three times, in front of witnesses, becomes a Muslim.

➜ **Salat** The obligation to pray to God, without an intermediary, five times a day (dawn, midday, late afternoon, sunset and night). Prayers are performed facing Mecca and can be undertaken anywhere, except on Friday at noon, when men must attend congregational prayers in a mosque.

➜ **Zakat** Muslims are required to give alms to the poor worth one-fortieth of their income. The West Bank and Gaza have around 80 *zakat* committees that oversee the distribution of charitable donations.

➜ **Sawm** During Ramadan, the ninth month of the Islamic calendar, nothing must pass through the lips (food, cigarettes or drinks), and sex is prohibited, from dawn until dusk.

➜ **Hajj** The pilgrimage to Mecca, which every Muslim who is able should make at least once in their lifetime.

Because of their close scriptural links, Muslims consider both Jews and Christians to be an *ahl al Kitab,* a 'people of the Book'. Judaism has always seen Islam as a fellow monotheistic faith (because of the Trinity, Jewish sages weren't always so sure about Christianity).

Muslims believe that Muhammad visited Jerusalem on his 'Night Journey', during which his steed Buraq took him from Mecca to Jerusalem in a single night. He then ascended to heaven from the stone around which the Dome of the Rock was later built, returning with revelations for the faithful. For a brief period, Muhammad instructed Muslims to pray towards Jerusalem.

Almost all Palestinian Muslims belong to Sunni Islam, by far the religion's largest branch; so do the vast majority of Egyptians, Jordanians and Syrians. The Lebanese Hezbollah movement, like its patrons in Iran, is Shiite. Syria's ruling elite belongs to a heterodox offshoot of Shiite Islam known as Alawite (Alawi).

In 1993 the late King Hussein of Jordan – out-manoeuvring the Saudis – donated funds to refurbish the golden dome of Jerusalem's Dome of the Rock. The exterior is now covered by 80kg of 24-carat gold leaf.

Arts

The diverse range of people that call Israel home – from Arab to Druze to Mizrahi and Azhenazi Jews – has always found its expression in literature, music, film or visual arts. In most towns and cities visitors will find small galleries, which are a great place to see the latest in Israeli art. When it comes to music, Israel has hosted high-profile artists from Guns N' Roses to the Rolling Stones in recent years. The West Bank has a thriving art scene, and cultural centres in the major cities often have both temporary and permanent exhibitions, featuring mostly local artists. Street art by local and international artists (yes, including Banksy) appears on large swaths of the Palestinian side of the separation wall near Bethlehem.

Literature

Israeli Literature

The Hebrew Book Week (www.sfarim.org.il), an incredibly popular carnival of the printed word, brings scores of publishers' book stalls – and steep discounts – to public squares and bookshops in a number of Israeli cities in mid-June.

Israelis across the political spectrum see the revival of the Hebrew language and the creation of modern Hebrew literature as the crowning cultural achievements of the State of Israel. Some names to keep an eye out for (their major works are available in English translation):

Shmuel Yosef Agnon (1888–1970) Israel's Nobel winner examined the dichotomy between traditional Jewish and modern life.

Yehuda Amichai (1924–2000) His poetry, written in colloquial Hebrew, captured the public's imagination with its gently ironic explorations of daily life.

Ephraim Kishon (1924–2005) The works of the brilliant Hungarian-born satirist skewer Israeli society and universal human foibles.

Aharon Appelfeld (1932–2018) In novels such as *Badenheim 1939* (1978), the Holocaust hovers just off stage.

AB Yehoshua (b 1936) Caught between intentions and their implementation, his characters struggle to break out of their loneliness.

Amos Oz (b 1939) His works paint compelling, if sometimes bleak, pictures of an Israel few visitors encounter.

Meir Shalev (b 1948) Often set in Israel's recent past, Shalev's highly acclaimed novels deal with vengeance and masculinity.

David Grossman (b 1954) The novelist established his reputation with *The Yellow Wind* (1987), a blistering and prescient look at Israel's occupation of the Palestinian Territories.

Zeruya Shalev (b 1959) Through her characters' inner life, Shalev explores family ties, yearning, the compromises people make and the pull of the past.

Orly Castel-Bloom (b 1960) Known for postmodern sensibilities and irony, with characters suspended between meaninglessness and moments of belonging.

Etgar Keret (b 1967) Dubbed 'the voice of his generation' for his often humorous postmodern short stories, screenplays and graphic novels.

Dorit Rabinyan (b 1972) Israeli writer whose controversial novel *All the Rivers Run* was banned by Israel's education ministry for its portrayal of an Arab-Jewish love affair.

Sayed Kashua (b 1975) Israeli-Arab humourist known for his tongue-in-cheek portraits of the lives and travails of Arab Israelis.

Palestinian Literature

The most widespread form of literary expression among Palestinians has long been poetry, whose leading voice remains Mahmoud Darwish (1941–2008). His lyrical collections, dealing with loss and exile, include *Why Did You Leave the Horse Alone?* (1995) and *Unfortunately, It Was Paradise* (2003). Prominent themes in the poetry of Tawfiq Ziad (Zayyad; 1929–94) include freedom, solidarity and Palestinians' connection with the land.

It wasn't until the 1960s that narrative fiction appeared on the Palestinian literary scene. Emile Habibi (1922–96) – like Ziad, a Knesset member from the Israeli Community Party – was the author of seven novels, including *Secret Life of Saeed the Pessoptimist* (1974), a brilliant, tragicomic tale dealing with the difficulties facing Palestinians who became Israeli citizens after 1948.

The stunning debut work of Ghassan Kanafani (1936–72), *Men in the Sun* (1963), includes a novella and a collection of short stories that delve into the lives, hopes and shattered dreams of its Palestinian characters. In *The Inheritance* (2005), Nablus-born Sahar Khalifeh (b 1942) provides frequently chilling insights into the lives of Palestinian women, both in the Palestinian Territories and abroad.

Music

Israeli Music

Israeli music encompasses a rich tapestry of modes, scales and vocal styles inspired by the musical traditions of both the East and West.

Israelis of all ages listen to songs from decades past without necessarily thinking of them as 'retro'. Among the still-popular greats of the mid-20th century is the Yemen-born singer Shoshana Damari (1923–2006), renowned for her peerless pronunciation of the guttural letter '*ayn*. Naomi Shemer (1930–2004) composed much of the soundtrack of Israel's 1960s, 1970s and 1980s, including the iconic – though rarely heard – 'Jerusalem of Gold' (1967).

Despite the 1965 banning of a Beatles tour by Israel's cultural commissars, rock quickly made itself a fixture on the local music scene thanks to groups such as Poogy (Kaveret), Mashina, Teapacks (named after Tipp-Ex, the correction fluid) and Benzin. Rock has inspired many of the anthems of classic Israeli pop – names to listen for include Shlomo Artzi, Arik Einstein, Matti Caspi, Shalom Hanoch, Yehudit Ravitz, Assaf Amdursky and Aviv Geffen. Idan Raichel introduced Ethiopian melodies to a mainstream audience.

Among the Israeli hip-hop artists and groups you may come across are Shabak Samech, HaDag Nachash, Subliminal, and militant right-wing rapper The Shadow. One of the most exuberant performers of dance

Attended by 600 publishers from 30 countries, the huge Jerusalem International Book Fair (www.jerusalembookfair.com) has been held in odd-numbered years since 1963. It's here that the prestigious Jerusalem Prize for Literature is awarded.

Musical festivities in Israel include the twice-a-year Abu Gosh Vocal Music Festival (www.agfestival.co.il), Eilat's Red Sea Jazz Festival (https://en.redseajazz.co.il) and, for dance music, Tel Aviv's annual Love Parade.

TRADITIONAL & MODERN DANCE

Israel has several world-renowned professional dance companies. The acclaimed Bat Sheva Dance Company (www.batsheva.co.il), founded by Martha Graham in 1964, is based at Tel Aviv's Suzanne Dellal Centre (p145); from 1990 to 2017 it was led by celebrated choreographer Ohad Naharin (b 1952). The Kibbutz Contemporary Dance Company (www.kcdc.co.il) performs around the country.

In the realm of folk dancing, Israel is famous for the *hora*, brought from Romania by 19th-century immigrants. The best place to see folk dancing is at the Karmiel Dance Festival (www.karmielfestival.co.il), held over three days in early July in the central Galilee.

The most popular Palestinian folk dance is a line dance called the *dabke*. One of the best Palestinian dance groups is El Funoun (www.el-funoun.org), based in Al Bireh in the West Bank.

music has been Dana International (www.danainternational.co.il), a half-Yemenite transsexual who won the Eurovision Song Contest in 1998.

Mizrahi (Oriental or Eastern) music, with its Middle Eastern and Mediterranean scales and rhythms, has its roots in the melodies of North Africa (especially Umm Kulthum–era Egypt and mid-century Morocco), Iraq and Yemen. Many modern works, though, are inspired by musical styles from the Mediterranean basin, especially Turkey and Greece. For decades Mizrahi music was banned from the radio – the Ashkenazi cultural elite feared 'Levantinisation' – so to find the work of artists such as Zohar Argov (1955–87) and Haim Moshe (b 1956) you had to head to grungy cassette shops around Tel Aviv's (old) central bus station.

These days, though, Mizrahi music may be Israel's most popular genre. Old-timers Shlomo Bar (www.shlomobar.com) and Yair Dalal (www.yairdalal.com), inspired by the traditional Jewish music of Morocco and Iraq respectively, are still performing, joined more recently by superstars Sarit Hadad (www.sarit-hadad.com), who has been described as Israel's Britney Spears, and Amir Benayoun, whose genre-defying concerts mix love songs, medieval Jewish liturgical poems and strident nationalism. Moshe Peretz enjoys crossing the line from Mizrahi to mainstream and back again.

Another popular trend is to use Jewish religious vocabulary and soundscapes to express latent religious feelings. Over the last few years, performers such as Etti Ankri, Ehud Banai, David D'Or, Kobi Oz, Berry Sakharof and Gilad Segev have turned towards traditional – mainly Sephardic and Mizrahi – liturgical poetry and melodies to create works with massive mainstream popularity.

Mizrahi music's traditional Ashkenazi counterpart, Klezmer, has not enjoyed as much crossover popularity. Born in the *shtetls* (ghettos) of Eastern Europe, Jewish 'soul' can take you swiftly from ecstasy to the depths of despair – check it out at the Tsfat Klezmer Festival.

Israel has a strong Western classical tradition thanks to Jewish refugees from Nazism and post-Soviet immigrants from Russia. The Israel Philharmonic Orchestra (www.ipo.co.il) – whose first concert, in 1936, was conducted by Arturo Toscanini – is world renowned.

Palestinian Music

In addition to catchy Arabic pop from Beirut and Cairo, visitors to the West Bank and Arab areas of Israel may come across traditional folk music featuring the sounds of the oud (a stringed instrument shaped like half a pear), the *daf* (tambourine) and the *ney* (flute).

For something completely different, check out the love ballads and nationalist hymns of Mohammed Assaf, a Gazan who won the second season of *Arab Idol*.

As for alternative music, the genre most closely associated with the Palestinian Territories is hip-hop, pioneered by Lod-based rappers DAM and later by artists such as Palestinian Rapperz (from Gaza) and Ramallah Underground. Shows in the West Bank are infrequent (they are more common in Israel) but an incredible experience if you are lucky enough to catch one.

Theatre

Israeli Theatre

Israelis attend the theatre more often than almost any other people. Tel Aviv, Jaffa, Jerusalem and Haifa have a profusion of companies, venues and festivals both large and small. The Acco Festival of Alternative Israeli Theatre (www.accofestival.co.il) brings innovative fringe productions to Akko each fall.

The best places in Israel to find creative Judaica (Jewish ritual objects) are Jerusalem (eg Yoel Moshe Salomon St), Tsfat (the Synagogue Quarter and the Artists' Quarter) and Tel Aviv's Nahalat Binyamin crafts market (Tuesday and Friday).

To hear some genuine Palestinian folk music, go to www.barghouti.com/folklore/voice. Many of the songs were recorded live at Palestinian weddings, where the art form is particularly appreciated. Another prominent Palestinian folk singer is Reem Kelani, who lives in Britain.

BANKSY ON THE WEST BANK

Bristol artist Banksy's connection with the Palestinian Territories dates back to 2005, when the secretive Briton stencilled his first work of art near the recently completed Separation Wall that has cut Bethlehem off from Jerusalem since the Second Intifada (2000–2005).

That year, Banksy produced nine pieces of work in the West Bank, including a dove wearing body armour with an olive branch in its teeth, an Israeli Defence Forces soldier being frisked by a young girl, and a girl rising to the top of the barrier with a bunch of balloons.

Banksy reported that he was threatened by an Israeli soldier and criticised by an elderly Palestinian man who said that it was wrong to make the wall beautiful with art.

In 2015, Banksy was smuggled into Gaza via illegal tunnels under the border with Egypt and stencilled a number of works in the strip, releasing a mock documentary that highlighted the destruction of the 2014 war via his website.

Two years later, Banksy opened the Walled Off Hotel (p272), which had been under construction just a few metres from the Separation Barrier for 14 months. As well as his own artworks, it showcased local and international artists and sought to highlight the plight of the Palestinians.

Ever since Banksy first began working in the Palestinian Territories, news stories have claimed that some Palestinians have felt that his work belittles their struggle against the Israeli population, but on the ground in Bethlehem that viewpoint is difficult to find.

Most Palestinians feel that the Walled Off Hotel and Banksy's work generally – most of which is still visible – has helped bring both attention and tourist dollars to Bethlehem, translating into more money for taxi drivers, restaurants and myriad guides that offer tours of his artworks.

Banksy, along with local and international artists, has also helped to spark a street-art scene in Bethlehem and elsewhere in the West Bank, ensuring that – if nothing else – Israel's towering separation wall and its impact appears in tens of thousands of holiday snaps every year.

Every taxi driver in Bethlehem will clamour to drive you to the various Banksy works in the city, but for a more organised tour, ask either in the Walled Off Hotel or the Banksy Shop next door.

Most performances are in Hebrew, though you can also find plays in Arabic, Russian and Yiddish. Some companies offer English subtitled translations once a week or more.

Many contemporary Israeli plays tackle the hot political and social issues of the day. In recent years, the Holocaust, *refuseniks,* the West Bank occupation, suicide and homosexuality within Orthodox Judaism have all been explored onstage. Playwrights to keep an eye out for include Hanoch Levin (1942–99), provocative enough to have had several of his plays censored in the 1970s, Nissim Aloni (1926–98), Yehoshua Sobol (b 1939), Hillel Mittelpunkt (b 1952) and Shmuel Hasfari (b 1954).

Attending a musical performed by the Yiddish troupe Yiddishpiel (www.yiddishpiel.co.il) is like a quick trip to pre-Holocaust Warsaw, though performances are heavy on nostalgia and the subtitles are in Hebrew and Russian, not English.

For something unusual and poignant, head to Jaffa's Nalaga'at Centre (p146), home to the world's only deaf-blind theatre company.

Israel's grandest performing-arts festival, the Israel Festival (www.israel-festival.org.il), is held every year in May and June in Jerusalem.

Palestinian Theatre

Long an important expression of Palestinian national aspirations, Palestinian theatre has been censored by the British, suppressed and harassed by the Israelis, battered by conflict and closures and, most recently, targeted by Islamists.

CONFLICT FLICKS

A host of powerful, award-winning documentaries by Palestinians and Israelis – in some cases working together – have emerged from the Israeli–Palestinian conflict:

➡ *Arna's Children* (Juliano Mer-Khamis; 2003) About a children's theatre group in Jenin.

➡ *Death in Gaza* (James Miller; 2004) A harrowing film about the lives of Palestinian children and the death of the director, shot by an IDF soldier during production.

➡ *5 Days* (Yoav Shamir; 2005) Looks at the Israeli pull-out from Gaza in 2005.

➡ *Precious Life* (Shlomi Eldar; 2010) Examines the relationships formed during a Gaza baby's medical treatment in Israel.

➡ *Law in These Parts* (Ra'anan Alexandrowicz; 2011) About Israel's military legal system in the West Bank.

➡ *5 Broken Cameras* (Emad Burnat; 2011) On the anti–Separation Fence protests at Bil'in.

➡ *The Gatekeepers* (Dror Moreh; 2012) Based on interviews with six former heads of Israel's Shin Bet security service.

To take the edge off these tension-filled flicks, check out Ari Sandel's zany *West Bank Story* (2005; www.westbankstory.com), a spoof of the musical *West Side Story*.

Nevertheless, Palestinian actors and directors carry on. Juliano Mer-Khamis (1958–2011), the Palestinian-Israeli founder of Jenin's Freedom Theatre (p290), was murdered by masked gunmen in Jenin, but the theatre continues to function in the city's refugee camp to this day.

Visual Arts

Israeli Visual Arts

Jerusalem's Bezalel Academy of Arts & Design (www.bezalel.ac.il), established in 1906 to provide training for both European-educated artists and traditional Yemenite artisans, developed a distinctive style combining biblical themes with the sinuous, curvaceous lines of art nouveau (Jugendstil). Today, the academy remains one of the most exciting forces in Israel's art scene.

During the 1930s, German-Jewish artists fleeing Nazism brought with them the bold forms of German expressionism. The New Horizons group, which strove to create visual art in line with European movements, emerged after 1948 and remained dominant until the 1960s. Romanian-born Marcel Janco, one of the founders of the Dada cultural movement, immigrated to Palestine in 1941 and later established the artists' village of Ein Hod, where a museum features his work.

In Israel's cities, keep an eye out for modern sculpture – works range from provocative to whimsical.

Israel's leading art museums, Jerusalem's Israel Museum (p86) and the Tel Aviv Museum of Art (p116), have superb permanent collections and often showcase contemporary Israeli artists. For details on the country's many museums, check out www.ilmuseums.com.

Shashat (www.shashat.org), a Palestinian NGO focusing on women in cinema, holds a Palestinian women's film festival each autumn.

Palestinian Visual Arts

Contemporary Palestinian art became distinct from traditional craft-based art during the 1960s. In the West Bank, the best places to see visual art are Ramallah's Khalil Sakakini Centre (p278) and the International Centre of Bethlehem (p269).

Cinema

Israeli Film

Israeli cinema has come a long way since the silent footage of the late Ottoman era, the heroic documentaries of the 1930s and 1940s, and the comic *borekas* movies (named after the flaky Balkan pastry) that dominated big screens during the 1970s. In recent years, Israeli feature films and documentaries – many of which take a highly critical look at Israeli society and policies – have been garnering prizes at major film festivals, including Cannes, Berlin, Toronto and Sundance. Israel's 10 Oscar nominees include Ephraim Kishon's *Sallah* (*Sallah Shabati;* 1964), a comedy set in a 1950s transit camp for Mizrahi Jewish immigrants, and Ari Folman's *Waltz with Bashir* (2008), an extraordinary animated documentary about Israel's 1982 First Lebanon War.

The country's first cinema, the Eden, opened in 1914 in Tel Aviv, on the edge of Neve Tzedek. Today, there are thriving cinematheques in Haifa (www.haifacin.co.il), Jerusalem (www.jer-cin.org.il) and Tel Aviv (www.cinema.co.il).

Israeli celebrations of the Seventh Art include the following:

Docaviv International Documentary Film Festival (www.docaviv.co.il) In Tel Aviv.

Haifa International Film Festival (www.haifaff.co.il)

Tel Aviv International Student Film Festival (www.taufilmfest.com)

Jerusalem Film Festival (www.jff.org.il)

Other Israel Film Festival (www.otherisrael.org) Focuses on Israel's minorities, including its Arab citizens.

Tel Aviv International LGBT Film Festival (www.tlvfest.com)

For a complete database of made-in-Israel movies, see the website of the Manhattan-based Israel Film Center, www.israelfilmcenter.org.

Palestinian Film

Cinema in the Palestinian Territories is hampered by a dearth of resources and film schools, a lack of funding and by threats from Islamists.

Most feature-length Palestinian movies are international co-productions. The first Palestinian film nominated for an Oscar was the controversial *Paradise Now* (2005), directed by Nazareth-born, Netherlands-based Hany Abu Assad, which puts a human face on Palestinian suicide bombers.

Elia Suleiman's *Divine Intervention* (2002) tells the story of lovers from Jerusalem and Ramallah who have to negotiate checkpoints to arrange their clandestine meetings.

Omar, also by Hany Abu-Assad, is a political thriller about trust and betrayal, and garnered an Oscar nomination in 2014.

Sadly both of the West Bank's movie venues – the Al Kasaba Theater & Cinematheque in Ramallah and the internationally supported Cinema Jenin – had closed as of 2017, with the latter bulldozed to make way for a shopping mall.

Each autumn, the Israeli Academy of Film & Television (www.israel filmacademy. co.il) chooses the winners of the Ophir Awards, Israel's equivalent of the Oscars.

Environment

Situated at the meeting point of two continents (Asia and Africa) and very near a third (Europe), Israel and the Palestinian Territories' environment is like nowhere else on earth. Asian mammals such as the Indian porcupine live alongside African tropical mammals such as the rock hyrax (dassie). In the Mediterranean forests of the Galilee, the oaks and sycamores recall biblical-era landscapes while the arid deserts of the Negev are home to species usually associated with Africa.

Habitats & Animals

A dozen species of bat, two of them critically endangered, have found cool, secluded warm-season shelter in abandoned Israel Defence Forces bunkers along the Jordan River, unused since the 1994 Israel-Jordan peace treaty.

Human beings have been having an impact on the habitats and creatures of Israel and the Palestinian Territories since the dawn of history, but the innovations of the past few centuries have been particularly damaging. The introduction of firearms during the 19th century led to the devastation of the country's large mammals and birds – cheetahs, bears, ostriches and crocodiles are just a few of the animals hunted to extinction in the area. Since the 1950s, Israeli ecologists have been working to protect the country's remaining biodiversity and have even reintroduced a few mammal species.

Much of the lush (and malarial) wetlands that once covered large areas of central and northern Israel were drained over the course of the 20th century, destroying important habitats for mammals and – especially – birds. Today, small sanctuaries such as the Hula Nature Reserve, Agamon HaHula and En Afek Nature Reserve (north of Haifa) preserve some of the original swamp habitats, providing important rest stops and feeding grounds for migrating birds. Like a number of other sites around the country, they are world-class spots for birdwatching.

Israel's 128 surviving indigenous mammal species are, for the most part, holding their own thanks to restrictions on hunting and a system of nature reserves and protected areas that encompass some 25% of Israel's land. However, protected areas are hardly a panacea for biodiversity loss. Many are quite small and isolated and can therefore offer only limited protection for endangered species. Moreover, many of the reserves in the south are also used for military exercises. Sometimes this overlap works to nature's advantage because civilian visitors are allowed in only on weekends and holidays, but the soldiers, tanks and jets cause significant disruption, especially for mammals.

The Israel Nature & Parks Authority (www.parks.org.il) administers most of Israel's national parks and nature reserves. Save money by buying a six-park 'Green Card' for 110NIS or an all-park card for 150NIS, both valid for 14 days.

Wildflowers

The hillsides of Israel and the Palestinian Territories are carpeted with yellow, orange, red, pink, purple and white wildflowers from about January to March (later at higher elevations, eg on Mt Hermon). The anemones and cyclamens of the Be'eri Forest in the northern Negev and the Beit Keshet Forest near Nazareth are particularly astonishing. Irises can be found on Mt Gilboa, and native orchids in the Jerusalem Hills.

During the 1960s, Israel's first-ever environmental campaign succeeded in persuading Israelis to refrain from picking wildflowers, an act that remains illegal.

Water, Source of All Life

In the arid Middle East, no resource is more precious than water – without it humans, animals and plants quite simply cannot survive. That's why King Hezekiah (8th century BCE) put so much effort into building a tunnel to ensure Jerusalem's water supply in time of siege, and why similar technology was employed by the Israelites at Tel Hatzor (9th century BCE); both sites are open to the public. And that's why in Palestinian-Israeli peace negotiations, most scenarios have left the three most difficult issues for last: Jerusalem, the fate of Palestinian refugees and...water.

As soon as Israel declared independence, it began to plan the transport of water from the Galilee, with its relatively plentiful rainfall, to the dryer south. By the 1960s, thanks to the reservoirs, tunnels and open canals of the 130km National Water Carrier – visible as you drive through the Lower Galilee – prodigious quantities of water were being piped to central Israel and the Negev Desert.

But water was still in short supply – today, rain supplies only about half of Israel's needs. It was this chronic shortfall that inspired Israeli researchers to invent modern drip irrigation, now a common sight in fields around the world, and that led to the construction of infrastructure that allows almost 90% of Israel's waste water to be recycled for use in agriculture.

Since 2005 Israel has built five enormous reverse-osmosis desalinisation plants along the Mediterranean coast that will soon supply 40% of Israel's drinking-quality water – and use some 10% of the country's electricity. For the first time in the history of the Middle East, water is no longer a zero-sum game. In the mid-1960s, clashes between Israel and Syria over water rights almost led to war, and Israel has disagreements over water both with Jordan, which shares water rights to the Jordan River, and with the Palestinians, who accuse Israel of taking the lion's share of West Bank water. Plentiful desalinated water – at a cost of about US$0.60 per 1000 litres – may defuse a key source of regional tension and even create opportunities for Arab-Israeli political and economic cooperation, in addition to freeing everyone from dependence

In *The Natural History of the Bible* (2007), Daniel Hillel, a world-renowned soil physicist and water-management expert (he was one of the creators of drip irrigation), examines the influence of local ecology on the people and world of the Scriptures.

ENVIRONMENT WATER, SOURCE OF ALL LIFE

ANIMALS OF THE BIBLE

An initiative known as Hai-Bar (literally 'wildlife') has, since 1968, taken on the challenge of reintroducing animal species that appear in the Bible but later became extinct in the Holy Land.

The Hai-Bar program's modus operandi has been to bring together a small number of animals from other parts of the region and breed them in captivity until their offspring can gradually be reintroduced to their natural habitats. In a parallel initiative, birds of prey, their populations ravaged by pesticides, have also been bred and returned to the wild.

While some zoologists question the historical accuracy of a few of the selected mammal species, the Hai-Bar program has largely been a success. Starting with the Asian wild ass, which appears in Isaiah's prophesies, a variety of endangered animals have been quietly reintroduced to the country's open spaces. A small group of Persian fallow deer was secretly airlifted from Iran in 1978 on the last El Al flight out of Tehran before Khomeini's revolution; these shy animals have taken hold in the Galilee reserve of Akhziv and in the hills west of Jerusalem. The Arabian oryx, whose straight parallel horns, viewed from the side, gave Crusaders the impression that they were unicorns, are also back.

The two Hai-Bar breeding and reacclimation centres – one at Yotvata in the Arava, the other on Mt Carmel, near Haifa – are being downsized, having completed most of their planned reintroductions, but are still well worth a visit for fans of Middle Eastern mammals.

Israel's first solar power station, the Solar Flower Tower, consists of a 30m tower and 30 tracking mirrors (heliostats) that focus the sun's rays. Situated 34km north of Eilat at Kibbutz Samar, it can generate enough electricity for 50 households.

on unreliable rainfall and aquifers threatened by seawater infiltration (Gaza's groundwater is already severely compromised by high levels of salinity, fertilisers and sewage).

Israeli scientists have also tried to find less costly ways to maximise water use. The ancients – especially the Nabataeans – developed sophisticated techniques to channel rare desert cloudbursts in ways that made agriculture possible even in the arid central Negev. Near the ruins of ancient Avdat, researchers at the Even-Ari Research Station began working in the 1960s to rediscover Nabataean techniques of terracing and water storage.

Wetlands Conservation

During the 1950s – a period of unbounded faith in the ability of technology to bring 'progress' – the Hula wetlands in the northeastern Galilee were drained to create farmland, destroying hugely important bird habitats and a key nutrient sink for the Sea of Galilee basin. The diversion of spring water and winter run-off for agriculture, industry and home use has degraded the aquatic habitats of many of Israel and the Palestinian Territories' streams and rivers, including the Jordan, a situation made worse by sewage run-off from Palestinian cities in the West Bank.

But not all is bleak for Israel's wetlands. Parts of the Hula swamps have been restored, and the Alexander River (www.restorationplanning. com/alex.html), 13km south of Caesarea, has been cleaned up and rehabilitated. In 2003 the latter project won the prestigious Thiess International Riverprize, awarded by the Australia-based International River Foundation (www.riverfoundation.org.au).

Is the Dead Sea Dying?

Because of pumping from the Jordan River, its tributaries and the Sea of Galilee by Israel, Jordan and Syria, the amount of water flowing annually into the Dead Sea is 1 billion cu metres (more than 90%) less than it would be naturally. As a result, evaporation is causing the sea to shrink rapidly, with the water level dropping some 1.2m per year – the surface

MIGRATION: A BILLION BIRDS A YEAR

Twice a year, 500 million birds from an unbelievable 283 species migrate through Israel and the Palestinian Territories: in the autumn as they head south from Europe and northwestern Asia to wintering grounds in Africa; and in the spring as they return to their summer breeding grounds.

Most migrating birds prefer to fly over land, where they can conserve energy by catching thermals. As a result, the Mediterranean and Caspian Seas end up funnelling huge numbers of Africa-bound birds to Israel's Mediterranean coast and the Jordan Valley (the Syrian-African Rift Valley), turning the latter into the largest avian fly-way in the world – some describe it as a 'superhighway' for birds.

Having so many birds flying through a narrow corridor along the eastern edge of Israel and the Palestinian Territories creates some of the world's most outstanding opportunities for birdwatching. Websites worth a look:

Israel Birding Portal (www.birds.org.il) Details on Israel's six main birding centres.

Agamon HaHula (www.agamon-hula.co.il) These reconstituted wetlands in the Upper Galilee are so popular with migrating cranes that some stay all winter.

Lotan Nature & Bird Reserve (www.kibbutzlotan.com) Kibbutz Lotan offers migrating birds a lush sanctuary in the heart of the Arava desert.

International Birding & Research Center (www.eilat-birds.org) An old garbage dump near Eilat has been turned into a salt marsh where exhausted birds can refuel.

ONLINE ENVIRONMENTAL RESOURCES

For more information on the state of the environment – and what's being done about it – in Israel and the Palestinian Territories, check out the websites of the following environmental organisations:

Adam Teva v'Din (www.adamteva.org.il) Israel's premier environmental advocacy organisation plays hardball in the courts, suing polluters and lethargic government agencies.

Applied Research Institute of Jerusalem (www.arij.org) An independent Palestinian research and advocacy organisation.

Arava Institute for Environmental Studies (www.arava.org) A teaching and research centre that brings Israelis, Palestinians and Jordanians to Kibbutz Ketura near Eilat.

Friends of the Earth Middle East (www.foeme.org) Promotes cooperation between Israeli, Palestinian and Jordanian environmentalists.

Israeli Ministry of Environmental Protection (www.sviva.gov.il) An increasingly powerful government ministry responsible for environmental regulation and enforcement.

Life & Environment – The Israeli Union of Environmental NGOs (www.sviva.net) Umbrella organisation for more than 130 Israeli environmental groups.

Palestine Wildlife Society (www.wildlife-pal.org) An educational and research NGO focusing on nature conservation.

Palestinian Ministry of Environmental Affairs (www.mena.gov.ps) Charged with environmental regulation and education.

Society for the Protection of Nature in Israel (www.natureisrael.org) Israel's oldest and largest environmental organisation.

---

area is now just 70% of what it was two decades ago. Thousands of sinkholes have appeared around the shoreline, posing a safety hazard and threatening both agriculture and tourist sites.

Proposals to refill the Dead Sea with seawater have been floating around for years. One idea calls for bringing in water from the Mediterranean through a 'Med–Dead Canal', while another proposes a 'Red–Dead Canal' from the Red Sea. The difference in altitude (more than 400m) could be used to generate hydroelectricity and produce desalinated water.

In 2013 an agreement was signed by Israel, the Palestinian Authority and Jordan to build a 110km-long canal through Jordan that would deliver 100 million cu metres of water to the Dead Sea and desalinate a similar quantity of water at a plant in Aqaba. Environmentalists are concerned about the impact on the Dead Sea of introducing seawater carrying a different mix of minerals as well as living organisms.

The Perils of Development

The population of Israel and the Palestinian Territories has grown by more than two million people and every decade since 1948, making today's population roughly seven times larger than it was seven decades ago. Over the same period Israel, initially a poor developing nation, has grown into a prosperous Western economy. The country's industrialisation, construction boom and enthusiasm for highways have generated pollution and sprawl comparable to those in the West – but because of Israel's small size, environmental ramifications are often felt more acutely. While Israel has been a world leader in water management, it has fallen far behind in other areas.

Tel Aviv has had remarkable success in convincing city residents to cycle rather than drive, thanks in part to two decades of grassroots activism by the Israel Bicycle Association (www.bike.org.il). The city now has some 120km of dedicated bike paths.

Air pollution in many Israeli and Palestinian cities is worse than almost anywhere in Europe and periodically reaches dangerous levels. On the solar-energy front, little has improved since a 1970s building code required that all Israeli apartments and homes install passive solar panels to heat water. Local waste management is surprisingly underdeveloped, with recycling rates well below those in Western Europe. Burial of rubbish at inexpensive municipal landfills is the default option, despite the dwindling reserves of available real estate. (Maybe policymakers just want to be generous to future archaeologists...)

Sprawl has also emerged as a serious problem, as more affluence has generated inefficient land-use patterns. In the past, most Israelis lived in apartment buildings, but their aspirations to move 'up and out' into 'villas' (single-family homes) have led to a proliferation of low-density communities based on a two-cars-per-family lifestyle. Open spaces have given way to roads and suburbs. Environmentalists have fought hard to stop this trend, but with only isolated success. However, a campaign to curb construction near beaches has produced dramatic results: laws now protect the coastline, banning most construction within 300m of the waterline and guaranteeing public access to all beaches.

Israel's environmental movement has grown bolder and more powerful in recent years. At the local government level, 'green' parties have begun to find a constituency.

Conflict with Israel, fuel shortages and intra-Palestinian political rivalries have shut down Gaza's sewage-treatment system. As a result, some of Gaza's streets are awash with human excrement, and 100,000 cu metres of raw sewage pour into the Mediterranean every day.

Survival Guide

Safe Travel

Is it safe? This is a question friends and family are likely to ask when you announce your plans to travel to Israel and/or the Palestinian Territories. The answer will always depend on current events, and can change within the space of a few days. The one certainty is that it's always a good idea to pay attention to advice from your country's foreign affairs department or ministry. You should also ask questions of any contacts you may have in this part of the world before you head here.

Travel Advisories & Information

A number of government websites offer travel advisories and information on current hot spots. Be sure to register your travel plans with your country's foreign affairs department or ministry so that they can email you security updates and advice if necessary. The best way to register is online.

Australian Department of Foreign Affairs (www.smartraveller.gov.au)

British Foreign Office (www.gov.uk/foreign-travel-advice)

Canadian Department of Foreign Affairs (http://travel.gc.ca)

US State Department (http://travel.state.gov)

News in English

When travelling in this region, you should regularly check the media for news about possible safety and security risks.

Haaretz (www.haaretz.com) The English edition of Israel's left-of-centre newspaper is sold at most newsstands.

Israeli Public Broadcasting Corporation (www.kan.org.il) Has an English radio broadcast daily from 8pm to 9pm in major cities.

Jerusalem Post (www.jpost.com) Right-of-centre and widely available.

Jerusalem Report (www.jpost.com/Jerusalem-Report) Bi-weekly, analyses current affairs.

Yediot Aharonot (www.ynetnews.com) Has an English-language news website.

Security Measures in Israel

Israel has some of the most stringent security policies in the world. Streets, highways, markets and public facilities can be cordoned off on the basis of intelligence (eg regarding a possible suicide bombing) and abandoned shopping bags, backpacks and parcels are picked up by bomb squad robots and blown up. Vehicles can be pulled over by the military and inspected for weapons or fugitives, especially near checkpoints. In recent years the number of terrorist attacks inside Israel has dropped, but it pays to remain vigilant about suspicious people or packages, especially when travelling by public transport.

When entering bus or rail terminals, shopping malls, supermarkets and other public venues, your bags may be searched or X-rayed. You may also be checked with a metal-detector wand or asked '*Yesh lecha neshek?*' ('Do you have a gun?'). It's amazing how quickly you'll get used to this.

In 2011, the Israel Defence Forces (IDF) deployed the Iron Dome (Kippat Barzel) mobile air defence system for the first time. Used to protect populated areas (especially cities such as Ashdod, Ashkelon, Be'er Sheva, Tel Aviv and Jerusalem), the system can intercept and destroy short-range rockets and artillery shells fired from distances of 4km (2.5 miles) to 70km (43 miles). It has proved to be highly effective and was utilised extensively and successfully during the 2014 Israel–Hamas conflict, intercepting and disabling 735 rockets fired from Gaza, 90% of the total number targeted at populated areas.

Safe Travel in the Palestinian Territories

The Gaza Strip is off-limits to travellers, but travel in the West Bank is generally very safe, and Palestinians are welcoming to tourists. Like other regions that are not widely visited, foreigners are often the object of curiosity, and hostility towards visitors to the West Bank is almost unheard of.

That said, the West Bank is under military occupation, and clashes between the Israeli military and Palestinian youths at checkpoints and in some of the more restive cities are common, particularly on Fridays and after major events, such as Palestinian funerals.

Steer clear of protests and, as much as possible, areas where protests are common – these include a number of villages next to Israeli settlements in the Hebron Hills and, at times, Qalandia Checkpoint. Ask ahead at your hotel or hostel before travelling.

Be aware that while organised tours are a great way to see the West Bank, offers of trips to the weekly protests at Bilin (or any demonstration, for that matter) should be declined.

Here are a few tips for safe travel in the West Bank:

➜ Always carry your passport. You will not need it when entering the West Bank, but you will need it, as well as your loose-leaf Israeli visa, to leave.

➜ Don't wander into the refugee camps on your own. Go with a local guide.

➜ If you wear any outward signs of Judaism, you may be mistaken for an Israeli settler (settlers are deeply resented by most Palestinians).

➜ Always avoid areas where demonstrations are being staged. Do not under any circumstances photograph Palestinian protestors (or, indeed, Israeli soldiers) without their express consent.

➜ Travel during daylight hours. Poor road signage, roadblocks and checkpoints make the West Bank disorienting enough in the daytime; travelling after dark will only add to the confusion.

➜ Use caution when approaching road blocks and checkpoints – Israeli soldiers are on high alert at all times, and causing unnecessary anxiety could lead to all sorts of problems and confrontations. Remember: they have no idea that you're just a curious visitor.

Political Protests

Israel is a democracy, where political protests are a legally protected right. But residents of West Bank areas administered by the Israeli army (ie under military rule) aren't protected by those same rights. This means that harsh measures – including truncheons, tear gas, stun grenades and rubber bullets – are often used against Palestinian protesters and

---

WHAT TO DO IN A ROCKET ATTACK

If you hear an air-raid siren (a rising and falling tone) while in Israel, you should immediately head to the nearest Mamad (reinforced concrete room) or conventional bomb shelter and close all doors and windows. Depending on how far from the launch site in Gaza, southern Lebanon or Syria you are, and depending on what type of missile it is, you may have as little as 10 seconds to get ready for impact (in Tel Aviv, for instance, the warning time for a Gaza-launched missile is 90 seconds).

If you're in a building without a Mamad (only buildings constructed after the First Gulf War of 1991 have them), head to a room situated furthest from the direction of the threat with the smallest possible number of outside walls, windows and openings. (In Eilat, the threat will usually come from Sinai; in Tel Aviv, it will come from Gaza; and in the north, it will usually come from Lebanon.) Another option is to take shelter in an interior staircase or a corridor as far away from windows and doors as possible. If you're on the top floor of a building, descend two floors – but not all the way to the ground floor.

If you are outdoors or in a vehicle, enter the nearest building and follow the above instructions. If you're in an exposed area, lie on the ground face down away from your car and cover your head with your hands.

If there are no additional instructions (eg on the radio), you can exit the shelter or get back into your car after 10 minutes.

This advice applies year-round, not just when there is an active conflict. The website of Israel's Home Front Command, www.oref.org.il, has advice about what to do in a rocket, missile, chemical or biological weapon attack, plus training videos and a map of early warning alerts.

the supporting Israelis who sometimes join them at demonstrations.

Be warned that if you show up at a protest rally, even just to watch, you stop being an innocent outsider and become a participant in the conflict.

Demonstrations can get out of hand. This is particularly the case when ultra-Orthodox Jews clash with police in places such as the Mea She'arim neighbourhood in Jerusalem or the city of Beit Shemesh. There have also been situations when members of extreme right-wing groups have assaulted left-wing activists at demonstrations in support of territorial compromise or against the Israeli settlements.

Temple Mount/Al Haram Ash Sharif in Jerusalem's Old City is a major flashpoint for demonstrations. Although Jordan has administrative control of this holy site, the Israelis are in charge of security and sometimes deny Muslim men under the age of 45 access to the compound (and hence to Al Aqsa Mosque) when the security situation is judged to be unsettled. This can trigger violent demonstrations in the Old City's Muslim Quarter, around Damascus Gate and in East Jerusalem, particularly on Fridays after noon prayers. It's best to avoid these areas when the political situation is tense.

Non-Muslims are not permitted to pray in the compound, something that infuriates ultra-nationalistic Jews and has led to violent confrontations between security forces and demonstrators in the past.

A number of commemorative days, often accompanied by protests, are marked by Palestinians. These days are sometimes marred by violence (from both sides) so

travellers are advised to be vigilant if in the West Bank or nearby.

Land Day A day of protest against Israel's expanded settlements dating from 1976. Called Yom Al Ard in Arabic and Yom HaAdama in Hebrew and occurs on 30 March.

Palestinian Prisoners Day Palestinians remember their compatriots imprisoned in Israeli jails on 17 April.

Nakba Day Commemoration of Al Nakba ('the catastrophe' to Palestinians) happens the day after Israel's Independence Day on 15 May.

Naksa Day Remembrance day of the *naksa* (what Palestinians call the 'setback') of the 1967 Six Day War on 5 June.

Minefields

Some parts of Israel and the Palestinian Territories – particularly along the Jordanian border and around the periphery of the Golan Heights – are still sown with anti-personnel mines. Fortunately, known mined areas are indicated in pink on topographical maps and are fenced with barbed wire sporting dangling red (or rust) triangles and/or yellow and red 'Danger Mines!' signs.

When hiking, don't stray from marked trails and never climb over or through a barbed-wire fence. In the Jordan Valley and the Arava, flash floods sometimes wash away old mines, depositing them outside the boundaries of known minefields – wherever you are, never, *ever* touch anything that looks like it might be an old artillery shell, grenade or mine.

If you find yourself in a mined area, retrace your steps only if you can clearly see your footprints. If not, stay where you are and call

for help. If someone is injured in a minefield, do not rush in to assist even if they are crying out for help – instead, find someone who knows how to enter a mined area safely.

Theft

Theft is no more and no less of a problem in Israel and the Palestinian Territories than anywhere else, so take the usual precautions: don't leave valuables in your vehicle or hotel room, and keep important documents and cash in a money belt. In hostels, check your most valuable belongings and documents into the front-desk safe. On intercity buses, it's fine to stow large bags in the luggage hold but keep valuables with you. Pickpockets have been known to lurk in crowded tourist spots and busy markets, so keep alert and stay aware of what's happening around you. Bike theft is rampant so use a massive, reinforced steel chain lock (not a cable), and never leave an expensive bike on the street overnight.

Traffic Accidents

The number of traffic fatalities in Israel has fallen in recent years (362 traffic deaths in 2017 compared with an average of more than 600 per year in the 1990s) and the percentage of fatalities per population is considerably lower than in many other countries (3.3 fatalities per 100,000 inhabitants as opposed to Australia's 5.2 and the United States' 11.6). That said, driving here can be dangerous, particularly on rural roads and highways where drivers often speed and take risks when overtaking. Stick to speed limits and always drive defensively.

Directory A-Z

Accommodation

Hotels

Both Israel and the Palestinian Territories offer accommodation options for every budget and style of travel. In Israel, expect prices – though not always standards – on par with Western Europe. In recent years an increasing number of small, stylish boutique hotels have opened. The West Bank is quite a bit cheaper, with many of the best options clustered in Ramallah and Bethlehem.

Israeli hotels are famous for their generous buffet breakfasts. Although most hotel restaurants serve only kosher food, they remain open on Shabbat and Jewish holidays.

Kibbutz Guesthouses

Capitalising on their beautiful, usually rural locations, quite a few kibbutzim offer midrange guesthouse accommodation. Often constructed in the socialist era but significantly upgraded since, these establishments allow access to kibbutz facilities (including the swimming pool), have a laid-back vibe and serve deliciously fresh kibbutz-style breakfasts. Prices are sometimes as low as 350NIS for a double without breakfast. For details and reservations, check out the Kibbutz Hotels Chain (www.kibbutz.org.il).

B&Bs (Tzimmerim)

The most common form of accommodation in the Upper Galilee and Golan is the *tzimmer* (or *zimmer*). No one really knows how the German word for 'room' came to symbolise for Israelis all that's idyllic about a cabin in the country, though the term may have been inspired by the 'Zimmer frei' signs you often see at German guesthouses. Prices are generally upper-midrange or higher. It's not always possible to check in late at night.

A *tzimmer* is often a room or cabin in a rural area with rustic, varnished pine decor, satellite TV, a kitchenette and – in more luxurious units – a spa bath. Some places serve great breakfasts but others offer beds without breakfast.

To find a *tzimmer*, keep an eye out for signs on the street or check the following websites:

→ www.zimmeril.com
→ www.israeltours.co
→ www.weekend.co.il (in Hebrew)
→ www.zimmer.co.il (in Hebrew)

Hostels & Field Schools

Almost three dozen independent hostels and guesthouses belong to Israel Hostels (www.hostels-israel.com), whose members offer dorm beds for 100NIS, good-value doubles and unmatched opportunities to meet other travellers.

Israel's 19 official Hostelling International (HI) hostels and guesthouses – significantly upgraded since the days of no-frills dorms and timer-activated communal showers – offer spotless, institutional rooms that are ideal for families, and also offer copious breakfasts. For details, check out the website of the Israel Youth Hostels Association, www.iyha.org.il.

The Society for the Protection of Nature in Israel (www.natureisrael.org) runs nine field schools (*beit sefer sadeh*) in areas of high ecological value. Offering basic but serviceable accommodation, they're popular with school groups and families. Book

---

BOOK YOUR STAY ONLINE

For more accommodation reviews by Lonely Planet authors, check out http://lonelyplanet.com/hotels/. You'll find independent reviews, as well as recommendations on the best places to stay. Best of all, you can book online.

SLEEPING PRICE RANGES

Israel: the following prices are for double rooms with breakfast on weekends and in high season. Prices are slightly higher in Tel Aviv compared with the rest of the country.

$ less than 350NIS

$$ 350NIS to 600NIS

$$$ more than 600NIS

Palestinian Territories: the following price ranges are for double rooms with breakfast on weekends in high season.

$ less than 200NIS

$$ 200NIS to 400NIS

$$$ more than 400NIS

well ahead, especially during school vacation periods.

Pilgrims' hostels run by religious organisations serve mainly, but not exclusively, religious travellers. As you would expect, they lack the party atmosphere of some independent hostels but offer solid value.

Camping

If you're on a tight budget, staying in a tent (or at least a sleeping bag) is a great way to save some serious shekels.

Camping is forbidden inside Israeli nature reserves, but various public and private bodies run inexpensive camping sites (www.campin gil.org.il) at about 100 places around the country, including 22 operated by the Israel Nature & Parks Authority (www.parks.org.il) next to nature reserves. Some are equipped with shade roofs (so you don't need a tent), lighting, toilets, showers and barbecue pits. In Hebrew, ask for a *chenyon laila* or an *orchan laila*.

Camping is particularly popular on the shores of the Sea of Galilee. Some organised beaches – offering toilet facilities, a decent shower block and security – charge per-person admission fees,

but others are free if you arrive on foot (visitors with wheels pay a per-car fee).

In the Palestinian Territories, camping should be avoided because of general security concerns.

Seasonal Rates
ISRAEL

Accommodation prices vary enormously with the day of the week and the season.

Weekday rates generally run from Saturday or Sunday night through Wednesday or Thursday night. Weekend rates apply on Friday and sometimes Thursday (many Israelis don't work on Friday) and/or Saturday night.

High-season pricing is in force during July and August in most parts of the country. The exceptions: extremely hot areas such as the Dead Sea and the Sea of Galilee.

High-high-season prices occur on Jewish holidays such as Rosh HaShanah, Shavu'ot and the weeklong Passover and Sukkot festivals, especially in popular getaways such as the Galilee, the Golan Heights and Eilat. At these times, book well in advance.

Accommodation prices given in shekels include Israel's value-added tax (VAT) of 17%, which foreign tourists

do not have to pay, so most places (though not some B&Bs) charge non-Israelis significantly less than their shekel prices.

Prices given in US dollars, and those generated by hotel booking websites, do not include VAT so Israeli citizens will find an extra 17% tacked on at checkout.

PALESTINIAN TERRITORIES

Room prices remain fairly constant year-round, the exception being Bethlehem, where rates rise around Christmas and Easter. Book well ahead if you are planning to travel at these times.

Customs Regulations

Israel allows travellers 18 and over, including those heading to the West Bank, to import duty-free up to 1L of spirits and 2L of wine, 250ml of perfume, 250g of tobacco products (200 cigarettes) and gifts worth no more than US$200. Pets can be brought into Israel but require submitting advance paperwork to the Ministry of Agriculture.

Bringing drugs, drug paraphernalia, mace (self-defence tear gas), laser jammers (to confuse police-operated laser speed guns), fresh meat and pornography are prohibited.

Dangers & Annoyances

Israel is generally a very safe place to travel and violent crime against tourists is extremely rare. However, the country has some unique challenges visitors should be aware of.

➡ Be careful when visiting border regions, particularly those close to Syria and Lebanon or between Israel and the West Bank.

➡ Keep your eye on the news and don't be afraid to ask

at your hotel or hostel for advice.

➡ Avoid demonstrations, particularly in Jerusalem, which can quickly descend into rioting.

➡ If you are asked about the political situation, be aware that feelings run high and discussions can quickly get heated.

➡ Use hotel safes where available. Don't leave valuables unattended, particularly on the beach.

➡ In the West Bank, hostility towards visitors is almost unheard of. However, visitors should exercise caution as the area is under military occupation and clashes between the Israeli military and Palestinian youths (eg at checkpoints and in some of the more restive cities) are common, particularly on Fridays and after major events such as Palestinian funerals. Steer clear of demonstrations and, as much as possible, areas where protests are common.

➡ Smoking is very common in the West Bank, and nonsmoking areas in bars and restaurants are very much the exception. That said, an increasing number of hotels and hostels have banned smoking in rooms and even in common areas.

Discount Cards

A Hostelling International (HI) card is useful for discounts at official HI hostels. An International Student Identity Card (ISIC) doesn't get anywhere near as many discounts as it once did – none, for instance, are available on public transport.

Some museums and sights offer discounts to senior citizens, though to qualify you may not only need to be senior but also a citizen.

If you're visiting lots of the national parks and historical sites run by the Israel Nature & Parks Authority (INPA; www.parks.org.il), you can

save by purchasing a Green Card, valid for 14 days, that gets you into all INPA sites for just 150NIS (a six-park version costs 110NIS). With membership of the Israel Society for the Protection of Nature in Israel (www.natureisrael.org) you'll get discounts on accommodation at field schools and outings.

Electricity

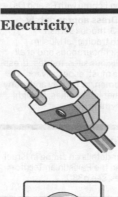

Type C
220V/50Hz

Type H
230V/50Hz

Embassies & Consulates

While Israel may claim Jerusalem as its capital, unresolved political issues have led most diplomatic missions to set up shop in or near Tel Aviv. A few countries maintain consulates in Jerusalem, Haifa and/or Eilat.

Australian Embassy (Map p118; ☎03-693-5000; www.israel.embassy.gov.au; 28th fl, Discount Bank Tower, 23 Yehuda HaLevi St; ⊗8am-12.30pm & 1-4pm Mon-Thu, to 1pm Fri)

Canadian Embassy (☎03-636-3300; www.canadainternational.gc.ca/israel; 3 Nirim St; ⊗8am-4pm Mon-Thu, to 1.30pm Fri)

Egyptian Embassy (☎03-546-4151; www.egyptembassy.net; 54 Basel St; ⊗9-11am Sun-Tue) There's also a consulate in **Eilat** (Map p336;☎08-637-6882; 68 Efroni St; ⊗9.30-noon Sun-Thu).

French Embassy (Map p122; ☎03-520-8500; www.ambafrance-il.org; 112 Herbert Samuel Esplanade; ⊗8am-12.30pm Mon-Fri) There's also a **consulate** (Map p80;☎02-629-8500; www.consulfrance-jerusalem.org; 5 Paul Émile Botta St) in Jerusalem.

German Embassy (Map p118; ☎03-693-1313; www.tel-aviv.diplo.de; 19th fl, 3 Daniel Frisch St; ⊗8-11.30am Mon, Tue, Thu & Fri)

Irish Embassy (☎03-696-4166; www.embassyofireland.co.il; 2 Jabotinski St, Ramat Gan; ⊗10am-12.30pm Mon-Thu)

Jordanian Embassy (☎03-751-7722; 10th fl, 14 Abba Hillel St, Ramat Gan; ⊗9.30am-3pm Sun-Thu)

Netherlands Embassy (☎03-754-0777; www.netherlandsworldwide.nl/countries/israel; 13th fl, 14 Abba Hillel St, Ramat Gan; ⊗9am-4pm Mon-Thu, to 1pm Fri)

Turkish Embassy (Map p122; ☎03-524-1101; 202 HaYarkon St; ⊗9am-noon Mon-Fri) There's also a **consulate**

(☎02-591-0555; http://jerusalem.cg.mfa.gov.tr; 87 Derekh Shchem (Nablus) Rd, Sheikh Jarrah; ⊗8am-5pm Mon-Fri) in Jerusalem.

UK Embassy (Map p122; ☎03-725-1222; www.ukinisrael.fco.gov.uk; 192 HaYarkon St; ⊗8am-4pm Mon-Thu, to 1.30pm Fri) There's also a **consulate** (☎02-541-4100; www.ukinjerusalem.fco.gov.uk; 15 Nashashibi St, Sheikh Jarrah; ⊗8am-4pm Mon-Thu, to 2pm Fri) in Jerusalem.

US Embassy (Map p122; ☎03-519-7475; https://il.usembassy.gov; 71 HaYarkon St; ⊗8am-noon Mon-Fri by appointment only) There are also consulates in **Haifa** (Map p160; ☎04-853-1470; 26 Ben-Gurion Ave, German Colony) and **Jerusalem** (America House; Map p72; ☎02-622-7230; https://jru.usconsulate.gov; 18 Derekh Shchem (Nablus) Rd, East Jerusalem).

Etiquette

Israel and the Palestinian Territories can sometimes feel like a bit of a minefield when it comes to etiquette, but there are a few rules that will help you to avoid offending local sensibilities.

➡ **Avoid politics** Unless you know someone well, it usually pays to avoid expressing an opinion on the

conflict – or at least consider your audience when doing so. Pro-Israel standpoints will be unpopular in the West Bank and are best kept to yourself.

➡ **Be polite** Even if it feels like nobody else is! Israelis are famously brusque – almost proudly so – so don't be surprised if interactions don't come with Ps and Qs.

➡ **Dress appropriately** In Orthodox Jewish and traditional Muslim neighbourhoods and at *all* religious sites, modest dress is a must, especially for women. In Tel Aviv and many other Israeli cities, though, anything goes.

Food

For details on eating in Israel and the Palestinian Territories, see p380.

Gay & Lesbian Travellers

Israel has a very lively gay scene. Tel Aviv has plenty of rainbow-coloured flags, a huge Gay Pride Parade and plenty of hang-outs. Haifa and Jerusalem have smaller gay communities. The resort town of Eilat is gay-friendly, although the scene is mostly Israeli tourists. Most local

organisations offering support, information, contacts and events are based in Tel Aviv and Jerusalem.

Orthodox Judaism, Islam and almost all of the Holy Land's Christian churches adamantly oppose homosexuality, so it's appropriate to be circumspect in religious neighbourhoods. There are no laws in Israel against homosexuality. Israel does not have gay marriage but recognises gay and lesbian marriages performed abroad.

Outside of Ramallah, the West Bank is conservative, and homosexuality and gay culture are very much taboo. Even in Ramallah and Bethlehem, there is no LGBT nightlife scene as such, and just as elsewhere in the Arab world, open displays of affection would certainly be frowned upon – and could be quite dangerous.

Insurance

It's always a good idea to take out a travel insurance policy before leaving home. In addition to the usual coverage for sickness (visiting an emergency room/casualty ward can be expensive) and theft, make sure that your coverage is appropriate for your specific needs. For instance, if you plan to scuba dive, skydive or ski, make sure your policy covers these activities. Almost all policies exclude liabilities caused by 'acts of war'.

Worldwide travellers' coverage is available online at www.lonelyplanet.com/travel-insurance.

Even as a tourist, it's possible to get pretty complete medical coverage at reasonable rates through one of Israel's excellent HMOs provided you'll be staying for at least three to six months. For details, drop by one of the offices of these organisations:

Maccabi Healthcare Services (www.maccabi4u.co.il) Look

EATING PRICE RANGES

Israel: the following price ranges refer to a main course. Prices are slightly higher in Tel Aviv compared with the rest of the country.

$ less than 35NIS

$$ 35NIS to 70NIS

$$$ more than 70NIS

Palestinian Territories: the following price ranges refer to a main course.

$ less than 35NIS

$$ 35NIS to 55NIS

$$$ more than 55NIS

for details on its Well-Come program.

Me'uchedet (www.meuhedet.co.il) Provides coverage under its Foreign Members Plan.

Internet Access

Wi-fi hot spots can be found all over Israel, including in almost all cafes and many restaurants. Wi-fi is also available on many intercity buses and trains, though it's rather slow. Tel Aviv offers free wi-fi in dozens of public spaces all over the city. HI youth hostels and more than a few fancy hotels charge for wi-fi and/or the use of internet computers; at ILH hostels and B&Bs and in midrange hotels, wi-fi is usually free.

Israeli and Palestinian SIM cards can be used in the West Bank, although the former will only work in areas close to Israeli settlements or the border. SIM cards can be bought cheaply in the major cities (you'll need your passport), and data costs are relatively low compared to Europe. Wi-fi is widely available in cafes, restaurants, bars and hotels throughout the West Bank.

Legal Matters

The Israeli police have been known to arrest people for having minute quantities of drugs in their possession, despite official policy being more lenient.

Visitors – unlike Israeli citizens – are not allowed to proselytise. Religion is a sensitive matter, so sharing your faith's 'good news' too enthusiastically can lead to angering locals and complications with the police.

Palestinian police are not permitted to arrest tourists, but they can detain a tourist before turning them over to the Israeli security forces.

If you're arrested, there's little your embassy can do for you while the legal process

plays itself out, other than sending a low-ranking diplomat to visit you.

Maps

Tourist office maps, when available, tend to be rudimentary. Excellent road maps are published by a Tel Aviv–based company called Mapa (www.mapa.co.il/maps) and sold at all bookshops in Israel; its website has a detailed Hebrew-language map of the whole country. The databases used by Google Maps and GPS-based navigational devices are not as developed as in most Western countries.

For hikers, the Society for the Protection of Nature in Israel (www.natureisrael.org), known in Hebrew as HaChevra l'Haganat HaTeva, publishes a series of 20 1:50,000-scale topographical trail maps (mapot simun shvilim), available only in Hebrew. Not only do they indicate nature reserves (shown in green with the name in purple) and all marked hiking trails, but they also show areas used by the IDF for live-fire military exercises (shitchei esh; indicated in pink) and the location of old minefields (sdot mokshim; in pink with a border of red triangles). The maps can be purchased directly from the SPNI (eg at field schools) and are also available at bookshops and come in waterproof versions.

Money
ATMs

ATMs are widespread, and Visa, MasterCard and, increasingly, American Express and Diners cards are accepted almost everywhere. Most – but not all – ATMs do Visa and MasterCard cash advances.

Note: ATMs are not available at border crossings with Jordan and Egypt.

Bargaining

Most of your bargaining experiences will happen at souqs, flea markets or in taxis, which despite being required by law to use a meter, rarely miss the chance to fleece tourists for a few shekels. As with bargaining across the world, it pays to keep your cool and – particularly with souvenirs – remember that as the buyer you ultimately have the advantage.

Cash

The shekel is divided into 100 agorot. Coins come in denominations of 10 and 50 agorot (marked ½ shekel) and one, two and five NIS; notes come in denominations of 10, 20, 50, 100 and 200NIS.

In late 2017 new bills featuring women literary figures were issued. Rachel the Poetess (Rachel Bluwstein; 1890–1931) appears on the 20NIS, while Leah Goldberg (1911–70) is on the 100NIS.

Moneychangers

Banks charge a hefty commission so the best exchange deals are usually available at post office branches able to handle foreign currency and from independent exchange bureaux, neither of which charge commissions.

Tipping

Tipping is not expected in most circumstances. However, it is becoming increasingly common in Israel and at touristy places in the West Bank.

Restaurants Waiters and waitresses expect a tip; 10–15% is fair.

Pubs Usually have tip jars on the bar; 10–15% of your bill is fair.

Guides It's always good to tip guides. Organise a whip around among other guests; 10–20NIS each is probably fair.

Hotels 10NIS to 20NIS a night for housekeeping is a nice touch.

Taxis Will not expect tips, but you can round up the price of the fare.

Post

Letters and postcards sent with Israel Post (www.israel-post.co.il) to North America and Australasia take seven to 10 days to arrive; to Europe it's a bit less. Incoming mail takes three or four days from Europe and around a week from other places; packages are much slower.

For express service, options include DHL (www.dhl.com) and UPS (www.ups.com); Israel Post's EMS (Express Mail Service) is cheaper but slower and not as reliable.

In the West Bank there are post offices in most of the main cities but your safest bet is to ask your hotel or hostel.

Public Holidays

Israel

Between the myriad Jewish and Muslim festivals and holy days that are marked (both officially and unofficially), it can often feel like there is a rarely a day in the calendar that isn't some sort of national holiday.

Bear in mind that during Jewish holidays such as Passover, most restaurants, bars and even supermarkets will close in Jerusalem and other religious areas, while Yom Kippur makes travelling by road anywhere in the country virtually impossible.

As well as the religious holidays, there are a number of national holidays that can have a impact on your stay.

Holocaust Memorial Day Yom HaSho'ah is a solemn remembrance of the six million Jews, including 1.5 million children, who died in the Holocaust. Places of entertainment are closed. At 10am sirens sound and Israelis stand silently at attention wherever they happen to be. (1–2 May 2019, 20–21 April 2020, 8–9 April 2021)

Memorial Day Commemorates soldiers who fell defending Israel and the victims of terrorism. Places of entertainment are closed. At 8pm and 11am sirens sound and Israelis stand silently at attention wherever they happen to be. Falls on the day before Israel Independence Day (7–8 May 2019, 27–28 April 2020, 14–15 April 2021).

Israel Independence Day Ha'Atzma'ut celebrates Israel's declaration of independence in 1948. Marked with official ceremonies, public celebrations with live music, picnics and hikes. (8–9 May 2019, 28–29 April 2020, 15–16 April 2021)

Yom Kippur The Jewish Day of Atonement is a solemn day of reflection and fasting – and cycling on the empty roads. In Jewish areas, all businesses shut and transport (including by private car) completely ceases; Israel's airports and land borders close. (8–9 October 2019, 27–28 September 2020, 16–17 September 2021)

WHAT'S OPEN ON SHABBAT

The Jewish Sabbath, known in Hebrew as Shabbat, begins 18 minutes (36 minutes in Jerusalem) before sundown on Friday and lasts until an hour after sundown on Saturday.

Halacha (Jewish law) prohibits the conduct of business on Shabbat, but in many Jewish-majority areas of Israel, including West Jerusalem and Tel Aviv, 'status quo' agreements allow restaurants, places of entertainment (theatres, cinemas, discos, bars), museums and small groceries – but not retail shops or full-size supermarkets – to stay open on Shabbat.

On land owned by kibbutzim (eg Kibbutz Shefayim) and in parts of Tel Aviv (eg in the Namal/Port area), boutiques and shops sell things on Shabbat, using non-Jewish staff to avoid fines from the Ministry of Labor and Social Affairs, which – to avoid employing Jews on the Sabbath – sends out only non-Jewish (usually Druze) inspectors!

In general, public transport in Israel does not run from mid-afternoon on Friday (the exact time depends on when sundown is) until sometime on Saturday afternoon or evening. Exceptions: certain bus lines in the religiously mixed city of Haifa that have been running seven days week since the time of the British Mandate; some long-distance intercity buses, eg to Eilat; and bus lines that serve mainly non-Jewish towns. However, many intercity sherut lines do run on the Sabbath, as do regular taxis.

In predominantly Muslim areas (East Jerusalem, Akko's Old City, parts of Jaffa, the West Bank and Gaza) many businesses remain open on Saturday but are closed on Friday. In mainly Christian areas (eg Haifa's Wadi Nisnas, Nazareth, Bethlehem and the Armenian and Christian quarters of Jerusalem's Old City) businesses are usually closed on Sunday.

In Israel, national parks, nature reserves and most museums are open seven days a week but close an hour or two earlier on Friday afternoon. Christian religious sites may be closed on Sunday morning, while mosques are often closed to visitors on Friday.

Hanukkah During the Jewish Festival of Lights, expect Shabbat-like closures on the first and last days only. Some Israelis go on holiday, so accommodation is scarce and room prices rise. (2–10 December 2018, 22–30 December 2019, 10–18 December 2020, 28 November–December 6 2021)

Palestinian Territories

The main Islamic holidays have variable dates and depend on sightings of the moon.

Islamic New Year First Day of Muharram.

Prophet's Birthday Celebrated on 12 Rabi' Al Awal.

Lailat Al Miraj Commemorates the Prophet Muhammad's 'Night Journey' from Mecca to Jerusalem and from there to heaven. One of Islam's holiest days; thousands flock to the Dome of Rock in Jerusalem.

Ramadan Holy month of dawn-to-dusk fasting by Muslims. Many shops and restaurants in East Jerusalem (including the Old City), the West Bank and Arab towns in Israel close during daylight hours, but sunset ushers in a lively atmosphere as Muslims head out to eat.

Eid Al Fitr Marks the end of Ramadan with one to three days of celebrations with family and friends. Most shops and services will be closed in Arab areas.

Eid Al Adha Commemoration of Allah sparing Ibrahim (Abraham in the Bible) from sacrificing his son, Isaac. It also marks the end of the hajj.

Taxes & Refunds

Israel has value added tax of 17% that is included in all purchases. Israeli citizens have to pay VAT when staying in hotels, but tourists are exempt.

VAT Refund

Foreign tourists are entitled to a VAT refund on items worth a total of at least 400NIS purchased from certain shops (look for a sticker reading 'tax refund for tourists' in the window). Purchases must be sealed in partially transparent plastic and accompanied by a tax-refund invoice (a standard receipt will not suffice). Claim your refund – subject to a handling fee of up to 15% – when you exit the country by air or land. At Ben Gurion Airport, the refund desk is in the Check-In Hall; tax officials must see your purchases so take care of refund formalities before going through security.

Telephone

In Israel domestic landline-to-landline calls are cheap, but depending on the company and the plan involved, calling a mobile phone from a landline or another mobile can cost 0.80NIS a minute or more. Be careful when you use the phone in your hotel room – hotels often charge exorbitant rates.

Mobile Phones

Although overseas mobile phones and smartphones work (on gadgets that can handle 900/1800 MHz), roaming charges can be ruinous. Fortunately, Israel's various mobile phone operators, including Orange (www.orange.co.il), Pelefone (www.pelephone.co.il), Cellcom (www.cellcom.co.il), Hot Mobile (www.hotmobile.co.il) and Golan Telecom (www.golantelecom.co.il), offer pay-as-you-go SIM cards as well as cheap monthly plans with a variety of data options. A number of online companies sell Israeli SIMs internationally.

Mobile phone numbers start with 05 plus a third digit. When calling a local landline from a mobile phone, always dial the area code.

If you are near Israel's borders (especially with Jordan), you may discover that your mobile phone has switched to a Jordanian network. Manually switch your gadget back to your Israeli network or you may clock up pricey roaming charges.

In the Palestinian Territories, SIM cards can be easily bought from either Jawwal and Wataniya – the two Palestinian networks – and used in unlocked phones.

Phone Codes

Israel's country code is 972, while the Palestinian Territories use both 972 and 970. To call from abroad, dial your international access code followed by the country code, the local or mobile phone area code (minus the zero) and the subscriber number.

In Israel, several competing companies, each with its own three-digit international access code, offer international dialling. International direct-dial rates can be as high as 3.80NIS a minute, but if you sign up in advance, fees can be remarkably cheap (as little as 0.05NIS a minute). Companies include 012 Smile (www.012.net), Netvision (http://netvision.cellcom.co.il), Golan Telecom (www.golantelecom.co.il) and Hot Mobile (www.hotmobile.co.il).

Phonecards

Prepaid local and international calls can be made using a variety of phonecards, sold at post offices, lottery kiosks and newsstands.

Time

Israel and the Palestinian Territories are two hours later than GMT/UTC (three hours later during daylight savings time), seven hours later than New York, 10 hours later than Los Angeles and eight or nine hours earlier than Melbourne. Israel goes on and off daylight savings time on almost the same dates – in very late March and very late October – as Europe.

Tourist Information

Nearly every major city in Israel has a tourist office offering brochures and maps; some also organise city walking tours.

Jaffa Gate (📋02-627-1422; www.itraveljerusalem.com; Jaffa Gate; ⏰8.30am-5pm Sat-Thu, to 1.30pm Fri) Helpful office in Jerusalem.

Free Tours Haifa (📋058 604-8428; www.facebook.com/free-tourshaifa; ⏰10.30am most Wed) Great place to start your visit to Haifa.

Useful websites:

➡ www.goisrael.com – Israel's Ministry of Tourism.

➡ www.iggoogledisrael.com – Tips on travelling and living in Israel.

➡ www.parks.org.il – Israel Nature & Parks Authority.

➡ www.travelujah.com – Comprehensive information for Christian travellers.

Most West Bank cities now have tourism offices, some of which are very high quality, including in Jenin, Jericho and Bethlehem. Hotels and hostels are a wealth of information on what to do and where to go.

Travellers with Disabilities

In Israel, access to public amenities for people with disabilities, including those in wheelchairs, is approaching the levels of Western Europe and North America. Almost all hotels and HI hostels are required to have one or more rooms outfitted for wheelchair users, and many tourist attractions, including museums, archaeological sites and beaches, are wheelchair accessible to a significant degree. Quite a few nature reserves offer trails designed for wheelchairs (see www.parks.org.il and www.kkl.org.

il), with new ones are being added each year. Restaurants are a mixed bag because few have fully wheelchair-accessible bathrooms. Kerb ramps for wheelchairs are widespread.

For details on accessibility, check out the website of Access Israel, www.aisrael.org. Yad Sarah Organisation (www.yadsarah.org) lends wheelchairs, crutches and other mobility aids free of charge (deposit required).

The Palestinian Territories are less well equipped than Israel, and getting around is made more difficult by Israel Defense Forces checkpoints, which often have to be crossed on foot and sometimes require moving over and around barriers.

Download Lonely Planet's free Accessible Travel guide from http://lptravel.to/AccessibleTravel

Visas

Israel

Israel no longer stamps tourists' passports (though it retains the right to do so). Instead, visitors are given a small loose-leaf entry card to serve as proof of lawful entry. It's easy to lose, but keep it somewhere safe as it's your only proof that you're in the country legally (eg to avoid paying VAT at hotels or to pass through a roadblock to/from the West Bank).

We've heard reports of Israeli authorities at Allenby/King Hussein Bridge and Ben Gurion Airport issuing 'Palestinian Authority Only' entry permits to travellers with family or personal connections in the West Bank, making it difficult or impossible to get past the IDF roadblocks that regulate traffic from the West Bank into Israel, including Jerusalem.

Students require a student (A/2) visa; kibbutz volunteers must arrange, through

their host organisation, a volunteer's (B/4) visa.

On-Arrival Tourist Visas

In general, Western visitors to Israel and the Palestinian Territories are issued free on-arrival tourist (B/2) visas by Israel. For specifics on who qualifies, visit www.mfa.gov.il (click on 'Consular Services' and then 'Visas'). Your passport must be valid for at least six months from the date of entry. Officials can demand to see proof of sufficient funds and/or an onward or return ticket, but rarely do so.

On-arrival visas are usually valid for 90 days. But some travellers, such as those entering by land from Egypt or Jordan, may be given just 30 days or even two weeks – it's up to the discretion of the border control official. If there is any indication that you are coming to participate in pro-Palestinian protests, plan to engage in missionary activity or are seeking illegal employment, you may find yourself on the next flight home.

Visa Extensions

To extend a tourist (B/2) visa, you have a couple of options:

➡ Do a 'visa run' to Egypt, Jordan or overseas. This might get you an additional three months – or just one. Ask other travellers for the latest low-down.

➡ Apply to extend your visa (90NIS). Extensions are granted by the Population & Immigration Authority (www.piba.gov.il), part of the Ministry of the Interior, whose offices include bureaus in Jerusalem, Tel Aviv and Eilat. Bring a passport valid for at least six months beyond the requested extension period, a recent photo, a letter explaining why you want/need an extension (plus documentation), and evidence of sufficient funds for the extended stay. Offices in smaller towns are often easier and faster to deal with.

If you would qualify for an *oleh* (immigrant) visa under Israel's Law of Return – ie you have at least one Jewish grandparent or have converted to Judaism and have documentation demonstrating this – it's easy to extend your tourist visa for as long as you'd like, or even become an Israeli citizen.

You can be fined if you overstay your visa. Travellers who overstay by just a few days report no hassles or fines but it's best not to risk it.

Jordan

Visitors from most Western countries are eligible to receive single-entry, three-month visas for Israel at the three border crossings with Jordan.

Going the other way, Jordanian visas on arrival are only available at the Jordan River–Sheikh Hussein crossing, 30km south of the Sea of Galilee.

As of 2017, the Yitzhak Rabin–Wadi Araba crossing, a few kilometres north of Eilat and Aqaba, and the Allenby/King Hussein Bridge crossing, did not give Jordanian visas on arrival.

Contact a Jordanian embassy or consulate (abroad or in Ramat Gan, near Tel Aviv) for a visa in any of the following cases:

➜ You want to enter Jordan via Allenby/King Hussein Bridge.

➜ You need a multiple-entry visa.

➜ At-the-border visas are not available to people of your nationality.

Single/double/multiple entry visas, valid for two/three/six months from date of issue, cost a hefty JD40/60/120.

Note: if you crossed into the West Bank and/or Israel through Allenby/King Hussein Bridge *and* re-enter Jordan the same way, you do not need to apply for a new Jordanian visa, provided you return while your Jordanian visa or its extension is still valid. Remember to keep the stamped exit slip and present it on returning.

Volunteering

Israel abounds with volunteer opportunities. These are often on archaeological digs, at ILH hostels or environmental organisations. Check the websites of The National Council for Volunteering in Israel (www.ivolunteer.org.il), Israel Hostels (www.hostels-israel.com/volunteer-in-a-hostel).

If you're between 18 and 35, it's also possible to volunteer on a traditional kibbutz in Israel. Volunteers interested in a taste of the lifestyle at these communal agricultural centres can expect to spend two to six months helping with manual labour, which could include anything from gardening to washing up or milking cows. Food and accommodation are provided and sometimes

---

---

a small weekly allowance. For more information, visit www.kibbutz.org.il/eng or read about one Brit's personal experience at www.kibbutz-volunteer.com.

In the Palestinian Territories, volunteer opportunities often involve helping the many NGOs working to improve everyday life for Palestinians, such as Medical Aid for Palestinians (www.map-uk.org). Groups that welcome volunteers include the following:

Al Rowwad Centre (www.alrowwad.org)

Freedom Theatre (www.thefreedomtheatre.org)

Hope Flowers School (www.hopeflowersschool.org)

Ibdaa Cultural Centre (http://en.ibdaa1948.org)

Palestinian Circus School (www.palcircus.ps)

Tent of Nations (www.tentofnations.org)

Doing due diligence before travelling to the West Bank as a volunteer is essential as some outfits are more reputable than others.

Women Travellers

Female travellers will generally feel as safe and comfortable as they would in any Western country. On some beaches foreign women may attract unwanted attention.

When you plan your day, keep in mind local expectations regarding modest attire. While tight-fitting, revealing outfits are common in urban centres such as Tel Aviv, they are inappropriate in more conservative areas and are likely to be met with overt hostility in ultra-Orthodox Jewish neighbourhoods such as Me'a She'arim in Jerusalem. When visiting conservative areas and when visiting all religious sites – Jewish, Muslim, Christian, Druze and Baha'i – wear clothing that covers your knees and shoulders. In Muslim and Christian areas, long trousers are OK, but in some Jewish areas – and at

all Jewish holy sites – only a long skirt is acceptable.

It's a good idea to carry a shawl or scarf with you at all times. You will need this to cover your head and shoulders when visiting Muslim holy sites (mosques, tombs and Temple Mount/Al Haram Ash Sharif), and it can come in handy if your definition of modest attire doesn't align with that of the caretaker in charge of a religious site.

In buses and sheruts, a woman sitting next to an ultra-Orthodox Jewish man may make him uncomfortable. Depending on how you look at it, that's either his problem or a local sensitivity you should respect.

Work

Working legally in Israel requires a permit from the Ministry of the Interior and, as in North America or Western Europe, these aren't easy

to get – with one exception. If you would qualify for an *oleh* (immigrant) visa under the Law of Return – ie if you have at least one Jewish parent or grandparent and have documents to prove it – you can arrange a working visa with relative ease.

Because of the occupied status of the Palestinian Territories, those finding work in the West Bank need both Israeli work permits and permission from the Palestinian Authority (PA). Israel has been known to reject work permits for foreigners who plan to work for Palestinian NGOs and, as a result, some workers choose to enter the country on a tourist visa, cross into the West Bank and leave Israel every three months in order to renew their visas. There have been cases of individuals being barred entry by Israel if authorities suspect they are working without a visa.

Transport

GETTING THERE & AWAY

Israel has peace treaties with Egypt and Jordan, so it's easy to combine a visit with a trip to Petra and/or to the Red Sea coast of Sinai. Western governments advise against all travel to northern Sinai for security reasons.

Flights, cars and tours can be booked online at www. lonelyplanet.com/bookings.

Air

Israel's main gateway is **Ben Gurion International Airport** (TLV; www.iaa.gov.il), 50km northwest of Jerusalem and 18km southeast of central Tel Aviv. The airport handles about 20 million passengers a year. For up-to-the-minute details on arrivals and departures, go to the airport's English website.

Ramon International Airport (www.iaa.gov.il), situated in the Arava Valley 18km north of Eilat, is scheduled to open sometime in 2018 as Israel's second international airport. It replaces Eilat's city-centre airport (no more turboprops swooping in low over North Beach), handling the low-cost flights that previously used **Ovda** (Uvda; ☑08-367-5387; www.iaa.gov.il) airbase. Ramon International Airport will also be used by flights to Ben Gurion that have to be diverted, eg because of the threat of missiles.

Israeli airport security is very tight so international travellers should check in at least three hours before their flight – when flying both to and from Israel.

Israel's privatised flag carrier, El Al (www.elal.co.il), has direct flights to several dozen cities in Europe, as well as long-haul services to the US and Canada, South Africa, India, Thailand and China.

Known for having the tightest security in the business, El Al's aircraft – like those of other Israeli airlines – are reportedly equipped with technology to foil heat-seeking anti-aircraft missiles.

The only Middle Eastern cities with direct air links to Tel Aviv are Amman, served by Royal Jordanian (www. rj.com); Cairo, served by Air Sinai (a low-profile but astonishingly expensive subsidiary of Egyptair); and Istanbul, served by Turkish Airlines (www.turkishairlines.com).

There is no airport in the Palestinian Territories so the only way to get to the West Bank by air is to fly via either Israel or Jordan.

Land

For details on land travel to/from Jordan and Egypt, see p36.

The West Bank has a land crossing with Jordan via the Allenby Bridge, but it is an an area under full Israeli occupation and therefore effectively like crossing the border into Israel.

CLIMATE CHANGE & TRAVEL

Every form of transport that relies on carbon-based fuel generates CO_2, the main cause of human-induced climate change. Modern travel is dependent on aeroplanes, which might use less fuel per kilometre per person than most cars but travel much greater distances. The altitude at which aircraft emit gases (including CO_2) and particles also contributes to their climate change impact. Many websites offer 'carbon calculators' that allow people to estimate the carbon emissions generated by their journey and, for those who wish to do so, to offset the impact of the greenhouse gases emitted with contributions to portfolios of climate-friendly initiatives throughout the world. Lonely Planet offsets the carbon footprint of all staff and author travel.

DEPARTURE TAX

There is no departure tax when leaving Israel by air, only at land crossings with Egypt and Jordan.

Sea

Unless you have your own yacht, it is not possible to get to Israel by sea.

GETTING AROUND

Air

Daily flights to Eilat from Ben Gurion Airport's domestic terminal are handled by Arkia (www.arkia.com) and Israir (www.israirairlines.com). Arkia also flies to Haifa.

Deals are often available online, with one-way tickets sometimes going for as little as US$25 to or from Ben Gurion – the price of a bus ticket!

Bicycle

Cycling is a great way to get around Israel. The distances between cities, villages, nature reserves and archaeological sites are relatively short; many highways have wide shoulders (though drivers can politely be described as erratic, and cycling is forbidden on some major intercity routes); and there is a growing number of off-road bike trails and scenic byways. Biking is also a great way to meet people and experience the country at ground level. Best of all, it's free and environmentally friendly.

The main drawback to cycling, other than the risk of being run over, is the heat. Always set off as early in the day as possible and carry plenty of water. Choose your route carefully: while the coastal plain is flat enough,

the Upper Galilee, the Golan and the Dead Sea region have lots of steep hills, and the Negev Desert and the Jordan Valley can be mercilessly hot. One of the best one-day bike trips is around the Sea of Galilee (bikes can be hired in Tiberias).

Bicycles can be taken on intercity buses for no charge and are allowed on all trains – including those serving Ben Gurion Airport – except during rush hour (6am to 9am and 3pm to 7pm) Sunday to Thursday and on Saturday evening (there's no rush hour on Friday and the eves of Jewish holidays so all trains are bike-friendly then). Folding bikes can travel with you inside buses and can be taken on all trains.

Some bike shops will rent out bikes by the week, and may agree to buy a bike back from you at a reasonable price if you purchase it new from their shop. You'll find plenty of bike shops in Tel Aviv (eg along HaHashmona'im St), Jerusalem, Haifa and other cities; the two largest chains are Rosen & Meents (www.rosen-meents.co.il) and Matzman & Merutz (www.matzman-merutz.co.il).

Some airlines allow you to bring along your bicycle for a reasonable fee while others charge a small fortune so check before you book.

Bike paths have been going up in cities all over Israel but the most developed network is in Tel Aviv, which has a municipal bike rental program called O-Fun (http://ofun.co.il).

Palestinian roads are not designed for cycling, and it is relatively rare to see bicycles in the West Bank. But a growing number of tour groups cater to cyclists, including Bike Palestine (www.bikepalestine.com).

Bus

Buses reach every corner of Israel and every part of major cities, but if you don't read

Hebrew it can be a challenge to figure out the bus routes – just ask locals or any passing bus driver.

Almost every town, village and kibbutz in Israel has bus service at least a few times a day – except, that is, from mid-afternoon on Friday until Saturday in the late afternoon or evening, when the vast majority of intercity lines don't run at all (exceptions include services to Eilat and Majdal Shams).

Tickets are sold at bus-station ticket windows and by bus drivers; exact change is not needed. Return tickets, available on a few lines (eg to Eilat), cost 15% less than two one-way tickets.

Most discounts are available only if you have a rechargeable Rav-Kav smartcard, which comes in two versions: personalised (ishi), which has your picture on it and requires you to fill out an application; and anonymous (anonimi), which is sold at stations (5NIS) and by drivers (10NIS) and is transferable but qualifies you for only limited discounts. The good news is that both get you 20% off all fares; the bad news is that at present, you need a separate Rav-Kav account for each bus company (a single card can hold up to eight accounts).

Israel no longer has a bus duopoly (the Egged and Dan cooperatives used to divide the country between them). Rather, there are now about 20 companies, including Egged and Dan, that compete for routes in Ministry of Transport tenders. The **Public Transportation Info Center** (www.bus.co.il), a snap to use once you figure it out, provides details in English on all bus companies' routes, times and prices. Smartphone apps for Android and iPhones can be downloaded from the website. To get information via SMS (text message), send a question (in Hebrew) beginning with the word otobus to 4949.

Bus companies you're likely to run across:

Afikim (www.afikim-t.co.il)

Dan (www.dan.co.il)

Egged (www.egged.co.il)

Kavim (www.kavim-t.co.il)

Metropoline (www.metropoline.com)

Nateev Express (www.nateevexpress.com)

Nazareth Tourism & Transport (www.ntt-buses.com)

Rama (www.golanbus.co.il)

The only bus tickets that need to be (or can be) ordered in advance are Egged tickets to/from Eilat, which can be reserved up to 14 days ahead via www.egged.co.il, by smartphone app or by phone (dial 2800 or 03-694 8888). Note: the system may only accept Israeli credit cards; PayPal may also be an option.

In East Jerusalem and the West Bank, a number of small, Arab-run bus companies provide public transport. Unlike their counterparts in Israel, they operate right through the weekend.

Car & Motorcycle

To drive a vehicle, all you need is your regular driving licence; an international driving licence is not required. Israel's automobile association is known as Memsi (www.memsi.co.il).

In the West Bank, the highways that link Israeli settlements are usually modern and quick, but on other roads traffic is often held up by donkey carts, traffic jams and army checkpoints.

Car Hire

Having your own wheels lets you travel at your own pace, stay in out-of-the-way B&Bs, get lost along back roads and – if necessary – cover a lot of ground in a short amount of time. It doesn't make much sense to have a car in Jerusalem or Tel Aviv – parking can

be a huge hassle – but it's a great idea in hilly Haifa and in the Galilee, Golan and Negev, where many towns and villages are served by just a handful of buses a day.

The biggest concentration of rental agencies is along Tel Aviv's HaYarkon St (one block in from the beach), but most companies have offices around the country, including the following:

Avis (www.avis.co.il)

Budget (www.budget.co.il)

Cal Auto (www.calauto.co.il)

Eldan (www.eldan.co.il) The only company with an office in Kiryal Shmona.

Green Peace (www.greenpeace.co.il) Based in East Jerusalem; pick-up possible at Allenby Bridge.

Hertz (www.hertz.co.il) The only company with a Dead Sea office.

Car hire with insurance and unlimited kilometres costs as little as 140NIS per day, US$200 per week or US$600 per month (the incredibly cheap prices advertised online don't include insurance). Israelis, unlike tourists, have to pay VAT/sales tax (18%). Significant discounts are available online, eg through the sort of websites that sell aeroplane tickets. Remember that

gasoline/petrol costs about US$2 per litre/US$7.60 per US gallon.

There's a surcharge for airport pick-up. If you get parking or traffic tickets, the rental company may forward them to you, including a handling fee of 60NIS. Some companies require that renters be at least 25 years old.

Read the fine print on your insurance contract carefully, especially regarding the excess (deductible), which can be US$400 or more – though for an additional fee (eg US$18) you can reduce that to zero. Some credit cards give cardholders free CDW (collision damage waver) coverage, but you may still have to purchase liability (third party) insurance – check with your card issuer. Even insurance policies sold by rental companies don't usually cover damage to the car's undercarriage or tyres.

Note that rental agencies generally forbid you to take their cars into parts of the West Bank defined in the Oslo Accords as Areas A and B – Dallah (www.dallahrentacar.com) and Goodluck (www.goodluckcars.com) are notable exceptions. It's no problem, though, driving on Rte 1 from Jerusalem to the Dead Sea or Rte 90 from the Dead Sea to the Sea of Galilee.

DRIVING ON SHABBAT

According to most interpretations of Halacha (Jewish law), driving a motor vehicle violates the sanctity of Shabbat (the Sabbath), in part by contravening prohibitions against lighting fire and travelling more than 2000 cubits. As a result, certain streets, neighbourhoods and villages populated almost exclusively by Orthodox and ultra-Orthodox Jews are closed to traffic from sundown on Friday until an hour after sundown on Saturday, as well as on many Jewish holidays. If you come upon a street blocked by a barrier, don't drive around it or you may find yourself facing angry locals or even having stones thrown at you.

By tradition (though not law), no one in Jewish areas – except for emergency services – drives a motor vehicle on Yom Kippur.

In Tel Aviv and its inner suburbs, Car2Go (www.car2go.co.il) hires out cars by the hour, charging 140NIS for an annual membership plus 20NIS per hour (180NIS per day) and 2NIS per kilometre (1NIS per kilometre after the first 50km).

Road Conditions

Most roads are in pretty good shape, but the newer ones, built to the latest safety standards, are safest. A visible minority of Israeli drivers are aggressive and/or unpredictable so drive carefully – and defensively – at all times.

North–south highways are designated using even numbers, while east–west routes have odd numbers; in general, numbers rise as you go south-to-north and west-to-east. Thus, Rte 2 runs along the Mediterranean coast while Rte 90 hugs the country's eastern border with Jordan; Israel's northernmost road, almost on the Lebanese border, is Rte 99. Rte 1, an exception to this sequencing, links Tel Aviv with Jerusalem and the Dead Sea.

Israel has three toll roads:

Rte 6 (Kvish Shesh; www.kvish6.co.il) Runs up the centre of the country for 140km. Bills for tolls – up to 33NIS – are sent to car owners on the basis of a national database of licence plate numbers. Some rental agencies charge a premium for paying these tolls, some up to 60NIS. The only way to avoid this is by paying the charge yourself via the website.

Carmel Tunnels (www.carmel tunnels.co.il; one/two sections 7.50/14.90NIS) Runs under Mt Carmel south of Haifa. Payment can be made in cash or by credit card.

Fast Lane (Nativ Mahir; www.fastlane.co.il) A 13km express lane from Ben Gurion Airport to Tel Aviv. Tariffs vary based on traffic conditions – the worse it is, the more you pay.

Road Rules

Vehicles drive on the right-hand side of the road; seat belts are required at all times. Unless you have a hands-free set, using a mobile phone while driving is illegal and subject to a fine of 1000NIS.

Road signs are marked in English, Hebrew and (usually) Arabic; be prepared for some quirky transliterations. The best road maps are produced by Mapa (www.mapa.co.il/maps) and are available at all bookshops.

From November to March, car headlights must be turned on whenever you're driving on an intercity road.

Police cars always have their blue (sometimes red and blue) lights flashing, so seeing police lights in your rear-view mirror doesn't mean you're in trouble (if you are, they'll make that clear with a megaphone).

Hitching

Although hitching was once a common way of getting around, recent reports of violent crime, including kidnapping, make this a risky business and we do not recommend it. The local method of soliciting a lift is simply to point an index finger at the road. Hitching is most common in the Upper Galilee and Golan regions.

Sherut

Sheruts (sheh-*roots*), known in the Palestinian Territories as a servees (sehr-*vees*), are a useful way to get around. These vehicles, often 13-seat minivans, operate on a fixed route for a fixed price. They're like a bus except that they don't have pre-set stops. If you don't know the fare, ask your fellow passengers.

Sheruts (Hebrew plural: *moni'ot sherut* – the word *sherutim* means 'bathrooms'!) are generally quicker than buses. They begin their runs from a recognised taxi rank and leave only when they're full so you may have to hang around for a while, though rarely more than 20 minutes. You can get out anywhere you like but will probably have to pay the full fare to the final destination. Many sheruts operate 24/7 and are the only means of public transport in Israel on Shabbat and Jewish holidays, eg between Tel Aviv and Jerusalem. Prices are the same or slightly lower than buses except on Shabbat, when they rise slightly.

Local Transport

Taxi

Taking a 'special' (*speshel*; ie nonshared) taxi can be very convenient but, at times, a bit of a hassle because some unscrupulous drivers overcharge tourists. The best way to avoid getting ripped off is to sound like a confident old hand as you give the street address, including a cross street. It's almost always to your advantage to use the meter (by law the driver has to put it on if you ask); make sure it is reset to the flag-fall price after you get in.

In Israel, flag-fall is 12.30NIS (10.50NIS in Eilat). Tariff 2 (25% more expensive than Tariff 1) applies between 9pm and 5.30am and on Shabbat and Jewish holidays. Wait time costs 94NIS per hour. Legitimate surcharges include the following:

➡ Pick-up at Ben Gurion Airport – 5NIS

➡ Piece of full-size luggage – 4.40NIS

➡ Third and fourth passengers – 4.90NIS each

➡ Phone order – 5.20NIS

Many Israelis now use the mobile phone app GetTaxi (www.gettaxi.co.il), available in Android and iPhone versions, to order and pay for taxis in all parts of Israel (except Eilat). Uber launched in Israel in 2014.

Taxi drivers do not expect tips, but in the absence of a rip-off attempt, it's fine to leave a shekel or two in change.

Tours

Tours are great if you're short on time (eg you want to make a quick trip to Petra) or if you have a special interest.

Society for the Protection of Nature in Israel (http://natureisrael.org) Runs highly regarded nature hikes (eg to see spring wildflowers) suitable for the whole family; they are mainly for Israelis so tour guides speak Hebrew – but SPNI outings are a good way to meet locals. Only the Hebrew website lists trips.

Abraham Hostel (www.abrahamtours.com) Runs excellent day tours of Jerusalem, the West Bank (including Bethlehem, Nablus and a 'dual-narrative tour' of Hebron), the Dead Sea, Masada, Haifa, the Galilee and the Golan. Also goes to Petra.

Bein Harim Tours (www.beinharimtours.com) Custom tours and trips to Petra, Jordan.

Touring Israel (www.touringisrael.com) Tailor-made, top-end trips.

United Tours (www.unitedtours.co.il) Large operator with one- and two-day trips all over the country.

A variety of companies offer tours (p265) of the West Bank.

Train

Israel Railways (www.rail.co.il) runs a comfortable and convenient network of passenger rail services; details on departure times are also available from the Public Transportation Info Center (www.bus.co.il). Trains do not run from mid-afternoon Friday until after sundown on Saturday. Return tickets are 10% cheaper than two one-way tickets; children aged five to 10 get a 20% discount. Unlike buses, Israel's rail system is wheelchair accessible.

Israel Railway's oldest line, inaugurated in 1892 and famously scenic, links three Tel Aviv stations with southern Jerusalem (23.50NIS, 1½ hours). The system's heavily used main line runs along the coast at least twice an hour, affording fine views of the Mediterranean as it links Tel Aviv with the following locations:

Akko (41.50NIS, 1½ hours)

Haifa (32NIS, one hour)

Nahariya (46.50NIS, 1½ hours)

Other useful services from Tel Aviv:

Be'er Sheva (31.50NIS, 1½ hours, hourly)

Ben Gurion Airport (16NIS, 18 minutes, at least hourly 24 hours a day except Shabbat)

A new train line is scheduled to open in April 2018 that will shorten the travel time between Tel Aviv and Jerusalem to just 28 minutes, thanks to a US$2 billion high-speed rail line that will also serve Ben Gurion Airport. A rail line linking Haifa with Beit She'an opened in 2016.

The West Bank has not had rail services since 1940s.

Health

While it's never nice to be injured or become sick while you're travelling, you can at least take some comfort in the knowledge that Israel has world-class medical facilities.

While standards of health are high in Israel, there are several location-specific conditions for travellers to be aware of, particularly dehydration, heat exhaustion and sunburn.

BEFORE YOU GO

Recommended Vaccinations

Israel does not require any vaccinations before arrival.

Health Insurance

Health insurance policies may not cover visits to the border regions with Gaza and Lebanon (although the Golan Heights is usually included).

Be aware that health insurance for Israel will generally not cover the Palestinian Territories, but some providers will offer cover for both.

Websites

It's usually a good idea to consult a government travel health website before departure.

Australia (www.smartraveller.gov.au)

Canada (www.hc-sc.gc.ca/hl-vs/travel-voyage/index-eng.php)

UK (www.doh.gov.uk)

USA (wwwnc.cdc.gov/travel) Search for the booklet *Health Information for International Travel* ('Yellow Book').

World Health Organization (www.who.int/ith/en) You can download the book *International Travel & Health*.

MD Travel Health (www.mdtravelhealth.com) Provides country-by-country travel health recommendations.

IN ISRAEL & THE PALESTINIAN TERRITORIES

Availability & Cost of Health Care

Israel has first-rate state-funded hospitals across the country, plus a number of private hospitals and clinics. For a list of hospitals, see www.science.co.il/hospitals.asp.

Pharmacies *(beit merkachat)* are a common sight on city streets; pharmacists speak English and can give advice about what medicine to take if you describe your problem. In cities, at least one pharmacy is always on call *(beit merkachat toran)* – phone 106 (the local municipal hotline) for details, or check out the links

at www.onlineisrael.info/search-internet/health/city (in Hebrew). Some branches of Super Pharm are open 24 hours. In the Palestinian Territories, medicine may be expired so check the date.

If you require any pre-scribed medication, take enough from home to get you through your trip and bring a copy of the prescription details in case you need a refill. Note: Israeli pharmacies can accept only prescriptions issued by Israeli doctors.

Private dental clinics are found everywhere from suburban streets to shopping malls. Standards of dental care are high, but keep in mind that your travel insurance will not usually cover you for anything other than emergency dental treatment.

Medical services available in the Palestinian Territories are not quite as advanced as in Israel, but you can rest assured that in an emergency a hospital in Israel is never too far away. Palestinian hospitals are by no means as bad as in some parts of the Arab world, but as a foreigner you will need to pay upfront, in cash, and claim any costs back on insurance.

Infectious Diseases

Leishmaniasis

Spread through the bite of an infected sandfly, leishmaniasis – endemic to this region – can cause a slowly growing skin lump or ulcer. It may develop into a serious life-threatening fever, usually accompanied by anaemia and weight loss. Infected dogs and animals such as rock rabbits (hyraxes or dassies) are also carriers of the infection. Sandfly bites should be avoided whenever possible.

Middle East Respiratory Syndrome

Since 2012, cases of MERS (Middle East Respiratory Syndrome) have been confirmed in the Arabian Peninsula, Jordan and Lebanon but not here at this stage. Symptoms of MERS include fever, coughing and shortness of breath; the illness is spread through close contact, meaning most people are not at risk. Almost one-third of those with confirmed cases of MERS have died, though most of those people had an underlying medical condition. For more details, see www.cdc.gov/coronavirus/mers.

Rabies

Rabies is rare but present so avoid contact with stray dogs and wild animals such as foxes.

Spread through bites or licks on broken skin from an infected animal, rabies is fatal. Animal handlers should be vaccinated, as should those travelling to remote areas where a reliable source of post-bite vaccine is not available within 24 hours. Three injections are needed over a month. If you have not been vaccinated, you will need a course of five injections starting within 24 hours or as soon as possible after the injury.

Vaccination does not provide you with immunity; it merely buys you more time to seek appropriate medical help.

Traveller's Diarrhoea

Traveller's diarrhoea can occur with a simple change of diet, so even though food and water are generally healthy you may get an upset stomach simply because your body is not accustomed to the new foods – it may take a few days to adjust. Keep in mind that in summer outdoor food spoils quickly, so this is a good time to avoid hole-in-the-wall shawarma and falafel joints because hummus goes bad quickly. (Eating hummus in an indoor restaurant is likely to be safer.)

If you develop diarrhoea, be sure to drink plenty of fluids, preferably an oral rehydration solution containing salt and sugar. A few loose stools don't require treatment, but if you start having more than four or five stools a day you should start taking an antibiotic (usually a quinolone drug) and an antidiarrhoeal agent (such as loperamide). If diarrhoea is bloody, persists for more than 72 hours, or is accompanied by fever, shaking chills or severe abdominal pain, you should seek medical attention.

Environmental Hazards

Heat Illness

Heat exhaustion is one of the most common ailments among travellers. This occurs following heavy sweating and excessive fluid loss with inadequate replacement of fluids and salt. It is particularly common in hot climates when taking unaccustomed exercise before full acclimatisation. Symptoms include headache, dizziness and tiredness. Dehydration is already happening by the time you feel thirsty – aim to drink enough water that you produce pale, diluted urine. The treatment for heat exhaustion consists of replacing fluid with water or fruit juice or both, and cooling by cold water and fans. The

---

IF YOU REQUIRE MEDICAL CARE

For emergency first aid or evacuation by ambulance to a hospital in Israel, call the country's national emergency medical service, Magen David Adom, on any phone by dialling 101. Magen David Adom stations also provide after-hours first aid.

For less urgent matters, you can do one of the following:

➜ Ask at your hotel for a nearby physician's office.

➜ Check the list of doctors on the website of the US Embassy (http://israel.usembassy.gov/consular/acs/doctors.html).

➜ In the Jerusalem area, contact Terem Emergency Medical Centers (www.terem.com) or the Family Medical Center – Wolfson (http://fmcwolfson.com).

➜ In Tel Aviv, contact **Tel Aviv Doctor** (Map p122; ☎054-941-4243, toll-free 1-800-201-999; www.telaviv-doctor.com; 46 Basel St, near Basel Sq).

If you become seriously ill, you may want to contact your embassy or consulate.

BOOKS ON TRAVEL HEALTH

Recommended references include *Traveller's Health,* edited by Dr Richard Dawood (Oxford University Press), and *The Travellers' Good Health Guide,* by Ted Lankester (Sheldon Press), an especially useful guide for volunteers and long-term expatriates working in the Middle East.

treatment of the salt-loss component consists of salty fluids as in soup or broth, and adding a little more table salt to foods than usual.

Heat stroke is much more serious. This occurs when the body's heat-regulating mechanism breaks down. An excessive rise in body temperature leads to the cessation of sweating, to irrational and hyperactive behaviour, and eventually to loss of consciousness and death. Rapid cooling by spraying the body with water and fanning is an ideal treatment. Emergency fluid and electrolyte replacement by intravenous drip is usually also required.

Insect Bites & Stings

Mosquitoes may not carry malaria but can cause irritation and infected bites. Using DEET-based insect repellents will prevent bites. Mosquitoes also spread dengue fever.

Bees and wasps cause real problems only to those with a severe allergy (anaphylaxis). If you have a severe allergy to bee or wasp stings you should carry an adrenaline injection or similar.

Sandflies are located around the Mediterranean beaches. They usually cause only a nasty itchy bite, but can carry a rare skin disorder called cutaneous leishmaniasis. Bites may be prevented by using DEET-based repellents.

The number of jellyfish has been increasing over the years, thanks to overfishing in the Mediterranean (fish eat jellyfish, and in the absence of predators the jellyfish have boomed). A jellyfish sting is irritating, but in most cases it wears off in about 10 or 15 minutes. A particularly strong sting (or a sting to the face or genitals) requires an evaluation by a physician.

Scorpions are frequently found in arid or dry climates. They can cause a painful bite that is rarely life threatening.

Bedbugs are occasionally found in hostels and cheap hotels. They lead to very itchy, lumpy bites. Spraying the mattress with an appropriate insect killer will do a good job of getting rid of them.

Scabies are also sometimes found in cheap accommodation. These tiny mites live in the skin, particularly between the fingers. They cause an intensely itchy rash. Scabies are easily treated with lotion available from

pharmacies; people who you come into contact with also need treating as they may become asymptomatic carriers.

Snake Bites

The vast majority of the snakes are not poisonous – but some, such as the Palestine viper (*tzefa*; *Vipera palaestinae*), are. Do not walk barefoot or stick your hand into holes or cracks.

If bitten by a snake, do not panic. Half the number of people bitten by venomous snakes are not actually injected with poison (envenomed). Immobilise the bitten limb with a splint (eg a stick) and apply a bandage over the site with firm pressure, similar to a bandage over a sprain. Do not apply a tourniquet, or cut or suck the bite. Get the victim to medical help as soon as possible so that antivenene can be given if necessary.

Water

Tap water in Israel is safe to drink but sometimes has an unpleasant taste (in some areas it is slightly saline) so many locals use filters or spring-water dispensers at home. Bottled water is available everywhere. Do not drink water from rivers or lakes as it may contain bacteria or viruses that can cause diarrhoea or vomiting.

In the West Bank, most locals drink bottled water, which is cheap and sold everywhere.

Language

HEBREW

Hebrew is the national language of Israel, with seven to eight million speakers worldwide. It's written from right to left in its own alphabet.

Read our coloured pronunciation guides as if they were English and you'll be understood. Most sounds have equivalents in English. Note that a is pronounced as 'ah', ai as in 'aisle', e as in 'bet', i as the 'ea' in 'heat', o as 'oh' and u as the 'oo' in 'boot'. Both kh (like the 'ch' in the Scottish *loch*) and r (similar to the French 'r') are guttural sounds, pronounced at the back of the throat. The apostrophe (') indicates the glottal stop (like the pause in the middle of 'uh-oh'). The stressed syllables are indicated with italics.

Basics

Hello.	שלום.	sha·*lom*
Goodbye.	להתראות.	le·hit·ra·*ot*
Yes.	כן.	ken
No.	לא.	lo
Please.	בבקשה.	be·va·ka·*sha*
Thank you.	תודה.	to·*da*
Excuse me./ Sorry.	סליחה.	sli·*kha*

WANT MORE?

For in-depth language information and handy phrases, check out Lonely Planet's *Middle East Phrasebook*. You'll find it at **shop.lonelyplanet.com**, or you can buy Lonely Planet's iPhone phrasebooks at the Apple App Store.

How are you?

מה נשמע?   ma nish·*ma*

Fine, thanks. And you?

טוב, תודה.   tov to·*da*

ואתה/את?   ve·a·*ta*/ve·at (m/f)

What's your name?

איך קוראים לך?   ekh kor·*im* le·*kha*/lakh (m/f)

My name is ...

שמי ...   shmi ...

Do you speak English?

אתה מדבר אנגלית?   a·*ta* me·da·*ber* ang·*lit* (m)

את מדברת אנגלית?   at me·da·*be*·ret ang·*lit* (f)

I don't understand.

אני לא מבין/מבינה.   a·*ni* lo me·*vin*/me·vi·*na* (m/f)

Accommodation

Where's a ...?	?... איפה	e·fo ...
campsite	אתר הקמפינג	a·*tar* ha·*kemp*·ing
guesthouse	ריח ההרחה	bet ha·'a·ra·*kha*
hotel	בית המלון	bet ma·*lon*
youth hostel	נוער אכסניית	akh·sa·ni·*yat* no·ar
Do you have a ... room?	יש לך ?... חדר	yesh le·*kha*/lakh khe·der ... (m/f)
single	ליחיד	le·ya·*khid*
double	זוגי	zu·*gi*

How much is it per ...?	כמה זה ?... עולה ל	ka·ma ze o·le le ...
night	לילה	*lai*·la
person	אדם	a·*dam*

NUMBERS

1	אחת	a·khat
2	שתיים	shta·yim
3	שלוש	sha·losh
4	ארבע	ar·ba
5	חמש	kha·mesh
6	שש	shesh
7	שבע	she·va
8	שמונה	shmo·ne
9	תשע	te·sha
10	עשר	e·ser
100	מאה	me·a
1000	אלף	e·lef

Note that English numerals are used in modern Hebrew text.

Eating & Drinking

Can you recommend a ...?	אתה יכול להמליץ על ...?	a·ta ya·khol le·ham·lits al ... (m)
	את יכולה להמליץ על ...?	at ye·cho·la le·ham·lits al ... (f)
cafe	בית קפה	bet ka·fe
restaurant	מסעדה	mis·a·da

What would you recommend?
מה אתה ממליץ? ma a·ta mam·lits (m)
מה את ממליצה? ma at mam·li·tsa (f)

What's the local speciality?
מה המאכל המקומי? ma ha·ma·'a·khal ha·me·ko·mi

Do you have vegetarian food?
יש לכם אוכל yesh la·khem o·khel
צמחוני? tsim·kho·ni

I'd like the ..., please.	אני צריך/ צריכה את ..., בבקשה.	a·ni tsa·rikh/ tsri·kha et ... be·va·ka·sha (m/f)
bill	החשבון	ha·khesh·bon
menu	התפריט	ha·taf·rit

Emergencies

Help!	הצילו!	ha·tsi·lu
Go away!	לך מפה!	lekh mi·po

Call ...!	תקשר ל ...!	tit·ka·sher le ...
a doctor	רופא	ro·fe/ro·fa (m/f)
the police	משטרה	mish·ta·ra

I'm lost.
אני אבוד. a·ni a·vud (m)
אני אבודה. a·ni a·vu·da (f)

Where are the toilets?
איפה השירותים? e·fo ha·she·ru·tim

I'm sick.
אני חולה. a·ni kho·le/kho·la (m/f)

Shopping & Services

I'm looking for ...
אני מחפש ... a·ni me·kha·pes ... (m)
אני מחפשת ... a·ni me·kha·pe·set ... (f)

Can I look at it?
אפשר להסתכל ef·shar le·his·ta·kel
על זה? al ze

Do you have any others?
יש לך אחרים? yesh le·kha/lakh a·khe·rim (m/f)

How much is it?
כמה זה עולה? ka·ma ze o·le

That's too expensive.
זה יקר מדי. ze ya·kar mi·dai

There's a mistake in the bill.
יש טעות בחשבון. yesh ta·ut ba·khesh·bon

Where's an ATM?
איפה יש כספומט? e·fo yesh kas·po·mat

Transport & Directions

Is this the ... to (Haifa)?	האם זה/ זאת ה ... ל(חיפה)?	ha·im ze/ zot ha ... le·(khai·fa) (m/f)
boat	אונייה	o·ni·ya (f)
bus	אוטובוס	o·to·bus (m)
plane	מטוס	ma·tos (m)
train	רכבת	ra·ke·vet (f)

What time's the ... bus?	באיזו שעה האוטובוס ה ...?	be·e·zo sha·a ha·o·to·bus ha ...
first	ראשון	ri·shon
last	אחרון	a·kha·ron

SIGNS – HEBREW

Entrance	כניסה
Exit	יציאה
Open	פתוח
Closed	סגור
Information	מודיעין
Prohibited	אסור
Toilets	שירותים
Men	גברים
Women	נשים

One ... ticket, please.	כרטיס	kar·tis
	אחד ...	e·khad ...
	בבקשה.	be·va·ka·sha
one way	לכיוון אחד	le·ki·vun e·khad
return	הלוך ושוב	ha·lokh va·shov

How much is it to ...?

| | כמה זה ל ...? | ka·ma ze le ... |

Please take me to (this address).

	תיקח/תיקחי אותי	ti·kakh/tik·khi o·ti
	(לכתובת הזאת)	(lak·to·vet ha·zot)
	בבקשה.	be·va·ka·sha (m/f)

Where's the (market)?

| | איפה ה (שוק)? | e·fo ha (shuk) |

Can you show me (on the map)?

	אתה/את	a·ta/at
	יכול/יכולה להראות	ya·khol/ye·kho·la le·har·ot
	לי (על המפה)?	li (al ha·ma·pa) (m/f)

What's the address?

| | מה הכתובת? | ma hak·to·vet |

ARABIC

The type of Arabic spoken in the Palestinian Territories (and provided in this section) is known as Levantine Arabic. Note that there are significant differences between this colloquial language and the MSA (Modern Standard Arabic), which is the official written language in the Arab world, used in schools, administration and the media. Arabic is written from right to left in Arabic script.

In our pronunciation guides a is pronounced as in 'act', aa as the 'a' in 'father', ae as the 'ai' in 'air', aw as in 'law', ay as in 'say', e as in 'bet', ee as in 'see', i as in 'hit', oo as in 'zoo', u as in 'pul', gh is a guttural sound (like the Parisian French 'r'), r is trilled, dh is pronounced as the 'th' in 'that', th as in 'thin' and kh as the 'ch' in the Scottish *loch*. The apostrophe (') indicates the glottal stop (like the pause in the middle of 'uh-oh').

Basics

Hello.	مرحبا.	mar·ha·ba
Goodbye.	خاطرك.	khaa·trak (m)
	خاطرك.	khaa·trik (f)
Yes.	ايه.	'eeh
No.	لا.	laa
Please.	اذا بتريد.	'i·za bit·reed (m)
	اذا بتريدي.	'i·za bit·ree·dee (f)
Thank you.	شكراً.	shuk·ran
Excuse me.	عفواً.	'af·wan
Sorry.	آسف.	'aa·sif (m)
	آسفة.	'aas·fe (f)

How are you?

| | كيفك؟/كيفك؟ | ki·fak/ki·fik (m/f) |

NUMBERS

1	١	واحد	waa·hed
2	٢	اثنين	'it·nayn
3	٣	ثلاثة	ta·laa·te
4	٤	اربع	'ar·ba'
5	٥	خمسة	kham·se
6	٦	ستة	sit·te
7	٧	سبعة	sab·'a
8	٨	ثمانية	ta·maa·ne
9	٩	تسعة	tis·'a
10	١٠	عشرة	'ash·ra
100	١٠٠	مءة	mi·'o
1000	١٠٠٠	الف	'elf

Note that Arabic numerals, unlike letters, are written from left to right.

Fine, thanks. And you?

| | منيح./منيحة. | mneeh/mnee·ha (m/f) |
| | وأنت/أنتي؟ | oo 'ent/'en·tee (m/f) |

What's your name?

| | شو اسمك؟ | shoo 'es·mak (m) |
| | شو اسمك؟ | shoo 'es·mik (f) |

My name is ...

| | اسمي ... | 'es·mee ... |

Do you speak English?

| | بتحكي انكليزي؟ | btah·kee ing·lee·zee |

I don't understand.

| | ما فهمت. | maa fa·he·met |

Accommodation

Where's a ...?	وين ...؟	wen ...
campsite	مخيم	mu·khay·yam
guesthouse	بيت الضيوف	bayt ld·du·yoof
hotel	فندق	fun·du'
youth hostel	فندق شباب	fun·du' sha·baab

Do you have a ... room?	في عندكن غرفة ...؟	fee 'ind·kun ghur·fe ...
single	بتخت منفرد	bi·takht mun·fa·rid
double	بتخت مزدوج	bi·takht muz·daw·wej

How much is it per ...?	قديش هقه...؟	'ad·deesh li·...
night	ليلة	lay·le
person	شخص	shakhs

SIGNS – ARABIC

Entrance	مدخل
Exit	مخرج
Open	مفتوح
Closed	مغلق
Information	معلومات
Prohibited	ممنوع
Toilets	دورات المياه
Men	الرجال
Women	النساء

Eating & Drinking

Can you recommend a ...? بتوصي بـ...؟ bit·waa·see bi·...

cafe مقهى ma'·ha
restaurant مطعم mat·am

What would you recommend? بشو بتوصي؟ bi·shoo btoo·see

What's the local speciality? شو الوجبة الخاصة؟ shoo il·waj·be il·khaa·se

Do you have vegetarian food? في عندكن طعام نباتي؟ fee 'ind·kun ta·'aam na·baa·tee

I'd like the ..., please. بدي ....، لو سمحت. bid·dee ... law sa·maht
bill الحساب il·hi·saab
menu قائمة الطعام 'ae·'i·met it·ta·'aam

Emergencies

Help! ساعدني! saa·'id·nee (m) / ساعديني! saa·'i·dee·nee (f)

Go away! (to a man/woman) روح!/ rooh/ روحي! roo·hee

Call ...! اتصل بـ...! 'it·ta·sil bi·...
a doctor دكتور duk·toor
the police الشرطة ish·shur·ta

I'm lost. أنا ضائع. 'a·na daa·'i' (m) / أنا ضائعة. 'a·na daa·'i·'e (f)

Where are the toilets? وين الحمامات؟ wen il·ham·maa·maat

I'm sick. أنا مريض. 'a·na ma·reed (m) / أنا مريضة. 'a·na ma·ree·de (f)

Shopping & Services

I'm looking for ... بدور عن ... bi·daw·wer 'an ...

Can I look at it? ورجني ياه؟ war·ji·nee yaah (m) / ورجيني ياه؟ war·jee·nee yaah (f)

Do you have any others? في عندكن غيره؟ fee 'ind·kun ghay·ru

How much is it? قديش هقه؟ 'ad·deesh ha'·'u

That's too expensive. هيدا غالي اكتير. ha·da ghaa·lee 'ik·teer

There's a mistake in the bill. في خطأ بالحساب. fee kha·ta' bil·hi·saab

Where's an ATM? وين جهاز الصرافة؟ wen je·haez is·sa·raa·fe

Transport & Directions

Is this the ... to (Petra)? هدا الـ ... لـ(بيترا)؟ ha·da il·... la·(bee·tra)?
boat سفينة sfee·ne
bus باص baas
plane طائرة taa·'i·re
train قطار 'i·taar

What time's the ... bus? أمتى الباص الـ...؟ 'em·ta il·baas il·...
first اول 'aw·wel
last اخر 'aa·khir

One ... ticket, please. تذكرة ... اذا بتريد taz·ki·re ... 'i·za bit·reed
one way ذهاب za·haab
return ذهاب واياب za·haab oo 'ee·yaab

How much is it to ...? قديش الاجرة لـ...؟ 'ad·deesh il·'uj·re la ...

Please take me to (this address). اوصلني عند (هيدا العنوان). 'oo·sal·nee 'ind (ha·da il·'un·waan)

Where's the (market)? وين الـ (سوق)؟ wen il·(soo')

Can you show me (on the map)? بتورجني (عالخريطة)؟ btwar·ji·nee ('al·kha·ree·te)

What's the address? شو العنوان؟ shoo il·'un·waan

GLOSSARY

The language origin of non-English terms is noted in brackets: Hebrew (H) and Arabic (A). Singular and plural is noted as (s) and (pl) while masculine and feminine terms are noted as (mas) and (fem).

ablaq (A) – in architecture, alternating bands of light and dark stone

abu (A) – father (of), often used as part of a name; see also *umm*

agorot (H) – smallest unit of the shekel; 1 shekel = 100 agorot

ain (A) – water spring or source; also *ein*

al (A) – the definite article, 'the'; also spelled 'el-' or with the L replaced by the letter that follows it, eg ash-sharif

aliya (H) – immigration to Israel (literally 'going up')

b'seder (H) – OK

bab (A) – door, gate

bakashot (H) – a cycle of petitionary prayers sung in synagogues that follow some Sephardic rites (eg those from Aleppo, Syria) in the early hours of Shabbat during the winter months

be'er (H) – well

beit knesset (H) – synagogue

beit merkachat (H) – pharmacy

beit/beth (H) – house

bimah (H) – central platform in a synagogue

bir (A) – well

burj (A) – fortress or tower

caravanserai (A) – see *khan*

daf (A) – tambourine

derekh (H) – street or road

ein (H) – spring

Eretz Yisra'el (H) – the Land of Israel

Eretz Yisra'el HaShlema (H) – the Greater Land of Israel, a term once used by the Jewish settler movement to refer to the territory that they believe God promised the People of

Israel (includes the West Bank and the Golan Heights and, for some, Gaza)

gadol (H) – big

gan (H) – garden or park

Haganah (H) – literally 'defence'; the Jewish underground army during the British Mandate; the forerunner of the modern day Israel Defense Forces (IDF)

hajj (A) – annual Muslim pilgrimage to Mecca

Hamas (A) – Harakat al-Muqaama al-Islamiya; militant Islamic organisation that aims to create an Islamic state in the pre-1948 territory of Palestine

hammam (A) – public bathhouse

har (H) – mountain

haraam (A) – literally 'forbidden'; holy sanctuary

Hared/Harediya/Haredim/ Harediyot (H, mas s/fem s/ mas pl/fem pl) – an ultra-Orthodox Jew, a member of either a Hasidic group or one of the groups opposed to Hasidism, known as Litvaks ('Lithuanians') or 'Misnagdim' ('opponents')

Hasid/Hasidim (H, mas s/ mas pl) – member of an ultra-Orthodox group with mystical tendencies founded in Poland in the 18th century by the Ba'al Shem Tov

hazzanut (H) – Jewish liturgical singing

Hebrew Bible – the Old Testament

Hezbollah (A) – Iranian-backed Shiite political party and militia active in Lebanon

hof (H) – beach

hurva (H) – ruin

IDF – Israel Defense Forces; the national army

iftar (A) – the daily, dusk breaking-of-the-fast feast during Ramadan

intifada (A) – literally 'shaking off'; term Palestinians use to describe an uprising against Israel; the First Intifada lasted

from 1987 to 1990. The Second Intifada lasted from 2001 to 2005

Islam (A) – literally 'voluntary surrender to the will of God (Allah)'; the religion of the vast majority of Palestinian people

israa' (A) – the 'Night Journey' of the Prophet Mohammed from Mecca to Jerusalem

juhhal (A) – literally 'the ignorant'; members of the Druze community who are not *uqqal*

kafr (A) – village

kashrut (H) – religious dietary laws, ie the rules of keeping *kosher*

katan (H) – small

keffiyeh (A) – the black-and-white chequered Palestinian Arab headscarf

ketuba (H) – Jewish wedding contract

kfar – village

khan (A) – also called a *caravanserai*, a travellers' inn usually constructed on main trade routes, with accommodation on the 1st floor and stables and storage on the ground floor around a central courtyard

khirbet (A) – ruins (of)

kibbutz/kibbutzim (H, s/pl) – a communal settlement run cooperatively by its members; kibbutzim, once based solely on farming, are now involved in a wide range of industries; see also *moshav*

kibbutznik (H) – member of a *kibbutz*

kikar (H) – square; roundabout

kippa/kippot (H, s/pl) – skullcap worn by observant Jewish men (and among reform and conservative Jews, sometimes by women); known in Yiddish as a *yarmulke*

Klezmer (H) – traditional music of Eastern European Jews, often described as traditional Jewish soul music

Knesset (H) – Israeli Parliament

Koran (A) – see *Quran*

kosher (H) – food prepared according to Jewish dietary law; see also *kashrut*

ma'ayan (H) – spring, pool

madrassa (A) – theological school, especially one associated with a mosque

majdal (A) – tower

makhtesh (H) – erosion cirque

matkot (H) – Israeli beach tennis

menorah (H) – a seven-branched candelabrum that adorned the ancient Temple in Jerusalem and has been a Jewish symbol ever since; it is now the official symbol of the State of Israel

mi'raj (A) – the Prophet Mohammed's ascent from Jerusalem to Heaven

midrahov (H) – pedestrian mall

mihrab (A) – prayer niche in a mosque, indicating the direction of Mecca

mikveh (H) – Jewish ritual immersion bath

minaret (A) – the tower of a mosque; from which the call to prayer is traditionally sung

mitzvah (H) – a commandment or obligation; a good deed

Mizrahi/Mizrahim (H, s/pl) – a Jew from one of the Middle East Jewish communities, eg from one of the Islamic countries such as Morocco, Yemen or Iraq; this term is often used interchangeably with Sephardi, though technically only the descendants of Jews expelled from Spain are Sephardim

moshav/moshavim (H, s/pl) – cooperative settlement, with a mix of private and collective housing and economic activity; see also *kibbutz*

moshavnik (H) – a member of a *moshav*

muqarna (A) – corbel; architectural decorative devices resembling stalactites

nahal (H) – river

Naqba (A) – literally the 'Catastrophe'; this is what the Palestinians call the 1948 Arab–Israeli War

nargileh (A) – water pipe; see also *shisha*

ney (A) – flute

oleh/olah/olim/olot (H, s mas/s fem/pl mas/pl fem) – immigrant

PA – Palestinian Authority

PFLP – Popular Front for the Liberation of Palestine

PLO – Palestine Liberation Organisation

PNC – Palestinian National Council, ruling body of the PLO

Quran (A) – the holy book of Islam

ras (A) – headland

refusenik (H) – originally a Jew in the Soviet Union who was denied permission to emigrate to Israel; sometimes used today to refer to Israelis who refuse to serve in the IDF in the West Bank

rehov (H) – street

ribat (A, H) – pilgrim hostel or hospice

sabil (A) – public drinking fountain

sabra (H) – literally 'prickly pear'; native-born Israeli

servees (A) – term used for small bus or service taxi in the Palestinian Territories, see also *sherut*

settler – a term for Israelis who have created new communities on territory captured from Jordan, Egypt and Syria during the 1967 Six Day War; the Hebrew word for settler is *mitnachel*

sha'ar (H) – gate

shabab (A) – literally, 'youths'; young Palestinians who formed the backbone of the intifadas by confronting the IDF and throwing stones

Shabbat (H) – the Jewish Sabbath observed from sundown on Friday evening to an hour after sundown on Saturday

shalom (H) – peace; hello; goodbye

Shari'a (A) – Muslim law

Shechina (H) – divine presence

sheikh (A) – learned or old man

shekel/sh'kalim (H, s/pl) – Israeli monetary unit

Shema (H) – Judaism's central statement of belief in the oneness of God

sherut (H) – shared taxi, service taxi; Israeli minivans that

operate on fixed routes, in or between cities; see also *servees*

shisha (A) – water pipe, term used in Egypt; see also *nargileh*

shiva (H) – ritual weeklong period of mourning for first-degree relatives

shofar (H) – ram's horn traditionally blown on Rosh HaShana and Yom Kippur

shtetl (H) – small, traditional Eastern European Jewish village

sukkah/sukkot (H, s/pl) – small dwellings built during the feast of Sukkot

taboun (H) – a clay oven

tel (H) – a hill; in archaeology, a mound built up as successive cities were built and destroyed on the same site

Torah (H) – the Five Books of Moses, ie the first five books of the Hebrew Bible (the Old Testament); also called the Pentateuch

Tzahal (H) – Hebrew acronym for the Israel Defense Forces (IDF)

tzimmer (H) – literally 'room' in German; B&B or holiday-cabin accommodation; also spelled *zimmer*

tzitzit (H) – white tassels worn by Orthodox Jewish men, attached to the four corners of a square undergarment; also the knotted fringes on the prayer shawl

ulpan/ulpanim (H, s/pl) – language school

umm (A) – mother (of); feminine equivalent of *abu*

UNRWA – UN Relief & Works Agency for Palestine Refugees

uqqal (A) – the wise; the select inner core of the Druze community; see also *juhhal*

wadi (A) – river that's dry except during downpours

WZO – World Zionist Organisation

ya'ar (H) – forest

yad (H) – hand; memorial

yeshiva/yeshivot (H, s/pl) – Jewish religious seminary or school

zimmer (H) – see *tzimmer*

Behind the Scenes

SEND US YOUR FEEDBACK

We love to hear from travellers – your comments keep us on our toes and help make our books better. Our well-travelled team reads every word on what you loved or loathed about this book. Although we cannot reply individually to your submissions, we always guarantee that your feedback goes straight to the appropriate authors, in time for the next edition. Each person who sends us information is thanked in the next edition – the most useful submissions are rewarded with a selection of digital PDF chapters.

Visit **lonelyplanet.com/contact** to submit your updates and suggestions or to ask for help. Our award-winning website also features inspirational travel stories, news and discussions.

Note: We may edit, reproduce and incorporate your comments in Lonely Planet products such as guidebooks, websites and digital products, so let us know if you don't want your comments reproduced or your name acknowledged. For a copy of our privacy policy visit lonelyplanet.com/privacy.

OUR READERS

Many thanks to the travellers who used the last edition and wrote to us with helpful hints, useful advice and interesting anecdotes: Aileen Oerloff, Anna Thanou, Bill Davis, Caroline Guibet Lafaye, Dominik Armellini, Eran Globus, Frederik de Smedt, Isabela Vera, Jannik Zijlstra, Jeroen van der Zeeuw, Kirsty Westra, Nikolaj Albrecht, Petra Bischofberger, Sophie Millner, Thorsten Nieberg, Vibhor Garg

AUTHOR THANKS

Daniel Robinson

Special thanks to (from south to north): Chini Da-Silva, Gili Bat-Sara, Eran Hejams, Jody Sirota and Michael Chen (Eilat); Yair Sela (Samar); Alex Cicelsky, Doria Pinkas and Maya Galimidi (Lotan); Anat Sha'ul (Ne'ot Smadar); David and Ofra Faiman (Sde Boker); Gil Shkedi (Ne'ot HaKikar); David Lew (Masada); Lee, Meitar and Shani (Ein Gedi Field School); Sliman (Ein Gedi Nature Reserve); Eldad Hazan (Ein Feshkha/Einot Tzukim); Nisim Bados (Beit She'an); Nati and Ofer (Banias); Rachel Eshkol (Tzipori); Ido Itai and Amir Aviram (Gamla); Gregory and Hanoch (Yehudiya); Alon Malichi (Katzrin); Omer Feldman and Ya'akov Leiter (Tsfat); Ron Tsvi, Amihai and Tehila (Rosh Pina); HaKupa'it Vera (Tel Hatzor); Mordechai Kohelet Israel (Dalton); Tony (Jish); Inbar Rubin (Agamon HaHuleh); Anat Nissim (Galil Nature Museum);

Shadi (Tel Dan); Talal (Mt Hermon); and, most especially, my wife Rachel and my sons Yair and Sasson for their support, understanding and patience.

Orlando Crowcroft

I would like to thank my friends Nigel Wilson and Mary Pelletier in Ramallah, MC in Jerusalem and Heidi Levine in Tel Aviv. A big shout out to all the staff at Area D Hostel, Ayman at the Cinema Guesthouse in Jenin, Canaan Khoury and family in Taybeh and all those who made me feel welcome during my stay in the Palestinian Territories. I'd also like to thank my editor Lauren Keith and fellow authors Anita Isalska, Daniel Robinson and Dan Savery Raz. And my wife, Helen, for everything.

Anita Isalska

Countless chance encounters and conversations enriched my research; thank you to everyone who knowingly or unknowingly guided my travels. I'm especially grateful for the suggestions and insights from Noga Tarnopolsky, Riman Barakat, Linda Gradstein, the Educational Bookshop & Cafe crew, and for Slavica and Einav, who pointed me to some excellent tips. Deep thanks to Anna Heijblok, whose stories of her Jerusalem will stay with me. And, as ever, heartfelt gratitude to Normal Matt for cheerleading from the wings.

THIS BOOK

This 9th edition of Lonely Planet's *Israel & the Palestinian Territories* guidebook was researched and written by Daniel Robinson, Orlando Crowcroft, Anita Isalska, Dan Savery Raz and Jenny Walker. The previous edition was written by Daniel Robinson, Orlando Crowcroft, Virginia Maxwell and Jenny Walker. This guidebook was produced by the following:

Destination Editor Lauren Keith

Product Editors Carolyn Boicos, Elizabeth Jones, Anne Mason, Saralinda Turner

Senior Cartographer Valentina Kremenchutskaya

Book Designer Katherine Marsh

Assisting Editors Sarah Bailey, Carly Hall, Gabrielle Innes, Helen Koehne, Lou McGregor, Rosie Nicholson, Charlotte Orr, Christopher Pitts

Assisting Cartographers Gabe Lindquist, Alison Lyall

Cover Researcher Naomi Parker

Thanks to Nicholas Colicchia, Gwen Cotter, Helen Elfer, Sandie Kestell, Virginia Moreno, Ilana Myers, Lauren O'Connell, Martine Power, Alison Ridgway, Kathryn Rowan, Jacqui Saunders

Dan Savery Raz

Thanks to destination editor Lauren Keith for kicking this project off and making it run so smoothly. Also thank you to Maoz Inon (travel entrepreneur and peace warrior), Yoram Hai (for vegan tips) and Bea Hemming (for recommending Bicicletta). Biggest thanks goes to my wife, Shiri, for looking after the kids while I tapped away on my laptop, and my two girls, Hila and Maya, for always making me smile.

ACKNOWLEDGEMENTS

Climate map data adapted from Peel MC, Finlayson BL & McMahon TA (2007) 'Updated World Map of the Köppen-Geiger Climate Classification', *Hydrology and Earth System Sciences*, 11, 163344.

Cover photograph: Dead Sea, vvvita/Shutterstock ©.

Illustrations pp56–7 by Javier Martinez Zarracina, pp350–1 by Michael Weldon.

Index

Map Legend

Sights

- Beach
- Bird Sanctuary
- Buddhist
- Castle/Palace
- Christian
- Confucian
- Hindu
- Islamic
- Jain
- Jewish
- Monument
- Museum/Gallery/Historic Building
- Ruin
- Shinto
- Sikh
- Taoist
- Winery/Vineyard
- Zoo/Wildlife Sanctuary
- Other Sight

Activities, Courses & Tours

- Bodysurfing
- Diving
- Canoeing/Kayaking
- Course/Tour
- Sento Hot Baths/Onsen
- Skiing
- Snorkelling
- Surfing
- Swimming/Pool
- Walking
- Windsurfing
- Other Activity

Sleeping

- Sleeping
- Camping
- Hut/Shelter

Eating

- Eating

Drinking & Nightlife

- Drinking & Nightlife
- Cafe

Entertainment

- Entertainment

Shopping

- Shopping

Information

- Bank
- Embassy/Consulate
- Hospital/Medical
- Internet
- Police
- Post Office
- Telephone
- Toilet
- Tourist Information
- Other Information

Geographic

- Beach
- Gate
- Hut/Shelter
- Lighthouse
- Lookout
- Mountain/Volcano
- Oasis
- Park
- Pass
- Picnic Area
- Waterfall

Population

- Capital (National)
- Capital (State/Province)
- City/Large Town
- Town/Village

Transport

- Airport
- Border crossing
- Bus
- Cable car/Funicular
- Cycling
- Ferry
- Metro station
- Monorail
- Parking
- Petrol station
- Subway station
- Taxi
- Train station/Railway
- Tram
- Underground station
- Other Transport

Routes

- Tollway
- Freeway
- Primary
- Secondary
- Tertiary
- Lane
- Unsealed road
- Road under construction
- Plaza/Mall
- Steps
- Tunnel
- Pedestrian overpass
- Walking Tour
- Walking Tour detour
- Path/Walking Trail

Boundaries

- International
- State/Province
- Disputed
- Regional/Suburb
- Marine Park
- Cliff
- Wall

Hydrography

- River, Creek
- Intermittent River
- Canal
- Water
- Dry/Salt/Intermittent Lake
- Reef

Areas

- Airport/Runway
- Beach/Desert
- Cemetery (Christian)
- Cemetery (Other)
- Glacier
- Mudflat
- Park/Forest
- Sight (Building)
- Sportsground
- Swamp/Mangrove

Note: Not all symbols displayed above appear on the maps in this book